P9-DBX-677

JEWISH WOMEN/JEWISH MEN

JEWISH WOMEN/
JEWISH MEN

The Legacy of Patriarchy
in Jewish Life

AVIVA CANTOR

HarperSanFrancisco
A Division of HarperCollins*Publishers*

JEWISH WOMEN/JEWISH MEN: *The Legacy of Patriarchy in Jewish Life.* Copyright © 1995 by Aviva Cantor. All rights reserved. Printed in the United States of America. No part of this book may be used or reproduced in any manner whatsoever without written permission except in the case of brief quotations embodied in critical articles and reviews. For information address HarperCollins Publishers, 10 East 53rd Street, New York, NY 10022.

Book design by Jaime Robles
Set in Poppl-Pontifex with Post-Mediäval titling

FIRST EDITION

Library of Congress Cataloging-in-Publication Data:
Cantor, Aviva.
Jewish women / Jewish men : the legacy of patriarchy in Jewish life / Aviva Cantor. —1st ed.
  p.   cm.
Includes bibliographical references and index.
ISBN 0–06–061376–9 (cloth)
ISBN 0–06–061359–9 (pbk.)
1. Women in Judaism.   2. Patriarchy—Religious aspects—Judaism.   3. Judaism—United States.
4. Jews—United States—Cultural assimilation.   5. Feminism—Religious aspects—Judaism.
I. Title.
BM729.W6C36   1995
296'.082—dc20   92–53918

95 96 97 98 99 ❖ RRD(H) 10 9 8 7 6 5 4 3

This book is dedicated to my devoted parents:

Joseph Cantor, who imparted to me his love of the Jewish people, its values and tradition, and of Israel, of Hebrew and Yiddish, of *chazzanut* (cantorial music) and Jewish humor, and of books, the theater, music, movies, and animals. A "practical dreamer," he truly understood that "life is with people," and he embodied the highest ideals of Jewish ethics and *mentschlichkeit*.

Naomi Freedman Cantor, who imparted to me her love of art, music, and literature, her faith in education and scholarship, her fierce loyalty to family, and her strong belief that "it is better to know than not to know."

May their memory be blessed.

I remember therefore I am.

BRIAN MOORE

Difference is ... the condition requisite to all dignity and to all liberation. To be aware of oneself is to be aware of oneself as different. To be is to be different.

ALBERT MEMMI

CONTENTS

ACKNOWLEDGMENTS

The genesis of this work—which took six years to complete—goes even further back in my life than the beginnings of the Jewish feminist movement in which I have participated, whose activities I chronicled in the pages of *Lilith* magazine as its longtime (co-founding) editor, and whose issues I attempted to analyze there, in other publications, and in lectures.

My interest and involvement in Jewish history, culture, and sociology goes back, as well, beyond the Jewish movement of the late 1960s to early 1970s, in which the Socialist Zionist theoretical framework of my views was forged and beyond my career in journalism, during which time I covered the American Jewish community as well as others abroad and Israel.

My passion for and commitment to Jewish culture and the Jewish people are rooted in my experiences in the traditional home in which I was raised in the East Bronx by devoted parents who had immigrated to North America from Russia after World War I.

My father, Joseph Cantor, who grew up in the *shtetl* (townlet) of Vizneh (Slutzk region of Belarus), was a Hebrew scholar conversant in six other languages as well. A lifelong Zionist, he wept with joy when Israel was born in 1948, a memory I cherish. As a youth, he had studied in the famed Volozhin Yeshiva; he helped me with my studies of Talmud, Hebrew language and literature, and Jewish history, took me to sit by his side in shul to hear *chazzanut* (cantorial music), told me numerous Yiddish stories and jokes, and was the exemplar of a *mentsch,* a kind and ethical human being.

He was proud of the writers in the family, including his brother, Israel, a Yiddish poet, and his uncle, the scholar, Meyer Waxman.

My mother, Naomi (Nechama) Freedman Cantor, was descended from a long line of Jewish businesswomen in Dubno (Russian Poland, now Ukraine). A practical and resourceful realist, she implemented my father's ideals by initiating my enrollment at the Ramaz (Hebrew day) school and the Massad (Hebrew-speaking summer) camp to provide me an intensive Jewish education. Her conviction that "it is better to know than not to know" was undoubtedly a factor in my choosing journalism as my profession to live up to my father's ethic of doing *mitzvot* (commanded deeds) to help better the world.

My teachers at Ramaz elementary and high school were gifted and devoted. Many on the secular teaching staff believed that students must be taught to think for themselves, and they encouraged us to do so. The Jewish studies staff was committed to Jewish continuity. I was also fortunate to study at the Hebrew University of Jerusalem with noted scholars such as professors J. L. Talmon (in history, my major) and Gershom Scholem; and at YIVO, under the wise leadership of Shmuel Lapin, with Isaiah Trunk.

My friend Nadia Borochov (Ovsey) enriched my store of knowledge with tales of her brother, Ber Borochov, the Socialist Zionist theoretician, and of her youth in Czarist Russia.

My mentor, Richard Yaffe (my boss at the American office of the London *Jewish Chronicle*), not only helped me hone my journalistic skills and apply them to covering the Jewish community but also brought me into the Socialist Zionist movement. Judah Shapiro, through his classes and in personal discussions about Zionism and the Jewish community and its democratization, was another beloved mentor.

To all of these cherished individuals who are no longer among us, I owe a debt of gratitude that can never be repaid.

I am also indebted to my *chaverim* (comrades) in the Jewish Liberation Project and the Jewish sixties movement generally, who addressed in theory and in activism the issues of assimilationism, communal democracy, and Jewish cultural revival. I am deeply grateful, as well, to the women in my Jewish consciousness-raising group, to the scholars and the activists in the Jewish feminist movement, and to my colleagues at *Lilith*. Discussions with these individuals in person, at conferences, and through correspondence were important in the evolution of my ideas.

❧ This work would never have come into being were it not for Doris B. Gold, my longtime friend, literary agent, and publisher of my *Bibliography on the Jewish Woman*. It was Doris who initiated this book project and who sustained me throughout its long gestation with her sage words of counsel, her boundless energy, and her unfailing empathy. She never lost faith, patience, or confidence in me; she spurred me ever onward when the going got rough; she was a rock of support.

I doubt that this work would have been possible without my husband, Murray Zuckoff. My mentor in Socialist theory, he placed his entire knowledge of history and his journalistic experience at my disposal. He read every draft (except for the first, handwritten one), made incisive and often critical comments, asked very difficult questions, and spent hours arguing with me over thorny points, thus challenging me to ever more strenuous efforts to refine/redefine and clarify my views. His infinite patience, his emotional support, his confidence in my work—not to speak of his endless stream of Yiddish jokes to keep up my morale—were indispensable. Murray also supported me financially when the demands of this project precluded outside employment.

I was very fortunate, too, in having the emotional support of dear friends who were unfailingly empathetic, kind, and interested in the progress of this work, as were my relatives from the Dror (Israel), Waxman (New York), and Nickin and Binder (Canada) families. A by-no-means complete list of these supportive friends includes Judith Ackerman, Bonnie Anker, Adena Berkowitz, Joyce Rosman Brenner, Aphrodite Clamar, Esther Cohen, Elie Faust-Lévy, Ted and Beverly Fettman, Eva Fogelman, Shirley Frank, Frieda Forman, Nora Gold, Beryl Goldberg, Susannah Heschel, Miriam Hipsh, Miriam Hoffman, Carmela Ingwer, Carol Jochnowitz, Stefi Kirschner, Julia Mazow, Isabella Meltz, Cheryl Moch, Barbara Spaulding Murray, Nina Natelson, Sonia Nusenbaum, Norma Fain Pratt, Harriet Rochlin, Rochelle Saidel, Judith Sokoloff, Amy Stone, Grace Weiner, and Karen Yaeger. Phyllis Chesler, Esther Cohen, Carol Klein, Irena Klepfisz, Israel Levine, Cynthia Ozick, Norma Fain Pratt, Nessa Rapoport, Harriet Rochlin, and Henny Wenkart provided invaluable advice regarding the publishing process, as did the National Writers Union. Counseling by Eileen Setzman and Norbert Fliegel helped bolster my courage to create.

Two friends, Richard Cohen and Aphrodite Clamar, generously gave me free use of their Xerox machine so I could photocopy thousands of pages of the various incarnations, revisions, and inserts of the manuscript. Their warmth and support—and that of their firm's staff—made their office a home away from home.

Several generous patronesses—Linda Bronfman, Barbara Dobkin, Nora Gold, and Fanya Heller—provided gifts/grants/support that made it possible for me to complete this project. Miriam Hipsh, and the Rita Poretsky Foundation with Arlene Agus as its executive director, made possible my publication of *The Egalitarian Hagada,* which was a source of *parnosseh* (support) when I was working on the book. Blu Greenberg, Eva Fogelman, Lisa Palmieri-Billig, and Susan Weidman Schneider used their good offices on my behalf in regard to grants and *parnosseh.*

꙳ At various phases, friends and colleagues—Adena Berkowitz, Jerome Chanes, David Kaufman, Leonard Levy, Hillel Schenker, Amy Stone, and Ruth Weinrach—provided needed source material. Mitchell Cohen and Steve Zipperstein pointed me to noted experts on various subjects; Shabtai Teveth enlightened me on a Ben Gurion statement; and Jehuda Reinharz, the president of Brandeis University and an authority on Weizmann, kindly retrieved the final piece of the puzzle on a very elusive quote. Dov Noy, head of the Folklore Department of the Hebrew University of Jerusalem, shared his insights on female roles and angles in Jewish folklore and encouraged my work.

Several librarians gave me vitally needed assistance in digging out often obscure and otherwise unavailable source materials. Michele Anish of the American Jewish Committee library was always just a phone call away when I needed instant information. Librarians Dina Abramowicz and Zachary Baker of YIVO, Emily Milner of the Jewish Women's Resource Center, Ida Cohen Selavan at the Hebrew

Union College, Yael Penkower and Annette Botnick of the Jewish Theological Seminary, Esther Togman of the Jewish Agency, and Salome Cory at Temple Emanuel (who also made her library, typewriter, and coffee machine available in the preliminary phase of this project) were also enormously helpful. Tamara Cohen did important research and fact checking for the notes. Miriam Jochnowitz compiled the initial version of the bibliography, and Julia Mazow proofread it in its second stage. JTA's Susan Birnbaum helped track down an extremely elusive date, and Larry Yudelson unearthed another source.

Kandace Hawkinson, my editor, read and reread various drafts and revisions. Her questions and comments were invaluable in compelling me to be ever more precise and to structure chapter contents appropriately. I deeply appreciate production editor Rosana Francescato's precision and attention to detail and nuance as well as her encouragement and understanding in guiding me through the final stages of this project.

Bernice (Bunny) Saibel, who typed the final drafts, was patient and understanding, especially regarding my endless stream of inserts and revisions. Her husband, Joel Saibel, uncomplainingly served as courier to transport many thousands of pages to and from his home and office. I greatly appreciate, as well, the careful and expeditious computer work by writer colleague Ari Salant in finalizing last-minute revisions of the notes and bibliography.

Finally, our cat, Zorro (like his predecessor companion animals in our lives: Ktantan, Samson, Jenny, and Sputnik), kept me company during the long and often lonely hours of writing and rewriting. His playfulness gave me great cheer, and his mellowness soothed my fevered brow. His presence kept me aware of the existence of God's beautiful natural world beyond the confines of my desk, a world that we must preserve and protect for all its creatures, human and non-human.

INTRODUCTION

It is not up to you to complete the work, but neither are you free to desist from it.

RABBI TARFON,
Pirké Avot (SAYINGS OF THE SAGES)

"Is it 'good for the Jews'?"

Jews used this yardstick throughout the centuries to try to get a correct reading of reality—and thereby to survive. This question was asked again and again during the initial ("civil rights") phase of Jewish feminism (1972–83), when its focus was on the struggle for equal access to the responsibilities commensurate with Jewish adulthood. For many years (and in some sectors even today), the resounding answer from the Jewish community was, *No:* Feminism is a threat to Jewish survival.

Why, we need to ask, did the antifeminist opposition assume this specific character? Why were Jewish feminists' efforts libeled as being "bad for Jews" when increasing the pool of active, committed Jews was supposedly an aim of communal leaders? Why were Jewish feminists perceived as trying to separate themselves from the community when what they wished was to be an integral part of it? Why was it alleged that if Jewish women won equality in the synagogue and in Jewish organizations, the men would defect in droves? Why were Jewish feminists pictured as selfish and narcissistic when they were so obviously altruistically motivated by the love of Judaism and the wish to contribute to Jewish continuity?

To understand why Jewish women were excluded from the public religious and secular spheres of communal life and why there was so much resistance to integrating them in the community as equals requires an in-depth analysis of Jewish society from its ancient beginnings, when the patterns of its culture were shaped, through all of history to today. Although these patterns began to break down in the modern period, the "Is it good for the Jews?" question still carries considerable weight.

This work attempts to provide such an in-depth analysis of Jewish patterns of culture by using feminism as the key to unlock and to solve its mysteries.

1

Feminist theory will allow us to explore some questions that have puzzled and intrigued both Jews and non-Jews. Some of these questions are

- What has enabled Jews to survive two thousand years of oppression, physical and psychological?
- What is the real motivation behind anti-Semitism?
- What caused Jews to envision a monotheistic God?
- Why is there an impression that Jewish life has always been a matriarchy or "crypto-matriarchy"?
- Why are American Jewish women and men having such difficulties in their interpersonal relationships today?
- Why are Jews culturally invisible in American society even as it is becoming pluralistic and multicultural?

While the initial purpose of this work was to apply feminist theory to Jewish society and culture and to religious, political, family, and communal life, it became clear as it progressed that such a feminist analysis of Jewish life would also provide clues to the resolution of fundamental questions raised by feminist theorists. Among these questions is that of nature versus nurture, which feminists have been grappling with for several decades and which various social scientists have been wrestling with for over a century. Related questions include

- Can male violence be eradicated, and if so, how?
- Is women's economic independence the key to their social and political equality?
- Can discrimination against women be abolished under a system dominated by men?

Neither feminist theoreticians nor other historians, sociologists, and anthropologists have explored/analyzed the Jewish experience with a view to discerning if it casts some light on these issues. Part of the reason is that the Jewish experience has never been part of mainstream culture, nor its literature or other forms of artistic expression integrated into it. Jews are as invisible in most present-day feminist works as they are in those of the past dealing with history and anthropology. As Heine once wrote, "The deeds of the Jews are as little known to the world as is their real character."

THE REFORMED PATRIARCHY

The starting point of this exploration of the patterns of Jewish culture is the recognition that Jewish life is and always has been a patriarchy, a society dominated by men. Men made the rules and enforced them; men created the structures and upheld them; men had the power, and women were powerless.

Because patriarchy exists on a continuum, with considerable variations in different eras and territories, it is necessary to analyze the specific character of patriarchy as it unfolded/evolved in a specific group in order to understand that group's patterns of culture. What is necessary in the case of the Jewish nation, therefore, is a feminist anthropology.

Such an anthropology reveals that the Jews' experience with patriarchy differs in two significant respects from that of other nations. One difference is that it was a *reformed* patriarchy, male dominated but unlike classic patriarchy, whose organizing principle is power exercised through three strategies: the club (violence), the yoke (slavery and exploitation), and the leash (psychological oppression). The second difference lies in the specifics of normative gender roles and behavior.

Both of these differences, to be described subsequently, derived from the reality of Jewish life in Exile and the perception of it as a national emergency. For the better part of two thousand years, Jews lived in Exile from their homeland of Eretz (the Land of) Israel after the Romans destroyed the Second Jewish Commonwealth (73 C.E.) and deported most of its residents. In the many territories in which Jews subsequently resided in small communities, often among hostile populations, they constituted a marginal, beleaguered minority and lacked the possibility of defending themselves from attack.

In many ways, the experiences of Jews under patriarchy paralleled those of women, as did their survival strategies, collective fantasies, and value system.

The relationship Jews experienced with the general society often degenerated into an abusive relationship, with Jews being used by the power structure as lightning rods to absorb the rage of other oppressed groups and to deflect it from the ruling class. Jews, like women, were treated as a pool of instantly available victims, and both were subjected to blame-the-victim myths and accusations of provoking violence and overreacting to threats of it.

The survival strategies Jews developed over centuries bear a striking resemblance to those that individual women employed: They have tried to cultivate powerful male protectors; to be economically useful to them to obtain protection (i.e., the privilege of living); and to psych them out as to appropriate tactics to employ.

The survival strategies had only limited success. This was, after all, a variation of the classic protection racket. More often than not, the powerful men whom Jews looked to for protection betrayed or abandoned them when this was expedient. The Holocaust proved the total bankruptcy of the classic Jewish survival strategies.

The condition of Jews and women as powerless, and the experiences of both in suffering attack and abandonment, were factors in the rescue fantasies developed in both groups. Just as some women individually harbor fantasies of being rescued, Jews collectively harbored a mass rescue fantasy. They projected it onto one omnipotent deity who would liberate them from Exile and its torments through the instrumentality of His Messiah. Obviously, to be all-powerful under patriarchy, such a rescuer God had to be male. The continuing psychological need for a male rescuer God accounts for much of the resistance to changes in God-language in prayer proposed by feminists today. Jews saw their relationship with God as a patriarchal marriage: God would keep His part of the contract to rescue them if they lived up to the ethical demands of the Torah (Scripture and Jewish Law).

When rescue from Exile was not forthcoming after centuries during which oppression worsened—and abandonment by God was too terrifying to contemplate—Jews incorporated into their folk culture various mystical concepts, including the notion that God was flawed and required repair through their ever more stringent observance of the Torah in order to be able to effect rescue. At the same time, Jews expanded the old idea of the Schechinah, a female element of the Godhead that suffered along with them in Exile and never abandoned them.

The mass rescue fantasies Jews traditionally projected onto God and the Messiah were directed in the modern era to various "liberal" and "enlightened" nations and radical movements. Here, too, there was a striking similarity with rescue fantasies of individual women under patriarchy: Jews "fell in love" with these nations and movements, believing that "this time it will be different," but their blind love was unrequited.

Finally, the value system: To help them survive patriarchy, women have developed a value system that stresses cooperation, altruism, mutuality and interdependence, and an emphasis on relationships, emotionalism and compassion, reverence for life, conflict resolution through consensus, and nonviolence.

Because the only way Jews could survive patriarchy was through communal cohesion, they incorporated these values in order to create and maintain it. They institutionalized them through *Halacha* (Jewish Constitutional Law), which was studied, interpreted, and amended by legislative bodies, including rabbinical arbiters who adjudicated disputes. Halacha was enforced by local community councils in the internally autonomous Jewish communities. The open debate in these communities, the resolution of conflicts through consensus, and the election of (male) council members were some of their protodemocratic elements, as was the educational system.

Thus traditional Jewish society was a reformed patriarchy standing on three pillars: the female value system, Halacha, and the community as the context for the institutionalization of the value system through Halacha.

GENDER ROLE VARIANTS

The need for communal cohesion to ensure survival under patriarchy necessitated several important variations in gender role definition. It was primarily because survival during the national emergency of Exile required the community to be a safe haven that male violence had to be eliminated. While Jewish male domination of the community was upheld, male power was stripped of the use of force and was redefined as the power of the mind and intellect. Masculinity was redefined as spiritual resistance: the intellectual labor of studying Torah and developing Halacha, and the public performance of important rituals, including conducting prayer services and ceremonies.

The second variation in gender role definition under the reformed Jewish patriarchy related to the changes instituted in the enabler role women are tracked into under all patriarchal systems. This role has two components: to facilitate what men decide is their work, which is always considered the most important work in the society; and to accept/endure exclusion from this work turf so that, in the absence of women from it, it can define manhood. When masculinity was redefined as spiritual resistance, women's enabler role was to facilitate it and to accept exclusion from it.

Facilitating involved maintaining the complex home-support system. Exclusion from spiritual resistance, especially from learning Torah, was rationalized on the grounds that women were unsuited to intellectual pursuits and needed to channel their energy into home support. Exclusion from learning meant that women were deprived of a role in shaping the evolving Halacha and in legislating and implementing it in the community. Jewish patriarchy took the "dowry"—the female value system—but banished the "bride," women, from major communal public roles.

The third basic difference is that breadwinning, which defines masculinity under classic patriarchy, was gender-neutral in most periods of Jewish history. Women functioned in the economic sphere of the public realm and were neither marginalized there nor privatized in the home. In fact in various periods and places, especially in the East European *shtetl* (townlet), women were responsible for the entire support of the family as part of their enabling role; this allowed the men to devote themselves to spiritual resistance. However—and this is an important lesson for feminists—the women's public economic role did not serve as their visa into the male turf of spiritual resistance, nor did it propel them into communal leadership.

The fourth difference in gender role definition relates to female and male behavior. The Jewish variant of enabling was so complex and so important that women were encouraged to be strong, assertive, and resourceful in carrying it out rather than passive, helpless, and dependent. This prescribed behavior has led to the erroneous perception of Jewish life as a matriarchy or a crypto-matriarchy. This is a false interpretation because female assertiveness was allowed only as long as it was altruistic, that is, in the interests of the community ("good for the Jews") as the men perceived and defined these interests.

Reinforcing the channeling of women's energy into altruistic-assertive enabling required the creation of positive role models, such as Queen Esther. Negative role models, such as Lilith, were created to warn of the dire consequences of role breaking.

To allow women to function successfully as altruistic-assertive enablers, their "working conditions" in the home and their "job security" had to be improved. Male power to abuse or to humiliate wives was limited, and divorce without a wife's consent was abolished, though the central stipulation that only the husband can grant the divorce has remained to plague observant women to this day. Jewish marriage was idealized as a monogamous partnership in which each spouse had defined entitlements and responsibilities. The sexual fulfillment of the wife was one of her entitlements and precluded the emergence of a Madonna/whore complex.

✦ The Israeli experience, however, demonstrates how easily all these reforms can fall by the wayside when the men, who instituted them, no longer deem them necessary. The pioneering sector of the *Yishuv* (Jewish community in pre-state Israel) was also a reformed patriarchy incorporating many female values, especially on the kibbutz. But when the male pioneers sought to recapture the turf of agricultural labor that Jews had been excluded from in the Exile and to use it, along with self-defense, to redefine masculinity, they tried to track the female pioneers into facilitating and withdrawing from this important work. The women fought against the repositioned enabler role but, as in the shtetl, they did "men's work," while the men never did "women's work" (cooking, laundry, child care).

After the establishment of the State of Israel in 1948, women were successfully eliminated from agricultural labor and light industry on the kibbutz and from various urban job sectors. A combination of circumstances, including the ongoing state of siege, produced a recrudescence of traditional normative patriarchal roles and macho behavior in men and "nurturing" and subservience in women.

ANTI-SEMITISM AND ASSIMILATIONISM

It is precisely because Jewish communities were infused with female values and were violence-free zones that patriarchal power structures considered them a threat and sought to keep their own oppressed masses separated from Jews to prevent defection or rebellion. The Jewish presence was often eradicated through massacres and expulsions (the High Middle Ages in Europe) or incarceration in ghettos (early modern period). Because the Jews' economic roles, including that of cultural intermediary, brought them in contact with members of all classes, Judeophobic myths were invented to engender psychological separation. The myth of Jewish power and influence—still being recycled today—deluded the masses into believing Jews were their real enemy.

The Holocaust is an extreme but by no means aberrant example of the deployment of these strategies to eradicate Jews and the female values that informed their communities.

❧ The strategy adopted by ruling classes in the West from the mid-eighteenth century on was to eradicate Jewish "influence" by making Jews invisible. Jews were conned into relinquishing the distinctive aspects of Jewish culture, especially their exhibition in the public sphere, and to accept the majority culture, which the ruling class shapes and dominates. The con took the form of the assimilationist contract: "Don't behave as Jews have always behaved and you won't be treated as Jews were always treated" (i.e., persecuted). The promise of an end to persecution propelled Jews into taking over the task of making themselves invisible, thus unconsciously colluding in their collective cultural suicide. Fear of breaking the assimilationist contract and thereby reigniting anti-Semitism has escalated since the Holocaust because to "be treated as Jews were always treated" now includes genocide.

Most of the Jews who immigrated to America from Eastern Europe (1880s–1924) jettisoned their culture piece by piece like the pioneers of overloaded westward-heading wagon trains abandoned property by the side of the trail to allow them to move ahead faster. They rationalized this behavior with the excuse that the national emergency that had necessitated spiritual resistance no longer existed, because "America is different" from the toxic exiles in which Jews had lived previously. They ignored the contradiction between adhering to this belief and accelerating invisibility to avoid "provoking" anti-Semitism, even during and after the 1960s, when diversity, pluralism, and multiculturalism began to replace the original American melting-pot concept.

Despite Jews' strenuous efforts at assimilation, many traditional Jewish values, survival strategies, and behavior patterns continue to be transmitted during socialization and are expressed in the family and in the communal life. The pillar of this value system, however, stands shakily now that the other two, Halacha and the communal context for its institutionalization, have been so weakened. This leaves individuals in a state of confusion and inner conflict, unable to give up Jewish cultural patterns completely but vulnerable to low self-esteem because they have also internalized the patriarchal general society's denigration of Jewish culture, especially its female value system.

❧ Assimilationism has had a profound effect on gender roles and consequently on male-female relationships, especially in marriage.

Most Jewish men internalized the American (middle-class) definition of masculinity: material success through breadwinning, and physical aggression and machismo. To live up to the material success component, they had to relinquish

Torah study and marginalize their participation in the public performance of ritual. They also had to recapture from women the turf of breadwinning. While they managed to eject women from this turf, their material success could not, for a variety of reasons discussed subsequently (see chapter 10), be conclusively validated. Nor, given Jews' continuing aversion toward physical aggression, could they live up to the macho behavior component. This led many Jewish men to obsess over the myth that European Jews had gone "like sheep to the slaughter" during the Holocaust, and to seek vicarious validation of their masculinity by identifying with Israeli men as fighters.

Suffering from low self-esteem because their masculinity could not be validated, these men blamed their mothers for having instilled in them behavior that precluded their being considered sexy. They projected their anxieties about masculinity onto their lovers and spouses, and they increasingly sought non-Jewish women as trophy wives.

These actions contributed to the erosion of Jewish women's already low self-esteem. They, too, suffered from an absence of validation, but for different reasons. They failed to live up to the majority culture's standards of beauty (blond, straight hair, thin body) and behavior (a restrained and cool demeanor). Turning to the men of their own group for validation, they experienced vilification as "Jewish mothers" and "Jewish American Princesses" ("JAPs").

COMMUNAL LIFE

Jewish men attempted to attain validation, self-esteem, and an ersatz definition of masculinity through organizational endeavors. The undemocratic and hierarchical communal structure they established, however, provided these only to the plutocracy of wealthy men, who disempowered everyone else. These men incorporated into the communal structure the patriarchal values of domination, status, and exploitation, and tried to suppress the female values of cooperation, interdependence, altruism, and compassion. They became fixated on fund-raising, involved in jurisdictional disputes over glamorous projects and issues, and engaged in efforts to suppress debate.

The use of the organization as an arena in which to define and validate masculinity necessitated the exclusion of women volunteers and professionals from anything other than token positions of responsibility and power. This accounts in part for Jewish organizations' lack of interest in issues affecting women's lives, such as day care, which are in actuality—like the equally neglected issue of Jewish education—concerns that affect the continuity of the entire community.

Men relegated women to women-only independent and auxiliary organizations. Women acceded to this communal separation because these organizations allowed them to use their energy, to behave assertively, and to have a public role, however indirect, in the community.

Many men in Jewish organizational life feared that Jewish feminism would motivate the women to take over their turf and crowd them out. Many women in the separate female organizations feared that feminism would cause their members to defect (as indeed it did). This dynamic accounts in large part for the opposition of organizational men to Jewish feminist demands and the initial lack of interest by most of the women's organizations in advancing them.

Jewish feminists, most of them well educated and involved in religious life, experienced the 1983 victory on the rabbinical ordination of Conservative women as the end of the struggle for equal access to the rights and responsibilities of adult Jews. While a few Orthodox feminists struggle for the reform of Halacha and for equal access to Jewish education, most Jewish feminists have turned their attention to changing the liturgy and creating new ceremonies to validate their participation as adults in religious life. Although aware of the contradiction implicit in attaining (limited) equality under a still-powerful patriarchal structure, they are unwilling to direct energy to dismantling it or to analyzing the dynamics of its continued existence.

FEMINIST LESSONS FROM THE JEWISH EXPERIENCE

If Jewish communities functioned for two thousand years in accordance with female values, including nonviolence, this demonstrates, in the words of the old Yiddish saying, that "if it happened, it's possible." Regardless of whether men are afflicted with "testosterone poisoning," biology is not destiny, and nurture can override nature in determining human behavior.

It must be noted, however, that while the reforms instituted in Jewish patriarchy eliminated the worst abuses of male power, they did not eliminate male power or the concept of its legitimacy. No equality was instituted for women, even when they attained prominence in public economic endeavors.

The fragility of the gender-role reform can be seen most conclusively in the case of Israel. What its reversion to traditional patriarchal roles and behavior means is that the men have the power even under reformed patriarchy to give and to take away when they perceive their interests to lie in either direction. Thus an analysis of the Jewish experience leads to the inescapable conclusion that while it is possible to reform patriarchy—even to instill female values into it and to proscribe male violence—this reform leaves patriarchy intact and women still vulnerable to male power.

Such an analysis also shows that there were three conditions under which male behavioral change occurred: a national emergency; the channeling of male aggression into a high-status activity considered necessary for group survival; and this activity's serving as the new definition of masculinity. Questions feminists need to explore are

- Do all three of these conditions need to be present for men to become nonviolent?
- Will men always need a definition of masculinity, and if so, why?
- How is an egalitarian society to be created if the existence of an alternative definition of masculinity in and of itself will necessitate the exclusion of women from the most important work in society and continue their functioning as men's enablers?

One is forced to recognize that infusing patriarchy with female values—even ending economic and social discrimination against women—is not going to transform society fundamentally. Even eliminating patriarchy is not enough. It is the idea of the legitimacy of power as the organizing principle of society, and its exercise by any individual or group over others and over nature, that must be challenged and overcome. A completely different ethos must be envisioned as the organizing principle for human society, one based not on power but on female values.

If the human race and the animal nations of our planet and Earth itself are to survive and flourish, the vision expressed over twenty-five hundred years ago by Isaiah must be midwifed into reality. The prophet wrote:

Nation shall not lift up sword against nation. . . .
The wolf shall dwell with the sheep
And the leopard with the goatling. . . .
The cow and the bear will graze [side by side]
And their young will repose together. . . .
And people will joyously draw water
from the wells of redemption.

1

PATTERNS OF TRADITIONAL JEWISH CULTURE

In the very heart of the nation women, as women, have almost no position: the history of all nations is a purely masculine history. In that masculine world, also, there are rich and poor. Historical memory seems to be dispensed according to power; only the leaders and men of importance have a right to a specified past.... The Jew does not even have the right to vague collective participation.... If it were not for a few accidental references in the archives of the non-Jews to such and such a collective slaughter or such and such an extraordinary tax imposed on him [sic], one might doubt that the Jew had ever lived in the land.... Did he even have a past at all? Did he even exist?

ALBERT MEMMI

ONE ❧ POWERLESS UNDER PATRIARCHY: THE NATURE AND DYNAMICS OF EXILE

Since the Jew is nowhere at home, nowhere regarded as a native, he [sic] remains an alien everywhere. That he himself and his ancestors as well were born in the country does not alter this fact in the least.

LEON PINSKER (1882)

"What makes Jews different?" asks Norma Rae, the young textile worker and union activist in the film of the same name. Union organizer Ruben Warshavsky, her mentor, answers in one word: "History."

Clues to the evolution and development of Jewish culture—the synthesis of Jewish values, attitudes, and behavior patterns—can all be found in that "black box" called recorded history. In that black box are the keys to the way Jews perceive themselves and the world and their relationship to it, how they behave in their female-male relationships and in their families and communities, and how they express their values and views in religious and ceremonial life, literature and folklore, music, crafts, and architecture.

And for Jews, the central experience in history has been that of living in Exile.

Exile is a specific form of national oppression endured by Jews three times in the past thirty-five hundred years. The first exile, in Egypt, probably began some time in the sixteenth century B.C.E. with the voluntary migration of people whose descendants were enslaved. The subsequent two exiles began with the political act of the expulsion of the majority of the Jewish nation from their homeland of Eretz (the Land of) Israel following military defeats and rebellions crushed by great powers. The second exile started with the deportation of the Jews by and to Babylonia in 586 B.C.E., the third exile with their expulsion by the Romans in 70 C.E. Following this latter expulsion, Jews lived in small communities dispersed throughout the globe. They lost control over their national destiny and over the most elemental parts of their present—including, at times, where they lived, how they earned a living, and even what they wore.

All these exiles have taken place under patriarchy, a system whose organizing principle is power. Under patriarchy, men wield power over women, children, and the natural world and engage in power struggles with one another as individuals and in groups along class, ethnic, and/or territorial lines. Any group that lacks power or the possibility of resisting it can be subjected with impunity to any of the strategies men employ in using power: the club (force and violence), the yoke (enslavement), and the leash (psychological oppression).

Patriarchy thus makes collective self-defense imperative. But Exile made it virtually impossible for Jews.

Jews in Exile lacked power or the possibility of attaining it. They lacked a territory as a home base in which to establish a political and economic structure based on their own needs and values and to organize a military to conduct its defense.

Jews lived "perpetually in enemy territory," as Theodor Herzl, the founder of political Zionism, put it. They were not members of the majority ethnic group in any territory or even of a large ethnic minority there. They did not share the ideology (religion, culture, feeling of common national origin) or language of any of them. Nor were they members of these groups' classes. They were thus outside the ethnic and class struggles occurring in various territories but were often exploited and viewed with suspicion by parties to a power struggle and trapped in the cross fire between them. The life Jews endured in the Exile was comparable to that of civilians in a neighborhood wracked by ongoing warfare between armed gangs. They were often suspected of aiding and abetting one side or another in a class or ethnic conflict, and the gangs tended to shoot first and ask questions later. Above all, the Jews were expendable.

∜ The Jews' condition in Exile is analogous in many ways to the oppression of women, who are also powerless under patriarchy and are affected by power struggles they are not part of and by their outcome. Lacking self-determination over their own destinies, Jews were, as are women, object rather than subject, forced to be reactive rather than active and to respond to others' demands.

Like women, Jews have not been allowed to define themselves. Those who have power over them define their nature and character and attempt to compel them to behave in accordance with these definitions and to fulfill certain roles.

Women under all patriarchal systems are programmed to be enablers. One of the two components of this female role is to facilitate the work that men designate as theirs, which is defined by men as the most important and prestigious in the society and as that which gives men power. The other element is to withdraw or accept/endure exclusion from that work turf, which, in women's absence, defines manhood.

Jews in Exile have often been forced to be enablers of the society's ruling class. The ruling class tries to track them into occupations and roles that it believes will facilitate its wielding economic, political, and military power; and tries to exclude them from those it believes could provide a viable basis for self-defense against its power.

Both Jews and women have constituted a pool of potential victims of violence. Jews for centuries constituted a kind of game preserve whose gates the ruling class could open to hunters at will. The ghetto, noted historian Israel Abrahams, enclosed Jews "in a defenseless pen where anyone who wanted to kill Jews knew precisely where to find them." (And, indeed, Jews in ghettos were victims of massacres as well as of criminal acts of sadism and humiliation, including body snatching and grave desecration.) A later writer described conditions in the Warsaw Ghetto during World War II as "comparable only to those faced by a trapped bear in a bear pit." The unconscious understanding by non-Jews of the parallels between the oppression of Jews and that of animals is the reason behind a law passed in thirteenth-century England proclaiming Jews to be "men *ferae naturae,*" wild animals ("like the roe and the deer, they are an order apart"); the call by Martin Luther for Jews to be expelled as if they were "mad dogs"; and the Nazis' characterization of Jews as "vermin" that had to be "exterminated."

Jews always faced the possibility that their relationship with the ruling class and the general society as a whole could degenerate into a physically abusive relationship. Violence against Jews, like violence against women—rape, battering, witch burning, suttee, and other forms of gynocide—has served as a safety valve to allow lower-class men trapped in an economic and political pressure cooker to let off steam when their rage against their own oppressors reached the boiling point. The powerless masses were thus co-opted with ersatz power over an even more powerless group than themselves. Periodic massacres of Jews—"pogroms," as they were called in Czarist Russia—also functioned as a campaign of terrorism designed to destabilize Jewish communities or, at the very least, to keep them off balance and insecure.

Finally, just as women are accused of "provoking" crimes against them (rape and battering, sexual harassment) by their behavior, so, too, Jews have been accused of "provoking" the crimes committed against them (pogroms, expulsions, incarceration in ghettos, as well as economic and social discrimination). Various blame-the-victim myths, endlessly recycled, have served to keep alive the hostility that fuels and is expressed through physical assault and to justify the attacks. The blame-the-victim myths are also a form of verbal abuse designed to try to break the morale of the oppressed, cause them to experience self-blame, and wear down their emotional resistance.

Jewish women, as we shall see in future chapters, have experienced double jeopardy, being oppressed as Jews and as women.

❧ Several modern Jewish historians and political and religious movements have advanced the concept that Exile is really a good thing, a blessing in disguise, a natural condition, or, at the very least, a necessary evil, or maybe, in modern parlance, a "growth experience." When proponents of these views use the term *diaspora,* they attempt thereby to cover up or deny the origin and character of Exile. (Most Jews today use the word *diaspora* without consciousness of its political implication that Exile was/is a benign condition.)

These views, however, are not a correct reading of reality. Exile has put the survival of Jews, individually and collectively, in jeopardy. Until recent times, Jews recognized this; they incorporated this understanding into the story of their enslavement in Egypt. The Scriptures relate that the Jews remained in Egypt long after the famine in Canaan that originally drove them there had abated, because life was comfortable. But, the story warns, Exile is a condition of powerlessness, and a nasty turn of events—such as that experienced by the Jews in Egypt when a new pharaoh decided it was expedient to enslave them—should never be unexpected.

Put another way, living in Exile was like living under a condition of pollution. When it reached levels of lethal political toxicity, Jews had to flee (if they could) or they ended up dead.

THE MEANING OF MARGINALITY

The eternal wandering outsiders, the Jews were never part of the classes that had evolved in various territories over centuries. They did not belong to the ruling classes, who owned the means of production, nor to the working classes, who produced goods the society regarded as essential.

Under feudal systems, the ruling class—kings, princes, nobles, the church—derived power in large part from the ownership of land, which is why Jews were forbidden to own it in most places and periods, including the European High Middle Ages (eleventh to fourteenth centuries). But neither were Jews part of the peasant class, which worked the land under the medieval manorial system and Czarist serfdom.

In the modern era, Jews were not an integral part of the Western bourgeoisie, which became the ruling class through its ownership of heavy industry, mines, and iron and steel mills. Nor were Jews part of the industrial proletariat, which worked in these industries. Even when and where Jews were part of the proletariat—in late nineteenth-century Czarist Russia and England and in early twentieth-century America—they worked primarily in light industries such as textiles, usually in small factories owned by other Jews.

Ber Borochov, the Socialist Zionist theoretician who died in 1917 at the age of thirty-six, analyzed this condition of Jewish marginality:

> Historically the Jewish worker has been torn away from nature
> (agriculture), from the natural resources (mines, quarries and forests) and
> from those industries which produce the means of production and

transportation facilities. . . . The Jews have been removed for centuries from the basic branches of production *upon which the economic structure depends.* . . . Instead of concentrating about the vital center of economic life, the Jews are scattered on its periphery [italics mine].

Jews had to find niches in the interstices of existing economic structures. They have tended to be in the distribution end of the economy (merchants, importers, owners of department stores) rather than the production end; to be artisans and entrepreneurs in industries primarily directed at the consumer (e.g., ready-to-wear clothing, electronics, the media) rather than the producer (heavy industry: machines to make machines); and in services, such as the professions, that involve the use of the mind.

The job choices many Jews make even today are conditioned by the Jewish experience, wrote Rabbi Richard Israel. He listed six ideal job characteristics that make certain occupations attractive to Jews: independence, "portability" of livelihood, the opportunity to associate with other Jews ("there's safety in numbers"), an urban environment (it is considered safer "to be a Jew in the anonymity of the city than out in the country, where distinctive status is so much more obvious and where a person is more vulnerable"), intellectual rather than manual labor, and providing high status among other Jews.

Having whittled the economic possibilities open to Jews down to the size that fit in their Procrustean bed, the ruling classes channeled Jews into occupations in which Jews would function as their enablers. These were occupations power structures found useful to their needs and nonthreatening to their hegemony. When the ruling class thought that the skills Jews developed in these pursuits would facilitate its interests, Jews were initially welcomed to a territory. Wrote Borochov: "The new immigrant groups are forced to become 'useful' by turning to economic fields as yet unoccupied. They are tolerated as long as they are active in economic functions which no one has previously assumed. But when the development of the forces of production has reached a stage wherein the native population can itself perform [them], the foreign nationality becomes 'superfluous' and a movement is begun to rid the country" of them.

In the Middle Ages, when a merchant stratum was lacking in Europe, the power structure found it expedient to have Jews fill the niche of importing spices and luxuries (such as enamel) from the Middle East. By the eleventh and twelfth centuries, however, an indigenous merchant class had arisen, and it displaced them. Wrote historian Henri Pirenne of these Jewish merchants: "Their economic role cannot be considered as anything but that of accessories. Society lost nothing by their disappearance."

And when centuries later the German Jews were forced out of their occupations by the Nazis and either fled or were deported to their deaths, the Germany economy "lost nothing by their disappearance," either. This is the essential meaning of Jewish marginality.

TRAPPED IN ETHNIC AND CLASS CROSS FIRE

The interstitial nature of Jews' economic roles propelled them into the cross fire of other people's class and ethnic struggles. In the High Middle Ages in Western Europe, for example, after having been ejected from the Oriental trade, Jews were forced into money lending to the nobles. In this role they incurred the hostility of the indebted nobles as well as that of the nobles' class enemies, the merchants and peasants, who saw the Jews' activities bolstering the nobles' power at their expense. Later, when pushed into money lending and pawnbroking to the urban poor, Jews incurred their hostility as well as that of the guild masters and city burghers, who saw the Jews' role strengthening their class enemy.

Another interstitial role that has often gotten Jews caught in the struggles of others—in this case, those between different ethnic groups—was that of cultural intermediary. Jews discerned, transmitted, and popularized cultural values, expression, and information as translators, publishers, musical interpreters, and academics in various eras and places, and in the modern era, as filmmakers, journalists, teachers, and social workers as well.

It is not surprising, given their history, that Jews acquired a great deal of skill in recognizing quickly what were the main values and myths of a society and its power structure, and what were the ground rules, because discerning these was often a matter of life and death. "The deer sees the hunter before the hunter sees the deer," commented historians Paul Mayer and Maximilian Harden.

The exquisite antennae Jews developed in this regard made them acute cultural intermediaries. For example, early-twentieth-century American Jewish moviemakers "understood public taste and were masters at gauging market swings," wrote Neal Gabler. Jewish journalists in Western Europe and America had "a sensitivity to nuances, a fine ear for subtle differences and a nose for things to come," in the words of Mayer and Harden. This is why Jews could sense and popularize newly crystallizing values. The so-called Salon Jewesses of late-eighteenth-century Berlin popularized the works of Goethe, Victor Hugo, and Heine, which were to be so important in the cultural scene of the next century. Social critics such as Tom Lehrer, Harvey Kurtzman (creator of *Mad* magazine), and Lenny Bruce lay the groundwork in the 1950s for the values of the 1960s U.S. counterculture; rebels such as Bob Dylan, Abbie Hoffman, and (the young) Jerry Rubin popularized them. It can even be argued that Jewish women in the contemporary feminist movement—theoreticians such as Phyllis Chesler, Robin Morgan, Shulamith Firestone, and Andrea Dworkin and writer-activists Betty Friedan, Gloria Steinem, and Letty Cottin Pogrebin—have functioned as cultural intermediaries between the movement and the general public.

Jews also knew how to transmit information. They knew how to organize education from their long experience in studying and teaching (of which more in chapter 4), how to write (Jewish men had 100 percent literacy at a time when only monks knew how to read and write), and how to publish. Finally, Jews had a vast amount of experience in organizing social services. Throughout most of their history, Jews had internal autonomy in their communities, and even when this was taken away, they used their skills to organize and run charitable and mutual aid efforts. The smallest *shtetl* (Yiddish for townlet) in Eastern Europe had volunteer societies for visiting and sheltering the sick; providing alms, free loans, clothes; caring for orphans, the elderly, and for poor travelers; burying the dead; and financing dowries for indigent young brides.

In modern times, many individual Jews who identified with the cultural values of the ruling class or majority ethnic culture transmitted them to the rest of society through education, the social work profession, the press, and film and television. This was the case in nineteenth- and twentieth-century Western and Central Europe, in Communist Russia and the then-Soviet bloc, and in the U.S. Like the biblical Joseph, they were dream interpreters. Heine's "Lorelei," for example, was the quintessential expression of the dreams of the German romantic movement of his time; songwriter Irving Berlin's "I'm Dreaming of a White Christmas" similarly captured and spread the values of twentieth-century America's majority culture. The filmmakers, with their "peculiar sensitivity to the dreams and aspirations of other immigrants and working-class families, . . . a significant portion of the early movie-going audience, . . . idealized every old glorifying bromide" about America. So did the two artists who invented Superman ("truth, justice, and the American way") and Irna Phillips, who created the soap opera genre.

The preponderance and high visibility of individual Jewish cultural intermediaries often led oppressed ethnic groups to see all the Jews in a particular territory as agents, or at the very least allies, of the oppressive power structure and its culture regardless of whether or not Jews actually identified with its values. Jews in late-nineteenth-century Central Europe, for example, were seen by proponents of the Czech national movement in provincial Bohemia and Moravia as allies of the German-speaking dominant class because Jews sponsored and attended German-language schools there. Russian-speaking Jews in Soviet provincial republics were perceived by their ethnic majorities as "Russifiers." The Quebecois separatists identified Canadian Jews as Anglophones—and allies of the very same white Anglo-Saxon ruling class that had sealed the doors of Canada during the Holocaust.

❧ From the mid-nineteenth century on in Western Europe, Jews occupying the middle range of economic positions were in direct contact with consumers and were increasingly visible as cultural intermediaries. They got caught in the class cross fire between the upper bourgeoisie and the working class. An integral part of neither, they were regarded with suspicion by both. Members of the bourgeois ruling class resented competition from Jewish financiers and merchants. They loathed and feared Jewish leftist intellectuals, such as Ferdinand LaSalle and Rosa

Luxembourg, who they charged were fomenting revolution against them among the workers. But many in the working class also looked with suspicion at Jews, believing that all of them were capitalists.

OPPRESSOR SURROGATES AND
LIGHTNING RODS

The prime reason that Jews got trapped in class and ethnic cross fire was that the ruling class forced Jews to act as a buffer between it and the oppressed lower classes. It thrust them into the role of oppressor surrogate doing the dirty work of the oppressors as the front man shielding them from view—and attack.

Sometimes Jews functioned as the oppressor surrogate of one warring segment of the ruling class vis-à-vis another. The Jews who lent money to the nobles, as oppressor surrogate of the king, did the dirty work of accumulating income that could then be taxed exorbitantly or confiscated and poured into the royal coffers. This way the king did not need to confront the opposition involved in extracting this money from the nobles directly. (Rulers in the High Middle Ages, to protect this lucrative source of cash, designated the Jews as "the king's persons"; they had the legal status of chattel.) The Jews, Israel Abrahams observed, served as "unwilling sponges, sucking in the wealth of the land and then being squeezed dry by the rulers." This bolstered the power of the king not only in relation to the nobles but also to the church—and it led the church to attack the Jews to weaken the king.

A role related to that of oppressor surrogate was that of lightning rod that the upper classes could use to deflect onto the Jews the rage of oppressed groups and classes. Jews in the High Middle Ages absorbed the rage of the masses oppressed by the nobles, the church, and the merchants, being the victims of numerous pogroms in England, France, Germany, Austria, and Spain over a four-hundred-year period.

Sometimes the two roles worked in tandem. In seventeenth-century Poland, Jews served as the oppressor surrogate of the Polish nobles vis-à-vis the Ukrainian peasants. Originally welcomed into the country in the twelfth century to serve as a middle class, they were cut off from other avenues of employment and channeled into the trades of selling liquor, collecting taxes, and acting as agents of the often absentee landlords.

In 1648 the Ukrainians mobilized under Cossack chieftain Bogdan Chmielnitzki (to whom a statue stands in Kiev) in a peasant revolt against the Polish lords. They directed their rage at the Jews as the lightning rod the nobles had set up for precisely such an eventuality, massacring 300,000 individuals, raping and kidnapping women, pillaging, and torching. The bizarre and horrific atrocities they perpetrated augured and anticipated in their fiendish sadism those of the Nazis, the Croatian Ustashi, the Romanian Iron Guard, and the Hungarian Arrow

Cross about three hundred years later. An eyewitness reported that Cossacks "stabbed infants in the arms of their mothers and tore many to pieces like fish." They forced Jews to dig graves "into which Jewish women and children were thrown and buried alive." By the time the Chmielnitzki pogroms were over, seven hundred Jewish communities had been wiped out.

❧ In the nineteenth century, the West European bourgeoisie used Jews as a lightning rod to absorb the rage of members of the working class and to divert them from struggles for reform and revolution and from participating in workers' and Socialist parties. Their strategy was to depict the Jews as the powerful capitalists who were the workers' real enemy, the one they needed to overthrow. Anti-Semitism made such inroads among the Austrian working class that Karl Kautsky, a Marxist leader, wrote Engels in 1884, "We have difficulty in preventing our own people from fraternizing with the anti-Semites." This phenomenon prompted Socialist leader August Bebel to comment, "Anti-Semitism is the Socialism of fools." A related bourgeois strategy was to prevent the lower middle class from making an alliance with the workers by picturing the workers' parties as dominated by revolutionaries who were Jews.

In essence the bourgeoisie was promoting class collaboration through anti-Semitism (the we-have-a-common-enemy ploy). Hatred of Jews was a very effective organizing tool, as it later proved to be in Nazi Germany and post-Anschluss (1938) Austria after their anti-Semitic parties had prepared the groundwork for state persecution for over half a century.

Some left-wing parties bent over backwards to try to distance themselves from any taint of concern about Jews. The Social Democrats of pre–World War I Austria-Hungary, for example, announced that Austrian workers would never allow themselves to be used as a "battering ram against anti-Semitism."

Nor were some "radicals" loath to use anti-Semitism as an organizing tool. All but one of the major *narodnik* (Populist Revolutionary) papers in Czarist Russia hailed the peasant pogroms of 1881 as the first sign of a mass stirring. One faction of the *Narodnaya Volya* (The Will of the People) Party went even further, stating that "the Ukrainian people suffer above all from the *zhid*" (kike). "The *zhid* is sucking its blood. . . . The Czar has sided with the *zhid*. . . . Arise, laborers, avenge yourselves on the landlords, *plunder the Jews*, and slay the officials" (italics mine).

In the black ghettos of mid-twentieth-century America, Jewish cultural intermediaries—teachers and social and welfare workers—played the role of oppressor surrogate, and they and small retail business owners and pawnbrokers were highly visible and accessible lightning rods. When the ghettos rose in revolt in the 1960s, it was the Jewish teachers whom black "leaders" vilified as oppressors, and it was the Jewish mom-and-pop stores that were torched. Long after Jews had ceased to function as oppressor surrogates in black ghettos, some African American demagogues continued to use anti-Semitism as an organizing tool. The direct consequence of propaganda such as that of City College Professor Leonard Jeffries—that Jews ran the slave trade and deliberately excluded blacks from films—was the August 1991 riot in Crown Heights, Brooklyn, during which blacks victimized Hassidic Jews and Yankel Rosenbaum was murdered.

JUDEOPHOBIC MYTHS AND THEIR RECYCLING

To set Jews up to be lightning rods for the rage of other oppressed groups, the power structure had to separate/isolate them physically and psychologically from the rest of society. They were physically separated in the Middle Ages by being forced to wear bizarre clothing and identifying badges designed to make them appear strange, to allow them to be easy targets, and to humiliate them and try to break their spirit. Later, from the fifteenth to the mid-to-late eighteenth centuries, Jews were incarcerated in ghettos, primarily in Italy and Germany.

The power structure invented ugly myths that separated/isolated the Jews psychologically from the rest of the population and conditioned the latter to hate Jews. The myths were always kept in active circulation so that if an "emergency" necessitated directing hostility against Jews, all that was necessary was to push the right buttons. Keeping Jews physically apart from the rest of society ensured the acceptance of these myths by preventing any experience of reality from challenging their supposed accuracy.

The prime Judeophobic myths have been recycled over the centuries to our own day.

The church—whose pulpits constituted the main communications network of pre-modern times—transmitted to the population the myth that Jews had killed Jesus and were therefore, in Pope Innocent III's words, consigned to perpetual servitude. This Christ-killer myth was repudiated by the Catholic church only as late as 1965. A recent recrudescence of the myth appears in the works of some American feminists—"matriarchalists" who charge that the ancient Israelites murdered "the Goddess" and thereby "introduced violence and war, patriarchy and exploitation."

Another favorite myth, which dates back to Apion of Alexandria in the early Roman Empire, was that Jews murder Christians, particularly children, to use their blood in the baking of Passover *matzah* (Hebrew for unleavened bread). A recycling of this ritual murder/blood libel by American anti-choice extremists is that "Jewish abortionists kill Christian babies for profit."

Other Judeophobic myths were that Jews desecrate the host (the Communion wafer representing the body of Jesus), that Jews are parasites on the body politic, and that they poison Christians. The myth that Jews caused the bubonic plague of the fourteenth century by poisoning the wells was recycled by the Nazis, who charged that Jews were "dangerous carriers of sickness and pestilence." This was their rationale for confining Jews in occupied Poland to a "quarantine area," that is, ghetto. Recycling the myth yet again, the Lyndon LaRouche organization on the American far-right propagandized that an international Jewish oligarchy was running the drug trade; blacks were told to hate Jews because of this. Not to be outdone, a black rock star said in 1989 that "the Jews finance those experiments on AIDS with black people in South Africa." The related slander that Jewish physicians in the Middle Ages and the fifteenth and sixteenth centuries used sorcery in their cures and would employ it to kill Christian patients was recycled by Stalin when he charged in 1952 that there was a "Doctors' Plot" against him and his regime. It was recycled yet again by Steve Cokely, a black mayoral aide in Chicago, who stated in 1988 that "the AIDS epidemic is a result of doctors, especially Jewish ones, who inject AIDS into blacks."

The charges that Jews were allied with enemies of specific nations are too numerous to record here. The Middle Ages were rife with such accusations. This can be seen, for instance, in the interpretation that Rashi, the great scriptural commentator of eleventh-century France, gives to the story in the Book of Exodus of the origin of Pharaoh's plan to murder newborn Jewish baby boys. The Scriptures relate that Pharaoh says he fears the Jewish slaves will take advantage of an enemy attack to escape from Egypt. Rashi interprets Pharaoh's words as a euphemism for the ruler's real fear, which was that the Jews would constitute a Fifth Column, take over the country, and make the Egyptians leave it. His interpretation obviously derives from his knowledge of and reaction to the medieval Judeophobic myth that Jews betray and take over countries. This myth has been recycled over the centuries and was used with great success by the Nazis in charging that Germany lost World War I because the Jews had "stabbed us in the back."

⠦ Jews in the nineteenth and twentieth centuries faced the charge from anti-Semites attempting to recruit workers that they were all capitalists. Anti-Semites in the bourgeoisie accused Jews of being revolutionaries and Communists out to overthrow the state. A libel invented by the Czarist secret police in the late nineteenth century "resolved" the seeming contradiction: There was an "international Jewish conspiracy" by the "Elders of Zion," who placed troops in both camps to launch a two-front attack with the ultimate aim of taking over the world. This was a recycling of the medieval Judeophobic myth that all Jews were rich, powerful, and in league with Satan in his quest to dominate the planet.

This myth was recycled during the Argentine juntas' reign of terror (1976–83) by the generals, who (said they) believed that the Jews were conspiring against "Christian civilization" and that the military had a "mission" to save it. This brings to mind the cry of the Czarist pogromists, "Beat the Jews and save Russia!"—a slogan that resurfaced in the late 1980s in the anti-Semitic Russian organization Pamyat. One of Pamyat's "intellectual" leaders charged that Jews "killed God" and were responsible for the mass terror of the Stalinist regime.

In the 1980s, too, Japan was flooded with anti-Semitic literature charging that Jews controlled the world economy; a best seller claimed to reveal a "complex and deeply laid strategy by the Jews to stand astride the world." Fifty years before this, some members of the Japanese Foreign Ministry advanced this reason for their "Fugu Plan" to rescue Jews from the Nazis and settle them in conquered Manchuria: "We will gain the affection of the American Jews who control the press, the broadcast media, the film industry and possibly President Roosevelt himself." This was at a time when FDR was turning a deaf ear to Jewish pleas to rescue German Jews.

In today's Poland, another country with a minuscule population of Jews, the myth of Jewish media domination was embodied in the words of Jozef Cardinal Glemp, the Roman Catholic Primate: "Your power," he warned the Jews in 1989, "lies in the mass media that are easily at your disposal in many countries. Let them not serve to spread anti-Polish feeling."

The media myth was recycled in America, too. Truman Capote charged that a "Jewish Mafia in American letters" controls "much of the literary scene." Several black "leaders" expanded on this Judeophobic myth in 1990 and 1991 when they held the Jews' "domination of Hollywood" directly responsible for the lack of African American representation in the movies.

Charges that Jews dominate the media have often been voiced in the same breath with those that Jews control all the banks. This linkage characterized Nazi propaganda. In the U.S. it surfaced in a statement by Gen. George Brown, then-chairman of the Joint Chiefs of Staff: "Jews own, you know, the banks in this country, the newspapers," he told a college audience in 1974.

The bank-control myth was recycled in the ensuing decade by American extreme right-wing propagandists. Trying to use anti-Semitism as an organizing tool among midwestern family farmers who were in desperate straits, the extremists charged that the Federal Reserve and its banks were controlled by Jews plotting to drive farmers into bankruptcy and appropriate their land.

❧ It should not be surprising that so many Judeophobic myths reflect, spread, and augment the obsession with the "power" of the Jews as "an elite people, sure of itself and dominating" (De Gaulle's words in 1967). Since patriarchy is a system based on power, these myths jab the right nerve to activate or reinforce anxiety among the powerful, who fear that they may lose power, and among the powerless, who realize that they lack it. Moreover, the myths reinforce the power of the ruling class by providing the masses an easily acceptable "explanation" of their powerlessness, which they can act on by attacking the diversionary target of the Jewish people.

The refusal of most North American non-Jews to believe the reports in the wartime Jewish press of the mass murders of European Jews was rooted, in large part, in their conscious or unconscious acceptance of the myth of Jewish power.

Rather than confront their own internalization of this fantasy, they discounted the accuracy of the reports. By placing on back pages the few accounts they did publish about the mass murders, editors of daily newspapers reinforced the denial disease. (So much for the myth of Jewish control of the mass media.)

Because right-wing anti-Semitic extremists propagate the myth of Jewish power, they also need to deny that the Holocaust—the quintessential epitome of Jewish powerlessness—took place. This is a prime reason behind the revisionists' Holocaust-denial propaganda.

POGROMS AND THE POGROM MENTALITY

The function of the Judeophobic myths becomes apparent when we look at their direct connection with pogroms.

During the Crusades, which began in 1096, marauding bands of Christians were incited to murder the local Jewish "infidels" as a dress rehearsal for their future killing of Moslem "infidels" in distant Palestine. "Let us first of all take revenge ... upon the Jews whose forefathers crucified our Savior," was their cry, according to one chronicler. Thousands of Jews—ten thousand in the First Crusade alone—were put to the sword and the torch (and records of the loans some had made were burned as well); hundreds of communities were destroyed.

In the late Middle Ages in France, Germany, and Spain, local pogroms were touched off at a moment's notice by a blood or host-desecration libel against a Jewish individual or community or by the charge of well poisoning during the bubonic plague. The blood libel also triggered pogroms in Poland from the fifteenth century on. Its last *recorded* surfacing was in 1946 in Kielce, Poland, where it detonated the massacre of several dozen Holocaust survivors. The charge that Jewish radicals were undermining the state touched off the *Semana Trajica*, the "tragic week" of pogroms in Argentina in 1919.

✥ The pogrom reached its state of the art in Russia from the mid-nineteenth through the early twentieth century. The typical Czarist pogrom would begin after a local priest had given the standard "Jews killed Christ" sermon. The peasants, acting on the signal from the pulpit, would get drunk and descend on the Jewish quarter. There they hacked, pillaged, gang-raped, castrated, torched, murdered, and carried out other atrocities, such as hammering nails into Jewish heads—with the Czarist police refusing to lift a finger to stop them.

Following the paroxysm of mayhem lasting from a day or two to a week, the peasants, like typical wife-batterers, would apologize for their "excesses" and use the excuse, "We were drunk. Now it's over." Since relationships between Jews and peasants were civil before and after pogroms, where did the hatred to fuel murder come from? The answer is: It was always there—a virus that lived permanently in the body politic, one that could be easily reactivated and could flare into epidemic proportions and then subside until the next attack. This led to the bitter Jewish comment that non-Jews "imbibe anti-Semitism with their mothers' milk."

By the turn of the century, and especially after the onset of the 1905 Revolution, the Czarist government was no longer willing to rely on drunken freelance pogromists. It orchestrated a reign of terror against the Jews in hundreds of communities by organized groups such as the Black Hundreds, aiming, said the interior minister, to "choke the revolution in the blood of the Jews." Immediately after World War I in Russia and the Ukraine, over thirteen hundred pogroms—primarily carried out by soldiers in the armies of Poland and the Ukraine (under Petlura and General Denikin) and of the White Russians—left more than seventy thousand Jews dead, thousands raped, and hundreds of thousands homeless and "on the verge of madness," reported the Red Cross.

An essential feature of all pogroms is that they seemed to come out of nowhere and to run their course, however long. Historian Max Bein has observed, "Almost all periods of great violence, at least since the Middle Ages, have caught the Jews by surprise and found them unprepared. . . . The persecutions began with particular severity and intensity especially when Jews believed their position was so secure and their relationship to their environment so well-ordered that there was no thought of attacks and major violence—at least not in their country."

Centuries of pogroms engendered a Jewish pogrom mentality: "The storm will pass and everything will be back to normal"—similar to the battered woman's belief that every assault is the last one.

The Nazis used this pogrom mentality against the Jews in their implementation of the Final Solution. Massacres and deportations came in waves, stopped for a while, and then resumed. Most Jews realized too late that an *aktion* (German for mass shooting, roundup, deportation) was not a pogrom with a beginning, a middle, and an end, but one more step in the implementation of a cold-blooded plan of total annihilation.

SURVIVAL STRATEGIES

Jews developed several survival strategies over the centuries to try to mitigate the effects of their powerlessness; some were conscious and deliberate, others not. A number of these survival strategies have striking parallels to those women have used under patriarchy. So does the need Jews experience to be always acutely sensitive to the scene and able to determine which strategies are applicable, and to psych out the rulers and authorities—figure out their agenda and anticipate their next move.

One strategy was to cultivate protectors from among elements of the ruling class—unless, of course, it was undeniably hostile and murderous, as were Czarist Russia and Nazi Germany. Why look for protectors in the ruling class, which turns on the faucet of anti-Semitism? Why not seek allies among other oppressed classes or minorities? The answer is that the masses were feared because they were the ones with the axes, knives, and torches in hand. The ruling class, on the other hand, was perceived as being able to turn off the faucet of anti-Semitism should its leaders perceive this to be in their own best interests. Jews, therefore, wrote historian H. H. Ben-Sasson, "tried to find a strong protector whose hand could reach over the walls to defend them from the depredations of ... [the] mob."

The constant threat of pogroms and the recognition that civil strife would trap them in the cross fire between different groups made Jews generally tend to support a strong *central* authority.

Looking, as women have done, to powerful male protectors to keep other men from attacking them, Jews were dependent on staying in the protectors' good graces—trying to be on their good side or at least not antagonizing them.

A second and related strategy was usefulness. Jews tried to determine which of the warring factions in the ruling class was most in need of their skills and would therefore extend them a measure of protection. Since Jews really had no choice about being tracked into enabling roles or about what type of economic pursuits they could engage in, this strategy was really one of trying to figure out who should be the prime exploiter of their skills. (This is akin to a child's picking one schoolyard bully over the others and doing the bully's homework in exchange for protection from the rest.)

The usefulness strategy did not involve ideological identification with the protectors or their agendas, with some exceptions in the cultural intermediary role. The Jewish-owned liberal press of fin-de-siècle Vienna, for example, supported Emperor Franz Josef, whom Jews in Austria-Hungary regarded as their "guardian angel, custodian and patron saint."

These two strategies often triggered a vicious cycle. The more Jews were perceived to favor an element of the ruling class, the more enabling they did in the hope of gaining some protection, the more they incurred the hostility of that authority's enemies, which led them to seek its protection even more desperately.

Strategy number three was to rely on trusted Jewish individuals situated in high places, where it was hoped their economic usefulness would give them enough influence to sway the authorities to avert the "evil decree" when the ax was about to fall. This is the strategy of the "Court Jew" a.k.a. *shtadlan* (Hebrew for diplomatic advocate/pleader/interceder; pl., *shtadlanim*). The practice of *shtadlanut* (quiet, behind-the-scenes pleading) is, of course, reminiscent of the role mothers play in patriarchal families as interceders with the father on behalf of the children.

The first recorded shtadlan was Joseph, who helped his people in Egypt after his meteoric rise from prisoner to economic czar. The second was Nehemiah, cupbearer to Cyrus, the Persian king who gave the Babylonian Jews permission in 538 B.C.E. to return to Judea and rebuild the Temple. Queen Esther, whose intervention with the king saved the Jews of ancient Persia, as we shall see in chapter 5, was another of the shtadlanim in the Scriptures. In medieval Spain, Jewish viziers, financiers, and physicians to kings of the various city-states used their position to help the Jewish communities they were part of. The wealthy Jewish men appointed as "court factors" (primarily military suppliers) in seventeenth- and eighteenth-century Austria and the small German states were often turned to for help in times of stress and disaster by Jewish communities they were not part of.

Finally, there was the tried-and-true strategy of bribery (that is, protection money) Jews paid authorities to obtain permission for residence and for engaging in various economic pursuits and to avert expulsion. Bribery was also used to win the release of prisoners and captives.

The propagation of Judeophobic myths was an attempt to undermine these collective survival strategies and to block their effective implementation. Each myth constituted the negative flip side of a specific Jewish survival strategy. Once the myth became an intrinsic element of non-Jews' interpretation of Jewish behavior, when Jews were perceived as trying to employ one of the survival strategies, its flip side could be immediately invoked by anti-Semites. Floating up to consciousness, it could constitute a wall of resistance to any other interpretation of a survival strategy, including, of course, the truth.

The flip side of the strategy of seeking a powerful protector was the Judeophobic myth that Jews were themselves powerful and were involved in a conspiracy to rule the world; that of being useful, the myth that Jews were parasitic, disloyal, and dangerous (for instance, poisoners and Christ killers); that of the Court Jew attempting to influence the authorities to head off some disaster, the myth that Jews actually control the country; and that of the bribery strategy, that Jews were all rich gold-hoarders.

❧ Jews came to set great store by these survival strategies, but history has shown that in the final analysis there was nothing Jews could do once a power structure had decided to initiate or tolerate attacks against them.

The problem with looking to an element in the ruling class for protection is that it could lose power to another element; kings could lose control over their territory, as did the Polish monarchy. Trading on economic usefulness for protection is not only an unequal exchange but it is also predicated on the protectors' interests, which might change. They might, for example, wish to award the Jews' economic niche to a more useful group, or they might regard economic usefulness as less important than some political consideration. For example, Ferdinand and Isabella of Spain, after having exploited the Jews' skills to consolidate their monarchy, found them expendable and acceded to the church's demand that they be expelled in 1492.

Anticipating such eventualities and not wishing to foreclose their options, protectors do not want to be too closely identified as the Jews' patrons. And they never launch a consistent all-out attempt to eradicate the anti-Semitic virus from the body politic because they might need to reactivate it.

The classic survival strategies proved abject failures during the Holocaust. No great power was interested in protecting or rescuing the Jews, and the quisling regimes in occupied Europe turned them over to the Nazis. (The wartime Danish and Bulgarian regimes were alone in refusing to do so.) The American Jews in Roosevelt's government refused to function as Court Jews and intercede with him on behalf of their people.

In Nazi-occupied Poland, of course, there were no potential protectors to whom Jews could be useful. Still, having believed so long in the efficacy of economic usefulness, Jews found it almost impossible to conceive that the Germans would not wish to keep them alive in order to exploit their slave labor. This was the basis of some ghetto council leaders' belief in the policy of what they called "survival through work." The Germans reinforced this belief by their brutal deportations and mass shootings of "unproductive elements," such as the elderly and the very young. But the working-ghetto strategy failed during the Holocaust for the same reason that bribery on a mass scale was impossible: The Nazis were in the grip of a "glorious mission" to "cleanse" Europe of Jews, a mission that would allow nothing, not even the war effort, to stand in its way.

STAGES IN THE EXILES

Multiply the dangerous and depressing situation of one homeless person by millions over two thousand years and you have the Jewish condition of Exile: permanent homelessness. This is not to say that there were no temporary shelters or even what Zionist leader Max Nordau called "overnight hotels," some relatively palatial. Wealth and comfort, however, should not be confused with security or power. The key word was always *temporary*. It is "this inescapable state of insecurity that we have in mind when we designate the Jewish Diaspora as Exile," wrote Martin Buber.

✦ Jewish history in the different Exiles seems to operate in stages. At the beginning of stage one in a particular territory, Jews are invited or welcomed to fill a particular economic niche and/or given privileges and rights there.

In stage two, as economic and social changes throw the society into upheaval, the niche the Jews have filled is sought by a new class or ethnic group, which is often challenging the ruling class. The power structure attempts to buy it off at the expense of the Jews by awarding their niche to that group or to one they seek as an ally against that group. Sometimes Jews find another niche, generally even more marginal and less secure, usually involving their functioning as oppressor surrogate. If the rebellious class or ethnic group still poses a threat to the power structure or its allies, Jews may be used as lightning rods to absorb and deflect their hostility. Late stage two often involves pogroms.

The oppressed classes or ethnic minorities generally fall for these anti-Semitic ploys because they are either competing with Jews and wish to take over their niche (e.g., sixteenth- to seventeenth-century Poland); perceive Jews as identified with the power structure and seek to weaken it by attacking the Jews (the late nineteenth-century Austro-Hungarian Empire); are too weak to attack the enemy directly and compensate by attacking its surrogate (the High Middle Ages in parts of Western Europe); and/or simply wish to settle an old score with the Jews at this propitious juncture (a phenomenon that occurred at various points throughout Jewish history and also characterized the behavior of East Europeans under Nazi occupation in World War II). The oppressed non-Jews rationalize their co-optation by regurgitating and embellishing the Judeophobic myths.

At this point, debates often rage in Jewish communities as to what to do. Jews do not always correctly decode the handwriting on the wall, failing to see a pattern in the attacks (the pogrom mentality) and/or interpreting them as "excesses" that will end once a strong authority gets a handle on the situation or a different group of leaders comes to power. Most Jews refused to leave Germany after 1933 because they believed the Nazi regime was a temporary aberration that would blow over once Germany—"the country of Schiller, Goethe, and Beethoven"—came to its senses. The longevity and staying power of this type of interpretation is demonstrated by the fact that its first recorded appearance is in the scriptural story of the Exodus. The story, whose message is intended as a warning against the interpretation, is that the slaves did not raise their voices in protest until the pharaoh who had enslaved them had died *and the new one continued his predecessor's policy.* Only at this point did they realize that a change in rulers would not mean an end to their oppression, and they "cried out" to God.

A prime factor in Jews' decisions to leave a toxic Exile is whether they have places to immigrate to where conditions are better—*and whose doors are open.* Jews in interbellum Poland filled no economic niche and were the victims of an official economic boycott, university quotas, and pogroms. Zionist leader Vladimir (Zev) Jabotinsky warned them in 1937 to "make an end of the Exile before it makes an end of you." But where to go? The doors of every country were locked to them and, later, to all but a few thousand refugees from the Nazi genocide.

Millions of Jews could have been saved before and during the Holocaust had any country extended them political asylum, even on a temporary (wartime) basis. And Mandatory Palestine, where thousands tried to escape to in "illegal" vessels, was under the iron fist of the British, who ruthlessly sealed its doors in 1939 and blockaded the coast.

Israel's granting unequivocal no-questions-asked asylum to all Jews on the basis of "home is the place where, when you have to go there, they have to take you in," constitutes implementation of the most elemental principle of Zionism and is codified in Israel's Law of Return. Regardless of Israel's many problems, it has lived up to this basic element of the Zionist vision, as the welcoming of immigrants from the Soviet Union and the airlifting of the Ethiopian Jews in the early 1990s attest.

In stage three, Jewish communal life in a particular country comes to an end, either gradually (for instance, because of intense isolation, as in China) or precipitously—with expulsion (medieval England and France; Spain, 1492); or through exodus triggered by intensified persecution (Arab countries after 1948) or an untenable political or economic situation (Ethiopia, 1991); or through mass annihilation. The Final Solution was the most extreme example of persecution on the continuum of Exile dynamics leading to stage three.

"IS IT GOOD FOR THE JEWS?"

Because of their history, no matter how felicitous their present situation may be, Jews worry, sensing (albeit sometimes denying at the very same time) that they are on shifting sands, needing to be careful where they tread and to look behind them and watch their backs. In essence Jews have lived for centuries with a permanent case of a national variation of post-traumatic stress syndrome. It is kept under control, but it is there nonetheless, right under the surface, an integral part of Jewish psychology.

Many non-Jews and assimilationist Jews may pooh-pooh what they regard as the Jewish tendency to see an anti-Semite under every bed, just as many men dismiss/belittle the feelings of women that a potential rapist is lurking around every street corner or in every fraternity house. But Jews know that they must always be exquisitely sensitive to the political currents swirling around them—ever trying to determine if what's blowin' in the wind is a passing dust storm or a lethal tornado. They feel the need to know at every moment precisely where they stand in their relationship with the general society and its various component groups.

As a result of their experiences and memories, Jews diverge from non-Jews not only in their views on certain issues and events but also in their feelings—a phenomenon the nineteenth-century Yiddish writer I. L. Peretz called "seeing the world through Jewish eyes." It is hard for a conscious Jew, for example, to be nonchalant about outcroppings of anti-Semitism that non-Jews may genuinely believe to be the work of "harmless crackpots" (Hitler was not the first "crackpot" to take over a nation-state), to be overjoyed over German reunification, to celebrate 1492 wholeheartedly (the year of the tragic expulsion from Spain as well as the beginning of genocide against Native Americans), or to see Israel as "just another little country in trouble."

Because of their history, too, conscious Jews look at events around them and ask, "Is it good for the Jews?" This is not chauvinistic paranoia; it is the very essence of trying to get an accurate reading of reality—and thereby to survive.

The establishment of Israel has not appreciably altered the dynamics that obtain in Exile. Only a clear-eyed analysis can lead Jews who wish to continue living outside Israel to make decisions as to how to respond to these dynamics. But such an analysis requires a feminist perspective incorporating the understanding that it is patriarchy that has proved so lethal to Jews, and that it is Exile that puts them at its mercy. Calling Exile "diaspora" and prattling about its advantages while ignoring its dynamics is very dangerous.

TWO ❧ SPIRITUAL RESISTANCE, MONOTHEISM, AND MASS RESCUE FANTASIES

> *Exile is a state suspended between our lost beginning and a future which remains inscrutable.*
>
> VINTILLA HORIA

> *Jewish mythology situates the mythical birth of the people of Israel at the end of an oppression. "Remember the time when you were a slave in Egypt" is one of the most haunting refrains of our collective memory.... All Jewish history, written and oral—that is, the image Jews have forged of themselves—is constructed or reconstructed in this perspective: oppression-liberation.*
>
> ALBERT MEMMI

> *When will the Messiah come? When will we become a nation?*
>
> TRADITIONAL HAVDALAH
(POST-SABBATH CEREMONY) SONG

The only real defense Jews have had against the physical and the psychological threats to their survival in Exile under patriarchy was communal cohesion and the spiritual resistance necessary to sustain it and to shore up their psychological defenses against anxiety, hopelessness, and depression.

The condition of Exile not only put all Jews at physical risk but was also psychologically traumatic by its very nature. This was especially true of the third exile, which involved not only the dispersal of the majority of Jews throughout the Roman Empire and, later, the world, but also exiles from exiles within the larger exile. Jews often tried to settle down somewhere only to be expelled or forced to flee. The trauma of being uprooted first from Eretz Israel and then from different cities and countries never had much of a chance to wear off.

These recurring exiles gave rise to feelings of melancholy over the separation from a familiar territory and way of life and from family, friends, and support networks. One recalls here how the twelfth-century philosopher and law codifier Maimonides longed for his "Andalusian homeland" and spoke to his last days of life "back home in Andalusia"; the nostalgia for Spain that characterizes so many Sephardic folktales; and American immigrants' longings for the little shtetls of Russia. Repeated uprootings also engendered initial alienation from the new environment and difficulties in adapting to it.

Jews, wrote Maurice Samuel, are "a people which lives at the best of times in a perpetual, subdued panic." Exile caused ongoing stress arising from the inability to relax one's guard and from having to worry about what "the neighbors" will say or do or when the eviction notice or the 2:00 A.M. knock at the door will come. Even in stage one of Exile there was often free-floating anxiety that the benign would turn malignant; in stage two there was fear that the malignant would metastasize. And there were always feelings of depression arising from the sense of powerlessness, of lack of control over one's own destiny.

Spiritual resistance required the creation of national myths comprising memories of the past, interpretations of the present (an explanatory style), and visions linking both to the future. Only the hope that continuing to uphold in the bleak present a commitment to an identity and culture that had originated in a glorious past and that would lead to a bright future provided Jews the motivation and the courage to endure suffering and persecution without cracking individually or collectively.

THE JEWISH CONCEPT OF GOD

The myths the Jews created to account for the origin and continuation of the Exile and to envision its ending with their liberation involved a concept of God, of His role in Jewish history, and of the Jewish relationship with Him (and the specific use of male pronouns here is significant, as we shall see).

The story of the first exile, the centuries of slavery in Egypt, recorded hundreds of years after the Exodus in the book of the same name—the second of the Five Books (the "Torah of Moses" or "Pentateuch") of the Jewish Scriptures—has two prominent elements that persist throughout Jewish mythology. One is that there was a reason for the exile. The other element is an obsession with rescue-from-outside—and with proving worthy of/entitled to it—and with abandonment.

The reason for the exile in Egypt given in Exodus is that God had engineered it to set in motion the necessary process of the Jews' maturation into a nation. Exodus tells of the strategy employed by Moses at God's behest to effect the liberation of the Jews from slavery, the first step in this process. Moses, whom one cannot help but regard as a great revolutionary leader, makes a transitional demand of Pharaoh: Allow the Jewish slaves to hold a religious festival in the desert. When Pharaoh turns down this innocuous reformist demand, the Jews are radicalized: They understand, at last, Pharaoh's unrelenting tyranny. Then Pharaoh is brought to his knees by the Ten Plagues (the precise translation is "ten blows" or "strikes"), probably in reality acts of mass civil disobedience. The escape from Egypt thus undoubtedly involved organized mass resistance.

Nevertheless, the *Hagada* (text for the Passover seder, the ceremony where the story of the liberation is recounted every year, from the Hebrew verb "to tell") does not mention Moses by name. Rather, it repeats the rescue-from-outside myth in Exodus: It was God who "took us out of Egypt with a strong hand and an outstretched arm."

Here, as later, we see how against the power of their enemies Jews counterposed not their own temporal power—they had none in the Exile—but the power of a supernatural force. And while various nations in ancient times invented pantheons of gods, some of whom fought their battles with them, Jews, given their obsession with rescue, had only one. The God who carried out a mass rescue had to be omnipotent, all-powerful. And who could be more powerful than the God of the entire universe?

It was a foregone conclusion that the Jewish rescuer God had to be male: Given female powerlessness in a patriarchal society, how could Jews have envisioned a female God as an all-powerful rescuer?

Monotheism, aside from its ethical content, thus had its psychological roots in wish fulfillment. Jews sought to compensate for their powerlessness by envisioning an all-powerful God onto whom they projected the male role under patriarchy that the men most admired: that of wielding power to protect, defend, and rescue the community. Later, in subsequent exiles, Jewish men enlarged and expanded this projection onto God of patriarchal behavior they had once carried out themselves (when living in Eretz Israel) and/or wished they could engage in, as they perceived non-Jewish men doing. Every Shabbat, for example, they repeated in their prayers the words of Moses' song praising God for drowning the Egyptian army that was pursuing the escaping slaves: "God is a man of war."

The concept of God as rescuer was part of Jewish tradition through the ages. The first major aspect of God Jews stressed in times of danger was that He would save them from it, even if only at the eleventh hour. Whenever Jews survived a crisis, they attributed it to God's rescue.

THE CONTRACT

After the Exodus, Jews needed to be reassured that God was on their side permanently and would always rescue them if the need arose. They therefore developed the concept of a Jewish Contract (called the Covenant) with God. The Contract obviously had to precede the Egyptian exile and rescue mission, and so a backstory was created attributing it to Abraham and to Jacob. It was then fast-forwarded into the post-Exodus period with the story of its reaffirmation as the Covenant on Sinai.

The Contract with Abraham required primarily his faith and trust. One of the stories in the Five Books—obviously a folktale with such deep meaning for the people that it was finally committed to writing—was that of the *Akeydah*, the "binding of Isaac": Abraham's preparations to sacrifice on the altar the beloved son of his old age, as God had demanded. The story reflects and encapsulates the Jewish explanatory style: God is testing our faith and loyalty, as He did Abraham's, to see if we are deserving, and He will rescue us at the last minute, as He did Isaac.

Possibly because the Jews' faith and trust in God before and during the Exodus was not all that high (a consequence of enslavement), they unconsciously recognized that something more in the way of reciprocity, something more definitive/substantial than faith, was required of them after their rescue from Egypt. Jews now had to *do* something in return for rescue and protection, reflecting the value Jews have always placed on behavior (of which more in chapter 3): They had to make a commitment to a way of life that God had outlined for them *and follow through on it.*

The Scriptures relate that the Jews assembled at the foot of Mount Sinai to receive the Torah, a manual of ethical behavior and the methodology of ensuring its implementation, as the basis of the Contract. The *Midrash*—the body of interpretive legends that accreted to the Scriptures over the centuries (from the Hebrew verb "to seek"/"explore"/"investigate"; it also means "individual legend"; pl., *midrashim*)—relates that other nations had turned down the Torah when God offered it to them first because it was so difficult to live up to. This was a point in the Jews' favor, proving them worthy of/entitled to rescue and protection. Evidence that the Contract was perceived as signifying a permanent, ongoing relationship between God and the Jews comes from the midrash that all Jews of all times were assembled and accepted the Torah at Mount Sinai.

The Contract involved the values of reciprocity and mutuality: God would use His great power on behalf of the Jews and would reward them with good crops, long lives, and victories over their enemies as long as they kept up their end by behaving ethically. But if they strayed—worshiped pagan gods and engaged in "abominations" (including temple prostitution and child sacrifice), behaved unjustly in their relationships with other human beings—they would be punished.

But God, too, could be called to account for not living up to His commitment to rescue the Jews from their enemies and ultimately, from the Exile. Significantly, the name given Jacob after his struggle with the angel, "Israel"—meaning "one who wrestles with God"—is the name Jews chose for themselves as a nation (e.g., "the children/people of Israel" or sometimes simply "Israel"). Jewish folklore and literature are replete with examples of Jews arguing with and confronting God, epitomized by that of Rabbi Levi Yitzhok of Berditchev (the Berditchever Rebbe) of the eighteenth century. In his famous *Kaddish* (Hebrew for mourners' prayer reaffirming God's benevolence), he says he comes to God "in a lawsuit on behalf of Your people Israel. . . . Why do You oppress your people Israel? . . . There must be an end to this—it must stop!" Similarly, Mendel the bookseller in the 1939 Yiddish film *Fishkeh the Lame* (a.k.a. *The Light Ahead*) weeps and rails at God for His silence of thousands of years: "How long will You look and keep silent? How long will they torture us? When will there be an end?"

THE ABANDONMENT-RESCUE CYCLE

The Jewish patriarchal God was originally envisioned as stern, judgmental, strict, jealous, ready to mete out punishment as a way of teaching a lesson to His recalcitrant children: a father figure writ large. His modus operandi was not the unconditional love associated with the mother under the patriarchal system, but the conditional love expressed classically by the father, in this case, in terms of material rewards ("grass for your animals, rain in its season"). Jews recorded in the Torah the warning that if they abandoned God and the Contract with Him, God would abandon them to their enemies. They would also face His ultimate punishment, in the words of Deuteronomy: "The Lord will disperse you among the nations."

Jews interpreted the events that followed the acceptance of the Contract at Mount Sinai and their settlement in the Promised Land of Canaan through the prism of the myth of an abandonment-rescue cycle. Each story in the anthology-like Book of Judges is a variation on this theme. The cycle would begin when the Jews turned "wantonly to worship other gods and bowed down before them." God gets angry and sends or allows various Canaanite peoples to attack the Jews, who then repent. God designates judges who "rescue them from the marauding bands" (the terrorists of the day), whom He has unleashed as instruments of His punishment. Some years later, however, when "the land is quiet" again, the cycle begins anew. In essence, God's punishment is abandonment to their enemies' power, and His reward for good behavior is rescue from their enemies' power.

When the Jews try to take their destiny into their own hands by seeking to install a leader-king who will make sure Jews can defend themselves no matter how they behave, God tells Samuel, the last judge, more in sorrow than in anger: "They have not rejected you, it is I whom they have *rejected,* I whom they will not have to be their king. . . . They are now doing to you just what they have done to me since I brought them up from Egypt. They have *abandoned* me" (italics mine).

The abandonment-rescue cycle continues unabated throughout the First Temple (First Jewish Commonwealth) period (973–586 B.C.E.) in Judea (and in the breakaway northern kingdom of Israel until its destruction by the Assyrian Empire in 722 B.C.E.).

What we see here is reminiscent of the classic adolescent separation ("individuation") struggle in which the youth separates from the parents to develop an individual identity and then returns home to renegotiate the relationship on an adult-to-adult basis. (Classically it was the male adolescent who undertook this struggle to separate from his father. Females either did not fully separate from their mothers or were considered to have reached womanhood at menarche or through early marriage, but in any case were not considered "adult" under patriarchy. In modern times the separation struggle has changed considerably, as we shall see in chapters 9 and 10. In ancient times it was therefore the boy's separation struggle with the father that provided the psychological model for the nation's.)

The Jewish people, a powerless child in need of rescue by a powerful father God, becomes a rebellious teenager influenced by peers (the Canaanite peoples), whose gods are less demanding. The Jews test God's patience and love with their idol worship, much as adolescents test their parents with disobedience and rule breaking. God's punishment is to abandon them to their enemies until they come crying to Him on their hands and knees.

Thus the Books of Judges, Samuel 1 and 2, and Kings 1 and 2 convey the myth of an unsuccessful separation struggle. God — like typical Jewish parents — refuses to allow the adolescent (nation) to separate. There is no way they can renegotiate the relationship, the Contract sealed at Sinai.

But in the First Temple period, the nature of the Jews' rebellion and rule breaking now shifts primarily from the sin of worshiping other gods to that of social injustice. In this period, which is one of the emergence of classes, there arose a movement of prophets—social thinkers and activists—who castigated the rich and powerful landowners for oppressing the poor and powerless small farmers. The prophets warned that if the Jews did not "pursue justice and champion the oppressed," in Isaiah's words, the next punishment was going to be Exile.

The Jews, however, paid scant attention to the prophets' calls for repentance and behavioral reform (except for brief periods in Judea under Kings Hezekiah and Josiah) or to their astute political advice about refraining from military confrontations with superpowers such as Babylonia. In 586 B.C.E. most of the Jews of Judea were exiled to Babylonia after it conquered the country and crushed three successive and unsuccessful revolts.

The exiles now faced the most momentous decision in Jewish history. In the my-god-is-more-powerful-than-your-god olympics of the day, Jews could easily have interpreted their national defeat as a defeat of their God, abandoned Him, and chosen another who was more powerful, a then-common response to national disasters. Moreover, the Babylonian exile, after the initial trauma ("By the rivers of Babylon, we sat and wept") wore off, was rather pleasant as exiles go (stage one). Jews could easily have rationalized assimilation by faulting and then dumping a powerless god. But the will to survive as a nation precluded assimilation.

National survival, however, was felt to be predicated on rescue-from-outside. If the Jews in Babylonia gave up God, whose omnipotence made Him alone able to effect rescue, they would be relinquishing the hope of redemption as well. For who else could rescue them? Certainly not the local divinities, who were so pathetically limited in their areas of expertise and jurisdictions! Giving up God, then, would mean they were all alone, abandoned orphans, which was infinitely more psychologically threatening than believing that God was a justifiably angry father who could possibly be placated, as He had been during the abandonment-rescue cycles of the period of the Judges and the First Temple.

The revival of the mass rescue fantasy foreclosed any separation struggle by Jews from the father God for the next two and a half thousand years. Instead of separating, they opted for "returning," and, indeed, the Hebrew word for repentance, *teshuvah,* derives from the root "to return."

Jews began to advance explanations for their national tragedy: God was powerful and good, it was the Jews who had broken the Contract with Him and had gotten what was coming to them. The uniqueness of the Jewish explanation is that it was their oppressive and unethical societal behavior that had constituted their abandonment of God—and thereby caused God's (temporary) abandonment of them. What was necessary, therefore, was to repent and reform, and God would rescue them as He had the slaves from Egypt. "There is hope for your future," says the prophet Jeremiah. "The children shall return to their own borders."

The small community in Babylonia started, finally, to take the Torah seriously, seeking reassurance that their Exile would end in rescue. Cyrus's granting of permission to the Jews to return to Judea in 538 B.C.E. demonstrated that they were right in reforming their behavior to prove worthy of/entitled to God's rescue. During the Second Temple (Second Jewish Commonwealth) period (538 B.C.E.–73 C.E.), a movement of scholars—the Pharisees—began to work out a system of law (to be discussed in the next chapter) to make sure that the behavioral reform sunk in.

MESSIANISM AND MYSTICISM

The prophets wrapped the mass rescue fantasy in flesh and blood by envisioning a Messiah as God's instrumentality for carrying it out. The Messiah was portrayed as a man on horseback—or more accurately, on a white donkey—a descendant of the house of the beloved King David, who would extract Jews from the clutches of their oppressors and bring them back home from Exile.

The vision of the Messiah links the rescue of the Jews from Exile with the redemption of all humanity and with the institution of a reign of peace (Isaiah: "Nation shall not lift up sword against nation") and of just and nonhierarchical relationships between humans, among nations, between humans and animals, and among the animals as well: "The wolf shall coexist with the lamb."

By the end of the Second Temple period, the idea had taken root that the coming of the Messiah would be preceded by a period of great wretchedness and upheaval, followed by the "end of the world" as presently constituted, that is, mired in suffering and injustice. This idea of the "birth pangs of the Messiah" opened the way for generations of Jews to believe that precisely because things were so terrible in their era, it must be premessianic. This belief dovetailed with the older concept that God would rescue the Jews at the last minute of a crisis.

During the oppressive period of the Roman procurators (6–65 C.E.), various preachers predicted that the Messiah's arrival was imminent. This fevered expectation reinforced the tendency among the Zealots, who carried out the first uprising against Rome (66–73 C.E.), to engage in last-ditch fight-to-the-finish battles. In a later revolt against Rome (132–35 C.E.), Rabbi Akiva, the leading scholar of the age and the soul of the uprising, proclaimed the military leader known by the nom de guerre Bar Kochba (Son of a Star) to be the Messiah.

Belief in the Messiah continued after the end of this failed rebellion—Maimonides lists it among the thirteen cardinal principles of the Jewish faith—but the scholars tried to discourage apocalyptic messianism. It did not flare up again in a major way until linked with mysticism about a millennium later.

⤞ As the Jewish condition in Exile worsened in the High Middle Ages, especially in Europe, a mystical system called *Kabbala* (from the Hebrew verb "to receive," as in "received wisdom") arose and became the basis of a mass movement. The basic premise of the Kabbala was the old concept that the Torah is not only the law of the Jews but also "the cosmic law of the Universe," and that it embodied its mysteries and secrets, which could be fathomed, wrote Gershom Scholem, who devoted his life to the study of Jewish mysticism.

The mysticism of the thirteenth century on and especially its major work, the *Zohar* (Book of Splendor), focused on the Creation. It advanced the concept of a "primary world of the *Ein Sof*" (Hebrew for the unending, i.e., infinite) which "remains unintelligible to all but God," and another world, that of the *sefirot* (emanations). These are ten "fundamental attributes of God, and, at the same time ten stages through which the Divine life pulsates back and forth," which "enables man [*sic*] to perceive God"—the "King's faces," as it were.

The Kabbalists of the thirteenth to fifteenth centuries focused on retracing the path where the history of the universe began to evolve. But the Kabbalists who came after the catastrophic expulsion of two hundred thousand Jews from Spain in 1492 merged this trend with that of apocalyptic messianism. Their aim in "return[ing] to the starting-point of Creation" was to determine what had gone awry so it could be set right by the "releas[ing] of all the forces capable of hastening the End," of redemption, wrote Scholem. In other words, their aim was to set in motion a course correction, as it were.

Rabbi Isaac Luria of sixteenth-century Safed, known as the *Ari* (Holy Lion), was the originator of the Lurianic Kabbala, which Scholem calls the "great myth of Exile." Luria described three stages in cosmic development: *tzimtzum* (contraction), *shvirat hakeylim* (breaking of the vessels), and *tikkun* (repair). To summarize briefly at the risk of oversimplification: God "contracted" inward to make possible the creation of the universe, later sending out a ray of His light from the essence of the Ein Sof. But the vessels that were supposed to hold the light (corresponding to the highest sefirot) shattered into fragments from which evil emerged and got mixed in with the few sparks of this divine light.

The Lurianic Kabbala advanced an explanation of Exile:

> This is the secret why Israel is fated to be enslaved by all the Gentiles of the world: in order that it may uplift those sparks which have fallen among them.... And therefore it was *necessary* that Israel should be scattered to the four winds [italics mine].

When good and evil are separated and the original cosmic harmony restored, a "natural by-product" and symbol of this tikkun will be the coming of the Messiah.

THE "CHOSEN PEOPLE" COUNTERMYTH

The Kabbala, especially its Lurianic school, can be seen as an attempt to head off the possible explanation that the lack of rescue from Exile meant that God had abandoned His people, as pre-Lurianic martyrologies often lamented. To accept this would have deepened the Jews' depression and destroyed their will to survive. But neither could they accept the explanation that their suffering was deserved because of the enormity of their sins. That would have meant they were unworthy of rescue—and therefore doomed.

Hope for and expectation of rescue is often linked psychologically with the sense of entitlement (or an attempt to cultivate one), of deserving to be rescued. Jews needed to believe they were living up to the Contract with God by carrying out His laws and living ethically—including rescuing other Jews (ransoming captives was always high on Jewish communal agendas)—and that God would therefore keep His part of the Contract and rescue them. And for centuries, Jews blessed God in their daily prayers as "redeemer of captives." They could not afford to believe that they had broken the Contract.

A second major reason Jews could not accept the explanation that the magnitude of their sins was impeding rescue was that it would have meant succumbing to Christian blame-the-victim dogma, according to which Jews were meted out eternal punishment and Exile because they were intrinsically evil. To survive psychologically and emotionally their being constantly bombarded with this Judeophobic myth, Jews had to develop a countermyth: the myth that they were the Chosen People. It would not have sufficed simply to believe that they were not sinful, not inhuman, not evil. A negative myth can be offset/canceled out only by a countermyth that is its positive flip side—in this case, that Jews were better.

The Chosen People concept originally appeared in the Scriptures as part of the post-Exodus Covenant. It meant selected by God to live by the Torah's manual. But in the Exile, it expanded into what Raphael Patai calls the "Jewish self-stereotype": Jews "considered themselves the people chosen by God to observe and study the Torah, a peace-loving people, a people whose heart was filled with compassion, a people of high morality, a people of believers who loved God and whom God loved, a people unique in the world and standing high above all other nations." This self-image immunized Jews against self-hatred and the annihilation of their self-esteem and was necessary to their maintaining psychological equilibrium.

The Jewish countermyth infuriated Christian anti-Semites not only because they saw it as negating Christian chosenness ("supercessionism": the belief that they had replaced Jews as God's favorites) but precisely because it constituted a strong Jewish defense against total demoralization and the internalization of hostile negative stereotypes. The casting-off of this protective shield by assimilationist Jews (as we shall see in chapter 7) left them without a major defense against the modern Judeophobic myths that recycled the medieval ones.

Having rejected as explanations of their continued suffering the possibility that God had abandoned them permanently and that this was due to their intrinsic evil and sinfulness, the Jews' only choice was to develop the concept of God as not quite all-powerful and as therefore unable to effect rescue. The rabbis of the Talmudic era had speculated that God "shackles His omnipotence and becomes 'powerless' so that history may be possible," writes Rabbi Eliezer Berkovits. The Lurianic Kabbala expanded this ancient theme and envisioned a God whose "hands are tied," as it were, a God who, to put it bluntly, is flawed and in need of repair.

THE CONCEPT OF THE SCHECHINAH

It is worth noting at this point that if the Jewish God had been matriarchal rather that patriarchal, Jews might not have been so vulnerable to the fear of and obsession with abandonment by God. Jewish mothers have been traditionally seen by the culture as refusing to abandon their children no matter what they did, and a Jewish matriarchal God might have reflected this perception. The old idea that God could employ abandonment as a punishment and the threat of it to get Jews to shape up could have arisen only when God was seen as a father whose love was conditional upon behavior. Even the Kabbalistic concept that God could absent Himself—which arose in the European High Middle Ages, a period when Jewish husbands and fathers were often away from home for long periods of time—might have been unnecessary had God been envisioned as a traditional home-based mother who was always there, both literally and figuratively, for her children.

The Jews' deep psychological need for a loving and compassionate divine entity during this disastrous period in their history was undoubtedly the catalyst for the Kabbalists' concept of the Schechinah as the female element of God who was giving and merciful, ever-present and approachable, who never abandoned the Jewish people in the torments of their Exile. The Schechinah was a necessary maternal corrective to God Himself, who was not exactly there for the Jews, whatever the cosmic reason.

The Kabbalists built on and expanded the earlier concept of the Schechinah in the Talmud—that great compendium of Jewish legal debates and lore dating to the first few centuries C.E.—and the Midrash. The term *Schechinah* derives from the Hebrew word "to dwell," and in the Talmud, explains Patai, it means the tangible manifestation of God's presence on earth in a form capable of being perceived by the human senses.

The views of scholars quoted in the Talmud are that the Schechinah was with the Jews in the desert after the Exodus, dwelled in the Tabernacle and First Temple, and subsequently (there are differences of opinion here, typical of Talmudic speculation) dwelled in the Second Temple; rested on important synagogues in Babylonia, on every house of study, and on worthy individuals; comforted the sick, helped the needy, and aided repentant sinners.

The Schechinah eventually came to be identified with *Knesset Israel*, the entire Jewish people. Most important, the concept in the Talmud that filtered down to popular folk culture was that the Schechinah went and remained with the Jews in all their exiles and would be there with them until their redemption. The femaleness of the Schechinah (and of Knesset Israel) was implicit in the Talmud mainly because of the grammatical gender of the word.

But hundreds of years later, the Kabbala made the Schechinah explicitly female. She is usually referred to in its literature as the *Matronit* (Matron), a maternal figure who is deeply concerned with the welfare of the Jewish people. She is also identified with/as Mother Rachel, "crying for her children in Exile," Mother Zion, the Widow Jerusalem, and, later, the Shabbat bride. The Schechinah represents the Jews in both meanings of the word—as a symbol of the Jewish people and as their interceder with God (a kind of Court Jew, as it were). She thus assumes the classic female role in patriarchy, that of interceder, of ameliorator in family disputes, especially with the father.

In the Kabbala, the Schechinah/Matronit is one of the sefirot. The King, another of the sefirot, is her husband, from whom she was separated when the Temple, their "bedchamber," was destroyed. To reunite the Matronit and the King is, according to Lurianic Kabbala, the mystical function of human activity. Special prayers called *yichudim* (Hebrew for unifications) written by Kabbalists were prescribed for this purpose and incorporated into some prayer books as well as various ceremonies. Therefore, although the Schechinah functions as an interceder for the Jews, she cannot actually rescue them or bring about their liberation. It is the Jewish people who have to help reunite her with her "master," the only way a female can ultimately be rescued.

It is doubtful that the masses of Jews were aware of the complicated, esoteric, and often contradictory Kabbalistic descriptions of the relationships among the different sefirot. (Only serious scholarly men over the age of forty were supposed to study the Kabbala.) The basic idea that entered the folk culture was along these lines: The Schechinah was a female part of God who was tragically separated from Him and was thus in Exile, just as the Jews were in Exile. The Jews could help reunite God and the Schechinah, and once this tikkun was effected and the Schechinah was no longer in Exile/separated from God, the Jews would correspondingly be liberated from their Exile. Until that time, the Schechinah was with them in Exile, providing maternal consolation, warmth, and solace, and mitigating their suffering by sharing it.

The psychological importance of the Schechinah in the Jewish folk culture should not be underestimated.

MYSTICISM GIVES JEWS SPIRITUAL POWER . . .
AND GUILT

Another important factor in the acceptance of the Kabbalistic myth of Exile is that it gave Jews power in the spiritual sphere that they lacked in the temporal sphere (and that the men, living under oppressive patriarchies against which they were powerless to defend their communities, felt the absence of most acutely). The doctrine of tikkun, writes Scholem, "raised every Jew to the rank of *protagonist* in the great process of restitution. . . . The Jew . . . has it in his *power* to accelerate or to hinder this process . . . [of] the restoration of the original harmony" and thus speed up the nation's rescue (italics mine).

Every *mitzvah* (Hebrew for commanded deed/action; pl., *mitzvot*) correctly carried out by every Jew contributes to the repair of the cosmos, the objective correlative of which is the rescue of the Jews by the Messiah. Every action, large or small—from prayer with the proper *kavannah* (Hebrew for motivation/intent/feeling, from the verb "to direct/to channel") to sex with the proper kavannah—contributes to this goal. The *Zohar,* for example, indicates that "when a pious earthly couple" has sexual intercourse, they "set in motion all the generative forces of the . . . mystical universe," causing a sexual union between "the King and the Matronit." One seventeenth-century Kabbalist prescribed a three-part nightly meditation to enable the Schechinah, by dawn, to "unite with her husband *through the power which you added* to her during the night" (italics mine).

The idea that Jews had a prime role in the cosmic repair leading to their redemption formed a kind of synthesis with that of the rescue-from-outside fantasy: At the time the repair was completed, God would (be able to) send the Messiah to rescue the Jews. This Kabbalistic concept played an important role in Hassidism, the religious movement that arose in parts of Poland in the eighteenth century, giving poor, downtrodden Jews a role in cosmic repair—and thus in shaping their own ultimate destiny.

The popularized Kabbalistic idea that was incorporated into Jewish folk culture—that there is something wrong with/in the universe and that it can and should be corrected by people's actions—is a revolutionary concept. It unconsciously influenced the philosophies and ideologies of secular Jewish reformers and revolutionaries who had been raised in a Jewish environment, even though they rejected belief in God, in the Messiah, and in the Kabbalistic methodology of hastening rescue. The tales they had heard at home, in school, and in the discourses of Hassidic leaders and itinerant preachers about the efforts of Kabbalist folk heroes to "hasten the End" prepared them to accept the ideological concept that revolutionary upheaval could hasten the advent of a just society.

The myth of the Jewish role in repairing the cosmos, however, had the effect of intensifying the Jews' feeling of being, in Scholem's words, "responsible for the continuation of the Exile." If rescue had not taken place, then whatever they were doing was just not good enough. Here is a source of a lot of the free-floating guilt that is so characteristic of Jews, who "carry the weight of the world on their shoulders."

The concept of responsibility (and guilt) for their condition skirts perilously close to victim self-blame but veers off with the idea of the *collective* character of the task. The nagging sense of individual guilt for falling down on the job was mitigated by hope that some day the *cumulative* effect of the correct performance of mitzvot by all the Jews would repair the cosmos and effect rescue. As one folk-tale has it, if all Jews all over the world would observe two perfect Sabbaths, the Messiah would arrive.

In the modern period, especially in America, the sense of guilt for not doing enough was split off from its connection with a collective national assignment, which most Western Jews ceased to believe in. Transmitted during the socialization process, guilt became attached to the achievement of *individual* success. This, of course, meant that the psychological mechanism for mitigating guilt—the idea that the goal and task was a collective one—was gone. Every individual Jew was prone to feeling guilty for not living up to parental and communal expectations.

SECULARIZATION OF THE RESCUE FANTASY

The mass rescue fantasy fueled the eruption of movements of various false messiahs over the centuries, Shabbetai Zvi of the seventeenth century being the most infamous. It continued well into the nineteenth century, when many Russian Jews considered Herzl to be the Messiah.

The rescue-from-outside fantasy persisted after the onset of the so-called Enlightenment period in eighteenth-century Western Europe and of the Jewish *Haskalah* (pro-Enlightenment) movements there and in nineteenth-century Czarist Russia. But the rescuing agent shifted from God and the Messiah to specific nations and movements. Assimilationist Jews who rejected the idea of the Messiah and the concept of a return to a national homeland projected the implementation of Jewish rescue—which they called emancipation—onto nations such as France and Germany, which they perceived as liberal and cultured. This was especially obvious in the case of the *maskilim* (Hebrew for wise, cultured, enlightened, from the word for intelligence), the proponents of the Haskalah, in eighteenth-century Western Europe. "To the maskilim," commented David Biale, "the absolutist state was close to a *messianic redeemer* from the servitude of the Middle Ages" (italics mine).

In the nineteenth and twentieth centuries, many Jews looked to various radical/revolutionary movements, primarily Socialism and Communism, to rescue Jews by establishing a "classless society"—which was a secularized version of the vision of a messianic era of peace and justice—one of whose consequences would be the automatic solution of what was called The Jewish Question. "O workers' Revolution," exulted Communist writer Michael Gold in 1930, "you are the true Messiah."

The projection of the rescue-from-outside obsession onto nations and movements dovetailed with the old Jewish strategy of looking to those in power (or soon to be in power) for protection. But it also applied to the Jewish revolutionaries' attitude toward the oppressed masses, despite the fact that traditionally, it was these masses that Jews had sought protection *from*. Once these peasants and workers had formed or joined movements that were dedicated to midwifing a just society, they were unconsciously regarded by many Jewish revolutionaries as protectors and rescuers.

❧ There was a crucial difference between the classic strategy of looking to the power structure for protection and the modern fantasy of regarding liberal nations and revolutionary movements as rescuers. When Jews in ancient and medieval times sought protection from some authority, they were unencumbered with illusions of its benevolence and kept a wary and watchful eye on it—often sweetening their requests for help with hefty bribes. But when assimilationist Jews looked to Germany or France or the Soviet Union for rescue, these nations and their power structures and leaders were seen as embodiments of reason, tolerance, liberty, reformism, and/or revolution, values many Jews harbored and regarded as consonant with their own. That is why Heymann Steinthall could write in 1890 that "we can by now be good Jews only by being good Germans." Dedicating themselves to these Enlightenment values, Jewish cultural intermediaries, such as authors Stefan Zweig, Jakob Wasserman, and Emil Ludwig, transmitted them in their works.

But the Jews in Western Europe, especially Germany, were trapped in a time warp. In the nineteenth century, the Enlightenment values were in conflict with rising nationalism, and by the last two decades, wrote George Mosse, "narrow nationalism" had all but replaced them. But German Jews continued to look to these ideals of cosmopolitanism, love of humanity, reason, progress, and of *Bildung* (German for education as character formation) as their guiding light. They were blinded by gazing at this sun as it was being eclipsed and were unable to see the reality around them.

The strong nationalist movements that coalesced by the century's end assaulted whatever remained of the Enlightenment values in liberal regimes (such as Austria-Hungary), bourgeois democracies (such as France), and in the society in general (Germany). These movements encountered Jews on the front lines of defense of the Enlightenment values that they were attacking, especially in the Jews' cultural intermediary role. In separating themselves from this eighteenth-century value system, the nationalist movements attacked the Jews as its staunchest and most visible defenders. Anti-Semitic parties and movements in Germany and Austria-Hungary opened the sewer culvert to release recycled Judeophobic myths of Jewish power and malevolence. Reactionary forces in France, which also recycled such myths, framed army officer Alfred Dreyfus for treason in 1894 in an ultimately unsuccessful effort to thereby discredit the Second Republic. When he was sentenced and court-martialed, mobs in the street howled, "Death to the Jews!"

Clinging to their faith in these nations as their secular rescuers, Jews refused to lift the veil of fantasy in which they had enveloped them. Even after the Nazis came to power in 1933, most German Jews believed theirs was still a country informed by the values of Schiller and Beethoven and continued to deny that a sea-change that could cause them to drown had taken place.

During the Holocaust, Jews looked to the Allied powers for rescue. It was inconceivable, even to East European Jews who were far from assimilated, that Britain and the U.S., the "bastions of freedom and democracy," would allow mass murders to take place in the center of Europe. Jews have still not recovered from the shock of the revelations of the Allied nations' indifference to the genocide and their sabotage of rescue.

PARADOXES OF THE SECULAR CONTRACT

The projecting of the rescue fantasy onto liberal nations and revolutionary movements brought with it the old idea of a contract originally associated with the rescuer God. But while the Contract with God involved the Jews' behaving as Jews, when it was applied to the secular rescuer entities, it entailed their *not* behaving as Jews, their relinquishing cultural distinctiveness, as we shall see in chapter 7.

But even more dangerous to Jewish survival was the demand that Jews relinquish ethnic loyalty and concern with whether something was "good for the Jews" and that they think instead of whether it was "good for France/Germany/England" or "good for the movement/revolution."

Many bourgeois Jews acceded to this demand. Jewish revolutionaries did, too, some of them rationalizing their behavior as being in accordance with the movements' "universalism." Socialist Zionist theoretician Nachman Syrkin castigated the West European Jewish Socialists for whom, he said, "Socialism meant first of all the discarding of Jewishness." He continued: "Impelled by their Judaism towards the path of revolution, the Socialists in their revolutionary opposition to the class society [did not emphasize] their kinship with the most suppressed people of the world and designate their protest in the first place as specifically Jewish. . . . They robbed the protest of its Jewish character. They *suppressed* all reference to their Jewish origin and thus became merely another type of Jewish assimilationist" (italics mine).

Some Jews found it easy to close their hearts to their own people. The Polish-born German Jewish revolutionary Rosa Luxembourg, for example, rebuked a friend in a letter from prison during World War I with the words, "Why do you pester me with your Jewish sorrow? There is no room in my heart for the Jewish troubles."

But the perceived need to give up Jewish identification as a prerequisite for rescue (the euphemisms for which were emancipation or liberation) created a major paradox for most revolutionary Jews, especially those in Russia, as well as for most bourgeois assimilationist Jews. A prime reason they were enamored of and committed to various nations and movements, however much they might conceal, suppress, or deny it (even to themselves), was to effect the rescue of Jews. But engaging *directly* in activities to bring it to fruition, even publicly expressing concern about what was "good for the Jews," was precisely what they had to give up to be "true Frenchmen" or "good Germans" or "real Communists."

Because of this implicit contract, Jewish Communists and other champions of the Soviet Union, many of whom were deeply concerned over the fate of European Jews during the Holocaust, did not hold public demonstrations calling for American action to rescue them. Their priority was to campaign for a Second Front to relieve German military pressure on the Soviet Union. (Some of them believed or rationalized that this would also help save Jewish lives in Europe.)

Similarly, assimilationist American Jewish "leaders" refrained during World War II from demanding publicly that the government undertake efforts to rescue European Jews. This would have challenged the official government position that calling attention to the needs of any one persecuted group rather than emphasizing only the necessity of America's winning the war was "unpatriotic."

❧ Jews brought into the secular rescue fantasy from Kabbalist mythology the idea of the rescuer's being flawed and in need of repair. Members of a nation that could accept the idea of God's being flawed are not likely to be devastated by the hot news flash that a nation or movement is flawed, primarily by its anti-Semitism. But here they came up against the second intractable paradox: The flaw repairing they wished to carry out was very obviously in the Jews' interest of effecting their eventual rescue, but it was not seen by the nations/movements as being in *their* interests. The secular putative rescuers wished Jews to engage in the classic type of enabling—facilitating *their* agenda and withdrawing from advancing Jewish interests through flaw repairing or otherwise.

The Jewish struggle to deal with this paradox took two forms. One was to believe that the two agendas were one and the same, and that by repairing the nation's/movement's flaws they were really acting in *its* best interests, whether it recognized this or not. This is one of the reasons many Jews developed/adhered to the fantasy that the nation's/movement's values were consonant with their own, and why they attempted to promote these values, primarily as cultural intermediaries.

The second response was denial, not of the existence of the flaws but of their significance and shelf life, and thus of the need to actively engage in repairing them. Many radicals, for example, discounted the anti-Semitism in the revolutionary movements they were part of and in the Soviet Union as anachronistic holdovers or temporary aberrations. Many Jewish Communists and leftists denied the existence of anti-Semitism under Stalin—even after the 1930s purge trials (during which time Stalin himself, as well as the press, deliberately referred to Jewish opponents of the Soviet bureaucracy by their original surnames, e.g., Bronstein rather than Trotsky); the Nazi-Soviet Pact of 1939 ("Fascism is a matter of taste," said Soviet Foreign Minister Molotov); and the murder of hundreds of Soviet Yiddish writers and intellectuals, and the treason trials of Rudolf Slansky and other Jewish Communists in Czechoslovakia in the immediate post–World War II period.

PARALLELS AMONG THE POWERLESS
(JEWS AND WOMEN)

One cannot help but observe that the millennia-long Jewish faith in the coming of the Messiah, who, "though he may tarry" (Maimonides' words), would bring the Exile to an end, resonates with the female fantasy that "some day my prince will come" and inaugurate a similarly happy ending. This, in essence, is the Jewish Cinderella complex.

The Jewish terror of abandonment and the concept of a Contract with God to behave ethically in accordance with His will and instructions in return for rescue have their counterparts in women's experiences. Many women suffer from fear and anxiety about being abandoned by their protectors. They enter into marriage contracts by whose terms women are rescued from the status of being single, and thereby vulnerable to attack from other men (and to destitution), and from desertion by their husbands in return for obeying and being enablers to them.

It is no wonder, then, that Jews saw their relationship with God as a marriage, with God as the husband and Knesset Israel as the wife. This marriage concept first surfaces in the Prophets (Jeremiah: "I remember the devotion of your youth, the love of your bridal days / When you followed Me in the desert, in an unsown land").

The idea of the relationship between God and the Jews began to change from father-child to husband-wife, but the two views of the relationship ran parallel for a while. Even as some prophets were developing the new metaphor, others were using the old one of rebellious youth in criticizing Jewish behavior (Isaiah: "I have raised and elevated sons but they have sinned against Me").

The new concept of the relationship as one between husband and wife eventually triumphed. It derailed the resolution of the separation struggle because the Jewish people began to see itself not as a child who must eventually grow up and who needs to separate temporarily from the parent to do so, but as a wife who is supposed to behave obediently—to be, in essence, a permanent child. That is why Hosea and other prophets describe the Jewish nation as a disobedient wife and as a whore or adulteress. Whoring, wrote Rachel Adler, was seen as an act not only of betrayal but also of rebellion. The Jewish nation/whore is warned of the dire fate in store: God will forsake her, and she will be like a woman unprotected by a male and therefore vulnerable, a "homeless exile."

But the prophets also envision God and the Jews being reunited in the end (Hosea: "I will woo her, I will go with her into the wilderness and comfort her"). This metaphor continues in a midrash on the Book of Lamentations, which mourns the destruction of the First Temple. A wife, left behind by her king-husband (who goes on a long journey), is tormented by her neighbors' charges that he has abandoned her. When the man returns, she tells him how she found consolation by rereading their marriage contract. The midrash continues: "So the nations of the world vex the children of Israel: 'Your God . . . has abandoned you. Come! Join us. . . .'" But the Jews find consolation by reading in the Torah of God's Covenant with them and continue to hope for eventual redemption.

The husband-wife metaphor for the God-Jews relationship continues in the Talmud—Rabbi Akiva convinced the other scholars that the erotic Song of Songs was an allegory for it—and especially in the Kabbala, with its complicated separations and reunions between the King and the Schechinah/Matronit/Shabbat bride.

Although the God–Knesset Israel relationship is based on mutuality and interdependence and is, like ideal Jewish marriages, a partnership, it was obviously, like actual Jewish marriages, an unequal partnership. God had the real power—to accept or to reject, to rescue or to abandon—just as husbands did in real life. To defuse the fear of abandonment that intensified as the Exile continued, Jews had made God less powerful. The Kabbalistic concept of repairing a flawed rescuer God so He could protect/rescue them has parallels with traditional female enabling—facilitating men's work. Gathering up divine sparks and bringing the Schechinah and her "master" together through correctly performed daily mitzvot and yichudim were forms of enabling.

Just as God required the assistance of the Jews as enablers in tikkun—to become "together" enough to effect their rescue—so, too, did the men of the community need the assistance of women as enablers to help hold the group together in the interest of collective survival. And just as Jews needed to believe that God was less powerful in order to avoid feeling abandoned, so, too, did the Jewish people need to mitigate somewhat the men's total power over women so that *they* would not fear abandonment—by desertion or nonconsensual (i.e., unilateral male implementation of) divorce—and could function well as enablers, as we shall see in future chapters. The spiritual and communal processes, springing from the same root—the need to survive until the Exile was over—evolved together and reinforced each other.

❧ When Jews in the eighteenth, nineteenth, and twentieth centuries looked to various nations/movements rather than to God for rescue, they overcompensated for their concerns about the secular rescuers' flaws by idealizing and romanticizing them. They behaved, in short, like women who have experienced one or more abusive relationships and fall in love with someone new and believe that "this time it will be different." This time, Jews felt, they were dealing not with some uneducated pogrom-prone *zhlob* (Russian for crude, uncultured brute) but with an entity that was enlightened and tolerant (liberal nation) or passionate about justice (revolutionary movement). Emblematic of this blind, passionate love were the words of immigrant writer Alberto Gerchunoff in 1910 about Argentina: "It's a land where . . . the Christian won't hate us because there the sky is different and in his soul are found mercy and justice."

The love Jews felt for these societies, however, was unrequited. As Scholem wrote: "The love affair of the Jews and the Germans remained one-sided and unreciprocated. . . . The Jews . . . almost never [found] the love they were seeking." Nobody in West European society was writing paeans to the wonderful values the Jews had, to the beauty of their culture, the worth of the contributions they had made. (On the contrary, they were not supposed to bring into their "marriage" with the general society what Memmi calls their "Jewish dowry," what makes Jews culturally different and distinctive.) They were sometimes tolerated; admonished to mend their ways; made to understand they were receiving great favors in not being persecuted; told to keep their noses clean; constantly nagged to give up their dirty, silly, superstitious, unesthetic old customs; and prodded to relinquish their loyalty to their dirty, silly, etcetera, relatives, near and far.

It was not hard for Jews to deal with such verbal abuse masquerading at times as constructive criticism: They were used to Judeophobic myths. Some Jews tried to ignore them, some to counter them in their writings, others to overcome their persistence by trying harder to please. Nor were most Jews distressed by being held at a distance: After all, God, too, was distant. Not being physically battered was such a change for the better that Jews believed it reflected and derived from a real shift in attitude. They believed that, as in the traditional marriage where love is supposed to sprout after the spouses live together and get to know each other, the people of these societies would learn to love them.

Unfortunately, by the end of the nineteenth century in Western Europe, the attitude had become, "See, we gave you every chance, and now we realize that no matter what we do for you, you just don't measure up. It must be something genetic." In historical terms, racial anti-Semitism had arrived on the scene.

THE ZIONIST REVOLUTION

Zionism, which arose at this juncture, in addition to being a political movement with messianic undertones, was a revolution in Jewish history. By Trotsky's definition, revolution is the "direct interference of the masses into historic events." As a revolutionary movement, Zionism rejected the concept of intervention by God or other nations and movements to rescue the Jewish people. It postulated instead that the Jews must be their own rescuers: "auto-emancipation," Leon Pinsker called it.

Psychologically Zionism was a separation struggle from the Exile condition *and* the traditional and modern Jewish responses to it. Rejecting Exile as pernicious and anomalous, Zionists sought to liberate the Jewish people from its perpetual childhood of powerlessness and from dependence on the kindness of strangers—the support/goodwill/protection of other nations and movements—and from the unrelenting and stressful struggle to live up to their demands, to be "nice," and please them in the hope of being rewarded for good behavior.

Zionism was a struggle for an instrumentality to enable the Jewish nation to act as a national collectivity in accordance with its own needs and values, to be independent and autonomous, and to defend these rights. That instrumentality for "national adulthood" is the State of Israel. Zionism thus has parallels with feminism, which advances the idea that women as individuals have the right to be autonomous, independent adults acting in accordance with their own needs and values. The psychological impetus for both movements is the rejection of dependence on powerful protectors and of being at the mercy of individual men and various patriarchal systems.

The Zionist movement could not have arisen and succeeded were it not for the fact that for two thousand years Jews affirmed and reaffirmed in their prayers, ceremonies, and customs their emotional connection with Eretz Israel as the locus of redemption and their faith that they would return there some day. The mass rescue fantasy of messianic redemption should not be denigrated as having kept the Jews passive; rather, it should be understood as an act of collective spiritual resistance that allowed them to keep their hopes alive and their morale high during the darkest of centuries. Once Zionists detached the idea of national rescue from the concept of rescue *from outside,* they could act on Herzl's words: "If you will it, it will not remain a fantasy."

THREE ❧ EVOLUTION OF *HALACHA*, JEWISH CONSTITUTIONAL LAW

> *Even more than the Jews preserved the Shabbat, the Shabbat preserved them.*
>
> AHAD HA'AM

> *[Jews] snatched their Bible from the great conflagration of the ... Temple and dragged it about with them in exile as a portable fatherland.*
>
> HEINRICH HEINE

> *The national legislative genius would have been extinguished had the sages not occupied themselves with the living development of the law. It was to this occupation that Judaism owed ... its existence in the diaspora.*
>
> MOSES HESS

It would have been impossible for Jewish communities in often hostile Exile environments to maintain group cohesion, to sustain it with spiritual resistance, and to constitute psychologically nurturing alternatives to and havens from outside oppression without incorporating many of the values we identify today as female values.

These include a reverence for life and the paramountcy of its preservation; nonviolence; emotionalism; empathy and compassion for the unfortunate, the downtrodden, and the helpless (significantly, the Hebrew words for "compassion" and for "compassionate people" derive from the noun for "womb"); recognition of the importance of relationships; altruism; cooperation; and mutuality and interdependence. These values coalesced into the ethos expressed in the Talmudic statement, "All Jews are responsible for one another."

The incorporation of female values into Jewish behavior and communal life created a reformed Jewish patriarchy qualitatively different from the standard/classic patriarchies of other societies in recorded history.

The motivation for the reform derived from the rabbis' and scholars' recognition after the third exile began that the Jewish patriarchy had to be buttressed. Only a strengthened Jewish patriarchy could stand up against the hostile and lethal non-Jewish patriarchies of the general societies in which Jews lived as a beleaguered minority.

It was the genius of the Jewish scholars and rabbis—virtually all of them men—to understand that infusing female values into their patriarchy would strengthen it in the struggle for national survival. Recognizing that only in unity is there strength, they realized that female values such as altruism, interdependence, cooperation, and nonviolence would provide the basis of that unity. The other possible response to the national emergency of Exile—to go in the opposite direction and make Jewish patriarchy more macho to fight fire with fire—would have been dangerous and destructive and was thus counterindicated for group survival.

The female values rabbinic Judaism adopted had originated in the family, where Jewish women, like women everywhere, had developed them to help one another survive under patriarchy. These values initially appear in the vision of social justice and of ethical collective behavior in the Five Books and in the Prophets, written/edited after the exile in Egypt. Though this vision was all too often subsequently honored in the breach, the Jews' commitment to it as an ideal to live up to made it possible for the rabbinical leaders who survived the destruction of the Second Temple and Commonwealth to begin the long, arduous—and ultimately successful—educative process of making behavior based on it normative in Jewish communities.

❧ It was *Halacha,* the system and body of Jewish Law—a word deriving from the Hebrew verb "to walk" and meaning "The Path," "The Way," "The Pathway"—that was the instrumentality the rabbis developed to anchor these values in deeds: prescribed normative behavior. Halacha thus constituted the mechanism by which female values were institutionalized in Jewish communal life, thus making it possible for the communities to function as havens from outside oppression.

Halacha covers not only matters of ceremonial observance but also the practical matters of daily life. Its laws concern what Jews eat and wear, how they conduct business, organize social services, dump garbage, treat animals, raise children, mediate labor and neighbor disputes, try criminals, and contract marriages.

Halacha was the "law of the land" in the internally autonomous Jewish communities that existed throughout the third exile until dismantled in Europe by the absolutist regimes of the eighteenth century and the bourgeois and Czarist governments of the nineteenth. They continued, in modified form, in some Islamic countries into the twentieth century.

Halacha, by setting the standards of Jewish behavior to enable Jews in every community of the world to share a common tradition and to cement connections between them, to maintain group cohesiveness and to define criteria for leadership, to minimize their class struggles and resolve other interpersonal conflicts, and to reconstruct communal life when establishing themselves in new locations, was a prime factor in Jewish survival in the Exile.

The Jewish value system, Halacha, and the communal context for its implementation were the three pillars upon which traditional Jewish public life rested.

NATURE AND CHARACTER OF HALACHA

Unlike classic patriarchy, whose organizing principle is that of power, Halacha, and the Halachic system and its methodology, operate by many of the female values its shapers infused into normative Jewish behavior. Halacha's processes involve cooperation in deliberations and consensus in arriving at decisions rather than the imposition of rule by brute force or rigid fiat.

The character of Halacha can be seen from a statement in the Talmud by Rabbi Yannai: "Were the Torah given as a fixed rigid immutable code of laws, there would be no cause for holding court and passing judgment." He quotes from a tale about God's answer to Moses on what constitutes the Law: There is no fixed law, only rule by the principle of the majority. "The Law will be explained now one way, now another, according to the conception of the majority."

A living and evolving rather than a static or frozen body of law fixed forever, Halacha allowed Jews to respond to ever-changing and often stressful conditions in different exiles. Halacha's methodology is to link past laws and present realities through interpretation. The chain of law thus remains unbroken; it expands rather than becoming a choker around one's neck. This means that circumstances and the needs of the moment can be addressed by the system's legal mechanisms rather than by automatic adherence to past decisions; that explanations and reasons have to be advanced for new interpretations and modifications; that logic and reason have to be used to reach conclusions and to justify opinions; and that the decision makers need to be accountable to the Jewish people, not only those of the local community, but the nation in its entirety, past and present. For this system to work, debate is necessary, and learning and study are the keys to keeping the Law alive.

EVOLUTION OF JEWISH CONSTITUTIONAL LAW

Halacha should be seen as the Constitutional Law of the Jewish people. The rabbis, whose prime functions were to teach and to arbitrate—to render decisions in cases brought before them, whether problems or disputes—and the rabbinical courts constituted the judicial branch of the communal Jewish "governments-in-Exile," with the greatest rabbinical arbiters of any age being the equivalent of Supreme Court justices. Legislation was enacted by rabbinical arbiters and synods; academies of scholars; and local community councils composed of rabbis and *balebatim* (Hebrew for householders; sing., *ba'al bayit;* Yiddish, *balebos*), with structures varying in different eras and places. The council also constituted the executive branch.

Because arbiters had to know the entire body of legal literature and the methodology of decision making and conflict resolution, it was necessary for the community to support educational institutions that made it possible for the most brilliant Jewish men to become part of a cadre of rabbinical arbiters and for others—the balebatim who dominated the local community councils—to attain considerable knowledge.

✸ The Five Books of Moses (the Pentateuch) is the original Constitution and is called the Written Law. Just as the U.S. Constitution is constantly being reinterpreted with attention to the "original intent" of its framers, so, too, with this Jewish Constitution, as well as with all of Jewish Constitutional Law.

In the period of the Second Temple/Jewish Commonwealth and after their destruction, scholars gathered in academies such as Yavneh (established ca. 68 C.E.) to discuss and transmit interpretations of the Written Law and to make rulings on their basis—"amendments" to respond to new social and political conditions, technological advances, economic exigencies, and other changes in daily life. The "amendments" to the Written Law were gathered, written down, edited, and grouped by Rabbi Judah the Prince into the Six Orders of the *Mishnah* (from the Hebrew for "to repeat/review") in the second century C.E.

The Mishnah's rulings were the take-off point for centuries-long debates in academies in Eretz Israel and Babylonia on a wide variety of issues and problems arising in everyday life. These debates on Halacha—plus the *Agada* (folkloric material, legends, gossip), interspersed with them via free association—were collected and transcribed from students' memories (some may have kept stenographic notes as well), edited, and grouped under the relevant Six Orders of the Mishnah. This collection of Halachic debates and the Agada is known as the *Gemara* (from Aramaic for "to derive/understand one thing from another" and "to transmit"). The Mishnah and Gemara together constitute the Talmud, which is called the Oral Law. There are actually two Talmuds: the Jerusalem Talmud (finalized in the fourth century); and the more commonly studied Babylonian Talmud (ca. 500 C.E.). When traditional Jews spoke/speak of "studying Torah," they usually mean(t) the Babylonian Talmud, although the word originally referred to the Five Books (and is sometimes used to mean the Scriptures or all legal texts).

Halacha continued to evolve in Talmudic academies in Eretz Israel and in Babylonia. Until about the eleventh century, the Babylonian academies functioned as courts, legislatures, and universities combined. In later centuries and other locales, case decisions were made by a local rabbinical arbiter or *bet din* (Hebrew for law court; pl., *batei din*) or by a regional rabbinical synod. Local arbiters who found a case brought before them to be too thorny would usually dispatch a query to the leading sage of the era; his answer, called a *responsum* (pl., *responsa*), would be recorded and circulated.

The questions that rabbinical arbiters were asked to render case decisions on advanced the evolution of Halacha. This means that educated laypersons (mostly men, but occasionally women) who asked of the arbiters questions relevant to daily life were active participants in the Halachic process.

Sometimes, especially in the Talmudic era, the period when the Talmud was evolving (first to fifth centuries), various pressure groups tried to get laws enacted to favor their economic interests. Some disputes in the Second Temple era between Hillel, the "broad constructionist" who represented the common folk, and Shammai, the "strict constructionist" representing the landed aristocracy, reflect this clash of class interests. For example, Hillel argued that since bread was the poor people's staff of life, the blessing said before each meal had to be on this food (which everyone ate), not on others that only the rich could afford (as Shammai argued). The Law follows Hillel.

Halacha was always, as educator Judah Shapiro observed, "in a constant state of disputation." Conflicting opinions existed side by side in any one period, and even rulings of the greatest arbiters did not always win immediate or eventual acceptance. Gradually discussions, sometimes over centuries, resulted in a consensus that became binding and was incorporated into the body of Halacha and the various Codes of Law, the most notable of which were Maimonides' *Mishneh Torah* (1180) and Joseph Karo's *Shulchan Aruch* (Hebrew for Prepared Table) (1567).

At the same time, any of the legal methods of introducing new laws or abrogating old ones could be applied by leading rabbis. One method was the *takkanah,* a new ruling necessitated by economic or social circumstances (from the Hebrew verb "to repair"; pl., *takkanot*). Some laws were allowed to fall into disuse, others were reinterpreted out of existence. Customs that originated with the people often became part of Halacha—leading Rabbi Irving Greenberg to suggest in the 1970s that contemporary women use this approach to advance their struggle for equality in religious life.

⧫ Rabbinical arbiters needed to understand and respond to the needs of the community. Making things too difficult for a community under stress might cause it to crack under the strain; making things too easy for a community to which things already came too easy might cause cavalier neglect of observance and its eventual decline. Arbiters had to be not only jurists but also shrewd social psychologists, and the best of them were. They sometimes bent or circumvented the law, found legal loopholes, and invented legal fictions to cope with difficult situations.

It is a great tragedy that most of today's Orthodox arbiters lack the psychological insight, courage, and, sometimes, even simple humanity to apply the methodology for amending Halacha to the resolution of current problems, including the challenges posed by feminism. Today's "Torah world," wrote one critic, is disengaged from facing up to the real-life problems of Jews that sages of the past did not flinch from grappling with: "One wonders whether the poor and the weak in Israel know that the Torah was primarily a manifesto of social justice . . . [and] that ensuring safety on the roads and providing an effective health care system are also supreme commandments of the Torah."

Moreover, most of these "sages" betray the spirit of Halacha as an evolving system by treating it as a body of law frozen and rigid. (Additionally, there is no educated laity to question and challenge them, as in the past.) This situation has impeded the development of a great legal system, whose growth is stunted by the absence of the sun of open inquiry and the lack of the waters of debate. It has also caused great distress to many people living by Halacha, and to many Israelis, all of whom are subject to its "personal status" (e.g., marriage and divorce) laws because these are state laws. It has led other Jews to give up entirely on Halacha because the unresponsiveness of its current interpreters creates the mistaken impression that it is the system itself that is incapable of addressing their needs.

A question frequently heard by those who wish to reform and restore Halacha is, Why bother with a system that dates back several thousand years and does not seem responsive to today's needs? The same question is sometimes posed, with a few qualifying changes, regarding the U.S. Constitution. The answer lies not only in love of Torah but in the reality that it is Halacha which has defined for thousands of years what Jewishness is, what behavior makes a Jew a Jew. Without Halacha, the traditional Jewish values (still transmitted in family life) have no instrumentality for realization that has solid roots and continuity. And, because of the absence of an organic Jewish community, there is no *public* context for fulfilling and validating these values and no support system for living by them, consciously or unconsciously. Every individual Jew is on her or his own.

THE TALMUDIC WORKSHOP

Patterns of thought engendered by the Halachic system and methodology, and especially the Talmud, have permeated all of Jewish life and survive even in Jews who have never heard of the word *Halacha* and mistakenly believe the Talmud to be a theological work.

The great nineteenth-century historian Heinrich Graetz called the Talmud "the cohesive force that united [the] scattered members . . . of the Jewish people in all the lands of dispersion," and its "tutor." Jewish men immersed themselves in the "sea of the Talmud," as it was called, studying it full time if they could. Part-time study at set periods of time every day was the normative pattern until a few centuries ago. "Every Jew," wrote Rabbi Abraham Joshua Heschel (meaning, of course, every Jewish man), "felt himself a partner in the Torah" through studying it. "He struggled over a difficult question and, because of his kinship with the Torah, *felt entitled to an opinion.* He received the apparatus of study, consisting of various methods, and attempted to evolve a system of his own.... The result was that he became a thinker, not merely a guardian of facts" (italics mine).

⤳ The Talmud, Graetz wrote, "introduces one into the workshop of thought." Rather than state a general abstract principle that applies universally and then list exceptions to the rule, the Talmud uses logic and life experience to uncover underlying "intent"/meaning of a scriptural law, then it uses models to extrapolate categories and subcategories. For example, the Five Books forbid Jews to "labor" on Shabbat because God rested then after creating the world in six days. Interpreting forbidden "labor" as creative work, the scholars chose as its quintessential model the construction of the Tabernacle in the desert. Analyzing work carried out there, they came up with thirty-nine basic prototypes of labor, each of which spawned subcategories.

Similarly the rabbis of the Talmud came up with four prototypes of causes of injury (the ox, the pit, grazing, conflagration) and five categories of damages an assault victim could be compensated for with payment: pain, medical care, blemish or disfigurement, unemployment during convalescence, and humiliation. (Because of the inaccessibility of the Talmud and Halacha in general, most people are unaware that the rabbis substituted such fines for the scriptural "eye for an eye" type of punishment.)

After determining the rock-bottom irreducible subcategories, Talmud methodology then considers every possible irreducible specific circumstance of who, what, when, where, how, and why and applies them to the picked-apart subcategories, seeing the conflicts and the priorities and sometimes subjecting *them* to specific, irreducible "intervening variables." Thus the answer to a question of whether a certain action is allowed or forbidden is often, "It depends."

The Talmudic intellectual method, which characterizes Halacha, "endeavors to prove the validity of its conclusions beyond the shadow of a doubt... to search for incontrovertible evidence" from life experience, commented Rabbi Adin Steinsaltz. That is why the free expression of differences of opinion is so important in the Talmudic "search for truth."

Also present in the Halachic mind-set is the tendency to try to reconcile differences—to find the common denominator or missing link that reveals A and B to be two sides of a coin rather than different coins. The Midrash, too, is characterized by the attempt to reconcile contradictions between stories in the Scriptures. For example, in grappling with the two accounts of the Creation of humans—

"male and female He created them" and the Eve from Adam's rib tale—writers of different midrashim came to the conclusion that the existence of two accounts meant that there were two Eves. Gradually the "first Eve" was infused with characteristics of other myths and stories and emerged in the Middle Ages as the personage of Lilith (of whom more in chapter 5).

In the Halachic method of "searching for truth," which permeates all of Jewish life, things are never cut-and-dried, black or white; there are always many sides to any issue, many circumstances to be factored in, many variables to be carefully considered, many angles, detours, and possibilities. This is why Jews often answer a question with another question. Mark Zborowski and Elizabeth Herzog, who tried to do a retrospective anthropology of shtetl life based on interviews with one-time residents, wrote in *Life Is with People,* "The attitudes and thought habits characteristic of the learning tradition . . . [include] the tendency to examine, analyze and reanalyze, to seek for meanings behind meanings and for implications and secondary consequences."

Deliberations in business and politics in the shtetl, respondents told them, showed considerable resemblance to the discussion of a Talmudic problem in the *yeshiva,* the institution of higher Talmudic study (from the Hebrew verb "to sit"; pl., *yeshivot*). One example they cited was shtetl residents' use of deductive logic to figure out why the local Czarist official had ordered their houses to be painted. Reasoning that it was because a top government official was to visit, and that only military maneuvers would bring him to this particular border shtetl, they concluded that war was imminent.

The year was 1914.

This way of thinking makes Jews great worriers—always asking, "What does this mean? What caused it? Where will it lead?" Jewish patients are said to worry more about the "significance" of pain than about its alleviation. Halachic-type thinking also tends to make Jews (in the past, men, of course) good lawyers, doctors (especially diagnosticians), psychologists, sociologists, social and political theorists, journalists, scientists (especially theoretical physicists and mathematicians) and, when given the opportunity (for example, in Israel), military strategists. It is also a factor in Jews' succeeding as cultural intermediaries, able to pinpoint overall patterns and the way they interact; and as humorists and comedians, who are comfortable with paradox and ambivalence.

INTELLECTUAL EXPRESSION

The Halachic process reinforced the respect for words characteristic of Jews generally as the "People of the Book."

Some midrashic methodology used in the Talmud (as well as in the Kabbala, the Midrash, and various commentaries on the Five Books) to interpret scriptural passages rests on the assumption that the exact way everything was inscribed in the Five Books—including the use of specific words, repetitions, anomalous spellings, and the locations and juxtapositions of words, phrases, and sentences, that is, the relationships between them—had a divine purpose that required exploration. Some interpretations derived from the use of *gematria* (from the Greek word for geometry), a system based on the fact that each Hebrew letter has a numerical value and therefore the letters in some words add up to the same totals as others. Since this was "not accidental," reasons for these equivalencies could also be advanced.

Although the lack of accessibility of the Talmud may have been a factor in historians Walter and Ariel Durant's denigration of this particular interpretive methodology as "absurd" and "a weird exegesis," such a value judgment is unforgivable. So is the fact that the Talmud and Halacha in general have never become part of mainstream world culture.

◆ The written word means much more to Jews than the spoken word. Folklorist Dov Noy once observed that half of the Six Million might have been saved had they not put such store by the written word. They believed that a nation that had given birth to Goethe and Mann, whose works they had read, could not possibly be perpetrating mass murder. Having learned to take spoken words more seriously after the Holocaust, Israeli Jews have believed the threats by Arab leaders to "push them into the sea" or bomb them back to the Stone Age, regardless of how others dismiss such words as "Arab hyperbole."

Threatening and hostile words are taken especially seriously when they are written down and published. The importance to Jewish life of the advent of newspapers should not be underestimated, because they give spoken words the cachet of written ones. The Israelis' obsession with obtaining signed peace treaties with their Arab neighbors and with the PLO's unwillingness to abrogate the Palestinian Covenant, which calls for Israel's destruction, also derives, in part, from the Jewish belief in the power and reality of the written word.

One effect of the respect for words on Jewish behavior in political life was described by a fictional Irish police chief in a Harry Kemelman mystery: "When you argue or campaign for office, you [Jews] fight on the issues. . . . It must have been a Jew who said he'd rather be right than President." Taking words seriously, Jews often ignore the reality that political platforms are sometimes composed of planks of rotted wood and will collapse as soon as the election is over. At that point, they feel abandoned and betrayed.

There is an irreconcilable contradiction between the tendency to take words seriously and to "fight on the issues," and the opposing tendency in the Halachic mind-set of trying to find legal loopholes and convoluted ways out of a situation instead of simply cutting the Gordian knot. The latter tendency derives from the need (as perceived by rabbinical arbiters in the past) to avoid festering conflicts arising from resentment over Pyrrhic victories by one side and to prevent people's giving up on Halacha because it is too stringent and rigid (while also not conveying the feeling that anything goes). A contributing factor, of course, is the generally infelicitous Jewish experience with powerful secular authorities and the survival tactic of outwitting rather than confronting them.

✺ The Talmudic/Halachic mind-set accounts for the legitimization extended to every individual Jew's having an opinion on every issue—the classic quip is "Three Jews, four opinions"—and its right and, even more important, its *need,* to be heard. (This is probably the underlying psychological reason for Israel's adoption of the proportional representation system, which allows the opinions of political minorities to be factored into the electoral process.) Argument and controversy are consequently very important in Jewish culture. Jews learn in the bosom of the family how to persuade others with arguments based on reason and logic. This is another factor in their gravitating to the communications professions, law, and teaching. It is no wonder that Jews embraced the Enlightenment: Its emphasis on reason—and on tolerance and progress—seemed consonant with their own values.

Because Jews are used to and enjoy debate and are accustomed to being validated for expressing contrary and controversial opinions, and also because being unpopular was not an unfamiliar (and unendurable) experience during most of Jewish history, Jews, in Freud's words, have often been "prepared to be in the opposition and to renounce agreement with the majority." Countless other Jewish innovators, such as Albert Einstein and Ignatz Semmelweis, and revolutionaries such as Trotsky and Emma Goldman, were hardly traditional Jews, but they, too, had absorbed Jewish attitudes about their right—indeed, duty—to express their opinions, however unpopular.

✺ Jewish communal life, which is permeated with these attitudes, has always been disputatious. Maurice Samuel once noted that "the Jews have kept themselves alive by quarreling with one another"; as an elderly American Jewish woman explained to anthropologist Barbara Myerhoff, "We fight to keep warm." Marge Piercy, in her science fiction novel, *He, She and It,* captures this spirit in her description of the utopian Jewish town of Tikva (Hebrew for hope) and its council meetings:

> Here, politics was still a participatory rather than a spectator sport. Every last voter expected to voice her or his opinion at some length and to be courted or denounced. The right to stand up and make a speech for the guaranteed three minutes on any point was a birthright of all: the right to bore your neighbors, the right to spout utter nonsense while all around you groaned, the right to hiss and boo other speakers, to . . . pull out obscure rules and execute fancy maneuvers while everyone glared. . . . The [residents] were accustomed to deciding every detail of town policy and budget openly and at whatever length it took to reach agreement.

Jews could allow themselves the intellectual freedom to debate because it was a given that no matter how acrimonious the dispute became, or how intense the feelings it aroused, no one was likely to change their observance of the mitzvot or leave the community (which all Jews needed for their survival) or come to blows because of it. Since violence was proscribed, as we shall see in the next chapter, Jews could feel free to express differing or opposing views and know that physical mayhem would not ensue.

There were centuries-long debates in Jewish communities between many different schools of Halachic interpretation and, in the past century, proponents of opposing ideological and political views. Some debates became extremely acrimonious, with different parties sometimes excommunicating each other's followers (separation being the punishment of choice among Jews) or even betraying each other to the secular authorities. But the advantages of freedom of debate were seen as far outweighing its occasional liabilities.

The mantle of freedom of intellectual expression covered the expression of contrary opinions only as long as this occurred *inside* the community. Once such verbal expression occurred or became known outside it, where it could then engender negative reaction from non-Jews, the mantle was withdrawn. Here the powerlessness of the Exile—in which concern over non-Jewish reaction and possible reprisal is so acute—collided with and became paramount over the Jewish legitimization of debate. A prime example is the case of Spinoza, who was excommunicated by the Jewish community of seventeenth-century Amsterdam, said Shapiro, "not because Jews couldn't tolerate heresy—the *apikoras* (skeptic) always had a place in the community—but because his public denial of the divinity of the Bible was annoying the non-Jews, and Jews worried that they could come down on the community for it."

A tragic latter-day form of excommunication was practiced by Latin American Jewish communities in distancing themselves from individual Jews, such as publisher Jacobo Timerman, whom hostile dictatorships had labeled as enemies because of the views they expressed. This behavior derived primarily from terror for the safety of the entire community. Even more reprehensible was the behavior of many American Jewish organizations in distancing themselves from Jewish victims of McCarthyism, behavior that reached its nadir during the Rosenberg ordeal. Arnold Foster of the Anti-Defamation League admitted in 1988 that "Jewish defense agencies were themselves prompted more by *fear and insecurity* than principle in urging Jews to avoid allowing extreme left-wingers to use their facilities . . . to urge protests against the injustice. . . . It perhaps indicates the extent to which we were all *terrorized* by the frightening smear that Jews generally were Communists" (italics mine).

The only instance of the suppression of debate when a community has not been or seen itself under duress involves attempts by American Jewish organizations to cut off public criticism by Jews of Israel's policies. But here, again, the major factor is not the criticism itself but the fear of what non-Jewish Americans will think and do as a result of its public expression, a subject to be returned to in chapters 12 and 14.

NO AWE FOR AUTHORITY

Basic to the Halachic mind-set, and particularly to the study of Talmud, is the attitude of not accepting something as a given just become some "authority" said so. That "authority" has to submit incontrovertible proof. In the Talmud a statement by a leading rabbi is often followed with "but others say." Evocative of this attitude is the Talmudic story about the visit of a delegation of rabbis to Rabbi Yohanan, who was inconsolable over the death of Resh (Rabbi Shimon ben) Lakish. To console him, they agreed with everything he said. This had the effect of deepening his mourning over Resh Lakish, because "When I said something he'd bring up 24 questions and I'd have to give 24 answers." In shtetl life, concluded Zborowski and Herzog from recollections of their interviewees, "no matter how wise a scholar may be, his words will be weighed, examined and questioned. . . . Moreover, no authority is taken as final, for someone else may see an aspect not yet revealed."

When this mind-set comes to the fore in medical matters, it leads to Jews' tendency to question experts they seek out (a holdover from going to a religious arbiter for a definitive Halachic decision)—and to trot to another expert . . . and another. It was probably a Jew who originated the idea of a second opinion (and a third or a fourth).

This habit of mind has also reinforced skepticism toward all authority figures ("Seek no intimacy with the ruling power," advised the Mishnah) and dovetails with a healthy suspicion of their motives that is derived from experiences during centuries of persecution. The Jewish habit of questioning authority, of refusing to take some public figure's statements on faith, is another reason power structures wished to keep Jews separate from the general society. They feared that this kind of thinking might be catching. Jews also have a strong tradition of resisting authority when its actions or demands go against one's conscience. This tradition has continued in Israel, where soldiers who have refused to carry out military orders they believed to be unethical have been ultimately vindicated by the courts.

Because of their lack of awe for authorities, Jews tend not to be easily led: They need to know the reason for some policy, law, action; they demand accountability and uphold their right of dissent. Chaim Weizmann, the first president of Israel, once told a visiting head of state that while the latter was president of millions of people, *he* was the "president of two million presidents."

This critical faculty, however, seems to fade appreciably when the authority figure is perceived as a (potential) rescuer. This happened with false messiahs in Jewish history and when a liberal nation or its ruler or a revolutionary movement or its leadership was perceived as a (secular) rescuer. Part of the reason in the latter case is that Jews fell in love with secular rescuer nations/movements, and love, as we well know, is blind. Since the uncritical attitude conflicts with the traditional one of mistrust and suspicion of secular authorities, assimilationist Jews often repress the suspicion and overcompensate with exaggerated trust and adulation.

This dynamic has often involved Jews' believing that the secular nations/movements or their authority figures share their values. This belief/illusion was a central factor in American Jews' adulation of Roosevelt—whom they mistakenly believed was a reformer at heart who initiated the New Deal because he cared about alleviating the misery of the poor rather than about resuscitating capitalism—even when he was disregarding their pleas to rescue European Jews. However, once a secular authority is either divested of the mantle of rescuer or shown not to share Jewish values, the critical faculty can reemerge. This was the strategy young Jewish leftists and the Jewish Defense League used in demythologizing FDR during the 1960s.

THE RELEVANCE OF RELATIONSHIPS

Underlying the entire system of Jewish law, as it was originated by the social thinkers who wrote and edited the Scriptures and by the prophets, and developed by the rabbis over the centuries, is the concept that what makes a Jew a Jew is behavior in his or her relationships—with family members, neighbors, and co-workers, with the community, and, ultimately, with the entire Jewish nation, with history, and with God.

A Jew's relationship with God is rooted in one's *behaving* as a Jew rather than in faith or quests for personal salvation. This behavior is expressed through the mitzvot Jews are required to carry out, each of which is a building block in the relationship. Because the route to God is through mitzvot, most of which involve other people and/or their cooperation, Jews have tended to live close to one another rather than to retreat into the wilderness to commune with God. This attitude is perhaps best illustrated in the famous story by Peretz, "If Not Higher," where the secret place a rabbi occasionally disappears to is discovered by a skeptic to be not the heavens (as a fervent follower boasts) but "even higher"—the hut of a poor disabled woman he chops wood for.

Remove God from Judaism and you still have a system of values, principles, laws, and customs, and a methodology for keeping it responsive to current conditions. "If only they had abandoned Me and kept My Torah," says a Talmudic sage in a comment on a passage in Jeremiah. In a famous Talmudic tale about a dispute over a point of law between two rabbis, one invokes heaven, and a heavenly voice takes his side. His opponent then addresses God: "The Torah has already been given at Mount Sinai. . . . We pay no heed to any heavenly voice because . . . You wrote in the Torah, 'One must incline after the majority.'" At that point God smiled and exulted, "My children have bested Me, My children have bested Me!"

Judaism, in being a this-worldly religious philosophy concerned primarily with social behavior—how individuals should act in their relationships to contribute to society and ensure that it will be good for all its members—is closer in some ways to Oriental religious traditions, especially those of the Chinese, rather than to West European or Mediterranean ones. It is significant to note in this regard the similarity of the Hebrew word *Halacha* and the Chinese word *Tao*, both of which mean "The Path" or "The Way." Even the Buddhist *zazen* ("just sit," its form of intense meditation) brings to mind the Hebrew word *yeshiva* and its derivation from a verb meaning the same thing. It is no wonder, then, that both the Chinese and the Jewish traditions show such great respect for learning and for teachers of advanced texts, and that scholars of both nations played such an important role in public administration. These parallels constituted a major reason why Jews felt at home in prerevolution China and why many young American Jews from the 1970s on have been attracted to some of the Oriental religions.

THE PRIME DIRECTIVE

The principle of *Pikuach Nefesh,* saving and preserving life (rescue), is the Prime Directive in Judaism. The Talmud subordinated to it every law but three—those forbidding murder, incest and other forbidden sexual relationships, and idolatry. "Whoever saves one life, it is as if he [*sic*] saved an entire world" is the way the Talmud sums this up. A Jew can—*and must*—violate the Shabbat or even Yom Kippur (the Day of Atonement), the holiest of holy days, to save a life, and the rabbinic interpretations of what constitutes Pikuach Nefesh are rather permissive. The importance attached to Pikuach Nefesh can be seen from the midrash about how the beloved King David did not dip into the special Temple building fund to buy grain to feed his people during a three-year famine. When he gets ready to start building the Temple, God tells him: "You refrained from *rescuing* human beings from death to save your money for the Temple. The Temple is not to be built by you" (italics mine).

Adhering to the concept of Pikuah Nefesh, Jews regard suffering and pain as the enemy, to be avoided, overcome, or eliminated whenever possible, rather than as ennobling, as in the Catholic view. It is no wonder that Jews misunderstood the intent of the statement by John Cardinal O'Connor, "It may be that the Holocaust is an inordinate gift that Judaism and the Jews have given to the world," and were shocked and appalled by it.

"Sickness," noted Rabbi Eugene Borowitz, "must be defeated.... Every new therapy ... quickly attracts a disproportionate number of Jews seeking life." Jewish doctors are known to go to extreme lengths to reduce or eliminate pain and disease, and they are perceived as never giving up even in the face of implacable opposition (e.g., Semmelweis in his battle against childbed fever; Paul Ehrlich, who won the Nobel Prize for Medicine for his discovery of a syphilis cure; neurologist Oliver Sachs, who pioneered in aiding victims of Parkinson's disease).

The view that suffering must be relieved was one reason rabbis allowed contraception in many cases, for example, when the woman had endured previous painful childbirths. Abortions were permitted by most rabbinical authorities when the woman was suffering during pregnancy or would experience physical or psychological pain after the birth. There was no question that if the woman's life was in danger, abortion was not only permitted, it was required. It was on these grounds that rabbis in the Kovno Ghetto, where pregnancy was forbidden by the Germans on pain of death, permitted women to have abortions.

⇥ The paramountcy of preserving individual life and the commitment to group survival have led Jews to place a high value on food. The children have always gotten the best food. On the early kibbutzim (Hebrew plural for collective settlements in twentieth-century Eretz Israel), pioneers who managed to get by on stale pita bread and the occasional olive fervently believed they were building a new society, relinquishing all the values and customs that originated in the Exile, but they fed the youngsters well.

Of course, there are other factors behind Jews' attitudes toward food, attitudes that prompt them to provide mountains of it at weddings and Bar/Bat Mitzvahs, snacks at two-hour intervals on cruises, coffee and tea with fruit and cookies at meetings of Israeli government leaders and bureaucrats, and dinner at fund-raising affairs, and to feed guests practically as they walk into the house. Artie Shaw's quip about pre-modern Jewish life, "What else was there to do in the ghetto but eat?" although mistaken, points to the connection between food and resisting oppression. Eating served to keep up their strength and to replace energy lost when they "ate their hearts out" and to counter stress and anxiety. Through feeding, Jews symbolically gave themselves and each other the love, nurturing, and caring they needed to offset/counteract outside hostility.

⇥ The corollary to saving life is that inflicting suffering and causing death is anathema. This is not to say that Judaism is pacifist: The Sixth Commandment is not "Do not kill," as it is usually mistranslated, but "do not *murder.*" As in so many other cases, the context is the determining factor. Self-defense is one such context: "If someone comes to kill you, kill him first," the Talmud advises. Waging war also depends on context—which requires defining (and debating) whether the war is a just one (in self-defense) or an unjust one. This is why Jewish draftees had a hard time getting conscientious objector status, which was granted in the U.S. to those whose religions were across-the-board pacifist, which Judaism is not.

While capital punishment was mandated in the Five Books for certain crimes, such as murder, the stringent Halachic requirements for proof introduced by the rabbis made it rare. In a murder case, for example, written testimony, confessions, and circumstantial evidence were not acceptable as proof. The court accepted only oral substantiation by two disinterested adult witnesses after the alleged perpetrator had been warned that what he was about to do was a crime and had accepted responsibility for it. No wonder a Sanhedrin (highest judicial body in the Talmudic era) that executed one person in seven years was called a *Sanhedrin katlanit* (pernicious/bloodthirsty court).

It is partly because of the emphasis on life and its preservation that crimes against property—which can be replaced, while life cannot—are not punishable with death in the Five Books. The Talmud did not even impose a prison term for theft. (The guilty party had to return the stolen object and pay a fine or work off both.) Another factor in the attitude toward property, reflected in the Hebrew language's lack of the verb "to have," was the experience of Exile. Jews could not afford to get too emotionally attached to property, especially the immovable kind, which they could so easily be deprived of. They generally chose to keep their assets liquid, in coins and jewelry. This survival tactic made it easier for non-Jews to believe the myth that Jews "hoard gold" for nefarious conspiratorial purposes.

CONTEXTS AND BOUNDARIES

The rabbis' methodology for prescribing and ensuring correct behavior was to define its appropriate context and surround it with boundaries. To understand this methodology, we need to look first at the tendency in the Five Books and the Halacha to group matter and time into unambiguous categories and then to protect their authenticity, uniqueness, and specificity with boundaries and to define the relationships between the categories.

A prime example involves *kashrut,* Jewish dietary law (from the Hebrew word *kosher,* which literally means "prepared and ready"). Food that Halacha defines as kosher must not only derive from permitted categories (certain "clean" types of animals, for example) but must also be prepared correctly: animals slaughtered and their flesh cooked in accordance with specific laws. Some categories of food (e.g., meat and dairy) may not be eaten at the same time.

Jean Soler argues that kashrut, as well as the Creation myth, are "based upon a taxonomy in which man [*sic*], God, the animals and the plants are strictly defined *through their relationships* with one another." Animals considered "clean" (and thus edible) must conform unambiguously to the original plan of Creation whereby "the waters bring forth swarms of living creatures, . . . birds fly above the earth, . . . the earth bring[s] forth living creatures *according to their kinds*" (italics mine). Each animal, he continues, "is thus tied to the one element it issued from and must live there and have the organ of locomotion appropriate to that environment" to be considered kosher: fins for the fish, legs for mammals, wings for birds. Water creatures with legs (crustaceans) appropriate for land locomotion, birds without wings to fly in the air (ostriches) or who spend most of their lives in water (waterfowl) are therefore "unclean." Uncleanness, then, "is simply disorder." And, indeed, the opposite of kosher is *treif,* a word deriving from the same Hebrew root as those for disordered, deranged, and torn apart.

In addition, Judaism forbids humans to violate the order of Creation according to which each species has authenticity and integrity—whether by mating animals of different species to produce hybrids, sowing fields with two kinds of seeds together, or wearing cloth woven of two different kinds of material. Explaining the Halachic ban on intermingling seeds and on grafting, Rabbi Saul Berman said Judaism places "limits on the rights of humans to interfere with what Nature ordered." This ethos should be a factor in the Jewish attitude regarding gene-splicing and genetic engineering as well as environmental conservation generally.

✤ The tendency to put things in unambiguous categories and place boundaries around them applies even more obviously in the realm of time. Shabbat is differentiated from the six workdays of the week by the proscription of creative labor—that which interferes with the environment—and the prescription of specific joyful activities, such as singing Sabbath songs after the Friday evening meal. This makes Shabbat a "sanctuary in time" (Heschel's words)—psychologically necessary because Jews lacked a haven-in-space, a land where they were free.

Shabbat was experienced as a foretaste of the messianic era of liberation. Significantly, this preview was democratic and nonhierarchical: Spiritual replenishment and rest were mandated for all, including servants and animals who labored for Jews. Shabbat was/is a utopia in time rather than in space, a world of the future toward which Jewish life is progressing, however slowly. For one day a week, Jews dwell in this mental haven-of-the-future.

To further differentiate Shabbat from the workweek, it was surrounded by the ceremonial boundaries of *Kabbalat* (welcoming of the) Shabbat at its beginning and the rite of Havdalah (which literally means "separation") at its conclusion. The boundaries around this mental haven-of-the-future provided Jews an experience of closure that they needed in the open-ended limbo of Exile. If Shabbat had a beginning, a middle, and an end, if this closure were possible in the microcosm of the week, so, too, would it be possible in the macrocosm of history, however far away in the future that "End" might be.

The Midrash, too, is characterized by the tendency to seek closure. The folk-mind (as Noy calls it) and the scholars who committed the tales to writing were uncomfortable with the loose ends of stories in the Scriptures, particularly in the Five Books. They sought to put a definitive end to an "unfinished" story so that cause and effect are manifest; to link up different characters so that important figures have relationships with each other; and to fill in the gaps between different stories so they form one long narrative—just like Jewish history did, with its many chapters, and with a beginning, a middle, and a longed-for "End."

❧ The surrounding of behavior with boundaries has its roots in the Jewish view of human nature. This view is that people have both a *yetzer hatov* (drives that lead to good behavior) and a *yetzer hara* (the aggressive and libidinal drives that can lead to bad behavior, usually simplistically and wrongly translated as "the evil instinct") and can choose one or the other to guide their actions.

The rabbis, wise psychologists that they were, did not seek to eliminate the libidinal and aggressive drives; they regarded them as necessary. As the Midrash states: "Were it not for yetzer hara, no man [*sic*] would build a house, take a wife, father a child, or engage in business." Instead they sought to define the proper context within whose boundaries the drives could be harnessed for good behavior and then to create laws and customs to channel the drives into those contexts. Boundaries were drawn to separate the proper from the improper context; this is embodied in the Hebrew word for sin, *aveyrah,* which derives from the verb "to cross over." Additional boundaries ("fences") were placed outside the real boundaries to prevent accidental crossings of the latter.

Aggression, as we shall see in the next chapter, was channeled into the altruistic pursuit of learning and was not allowed to be expressed in violence. Sex was judged as good or bad depending in large part on the context in which it took place. As Rabbi Jacob Emden, a leading eighteenth-century religious arbiter, wrote: "There is nothing better than sex *in its proper circumstances.* . . . In the wrong circumstances, there is nothing worse" (italics mine). The proper context for sexual expression was defined as the legal marital relationship, which was surrounded with boundaries of time and place and infused with norms of ethical behavior. The Talmud records two sages as arriving in a new town and each asking, "Who wants to be my wife for the night?" It was acceptable for a married man to have a sexual relationship with an unmarried woman at a time when polygamy was permissible, but he had to marry her first, even if just for one night.

A male-female sexual relationship had to have an official beginning: the marriage ceremony, with all its documents (the obsession with getting things in writing) acting as a boundary/demarcation line to prevent the partners' straying into forbidden territory, that is, illicit sexual relationships. It is for this reason that the text for this ceremony includes a clause about the outlawing of incestuous relationships. If the marriage broke up and the couple separated, there had to be a divorce ceremony or, at the irreducible minimum, a *get* (Hebrew for divorce document) given by the soon-to-be ex-husband to the soon-to-be ex-wife. The get, which also reflects the Jewish obsession with getting things in writing, serves as the demarcation line of that (ended) marriage and provides the experience of closure.

❧ Another area where boundaries were placed on human drives relates to the pursuit of material possessions. The sages who shaped Judaism saw nothing intrinsically wrong with this pursuit, and they frowned on asceticism. One story tells of how they condemned a rich man for living on bread crusts: "If that's what *he* lives on, and he's rich, what does he expect the poor to live on?" Their concern that this pursuit be conducted within the context of ethical behavior toward others led the rabbis to set boundaries beyond which the rich could not venture when accumulating wealth—for instance, by engaging in behavior such as fraud, cheating, rent gouging, exploiting laborers—and even in ostentation, which is something Jews who throw today's lavish affairs might ponder on. (They might also reincorporate the traditional Jewish feature of inviting the poor of the community to the feast.) The rabbis tried to impose price controls, limit profit on basic commodities, and regulate employer-employee relations. Many laws protected laborers' interests: They could, for example, demand immediate payment of wages for a day's work. (Given current interest in alternative dispute-resolution, it would be very useful to set up a model bet din using Halacha in cases involving business relationships, labor and tenant-landlord disputes, and similar civil conflicts.)

The central principle of Jewish economic philosophy, wrote Meir Tamari, is that all wealth belongs to God, who gives it *temporarily* to humans on the "basis of stewardship." Since Judaism is a communally rather than individually oriented religious system, this means that the group at all levels—local, national, and international—is theoretically/ideally a partner in each individual's riches. This is another reason many Jews perceived the principles of revolutionary movements that sought to end private property and to redistribute wealth as being consonant with their own values.

This principle also informs the concept of *tzedakah,* which is rather anemically translated as "charity" but means something quite different. Deriving from the Hebrew word for "justice," it embodies the obligation of each individual—and the community as a whole—to carry out justice by the mitzvah of helping those in need. The emphasis on tzedakah and the experience of Jews in carrying it out was a factor in many twentieth-century Jews' taking up social work as a profession.

Tzedakah institutionalized the female values of compassion, altruism, and interdependence. In most places and eras, tzedakah operated on the principle of preserving the dignity of the poor and was often dispensed anonymously. In early twentieth-century Persia, for example, community heads would make discreet inquiries before major holidays as to who was in need of help, and they would leave bundles of food and clothes on those families' doorsteps before dawn. The preservation of the dignity of the poor was also expressed in burial customs. The practice of closed coffins at all Jewish funerals originated in the wish not to embarrass the poor, whose bodies would be thin and gaunt.

Tzedakah embodies the implication of the *entitlement* of the needy to assistance from wealthy individuals (and from the community). That is why there is a whole body of Jewish jokes about the chutzpah (Hebrew/Yiddish for unmitigated gall) of *schnorrers,* savvy types who regard handouts as their right. (Schnorrer to rich man who explains that the cutback in his regular weekly handout is due to business reverses: "You had a bad week, so *I* should suffer?!")

"LUSTING IN YOUR HEART" DOESN'T REALLY COUNT

The emphasis on behavior and on channeling human drives into contexts where ethical guidelines must obtain and be expressed through mitzvot led to the attitude that "it is the deed and not the thought that counts." Repentance means nothing unless it is followed by a change in behavior; that is why the word for it is *teshuvah,* which means "to return" (to the right path). Concern about some social problem means little unless it is a jump start to action; this principle, plus the Jews' long history of abandonment by putative protectors, has engendered in them a visceral feeling of repugnance toward bystanders. During the long agony of Bosnia the Jews were the only ethnic group in America that actively called for U.S. intervention to end the genocide.

Similarly, while it is better to perform a mitzvah with the proper kavannah, it is better to do it without any rather than do nothing while waiting around for inspiration. The rabbis firmly expected that "out of doing it not for its own sake, you will come around to doing it *for* its own sake," and even if you do it without the right motive or kavannah, it doesn't matter extremely much. When Maimonides encouraged giving tzedakah even with a surly attitude (the lowest rung on his eight-rung "Ladder of Tzedakah"), he conveyed this view. The concept that the performance of a mitzvah should be valued regardless of its motivation is one reason why critiques of present-day Jewish fund-raising—that it is done primarily to enhance the contributor's status—are largely greeted with a shrug ("So what else is new?").

Since Judaism, as shaped by the rabbis and scholars, has never been particularly interested in thought control, but, rather, in behavior control, individual Jews are not held accountable for their thoughts, however vile they may be, unless they act on them. The ethical irrelevance of unconsummated thoughts and emotions accounts for the Jewish lack of guilt about stray feelings of illicit lust or violence. The typical Jewish response to then-presidential candidate Jimmy Carter's confession of sin—that "I lusted in my heart"—was, again, "So what else is new?" And since Jewish communities, by methods to be discussed in detail in the next chapter, had virtually eliminated violence from normative behavior, it was not necessary for Jews to agonize over whether the subterranean existence of fantasies of violence in the nether regions of people's psyches would inevitably lead to *acts* of mayhem.

❧ The lack of interest by the religious leaders who shaped Jewish Law in the control of thoughts and feelings had a liberating effect on thinking and on feeling.

This dovetailed with and reinforced the validation accorded to the verbal expression of thoughts, ideas, and opinions, and with the incorporated female value of emotionalism. The open and public *verbal* expression of feelings—including those of anxiety, worry, and complaint—was given legitimacy in Jewish life.

This also accounts for the Jewish passion for cultural expression. The Austrian Jewish author Stefan Zweig once pointed out how the Jewish bourgeoisie of fin de siècle Vienna were the real supporters of Viennese culture, and this behavior has characterized many other Jewish communities in the West. Even in the long, dark night of the Holocaust, Jews incarcerated in Polish ghettos organized and attended plays, concerts, and lectures.

The absence of fear of the free expression of thought allowed the writers of midrashim to indulge in all kinds of imaginative and fanciful interpretations of and legends about scriptural characters and events, some contradicting others. (Here the relationship of the scriptural stories to the Midrash, including the Agada, is something like that of the original Star Trek series to the subsequent novels and fanzines.) By giving free rein to the imagination in this kind of interpretation of scriptural stories, the writers of midrashim allowed it—and the transmuted elements from other folk traditions—to be channeled *into* Jewish folklore, where insights from contemporary life enhanced interpretation.

Finally, Freud may have felt free to explore the monsters of the unconscious mind because of the lack of anxiety that delving into and acknowledging feelings would inevitably cause evil behavior. Add to this, of course, the Jewish love of learning for its own sake, the "search for truth" of the Talmud and the intellectual freedom inherent in the debates on Halacha and in the scriptural and Talmudic commentaries, the curiosity of the Midrash and its tendency to try to reconcile contradictions and trace the beginnings and ends of stories, the commitment to life in the here and now, the emphasis on relationships, the positive attitude toward emotionalism, the wish to understand and thereby eliminate suffering, violence, and persecution—and you have all the necessary ingredients for the creation and practice of psychoanalysis and its derivative therapies.

And countless Jewish patients.

THE FIVE BOOKS AS AN INSTRUCTION MANUAL

The Torah, the Written Law, is regarded in Judaism as a kind of blueprint or instruction manual, provided by God, as to how individuals should "choose life"—life-enhancing and life-preserving *behavior*—to create a good society, by which is meant one that is just.

The Five Books—particularly their social legislation and the stories of the Exodus and the wandering in the desert—embody the powerfully radical ideas that oppression is not part of the natural order of things, that people are entitled to make a good life for themselves, and that the way to do this is to establish a social structure based on ethical relationships. The Jewish passion for justice and the mandate in the Jewish ethos to pursue it have propelled individual Jews into the forefront of modern movements, revolutionary as well as reformist, to change social conditions and into human rights struggles in various countries.

There was a seeming contradiction in Jewish life for close to two thousand years between this idea of the establishment of a just society and the fantasy of rescue-from-outside by God and His Messiah. Jewish communities of the Exile did organize themselves to live by the female values of altruism, mutuality, cooperation, and nonviolence. But a powerless minority, marginal and often persecuted, could not by itself change the overall conditions under which it lived to "create justice in the midst of injustice," in Simone de Beauvoir's words. National rescue, to get Jews *out* of an oppressive situation where they were powerless to create a just society, was the prerequisite, as it was in the Egyptian "house of bondage."

THE PROPHET MOTIVE

The Five Books include the vision of an economically (though not sexually) egalitarian society, where, in the words of Peretz, "every man [sic] is to do his own work and have his share of the soil, which is to be divided equally among all"—a kind of Jeffersonian agrarian democracy, of each "man [sic] under his own vine and fig tree."

The Five Books, which drew on and included oral and written material from different periods, were edited during the First Temple era. It was during this time that the original vision of the continuation of the classless society that had prevailed in the desert was derailed by a new reality: the emergence of an economic system with classes—a ruling class of rich landowners with large estates created from family farms; a middle class of merchants; and a lower class of poor artisans and day laborers and increasingly beleaguered small farmers. There was also a caste of government bureaucrats and tax collectors.

The writers/editors of the Five Books included in these texts the original vision *and* later material showing the methodology they created in the face of the detour from it. This methodology was reformist: to mitigate the worst abuses of class society by placing boundaries on the behavior, particularly the use of power, of the rich and by instituting mini-course corrections such as the Sabbatical and Jubilee Years, when debts, land sales, and indentured servitude were canceled. Underlying the radical reforms was the concept that the entire community is the final arbiter of the uses of power and wealth and that all are accountable to it— and ultimately to God.

The writers and editors of the Five Books stressed that society as a whole had a responsibility to ensure that the unprotected, the helpless, defenseless poor—a population that would not have existed had the original egalitarian vision been implemented—would not be ground into the dust by the rich, the powerful, and the dominant.

The prophets, whose words also date to this period, did not seek to have the emerging ruling class overthrown. Instead they castigated the rich oppressors and, like the utopian Socialists, called on them to repent: to change their behavior toward members of the oppressed classes. The prophets did not hesitate to hold powerful people—even kings—accountable for their misdeeds.

Women gained some benefit from the emerging ethos that justice demanded that the "defenseless" be treated fairly, but the fair-treatment laws applied mainly to widows and to orphans (of both genders), who had no man to protect them. Since there was no original vision in the Five Books to institute *gender* equality—and therefore no detour from it that required radical reformism—there was no passion to institute justice for all women until the rise of Jewish feminism more than three thousand years later.

METHODS OF MOSAIC PERSUASION

While retaining the original vision of a just and egalitarian society, the rabbis who developed the Halacha from its scriptural roots did not actively try to implement it by the revolutionary methods of organizing the redistribution of wealth or overthrowing the system.

Instead they adhered to the Talmudic injunction, "Do not impose a decree on the community which the majority will not be able to tolerate." They did not, for example, outlaw certain popular social practices that were distinctly contrary to the spirit of the original vision, including slavery, polygamy, and (in the opinion of some) meat eating. Banning these, they realized, would have driven such behavior underground, triggered resentment and confrontations, and caused people to start breaking other laws as well.

The rabbis worked out a reformist methodology to bring people closer to the ideal. This was to "whittle away" at behavior they regarded as socially unbeneficial, to fence it in with all kinds of restrictions so that the area in which it could be practiced became so constricted that it left little room for people to maneuver. Meanwhile they subjected the attitudes underpinning this behavior to the water-on-the-stone type of propaganda, mainly involving praise of an alternative model. When the area where the behavior could be practiced became almost unbearably restricted, the rabbis could point to the alternative, which now appeared to be the line of least resistance.

The tendency toward pragmatic reformism dovetailed with and reinforced the traditional Jewish approach, which became so central to Kabbala, of repairing the world rather than destroying everything and starting again from ground zero. The resistance to the latter approach is embodied in the folktales included in the Five Books about the evil human behavior that followed both the Flood and the destruction of Sodom and Gomorrah. The message in these stories is that the obliteration of an evil society does not necessarily mean that the one that rises from its ashes will be any better. Drawing on this folk wisdom, the rabbis employed an evolutionary approach: "creeping reformism," a several-pronged chipping-away from different angles rather than a frontal attack.

Education was a key factor in the process of advocating behavioral change, incorporating various legal reforms to encourage it, and winning the voluntary compliance of the people. The success of this approach reinforced the belief among modern Jews that education to instill the values that their communities had lived by would help make the world a better place. This belief was another factor in modern Jews' gravitating toward the teaching profession.

PROTO-DEMOCRATIC ASPECTS OF TRADITIONAL COMMUNITIES

The communities (*kehillot*) of the past were run by local councils, which levied and collected taxes for funds to provide assistance to the poor; dowries for indigent brides, ransom for captives; operating expenses for hospitals, cemeteries, and lodgings for wayfarers. They administered all these social services, supported the law courts for conflict resolution, and meted out punishment to offenders.

Depending on the place and era, patterns varied as to the way the council's leaders were chosen and how they interfaced with the religious arbiters. In the classical period (900–1200 C.E.) under Islamic rule, the small size of the communities, centered around synagogues, "made it possible for everyone" (i.e., all the men) "to take part in the deliberations and often in the decisions," according to historian S. D. Goitein. In some communities in medieval Spain until 1391 (when the period of pogroms began), "even the majority [had] no right to do anything unless they consult[ed] all the people and obtained their consent," and a synod passed a takkanah in other countries along these lines. In most of medieval Western Europe by the High Middle Ages, each community had a "Council of Upright Men," which Abrahams described as "an aristocracy of merit and learning, not of property," headed by a rabbi. In medieval Poland, communities were headed by a council of leaders elected by a small selection committee. The rabbi, appointed and paid by the council, exercised "judicial review" of its takkanot and arbitrated disputes arising from their interpretation.

Women could not be elected to the councils, and, in most eras, neither could any poor Jews. This occasioned bitterness by poor men in some communities. In medieval Spain and eighteenth-century Poland, revolts by artisans and their guilds against the councils succeeded in winning them representation on these bodies.

That there was also bitterness in some periods on the part of poor scholars toward wealthy balabatim can be seen from an anonymous thirteenth-century

Kabbalistic work called *Raya Mehemna* (Aramaic for "The Faithful Shepherd"). The work interprets the *erev rav* (the "mixed multitude" of non-Jews who joined the Jews in their Exodus from Egypt) to mean the stratum of rich ignoramuses dominating the community. It portrays Moses as a poor mystic scholar who suffered from this erev rav as he did from the one of the Exodus era, and it envisions a redemption of the poor scholars and mystics from this plutocracy upon which they are economically dependent.

❧ Throughout most of Jewish history, there were built-in communal mechanisms to prevent the abuse of power by the balabatim. A custom that probably originated in twelfth- or thirteenth-century France and Germany was that of the interruption of the prayer services by an individual with a complaint; prayers had to be suspended until the case was examined. In Renaissance Italy, mothers of out-of-wedlock children threatened to bring the infants to the synagogue and interrupt the services unless they received child support from the fathers. (Contemporary women whose husbands withhold a get might consider reviving this custom today.) Rabbi Louis Finkelstein commented that in these "little democracies," the custom of prayer interruption had "the same effect in [the community] as an exposure of a crime in a modern metropolitan newspaper.... [Its] practical application was a bulwark of strength for the weak and oppressed against the powerful."

Traditional Jewish communities, of course, were not representative democracies any more than Athens was. All branches of the Jewish "government-in-Exile" excluded women, and the executive branch sometimes excluded poor men as well. But the legislative and judicial branches involved with Halachic decision making and review as well as the ambiance of communal life—as reflected in the prayer-interruption custom—were inherently democratic in process.

For this reason, Jewish immigrants to America could easily believe that its values, including majority rule, were consonant with theirs. The principle of freedom of speech entranced Jews, who were used to argument and debate; freedom of the press inspired them because they placed great value on the written and printed word. The American idea of progress toward a more tolerant and just society seemed consonant with Jewish messianism, and its pragmatic reformism appealed to Jews because this was the methodology of change used by the rabbinical leaders. Above all, the concept of the rule of law rather than that of capricious and cruel rulers struck a positive chord with Jews, who had lived for so many centuries by the system of Halacha in their own communities—and who had been persecuted for so many centuries by tyrants in the patriarchies of the general societies who had ultimate control over whether they lived or died.

FOUR ✑ FROM MACHO TO MENTSCH: REDEFINING JEWISH MANHOOD

> *Scholars increase peace in the world.*
>
> TALMUD

> *Jerusalem was destroyed only because people neglected to send their children to school.*
>
> TALMUD

> *My town was like one large family.... Should anything happen to a small town Jew, the entire community would share his joy or his sorrow.... Jews clung together like children abandoned in a desert.*
>
> MOISSAYE OLGIN

It is striking to observe how many of the female values enshrined in Judaism and institutionalized by Halacha are those associated with the extended family, especially one living under dangerous and unstable conditions.

Journalist Luigi Barzini described the traditional/classic Italian extended family as a "stronghold in a *hostile* land.... No Italian who has a family is ever alone.... Among its members, the individual finds consolation, help, advice, provisions, loans ... [and] allies.... He finds in it a *refuge*.... The family was the sacred ark in which Italians deposited and preserved against alien influences all their ancient ideals" (italics mine).

Substitute the word *community* every time the word *family* appears in Barzini's description and you get a fairly accurate portrait of the (ideal) traditional Jewish community. For only by functioning as classic extended families imbued with the values of altruism, interdependence, and cooperation originated by women could Jewish communities maintain the cohesion necessary for group survival. And, indeed, in the Middle Ages, Abrahams observed, "The community was in a very real sense of the word *one united and rather inquisitive family*" (italics mine).

Because of this community-as-extended-family dynamic, there was never any concept of individual solutions in the traditional Jewish worldview. Jews accepted the concept that they have one history and destiny which, their mythology relates, began when they undertook the collective responsibility of adhering to the Torah. The mystics who wrote and studied the Kabbala, as we have seen in chapter 2, focused not on individual salvation but on trying to bring about national—and universal—redemption. It is no wonder that many Jews found the collective and universalist values of revolutionary movements consonant with those of Jewish culture.

The idea of the Contract between God and the Jews reflects the ethos of mutuality and interdependence, as does the concern about what is "good for the Jews." One-time shtetl residents recalled, "A Jew is always concerned with the troubles of all other Jews and conscious of the fact that his [sic] personal lot is *dependent* on the way other Jews live or are treated" (italics mine). The corollary is that withdrawal from involvement with other Jews, whether physical or psychological, is, in the words of a former shtetl resident, "felt as an attack." Hillel instructs Jews: "Do not separate yourself from the community," and separation has always been regarded in the Jewish culture as a crime of abandonment and betrayal, feeding on and reinforcing the Jewish obsession with abandonment.

The comment in the Talmud about the type of character who says, "What's mine is mine, and what's yours is yours," is very revealing in this connection. After considering this type "neutral," the Talmud adds, "but others say, this is a character like that of Sodom," whose citizens' crimes, according to the Midrash, were lack of compassion for and assistance to the poor and to wayfarers. Thus, the type of person who only looks out for Number One is likened to an archcriminal.

The commitment to the values of interdependence, mutual assistance, and responsibility, and to their corollary—the condemnation of isolation, separation, and abandonment—characterized the youth in the Jewish Resistance during the Holocaust to an extraordinary degree. The outbreak of World War II on September 1, 1939, found many Zionist youth leaders at a World Zionist Congress in Switzerland. When the Congress concluded, these youth leaders, who could have sought asylum in that country or elsewhere, made their way back home to Poland to serve their people. Wrote Yitzhak Zuckerman, second-in-command of the ZOB, the Jewish Fighting Organization in the Warsaw Ghetto, of the Zionist youth: "There was *mutual* responsibility, we weren't just concerned for ourselves.... The possibility that one person could leave another and look after himself ... didn't exist among us." Because of this sense of responsibility, said Zuckerman, the youth in the Resistance agonized over whether to try to escape to the forests to fight as partisans. They asked themselves and one another, "Do we have the right to *desert* the ghetto in its extremity, depriving it of its young people, its fighting strength?" (italics mine).

Jews continue to behave even today as one large and fairly contentious family, and they refer to one another and to the nation as a whole as *mishpucha* (Yiddish/Hebrew for family). Many continue to feel that they can really be themselves only among other Jews. Their gravitating to other Jews, however, is often stereotyped as "clannishness"—a charge assimilationist Jews will go to great lengths to deny, demonstrating how they have internalized negative stereotypes of positive group behavior.

Jewish organizational life, as we shall see in chapters 11 and 12, tends to replicate many behavioral patterns associated with the family, as evidenced by the injunction, "Don't wash your dirty linen in public," that is, where non-Jews can see it. The community-as-family pattern also obtains in the relationship between American Jews and Israel, as exemplified by the statement by an Israeli Knesset (Parliament) member about some American Jews' criticism of his government's policies: "If you are really *part of a family,* you don't walk away and disown the member who is in trouble" (italics mine).

WHY VIOLENCE HAD TO BE VANQUISHED

Of all the female values incorporated into Jewish communal life, that of nonviolence had the most far-reaching consequences. Force, violence, and physical coercion and abuse had to be and were outlawed because survival in the Exile demanded it.

All violence had to be eliminated from the behavior of Jewish men to prevent their using it against non-Jews. (It is primarily in this specific ban on violence against people *outside the group* that the Jewish community-as-extended-family dynamic differs from that of the traditional/classic extended family under duress.) Violence was also counterindicated in order that the community function as a refuge/safe haven where Jews could regroup and heal from the hostilities inflicted upon them.

⋙ Rabbinical scholars who assumed the leadership of the Jewish nation in the first few centuries C.E. began the ideological and practical campaign against violence, which continued in subsequent eras. Their initiation of the antiviolence campaign was rooted in an understanding of the cause and consequences of the national disaster that ensued after the failure of the rebellions against the Roman Empire. The cause was the tendency on the part of Jewish men to resist tyranny militarily no matter what the cost, to engage in wildcat revolts, and to fight last-ditch battles during uprisings (e.g., at Masada, 73 C.E.; at Betar, 135 C.E.). This behavior was not "good for the Jews."

Moreover, the rabbis believed that spiritual rather than physical resistance was the best way to ensure the survival of the Jewish nation. They followed Isaiah, who believed, wrote Shmuel Eisenstadt, that "the best way for a small people like his to react to the menace of brute strength was to build its own inner life on foundations of justice, of decent relationships among its citizens." Like the prophets, who warned (in vain) against Judea's fighting the Babylonian Empire, the rabbis considered mass armed resistance to the overwhelming power of a foreign state counterproductive to group survival. This is also why the majority of the Talmudic sages condemned the Zealots who had led the revolt against Rome in 66–73 C.E. and called Bar Kochba (Son of a Star), the military leader of the uprising in 132–35 C.E., *Bar Keziva* (son of a lie).

Furthermore, the rabbis realized that if Jews could not succeed at physical resistance to oppression while they were still living in their own territory, they would most certainly fail at it in the Exile. There, living scattered in small communities, sometimes among hostile populations and often under inimical regimes—all armed to the teeth—they lacked the prerequisites of mass physical resistance, including the most crucial one: a territorial base. And, indeed, on the rare occasions when Jews did engage in physical resistance to attacks, they were slaughtered. This type of resistance took place when all other options were foreclosed and they would have been murdered anyway. What the rabbis were concerned about was making sure that physical aggression, if used, was the last resort for collective self-defense *in extremis* rather than the first knee-jerk response to the day-to-day problems of living in Exile.

But there was an even greater fear: that entire communities would be put to the sword had even a small number of Jewish men engaged in individual or collective physical aggression. Given the Jewish ethos of interdependence, this fear became, after centuries, a prime motivating factor in the normative Jewish response to outside attack. This is evident from the reaction of Jews defending the city of Tulczyn together with the Polish nobles in 1648, during the Chmielnitzki massacres. After their Polish "allies" turned them over to the besieging Cossacks, the Jews refrained from attacking the nobles and chose martyrdom instead when their leaders told them: "We are in Exile among the nations. If you lay hands upon the nobles, then all the kings of Christianity will hear of it and *take revenge on all our brethren in the Exile*" (italics mine).

About three hundred years later, the concern over German collective punishment of entire ghettos in occupied Poland for acts of resistance was a prime factor in the decisions of the various Jewish underground movements about whether and how to carry out such actions. In one case, in Vilna, the leader of the Jewish Resistance chose what amounted to martyrdom when the Germans threatened to liquidate the ghetto if he did not turn himself in.

THE COMMUNITY AS A VIOLENCE-FREE ZONE

Eliminating violence from male behavior also required banning it inside the community so that the men would not be psychologically revved up to use their hands rather than their minds to solve their national problem.

Rage against outside oppressors had to be repressed because it could lead to violence or, at the very least, loss of control under conditions where self-control was imperative. (This is the reason Jews believe drinking was frowned upon: Jews might lose control, engage in antisocial behavior, and be unprepared to deal rationally and effectively with attack.) Jews were often not even allowed to express their rage verbally against their oppressors. At various times in the Middle Ages, Christians actually cut out from the Jewish prayer book sentences such as "the informers shall have no hope" and banned the custom of burning Haman (initiator of a genocide plan in ancient Persia, according to the Purim story) in effigy.

The rabbis realized that oppressed people often direct their rage against each other physically because it is too dangerous to direct it against their enemies. They understood, as well, that such behavior could be both physically and psychologically destructive and could lead to communal breakdown. A Jewish community that functioned like Belfast or Beirut in the 1980s, in which lives and property are continually being wiped out, in which the best and the brightest dedicate themselves to warfare rather than to spiritual resistance, in which the next generation has as little hope as do children in the black ghettos of the U.S. today, would not have lasted long, certainly not under the adverse conditions that prevailed.

It would have also been impossible for a community plagued by internal warfare deriving from conflicts between classes (and between settled and immigrant populations) to maintain the mutual trust and cooperation necessary for its members to join together against a common enemy. In the Zealots' revolt against Rome, concomitant class struggle and armed warfare between the different resistance movements resulted in the burning of virtually the entire food supply of besieged Jerusalem. This had taught Jews that intracommunal violence was lethal. The psychological aspect was also important. Jews were already forced to endure a siege mentality because of outside persecution. It would have been psychologically destructive for them to have to endure the kind of anxiety that crime engenders in the large cities of late twentieth-century America.

In short, violence was counterindicated if the community was to be a haven in which Jews could feel the safety that they did not and could not feel as individuals or as a group in relation to the general society. The Exile community's functioning as an extended family meant that physical aggression against its own members had to be eliminated.

Physical aggression also had to be forbidden in order to allow Jewish men unrestrained freedom of expression in Halachic debates and discussions about changing or adding new laws and ordinances upon which communal survival depended. It is precisely because free expression of differences of opinion had to be encouraged in Jewish society that Jews made sure that verbal expression of conflict would not deteriorate into physical expression of conflict. Knowing that the expression of a controversial or unpopular view would not lead to violence gave the men the emotional security to engage in verbal attacks and acrimonious exchanges that enlivened and enriched the scholars' intellectual horizons and reinforced the free exchange of views elsewhere in the community. (Conversely, the outlawing of violence required safe spaces where negative feelings could be expressed verbally without fear of their escalating into physical aggression. The study house was one; the home, as we shall see in subsequent chapters, another.)

The struggle against all forms of violence had to be unrelenting. As one historian described it, "Only against rioters, violent men, rough attackers did the sages of Israel in Spain in every generation see it as their duty to fight ... *for the sake of the welfare of Jewry*. And if ... [they] saw danger of an outburst from within *that might harm the Jewish community,* they did not hesitate to take measures against those who had *lost control of themselves*" (italics mine).

The rabbis' struggle to eliminate violence was ultimately successful. Most of the memoirs and other archival materials that have come down to us point to Jewish communities' being violence-free zones. What began as a necessity for survival—although it may not have been acknowledged as such—became after many centuries an accepted and glorified philosophy of life: "From not doing it for its intrinsic value, they came around to doing it for its own sake." Nonviolence became part of the Jewish self-image, the countermyth that Jews were highly ethical, "compassionate people, children of compassionate people"—and peaceful.

◆ Being shrewd behavior psychologists, the rabbis understood violence in terms of the domino effect rather than as a safety valve. Therefore, the classic pattern so often found among oppressed people—after the powerful man beats the powerless man, the latter beats his wife, the wife slaps the kid, the kid kicks the dog—had to be smashed and every possible link eliminated.

One such link was between violence against and cruelty to animals and humans. While the Five Books did not contain the concept of animal rights and embodied the belief that animals could be used for "legitimate human needs," they did contain laws against what came to be called *tzaar ba'alei chaim,* causing animals pain and suffering, both physical and psychological. The concept behind laws such as allowing threshing animals to graze and not harnessing an ox and mule together to the plow was developed and expanded in the Talmud and responsa. Blood sports, including hunting for "pleasure," were outlawed, as was the spurring of horses. Hundreds of laws regulated *schechita* (ritual slaughter of animals for food) to ensure that it be swift, painless, and humane and that the *schochet,* the ritual slaughterer, be a person of the highest moral caliber. As one writer described schechita: "The [animal] sagged slowly down, dead before it could be surprised."

Jews were also required to prevent cruelty to animals. They were not allowed to eat a meal until they had fed their animals. Emblematic of this attitude of caring and compassion was an incident that took place in Slovakia during the Holocaust, recalled by Rabbi Michael Weissmandel. While being shoved onto a deportation train, a Jew named Itzik Rosenberg called out to his non-Jewish neighbors, who were watching the scene with glee, "I beg you—go to my home and feed the geese. They have had nothing to eat or drink all day."

Compassion toward animals became so normative in Jewish behavior—bordering on identification with them as hunted and abused with impunity, as were Jews—that a little boy in a story by the great Yiddish writer Sholem Aleichem says a particular individual cannot possibly be a Jew because he is cruel to animals.

PROSCRIBING VIOLENCE AGAINST WOMEN

Violence against women, particularly rape, had to be eliminated because of the domino effect, the need for communal cohesion, and the community's having to be a safe haven. The rabbis recognized that attacks on a woman "belonging" to another man could trigger multigenerational blood feuds. And, indeed, cases of rape are candidly documented in the Scriptures precisely from the angle of their causing struggles between men. Significantly, one midrash attributes to the rape of Dina, Jacob and Leah's daughter, the subsequent rift in Jacob's household and her brothers' becoming bloodthirsty savages when avenging the assault.

Additionally, the men's fears of assaults upon "their" women and their consequent need to protect them—plus the internecine warfare this would have engendered—could have siphoned off the men's energy from their important work of spiritual resistance (of which more below) and from seeking *parnosseh* (Hebrew/Yiddish for earning a living), which in many cases required long-term travel.

Finally, in the struggle for national survival, which had priority, women had to be able to do their part as enablers, which, as we shall see in the next chapter, often involved working in the marketplace and traveling around the countryside. The threat of intracommunal rape might have compelled the men to seclude women inside the home or, at the very least, made women weak, dependent, and clinging when they had to be resourceful and strong in order to pull a heavy load.

❧ Legislation in the Five Books considers rape from two angles: the financial payment due the father of the victim, the prototype being the "unattached virgin"; and sexual transgression, whose prototype was the "betrothed virgin" (betrothal was practically like marriage in ancient times).

The rapist had to pay the father of an unattached woman a fine for his loss of the going bride-price for virgins, and he had to marry the woman and never divorce her. In the patriarchal mind-set of the day, this was considered protection for the woman, who, having lost her most valuable asset, her virginity, might otherwise never find a husband. However, since rape was regarded in ancient times primarily as a "crime of passion," and as a way of compelling a match rejected by the woman and/or her father, this hardly seems like punishment for the man, who might also console himself with additional wives. Maimonides may have understood this and the woman's suffering when he ruled that she and/or her father could decline the match.

In the case of the "betrothed virgin," the element of illicit sexual relations outweighs assault and it is the crime for which the Five Books mandate that the rapist be executed. (So are adulterers, defined as men, married or unmarried, who have sexual relations with married women, and married women who have lovers.) The inescapable conclusion is that the severity of the punishment depends on who the woman is in relation to some man rather than on the nature of the sexual relations (coercive or consensual).

Rape of unattached women is punished more severely in the Talmud, which includes it with assaults resulting in bodily injuries. In the case of rape, monetary compensation is due the woman for pain, disfigurement, and humiliation.

There is considerable discussion in the Talmud and in later legal literature as to what precisely constitutes rape, mainly in the context of what determines consent. The crucial defining factor, writes Rachel Biale, is *initiation* of sex under duress: A woman does not need to resist physically or to scream throughout the attack to be considered a rape victim.

We should note in this connection that marital rape is forbidden in the Talmud and by Maimonides and other rabbinical sages. The twelfth-century scholar Rabbi Abraham ben David (a.k.a. Rabad) defines marital rape: The wife "does not reciprocate" the husband's advances, she "does not turn around and desire him, too," and finally she says, "I am being forced," and the husband does not heed her objections.

Contrast these latter two rather progressive views with one rabbi's statement in the Talmud that "when a grown man has intercourse with a little girl it is nothing, for when the girl is less than [three], it is as if one puts a finger into the eye." Regardless of whether this was an actual atrocity or one of the hypothetical cases—such as flying towers—that Talmud scholars loved to explore, the statement shows gross insensitivity to a child's pain and terror and a lack of interest in the man's moral culpability, issues that, writes Rachel Adler, are considered "nondata."

The discussions in the Talmud and in later works give no indication as to the actual prevalence of intracommunal rape at the end of the Second Commonwealth and in the third exile. We can observe only that there was comparatively little space allotted to it in the Talmud and the responsa literature, but this could mean that no especially difficult decisions were required. The lack of material on intracommunal rape in descriptive material such as memoirs and accounts of travelers—which are fairly candid about other communal problems, such as premarital pregnancy (e.g., in Renaissance Italy)—seems to point to this not being a burning communal issue, but further research is indicated.

That the proscription of rape became part of normative Jewish male behavior can be seen from testimony by women such as Vitke Kempner and Ruszhka Korczak, who fought as partisans in Poland during World War II. They reported no threat of rape in Jewish partisan units—in contrast to the situation that prevailed in non-Jewish fighting units, where "the opinion prevailed . . . that the task of women in the force was to satisfy the sexual needs of the fighters." Because of this, said Korczak, Jewish women constantly had to "defend their honor" against their non-Jewish male comrades.

While incidents of rape have increased in Israel (as we shall see in chapter 8), women can still walk on the streets of Jewish neighborhoods at night without fear.

DOUBLE JEOPARDY

Violence against women would have also led to the erosion of their loyalty and the shattering of their morale.

The necessity of maintaining the women's morale was especially important, because while all Jews faced and suffered persecution, the women faced double jeopardy because of the ever-present threat of rape by non-Jewish men. Sartre understood the pervasiveness of rape when he wrote that the phrase *Belle Juive* (beautiful Jewish woman) "carries an aura of rape and massacre. The '*Belle Juive*' is she whom the Cossacks under the Czars dragged by her hair through the streets of her burning village."

The prevalence of rape by non-Jewish men can be seen from legal discussions on the subject (and on the kidnapping of women) going all the way back to the Mishnah. Rabbis in the Middle Ages allowed Jewish women to dress as men (although cross-dressing was forbidden by Halacha) and even to sport false beards to avoid "molestation" on journeys.

The popular explanation among Jews of Halacha's definition of a Jew as an individual born of a Jewish mother demonstrates how pervasive the expectation of rape was. The explanation is that because Jewish women were at high risk for rape by non-Jewish men, to determine and trace Jewishness through the father's identity could have been impossible; painful and humiliating for women; and conducive, as well, to intracommunal conflict. It might have even led to the creation of a subgroup of Jews who, like *mamzerim* (Hebrew for bastards, meaning offspring of an adulterous union), are forbidden to marry non-*mamzer* Jews. Frequent expulsions and migrations would have made it eminently difficult to keep track of who was a Jew. Given the absence of a territory by which to define the nationality of group members, the only possibility left was to base it on the mother's identity.

Another indication of the acute awareness of the pervasiveness of rape by non-Jewish men is its being advanced by Jews as the reason they have so many different colors of skin, eyes, and hair (something that anti-Semites who spew forth propaganda about the Jewish "race" conveniently ignore).

❧ The danger and threat of rape was intensified in the Exile because of the hostility against Jews. Jewish women often served as lightning rods for this hostility. Rape and gang rape were standard features of Czarist pogroms and those perpetrated all over Eastern Europe after World War I. Evidence from recently recorded oral history has also revealed the perpetration of rape of Jewish women by Germans during the Holocaust. Because a perpetrator violated the "race purity" laws, he usually murdered his victim(s) to avert detection. Jewish women were also forced into prostitution in concentration camps and subjected to fiendish experiments, including sterilization, and other forms of torture and acts of sadism. During the reign of terror in Argentina, Jewish women political prisoners were twice as likely to be raped in the secret prisons as were non-Jewish women.

Hostility against Jews made the rapes especially brutal and sadistic in all eras. Accounts of the Chmielnitzki massacres are replete with stories of grisly rapes. One popular atrocity was to slash open the bellies of women and sew in live cats.

Jewish women could certainly not count on any non-Jews' moral objection to their rape or on being rescued as "damsels in distress" by knights in shining armor. While most lower-class non-Jewish women could not depend on such upper-class chivalry either, the prime difference for Jewish women was that they could be neither defended nor avenged by their own male relatives. A community that stood poised on the edge of a sword of annihilation if some non-Jew placed the body of a dead child on a Jewish doorstep and charged all the Jews with ritual murder could not possibly allow a Jewish man to kill or injure a non-Jewish man for any cause that might trigger a pogrom, let alone for rape, which the men did not perceive to cause any permanent injury.

The Jewish woman, like her black sister in the pre–civil rights movement South, was at risk for rape whether one or more men were with her or not. Worse yet, non-Jewish men were acutely aware that the crime was unlikely to be stopped or avenged by Jewish men. This made it so much more appealing than, say, the rape of a non-Jewish woman, whose male kinfolk might be armed and dangerous.

◆ Given the virtual absence of women's literature, it is impossible to know how Jewish women felt about the pervasive threat of rape by non-Jewish men and the inability of the men of their own group to defend and/or avenge them. (The only thing Jewish men could do was to try to ransom kidnapped women, who may or may not have been threatened with or subjected to rape, and the standard marriage contract consequently specifies ransom from captivity as one of the wife's entitlements.)

The men's inability to protect or defend the women—especially during pogroms—may have militated against Jewish women's harboring fantasies of chivalry by men of their own group. This probably affected the dynamic of the female-male relationship, making it less like the one under classic patriarchy in which the woman is physically and/or psychologically dependent on the man as her protector. (Moreover, the fact that all Jews looked to God for rescue precluded women's looking to "their" men as rescuers rather than seeing them as other potential rescuees.)

Another long-term effect of Jewish women's historical experiences of rape by non-Jewish men, and in particular its association with pogroms, is their lack of expectation of it in America, where no pogroms against Jews have taken place. This, plus the absence of a history of rape by men of their own group, has caused many of them to fail to be alert to the threat of rape and to develop effective techniques of rape avoidance. The result, believes feminist sociologist Pauline Bart, is that attacks on American Jewish women tend to be more likely to end in rape than those perpetrated against women of other ethnic groups.

❧ One clue as to how the men felt about their inability to prevent rape of "their" women comes from statements in the Talmud.

While the sages condemned David's wars, later scholars suggested that the king had waged them to prevent the capture and rape of Jewish women. This points to a yearning on the part of Jewish men to prevent such rapes. The yearning, however, was not acknowledged because it would have reinforced the men's anxiety about their powerlessness in the Exile and their shame about not fulfilling the classic role that defines masculinity under patriarchy: protecting and defending "their" women. These feelings were kept at bay by the defense mechanism of denial—not of the prevalence and threat of rape but of the men's responsibility to prevent it. The very fact that they allowed women to travel unescorted on long business trips during the chaotic and strife-torn period of the European Middle Ages and in pogrom-prone Eastern Europe is evidence of this attitude.

The denial dynamic often took the form of placing all responsibility for rape avoidance on the woman. The East European rationalization was that she could "take care of herself." If she was raped, therefore, it was because she did not resist or did not resist "enough," that is, make extreme, inordinate sacrifices to avoid it, of which more shortly.

The men's use of the blame-the-victim denial mechanism to avert shame about their powerlessness can be seen very clearly in midrashim faulting the biblical Dina, the prototypical rape victim, for being abducted and assaulted: She was "promiscuous," and her motive in leaving home was to seek sexual experience. Two scholars even stated that she had to be dragged out of her rapist's house kicking and screaming because she found pleasure in sex with an "uncircumcised" man. The charge of Dina's sexual interest in a non-Jewish man—one able to protect "his" women—reveals the men's underlying anxieties about their own lack of masculinity and its possible effects on women's spousal choices. These anxieties—and the anger that could not be directed at non-Jewish men—were repressed by projecting blame onto Dina. Similarly, the classic "joke" from Eastern Europe is that a child begs a Cossack to refrain from raping his mother. The woman turns to the kid and snarls, "Shut up, a pogrom is a pogrom!" (i.e., the woman does not want to resist).

Chaim Nachman Bialik, the poet laureate of the Hebrew national renaissance, understood well that the men's denial of their responsibility to prevent the women's rape kept shame at their powerlessness from surfacing. In his famous Hebrew poetic epic "In the City of Carnage," written after the Easter Sunday, 1903,

Kishinev pogrom, he excoriated the men for hiding when their wives, daughters, and sisters were being gang-raped: "They saw and they didn't move. They didn't gouge out their eyes or go out of their minds." Bialik also lashed out at the men for getting on with their lives after the pogrom by asking rabbis the question uppermost in their minds: When could they resume sexual relations with their violated wives? These passages in the poem were Bialik's deliberate attempt to make Jewish men feel ashamed of their powerlessness—and to do something about it instead of accepting the inevitability of pogroms. This attempt became part of the effort by Zionists to create a "new Jewish man" in Eretz Israel, one who would be willing *and able* to defend "his" women as well as the community as a whole.

❧ It was precisely the need to prevent Jewish men from feeling ashamed about their not living up to the classic definition of masculinity—and possibly adopting it—that extreme sacrifices were demanded of women to avoid rape. This meant that the Jewish woman had the responsibility not only to try to protect her own honor but also, by doing so, to protect the man's psyche.

Peretz's famous story "The Three Gifts" is emblematic of the behavior traditionally expected of women when assaulted. The story praises a medieval Jewish woman dragged through the streets tied to a horse's tail for pinning her garment to her skin. There are many accounts of actual women who avoided rape by martyrdom. In a medieval Spanish account, a rabbi's wife leaps into the sea to avoid rape by a pirate ship captain; in an oral Kurdish account, a woman escapes gang rape by seven "infidels" by drowning herself in a *mikvah* (ritual immersion facility). A story told in Brahilov, Russian Poland, relates how a widow wins a promise from a general to spare the town, then kills herself and her daughter to avoid their falling into his hands.

Folktales, as well, laud women's actions to avoid coerced sexual relations with non-Jewish men. These stories, whether based on actual events or drawing on the prevailing general reality, were probably told by men and among women to advance and validate an ideal model of behavior the men wished the women to fulfill. In one such story, recorded in Venice in 1600, a prince lusts for a "pious maiden" and brings her to his palace by force. When he tells her, "You have the eyes of a dove; they have taken me captive!" the maiden gouges out her eyes with a knife. Returning to the prince with them in hand, she murmurs, "Since you have such a great love for my eyes, you may have them. . . . Here they are. Do with them what you wish." Shaken, the prince lets her go home.

This grisly and horrific story, which shows the extreme to which the loyalty of Jewish women was expected to go in rape avoidance, brings us back to the question of upkeep of morale and its relationship to the banning of intracommunal violence against women. Since the men saw them as the gender that was weaker, especially intellectually, perhaps they feared that if women had to face violence from within the community in addition to that coming from outside it, especially in the form of rape, they would break under the strain of a two-front war. Intracommunal rape, therefore, had to be eliminated.

A final factor in the bolstering of Jewish women's morale was that the incorporation into Jewish society of female values such as nonviolence ensured a community where women felt more at home because these were *their* values. The success of the morale factor in upholding women's loyalty can be seen from the feeling prevailing among many Jewish women today, whether conscious or unconscious, that they have it better than their non-Jewish sisters.

REDEFINING MALE POWER

The rabbis' incorporation of female values, especially nonviolence, into Jewish society to ensure communal cohesion and thus, national survival, created a conflict that could have doomed their efforts to failure.

On the one hand, there was the necessity for Jewish men to compensate for having been deprived of power vis-à-vis the men of the general society. Exile deprived them of the ability to engage in physical aggression and of using it to defend women and children and the community from attack. Exile reduced men to the powerlessness associated with that of women.

Since men considered themselves the superior gender, it was vital to keep them committed to the struggle for survival. Had Jewish men felt like sissies—which, given their patriarchal mind-set, would have been the natural psychological consequence of the deprivation of power—they might have lapsed into despair and dropped out of the survival struggle. To prevent this, they had to be given more power *inside* the community. At the very minimum, they had to continue to dominate all aspects of communal life—legal, social, religious. That, at least, put them on par in this respect with non-Jewish men.

This perceived necessity for men's communal domination accounts in part for the fact that they took the "dowry" (the values created by women), but rejected the "bride" (women's active role in developing Halacha and executing laws based on these values). This is why one major line of argument used in the 1970s and 1980s against American Jewish women's equal participation in religious and communal life was that it would make the men "impotent" and cause them to defect from the community.

But on the other hand, another prerequisite for Jewish survival was that the Jewish community function as a safe haven and violence-free zone, which is why the female values had been incorporated to begin with. Taking away from Jewish men the possibility of recourse/access to the threat or use of force and violence meant that, in essence, they now had even less power—at least, less of the kind of power men traditionally wielded under patriarchy and which they saw non-Jewish men, even the most oppressed, as possessing. The incorporation of certain female values, especially nonviolence, was thus in direct conflict with the need to give Jewish men more power inside the community to compensate for their lack of power in relation to the general society.

Thus, at one and the same time, Jewish survival demanded that Jewish men have more power and less power.

❧ The rabbis ingeniously resolved this conflict by changing the concept of what constituted male power and, even more fundamentally (since power is part of the definition of manhood), what constituted masculinity. They stripped male power of the glorification and practice of violence, of rugged individualism, rapacious exploitation, machismo, rampant cruelty, conquest, military prowess, physical heroism, and of the abuse of women. They redefined power as knowledge, learning, and studying. They defined manhood itself in terms of commitment to and achievement in learning Torah. Thus they replaced the classic patriarchal definition of masculinity, man-as-macho fighter, with the alternative definition of man-as-scholar.

The rabbis went even further: They defined learning Torah not only as the Jewish man's work but also as the most important work in society, the work necessary for Jewish survival. This intellectual work and the public performance of ritual (particularly in the synagogue) were posited as the main components of spiritual resistance in the Exile.

By recasting the definition of masculinity, the rabbis accomplished two additional aims. They cooled out the men and got them to give up physical aggression, which was counterproductive to national survival; and they got them to engage instead in spiritual resistance, particularly in the study of Torah, which the rabbis had long believed to be the pathway to an ethical life as well as the method for the nation to guarantee its self-preservation and surmount the crises it faced.

❧ The rabbis' methodology for winning compliance with this new definition of masculinity as spiritual resistance, and particularly of its intellectual component, involved the standard Jewish approach to behavior modification: direct human aggressive drives (yetzer hara) away from violent expression—detach violence from aggression—and channel aggressive drives into a safe, constructive, and useful context. Study was that constructive context, which is why historian E. E. Urbach observed that Torah study was "the most potent" (his use of this word is instructive) means the sages had of "keeping the passions at bay." Heine aptly calls the disputatious sections of the Talmud "that famous school of *fighting* ... where athletes dialectic / Best in Babylon ... / Did their intellectual *tilting*" (italics mine).

This methodology is beautifully illustrated in the story in the Talmud about the time Rabbi Yohanan was bathing in the river and Resh Lakish, then an infamous bandit, jumped in after him. Yohanan, not losing his cool, said to the highwayman: "Your strength [should be used] for the [study of] Torah." Resh Lakish gave up his life of crime and eventually became the great and respected scholar

Rabbi Shimon ben Lakish, whose death left Rabbi Yohanan inconsolable.

This behavior modification process, which began to take hold at the beginning of the first millennium C.E., was so successful that Abrahams wrote about yeshiva students in the Middle Ages that "just as in Bible times wives were won by bold feats on the battlefield, so in the Middle Ages, the way to a maiden's heart was often made by the brilliant *exploits* of a young, budding Talmudist on the field of Rabbinical controversy.... The youths might display their intellectual *prowess* under the gaze of their future wives" on various public occasions (italics mine).

Study also provided an activity around which male bonding could coalesce, and stories of yeshiva study partners are therefore somewhat reminiscent of those about cops who are partners. Moreover, learning Torah involved male cooperation in an activity vital for the nation's survival and provided validation to participants without the strife that collective male endeavors usually entail. (It can be argued that part of the attraction of men to warfare, in addition to providing them the opportunity to engage in legally sanctioned and validated mayhem, is precisely the incorporation of the female values of cooperation and interdependence among a group of soldiers. These values are remembered fondly from their childhood in the family but suppressed in men's dealings with one another in ordinary daily life, which usually involve competition, isolation, and alienation.) At the same time, learning Torah reinforced the female values of the community, both because these were enshrined in the texts being studied and because the process itself involved cooperation.

By giving the men control over intellectual turf, which compensated for their lack of control over their physical lives, studying warded off depression and kept Jewish men sane. As Heschel put it, "Study was a technique of *sublimating* feeling and thought, ... of expressing pain in a question and joy in ... [finding] an answer to gnawing doubts" (italics mine). And it precluded the kind of alienation that Paul Goodman described in young twentieth-century American men: "If there is nothing *worthwhile,* it is hard to do anything at all. When one does nothing, one is threatened by the question whether one is nothing" (italics mine).

Because the study of Torah was the major component of the new definition of masculinity, its pursuit had to be democratized. It could not become the property of one class or age group or of an intellectual or political elite. At the same time, it obviously had to be closed to women, along with the public performance of ritual, a subject to be explored in the next chapter. Thus women, wrote Judith Romney Wegner, were excluded from "the life of the mind and spirit" in the Jewish "learning-based culture."

❧ As the new definition of Jewish manhood evolved in the Exile, so did the concept of God. This is most clearly demonstrated in the midrash that God spends a lot of His time learning Torah! Jews added female values such as compassion and interdependence onto their image of male God, just as they had incorporated them into their concept of the ideal Jewish man (and society). God remained male but became less stern, angry, and jealous and more of what is called in Yiddish a *mentsch*–someone who is caring, compassionate, responsible, reliable, serious, dependable, ethical, and kind–as the Exile dragged on.

At the same time God came to be viewed in the Kabbala and in the folk culture it permeated as limited in power, as we have seen in chapter 2, especially in His ability to effect immediate rescue. Thus Jewish men headed off their shame for not being able to defend/rescue "their" women from rape by non-Jewish men and their families and communities from pogroms by envisioning God, too, as "having His hands tied."

THE PASSIONATE PROJECT OF STUDY

The study of Torah–the Law: the Scriptures, the Talmud, the commentaries– became the collective national project of the Jewish people, with the men doing the actual work and the women serving as enablers, as we shall see in ensuing chapters. A Yiddish saying glorifies *Dee Aibige Torah,* "the eternal Torah"; studying it was the adhesive that bonded the Jewish nation together.

The centuries-long experience of learning Torah reinforced the respect accorded to learned people, scholars, and academics; the printed word and books; education; and the life of the mind. One scholar, Judah Ibn Tibbon, advised Jews to "make your books your companions" and "let your bookcases and shelves be your gardens and your pleasure-grounds"–and they did. Even in Polish ghettos under Nazi occupation, Jews operated schools, often illegally; secretly preserved their old public libraries as long as they could; and hid archival material from the Germans.

◄» Torah study became one of the highest mitzvot, not only a prerequisite to carrying out all the other ones–"An ignoramus cannot be pious," says the Mishnah– but also one greatly valued as an end in itself: *Torah lishma,* for its own sake. A Jewish man, to be regarded as a "real" man, had to be learned or at least involved in some way in studying or (the bare irreducible minimum) in supporting scholars and thus basking in the reflected light of their brilliance. The Yiddish term *yichhus,* which means high status derived from being related to or descended from someone important, is applied only to relatives of scholars.

Peretz's moving story "*Sholom Bayis*" (Yiddish/Hebrew for domestic tranquillity) tells of a poor worker who goes to a rabbi to find out how to express his love for learning. After the rabbi elicits the information that the man lacks the skills to study Talmud or even the Psalms, he tells the laborer to "serve those who study– bring a few buckets of water to the synagogue every evening so that the scholars have something to drink." The man returns home with great elation to tell this to his beloved wife.

Jewish mothers, as Maurice Samuel once pointed out, "dreamed of seeing their children learned rather than wealthy," and many of the lullabies they sang, their folk and children's songs, were "songs of learning."

The young men who were the most brilliant scholars were the most sought after by wealthy men as husbands for their daughters. The newly married couple was usually provided with *kest* (Yiddish for room and board) at the home of one set of in-laws (in Eastern Europe, the bride's parents) for up to ten years while the boy studied Torah. This system not only enlarged the pool of scholars and ensured the emergence of a cadre of the best ones, but also provided a kind of upward mobility for poor but brilliant boys.

The ideal Jewish boy was pale: This meant that he was spending his days in the study house as befitted a child of his gender and intellect. The boy in the story "The Calf," by Mendele Mocher Sforim (Mendele the Bookseller), becomes suntanned after spending his days romping with the animals in the fields and is berated for having developed a ruddy look unbecoming a Jewish child. Cultivation of boyish pallor also had economic motivations: It indicated that the boy was so brainy that someone (parents, in-laws, a wife, the community, a wealthy patron) was or should be eager to support him in his intellectual pursuits.

Gymnastics were discouraged, as Nordau noted when he urged Zionists to cultivate a "muscular Judaism." The ideal Jewish boy and man was mentally acute but not physically fit. This ideal and that of nonviolence would cause considerable conflict for Jewish men in America, where physicality and physical aggression were considered part of the definition of manhood, as we shall see in chapters 9 and 10.

❧ The education of male children—and adults—was a function not of the family but of the community, which supported elementary and higher Torah education, mostly through taxation. Universal elementary education for boys, according to the Talmud, officially dates to around 64 C.E., when Rabbi Joshua ben Gamala decreed that teachers be appointed in every district and city and boys of six and seven be enrolled in their schools regardless of their social or economic status. Rabbi Judah the Prince, compiler of the Mishnah, said, "One does not suspend the studies of the school children even for the building of the Temple."

The goal of universal elementary education for boys came close to 100 percent attainment except in periods of mass persecution or relocation. That is why in the world of Sholem Aleichem's Tevye the milk peddler, writes Cynthia Ozick, "it is not unusual for a milkman or carpenter to know the [Five Books] and the Psalms inside out and considerable other Scriptural and rabbinic territory as well."

Even in Poland between the two World Wars, when Jews lived in abysmal poverty and were threatened by pogroms, they maintained four academic school systems, not counting *cheders* (from the Hebrew word for room) and *Talmud Torahs* (private and communal elementary schools, respectively), and numerous yeshivot. The inspiring and moving film *Image Before My Eyes,* a documentary on interbellum Polish Jewry, shows a small provincial community's response to their terrifying situation at the end of the 1930s: It establishes a new school for the children.

◀▷ Higher Jewish education took place in Talmudic academies (which also functioned as legislatures and courts) in the Near East. Study attained such popularity
in first-millennium C.E. Babylonia that a *Kalla* system was instituted whereby two
times a year thousands of students would stream from all over the country and
even abroad to one of the several leading academies and spend a month at a time
in study there.

Every sizable Jewish community on the European continent sought to have
a yeshiva for the study of Talmud and its commentaries. The local community
supported its yeshiva, and no fees were charged students. In Eastern Europe the
community also arranged "scholarships" for the maintenance of the students, a
system called eating days (a student would eat every Tuesday with family X and
every Wednesday with family Y). Students studied independently or in pairs, with
the teachers occasionally listening to them arguing and advancing more arguments themselves.

The primary aim of the yeshiva, wrote one modern educator, was to produce
learned Jews who would live according to the Jewish Law and set aside daily periods for studying it all their lives (only a few became rabbis). A man might study at
home or in the *besmedrush* (Yiddish, from the Hebrew *bet midrash:* study house)
that existed in every East European community. This one room of the synagogue—with its library of books including the Scriptures, Talmud, commentaries,
and midrashim—would buzz with activity from early morning until late at night.
The *Chevreh Shas* (Talmud study circle) that met there two or three times weekly
included members of all classes: "Peddlers, shoemakers, tailors, all sorts of economic rag-tag ... belonged as naturally to such a circle as well-to-do merchants,"
wrote Samuel. The importance of study is reflected in the law that a synagogue
structure may be turned into a besmedrush but not vice versa because, as one educator wrote, "one is permitted to elevate an object from a lower to a higher state
of sanctity but not to reduce it from a higher to a lower one."

A young student could take up independent study in a besmedrush before
or instead of attending a yeshiva. Bialik, many years after his own study there,
paid a poetic tribute to the old besmedrush, which he called "the creative house /
foundry of the soul of the nation":

> Should you wish to know the well
> From which your brothers
> Crushed between
> the narrows of death and the torments of hell ...
> Drew holy consolation, trust, courage, patience ...
> to endure ...
> a life of suffering without end, without respite, with no other future in
>   sight. ...

If you desire to know the merciful mother
The old, doting, loyal mother
Who collected in her boundless compassion
The tears of her doomed son. . . :.
And . . . enveloped him in the shade of her wings. . . .
Oh my brother! . . .
Drop by the old decrepit study house. . . .
Even today you will see with your own eyes. . . .
Sad Jews . . . Sons of the Exile, carrying the weight of its yoke
Who forget their labor in a worn page of Gemara
Who bar thoughts of poverty with a story of bygone days
Who banish their worries with the poetry of the Psalms. . . .
Then your heart will tell you
That you tread upon the threshold of our very house of life.

RETROACTIVE ROLE MODELS

When being a scholar became the model for Jewish manhood, a body of literature sprang up picturing scholars as heroes and heroes as scholars. Rabbi Yochanan ben Zakkai, for example, is considered a great hero for having smuggled himself out of besieged Jerusalem during the Zealots' revolt against the Romans and gotten their general, Vespasian, to agree to his establishing an academy in the town of Yavneh. Other hero-scholars were the "Ten Martyrs of the (Roman) Empire," including Rabbi Akiva, who resisted the Emperor Hadrian's edict forbidding the teaching of Torah and were tortured to death. The Ten Martyrs, parenthetically, are heroes only in the Jewish culture, never having been mainstreamed into world history and literature. This prompted Rabbi Finkelstein to write, "This drama was worthy of having Plato as its chronicler and should have taken its place in the history of human civilization with the martyrdom of Socrates himself."

The Midrash and Agada created the new myth of the hero-as-scholar by making the pursuit of learning retroactive, as it were, to the three Patriarchs and to beloved scriptural heroes such as David, Solomon, and Elijah. While it was not necessary to do this with Moses, because this folk hero was already portrayed in the Five Books as a lawgiver, it is interesting to note that of all the many roles he played, the tradition emphasizes that of educator by always referring to him as Moshe *Rabbenu,* "our teacher."

Various midrashim relate that God revealed to Abraham "the new teachings which He expounded daily in His Heavenly Academy" (even God is portrayed as a scholar-teacher!), and that Abraham fulfilled all the mitzvot that were "revealed" later. Another midrash recounts how Jacob continued to study in the local bet midrash after his thirteenth year. He was "so simple and modest in his demeanor that if he came home from the bet midrash he would not disturb anyone to prepare his meal but would do so himself," a protofeminist behavior model, incidentally. Rashi expands on the retroactivity of commandment-fulfilling in his interpretation of the clause "I lived with Lavan" (his father-in-law) contained in the message Jacob sent to his estranged brother, Esau. Rashi relies on gematria, according to which the Hebrew word for "lived" adds up to 613—by tradition, the total number of mitzvot incumbent on Jews. The clause, he says, really means that Jacob "lived with Lavan but still observed all 613 mitzvot."

David, the warrior-king, emerges in the Midrash as rising at midnight to study Torah. Even after becoming king, he "sat at the feet of his teachers," submitting to one of them his decisions on religious questions "to make sure they were in accordance with the Law." Transforming Solomon into something greater than an instinctively wise judge, one midrash relates that he "analyzed the laws revealed to Moses and assigned reasons for the ritual and ceremonial ordinances of the Torah which, without his explanations, had seemed strange."

Jewish legends and folktales describe the fiery prophet Elijah after his ascent to heaven in a chariot as often reappearing on earth in disguises, such as jolly beggar, to provide assistance to the poor and advice to scholars on how specific issues were interpreted in the "Heavenly Academy."

The rabbis, by attributing to these scriptural heroes the qualities they admired and sought to instill in Jewish men, transformed them into role models whose exemplary scholarly qualities could be evoked during readings of the weekly Torah portion and invoked in sermons and in the education of the young. The retroactive transformation of hero-warriors into hero-scholars validated and reinforced the new definition of Jewish manhood.

◆ The efforts of the rabbis to create a "new Jewish man" were eminently successful. The power of Jewish men became the power of the mind and the intellect. Men whose brains had been honed razor-sharp through puzzling out, arguing over, and debating the Talmud, who could work their way through the maze of conflicting opinions, who could find legal loopholes and logical justifications, became the ones who made the major decisions on the internal life of Jewish communities and on their relationships with the general society, where sharp wits were necessary for group survival.

This was arguably the closest any society came to fulfilling Plato's ideal of the philosopher-king.

FIVE ❧ THE JEWISH WOMAN AS ALTRUISTIC-ASSERTIVE ENABLER

The Jews were liberated from Egypt because of the righteousness of the women.

TALMUD

The Jewish woman carried on her shoulders the weight of breadwinning for many years as the means of maintaining Torah study and she shall not be forgotten for that.

DI NATSION (RUSSIA, 1901)

The truth is that the Talmud is the collective endeavor not of the entire Jewish people, but only of its male half. Jewish women have been omitted—by purposeful excision—from this "collective endeavor" . . . from the main stage of Jewish communal achievement, . . . a loss numerically greater than a hundred pogroms; yet Jewish literature and history report not one wail, not one tear.

CYNTHIA OZICK

When study and the public performance of ritual—the components of spiritual resistance—came to be regarded as the most important endeavors in the Jewish struggle for survival, and the ones that defined masculinity, the role of the Jewish woman as enabler became to facilitate these pursuits *and* to accept/endure exclusion from them. It was the designation of spiritual resistance as the important work she was to facilitate and be excluded from that constitutes the major Jewish variation of the enabling role all women are supposed to fulfill in patriarchal societies.

The nature and character of the Jewish woman's enabling role can be seen clearly in the Talmudic stories about Rabbi Akiva and his wife, Rachel. These stories bring to mind the legends about Ulysses and Penelope and clearly show how female enabling patterns are predicated on male definitions of masculinity (hero-scholar vs. hero-warrior).

Akiva was a forty-year-old shepherd, poor and illiterate, working for a rich landowner in first-century Eretz Israel when Rachel, his boss's daughter, fell in love with him and proposed. "If I become betrothed to you," she asked him, "will you go and study?" Yes, he replied. When her father heard they were engaged, he threw her out of the house and cut her off without a *zuz* (penny).

Akiva and Rachel were married. That winter they lived in a hayloft, and he would gingerly tease out the hay from her beautiful long hair. When spring came, Akiva, at Rachel's urging, went off to the academy. One legend relates that she cut off and sold her hair to pay for his journey.

Akiva returned to town twelve years later. Standing near the door of Rachel's shack, he overheard a neighboring woman deride his wife for having let her husband desert her. Rachel replied, "Would that he stayed away for another twelve years if that's what it will take for him to become a scholar." Akiva tiptoed away without talking to his wife. He returned a dozen years later, flanked by an entourage of twelve thousand students. He did not go first to see Rachel but proceeded directly to the public square, where the town had rolled out the equivalent of a red carpet for this local-boy-made-good, the Jewish superstar scholar.

Rachel, of course, had aged—ground down by poverty and hardship. As she prepared to greet her husband, the neighbors urged her to adorn herself, fearing Akiva would not recognize the beautiful woman he married twenty-four years before. Replying to them in what is perhaps the most self-abnegating recorded statement by a Jewish woman, Rachel quoted from Proverbs: "A *tzaddik*" (righteous, pious man, from the Hebrew word for justice) "understands the soul of his animal." She then went out to greet her husband.

One can envision her—bent, hobbling, desperately trying to make her way in the crush of his scholarly groupies and the adoring townsfolk. Finally, close to the great man, she was overcome with emotion and fell on her face and kissed his feet. Akiva's students, seeing what appeared to them to be a crazy old woman, tried to push her away.

Suddenly Akiva looked away from the crowd and recognized her. Holding out his hands to Rachel, Akiva said to his students, "Honor her, for everything that is mine and yours" (that is, his and their learning) "is *hers*" (italics mine).

Akiva went down in Jewish history as a much-beloved hero: brilliant scholar, courageous rebel against Rome, brave martyr burned at the stake as one of the Ten Martyrs of the (Roman) Empire. He is the quintessential model of the Jewish man who makes great sacrifices in order to study and teach Torah.

Rachel, of whom Akiva said in that sublime moment of truth, "Everything that is mine is hers," is held up as a role model of what the Jewish woman should be—devoted, appreciative of her husband's intellectual possibilities and (later) his accomplishments, and provider of support in his academic endeavors to the point of self-sacrifice. The quintessential enabler, Rachel, wrote Rabbi Finkelstein, was "typical of a large number of pious women who made the preservation of the Torah in Israel possible amidst the perils that surrounded it."

MAINTAINING THE HOME SUPPORT SYSTEM

A prime reason for the specifically Jewish gender division of labor whereby men had a monopoly on spiritual resistance and women were their enablers in this most important work was that the men experienced the situation in the Exile as a national emergency that necessitated a long-term struggle for collective survival. This required that the most qualified people do the most important work, and obviously the men considered their gender the most qualified for learning Torah and for the public performance of ritual. Nothing less than national survival was seen to hinge on maintaining this specific division of labor.

The Jewish woman's facilitating of the men's spiritual resistance work went far beyond the traditional female role under patriarchy of responsibility for running the household. The home was one of the major support systems on which Jewish life rested. Facilitating in the home was particularly important because it was/is the locus for so many ritual observances and ceremonies, from those of kashrut to those of Shabbat and major holidays such as Passover. The crucial significance of home facilitating can be seen from the testimony of former shtetl residents, which applies to all eras, that "the mother is responsible for the physical aspect of [the home's] *Yiddishkeit*" (Jewishness, Jewish values and their expression), "by which is meant the *total* way of life of the 'real Jew.' ... All the intricate apparatus of domestic religious observance is in her keeping. Every member of the household *depends on her vigilance* to keep him [*sic*] a 'good Jew' in the daily mechanics of living" (italics mine).

If the woman was an efficient and skillful housekeeper, if she maintained a *Yiddishe hoyz* (Jewish home) with a warm Jewish atmosphere, where children absorbed much of the experience of and the feelings about what it meant to be Jewish, if, in addition, she kept harmony in the family, then she was known, they said, as a real *baleboosta* (Yiddish, from the Hebrew for householder), a complimentary term meaning a woman in total control of every aspect of home life.

◆ The crucial importance of women's skills in maintaining Jewishness in the home becomes apparent when we look at their role during the centuries of the Inquisition, among the crypto-Jews (a.k.a. Marranos) in Iberia and its New World colonies. Under these conditions, the home became the only context/center for the expression and transmission of Jewishness, and in this women played the key role. For example, Juana Enriques was the daughter of the matriarch of the largest secret Jewish group in Mexico City in the first half of the seventeenth century. The women slaughtered and koshered fowl according to Halacha and served as the *Chevra Kaddisha* (Hebrew for the "holy society" that washed and prepared the bodies of the dead for burial). Every day Enriques gave charity and visited and took food to Jewish hospital patients. Another noted Marrano woman of that era, Justa Mendez, observed kashrut, lit the Shabbat candles, fasted on prescribed days, and bought new dishes before Passover. She raised her children as Jews and made sure they married other observant secret Jews.

The survival skills women had sharply honed in running households were crucial during the Holocaust. In the earlier days of some of the ghettos, when younger men disappeared into forced labor camps or escaped, "the burden of sustaining the family fell on the woman's shoulders," said historian Isaiah Trunk. Their skills in cooking and nutrition were vital under ghetto conditions of hunger and starvation. Their housekeeping skills were important in some concentration camps (until 1941) because keeping the barracks clean lowered the epidemic death rate.

The emotional skills women had developed were possibly even more important in the ghettos and in the Resistance. Many women in the ghettos put their energy into organizing secret schools and public soup kitchens. They were the force behind the house committees (groups of tenants who cooperated in many ways, including child care), which later became important in the Resistance. They played an especially important role as couriers in the Underground. Marie Syrkin wrote that every ghetto had one young woman who was called its mother. She "flitted from dungeon to dungeon, from ghetto to ghetto, smuggling food, information or arms . . . always strengthening the [Jews'] capacity to endure and survive."

Women in death camps (those that survived the initial "selection" that marked most Jews for the gas chamber) and in concentration and labor camps helped each other survive by creating new "families" based on bonding as *lager-shvesters* (German, Yiddish for camp sisters). This phenomenon was not generally present among men, whose bonding, when it existed, was mostly along political lines. Survivors' testimony also indicates other gender differences in prisoner behavior. Eugen Kogon wrote that "many male prisoners became hardened" and some became "cruel to the point of sadism"; Primo Levi described the "entry ritual" by which veteran inmates of Auschwitz tormented new arrivals. By contrast, wrote Germaine Tillion, "In the women's camps, only the most selfish in character became so hardened, while for many, the incredible personal suffering only increased their concern for the needs of others." The story of what women experienced and did during the Holocaust and Resistance has never been incorporated into the history of the period and still remains to be fully researched and recounted.

EXCLUDING WOMEN FROM SPIRITUAL RESISTANCE

Women were excluded from the study of Torah lishma. They were not legally forbidden to learn Torah, and some women scholars in various eras and places, most of them taught by their fathers, attained considerable scholarship. The exclusion mainly took the form of prevention: They were not given the kind of elementary Jewish education universally required for boys, and thus they lacked the basic knowledge to continue studying on their own; the world of the besmedrush and the yeshiva was closed to them.

Females were usually taught just enough to know how to carry out their complex facilitating role, what to ask of a rabbinical arbiter when a difficult problem arose, and how to read the Hebrew prayers (and, in Eastern Europe, stories from the Torah and midrashim in Yiddish), but little more. Excluding women from Torah study, of course, prevented them from attaining the intellectual expertise necessary for their becoming legislators and arbiters; they were allowed no role in developing the Halachic system, even in contributing insights to legislation that impacted on their lives as women—those regarding marriage, property, divorce, assault, and "family purity," of which more in chapter 6.

Scholars of the Talmudic era believed women's exclusion from Torah study was "good for the Jews." Their justification/rationalization was that "women are light-headed"; they were adept at dealing with the practical matters of running a household, even engaging in business, but not qualified for the high-octane, intellectually creative work of study that was *the* prerequisite for Jewish survival.

Because of this, letting them study Torah was considered dangerous, as we can see from a debate on this subject beginning in the Mishnah. The discussion centers on whether women should be taught only specific laws on a "need to know" basis (Rabbi Eliezer's view) or also the underlying meanings and reasons behind them (Ben Azzai's position). Eliezer states that "whoever teaches his daughter Torah" (the Gemara adds here, "it is as though he") "teaches her *tiflut.*" He is later quoted as saying, "Let the words of the Torah be burned and not given to women."

It is impossible to know what tiflut actually meant in the usage of the day. The ensuing discussion in the Gemara, which stresses women's lack of "subtlety," seems to point to a translation of "nonsense" or, more accurately, useless information (along the lines of a little knowledge being a dangerous thing). It is usually translated as immorality and lechery. In any case, the debate, and the later commentaries on it, testify to the fear that dire consequences (lechery/immorality or misinterpretation leading to it, or both) will result if women are allowed to engage in the same process of learning as men.

❧ Women were exempted (i.e., excluded) from some of the positive time-bound mitzvot, most of which involve public performance of ritual at set times, such as praying in the synagogue at regular daily intervals and on Shabbat and holidays and performing various ceremonies there. They were excluded from participating in the *minyan,* the quorum of ten worshipers necessary to conduct an official prayer service, and from being called up for an *aliyah* (from the Hebrew verb "to ascend/go up") to read or bless the reading of the Torah portion in the synagogue.

Reams of apologetic rhetoric have been expended to "prove" that the exclusion of women from the public performance of ritual is unimportant because it is in the home, where women "reign supreme," that so many rituals are performed and holidays celebrated. But aside from the three prime female mitzvot—lighting Shabbat candles, observing the "family purity" laws (which also obviously involves the men), and pulling off and burning a piece of *challah* (Hebrew for white Shabbat egg bread) to symbolize the Temple tithe—all the ritual observances in the home are performed by men. These include their reciting the blessings on bread before eating, leading the grace after meals, making the blessings on the Chanukah candles, and conducting the Passover seder.

However, since women's enabling in the home, as we have seen, involved so much more than responsibility for the material aspects of the household, it is possible that the rabbis who made the rules and the female and male Jews who followed them may have sincerely believed that "exempting" women from some time-bound mitzvot was actually a boon to women.

◆ It is the privilege of being "burdened" with *all* the mitzvot that is always cited by apologists as the "real meaning" behind the men's daily morning prayer, "Praised be God that He has not created me as a woman." In commenting on the reason for this prayer, Rashi links it with another one, also mandated in the same Talmudic passage, expressing gratitude for not having been created as a slave (for whom total religious obligation is not required). A wife is like a slave in this regard, he writes, because she is "a servant to her husband like a slave [is] to his master." Apologists have softened this language and explained that women were exempted from certain time-bound mitzvot to free them up to perform their main function, caring for home and children, that is, enabling.

Women were also disqualified as witnesses in a bet din except in a few specific circumstances, although in many places (e.g., Egypt in the eleventh to thirteenth centuries and Renaissance Italy) they did appear in court to settle their own business matters. The prime rationale for their disqualification (along with children, idiots, and men with such shady job titles as pigeon racers, gamblers, and usurers) was not, as is sometimes stated today, that women's credibility was suspect; the courts did accept their testimony in cases of rape and battering. Rather, the justification was that this would conflict with their family responsibilities.

This brings us back to the connection between the perception of a national emergency and the exclusion of women from spiritual resistance. The link is revealed when we analyze the words and actions of the false messiah of the seventeenth century, Shabbetai Zvi. Addressing women, he lamented their situation: "Woe unto you, unhappy women, who for Eve's sin are *subject to your husbands* and all that you do depends on their consent" (italics mine). He then promised to liberate them from the "curse of Eve": "Blessed are you, for I have come to make

you free and happy like your husbands." One innovation he introduced was calling up women for an aliyah in the synagogue.

Shabbetai's dream of a radical reform of the status of women and his actions
on their behalf become comprehensible in light of his declaring himself to be the
Messiah. This meant that the age of redemption had dawned and, therefore, that
the national emergency—which had necessitated the division of labor excluding
women from the arena of spiritual resistance—was over.

SPIRITUAL RESISTANCE AND THE DEFINITION
OF MASCULINITY

Underneath the conscious perception of national emergency requiring the exclusion of women from spiritual resistance was an unconscious motivation of far
greater significance: to make this a turf that defined masculinity. This motivation
emerges when we juxtapose the two reasons the men advanced for excluding
women from this turf.

One reason was that women would "distract" men from spiritual activities,
especially from learning. This is the uniquely Jewish expression of the male fear
in all patriarchies of women's sexuality and sexual power. Evidence of this
anxiety comes from a revealing quote in the Talmud: "He who talks much with
womankind brings evil upon himself and *neglects the study of the Law*" (italics
mine). Further evidence comes from legends about gorgeous, seductive, and near-
irresistible females who tried to lure scholars away from their tomes.

Although Torah study, according to the Talmud, was supposed to be a prophylactic against men's acting on illicit libidinal cravings (and considered capable
of preventing their being "delivered into the power" of the yetzer hara), the Agada
relates that both Rabbi Akiva and Rabbi Meir, another famous scholar (husband
of the learned Beruriah, whom we shall discuss shortly), almost succumbed to a
seducer who looked like a woman but was actually Satan in drag. To catch up
with "her," Akiva clambered up a palm tree and Meir crossed a river on a shaky
rope bridge. Satan vanished when a heavenly voice conveniently warned him off
(a classic last-minute rescue if ever there was one).

Even more revealing is a Hassidic story about a married woman who,
dressed in a nightdress, entered the room where a famous rabbi was studying one
night and looked at him "as though she wanted to throw herself down" before
him. The rabbi, "attacked" by a "compulsion" that "used the forces of both [his] admiration and [his] *compassion for her humanity*," managed to escape by leaping
out the window (italics mine). Here, acknowledging a woman's "humanity" and
sexuality almost resulted in her stealing him away from Torah study.

(The fear of female "distraction" is also a prime reason given by Orthodox
apologists today for segregating women in the synagogue behind a *mechitzah,* a
partition between worshipers of the two genders, or in a balcony section.)

The second reason given for excluding women from spiritual resistance is embodied in the Talmudic statement, "All are qualified to be among [those who read aloud from the Torah] even a minor and a woman, but the sages said, 'A woman is not to come forward to read [publicly] from the Torah out of respect for the honor of the community.'"

The implication here is that the community would be "dishonored" by a woman's public reading from the Torah because if it had to scrape the bottom of the barrel by calling on a woman to do so, it must obviously lack a man—any man—who is capable of doing this "man's work." Such a community must be one where the men are unlearned and therefore unmasculine. This shameful state of affairs, when revealed in public by the woman's action, would impugn the "honor of the community."

The statement about the community's honor/dishonor reveals the precise nature of the men's anxieties that are embodied in the seduction-manqué legends and the distraction argument. The fear was that by losing *control* over study— through women's "distracting" them with their sexuality or through their participating in learning (proof of which would be the erudition exhibited in reading from the Torah in public)—the men would lose their masculinity. How acute must this psychological need have been for men to exclude women from the turf of study *so it could define their masculinity*—a need so acute that it superseded the practical necessity to include *half the nation* in the pool from which brilliant scholars and rabbinical legislators were drawn!

Preventing women's intrusion upon this turf involved the classic Jewish behavioral methodology of channeling women's love of Torah into enabling. This can be seen from the statement in the Talmud that women should "have their sons taught Torah and Mishnah and wait for their husbands until they return from the study house."

THE BERURIAH LIBEL

There is only one woman recorded in the entire Talmud as having been such a respected scholar, teacher, and debater of Halachic issues that her opinions were accepted as law. She was Beruriah, the daughter of a famous rabbi, who lived in second-century Eretz Israel after the harsh suppression of the Bar Kochba rebellion.

The stories about her in the Talmud and Midrash portray a woman of great intellectual and moral strength who has mastered the methodology of disputation and surmounted various family tragedies; who is diligent in studying and teaching Torah, and who lives by it; and who is empathetic to the sincere but is witheringly contemptuous of ignorant men with inflated egos.

Beruriah's formidable reputation, however, is later dragged through the mud. A mysterious Talmudic passage states that her husband, Rabbi Meir, ran away to Babylon possibly "because of the incident regarding Beruriah." Nothing further that we know of was written on this "incident" anywhere until about five hundred years later, when Rashi told this story in his commentary on the Talmudic passage: "Beruriah once again made fun of the saying of the sages that women are light-headed. Then Meir told her, 'With your life will you have to take back your words.' He sent one of his students to test her, to see if she would allow herself to be seduced. He sat [sic] by her ... until she surrendered herself to him. When she realized [what she'd done], she strangled herself. Then Rabbi Meir ran away because of the scandal."

The story is obviously preposterous. The behavior of both individuals is totally out of character: Beruriah was an exceptionally moral and ethical individual and too smart, as well, to fall into such a trap; Meir can hardly have been regarded as so unethical (and spiteful) as to have set it; and their marriage was exemplary for its mutuality of devotion and respect.

The Beruriah libel is designed to show that it is the intellectual woman who is the real threat to the Jews. It "proves" the wisdom of the rabbis who believed that allowing women to study Torah would lead to dire consequences (immorality being one). It was precisely because Beruriah mistakenly believed her mind "subtle" enough to understand the complexities of Torah that she regarded herself as immune to illicit lust and ignored the fact that *all* women are "light-headed." She thus brought herself (and her husband) to ruin.

There is no way to trace the origin of this chilling misogynist libel. Rashi was a student of a disciple of Rabbi Gershom, "The Light of the Exile" (960–1028), who unilaterally (or by convening a synod of rabbinical and communal leaders from France and Germany) improved women's situation in the West by banning polygamy and nonconsensual divorce. Rashi was not given to making up stories and tends to transmit midrashim by other scholars rather than invent his own. Touchingly modest, he frequently admits in his commentaries that "concerning this I have no tradition."

If the story was an oral legend passed on for hundreds of years, why wasn't it committed to writing before? And, new or old, why did Rashi, living in eleventh-century France and Germany, find it so necessary to disseminate it to (male) students of the Talmud?

A clue emerges from the responsa of the High Middle Ages, which testify to women's higher economic status. Many women in that era were involved in moneylending to nobles and peasants. Congregations as well as private families appointed them as trustees, and communal funds were given into their care for administration and investment at their discretion.

Their important economic position and their consciousness of its importance led a few prominent women to venture into the forbidden turf of public performance of ritual. Some began to observe mitzvot from which they were exempted, including wearing *tzitzit* (fringed undergarments), as one rabbi's wife, Bruna, did, or putting on tefillin (phylacteries), as Rashi's own daughters did.

Moreover, certain rabbis were acceding to these practices. In the twelfth century, Rabbi Abraham of Orleans encouraged his daughters to be part of the minyan chanting grace after meals, and Rabbi Simcha of Speyer allowed his wife to do so.

Some scholars, seeing this trend emerge, may have felt that an even greater danger loomed—of women invading the turf of study. They created a misogynist libel about how a learned woman came to grief as a warning to the men who were allowing women to participate in such rituals against permitting women to go too far. It was an attempt to set boundaries (a classic Jewish behavioral control method) beyond which women must not be allowed to venture.

Elizabeth Janeway argues that behind every positive role (e.g., the ideal pleasing woman) lurks a negative shadow role (e.g., shrew, bitch), which is its flip side. The negative role exists to be called up and attached to breakers of the positive role and is a threat of the dire consequences of not adhering to it. In the case of Beruriah, Rashi's libel flipped her from being a potentially positive role model for women of that day to being a negative one, thus showing the dangerous consequences of allowing women to break the gender division of labor.

BREADWINNING AS GENDER-NEUTRAL TURF

The Jewish division of labor between women and men did not extend to earning a living, which was gender-neutral turf. This was another crucial difference between Jewish patriarchy and classic patriarchy. In the shtetl, as elsewhere, paid work was "sexless." Unlike the synagogue, dominated by men, and the home, by women, "the marketplace belongs to both," said Zborowski's and Herzog's interviewees.

Breadwinning could not be allowed to define masculinity because the Jews could not afford to exclude women from participating in the fierce struggle for economic survival in the Exile. Evidence for this motivation comes from accounts of women embroiderers on silk in Egypt (ca. twelfth–thirteenth century). The rabbis "viewed with concern" the women's having to work at the palaces of princely families, wrote historian Mark Wischnitzer, "but to no avail. The women argued that *poverty compelled them to earn a living* and that they had their husbands' permission to work away from home" (italics mine).

⤎ Jewish women were not excluded from the economic sphere of the public realm nor were they marginalized or invisible on this turf. Their role in paid work goes back to First and Second Jewish Commonwealth Eretz Israel. Their spinning and weaving of fabrics for sale grew out of household tasks, as did basket weaving, a field they dominated. Along with men, they also produced pottery, some for export. In the Second Temple era, women bakers were the principal confectioners, and women (and men) prepared cosmetics. Another occupation women engaged in was that of professional mourner, which often included composing elegies on the merits of the deceased.

In the Exile, Jewish women's occupations expanded across the realm of public economic life and included both craftwork and business.

Except where Jews constituted a small percentage of the total population of a territory and were excluded from working at crafts (e.g., northern Europe in the Middle Ages), Jews, women as well as men, could be found working as artisans. This was true of Mediterranean communities, Spain, and Eastern Europe from the end of the fifteenth century. Jewish women artisans worked in weaving in thirteenth-century Palermo; in producing apparel in sixteenth- to eighteenth-century Rhodes; as tailors, quiltmakers, glovemakers, beauticians, and painters of playing cards in medieval Rome; in cloth making in sixteenth-century Salonika; and as shoemakers, tailors, furriers, milliners, and producers of buttons, cords, trousers, and gloves in eighteenth-century Prague, to cite just a few examples from Wischnitzer's exhaustive research on Jewish crafts and guilds. Close needlework made some women blind or impaired their vision, and tobacco work caused them intestinal disorders.

Wischnitzer also unearthed information about women's work in what we might consider nontraditional occupations. In pre-1391 Navarre (Spain), women worked in the building trades, where, in accordance with traditional economic practice, they were paid about three quarters of the salary of Christian male employees. Women in isolated Italian Renaissance communities were allowed to be ritual slaughterers (this was justified on grounds that they needed to be able to provide food for their families). During the late Middle Ages in Europe and in the Renaissance, Jewish women worked as copyists (as they had in medieval Egypt), scribes, translators, and, later, typesetters and publishers in the newly established printing industry. In Renaissance Italy, as in medieval Spain and eighteenth-century Prague, they were also physicians. In seventeenth-century Holland, wives turned the grindstones in the home-based diamond cutting-and-polishing industry.

Selling was another important occupation of Jewish women in different eras. The Mishnah states that a man may "set his wife up as a *chenvanit*" (stall keeper) in the market. From these market stalls, women in Second Temple–era Judea sold bread, and women in the shtetl centuries later sold a variety of other products. Fairs and country markets were the venue where Jewish women peddled their wares in fourteenth-century Navarre and Renaissance Lombardy, and the garments and collars they produced in late-fifteenth-century Cracow. Jewish women worked as merchants in many different times and places, including Asia Minor in the first centuries C.E., Islamic Spain, England in the High Middle Ages, Renaissance Italy, fifteenth- and sixteenth-century Turkey, and Poland.

The Jewish woman often became a businesswoman in medieval France and Germany during and because of her husband's absences from home, usually to study. The absent-husband pattern continued in Eastern Europe: Some men went on the road for long periods of time to try to eke out a living; others lived for years at a yeshiva or at a Hassidic court; later, many immigrated to America. Widows, among them the seventeenth–eighteenth-century memoirist Gluckel of

Hameln, often continued the businesses of their husbands, a role epitomized by Mirele Efros, the heroine of Jacob Gordin's Yiddish play of that name.

The expectation that the woman would play an active role in supporting the family was taken into account during negotiations of a *shidduch* (Hebrew/Yiddish for match, arranged marriage). It also determined the character of the secular education given to daughters in many middle-class European families, which included instruction in indigenous languages.

From late in the Second Temple era, women's involvement in working for pay was regarded as a form of enabling that would facilitate the men's being able to study. This emerges from the description of the "Woman of Valor" in Proverbs (an alphabetical acrostic traditionally ascribed to King Solomon but believed to have been compiled around 300 B.C.E.). The long list of this valorous (and overworked) woman's accomplishments—"After careful thought, she buys a field and plants a vineyard *out of her earnings.* She weaves linen and sells it, and supplies merchants with their sashes" (italics mine)—is given in no special order. But in the middle lies the key to its raison d'être: "Her husband is well known in the city gate, where he takes his place with the elders of the land" (i.e., scholars and lawmakers). The writer(s) of Proverbs exhort(s) the readers to "let her labors bring ... honor" to this precursor of today's Superwoman because what she does enables her husband to sit with the elders and study.

In Western Europe a custom began to evolve around the fifteenth and sixteenth centuries of women, in the words of a contemporary traveler, "doing all kinds of handiwork for the [nobles] and in this way *support[ing] their husbands*" while the men studied Torah (italics mine). The pattern of the woman's being the *sole* supporter of the family came to its apotheosis in the shtetl. The wives of five leading Hassidic rabbis, for example, were a cloth vender, a sugar merchant, an estate supervisor, a clothes dealer, and an itinerant peddler. Wives of non-Hassidic rabbis and scholars had similar work experiences.

DOWNGRADING BREADWINNING AS "WOMEN'S WORK"

While the pattern of wife as sole provider gradually ebbed in Western and parts of Central Europe as economic conditions improved in the modern era, East European Jews remained mired in abysmal poverty well into the nineteenth and even twentieth centuries. Most lived on a primarily vegetarian and dairy diet consisting mainly of bread, potatoes, kasha (buckwheat groats), noodles, eggs, milk from goats and cows, plus the occasional herring. The "joke" was that "if a Jew ate a chicken, one of them was sick." An orange was such a rarity that it was treasured by an entire shtetl.

Reading the history of the cruel and unremitting persecution of the Jews by the Czarist regime in the nineteenth century leaves one amazed at their ability to survive at all. Czarist oppression included forcing Jews to live in the "Pale of Settlement" (essentially the provinces in the area annexed in the late eighteenth century from Poland, later reduced in size); periodically rounding up Jews caught living in cities outside it; banning Jews from traditional sources of livelihood; and expelling them from the shtetls to towns and cities. It also included the drafting of boys, most of them poor, for twenty-five years of what Simon Dubnow, the great Russian Jewish historian (murdered by the Nazis in 1941), called "military martyrdom": harsh and brutal army servitude, during which they were tortured into forced conversion to Russian Orthodoxy. These were the "cantonists," a group of whom Alexander Herzen encountered in 1835 and for whom he begged the army officer in charge of the deportation, in vain, for mercy. They were, he wrote, "children of eight and ten, ... pale, emaciated, terrified. ... Their lips were bloodless and the blue circles under their eyes spoke of fever and chills. So the poor children, deprived of all love and care ... trudged toward the grave."

In addition to this persecution, there were pogroms. Incredibly, the Russian Jews did not crack under these blows.

Many men, failing to earn a living under these conditions of unremitting poverty and unrelenting stress, simply gave up (just as they had long ago given up on defending "their" women from rape by non-Jewish men). They abandoned the turf of breadwinning to the women, who were not expected to crack under the strain, not even when their burden doubled because of the men's passivity. The women became super-enablers, responsible for the entire physical existence of the family, while the men retreated into the world of study, a socially approved activity that provided ample validation, or of Hassidic activities. There was also alcoholism among the Hassidic rank and file, particularly in southwest Russia, according to Dubnow. This drinking at Hassidic gatherings "resulted in drowsiness of thought, idleness and economic ruin. ... [Many Hassidim] neglected their business affairs and their starving families."

In patriarchal societies, men are supposed to be the primary providers or at least to do remunerative work; wives sometimes supplemented the family income (or worked alongside their husbands, as in farm families). It is partly because poor women have to work that poor men define their masculinity on the basis of men's specific types of physical labor—in the urbanized West, those that require brawn, strength, and muscle—from which women are excluded.

Jewish men in the past did not look to non-Jewish men of any class in the general society as their reference group (the sector of society that one regards as a model for one's own behavior) in this or any other area of life. Abrahams writes that in the Middle Ages, the Jewish businesswoman often supported her husband "despite the contempt in which a Jew was held for allowing his wife to *play the man* for him" (italics mine). Jews in Russia certainly did not look to peasants as their reference group, regarding them as drunks, wife-beaters, and pogromchiks at worst, uneducated and uncultured hard-luck cases at best. They did not feel demeaned as men for not laboring as the peasants did.

While being a "good provider" did not define masculinity for Jewish men, they did know that they should have (taken) responsibility for supporting their wives and children—or, at the very least, themselves. The Talmud instructs a man to brave embarrassment and "Skin a carcass in the public square rather than become a burden to the community," and Maimonides ranks assisting someone to become self-supporting as the highest rung on his "Ladder of Tzedakah." The material support the husband was obligated to provide his wife was spelled out in the marriage contract he signed.

To maintain their self-respect despite their having relinquished responsibility for providing, the men downgraded breadwinning as inappropriate work for their gender. They took refuge in the rationalization provided by the Vilna Gaon, the leader of the religious opponents of the Hassidim in the eighteenth century, who wrote, "True heroes are men ... meditating on Torah day and night even though their home be without bread and clothing." The downgrading of providing was thus not the result of an authentic belief in its inappropriateness as a male activity. This is borne out, for instance, by the haste with which East European men who immigrated to America reestablished themselves on the work turf once they saw its doors open to them.

The more women entered the breadwinning turf, of course, the less status it had for men—a typical pattern when women proliferate in a field of endeavor. This allowed the men to regard it as "women's work" and thereby rationalize their being disinclined to engage in it. This attitude is represented in the comment of a young Hassid in a nineteenth-century novel by Peretz Smolenskin: "Is my mother-in-law paralyzed that I should have to earn a living? Until the day the worms take up residence in her corpse, she will go on working and supplying our needs."

The women colluded with the men in this rationalization to allow their husbands to retain their self-respect (just as they had done in taking responsibility for rape avoidance). They behaved as women were advised to do by an early seventeenth-century German guidebook for women, which urged that "wives of scholars who support the entire family with their earnings must not disparage their husbands who are *unsuited to everyday tasks*" (italics mine).

These four words provide another clue about the reason for the women's collusion. The women had little choice but to accept the burden of supporting the family; the alternative was to see their children starve. The idea that breadwinning was women's work and that it was their duty, privilege, and honor to support their scholarly husbands and their children served as a rationalization of what might have otherwise been experienced as an unjust and intolerable burden/imposition. The validation they received from the community for fulfilling this role enhanced their self-esteem: They knew that what they were doing was necessary and important.

❧ Another factor may have also been operating here. The men may have unconsciously perceived that only "total immersion" in spiritual resistance would provide them the emotional strength and mental sanity to resist Czarist tyranny and avert the Jews' having a collective nervous breakdown from the blows it inflicted. "The reactionary force of Hassidism," Dubnow acknowledged, "acted as the only antidote against the reactionary force from the outside."

While "total immersion" was Draconian and its cost high, perhaps it was a necessary transition, a holding-pattern stage, until movements coalesced that advanced political solutions Jews could work for actively, which happened at the end of the century. As Dubnow concluded:

> The sledgehammer of Russian reaction [that] had been descending with crushing force upon the ... community, ... instead of shattering the national organism of Jewry, had only helped to steel it and to harden its indestructible *spiritual* self. The Jewry of Russia showed to the world that it was endowed with an iron constitution [italics mine].

FORGING THE FEMALE ALTRUISTIC-ASSERTIVE ENABLER

Assertive behavior in women sometimes comes to the fore under conditions of harsh oppression. This is probably what happened with Jews in the Exile. The men, responding to its emergence with the classic Jewish behavioral methodology, sought to direct this assertiveness into appropriate channels—altruistic activities (i.e., enabling) to benefit Jewish survival: "good for the Jews," as defined by them.

Harnessing the Jewish woman's assertiveness to altruism produced a truly outstanding type of enabler: the altruistic-assertive enabler, epitomized, above all, by Queen Esther.

It is significant to note here that Esther, whether or not she actually existed, and the *Megillah* (scroll) bearing her name (which dates to the Second Temple era and is read in the synagogue on the holiday of Purim) deal with the experience of Exile. The Megillah relates how Jews seemed to be living in peace and security in Persia but their reading of reality was incorrect. The message of the Megillah is essentially the same as the one in Exodus: Anything can happen in an exile, so don't be surprised; Judeophobia is an irrational, chronic disease, so it is pointless to advance logical counterarguments against it.

To recap the story briefly: Haman, the grand vizier, seeks to convince King Ahashverosh to have all the Jews killed because one of them, Mordechai, refuses to bow to him. His argument draws on the classic Judeophobic myths going back to Pharaoh's times: Jews are threatening, powerful, disloyal, alien: "There is a certain people scattered abroad and dispersed among the peoples in all the provinces of your realm. ... They do not observe even the King's laws. Therefore, it is not befitting the king to tolerate them. ... Let it be recorded that they be annihilated."

Giving Haman's Final Solution nary a stray thought, Ahashverosh acts like M.A.S.H.'s Colonel Blake when Radar shoves some papers under his nose to sign.

He orders a decree designating a particular date as D (Destruction of the Jews)-Day to be drawn up and dispatched throughout the kingdom. There is no recorded protest from anyone now or when the genocidal action (or should we use the Nazi term *aktion?*) is attempted.

What–or who–saves the Jews? First, Mordechai, the *éminence grise* of the Megillah, who has had the prescience to employ the Court Jew survival strategy: making his orphaned niece and ward, Esther, audition (successfully) for queen. As he tells her after the evil decree is issued: "Who knows if it was just for a time like this that you attained the royal position."

Esther is initially pictured in the Megillah practically as a puppet of Mordechai's. She "told nothing of her kindred and her people as *Mordechai had instructed*" (italics mine). The Midrash goes to great lengths to show how Esther observed Jewish Law at the palace while remaining in the closet. She is at first reluctant to obey Mordechai's instructions to go to the king and get him to repeal the decree because, she writes her uncle, people rarely approach the king unsummoned and live to tell the tale. Mordechai shoots back with, "Do not imagine that you will be able to escape in the king's palace any more than the rest of the Jews."

Aside from being a dig at assimilationist Jews who think they can pass unscathed during a pogrom, these words were included to transmit the message that Jewish women really don't understand too well what is at stake in the Exile ("Women are light-headed"), and require motivation, instructions, and training from men. In addition, Esther is seen as a rescuer who is flawed and must be repaired to do rescuing. In one midrash, God refers to her thus: "The *redeemer* I shall send to you in [Persia] shall also be an orphan, fatherless and motherless" (italics mine).

Once pointed in the right direction by Mordechai (repaired), Esther puts her life on the line, revealing herself to be an inspired and consummate strategist, as the Midrash points out. Because of her intercession, the king orders Haman hanged. But since the genocidal decree, like those famous letters of transit in *Casablanca,* cannot be rescinded, the king now has to dispatch another decree permitting the Jews to defend themselves on D-Day. The Megillah writer(s) probably included this element of the story to discourage physical resistance in cases where overwhelming state power is lined up against them. Parenthetically, the second decree does not discourage the Persians in the least from trying to perpetrate a pogrom–another message about what to expect in the Exile.

Esther's assertiveness has thus saved the day. But the writers of the Megillah realized the danger in encouraging assertive behavior in women: It might ignite independence of mind and spirit; they might become uppity and rebellious and refuse to stay on a leash and follow orders. Therefore Jewish women had to be given precise boundaries (again, part of classic Jewish behavior control) for their assertiveness. They had to learn where the fine line was between altruistic-assertive enabling (like Esther's) and garden-variety assertiveness, and not to cross over it.

One way to do this was to present a negative role model showing the dire consequences of "going too far." It is primarily for this reason that the Megillah opens with and features so prominently the story of how Esther's predecessor, Queen Vashti, disobeyed the king's order to attend a banquet, and it quotes the reaction of one of his advisers: "It is not only the King whom Vashti has wronged but also all the officials and all the people in all the provinces. . . . For this deed of the Queen's will come to the attention of all women, *making their husbands contemptible* in their eyes" (italics mine).

The adviser suggests a decree banning Vashti be proclaimed everywhere so that "all the wives will show respect to their husbands, great and small alike," and that it include the proviso that "every man should rule in his own home."

Thus the lessons of the Megillah about women are very clear: Since their intellectual understanding of what is necessary for Jewish survival in the Exile is limited, they need to be properly motivated and directed, as Esther was. (Significantly, one scriptural commentary blames Adam for the serpent/apple disaster because he failed to instruct Eve properly.) Women are to be allowed a fairly wide behavioral range in order to be able to carry out their demanding enabler role, but they are to be discouraged from acts of assertiveness that, like Vashti's, are selfish and only in the interests of the woman herself.

THE MARTYR AS ROLE MODEL

The need to control women's assertiveness is behind the tendency on the part of some late- and post–Second Commonwealth sages to deglorify the strong women in the Scriptures to ensure they not be viewed by women as positive role models.

The Jewish women in the early Scriptures fall into two basic categories: protagonists—the four Matriarchs (Sarah, Rebecca, Leah, and Rachel); Miriam the prophet; Deborah the judge; Samuel's mother, Hannah; and David's wife, Abigail—and victims—Dina; David's daughter, Tamar; his first wife, Michal; and Jepthah's unnamed daughter.

The protagonists are assertive, resourceful, good strategists, and by no means shrinking violets, although only Miriam actually rebelled openly against patriarchy (and only in one case involving her criticizing Moses). They either tried to beat it at its own game, found ways to circumvent it, or manipulated it and the men in their lives, sometimes using sexual wiles. But what apparently disturbed some of the scholars who are quoted in the Midrash and the Talmudic Agada was that these women's *motivations* were not purely altruistic (or not altruistic at all) and, moreover, that they took much too much initiative. Their assertiveness had to be criticized as inappropriate female behavior.

A prime target of this methodology is Deborah, who is always trotted out by antifeminist apologists as proof of Judaism's "positive attitude" toward women. The midrashim about Deborah, however, testify otherwise: "Prophet though she was, she was subject to the *frailties* of her sex. Her *self-consciousness* was inordinate. She sent for Barak [the general] to come to her instead of going to him, and in her Song she *spoke more of herself than was seemly.* The result was that the prophetical spirit departed from her for a time when she was composing her Song" (italics mine).

The Agada, too, transmits negative comments about Deborah, as well as about Hulda the prophet. Hulda, it should be pointed out, was an important spokesperson for the prophet movement of the First Temple era and was instrumental in bringing about fundamental reforms beginning in the eighteenth year of King Josiah's reign (around 621 B.C.E.). A delegation of five important officials, headed by the high priest, called on Hulda at the king's request. Acting on her prophecy that the people's crimes would lead to their doom, Josiah repented and "made a Covenant . . . to walk after the Lord and to keep His commandments . . . and all the people joined in the Covenant." But the comments in the Agada denigrate these two courageous women. Deborah (which means bee) and Hulda (which means weasel) were, they said, named for "nasty animals" because they displayed haughtiness and disrespect toward men. (When male prophets such as Nathan, Elijah, and Jeremiah confront kings over their evil deeds, they are considered heroes.)

❧ Writers of literature in and after the Second Commonwealth era provide as role models the "modest" Esther (who, unlike Deborah, did not blow her own horn) and two female martyrs, mothers of seven martyred sons. One mother was from the early years of the period of the Maccabees, leaders of a successful revolt—which the holiday of Chanukah celebrates—against the Hellenistic Syrian rulers of Judea beginning in 168 B.C.E., and founders of a royal dynasty that came to an end when the rule of the quisling and Roman collaborator Herod began in 37 B.C.E. The other was from Roman times.

The Second Book of Maccabees (first century B.C.E.) relates the ordeal of the "surpassingly wonderful" Hannah, mother of seven sons whom she encouraged to die rather than violate Jewish Law, "for she was filled with a noble spirit and stirred her woman's heart with *manly* courage" (italics mine). Hannah herself was martyred following her youngest son's death. The Fourth Book of Maccabees, written a century later, goes even further in praise, equating Hannah with Abraham in her willingness to sacrifice her sons for the Law. A story with an almost identical cast of characters and sequence of events is recounted in the Agada about a female martyr in the last days of the Bar Kochba rebellion.

As with all such legendary folk heroes, it is important to note what characteristics the nation chose to endow them with. And in these two cases, what is extolled is self-sacrificing altruism. Historian Shlomo Noble understood this when he commented on a tenth-century work exalting the Jewish woman martyr: She manifests, he wrote, "a *profound contempt for self-interest,* a boundless devotion to her people, and stoic defiance of death and suffering" (italics mine).

🖎 Jewish chroniclers recount with encomiums stories about female martyrs during the High Middle Ages, a period Noble called "the finest hour of the Jewish woman."

When Robert the Pious, king of France, forced the Jews to choose in 1007 between conversion and death, related a contemporary chronicler, "there arose noble women [who] took ahold of one another's hands saying, 'Let us go to the river and drown ourselves so that the Name of God be not desecrated through us, for the sacred [Torah] is trodden down in the mire of the streets and . . . burned in fire, and altogether death is better for us than life.'" Chroniclers from the era of the Crusades reported similar scenes in countless Rhineland communities. The women are described in the period's literature as going to their martyrdom as if to their wedding canopy: "The brides bid farewell to their bridegrooms with a kiss and rush off to be slaughtered."

Dreading most the seizure and forced baptism of their sons and daughters, the "compassionate women strangle[d] their children." Some tied their children to their bodies so they would have to be burned together. Jewish chroniclers praised the women's resourcefulness: "Knowing the greed of the adversaries, they would cast out to them through the window money, silver, and other valuables to keep them busy with picking up the treasure so that [the women] could complete the slaying of their children." Another delay tactic was to hurl stones through the window at the attackers.

One Spanish Jewish chronicler related that women led the way in *Kiddush HaShem* (Hebrew for Sanctification of the Name of God by choosing martyrdom over conversion or idolatry). The Crusaders actually blamed their failure at forced conversion of the Jews on the women who "enticed their husbands" to repudiate it. The women, observed Noble, were the first to perceive the *nature* of the Crusaders' onslaught—"Quite early it dawned upon them that the aim of the Crusaders was to extirpate Judaism rather than annihilate the Jews"—and to sound the alarm to the men. (In some ways, this brings to mind the experiences and actions of many Jewish women in pre-1938 Nazi Germany. Their early warning alarm systems allowed them to perceive early on the nature of the onslaught, wrote historian Claudia Koontz, and to pressure their husbands to have the family emigrate while there was still time.)

These women of steel courage and resourcefulness whose loyalty and devotion to Judaism extended to voluntary martyrdom were real. Their names—for instance, Dulcie of Worms, Minna of Speyer, Minna of Worms—and actions were known. Jewish women's extreme demonstrations of altruism should have left no doubt in the minds of the men as to their commitment and adherence to this value. There should have been no perceived need to threaten them with negative role models showing the dire consequences of their abandoning altruistic-assertive enabling. Yet this is precisely what happened.

THE REAL LESSON OF THE LILITH LEGEND

While the women in the Scriptures are somewhat discredited in the Midrash and Agada, they never actually become negative role models for Jewish women. Even Eve is pictured in the Midrash as a "light-headed," irresponsible, and easily manipulated female (as contrasted with the Christian view of her as evil incarnate).

The prime negative female role model in Jewish mythology is Lilith, who is the flip side of Esther, the altruistic-assertive enabler. Esther is the epitome of enabler, Lilith of *dis*abler.

The story of Lilith draws on various midrashim that attempted to resolve the contradiction between the two stories in Genesis about the creation of the first woman. One was that God created her from the earth together with Adam, the other that God fashioned her from Adam's rib. Midrash writers speculated that there were two Eves, and that the "First Eve" was the one created from the earth. Meanwhile, in the Talmud, Lilith is mentioned several times as a wild-haired winged creature with nymphomaniac tendencies and as the mother of demons.

The author of the *Alphabet of Ben Sira,* which scholars believe was written sometime between 600 and 1000 C.E., merged the two traditions, giving us the demon Lilith as Eve's predecessor. The *Alphabet* relates how after God created both Adam and Lilith from the earth, they immediately quarreled because she refused to lie beneath him. Lilith told Adam: "We are both equal because we both come from the earth." Realizing that it was as futile to use logic to argue with him as it was with anti-Semites, Lilith uttered God's secret Name and flew away from Eden. The *Alphabet* tells of her refusal to return to Adam after three angels God had dispatched asked her to. She accepted the punishment that one hundred of her "demon children" would die every day.

Early Kabbalistic works, starting with the thirteenth-century *Zohar,* embellished Lilith's demon reputation with sundry legends, often contradictory, of her vengeful activities to harm or kill: newborn babies; women who give birth and nurse in rooms without industrial-strength amulets to ward her off; and men, whom she robs of sperm in their sleep to manufacture demon children or whom she seduces and afflicts with illness. In later Kabbalistic works, she is portrayed as the bride and partner of Samael, the archdemon and chief evil force in the universe, who is blocking national redemption. These stories became part of Jewish folk culture, and anti-Lilith amulets are still enjoying brisk sales in some Orthodox communities.

To understand the motivations behind the Lilith myth, we must separate the *Alphabet* story, which is an almost entirely gynophilic one, from the Kabbalistic legends, which are totally misogynist. In the *Alphabet,* Lilith is an independent, courageous woman and a strong character. Her self-esteem is high: She perceives her equality with Adam as part of the natural order of things, a result of their having been created from the same element. She immediately recognizes Adam's tyranny as injustice and immediately and decisively resists it ("I will not lie beneath you"). She is willing to take risks for her integrity and to relinquish a life of security in the Garden of Eden in order to uphold it, and she accepts uncomplainingly the consequences of her decision.

Only at the end of the story is there an O'Henry twist: She is referred to as a demon. This instantly converts all of these attributes, which may have seemed positive to women, into negative ones. But still, the unavoidable implication is that had her struggle for equality with Adam succeeded, she would not have had to leave him and become a vengeful and dangerous creature.

Jewish tradition is replete with folktales that have female endings when told by women and male endings when recounted by men (plus some for both genders). The female folktales were transmitted orally, the ones with the male endings were generally written down. What may have happened with the Lilith story in the *Alphabet* is this: The core of the story may have been a folktale told by women to women over many generations, a story praising women's assertiveness under the adverse conditions that had brought it to the fore. The author of the *Alphabet* may have cribbed this female story and added a negative ending, making it into a male story (or, more probably, one directed at both genders).

The reason for the negative O'Henry twist at the end is to flip Lilith from positive to negative role model. Her refusal to be subservient ("I will not lie beneath you") and her escape from Adam provoked too much anxiety in the men to allow this behavior to stand. A woman who "withholds herself" from a man—either by refusing to be subservient or by denying him her very presence, thereby committing the great crime in Jewish life, abandonment—is a role breaker and must be transformed into a creature who is innately evil/demonic. (The anxiety about emotional abandonment is also behind the charge of Lilith's "frigidity" in the demon legends.)

The misogynist demon stories, written by men several hundred years after the *Alphabet,* reflect an intensified anxiety about Jewish survival and about the men's ability to ensure it. This anxiety is at the root of the specific crimes the stories attribute to Lilith: She is a slayer of babies and injurer of their mothers—thus threatening the physical survival of the Jewish nation. She also commits crimes against men: She steals sperm from them. By sapping the men's "life fluid" while they are asleep—a metaphor for reducing them to powerlessness—she weakens their ability to function as men, that is, she damages their masculinity. By thus impairing them psychologically, she impedes their ability to fulfill their role as men in ensuring Jewish survival.

It is not surprising that men's anxiety about Jewish survival should be expressed in late medieval stories since, as we have seen, the High Middle Ages were extremely lethal for Jews in Western Europe. The men's anxiety about their ability to ensure Jewish survival, however, is not expressed directly. To do so would have involved questioning the logic of the gender division of labor they had established. Given that the women's rates of conversion were lower than the men's during this period (and that in the Marrano era, women endured the tortures of the Inquisition with more fortitude than men), the implication would have been that perhaps men were not, after all, the gender best qualified for the job of spiritual resistance.

The men, therefore, projected their anxieties about fulfilling their role onto the women, as represented by Lilith. It is the women, not the men, who are depicted as having the power to derail Jewish survival by not fulfilling *their* role.

Seen as a totality, the Lilith myth transmits the message that if a woman refuses to be an altruistic enabler, if she selfishly chooses independence over subservience, she will destroy the man's masculinity at a time when he has already been reduced to powerlessness. He will consequently not be able to play his role in advancing Jewish survival.

By making an independent woman a destroyer of Jewish manhood and Jewish lives, and an ally of the Jews' worst foe, who blocks Jewish liberation, the Lilith libel clearly tells us that *nothing less than Jewish survival hinges on the woman's behavior:* Jewish men will lose their manhood and the Jewish nation will consequently be destroyed if Jewish women refuse to stay in the subservient enabler role.

As if this warning were not enough, the authors of the demon tales of Lilith made sure to emphasize again and again her specific crimes against women. As baby slayer and mother injurer, she posed a danger to them at a time when infant mortality was high and the death of mothers in and after childbirth was common. Here Lilith is the flip side of the midwives in Egypt, who disobeyed the genocidal orders of the Pharaoh to kill newborn boys and instead, the Midrash relates, took special care of them and their mothers. By picturing Lilith as a threat to individual women who were carrying out their prescribed wife-and-mother enabler role under difficult conditions, the male authors were attempting to keep them away from assertive women role breakers, just like the anti-Semites who created Judeophobic myths attempted thereby to keep oppressed non-Jews away from Jews. This divide-and-conquer technique was also designed to mobilize women to keep possible troublemakers in line by pitting "good" women against "evil" ones.

ᐧᐧ The Lilith myth tells us something even more chilling. In the gynophilic core of the story in the *Alphabet,* Lilith upholds the Jewish values at the heart of spiritual resistance in demanding mutuality in her relationship with Adam. Moreover, in arguing with him, she provides intellectual substantiation for her opinion as Talmudic scholars do: with evidence from life experience ("We were both created from the earth").

When this approach fails, she forsakes the economic security of the Garden of Eden and accepts exile from society and a pariah status. In resisting oppression, in being highly conscious of her equality, in accepting outsider status in order to maintain her integrity, she behaves much like . . . the Jews! In fact, when she flies off from Eden, it is to the Red Sea, the precise scene of the Jews' consciously elected transition from the oppression *and security* of their bondage in Egypt to the insecurity and risks of freedom in the desert.

In her subsequent demonic incarnation, Lilith becomes a metaphor for the general societies of the Exile, which show different and sometimes contradictory "faces" to Jews, all of which ultimately threaten their survival. The faces are the three strategies of oppression: the club, the yoke, and the leash.

The "club" strategy is annihilation: Lilith the baby slayer and mother injurer destroys the nation's continuity of generations and thus its future. Significantly, the men are unable to protect "their" women and children from Lilith's mayhem any more than they could defend them against rape and pogroms in the Exile.

The "yoke" strategy is the reduction of Jews to slavelike powerlessness— being the "king's persons" with the status of chattel and in this and other ways, being forced to act in the interests of the rulers, not their own. Lilith saps men's "life fluid," a metaphor for power. In the context of medieval Europe, this is also a metaphor for draining the Jews' economic resources (one recalls here Abrahams's description of them as "sponges" for the king).

The "leash" strategy of deceit is that of assimilation: Lilith is seductive but frigid, alluring but unresponsive to the man's psychological need for emotional support, and she ultimately abandons him. Assimilation (which in the Middle Ages took the form of conversion) is seductive; it holds out but ultimately withholds the brass ring of acceptance, as the Spanish *conversos,* Jews who became "New Christians" in the fourteenth and fifteenth centuries, learned. The nations Jews were so attached to did not reciprocate their love and devotion (the Jews, who adored Spain, were summarily expelled in 1492).

Ultimately all three "faces" of the demonic Lilith, all three strategies of oppressive exiles, are variations of one: the face of the enemy working against, preventing, and/or delaying national redemption, the face of the "consort of Samael."

By juxtaposing these two images—Lilith as Exile, Lilith as Jew in Exile—we come to the true meaning and message of the Lilith libel: A Jewish woman who behaves in relation to a man in the courageous, independent-minded, unyielding ("stiff-necked") way that the Jewish nation behaves in relation to the general societies of the Exile is advancing the interests of those who wish to destroy Jewish identity, derail Jewish survival, and block Jewish liberation.

A woman behaving as a Jew in the community—who takes upon herself the role of ensuring Jewish survival by engaging in spiritual resistance (the way Lilith did at the outset)—is acting not in the interests of Jewish survival but of national destruction (as Lilith does later, when she shows her true demonic colors). If she is a "good Jewish daughter," she will not try to be a "real Jew." She will not engage in the study of Torah, as Beruriah did, or in the public performance of ritual, as some prominent medieval women did, because such participation will undermine the men's definition of masculinity (sap their "life fluid") and thereby render them psychologically incapable of engaging in this spiritual resistance work designed to ensure Jewish survival. Instead she must accept exclusion from this turf and adhere to the prescribed role of subservient, altruistic enabler. If she refuses to be an enabler, she flips over to the shadow role: disabler and enemy of the Jewish nation.

SIX ❧ THE INSTRUMENTALITY OF DOMESTIC TRANQUILLITY: SEX, MARRIAGE, LOVE, AND JEWISH FAMILY LIFE

Women are a nation unto themselves.

TALMUD

Woman's weapons are on her [body].

TALMUD

[The traditional Jewish family was] a mighty fortress in whose tranquility the Jew built his [sic] own world of love and peace.

ARTHUR RUPPIN

The role of altruistic-assertive enabler evolved as the institution of marriage was reformed/transformed from a male autocracy into a monogamous partnership in which companionship, affection, and mutual respect were (ideally) to obtain.

The main motivation for this radical change was that the rabbis during and after the late Second Commonwealth era realized that the institution of marriage had to be strengthened because of the national emergency. Just as cohesion was crucial if the community was to become a successful counterforce to and haven from outside oppression, so, too, with the family. And cohesion required that the basis of marriage be a genuine bond, a cooperative relationship/partnership between wife and husband, with each spouse fulfilling his or her role in the gender division of labor.

We can see this view of the intrinsic value of the marital pair-bond emerging in the Talmud, with its statements about marriage being a mitzvah, and in the blessings it included for the wedding ceremony. These blessings, recited to this day, celebrate the marital state as one of "joy and gladness . . . mirth and exaltation, pleasure and delight, love, friendship, peace, and companionship." Marriage is defined as a partnership in the Jerusalem Talmud and in documents from the eleventh-century Islamic world found in the Cairo *Genizah* (Hebrew for storehouse for discarded religious texts and legal papers). The acceptance of the partnership ideal is evident from the Yiddish word for parents, which is *tateh-mameh* (daddy-mommy) used in the singular form ("the *tateh-mameh* says ... ").

The marital bond became more and more important in the Exile in the face of the breakup of extended families through migrations and expulsions. (The pattern of extended families sharing a household became less common in the Exile. In the High Middle Ages in Egypt, for example, it is estimated that half of newly-wed couples lived in nuclear households; similarly in early modern Europe.) Since neither alliances between powerful extended families, property considerations, nor the need to produce heirs to large landed estates figured as extrinsic reasons for marriage, the bond itself assumed greater importance.

Strengthening the pair-bond necessitated ensuring that sex be channeled exclusively into the marriage to enhance the relationship. This also helped prevent extramarital straying, which damages the mutuality and trust necessary in a partnership.

The pair-bond ideal obviously required the discouraging of polygamy. The stories in the Scriptures of how competition and conflicts between co-wives (e.g., Rachel and Leah) damaged marital trust and made relationships with their husbands into an endless tug-of-war provided ample evidence against polygamy. Moreover, the time and energy spent in coping with these inevitable conflicts had to be channeled into partners' fulfilling their defined survival roles.

The rabbis discouraged polygamy primarily by counterposing monogamous partnership as the marital relationship that was the most harmonious and felicitous, and by setting an example; none of the rabbis who shaped the Talmud lived in polygamous marriages. (Of course, economic and political factors also contributed to the decline of polygamy. This system is most useful in an agrarian society, where production of large numbers of offspring as labor power is necessary. Agrarian life declined among Jews around the end of the eighth century C.E., when the largest community was in Babylonia. Another factor in the West was the wish not to give Christians, who mandated monogamy, another excuse for persecution.) By the time Rabbi Gershom and/or the synod he convened placed a millennium-long moratorium on polygamy for Ashkenazic Jews in 1000 C.E., it had pretty much fallen into disuse. Nor was it the norm among Sephardic Jews, but rather an exception sometimes practiced by the very wealthy.

ﺴ The partnership ideal, carried to its logical conclusion, would have meant abrogating the ancient concept of *kinyan* (from the Hebrew word for acquisition or purchase). Kinyan defines the initiation and dissolution of a marriage as unilateral transactions by the man and implies absolute power over his wife as his possession. This is obviously incompatible with the partnership ideal, which defines the marital relationship as one of mutuality and interdependence, of "love, peace, and companionship."

Kinyan, however, could not be abrogated because of the perceived need to uphold male power in the home (as in the community). Some way had to be found to allow it to coexist with the evolving partnership ideal, which was the key to couple cohesion.

What the rabbis did was to employ classic behavioral methodology to limit the absolute power given the man by kinyan. They whittled away at this power by placing boundaries on it. Various laws took away the husband's life-and-death power over his wife (and children). The legal status of the woman was changed from her being little better than a slave in biblical times to one of junior partner with specific responsibilities, rights, and entitlements.

At the same time, the rabbis tried to redefine male power in the home. While the husband was expected to dominate—as Maimonides wrote, "Every man is a king in his own house"—he was reduced from the autocratic ruler of biblical times to a kind of constitutional monarch under Halacha as Jewish Constitutional Law. The rabbis redefined the kind of behavior expected of this "king": He was to be benevolent and wise rather than tyrannical and cruel. Through laws, examples, and unrelenting propaganda, the rabbis sought to create this "new Jewish husband" as they had created the new model of Jewish man-as-scholar.

The concepts of kinyan and partnership coexisted uneasily, with the pendulum of rabbinical decision making on marriage swinging back and forth between them. The rabbis would strengthen partnership by limiting kinyan, then strengthen kinyan by limiting partnership. In engaging in this process, which runs throughout Halachic debates, they tried to make sure the pendulum never swung so far in either direction as to reach its polar extreme.

◆ The wife's fulfillment of the responsibilities inherent in her role as junior partner was a key motivation for limiting and redefining male power in the home.

The rabbis apparently realized that the woman's enabling skills had to be harnessed for survival; they were too useful to have their effectiveness jeopardized by denying her breathing space or room to maneuver, or by destroying her morale and loyalty. Improvements had to be introduced in the wife's "working conditions" at home, including mitigation of some of the worst abuses of male power, such as battering; in bolstering "job security" through divorce reform; and with the incorporation of incentives and rewards, one of which was sexual satisfaction, of which more presently. Acknowledging the link between the importance of enabling and the improvement of "working conditions," the rabbis in the Talmud urged the husband to "be careful to respect his wife because all blessings on his [sic] house are due to her."

There was apparently an inchoate realization of the vast difference between an energetic and loyal subordinate and a passive, sullen slave, between a fairly well treated employee who thinks "working conditions" are really not that bad and a resentful and alienated worker who feels she has nothing to lose. What we see here is thus somewhat analogous to the good employee relations policies instituted by some American corporations in the 1950s, which gave workers a more pleasant workplace and some benefits but left the power in the hands of the boss.

LIMITING MALE POWER

While transforming marriage into a partnership, albeit unequal, required limiting male power in the home, other survival factors also contributed to the need for this limitation. One was that the role of all-powerful patriarch of a strong extended family on the Italian or Chinese model was both unnecessary and dangerous. The powerful extended family as a state within a state was impossible for Jews, associated as it was with land ownership and the ability to form alliances with other powerful families and institutions in the general society based on the ability to join with them in warfare against a common enemy. Jews were not allowed to own land in most periods; non-Jews did not see anything to be gained from alliances with Jews, especially since defending them, should the need arise, might subject them to the same persecution.

Additionally, the Jewish community could not allow individual families to take the law into their own hands, so to speak, in implementing "foreign policy" by making allies in the general society without the community's deciding whether this was "good for the Jews." And there was certainly no wish to encourage men to try to defend their families by the use of physical aggression. Moreover, such families might have constituted a dangerously competitive counterforce to the rabbinical leadership.

Since powerful extended families were not the norm, there was no need for the role of patriarch to serve as their government heads or generals, with total power over "their" women and children.

The second reason men could not be allowed life-and-death power inside the home is that it would have required the use of force, which could not be allowed anywhere in Jewish life because of the domino effect. Nor could Jews afford the kind of situation prevalent in the U.S. today, where, said a sociologist, "the family is the most violent group in society, with the exception of the police and the military. You are more likely to get killed, injured, or physically attacked in your home by someone you are related to, than in any other social context." Such violence would have made homes into desperately unhappy battlefields—counterindicated if cohesion was the goal and the loyalty of women and children was to be maintained.

On the contrary, the home had to be a "haven of rest from the storms that raged round the very gates of the ghettos," in Abrahams's words. A prime rationale for many rabbinic decisions on marriage, therefore, was to engender *shalom bayit* (Hebrew; *sholom bayis* in Yiddish), a peaceful and harmonious home life.

That the motivation for treating the women kindly was to ensure shalom bayit can be seen from the Talmudic quote, "Whoever loves his wife as himself and respects her more than himself . . . of him the sages say, 'And you shall know the *peace* of your tent'" (italics mine).

The home also had to be safe space where accumulated feelings of rage arising from oppression, however repressed they were, could be expressed without any danger of their escalating into violence. The Jewish home often became the scene of a great deal of verbal expressiveness, some of it antagonistic. Arguing, yelling, and interrupting have usually been considered a natural part of Jewish family (and communal) life. One has only to recollect in this connection how Woody Allen depicted this behavior in his 1977 film *Annie Hall:* A split-screen scene contrasted the wild and passionate arguing around Alvy's parents' dinner table with the low-key, restrained, and unemotional conversation of Annie's non-Jewish family at Thanksgiving.

Moreover, the father could not be allowed life-and-death power over the children because the fate of the entire people was at stake in their physical survival. And, indeed, the Greeks and Romans, including Tacitus, thought it "peculiar" that Jews did not "expose" their children—leave newborn babies to die outside—but raised them all.

Finally, the home was where the children's commitment to becoming good Jews and their loyalty to the nation were forged. Physical and sexual abuse might have led to defection, psychological illness, and/or rebellion. Anecdotal evidence confirms the generally good treatment of children. For example, medieval moral guidebooks frequently lamented that "the children are allowed too much license at the table, in the synagogue, and in the presence of their elders generally."

IMPROVING "WORKING CONDITIONS"

The rabbis walked a fine line between strengthening marriage as an institution—which required some limitation of male power—and weakening/destroying it as a patriarchal institution, which required maintaining male power. Knowing how far to go in limiting it was a difficult enough balancing act. When a necessary reform came near to crossing the line between being a limitation of male power and a threat to it, they pulled back to ensure that male power was maintained.

Therefore, although strengthening the institution of marriage generally dovetailed with the protection of women, this protection fell by the wayside if it came close to colliding with the need to maintain male dominance. We can see the operation of this dynamic in the evolution of the laws regarding woman's entitlements and property and in the debates on wife-beating.

❧ The *ketubah* (marriage contract, from the Hebrew verb "to write"; plural, *ketubot*) spelled out the wife's entitlements. These included the husband's obligation to provide clothing for the wife in accordance with her "station" in life, pay her medical bills, ransom her from captivity, and give her a proper burial.

Shimon ben Shetach, head of the Sanhedrin in the first century B.C.E., is credited with originating the standard ketubah as well as some of the laws on compulsory elementary education for boys. The connection between these two actions is not accidental: Both were regarded as instrumentalities of Jewish survival.

The Talmud stipulates that the wife continue to own any property she brought into the marriage, but the husband was to manage it as well as her dowry; income from both belonged to him. Anything a married woman found or earned (except for compensation for injuries) belonged to the husband, although the Talmud states that the wife could retain her earnings if she gave up her right to be supported. The wife could not inherit the property of her husband or of her son or daughter, either. If the husband died, she was to be supported by his male heirs from his estate and remain in "his" home. As long as they supported her, her earnings belonged to them.

These Talmudic laws, however, were overridden during the first millennium C.E. by the introduction of tailor-made ketubot. These could include virtually any condition the spouses or their parents wished (for example, that the wife's children and not her husband would inherit her property; that she could keep her earnings and waive all or part of her husband's support; and regarding divorce and the divorce settlement, which will be discussed subsequently). The most popular of these conditions became takkanot of different communities.

Documents from the eleventh to thirteenth centuries found in the Cairo Genizah show that women participated in public commercial life; inherited and managed property; gave loans to their husbands, fathers, and brothers or stood security for them; left wills and bequeathed their property to whomever they wished; and served as executors of their husbands' wills and guardians of the couple's children.

Stipulations regarding a wife's earnings begin appearing in these Genizah documents toward the beginning of the twelfth century. There was a wide variety in these conditions. Goitein believes that the incorporation of stipulations regarding who provided the wife's clothing when she or the husband kept her earnings reflected the reality that women had fewer options for earning a living outside the home in these times than in late antiquity. The reason was that in Islamic times, women were more confined to the home, where they often engaged in needlework and the dyeing of textiles. While the wife could not always support herself, she could provide her own clothing.

The practice of tailor-made ketubot and communal takkanot regarding stipulations to be included in them declined around the fourteenth century. One theory recently advanced for this decline asserts that some rabbis were concerned that the plethora of different takkanot would undermine the stability of marriage. But the real reason is obvious: The rabbis felt they had given women too much power and that they had to pull back before male dominance in the home was destroyed. They pulled back so far that when Rabbi Ezekiel Landau of eighteenth-century Prague was asked whether one could accept tzedakah from a woman who managed her husband's business if it was known that he was a miser, his responsum was, "God forbid the acceptance of such charity; it is plain robbery. To be sure, the bet din has the power to force one to give tzedakah, but who invested the wife with the authority of judge? Her sex is barred by law from dispensing judgment."

֍ The Mishnah stipulated rules designed to protect the wife's dignity. The husband was not allowed to subject her to "petty tyrannies" or to restrict her social contact "more than is customary [sic]," or to degrade her for his convenience or "entertainment."

The rabbis quoted in the Talmud urged the man to "spend above his means on his wife and children," be "ever attentive to the needs of his wife," and to "honor your wives that you may be blessed with wealth," another acknowledgment of the link between "good working conditions" and successful enabling.

The husband was also urged "not to make a woman weep, for God counts her tears." Jewish medieval literature warned the husband "not to be a terror at home," wrote Abrahams, and the ethical will of a medieval rabbi urged the men to "love and cherish their wives, not to vent their anger on them."

֍ The Jew who engaged in the physical abuse of his wife was regarded as a "monstrosity" in the Middle Ages, wrote Abrahams. The twelfth-century Rabbi Jacob Tam called wife-beating "a thing not done in Israel." The reality, however, was otherwise, as the words of Rabbi Peretz ben Elijah of thirteenth-century Corbeil (France) testify:

> The cry of the daughters of our people has been heard concerning the sons
> of Israel who raise their hands to strike their wives. Yet who has given a
> husband the authority to beat his wife? Is it not, rather, forbidden to strike
> any person in Israel? . . . We have heard of cases where Jewish women
> complained regarding their treatment before the kehillot and no action was
> taken on their behalf.

While wife-beating is not dealt with in the Talmud (possibly because it is subsumed under the general assault laws), later rabbis fought it tooth-and-nail, especially in the Middle Ages in Europe. Batei din in the ninth and tenth centuries fined the guilty man to the utmost limit of his resources. In the following century, Rabbi Simhah ben Shmuel of Vitri (northern France) prescribed this punishment for the wife-beater: "We must excommunicate him, scourge him, chastise him with all kinds of punishment, even cut his hand off." Rabbi Meir of thirteenth-century Rothenberg (Germany) insisted that the community treat battering husbands more stringently than men guilty of other types of assaults. One rabbinical synod in that century prescribed flogging and excommunication.

Rabbi Peretz tried to institute a takkanah through correspondence with his rabbinical colleagues mandating that "any Jew [*sic*] may be compelled on the application of his wife or any of her near relations to undertake [on pain of excommunication] not to beat his wife in anger or cruelty or so as to disgrace her for that is against Jewish practice." If the husband refused to obey the bet din receiving the complaint, she would be entitled to separate maintenance "according to her station . . . as though the husband were away on a journey." Why his proposal failed, we do not know.

Rabbinical opinion on the issue, however, was not unanimous. Despite the fact that batei din in twelfth-century Egypt sided with the wife in cases of wifebeating, Maimonides, who lived there in that era, allowed limited beatings as a form of discipline, as did Rabbi Moses Isserles, a leading rabbinical arbiter in sixteenth-century Poland. Maimonides wrote that the wife who refuses to perform any of her obligatory chores "may be beaten even with a rod until she does it."

Wife-beating was the flash point of the conflict between the need to ban violence because of the domino effect and the home-as-haven ethos—both of which required mitigating male power in the family—and the psychological need to maintain male domination there. The rabbis who fought wife-beating considered the banning of violence and the haven ethos the more important needs. The others, unwilling to reduce male power by eliminating all wife-beating but unable to reconcile it with these ideals, rationalized by defining wife-beating that resulted from male aggression as abuse, and banning it. Then they redefined limited beatings as "punishment" for the wife's serious offenses, and once these were supposedly no longer due to male aggression, they were allowed. Interestingly, Isserles states that the testimony of the woman overrides that of the man when a bet din has to decide what category the beating fell under.

That some rabbinical arbiters had to create elaborate rationalizations to justify limited beatings means that a consciousness already existed that the physical abuse of women was "a thing not done in Israel." This normative ideal was incorporated into the Jewish self-image to the extent that reports of wife-beating in Jewish families in North America and Israel today are often greeted with incredulity: "Jews don't do that."

◆ As the concept of the husband evolved, God began to take on some of the attributes of this "new Jewish husband" and "family man" who had (limited) power in the home and was a wise, learned, and kind mentsch rather than a shorttempered ruler who would "vent anger" and whose punishment could take the form of abandonment.

(The experiencing of God as a deity with some of the characteristics of the Jewish husband was a factor in the synagogue's becoming a structure with a homelike atmosphere: cozy, warm, and noisy—witness the Polish expression "noisy as a Jewish synagogue"—rather than forbidding and awe-inspiring. Obsessed with abandonment, Jews wanted to feel that God was there for them and with them, and they yearned to bring Him closer rather than to create emotional distance, which they equated with separation and abandonment. Calls for synagogue decorum from the Middle Ages on went unheeded until the rise of Reform Judaism in the nineteenth century.)

It is fascinating to note how the image of God in the Kabbala began to reflect the ideal of the Jewish "family man." Four of the sefirot constituted the "divine Tetrad": Father, Mother, Son (a.k.a. the King), and Daughter (a.k.a. Schechinah/ Matronit). The Jewish man, writes Patai, derived great emotional satisfaction from knowing that "God, too, lived on high in a family of His own." The Talmudic idea that "a man without a wife is not called a man" also applied to the situation of the King when separated from the Schechinah. "The King without the Matronit is not a king, is not great, and is not praised" is a sentiment expressed repeatedly in the Kabbala. There is also a parallel, however faint, between the limitation on the man's power in the marriage and the Kabbalistic concept of *tzimtzum* (contraction), the prerequisite for and first stage of Creation: "Since the All was up to that time totally filled with [God's] being, He contracted Himself so as to make room for the created universe."

As we have seen in an earlier chapter, the relationship between God and the Jewish people was perceived as that of husband and wife and was based on a Contract, the Covenant. Just as the wife was allowed to be assertive with her husband when her motive was altruistic, so, too, the Jews were allowed to argue with and talk back to God when this was in the interests of the nation. The Jewish wife was allowed to summon her husband to a bet din when he was not living up to the marriage contract; the Jewish people, too, could insist, as did the Berditchever Rebbe, that God live up to His Contract with them.

However, when Jews projected God's rescuer role onto secular nations/movements, "altruistic" was defined as being in the latter's interests, not in that of the Jewish people. Jews therefore felt they could be assertive only when it was good for these nations or movements, not when it was "selfishly" only "good for the Jews," and they censored themselves accordingly.

"JOB SECURITY"

In looking at the limitation on male power in marriage, we can see the tug-of-war between kinyan and partnership most clearly in the evolution of the marriage and divorce laws.

The rabbis left kinyan intact: Two thousand years ago and today, it is still the man who "acquires" the wife in marriage by giving her a ring or a coin and saying in the presence of witnesses, "By this you are consecrated unto me." And it is the man who gives the get to the soon-to-be ex-wife. "Women cannot be allowed to destabilize the system by arbitrarily releasing themselves from the husbands who selected them," wrote Judith Wegner.

While the rabbis upheld kinyan, they amended the circumstances and conditions of its implementation at both ends, reducing the father's power to sell/ marry off his daughter and the husband's to divorce his wife.

In the society portrayed in the Scriptures, a father could sell his daughters until puberty to become wives or slaves/indentured servants or offer them to strangers, as Lot did when he sought to deliver his daughters to the Sodomites to "do to them what you like." The Mishnah required the father to redeem at puberty the minor daughter (under twelve years of age) he had sold as a slave. The rabbis, according to the Jerusalem Talmud, found selling daughters into slavery to raise money for settling in Eretz Israel so abhorrent that they forbade such immigration. The Gemara stated that the father could not marry off his daughter as a minor but had to wait until she came of age and said, "I want this man." Perhaps this was advanced as an ideal to live up to; it could not possibly have obtained when the female age of majority was twelve and a half years and one day. But it should also be noted that as the age of arranged marriages declined in the West to pre-puberty, as we shall see, the son had no say in such matches, either.

❧ To reduce the man's power to divorce, which is virtually unlimited in the Five Books, the rabbis propagandized against frivolous divorce and whittled away at some aspects of the process. The Talmud records various sentimental statements about not abandoning the "wife of one's youth," about a man's "finding contentment" only with his first wife, and about how "even the altar sheds tears" when he divorces her.

Whittling away involved including in the standard ketubah the financial settlement the husband had to pay the wife if he divorced her "so that it shall not be a slight matter for him to repudiate her." Another tactic concerned the get, which is mentioned only fleetingly in the Five Books. Its formalities, noted Orthodox feminist Blu Greenberg, were made quite complicated, as were the divorce proceedings themselves. This supposedly militated against a man's hasty and impulsive action.

Nevertheless, the Talmud states flatly that "a woman may be divorced with her consent or without it." This meant that all the putative protection extended to women was as thin and fragile as the parchment the ketubah was written on. In the Middle Ages this abuse was eliminated by a takkanah dated 1000 C.E., attributed to Rabbi Gershom. It decreed that a man was forbidden to divorce his wife against her will on pain of excommunication.

A clue to the reason behind the acceptance of this ban lies in a statement by Rabbi Peretz of Corbeil—significantly, the same rabbi who fought wife-beating—in the period of dislocation after the Crusades: "Now, when our numbers are reduced and our people scattered, we are in the habit of marrying [off] girls under the age of 12 should an eligible husband present himself ... because day after day the [oppression of the] Exile increases." The intensified precariousness of Jewish life thus caused Jewish leaders to encourage young people's early marriages so they could be spoken for and to try to keep long-term marriages together by abrogating nonconsensual divorce. This went hand in hand with improvements in "working conditions" in the home to keep women functioning there as satisfied and loyal enablers.

⤖ While in the Scriptures the divorcing man was virtually unaccountable to anyone, the rabbis of the Talmudic era believed the man had to have grounds for divorce. One long debate between the schools of Shammai and Hillel was over what constituted legitimate grounds. The Shammai school held out for adultery, the Hillel school "for the slightest inconvenience, even spoiling his soup." Some scholars attribute the latter opinion to economic conditions: The Hillel school stood up here, as elsewhere, for the "common man" who was unable to afford a second wife unless he had divorced the first one. Moreover, in the evolving urban society of the Second Temple era, where the Hillel school's "common man" lived, divorce supposedly did not mean destitution for the woman, as it did in the agrarian environment that many of the Shammai school patricians came from. Presumably in the city a divorced woman could support herself.

Rabbi Akiva, husband of the self-sacrificing Rachel, followed the Hillel school. He stated that no greater reason for divorce was needed than a man's finding a prettier woman to marry. The statement seems strange coming from a sage who had answered the question, "What is true wealth?" with "A wife who is beautiful in her deeds" and who advocated that a man should marry a woman suited to him. But it was precisely because Akiva viewed mutual affection as the basis of marriage that it logically followed that a man was obligated to divorce his wife once he had taken a dislike to her for whatever reason and marital harmony was consequently broken.

The general impression that emerges from the legal literature is that the rabbis' main concern was to ensure stable marriages and families as a component/prerequisite of Jewish survival. By this criterion, "unendurable" marriages had to be ended because they were "bad for the Jews" as a collectivity. This underlying motivation comes into focus when we look at the "unendurable" conditions that rabbinical arbiters regarded as legitimate for a bet din to compel the husband to give his wife a get. According to the Talmud, if a man did not fulfill certain conditions that made the marriage "viable"—if he refused to fulfill her conjugal rights (of which more shortly), was impotent, had a serious disease or a foul smell, did not support her appropriately (later authorities added licentious behavior and petty tyrannies to the list)—the wife was entitled to a divorce.

The procedure involved her presenting her case to a bet din, which could compel the husband to reform his behavior. If he failed to do so, it could order him to divorce her by resorting to various economic or social sanctions (e.g., the threat of excommunication or of refusing to bury him in a Jewish cemetery), using "coercion until he says, 'I am willing,'" to quote both the Talmud and Maimonides. With the dismantling of the autonomous communities, today's rabbis have no such powers of coercion.

Some ancient marriage contracts found in the Cairo Genizah indicate that in the third and fourth centuries C.E., stipulations were included in the ketubah to allow the bet din to mandate a divorce if either party found the other "distasteful." Documents from the eleventh-century Islamic world reveal that women were given the right to initiate divorce proceedings for no other reason than hatred of the husband. The courts were required to compel the man to give her a get. In first-millennium C.E. Babylonia, the courts forced the husband to grant his wife a divorce if she found sex with him so repellent that she refused to have relations with him. Maimonides agreed, stating that "she is not a captive that she should consort with one who is hateful to her."

Ahad Ha'am, the nineteenth-century Russian theoretician of Spiritual Zionism, considered this statement an example of the "tendency to emancipate the wife." It exemplified, he said, the Jewish attitude toward marriage as "a social and moral cord, the two ends of which are in the hearts of husband and wife; and if the cord is broken at either end . . . the marriage has lost its value and it is best that it should be ended." But he acknowledged that most of the sages did not accept Maimonides' view. Actually it was the Ashkenazic rabbinical arbiters who debated the issue for centuries. The consensus that finally emerged was that the husband could not be compelled to divorce his wife in these cases. That, notes Rachel Biale, would have given the woman too much power.

Even more revealing in this connection is the debate among Ashkenazic rabbinical arbiters on whether a woman who deserted her husband could receive with her get the property she had brought into the marriage. Rabbi Meir of Rothenberg—who (along with some courts in Renaissance Italy) advocated forcing a wife-batterer to grant a divorce—finally became opposed to the property-restoration provision. Rabbi Finkelstein's hypothesis for Meir's view (itself very revealing) goes back to the participation of a large number of women in the economic life of medieval Germany: "It was not unusual for a wife to support her scholarly husband while he devoted himself to his studies. . . . Under such conditions it was likely that the number of women who would express dissatisfaction with their husbands would increase," and this expression, leading to desertion, could not be countenanced. In other words, the women's economic power could not be allowed to adversely affect male domination in the home any more than it could be allowed to serve as a woman's visa into the turf of spiritual resistance, especially study.

◄● A woman whose husband refused to grant a get because he was malicious or insane, or who deserted her or was otherwise missing, became an *aguna,* an "anchored woman" who could not remarry. The rabbis went to great lengths to prevent a woman's becoming an aguna and to release her from this state. In the Middle Ages in Europe, men were encouraged to write "conditional divorces" that would take effect if they failed to return from an absence after a certain period of time. The *Shulchan Aruch* states that "it is permissible for the bet din to desecrate the Shabbat in order to hear the evidence of witnesses and imprison a husband who intends to desert his wife."

As for the confirmation of a man's death (there being no presumption of death in Jewish Law), the Mishnah allowed testimony from one witness rather than the usually required two witnesses, even from the wife. Many rabbis went even further after the Holocaust. For example, Rabbi Jacob Avigdor, the former chief rabbi of Drohobicz, Galicia, and himself a survivor of several camps, wrote a responsum on the aguna issue that began by describing the steps in the annihilation of European Jewry. On the basis of his own detailed knowledge of how small a percentage could possibly have escaped, he said he could "declare the overwhelming probability to be that any particular missing man may well be presumed dead."

REWARDS

The generally accepted view that a wife's or a husband's refusal to have sexual relations with the spouse made the marriage unviable derives from the Jewish attitude toward sex. "The sexual act," wrote Rabbi Emden, "is worthy, good and beneficial even to the soul"—in the proper context of the legal marriage. Here we see clearly the interweaving of several Jewish cultural values, including the channeling of human drives into a proper context and the emphasis on relationships.

Illustrating this approach as well as the divergent attitudes toward sex of the Jewish and the Christian religious traditions—and the stunning inaccuracy of the term *Judeo-Christian*—is this statement in the anonymous thirteenth-century Kabbalistic work, *Iggeret Hakodesh* (Holy Letter):

> If we were to say that intercourse is repulsive then we blaspheme God who made the genitals.... All organs of the body are neutral; the use made of them determines whether they are holy or unholy.... *Marital* intercourse, *under proper circumstances,* is an exalted matter ... holy and pure *when carried on properly,* in the proper time and with the proper intentions [italics mine].

The glorification of marital sex prevented the emergence of a Madonna/whore complex in Jewish life. Since sex was regarded as good, the man could engage in it with his wife, a "good" woman, rather than desexualize her because sex was bad/dirty/repulsive and then seek recreational encounters with "bad," that is, sexual, women outside marriage.

The Jewish woman was not only allowed to be sexual in marriage ("There are no convents in Jewish life," as the saying goes) but was also legally *entitled* to sexual satisfaction.

A clue to the motivation for this entitlement comes from centuries-long discussions among scholars about women's "nature." A popular story in the Midrash tells how God, after much thought, created woman from the "chaste" rib because other organs were associated with faults: the eye (with coquettishness), the ear (eavesdropping), the mouth (loquacity), the heart (jealousy), the foot (gadding about). It concludes: "Yet, in spite of all this reflection and precaution, woman possesses the very faults God sought to prevent."

Significantly, that legend begins with the sentence, "God reflected on which part of man would *influence the natural propensities of woman for good*" (italics mine). This line provides the key to the reason behind the debate on woman's "nature." That reason was to enable the rabbis and scholars to draw up a kind of collective psychological profile to allow them to create laws that would work with rather than against women's "nature" *in order to control it.*

In deliberating about women's so-called nature, the scholars concluded that "a woman's passion is greater than a man's." Women, said the Talmud, "prefer a life of poverty with a husband who gratifies their sexual cravings to a life of plenty and ease with a husband who is temperate in sexual intercourse." Nachmanides, the leading scholar of the thirteenth century, wrote that Eve's curse/punishment was "that her desire for her husband would be so exceedingly great that she would not be deterred ... *because he keeps her as a maidservant.* ... [God] punished her that [the husband] should *command* her, entirely at his will" (italics mine). In other words, a woman's sexual satisfaction would keep her happy in her enabler (maidservant) role, which helped the man carry out *his* important work, thus ensuring the partners a tranquil and harmonious home life. And significantly, a Talmudic sage called his impotence in old age "the cessation of the instrumentality of shalom bayit."

Regardless of its motivation (the deed is paramount over the thought), the rabbinic law that the husband was obligated to provide his wife with sexual satisfaction seems strikingly progressive. This duty is the mitzvah of *Onah.*

⊷ The laws of Onah, meaning women's conjugal rights (from the Hebrew for season/time period/set time), outline the quantity (frequency) and quality (physical intimacy, appropriate surroundings, attitude) of sexual relations the wife is legally entitled to. The Mishnah prescribed a timetable of minimum frequency according to the husband's trade. When Rabbi Moshe Feinstein, a noted American Orthodox arbiter, increased scholars' frequency from once to twice a week, his argument was that contemporary women's sexual needs are greater than their predecessors' and that "the main point of the mitzvah of Onah" is suiting it to "what the woman desires and wants." It is fascinating to note here that one reason Rabbi Feinstein gave for expanding Onah minimums is contemporary women's "jealousy for another woman's lot." Increased sexual satisfaction is apparently seen as a way to co-opt the Orthodox women who experienced such "jealousy" and thereby to ensure that they continue their enabling.

The Talmud also prescribes a man's initiation of sexual relations before periods of abstention, such as his leaving on a trip, and when, in the words of Rabad, "he sees that she is asking him for that act and that she has a need for it."

Nachmanides states that intercourse must be conducted with "close bodily contact." Other rabbinical authorities issued various exhortations against engaging in intercourse in a state of enmity or intoxication or by force. Rather, writes the author of the thirteenth-century *Iggeret Hakodesh* in words that make the average American marriage manual seem cold and technical by comparison,

> Engage her first in conversation that puts her heart and mind at ease and gladdens her. Thus your mind and your intent will be in harmony with hers. Speak words which arouse her to passion, union, love, desire, and lovemaking and words which elicit attitudes of reverence for God, piety and modesty.... Never may you force her for in such union, the Schechinah cannot abide.... Do not quarrel with her or strike her ... rather win her over with words of graciousness and seductiveness.... Do not hurry to arouse passion until her mood is ready.

Other sages advised the husband to let the woman have her "insemination" before him. (The sages believed that women experience a form of ejaculation; in any case, it was a recognition of the existence of female orgasm.)

That the guidelines of the rabbis were taken to heart by the average husband can be seen from a letter in the Cairo Genizah by a traveling husband to his wife: He wrote that he was "yearning after you and regretting to be unable to provide you with what I so much desire: *your legal rights on every Shabbat and holiday*" (italics mine).

MENSTRUAL AND POSTMENSTRUAL SEPARATION

The laws of *Niddah* (the menstruant or menstrual period, from the Hebrew verb "to separate" or "to distance oneself") reduced the time for marital sexual indulgence to about half the month. These "laws of family purity," recorded in the Talmud, require sexual abstinence during a woman's period (mandated in the FiveBooks); plus a half-day before (to avoid the accident of her getting her period during intercourse) and for seven days after, the so-called white days (usually explained as a precautionary "fence"). Another "fence" was the set of rules forbidding husband and wife from touching, sleeping in the same bed, or passing objects hand to hand during those weeks. At the conclusion of the Niddah period, the woman was required to immerse herself in a *mikvah* (Hebrew for ritual facility for this purpose, featuring free-running water) before the couple could resume sexual relations.

The central question here is why the law in Leviticus forbidding intercourse during menstruation was so greatly expanded after the end of the Second Jewish Commonwealth as to bring the total period of abstinence to about two weeks a month.

There is an even more intriguing question: The Five Books considered menstruation a ritual impurity that prevented the woman from entering the Tabernacle (later the Temple). Why is menstruation the only ritual impurity out of many (e.g., from skin eruptions) that remained in force for all Jews after the Temple no longer existed? Another question: Why did the Talmud make the woman's ritual purity—required by the laws of the Five Books before she could reenter the Tabernacle/Temple—into the prerequisite for a couple's resumption of sexual relations? And why should her purification ceremony take the form of immersion in a mikvah when Leviticus specified no such ritual for a woman after menstruation, not even as a prerequisite to reentering the Tabernacle?

৵ Since it was the men who created the Niddah (a.k.a. "family purity") system, it was obviously in their interest, and that interest was psychological in origin: to create a system of part-time abstinence for the men (which, of course, affected the women, too). This motivation derived from men's fear of female sexual power, common under patriarchy. Jewish men were vulnerable to the intensification of this fear because of their powerlessness in relation to the (men of the) general society. A comment by Philip Roth's antihero Alexander Portnoy illustrates the connection between these two phenomena: "Here in a Turkish bath, why am I dancing around? There are no women here. No women—and no *goyim* [non-Jews]. There is *nothing to worry about!*" (italics mine).

Jewish men did not, apparently, seem overly anxious about the woman's power to withhold herself sexually (as rabbinical comments on her great "passion" and sexual neediness show). Rather, they harbored the fear of being overwhelmed by her sexual power (as seen in the stories about scholars' hair-breadth escapes from seductive females). Having compensated for their powerlessness by redefining masculinity as the power of the mind, they feared that this new definition could be undermined by women's sexual power. As the earthy Yiddish saying goes, "When the prick stands up, the brains are buried in the ground."

Jewish men's fear of women's sexual power, therefore, is often expressed as the anxiety that women will take them away from the study of Torah, as we have seen. It is significant in this connection that the study of Torah away from home was considered a legally acceptable reason for overriding the mitzvah of Onah. Ben Azzai, the same Talmudic sage who would have allowed women to study Torah, stated that he did not marry because he loved Torah (study) so much.

The implication here is that a man, to totally immerse himself in study, would have to absent himself totally from women and their sexual power. Total abstinence, however, was counterindicated for Jewish survival because of the need for children, for the solace of family life, for release of tension, for some pleasure. There had to be some other way that the men could both engage in sex but not be overwhelmed by it and by the women's sexual power.

Niddah provided that (partial) absence from female sexual power—in time rather than in space (a typical Jewish approach)—and thus helped defuse the men's fear of it.

Another way of looking at the Niddah-study connection is that the sexual separation and deprivation experienced by the men gave rise to frustration and tension that could be sublimated/channeled into Torah study—with its debates, intellectual competition, and validation. Sexual separation from women also intensified the male bonding involved in studying and in the Hassidic world.

◄ Niddah also served to reinforce monogamous partnership, the rabbis' ideal marriage model. The necessary restraint and the difficulties inherent in adhering to the Niddah laws—including observing the no-touching regulations—meant that the wife and husband had to cooperate to help each other fulfill this mitzvah, and this cooperation strengthened the partnership bond generally.

We can see the rabbis' motivation in the current literature by Orthodox authors glorifying Niddah because it causes the marriage bond to grow in intensity as the couple is led to "explore new avenues of communication." By controlling his libidinal urges (temporarily), the husband, they state, learns to appreciate his wife as an autonomous human being and not as an object for his own gratification.

Niddah promoted self-control generally, not only among the men, although Patai ignores women when he writes, "The Jew's sexual life, which he [sic] was commanded to enjoy, was in effect a lifelong training in deferred gratification." This guiding principle of Jewish existence enabled Jews to accept the "deferring" of redemption, says Patai. Since restraint, control, and order had to obtain in all areas of Jewish life, the sexual arena could not be exempt. On the contrary, experiences there had to reinforce self-control, which Niddah did.

There was also another unconscious connection between the acceptance of the deferral of redemption and the Niddah abstinence period. Niddah, with mikvah at its conclusion, dramatized symbolically the idea that separation always ends with reunion. Just as reunion followed separation in the microcosm of the individual marital relationship, so, too, would it occur in the macrocosm of the historical relationship between God and the Jews, which was seen as a marriage. Separation, then, was but a temporary thing, with temporary boundaries. Thus the Niddah period provided Jews another symbolic experience of closure in the open-ended limbo of Exile.

All of these factors, taken together, contributed to the decline of polygamy. Under a polygamous system, the man would have been unable to benefit from the defusing of women's sexual power through Niddah. Having several wives meant that, in essence, he would never be absent from female sexual power. The perception of the psychological benefits of Niddah made monogamy seem preferable to polygamy. So did the strengthening of the pair-bond that Niddah contributed to and the shalom bayit that marital cohesion helped create.

THE ONAH-NIDDAH CYCLE

The Onah and Niddah practices worked in tandem, and we can call this dynamic the Onah-Niddah cycle. This dynamic was designed to prevent the threat and/or practice of a husband's sexual withdrawal motivated by a wish to increase his power in the home, and by fear of being overwhelmed by his wife's sexual power.

Male sexual withdrawal could not be allowed in marriage because (in addition to the procreation factor, of course) sex was a major factor in enhancing the pair-bond and in promoting shalom bayit, and Onah was a kind of reward to women for their loyalty and commitment to fulfilling the demanding enabler role so necessary for Jewish survival. Moreover, male sexual withdrawal and/or its threat might have triggered a power struggle between the spouses, which would have jeopardized the trust and cooperation necessary in a partnership, destroyed sex as the "instrumentality of domestic peace," and possibly led to infidelity.

Onah prevented male sexual withdrawal by mandating legal minimums of sexual intercourse. Its legal character—the very fact that a bet din could compel a man to divorce his wife if he failed to fulfill his conjugal duties—also acted to prevent his sexual withdrawal. Niddah channeled the man's wish for sexual withdrawal into a regulated—and limited—time span.

But beyond this, the Onah-Niddah cycle gave the man the benefits of sexual withdrawal *without his having to engage in it.* It gave him increased power vis-à-vis his wife to compensate for its limitation in other areas of the marriage. Since the woman was seen by the rabbis as the more sexually needy spouse, the part-time abstinence of Niddah increased her sexual dependency on her husband. For it was up to the man to decide whether to adhere only to the minimum Onah requirements or to go beyond them. The rabbis prescribed that the husband be sensitive to his wife's needs and relieve her "sexual hardship," but, again, it was up to him to decide whether or not to do so.

The wife's sexual dependency carried over into other spheres of the marital relationship, because a woman was seen as willing even to be a "maidservant" to get sex beyond the Onah minimums. The connection between sexual dependency and subservience can be clearly seen in a statement by Rabad, which begins by stating that a man owes his wife as much sex as she desires, not just the Onah minimums. This seems very liberated until we read the comment in context: "Woman was created from the rib to serve man just like the other limbs of his body. A man must satisfy his wife's desires just as he must satisfy the demands of his own body but he must also *rule his wife* as he is commanded to rule his body" (italics mine).

This brings us to the tension between kinyan and partnership that exists in the Onah-Niddah cycle as it does in many areas of Halachic debate about women and marriage. The rabbis used the Onah-Niddah cycle to mitigate some of the aspects of kinyan by taking away from the man the unilateral right to engage in or refuse to engage in sex any time he wished, in order to advance the partnership ideal. He was not allowed to have sex during the Niddah period or to abstain from it in the weeks when Onah was in effect. But here again the rabbis pulled back from going too far away from kinyan. For while the husband was exhorted to be a mentsch with his wife in the spirit of the *Iggeret Hakodesh,* legally, wrote Maimonides, "whatever a man wishes with his wife he may do. . . . He may have intercourse in a natural or unnatural manner as long as he does not expend semen to no purpose," that is, he must have his ejaculation inside the woman's vagina. Several stories in the Talmud of wives' complaints to rabbis about their husbands' "unnatural" sexual proclivities elicited what amounts to a shrug. The husband was exhorted *but not legally required* to be a mentsch.

Finally, the Onah-Niddah cycle defused the man's fears of the woman's sexual power. The nature of Onah as a mitzvah prevented him from perceiving sex as a female demand he had either to give in to or resist. The standardized requirements of Onah together with Niddah reassured the man that he would not be overwhelmed by sex, because it had definite boundaries in time. And because the Niddah abstinence increased the woman's dependency, it also defused the man's anxiety that the assertiveness allowed the wife as part of her altruistic-assertive enabler role would be used for any "nonaltruistic" quest for power in the home. The husband could accept female assertiveness *and* the limitations on his power, knowing that neither would go too far.

Despite all this, male fear of women's sexual power remained, and a symbolic/ceremonial dramatization had to be created to further allay it.

SYMBOLIC REVIRGINATION

The men's anxiety about being overwhelmed by/in a woman's body is a key reason why a "purification" ceremony is required before spouses resume sexual relations and why it has taken the specific form of the woman's immersion in a mikvah. The man needs to be reassured that his wife is "pure," which in this context means virginal. The mikvah ceremony is the same rite that precedes the wedding of a (presumed) virgin, a woman whose sexual power is undeveloped and who is thus not sexually overwhelming. The mikvah ceremony allows a Jewish husband to affirm symbolically and in fantasy every month that he is not in danger of being dominated by his wife's sexuality and sexual power because she is a "pure" virgin—inexperienced, modest, shy, undemanding, uncritical.

A clue to the even deeper underlying psychological need for the woman to be "pure" before marital sex is resumed after Niddah comes from the Talmudic statement, "A man's wife is his home." Just as there are ceremonies in Leviticus for the purification of a house (after a "fungus infection") to enable people to dwell in it, so, too, should there be a ceremony for the purification of a woman's body for the sojourn there of a man's penis and "seed."

Impurity of all kinds, writes Rachel Adler (drawing on the work of anthropologist Mary Douglas), is connected with the fear of death. A person becomes impure at certain "nexus points" at which life and death are linked. Menstrual blood, "which sustains embryonic life ... is a token of dying when it is shed.... The dying ... makes room for new birth." For a man to be in contact with a menstruant, therefore, is to be tainted by contact with death.

The intensification of the Jews' fear of total annihilation after the destruction of the Second Jewish Commonwealth led them to strengthen symbolic dramatizations of distancing themselves from death. One was the adding on of the seven postmenstrual "white days," through regulations issued in the days of Rabbi Judah the Prince, who took office in 170 C.E. Another was the woman's post-Niddah immersion in the mikvah, a requirement that some scholars believe was initiated by Rabbi Akiva. This immersion symbolized her being "reborn" as a "new woman"—just as someone who immerses herself or himself in the mikvah as part of the Jewish conversion ceremony becomes a new person. She was thus "different" from the one tainted by contact with death; her body was a "home" that the man could now reenter because it had been "decontaminated."

At the same time, the rabbis prescribed a symbolic reaffirmation of the preservation of life via the prohibition on *hashchatat zera,* literally in Hebrew the "slaughter of seed" (sperm), which generally means any ejaculation outside the woman's vagina. The mystical tradition exhibits a sense of horror about hashchatat zera (especially through masturbation or seminal emissions), with the *Zohar* declaring it to be "a sin more serious than all the sins of the Torah" and actually calling it murder. This view had a profound influence on both legal authorities and the general population. It is hardly surprising that the obsession with "sperm slaughter" intensified during the High Middle Ages, when the dangers to Jewish life and survival intensified as well.

ABORTING FALLING IN LOVE

In the Onah-Niddah cycle we see how a nation that lacked boundaries in space created for itself boundaries in time, even in the area of sexual enjoyment. Just as one day, Shabbat, was carved out of the seven-day week and set apart for spiritual replenishment, so, too, the time when Onah applied was carved out of the month. In both cases this made those days special, and in both cases they were set apart with ceremonial demarcation lines (Kabbalat Shabbat/Havdalah and mikvah). It is not accidental that the Kabbalists, who were, wrote Scholem, "the true representatives of the living popular religion of the masses" and who were in touch with some of the deepest emotions of the people, referred in the prayers they wrote for Kabbalat Shabbat to the Sabbath "bride." Nor is it coincidental that hundreds of years before this, the rabbis who contributed to the Talmud had mandated Shabbat eve—which, in the words of the author of *Iggeret*, is "spiritual, holy unto the Lord"—as the optimum time for the "holy act" of sexual relations between wife and husband.

It becomes apparent that the prerequisite to making marital sex special (as Shabbat was special in relation to the week) was limiting the time available for its expression. This is a Jewish form of quality control: Limit the quantity and you can enhance the quality. The question is, Why did the rabbis feel the need to make marital sex something so special? Answering this question requires the classic Jewish approach of looking at the context, which was that of arranged marriages, a practice that prevailed well into the nineteenth century; child and teen marriages; and the struggle against the ideas of premarital and extramarital romantic love.

⊰ In traditional Jewish communities, all first marriages were arranged by the parents. The ages of the children entering marriage declined from between eighteen and twenty for boys and midteens for girls in first-millennium C.E. Babylonia to under ten for boys and even younger for girls in Western Europe until around the sixteenth century; at that time, they rose to eighteen and sixteen, respectively. But well into the nineteenth century in Russian Poland, boys were still married off at thirteen, girls at twelve.

A confluence of religious and economic reasons, and, above all, survival needs, especially in the Middle Ages, made arranged early-teen marriages desirable—and possible for the middle class. Persecution and dislocation made Jews wish to create some family stability to offset the disasters raining down on them, as we have seen from Rabbi Peretz's rationale for preteen marriage. Arranged marriages between children from different towns were also a kind of insurance: One had in-laws to flee to, if need be.

The economic factor was that the young couple would receive *kest* (room and board) in the home of one or another set of in-laws while the boy studied Torah. He was able to do this rather than train for work, according to historian Jacob Katz, because many of the occupations of middle-class Jews, such as engaging in business, did not demand specific training (like that required of artisans or professionals). During the time the boy was studying—adolescence—he was off the "job market," out of the competition. Thus the kest system was a form of warehousing, keeping a large number of middle-class youth out of the arena where competition for a livelihood was intense.

At the same time, the system enabled the community to educate its future political leaders—both the middle-class boys who might become rabbis or balebatim active in community councils; and the poor but brilliant boys, sought as sons-in-law by wealthy men, who might otherwise have had to apprentice themselves as artisans and thus be lost to the cadre of religious leaders.

The religious reason for a boy's early marriage was that he would be able to concentrate on his studies, because not only were his financial needs taken care of, but also his sexual ones. Marriage was seen as the method of keeping him free of the sins of hashchatat zera and illicit sexual relationships.

Above all, early arranged marriage headed off youthful rebellion of all kinds. The poor but brilliant boys were co-opted by kest, and both they and the middle-class boys were kept from earning a living, which would have made financial independence possible. The system obviously also engendered emotional dependency and delayed adulthood at a time when there was no concept in Western Europe of "adolescence."

Girls from middle-class families either remained under the control of their fathers (if postmarital residence was matrilocal, as in Eastern Europe) or passed directly into the control of their in-laws (if residence was patrilocal). They were saddled with too many responsibilities, such as child rearing and sometimes breadwinning, to dream of independence (which they had no model for anyway). Poor girls sometimes worked as servants in the homes of the wealthy until marriage or labored alongside their mothers in craft work or selling in the marketplace, and they sometimes continued these latter occupations after marriage.

➤ While Jews were hardly alone in arranging their children's marriages, they had different concepts of marriage, love, and sex than Christians, especially from the High Middle Ages on, when the cult of romantic love—which involved adultery, whether in fantasy or reality, consummated completely, partially, or not at all—began in Western Europe. For Jews, marriage was not debased as a loveless arrangement motivated by extrinsic reasons—as was the case with Christians in the nobility. Nor did they struggle psychologically or intellectually, as did Christians, with the idea of sex as something sinful or dirty, or extol abstinence or "continent marriage."

They did, however, greatly fear romantic love—with its wild, uncontrollable passion—as a destabilizing force. Jews, as Jabotinsky once wrote, "could not tolerate, for self-preservation's sake, such wild and *uncontrollable* factors as . . . passion in any form" (italics mine). The biblical story of Michal, Saul's daughter, and her unrequited love for David (who later abused her), was a warning to Jewish maidens that such passion was dangerous.

Feelings of *grande passion* could not be allowed to precede marriage and cause young people to wish to choose their own spouses, nor could it be allowed to be brought into marriage to determine the nature of the spouses' relationship. The social order was based on an individual's following not her or his own heart but a trajectory paved with mitzvot that included no voluntary detours or ruptures or the upheavals that come with falling in love.

The free choice of spouses (possibly even from different classes) would have undermined the whole structure of Jewish society: Young men might have abandoned study for the pursuit of happiness, and couples might not have wanted to tolerate the imposition of the Niddah period of sexual separation; the benefits of the Onah-Niddah cycle would have fallen by the wayside. The Onah-Niddah cycle was a form of social control designed to put a brake on the spontaneous expression of passion; falling in love, in Francesco Alberoni's words, is an "act of liberation," an attempt to smash institutional control. Obviously, the two are incompatible.

The rabbis, communal leaders, and parents understood full well that the purpose of early arranged teen and preteen marriages was to prevent any falling in love. While the Crusades and their dislocations were said to have prompted the drastic lowering of the marriage age, the fact that this phenomenon prevailed when the cult of romantic love was in full flower was hardly a coincidence.

In sum, the erotic force could not be allowed to run wild. It had to be channeled into and harnessed to work for stable marriages, families, and communities.

Early marriages meant that the sexual feelings that developed in adolescence (ideally) came to the fore within the context of marriage. Since the couple had a set of ready-made obligations and patterns of behavior to live up to, these experiences were not free and wild. And the fact that both spouses were presumably inexperienced virgins created a kind of equality in sexual matters whose psychological effect may have carried over into and influenced the partnership ambiance of the relationship in general. The ideal was that spouses would grow to love each other after being married. But such love was a far cry from the wild, mad passion being glorified by some Christians in the High Middle Ages as romantic love.

THE NIDDAH-ENDOGAMY CONNECTION

This brings us back to the question of why sex in marriage had to be made special, more entrancing (after the initial excitement wore off). Sex in arranged marriages might have become ordinary, mundane, tedious, pedestrian, and routine (which also happens in love marriages) and thereby incapable of being the "instrumentality of domestic peace."

Either partner might have been tempted to seek sexual recreation outside marriage, which could not be allowed. Extramarital affairs could have caused extreme enmity between men in conflicts over women, possibly leading to intracommunal violence.

The marital partnership would have been ruptured by mistrust, jealousy, and rage—possibly even leading to violence—as responses to either spouse's affairs, and the home-as-haven would have been disrupted/destroyed, as well.

The husband's affairs, even if they were with unmarried women (and therefore not considered adulterous according to Halacha), would have eroded the wife's morale, which the community wished to uphold. A Jewish wife's adultery was considered a criminal act, threatening not only the man's (and the community's) sense of security about the children's parentage (and thus their status in the community) but his "masculinity," as well. The medieval libel about Beruriah's (alleged) adultery reflected the men's anxiety about the possibility of a wife's succumbing to the temptations of adultery ("women are light-headed") at a time when extramarital romantic love was glorified in Christian society, and it embodied a message about its fatal consequences.

❧ A related need was to prevent sexual relations with non-Jews. Such relations were prohibited by Christians, sometimes on pain of death, and by Jews, who feared Christian retaliation. Intermarriage would, of course, have required either the conversion of the Christian partner to Judaism, which would have subjected the convert to persecution by former coreligionists in most periods; or of the Jewish partner to Christianity, which would have led to the loss of the Jew and his or her children.

Endogamy (marrying and/or having sexual relations only with members of one's own group), however, triggers anxieties about incest: The spouse is familiar, known, and thus reminiscent of one's parent and siblings of the opposite sex. The Hebrew euphemism for intercourse is *to know,* which points to the feeling in the Jewish culture that sex means knowing another human being intimately. A period of abstinence allays and defuses anxieties about incest by making the spouses a little less "known" to each other, a little less familiar, a little more mysterious. The grouping of the laws about Niddah with the laws against incest in Leviticus 18 points to the unconscious association of marital part-time abstinence with defusing incest anxieties.

Making the spouse less familiar also makes sex more interesting, thus heading off the temptation to engage in extramarital affairs. (Again, this unconscious association can be seen from the grouping of laws on Niddah with those on adultery in Leviticus 20.) As one of Arthur Miller's characters says in *After the Fall:* "I set aside five minutes a day just imagining my wife as a *stranger. . . .* You got to generate some respect for her *mystery"* (italics mine).

The rabbis understood the role of the Niddah abstinence period in generating mystery and unfamiliarity to make sex more exciting. This is evident from the following Talmudic passage: "Why did the Torah ordain [the Niddah period]? . . . So that he may not get too used to her, so that she will *become more desirable* to her husband *as she was when she entered under the chuppah"* (Hebrew for marriage canopy; italics mine).

Immersion in the mikvah waters symbolizes one's casting off an old self (virgin before marriage, non-Jew before conversion) and "rebirth"–the assumption of a new identity. The immersed woman becomes a "new person," a stranger, a mysterious and unknown individual, as it were, a new and desirable bride.

THE RISE OF ROMANTIC LOVE

Romantic ideas, despite the strenuous attempts to block them at the communal border, did seep into Jewish life. In medieval Spain, Hebrew poets, including Moses Ibn Ezra and Yehuda Halevi, wrote poems and songs about unrequited love, the sterling qualities of the beloved, and romantic passion. In Central and Eastern Europe, the ideas of romantic love found their way into Jewish life through ballads by wandering minstrels and in folk songs (some of them sung as lullabies).

The Jewish community fought vigorously against romantic love and the free choice of spouses. Jewish legal and communal literature is replete with cases of clandestine marriages (sometimes of young people from wealthy homes with servants) and the struggle against them. For example, the Council of Four Lands (the umbrella governing body of Polish Jewry in the sixteenth to eighteenth centuries) legislated that youths below twenty who married without their parents' consent "shall have their engagement contracts declared void." Similarly, legislation in sixteenth-century Lithuania stipulated that anyone who married secretly would be "excommunicated and ostracized." It mandated severe court punishments as a means of preventing the "promiscuity of this generation." These last four words indicate that the practice of secret marriage might not have been uncommon.

By the nineteenth century in Eastern Europe, love was featured in many novels in Yiddish, often read clandestinely by young women. A common theme was that of predestination: The girl and boy fall in love and believe it is their free choice, only to discover that they were destined to marry by a vow taken by their parents. The predestination theme was an obvious attempt on the part of writers in touch with the yearnings of the youth for free choice in marriage to "prove" to the community that this was "good for the Jews," that it would buttress rather than rock the established order.

But by the middle of the nineteenth century, many youth had become restless as currents of revolutionary thought began sweeping Czarist Russia. Many, too, were influenced by the maskilim, who made the campaign for love and against arranged marriage (and its abuses) an important part of their agenda. What they sought to do was to detach the erotic force from arranged virginal marriages and harness it to their cause: to break the control of communal institutions and, as they saw it, bring Jews into the modern world.

THE IMPACT OF ASSIMILATIONISM ON JEWISH PUBLIC AND PRIVATE LIFE

The Jews are probably the only people in the world to whom it has ever been proposed that their historic destiny is—to be nice.... As applied to an individual, the word nice indicates a pleasing absence of character.... In the philosophy of many Western Jews ... anti-Semitism is the result of a lack of niceness in the Jew. If the Jews would only temper their voices, their table-manners and their ties, if they would be discreet and tidy in their enthusiasms, unobtrusive in their comings and goings, and above all reticent about their Jewishness, they would get along very well.... The nice Jew ... is in the curious position of the diplomat who does not say what he means, but has come to mean what he says. He has ... talked himself out of his soul.... Nothing remains for a man [sic] in this desperate position but to surrender his identity, too; and consciously or unconsciously, this is the intention behind the theory of niceness.

MAURICE SAMUEL

SEVEN ❧ THE NEW MARRANOS:
ASSIMILATIONISM AND ETHNIC AMNESIA

Be a Jew in your tent and a human when you leave it.

YEHUDA LEIB GORDON (1863)

America was ready to open its heart only to those who viewed themselves as "wretched refuse"—inferior cultures which they will discard.

LEONARD FEIN

Death and suicide are the most radical reliefs from disease. Similarly, assimilation is the most radical solution to the Jewish problem. If there were no Jews, there would be no suffering from the Jewish tragedy. Nevertheless, no medical expert would advise a patient to take poison for a cure.... Only to us Jews have self-appointed "physicians" had the audacity, the shamelessness, to preach national suicide.

BER BOROCHOV (1915)

The departure of over a million and a half Jews from Eastern Europe to America from 1881 to 1924 was more than a population shift—it was a sea change. This migration, unlike those of the past, led to the new immigrants' departure from many traditional values and customs as part of an effort to assimilate into the general society.

Assimilation means relinquishing the values, lifestyle, customs, languages, and behavior patterns of one's ethnic group and adopting those of the majority culture, which is molded by the ruling class.

Total assimilation would mean the disappearance of the Jews as a discrete ethnic group.

It is precisely for this reason that the ruling classes of modern Western nation-states, while pressuring Jews to one degree or another to assimilate, are not really interested in their complete and total assimilation. If the Jews ceased to exist as an ethnic group in these states, they would not be able to occupy/fill the interstitial niches and societal roles that the ruling class finds so necessary.

What the power structure is really interested in, therefore, is not assimilation but assimilation*ism*—getting Jews to *try* to assimilate and thereby become Jewishly invisible as individuals and as a group in the public sphere.

Assimilationism deflects the energy of individual Jews into trying to live up to the "superior" values and behavior patterns infused into the majority culture by the ruling class, and into seeking validation in the general society for their success in doing so. It involves them in efforts to eradicate differences in appearance and behavior that are negatively stereotyped by the ruling class and the majority culture and propels them to engage in extreme self-censorship to keep whatever remains of their Jewishness in the closet. The "best powers" of the assimilationist Jew, said Max Nordau, "are exhausted in the suppression or at least in the difficult concealment of his [*sic*] own real character." (At the same time, once Jews accept the ruling class's values, which inform the majority culture, they become more easily exploited as instruments for fulfilling the socioeconomic roles it finds necessary.)

Conditioning individuals to lose touch with their own feelings and concerns, to reject the legitimacy of their own interests, and to focus instead only on what reaction their behavior will elicit from others eliminates any possibility of their determining and acting on their own inner-directed agenda and makes them eternally insecure and ultimately powerless. Assimilationism, a form of psychological oppression, thus has its parallels with women's conditioning to be unaware of their own intrinsic needs and interests and to engage in behavior that others, especially men, will approve of and validate.

Assimilationism programs Jews to ethnic amnesia: to "forget"/become oblivious to/discount the fact that they are part of an ethnic group with specific concerns and interests that *continue to exist even as individual Jews' identification with the group is being eroded*. Ethnic amnesia breaks down group cohesiveness; this makes it possible for the power structure to deal with isolated individuals rather than a collectivity ("United we stand, divided we fall"). In the absence of a mechanism for working out collective solutions to the problems they face, Jews must constantly reinvent the wheel whenever they need to unite, engaging in time-consuming efforts to develop/retrieve trust, to build working relationships, and to reach an understanding that they share the same values and concerns—all on an ad hoc basis.

Assimilationism is a kind of domestication. When inflicted on animals, domestication involves, in the words of John Livingston, a professor of environmental studies, "a life on sufferance ... the acceptance of being dependent." The victim, denied contact with and the possibility of forming attachments to others of its species, suffers self-alienation, becoming a "social cripple" without a social identity. The creature is characterized by behavioral sameness and "manageability." Substituting the word *group* for *species* and *Jew* for *creature* in this definition of domestication provides a fairly accurate description of the assimilationist programming process.

Because complete assimilation is impossible, individual Jews continue to draw on classic survival strategies to cope with the problems they still face as Jews. The existence of these survival strategies (as we shall see in chapter 9) and of individuals who resist assimilation, as well as its ultimate impossibility, causes Jews to be suspended in a psychological twilight zone. They veer back and forth in vertiginous response to the gravitational pull of the general society and the centrifugal force of their own group and of whatever remains of their ethnic identity, however marginal or unconscious.

⮊ Assimilationism is thus the opposite of the kind of situation for which, significantly, no word (yet) exists, one in which each ethnic group in society contributes its creativity to a multicultural patchwork quilt rather than simply accepting a tightly woven blanket produced and proffered by the power structure and its culture, under which one can easily be smothered. It is what Peretz meant when he wrote: "I am not advocating that we shut ourselves up in a spiritual ghetto. On the contrary, we should get out of such a ghetto. But we should get out *as Jews,* with our own spiritual treasures. We should interchange, give and take" (italics mine).

The closest Jews have come to that situation was in the Golden Age (tenth to twelfth centuries) of medieval Islamic Spain. There a true "interchange"/cross-fertilization occurred. Drawing on their tradition, values, and culture, Jews participated in and contributed to the secular life of the general society. They also brought into Jewish life some of its artistic elements, developed and transformed them, and thus enhanced their group's cultural creativity—enabling them to contribute even further to the general society.

THE ASSIMILATIONIST CONTRACT

The assimilationist dynamic has applied in all modern Western societies where Jews have lived since the mid-eighteenth century, with variations in the degree of pressure to assimilate, the nature of rewards for success at and punishments for failure in doing so, and the responses of Jews to these phenomena.

Nowhere has assimilationism worked as well as in the United States. Within a few generations after the mass immigration of East European Jews to these shores, the vast majority suffered cultural/ethnic amnesia. As Cynthia Ozick observed, "In the rush to Americanization, the immigrants . . . ended by encouraging amnesia of the central motifs and texts of their civilization." Many forgot how to live as Jews, and it became difficult to tease out anything authentically Jewish in their daily lives. Many lost the ability to "see the world through Jewish eyes." And the changes they made in their gender roles to live up to ruling-class definitions transmitted by the majority culture caused intractable conflicts between women and men—and in the hearts of both.

To understand why the East European Jewish immigrants (and their descendants) shed like torn *shmattes* (Yiddish for rags) their putatively beloved values, lifestyles, and folk customs as disposable ethnicity, we must look at the historical events that changed Jewish life in Europe several centuries before their mass immigration.

The departure point for this exploration is the spiritual crisis that ensued in the mid-seventeenth century with the crash of the "revolution of rising expectations"—the flare-up of the mass rescue fantasy in the Shabbetai Zvi messianic movement of the 1660s. The movement spread rapidly from Turkey to the communities in the Mediterranean area and to Eastern Europe (where Jews were still reeling from the Chmielnitzki massacres). Jews experienced transports of ecstasy and expected to experience soon, as well, transports to Eretz Israel. The crash—Shabbetai Zvi converted to Islam in 1666 and gave up his messianic pretensions—forced Jews to confront forestalled redemption. East European Jews, as we shall see shortly, turned ever more inward, bolstering their spiritual resistance by the creation of the Hassidic movement about seventy years later.

Western Jews—those living in France, the Germanic states, and the Austrian Empire—began to direct their rescue fantasy outward, toward the absolutist regimes in these countries and to the Enlightenment movement of the eighteenth century, which propagated the ideas of reason, tolerance, and emancipation; later they looked for rescue from the nineteenth-century bourgeois nationalist states. The responses of the Western Jews, particularly those in Germany, created patterns of behavior that those Jews who immigrated to America after 1848 brought with them and continued to incorporate in their lives. To understand their experiences and responses, it is necessary to look closely at how assimilationist methodology worked in these West European societies.

⊰ The Western regimes of the past two and a half centuries have promoted an assimilationist contract with the Jews; this has also obtained in the U.S. Its terms were, in Leonard Fein's words, "Do not behave as Jews have always behaved and you will not be treated as Jews have always been treated." The contract looks like a carrot held under the Jew's nose, but it is really a stick with a heavy carrot covering. "Give up your distinctiveness and be rewarded—*or else*" is its real message. Its implication is that Jews will be tolerated only if they give up their differences, and that their refusal to do so will "provoke" anti-Semitism. Thus it is Jews who must bear the ultimate responsibility for anti-Semitism in the future as they did in the past. This, of course, is another variation of blaming the victim. *What it really means is that the only way Jews can avert physical annihilation is through cultural suicide.*

The assimilationist contract brings to mind a similar one by which men promised women that if they changed their sexual behavior—became more "accessible"—they would be more likely to be treated better by individual men. American women were barraged with "Sexual Revolution" propaganda to smash their old defenses (play hard to get, wait till you get married). Not only did sexual exploitation actually increase, but rape escalated, as well. Women were then blamed for "provoking" rape by giving out signals (e.g., through dress) of being sexually "accessible"—the precise kind of behavior the men had promised would lead to *better* treatment.

⊰ One prime motivation of the absolutist states of the eighteenth century in promoting the assimilationist contract was their wish to destroy Jewish collectivity. These states could not tolerate any alternative organized structures that they could not control. They therefore acted to break up such structures, including the autonomous Jewish communities that had existed for centuries.

To deceive Jews into acceding to the destruction of one of the instrumentalities of collective solutions, these states held out the carrot of individual solutions—granting emancipation (citizenship and, later, voting rights) to Jewish men. "The very power that had been invested in the communal structure was now to be returned to the individual Jew so he [*sic*] could reinvest it in the secular state," wrote David Biale.

A similar motivation and process obtained in the bourgeois nationalist states of the nineteenth century. These states could not tolerate ethnic differences any more than class consciousness, both of which involved identification with groups outside their borders. In revolutionary France, the policy, in the words of a delegate to the National Assembly, was that "Jews should be denied everything as a nation but granted everything as individuals."

The second prime motivation of these states was to promote the invisibility of Jews as Jews in the public sphere. It would have been impossible for them to use the assimilationist contract to do so had an autonomous Jewish community existed to teach, reinforce, and validate Jewish distinctiveness and to serve as the public context for its expression. A strong collectivity, by its very nature, cannot be easily forced to relinquish its distinctiveness. But individuals' wish and ability to retain their differences can be broken down by the digestive enzymes of economic and political incentives and the bile of "rationalist" critiques, as we shall see.

Jews acceded to invisibility because on the surface it seemed like a boon—a liberating opportunity rather than an oppressive demand. The reason it seemed so positive is that it contrasted so sharply with a strategy of the past: that of making Jews *hyper*visible by forcing them to wear weird clothes and hats and/or yellow badges and/or to live in ghettos. This strategy served to separate Jews from non-Jews, thereby fulfilling the power structure's aim and policy of eradicating Jewishness from the public sphere. What Jews did not understand is that *invisibility was not a reversal of the eradication policy but rather a new strategy of continuing it.*

Furthermore, because hypervisibility had made Jews easier to spot and attack, Jews in traditional communities had often tried to counter it with the survival strategy of being inconspicuous/unobtrusive, of maintaining a low profile to avert trouble for the entire community. Thus public invisibility seemed like a continuity rather than a discontinuity of classic Jewish behavior. It became internalized by assimilationist Jews to such a degree that it was no longer experienced as a demand emanating from outside but as a survival strategy. Training to "pass, to slip unnoticed into the non-Jewish community, to do nothing which would attract the notice *and so the wrath*" of non-Jews, in David Mamet's words, begins in childhood (italics mine). These words point to how the old fear of conspicuousness became intermeshed with the new fear of ethnic visibility deriving from the corollary of the assimilationist contract: If one behaved in the culturally distinctive way Jews had always behaved, one would be treated as Jews were always treated, that is, persecuted. It is this fear of "provoking" persecution that is the prime motivation behind Jews' adhering to the terms of the assimilationist contract.

✤ While the Jews' ethnic distinctiveness disappeared in the public sphere, they were still identifiable as Jews because of their prominence in the high-visibility socioeconomic roles they had been slotted into. The draining off of ethnic characteristics in their public behavior caused these roles to loom larger in and take over the vacuum/space vacated by the cultural characteristics. Many non-Jews tended to see these specific roles as the sole defining essence of Jewishness. This phenomenon can be seen very clearly in the following statement by Marx:

> What is the secular basis of Judaism? Practical need, self-interest. What is the worldly culture of the Jew? Bargaining. What is his worldly God? Money.... Money is the jealous God of Israel, beside which no other God may exist.... Very well. *Emancipation from buying and selling, that is to say, from practical and real Judaism,* would be the self-emancipation of our era.... An organization of society which abolished the necessary conditions for buying and selling ... would make the Jew impossible; his [*sic*] religious consciousness would evaporate [italics mine].

Some of the roles foisted upon Jews had already induced hatred of them for centuries and had thereby allowed them to be used as lightning rods to absorb the rage of the oppressed. Strangely and unfortunately, Marx did not (care to) understand that part of the ruling class's agenda in promoting Jewish cultural invisibility was to allow the Judeophobically stereotyped roles to *totally* define Jewish difference. Its success can be seen from the easy acceptance of the definition of Jews by Voltaire. This fierce critic of the Old Regime of France and the paragon of the Enlightenment envisioned a halcyon future when "these *wandering brokers,* ... no longer able to enrich themselves through our negligence" (the parasite myth) "and ignorant even of their own books ... will assimilate among the scum of other peoples" (italics mine).

Nor has there been any comprehension of how the eradication of difference creates the impression of an even greater difference between Jews and other human beings: the *absence* of cultural differences. Ethnic invisibility makes Jews appear unreal because real people do have ethnic differences—these are part of being human. This phenomenon makes it seem that Jews are mysterious, exotic, strange—not quite human. Nordau, a psychiatrist, understood this when he described the "emancipated Jew" as "externally *unreal,* and thereby always ridiculous and hateful to all higher feeling men [*sic*] as is everything that is *unreal*" (italics mine).

It is worth noting here what Richard Gruenberger wrote about the Holocaust. It was, he said, unreal to most Germans "because Jews were astronomically remote *and not real people*" (italics mine).

THE CON GAME

Getting Jews to accept the viability of the assimilationist contract has involved a con game of deluding them into believing that relinquishing distinctiveness will lead to an abatement of or even an end to anti-Semitism and, eventually, to their total acceptance into the general society. The ruling classes had to smash Jews' classic psychological defenses by convincing them that (a) their distinctiveness was not worth preserving and (b) that giving it up was indeed resulting in declining prejudice and increased "integration"—even when it wasn't.

In Western Europe, propagandists of Enlightenment ideology kept up a nagging barrage of criticism of Jewish distinctiveness as not only negative but also as the obstacle to "equality" and acceptance. Judaism was criticized for its "irrationality" and its ethics for their lack of "universality." In the nineteenth-century romantic era, Judaism was faulted for its lack of emotional warmth and gratification as well as on esthetic grounds: It was not only obscurantist, but also noisy, uncouth, superstitious, uncultured, and old-fashioned.

The Enlightenment-era critics also propagandized that Jews were morally inferior because of their occupations, a classic blame-the-victim charge (these were the only occupations Jews had been allowed to pursue). Recycling the old Judeophobic parasite myth, they especially scorned peddling as a "morally dangerous occupation."

This barrage of criticism helped smash a prime traditional inner defense against the classic anti-Semitic mythology that Jewish distinctiveness meant Jewish inferiority: the Chosen People countermyth and the self-image of Jews as being ethical, worthy, and good. This left Jews without a psychological barrier to the internalization of the various Judeophobic stereotypes recycled by the "social philosophers."

To get Jews to believe that the eradication of their distinctiveness was paying off, the ruling classes of the eighteenth and nineteenth centuries provided intermittent/partial reinforcement in the form of small rewards supposedly auguring larger ones. Citizens' rights were extended to Jews in bits and pieces, then sometimes withdrawn; ghetto walls were opened, then closed again. The last of the West European ghettos, that of Rome, was abolished only as late as 1885.

Jews who gave up their distinctiveness were never quite allowed to cross over the border into total acceptance. This made them desperately eager to give up more and more distinctiveness because they saw its remnants as the impediment to total acceptance. Jumping through one hoop after another, they were off balance and easier to exploit and manipulate.

The power structure also derided outcroppings of anti-Semitism as insignificant or tried to make Jews believe they were imagining them because they were paranoid or simply anachronistically insecure. It also continued to propagandize that any instances of discrimination were the Jews' own fault—they had not lived up to their end of the assimilationist contract by giving up distinctiveness or giving it up "enough." Jews were especially susceptible to believing they had not done enough because of their classic strategy of being better at something (i.e., more useful) to overcome discrimination and their old guilt—traditionally connected with trying to effect redemption—about not having done enough.

The ruling class thus broke down another traditional inner defense: that anti-Semitism derived not from Jewish behavior but from the irrational beliefs and/or self-serving needs of oppressors, the messages in the Books of Exodus and Esther.

With the old defenses broken, assimilationist Jews internalized the recycled Judeophobic stereotypes, and some blamed themselves for the anti-Semitism they had "provoked." Unable to totally erase their differences and thereby attain "acceptance," and suffering from an "unrequited love for their enemies" (Theodore Lessing's words), they experienced a neurosis new in Jewish history: self-hate. An extreme but by no means unusual example comes from the pen of Otto Weininger in fin de siècle Vienna. Weininger unconsciously recognized the parallels between the oppression of Jews and of women but blamed it on the victims' inferiority. He defined masculinity as positive, as Being, as the expression of all that is great, noble, and valuable, and as embodied in the "Aryan." He defined femininity as non-Being, as guilt, as "man's [sic] lower self." It was, he wrote, embodied most typically in the Jew who, "like Woman, is utterly devoid of genius and hence always mediocre and imitative."

THE "TRANSMISSION BELT"

The success of the con game required the services of a stratum of Jews who would try to live up to the assimilationist contract and ensure that more and more Jews did so, too. In essence, Jews of this stratum functioned as collaborationists, accepting the (limited) rewards of giving up distinctiveness in return for trying to "de-Semitize" the masses of Jews. This dovetailed with the pattern described by Maurice Samuel by which "rich Jews, obtaining favors from Gentile rulers for themselves and for their people, had to have a docile and obedient Jewry to deliver."

Jewish assimilationists in Western countries colluded with the ruling classes because they saw it in their interests to get the masses to try to assimilate. The visibility of the masses' distinctiveness made them—and any vestiges of their own Jewish behavior patterns—conspicuous. This is why assimilationist nineteenth- and twentieth-century German and Austrian Jews who were already well established in European (and American) cities harbored such loathing for the *Ostjuden,* the masses of nonassimilating poor Polish and Russian Jewish immigrants. (It is also why assimilationist Jews cringe at the sight of right-wing Orthodox Jews in their distinctive black coats and hats—correctly interpreting this dress code as a revolt against invisibility.)

✦ A considerable number of upper-middle-class Jews, as well as intellectuals, eagerly acted as the "transmission belt" of the Enlightenment philosophy/ideology into German and French communities. The intellectuals, calling themselves maskilim, accepted, internalized, and disseminated a great deal of the negative evaluation of Jewish culture. They and the wealthy assimilationist men were especially perturbed by the charge that the Jewish community's occupational profile was "abnormal" because it was a recycling of the old parasite myth. Wealthy Jews established organizations in virtually every major community from Alsace to Hungary to promote "occupational redistribution," wrote Jacob Katz, but these efforts had little effect.

They also strived to get the masses of Jews to give up their distinctive dress code and forms of religious expression, especially various ritual observances, such as kashrut, which were seen as an impediment to associating with and being accepted by non-Jews. Another such impediment they sought to convince the Jews to relinquish was their languages: Hebrew, which had become in the Exile the language of prayer and Halacha; and Yiddish, the everyday lingua franca of the Ashkenazim—northern, central, and East European Jews. (The Sephardim, Jews descended from the Spanish expellees, who lived in southern Europe, the Balkans, and Turkey, spoke Ladino; those living in North Africa and other Arab countries spoke Judeo-Arabic.)

✦ The assimilationists' ability to function effectively as a "transmission belt" required their direct access to the masses unimpeded by any rival communal structure committed to group cohesion and cultural distinctiveness. Their consequent wish to break the hold of the rabbinical establishment on the masses of Jews often made them unofficial allies of the absolutist and nationalist regimes that dismantled the autonomous communities.

Rejecting Halacha and Halachic authority, German assimilationist Jews of the nineteenth century created a new form/style of religious expression, Reform

Judaism. The Reform movement sought to reconstitute Judaism as a religious faith in a neo-Protestant incarnation, with "dignified" synagogue services in the German language.

Further colluding in the erosion of communal cohesion, the Reform Jews developed the ideology of Jews' being not a nation but only a religious faith. Having internalized the libel that the Chosen People countermyth was arrogant and clannish, they reworked it into the concept of a "Jewish mission" to pass on the message of God, revealed at Sinai, to all the nations and trumpeted the universality of the prophetic tradition.

Ahad Ha'am, in a scathing critique, wrote in 1889 that "if Western Jews were not slaves to their emancipation, it would never have entered their heads to consecrate their people to spiritual missions or aims before it had fulfilled that physical national 'mission' which belongs to every organism—before it had created for itself conditions suitable to its character, in which it could develop . . . its own particular form of life . . . in obedience to the demands of its nature."

German Jews who had reinvented themselves as "Germans of the Mosaic persuasion" also began to promote the idea that the family should fill the void that their neglect of religious tradition had created, wrote historian Marion Kaplan. This process came to fruition in imperial Germany, by which time most Jewish women were secluded in the home from the front lines of change. The observance of ritual, therefore, waned most slowly among them, and they were expected to "cushion the family from [the] shock waves" of assimilation.

Women Marranos of Iberia and its Western Hemisphere colonies had also played a key role in maintaining the home as the context for the expression of Judaism. This occurred when no public context existed, and they and the men wished to preserve Judaism. Among these "new Marranos" (as Nordau called them), it was not life-threatening to be Jewish in the public sphere, but the men wished to be invisible as Jews there. They relegated Judaism to the home to limit its expression to the private sphere. Having downgraded the importance of Jewish ritual observance, they made its transmission "women's work" but did not provide women the requisite Jewish education to be effective as teachers and role models.

(In reaction to the rise of Reform Judaism in Western Europe and to assimilationism generally, the rabbis who continued to adhere to Halacha regrouped and developed what is known today as Orthodox Judaism. Embracing Judaism in a bear hug, they thereby stunted its growth. Put another way: They froze Halacha in an effort to preserve it. Unfortunately, it is precisely this strategy that has made it too rigid to respond to the new challenges that face all Jews in the modern era. Orthodoxy consequently became a minority "denomination" in the community.)

◀▶ Germany's Jews never received the rewards promised them by the assimilationist contract. The initial emancipation of its Jewish population from the ghettos occurred only after the Germanic states were invaded by Napoleon's armies. For the next half-century, the Jews continued to experience social, economic, and political discrimination (which led some of them to embrace Socialism). Jews attained full civic equality in Germany in 1870. But they were never seen as part of the nation, because all Western states, wrote Katz, "continued to evince a Christian character."

This did not cause German Jews to give up their faith in assimilationism. Those who came to America after the failure of the 1848 Revolution believed that "this time it will be different." America, they believed, was the place where the assimilationist contract would work and where individual solutions would be possible.

RUSSIAN REACTION

Jews in Eastern Europe underwent a completely different metamorphosis in the mid-eighteenth century. To recover psychologically from the horrors of the previous century, Polish Jews had to find a way to maintain their spiritual resistance until their mass rescue fantasy would be realized in the far future. The Hassidic movement originated by the Ba'al Shem Tov (Master of the Good Name) in the 1730s and 1740s created a new variation of spiritual resistance.

Hassidism (from the Hebrew word for piety) began as a revolutionary mass movement. It emphasized that God could and should be worshiped with emotion and joy and through song and dance; it deemphasized the primacy of study of Talmud as the main expression of spiritual resistance.

The massacres of 1648–58 from which hundreds of communities never recovered economically—and the dislocation, homelessness, poverty, and despair the onslaught had left in its wake—impaired the ability of many men to return even to part-time Torah study. By emphasizing the role of even the most destitute Jewish man in helping to bring about cosmic repair and messianic redemption through the joyful fulfillment of everyday mitzvot, including prayer, Hassidism overcame the feeling of powerlessness reactivated by the pogroms and of its constant companion, depression. The Hassidic movement's egalitarian elements appealed to men who had to put their energies into eking out a subsistence living and who resented the rabbinical leaders and their bourgeois allies, the balabatim, who looked down on the unlearned.

At the same time, Hassidism challenged the old communal structure by elevating a new kind of religious leader. He went by various names: rebbe, *tzaddik* (Hebrew for saintly man), *ba'al shem,* all of which meant a combination of guru and wonder-worker with magical and healing powers. Unlike the rabbi, the charismatic rebbe/tzaddik was seen by his followers as their intermediary with God (a previously unknown concept in Judaism, which gives all Jews a direct line to the Almighty). His advice could not be rejected, and he could not be criticized.

It is precisely because the rebbe/tzaddik was experienced as a kind of rescuer that the critical faculty of his followers was deactivated.

The Hassidic movement can also be seen as an attempt to redefine masculinity by and for all those poor men who could not be or could not support scholars and who had therefore felt emasculated. The new definition of masculinity was ecstatic piety, carried out by a group of men led by the rebbe. Hassidic activities involved and promoted intense male bonding, with followers of a rebbe gathering at his table to listen to his fanciful tales, sing his unique melodies, and attain communion with the divine.

Women were totally excluded from such Hassidic activities so that these could define masculinity. They were allowed to function as enablers by supporting the family while the man of the house was away at the rebbe's court and, of course, by accepting exclusion from attendance at occasions such as *farbrengens* (Yiddish for joyous get-togethers around the rebbe's table). One woman attained considerable prominence among Hassidim for her erudite discourses: the "Maid of Ludomir," Hannah Rachel Werbermacher (1805–1892). She was eventually forced to give up her lectures.

The old leadership fought back by creating a kind of "Counter-Reformation" movement revivifying study. Its proponents called themselves *Misnagdim* (Yiddish plural, from the Hebrew *mitnaged:* opponent). Hassidism evoked intense opposition from the Misnagdim not only because it rejected the old leadership but also because it posited a new definition of masculinity, ecstatic piety, that challenged theirs, which continued to emphasize the primacy of study.

⤐ The end of the eighteenth century found the majority of East European Jews living in Czarist Russia, which got the lion's share of the Jews of partitioned Poland (Prussia and Austria got the rest). The Czarist form of control (except for a respite during the 1855–81 reign of Alexander II) was the spiked truncheon of persecution and pogroms rather than the carrot-covered stick of assimilationism.

The Czarist government was obsessed with Jewish "separatism" and was determined to eradicate it. Even under Alexander II (who emancipated the serfs), the regime's goal was what Dubnow called "forced enlightenment." A special commission was established in 1871 to promulgate "ways and means to weaken as far as possible the communal cohesion of the Jews." The regime dissolved the communal councils, established special schools to wean Jews from the cheders, and passed laws against the traditional dress code, including women's having shaved heads under their wigs. (Jewish women had always been required to cover their heads lest their hair tempt men to sin. The wearing of wigs was a custom, originated by women, that took root in Poland and was practiced in Russia among those who could afford it. It is practiced today among right-wing Orthodox Jews of European origin.)

Jews were unable to use any of their classic survival strategies: The ruling class was rabidly anti-Semitic, and none of its components saw it in their interest to extend the Jews protection. It used Jews as lightning rods to absorb and deflect the hostility and rage of the oppressed peasants. Jews had no way to be useful to this ruling class: Most were too severely fenced in (geographically in the Pale and economically) to fill traditional middle-class niches. The pencil-thin stratum of wealthy entrepreneurs given special privileges and allowed to live outside the Pale lacked the influence and connections to behave as classic Court Jews. Some put their class interests ahead of their ethnic consciousness.

✒ While the eighteenth-century *Haskalah* (pro-Enlightenment movement) in Western Europe was composed of rich men and intellectuals who sought individual assimilationist solutions, the nineteenth-century Haskalah movement in Russia was led by intellectuals, writers, and educators who sought a collective solution: the reform of the Jewish community. Another major difference was that the German Haskalah's assimilationism led to the elimination of the Jewish languages; the Russian maskilim lay the foundation for a national renascence of literature in Hebrew and, later, Yiddish.

The Russian maskilim were bitterly critical of the community's religious life and especially of Hassidism. They felt it kept the masses passive and unable/unwilling to take action to change their condition. Unlike their Western counterparts, these maskilim did not create or participate in a new religious movement. Instead they tried to revitalize Judaism by incorporating elements of modern culture and promoting a new educational system emphasizing European languages and the sciences in order to "productivize" the Jews. Some of them fell initially into the same trap that their Western counterparts did: They naively believed that the government's support could be enlisted to make reforms, such as establishing a network of secular Jewish schools; they were soon disabused of this fantasy, however.

The Russian maskilim were influenced to some extent by the ideas of the Western Haskalah, which had internalized the view of Jewish life's "obscurantism," "backwardness," and "superstition." They also accepted the critique of its occupational structure's being "abnormal." Such ideas, as well as that of the glorification of agricultural labor, were also current in the Russian culture, especially during the period of quasi liberalism under Alexander II and in the Populist movement, which saw the peasants as the hope for revolutionary change in Russia.

The belief in the power of agricultural labor to eliminate Jewish economic "abnormality" and isolation can be seen in the "Song of Bread" by M. M. Warshavsky, which attained the popularity of a folk song: "Brothers, gather together the sheaves. . . . Let us never go back! / Let our children learn / To enjoy *life in the world*" (italics mine). The 1937 Yiddish film *Green Fields,* the story of a yeshiva student who settles happily on a Jewish farm, captures and embodies this nine-teenth-century glorification of labor on the soil and its redemptive spirituality. This idea played an important part in the various attempts then and later to settle Jews as farmers in Argentina, the U.S., and the Crimea, as well as in the evolution of Socialist Zionist and Labor Zionist ideology, as we shall see in the next chapter.

The maskilim called for the destruction of the system of arranged teenage marriage with matrilocal residence and kest because it prevented Jewish "produc-tivization." They advocated that a boy marry only after learning a trade, which would make him able to support a wife, and that women be removed from the turf of breadwinning. While they propagandized about liberating Jewish women from the "yoke" of traditional arranged marriages, wrote David Biale, what they really wished was to "liberate" the men from the (economic) "domination" of the women.

❧ The maskilim tried to activate the masses of Russian Jews into joining their at-tempt at a separation struggle: to reject the domination of the rabbis and rebbes and to regroup and work out a new definition of Jewishness with which they could reenter Russian society. It was for this reason that so much of their focus was on the reform of education. What happened instead was that when Alexander II opened the *gymnasia* (academic high schools) and universities to Jews, many youths opted for the individual solution of Russification. The Jewish masses, by contrast, continued to adhere to the concept of the collective solution of mes-sianic redemption. Many young Jews who sought secular collective solutions for the Jews left the community and joined the Populist Revolutionary (*narodnik*) movement. Some, including female revolutionaries, converted to Russian Ortho-doxy to make it possible for them to organize the peasants. Historian Eliahu Cherikover writes that the women "truly uprooted themselves from their families and the Pale." Their lives were characterized by personal tragedy more than the men's. Some took their own lives out of suffering and despair, others were exe-cuted, murdered, or sentenced to hard labor or internal exile (Siberia), where some died.

The Jewish masses' obdurate opposition to any change that could possibly weaken their spiritual resistance to the Czarist regime led to a kind of war be-tween the maskilim and the Jewish masses, who refused to be reeducated, wrote historian Jacob Talmon. Another factor in the masses' resistance was that the maskilim impugned the men's definition of masculinity by criticizing a system in which the women were the main breadwinners. Such criticism threatened the mythology the men had created to downgrade providing as women's work and thereby retain their self-respect.

Despite this resistance, the ideas of the maskilim seeped into Russian Jewish life and, in the long run, helped break down the concept that there was only one right way for all Jews to live. By the middle of the nineteenth century, many Rus-sian Jews had come to feel that studying was a substitute rather than a mechanism for coping with the changing reality, and that it had curled in on itself like an ingrown toenail, impeding any forward movement. But what alternatives were there? Evocative of this dilemma is M. Z. Feierberg's story "Whither?" in which a yeshiva student returns to the besmedrush after finding nothing else of spiritual value to take the place of Torah study.

❧ The pogroms of the 1880s were an especially brutal shock to those young Jews who had sought individual (Russification) or collective (revolutionary) solutions to the problem of Jewish survival in Russia. They demonstrated that neither Russification nor peasant revolution was the answer: The peasant pogromists were equal-opportunity murderers.

It took about twenty years until the Jews who remained in Russia after these pogroms regrouped to work out new definitions of Jewish identity that celebrated their ethnic differences and created movements to advance collective solutions that made the community politically pluralistic and thus allowed Jewish revolutionaries to work for change within rather than outside it. These collective solutions—Zionism, Socialism, Socialist Zionism, Folkism, cultural autonomy, Territorialism—were obviously not available to the Jews who emigrated in the 1880s, and it was they who set the pattern for the responses of East European Jews to America.

AMERICANIZATION

What the new immigrants found in the U.S. was the ethos of individualism, of the entitlement of white males to the pursuit of happiness—defined as material success plus love—and the possibility of attaining this happiness. Having been trampled under the hobnailed boot of the Czarist regime, ground into the dust by its bloodthirsty pogromists, and near buried alive under the suffocating group discipline of a community that feared that action by any Jew could trigger dire consequences for all, they experienced the American concept of individual solutions as liberation.

The material success of their German brethren, who had arrived after 1848 with nothing, led them to conclude that they, too, could fulfill this American Dream. Since only white male Americans were entitled to (pursue) happiness (i.e., material success), the Jewish immigrant men had two out of three qualifications. They were led to believe that their material success was conditional upon the third prerequisite: being Americanized, a euphemism for assimilation. For this reason, in the immigrant period, wrote Judah Shapiro, "To speak Yiddish, to light candles on Friday night, to attend religious services on Saturday, to eat traditional foods, were challenges to one's *good standing as an American*" (italics mine).

❧ The pressure on the East European Jews to assimilate came from many quarters, including the newspapers—which published nasty stories about the unwashed—

and the public school system, where, wrote Margaret Mead, the immigrants were "taught to reject and usually to despise their parents' values." In college, even in the late 1930s, the Jewish students, wrote Leslie Fiedler, were "like a class in an occupied country.... We were forbidden Yiddishisms."

Pressure to assimilate also came from German Jews, who acted as a kind of "transmission belt" of the values of the upper middle class of the general society (their reference group). German Jews feared that "only disgrace and a lowering opening [*sic*] in which Israelites" (their euphemism for themselves) "are held ... has resulted from the continued residence among us of these wretches" (the Russian Jews), as one of their charity officials put it.

After the failure of their organizational attempts to limit the Russians' immigration and then to disperse them away from New York, German Jews turned to efforts to Americanize the uncouth and unwashed: to dust them off, clean them up, and get them to behave and look as much like "Americans" as quickly as possible, wrote Stephen Birmingham. The East Side settlement houses they established were originally little more than delousing stations. The purpose of the YMHA's and Jewish community centers was to "civilize" the immigrants: teach them English, civics, proper dress, and hygiene; and to uproot Yiddish and "free love." These institutions were also determined to stamp out Socialism and unions, not only because of the economic interests of their board members, some of whom were factory owners, but also because of the antiradical hysteria that was gathering momentum and that would result in the deportation of famed anarchist Emma Goldman and others after World War I. The Educational Alliance on the Lower East Side, by its own account, went out of its way to discourage all "isms" that "encouraged Jewish separation." No Yiddish books were allowed in its library.

What the German Jews feared most was that the high visibility of the Russians in "behaving as Jews have always behaved" would detonate anti-Semitism, and that it would be directed at *them,* as well. Even after the Russian Jews had given up many of their Old Country ways, German Jews continued to fulminate about the dire consequences of high Jewish visibility. This can be seen from the warning by arch-assimilationist Walter Lippmann that "the rich and vulgar and pretentious Jews of our big cities ... are everywhere *in sight*... and a thousand times more *conspicuous....* They are the *real fountain of anti-Semitism"* (italics mine).

The paternalistic attitude of the German Jews and their efforts to do a makeover of the Russians naturally generated a great deal of antagonism. The Russian Jews refused to accept German Jews' definition of them as charity cases, and they set up their own mutual aid institutions. The resentment against the German Jews, however, persisted for generations. While the differences between the descendants of both groups eventually became blurred, the hierarchical character of the institutions the German Jews established to "uplift" the Russian Jews has persisted, as we shall see in chapter 11.

NO LEGACY TO STAND ON

The assimilationist contract in America followed along the lines that had obtained in Western Europe, with "integration" and acceptance being the inducement proffered in return for Jews' sandpapering away their ethnic distinctiveness to the point of public invisibility. The one significant difference was that assimilationism in America was advanced in terms of the melting pot ideology, which applied to all white immigrants across the board, not only to Jews.

While most of the new immigrants wished to become Americanized, they also wished to retain their Jewish identity. They did not see the melting pot as a fiery cauldron that would boil their identity away, leaving an empty casing that could then be filled with WASP values and behavior. They saw it rather as a neo-mikvah where they would be purified only of their "backwardness," their "primitive" customs and idiosyncratic strangeness (stereotypes they had internalized), and from which they would emerge in a refined state, worthy of entering the tabernacle of the pursuit of happiness.

What they did not realize was that identity, like a soul, cannot exist in a disembodied state. It requires a body of customs and traditions to express it and an organic community as the context where that expression takes place. The East European Jews allowed this body of customs to undergo amputation limb by limb. As this process accelerated in subsequent generations, Jewish identity became so disembodied that it became insubstantial and seemed unreal. By the late 1950s, many young Jews, when asked about their identity, would say that they were "born Jewish" and attached no importance to that "accident of fate."

◆ The process began with the marginalization of traditional Jewish observances and of the synagogue, which had once been a major spiritual center of Jewish life. Ritual observance was almost completely relegated to the home, as in imperial Germany. By 1990, the National Jewish Population Survey revealed, attendance at seders and lighting Chanukah candles were the most popular forms of religious expression. While 86 percent and 77 percent of the respondents, respectively, told researchers that they observed these rites, only 11 percent said they participated regularly in synagogue services. Attending a seder and lighting Chanukah candles were the only rituals performed by Jewish M.B.A.'s from three eastern business schools surveyed by the American Jewish Committee in 1988. Half of the survey's respondents were unable to decode the letters of the Hebrew alphabet, and few had any Jewish vocabulary.

Some of the surviving rituals took on a completely different character and role in America. The prime function of the Bar (and, later, Bat) Mitzvah rite became to call attention to a family's material success, Chanukah to provide children a competitive alternative to the all-pervasive influence of Christmas.

American Jews constituted their own individual brands of Judaism, choosing one custom from Column A and another from Column B. This, Shapiro observed, was a complete reversal of the Jews' previous relationship with Judaism:

> Judaism once had its imperatives. The minute you said you were a Jew, so-and-such was what you believed and did. In America, if you chose to be a Jew, it did not mean there was a pre-determined pattern for your behavior. You could make it up as you went along. A Jew in America is no longer the product of Judaism, but its author. Today, if you want to [determine] what a Jew is, you do not look at the normative texts on what a Jew believes and does, you report on surveys.

◆ Having opted for individual solutions, the East European immigrants (like the German Jews before them) did not wish to reconstitute an organic community to work out collective ones. They rationalized this inaction and the abandonment of Jewish customs and traditions by choosing to believe that the danger to Jewish survival—the national emergency—had passed and that therefore communal cohesion and the lifestyle that bonded Jews together were no longer necessary.

In subsequent generations, this rationalization was encapsulated in the mantra "America is different": It is exempt from the classic dynamics of Exile societies. The key elements touted in what can be called the ideology of American exceptionalism are the absence of a history of physical persecution and of institutionalized anti-Semitism in America, and its being a nation of immigrants. The myth of the "hospitality" of the U.S. to the teeming masses of the pre–World War I period has all but covered over the reality of those years' xenophobia and successful anti-immigration agitation, as we shall see in chapter 13. This is but another example of how experiencing a nation as a secular rescuer depresses the critical faculty.

Assimilationist American Jews trumpet the good news that Jewish survival is no longer threatened because of American exceptionalism. At the same time, they engage in contortionist self-censorship to avoid trip-wiring the corollary of the assimilationist contract, the threat that if Jews do not stop behaving as Jews have always behaved, they will be treated as Jews have always been treated. They choose to ignore the obvious contradiction between these two actions.

It was precisely the fear this threat of persecution aroused that motivated the Jewish Hollywood studio heads of the early and mid-twentieth century to promote Jewish invisibility in the movies. A veteran screenwriter who worked for these moguls called them "accidental Jews, terribly frightened Jews," who wouldn't touch a story about a Jewish character. If they did happen to have one in a movie, they would cast a non-Jew in the part.

Films about American Jews (as well as about pre–World War II European Jews and about Israelis) are consequently rare: The moguls feared that dealing with Jewish subjects would call attention to their own Jewish identity and to vestiges of Jewish behavior they still retained—the same reason the German and Austrian Jews had been embarrassed by the *Ostjuden.* Advertisements for the handful of movies about Jews (e.g., *Romance of a Horsethief,* 1971; *Avalon,* 1990; *Mr. Saturday Night,* 1992) have omitted mentioning that they are about Jews.

As for television, many of whose producers, directors, and writers are Jewish men, only three of the six multiseason sitcoms about Jews to date (*The Goldbergs,* 1949–55; *The Gertrude Berg Show,* 1961–62; and *Brooklyn Bridge,* 1991–92) have featured nonassimilationist characters. Aside from these exceptions and one more—Ben Meyers in *The Trials of Rosie O'Neill,* 1990–91— none of the major Jewish characters on any popular TV show (all of them men) is as proudly, identifiably, and expressively Jewish as Abby Mann's Kojak was Greek. Only one soap opera, *Days of Our Lives,* has had any distinctly Jewish characters and story lines, and these (the creation of a female Jewish head writer) were short-lived.

There were and are a multiplicity of Jewish comedians; their Jewish identity is generally known, and much of their material derives from old Jewish jokes and routines. But, with a few exceptions, when they perform in the mass media, neither their roles nor their vehicles (shows, movies) are explicitly Jewish. Nor do Jewish artists, scientists, politicians, or sports figures publicly acknowledge, discuss, or express their Jewishness except on rare occasions (e.g., when baseball stars Hank Greenberg and Sandy Koufax refused to play on Yom Kippur). And the obituaries of well-known Jews omit stating their ethnicity.

The unconscious yearning by Jews for high-achieving Jews to be Jewishly visible expresses itself in an activity that Rabbi Albert Vorspan called Locate the *Landsman* (Yiddish, lit., person from one's hometown; by extension, another Jew). This game involves making the invisible visible: "Did you know that Leslie Howard was a Jew? Laurence Harvey? Ted Koppel? Bruce Springsteen?" But this activity takes place only in the safe spaces of the home and community.

MEN RECLAIM THE TURF OF BREADWINNING

Zvi Falk Widawer, a scholar and Hebraist who traveled in America in the 1880s, wrote that "the Jews who live in this land did not endure long journeys and untold hardships in order to ... busy themselves in the Torah in a free and untroubled place. Jews came here only to achieve the purpose which occupied their entire attention.... That purpose was money."

Jewish men's giving up full- and even part-time Torah study stemmed not only from the perceived need to free up time and energy for the pursuit of material success but also from the belief that the danger to Jewish survival had passed. Since communal cohesion was no longer necessary to try to ensure survival, they could feel justified in sloughing off the customs and traditions that had maintained it in the past. And learning Torah was the key to developing a communal leadership cadre and to maintaining the culture that bound the community together.

Giving up Torah learning—the heart of Judaism for over twenty centuries—left an empty space where once a heart had throbbed and pumped spiritual lifeblood to keep the body politic alive, making it easy for other, new values to take up lodging there.

❧ One American middle-class value most of the male immigrants accepted was that of the glorification of material success as an end in itself, deserving of high status, especially if its pursuit resulted in a man or his son's becoming a professional. The value of material success was then transmogrified into an American *Jewish* value, as worthy of individual and family sacrifice as learning Torah had once been. The distortion of reality involved in defining alien values (such as material success) and various behavior patterns as Jewish is the corollary of the belief that the secular rescuer shares the values of the Jewish culture.

Traditionally the Jewish attitude toward material success had been that, in Tevye's words, "Being poor is no shame, but it is no great honor, either." An East European Jewish man's penury under the prevailing late-nineteenth-century conditions of an "equality of poverty" or his being supported by his wife or relatives—or even by communal tzedakah (as were about one quarter to one third of the Jewish population in Russia in this period)—was not a source of shame or guilt. Wealth did not inspire awe, nor was its possession regarded as a sign of God's grace or as the proof of a man's worth. But in late-nineteenth-century America, "making it," succeeding for oneself rather than doing something of value for the entire community and its survival, came to be regarded as deserving of the kind of high status and honor that had once accrued to noted scholars and the men who supported them.

❧ Another new value the men accepted was the American definition of gender roles. In America a man's masculinity was defined in large part by his working and being a breadwinner and, in the middle class—the reference group of most East European Jewish men—attaining material success from it. Having accepted this definition as superior to their traditional one of spiritual resistance, especially through learning, the men measured themselves by it—and found themselves wanting. All classes regarded men who did not earn a living as wimps and/or gigolos and as parasites (triggering the fear of the recrudescence of the old Judeophobic myth) and believed that study was a pursuit for children and youths, not for adult men. One recalls in this connection the scene in the novel *Marjorie Morningstar,* by Herman Wouk, when Marjorie confesses that Noel, her lover, had gone to Paris to study philosophy. The reaction of her immigrant father is very revealing of the quick internalization of this new value: "Study?" (The father is absolutely incredulous.) "A man 32 years old?"

As long as Jews did not look for approval and validation to the men in various classes in societies where they lived, they did not feel emasculated by not living up to the standard patriarchal definition of man as provider. And as long as they believed that ("total immersion" in) study was necessary to ensure Jewish survival, they could let themselves relinquish the turf of providing to women without feeling demeaned or castrated and could devalue it as "women's work." Now, neither of these psychological mechanisms obtained.

⋙ Jewish men, therefore, sought to recapture from women the breadwinning turf so that it could define their masculinity, as it did that of other American men. Providing was no longer to be gender-neutral but an exclusively male arena.

The father of immigrant writer Anzia Yezierska was one of many older men who were unwilling to give up the old scholarly role. But most immigrant men quickly adopted working for a livelihood and providing for the family instead of learning Torah as their definition of manhood. Some were able to live up to the terms of the definition; many were ineffectual dreamers who couldn't quite get the knack of breadwinning (the women "minded the store," i.e., ran the business, with the men as titular heads). All the men, including those who could not adapt, invested their hopes in their sons' success.

The middle class rather than the working class (which defined masculinity as doing physical labor) was the reference group of most immigrant Jewish men, the majority of whom worked in factories, because they regarded themselves as a temporary proletariat. Their behavior in starting pushcart businesses as soon as they could scrape a few dollars together bore out Borochov's analysis of how the "natural gravitation of the Jew toward the occupations that require mental labor" drives Jewish workers to leave the proletariat and become small but independent entrepreneurs at the first opportunity.

Moreover, the immigrant man had a passionate commitment that "my son shall not work in the [sweat]shop" where he was trapped, wrote Irving Howe. But the commitment also drew on the traditional Jewish value that the son could exceed the grasp of the father. In the past this applied to the boy's becoming a scholar, which gave the entire family *yichhus* (prestige and status); in America, where secular learning was the rail on which Jewish men would ride to success, yichhus came from the son's becoming a professional.

The men's quick-study and quick-change artistry indicates that they had probably harbored all along the gnawing anxiety that there was something not quite kosher about being supported by their wives but had engaged in mass denial. Moreover, East European Jews had experienced several decades of Haskalah propaganda calling for the "productivization" of the Jews. The views of the Haskalah movement seemed to have sunk into the Jewish psyche and lay dormant there, like spores, until it was possible for them to sprout.

In America the maskilim's dream of "productivization" came true. With Torah study abandoned (except for some Orthodox men) and wealthy fathers-in-law absent (most immigrants were poor), the entire arranged marriage/kest system collapsed. Free choice in the selection of marriage partners, something the maskilim had long advocated, also became possible, validated by the American ideal of love as the prerequisite of marriage and as a key component of happiness.

❧ Gradually the men succeeded in recapturing the turf of paid work from the women and ejecting them from it. The process resembled the one by which Jews in various periods were ejected from trades they had been prominent in when the rise of "native cadres" made their presence unnecessary and their skills redundant.

In the first immigrant generations, the harsh struggle for survival in the urban ghettos necessitated women's continuing to work, which was already perceived and portrayed as "helping" the men support the family. Married Jewish women took in "home work" from the factories, cooked and cleaned for the paying (and nonpaying) boarders in their homes, and worked alongside their husbands at the pushcarts and in the mom-and-pop stores some started. But as soon as work outside the home was no longer desperately needed, the men insisted the women give it up. The first status symbol on the Lower East Side of New York was a nonworking wife.

RECASTING THE ENABLER ROLE

When Jewish men recaptured the turf of work, they recast the two-part enabler role of the women to bring it in line with the American values they had adopted.

Facilitating began to shift from helping to ensure the family's physical survival to assisting the men to achieve material success and high status. Women who had sacrificed in the Old Country to enable their husbands and sons to be Torah scholars were now encouraged to sacrifice to allow their brothers and sons to go to high school and, later, college and to enter the professions in the "Golden Land."

While enabling had once required Jewish women to withdraw from the arena of study and public performance of ritual so that, in their absence, it could define manhood, now it required them to withdraw from the turf of paid work—by becoming housewives, mothers, and "ladies of leisure"—so that *it* could define masculinity.

There were many younger immigrant women who attempted to break out of all forms of enabling—women who worked long hours in the sweatshops and then studied long hours in night school; women who were fervent Socialists, anarchists, militant union organizers; women like Clara Lemlich (Shavelson), Rose Schneiderman, Rose Pastor Stokes, Pauline Newman, Theresa Malkiel. Hutchins Hapgood, a non-Jewish journalist in this period, described them thus:

> They have in personal character many virtues called masculine [*sic*], are
> simple and straightforward and intensely serious.... It is from this class of

women . . . who are apt to throw the whole strength of their primitive [sic] natures into the *narrow intellectual channels that are open to them,* that a number of ghetto heroines come who are willing to lay down their lives for an idea or to live for them [italics mine].

These immigrant women, and the Yiddish writers among them, were truly inner-directed. Their reference group, if any, was the revolutionary movement in Russia they had left behind. In the beginning, they believed that in America, the "land of opportunity," they would be free, like their brothers, to pursue happiness, by which *they* meant to educate themselves to do meaningful and fulfilling work. In some inchoate way, they wanted to remain in the work arena and not be slotted into the old or the new enabler role.

Their struggle failed because of several obstacles. One was their double jeopardy as Jews and as women. All Jews faced job discrimination until the mid-1960s, and all women experienced sexism. American society was therefore even less predisposed to accept Jewish women as equals to men in educational and vocational endeavors than to accept non-Jewish women. Many colleges and professional schools did not admit women, and those which did had a quota for Jews and/or for women. Nor were jobs outside the blue-collar and pink-collar ghettos and elementary school teaching and nursing (all poorly paid) open to any but a few token females.

Sexism pervaded even the radical Jewish subculture, as can be seen from the bitter struggles of scores of women who wrote in Yiddish. Many had been deeply influenced by their participation in revolutionary movements in Russia and saw literature as a way to advance their Socialist ideals. But the Yiddish Socialist press in America, dominated by men, was not interested in publishing anything by women unless it was on a woman's issue, nor in putting them on staff. They were not accepted in literary circles unless involved with a man who was. Norma Fain Pratt, who researched the lives of fifty of these women—including Esther Luria, Fradel Stock, Yente Serdatsky, and Anna Rapoport—concluded that the prevalent "cultural asymmetry" meant that male activities "were always recognized as having greater importance, authority and value even when females were engaged" in the same activities. The Jewish male intelligentsia, in sum, continued to protect intellectual turf as a male-only preserve. The women could not earn a living from their writing, and many ended their lives in poverty, breakdowns, and despair.

The second obstacle the women faced was that the parents had always provided the best education, traditionally defined as religious studies, to the sons. Now their aim was to provide them the best higher *secular* education, seen as the route to material success. The daughters' education was traditionally focused on training them to be enablers (which is why many European middle-class families provided them the secular education necessary to their being able to support their families). Being enablers in America required their being kept *out* of the work arena.

Moreover, because of the economics of the patriarchal capitalist general society, only the sons had the possibility of earning a decent living (and even they experienced discrimination). Therefore, if a family had to choose between educating the son or the daughter, they educated the son. (Many black northern urban families educated the daughter for precisely the same reason.) Additionally, the parents had begun to expect that their daughters would be supported by their husbands and therefore saw their higher education as unnecessary. The daughters needed only the skills to help support their birth families until they married, to put their brothers through college (believing they would get their turn, which more often than not never came), and to have a trade "just in case anything happened" (the Jewish euphemism for death) to their husbands.

Since material success was closed to women, they did not need to try to assimilate in order to pursue it. Yet they did so (though to a lesser degree than the men) because they now had to strive for the only avenue of success open to women: marriage.

❧ Jewish men in America who were reclaiming the turf of paid work began to dream of acquiring, as well, all the psychological rewards they perceived non-Jewish men as having and that had long been denied them because of conditions in oppressive exiles and the need to survive them. These rewards included having wives more subservient, less assertive, more pliable and appreciative, less outspoken—unlike those of the shtetl, who, as altruistic-assertive enablers par excellence, were allowed so much leeway in verbal expression. They sought women like those in the non-Jewish urban middle class (as they perceived them): silent rather than active partners; women who did not yell and scream at home or in the street; women who were "nice"—women who were "ladies."

While the woman sought in marriage in the shtetl was and looked physically strong and resourceful—able to pull a heavy load—the woman now sought as a wife was not supposed to look *well* but to look *good*—and "good" was defined according to the American majority cultural ideal of beauty. Hefty immigrant Jewish mothers who wore *babushkas* (Yiddish for head-kerchiefs) or wigs or who dressed in classic Russian style began to give way in subsequent generations to daughters who straightened their curly hair (as Kate did by having it ironed in the memorable 1973 movie *The Way We Were*), their noses (there was a time when a nose job was considered a valuable sweet sixteen or Bat Mitzvah gift from one's parents), their figures, and their voices (accents and decibel levels). They did this not only because they, too, had internalized the majority cultural ideal of what was considered beautiful but also to compete for husbands with non-Jewish women.

For the more Jewish men sought "ladies" for wives, the more they began to seek them among non-Jewish women: Why settle for a poor copy when you can have the real thing? The non-Jewish wife became the ultimate status symbol and trophy for many Jewish men—proof that they had "arrived"—and a major source of validation of their masculinity. Philip Roth's Portnoy described his motivation for sex with a *shiksa* (Yiddish pejorative for non-Jewish woman) as "conquering" America. And again: "America is a *shikseh* nestling under your arm whispering love, love, love, love, love!"

Another psychological perk was that with a non-Jewish wife, the Jewish man could recast his image in the incarnation of a totally assimilated person, more American than other Americans. With the Jewish woman, reinventing himself was impossible. Intermarriage also became more psychologically appealing because of the recrudescence of the incest anxiety classically generated by endogamy. In America the Onah-Niddah cycle, which had defused this anxiety and those regarding the woman's sexual power and assertiveness, fell by the wayside along with arranged marriages.

❧ Non-Jewish women who married Jewish men struck terror in the hearts of Jewish women, similar to that felt by black women over white females who marry men from their group. To Jewish women they were like the scabs brought in by capitalists to force union workers to back down on their demands for fear of losing their jobs. Jewish men let Jewish women know that vast numbers of non-Jewish females were available and willing to make fewer demands, to be less pushy, more appreciative of having the "job," and to function as *Shabbos goys* (Yiddish for non-Jews who performed for Jews certain actions forbidden on the Shabbat, such as fire lighting) by engaging in sexual practices Jewish women purportedly disliked.

Conversely, because the non-Jewish woman was valued so highly, Jewish men were more afraid of losing her. The Jewish husband, therefore, tended to make fewer demands of her and to be more responsive to her wishes. This is possibly why Jewish men were and are so prized as good husbands by non-Jewish women, in addition to their image, as described by Portnoy, of always being "*around the house*. No bars, no brothels, no race tracks, no backgammon all night long . . . or beer till all hours" (italics mine).

❧ Jewish women in the early immigrant generations in America basically had two choices. One was to be independent, which almost always meant being single, an option few women would choose given their double jeopardy on the job market and their fear of loneliness in a family-oriented society. The other choice was to be married and acquiesce to the new enabler pattern men sought to fit them into, as into a dress several sizes too small. Most opted for marriage.

Finally, most Jewish women—like many African American women from the 1960s on—were relieved to unload from their aching backs the burden of supporting the family and to let the men, who were so eager to do so, heave it onto theirs. They were happy to be supported by their husbands—it constituted validation of the men's material success and of the woman's success in having "made a good marriage." This was the American Way—and wasn't the American Way the best way, after all?

EIGHT ❧ ISRAEL: "NEW JEWS" AND RECYCLED GENDER ROLES

> *Exile from the Land [of Israel] was conceived as an interruption, as a prelude to return, never as an abandonment or detachment. Bonds of hope tied us to the Land. To abandon these bonds was to deny our identity.*
>
> ABRAHAM JOSHUA HESCHEL

> *We will never have a normal nation here until there are Jewish thieves and prostitutes.*
>
> CHAIM NACHMAN BIALIK

> *Feminism has the power to get all women out of the kitchen into public places where only men are allowed. Now if they get there, they may act ... as anti-feminists, but they will be acting in public places where women are not now allowed. That is a feminist action. In the same way that we have a State of Israel and it turns out unfortunately not to be Utopia, does that mean that it should not exist? Because as long as you have Jewish people able to act just like other people, you have made a revolution.*
>
> PHYLLIS CHESLER

Unlike the Jews who came to the U.S. from Russia before and just after World War I seeking individual solutions, the young Jews who went to Eretz Israel as pioneers in that period brought with them a vision of creating a collective solution: the redemption of the Jewish people through the establishment of a just and free society there.

The men in both groups sought to redefine masculinity by recapturing the turf of work. The men coming to the U.S., whose reference group was the non-Jewish middle class, which defined manhood in terms of material success, sought to escape physical labor (factory work) as soon as possible and to work with their minds, a return to old Jewish (middle-class) occupational patterns. The reference group of the pioneers in Eretz Israel was the working class and, especially, agricultural laborers. They sought to reclaim the turf of agricultural labor Jews had long been absent from and to work with their hands.

While many American Jewish immigrants gradually peeled off what they saw as the barnacles of Exile culture to be able to move faster toward material success, the pioneers quickly stripped away this entire culture—religion, study, folk customs—to allow them to steer the ship of state in a new direction. In rejecting Yiddish as associated with the nightmare of oppression and powerlessness, the pioneers adhered to the contemptuous view of the early maskilim that it was the language of women and of the ignorant, which, wrote Cynthia Ozick, were "categories that frequently overlapped." (The later maskilim and the Jews who remained in Russia after the 1880s, and many who came to America, embraced Yiddish and the great literature being written in that language.)

The pioneers sought to build a new culture based on love of the land and of The Land (of Israel) and on Hebrew which harkened back to the glorious days of yore pictured in the major historical novels of the Russian maskil and early Zionist Avraham Mapu.

But despite the pioneers' belief that they had given up the culture of the Exile, its prime female values were the very cornerstone of their ethos. The collective communities they established functioned as extended families, just as the Jewish communities of the Exile had. And in these collectives, the old patriarchal pattern of the men excluding the women from the most important work—now redefined as agricultural labor—and having them function as enablers continued. When they spoke of creating a "new Jew," what they meant was a new Jewish *man*.

THE RELIGION AND "CONQUEST" OF LABOR

Zionists' use of the word *aliyah*, meaning "ascent" to live in Eretz Israel, was rooted in the traditional commitment to the age-old messianic dream of return to and redemption of and in the Jewish homeland.

The word *aliyah* entered official Zionist vocabulary with the First Aliyah (wave of immigration) of the 1880s. It was known as the aliyah of the Bilu movement, whose name was a Hebrew acronym for the prophetic exhortation, "House of Jacob, come, let us go." The Bilu was a group of Russian students who established several agricultural settlements in Eretz Israel. The catalyst for their aliyah was these young Jewish revolutionaries' agonizing reappraisal of their politics after the pogroms of the 1880s, the support given the massacres by some narodnik comrades, and their feelings of abandonment when the vast plurality of Russian intellectuals failed to protest. "Where are the Russian writers and preachers of love and brotherhood whom our youth idolized?" was the cri de coeur of a Jewish periodical of the day.

The harsh conditions the Bilu student *olim* (immigrants, also from the Hebrew verb "to ascend") faced in Eretz Israel ultimately compelled them to abandon the communal and Socialist principles they had originally intended to implement.

Their settlements became villages controlled by administrators from the Rothschild family, on whose largess they depended.

The young Jewish revolutionaries who came to Eretz Israel in the Second Aliyah (1905–14) had been traumatized by the pogroms of the early 1900s and the failure of the 1905 Revolution. Many were plunged into deep despair and apathy, and some did not leave their rooms for months on end. Their situation differed from that of their predecessors, however, in that they could join various ideological movements of Jewish regeneration that advanced collective solutions to the Jewish condition, among them Jewish Socialism (the organizing principle of the Jewish Labor Bund, officially established in 1897) and Zionism.

A Zionist movement that aimed to settle Jews in Eretz Israel and build a Jewish homeland there had existed in Russia from the days of the Bilu. It grew rapidly, given impetus in 1897 by Theodor Herzl's convening of the first World Zionist Congress, which adopted the official Basle Program—"Zionism strives to create for the Jewish people a home in Palestine secured by public law"—and established the World Zionist Organization as its representative body. While the movement was not monolithic and embraced many factions and political tendencies, there was unity in this diversity: All Zionists agreed that establishing a Jewish homeland would provide Jews a necessary refuge and enable them to develop there a "normal" life as a nation. Many Zionists believed, as well, that when Jews had a homeland, relationships between it and other states and between Jews and non-Jews generally would also be normalized. Some also believed that a state would enable Jews to build a society based on Jewish culture, one as "Jewish as England is English," in Zionist leader Chaim Weizmann's words.

The *Poale Zion* (Hebrew for Workers of Zion: Proletarian Zionists) developed a synthesis of Zionism and Socialism. These Socialist Zionists, like many Russian Jewish intellectuals of the period, accepted the Haskalah's critique of the "abnormality" of Jewish life in the Exile and especially of its occupational structure. Their analysis of the reasons for it in class terms was that in Exile Jews were separated from the land and from physical labor and forced into "middlemen" roles, which made their existence precarious. The Socialist Zionist program was to create a Jewish homeland where Jews could engage in labor, thereby normalizing the Jewish occupational profile and, ultimately, the nation. With a strong working class as its base, this society would be a Socialist one.

Many Socialist Zionists, especially the left-of-center ones who called themselves Labor Zionists, believed that agricultural workers were going to be the midwife of the Jewish homeland. These Socialist Zionists immigrated to Eretz Israel in the Second Aliyah—along with the disciples of just about every philosophical tendency in Russia: anarchists, Social Democrats, non-Marxist Socialists, Tolstoyans, pacifists, and vegetarians.

The pioneers of the Second Aliyah and of the Third (1919–23) faced enormous economic and psychological difficulties: They rarely found work in the villages of the First Aliyah settlers; they starved; they suffered from malaria; some died, and there were some suicides. Only 10 percent of the Second Aliyah pioneers remained in the country, according to kibbutz movement historian Muki Tsur. Those from both waves of immigration who stuck it out, whose passion, commitment, and sheer stiff-necked stubbornness were the strongest, became the founders of the Jewish State.

◆● The *chalutzim* (Hebrew plural for pioneers; lit., vanguard; a woman was a *chalutza,* women were *chalutzot,* a man was a *chalutz*) "were convinced that . . . the magic key to a true perception of self was physical labor . . . [and] it was worshipped," wrote Amos Elon. One of their charismatic gurus was A. D. Gordon, known in Zionist legend as the Prophet of the Religion of Labor. He wrote that Jews "lack the fundamental element—labor . . . by which a people becomes rooted in its soil and in its culture. . . . Our entire structure must be founded on labor. . . . Then we can consider that we have our own culture, for then we shall have life. . . . Labor will heal us." Labor, in short, was to be the new rescuer.

In defining physical labor as the most important work in their emerging society, the pioneers brought to it some of the behavior patterns that had characterized spiritual resistance in the Exile and the passion that had once informed it. Jews who had once been in love with the Torah were now in love with the earth. They accepted the idealized and romanticized myth of the peasants' mystical connection with the soil that Tolstoy had tried so hard to feel and experience through the character of Levin in *Anna Karenina,* and the narodnik, anarchist, and Slavophile adulation of the *obschchina,* the Russian peasant commune.

Significantly, the word *aliyah,* which had once meant being called up to bless the reading of the Torah, now meant "going up" to the land of Israel to rebuild it; and the word *avoda,* which had once meant the work of prayer—"services of the heart"—now meant the important work of manual labor. This is why the "hymns to labor" sung in the fields and around campfires during the Second and Third Aliyahs sound like prayers: "Work is a vision of glory, work is a serene [shelter]"; "A blessing descends from on high. . . . / Humans have returned to the earth"; "We have come to the Land / to regenerate [it] and to be regenerated."

The pioneers' glorification of manual labor was actually a return to the value placed on it by the rabbis of the Talmudic era, who had worked in charcoal burning, leather crafting, sandal making, and baking, among other trades. These rabbis had believed that "all study of the Torah without labor must in the end be futile and become the cause of sin," and that "a blessing alights only upon the work of a man's [*sic*] hands."

As in traditional Judaism, it was deeds—the new mitzvot of stone clearing, swamp draining, tree planting, farming—that counted and were validated. The traditional Jewish community had accorded high status to scholars; the pioneers validated and assigned high status to laborers. Road builders of the 1920s were the emerging society's folk heroes and elite; the most prestigious "addresses" for a

Third Aliyah pioneer were the Tiberias–Tzemach and Haifa–Jedda roads under construction. Manual work had such cachet that Premier David Ben Gurion, when asked his occupation in Israel's first census, replied, "agricultural laborer."

❧ A prime aim of the Second and Third Aliyahs was *Kibbush HaAvoda* (Hebrew for conquest of labor). The slogan's manifest meaning referred to Jews' becoming self-sufficient, laboring, as A. D. Gordon wrote, "with our very own hands at all things which make up life." Its deeper meaning was that the male chalutzim sought to recapture for Jews the turf of work, by which they meant physical labor. It would then become the definition of their masculinity as it was that of other working (class) men.

THE KIBBUTZ AS THE EMBODIMENT OF
FEMALE VALUES

The pioneers created a unique form of social organization: the *kvutza*, later called the kibbutz (from the Hebrew for "to gather together"), a settlement where all members worked a piece of land collectively and shared all property. The kibbutz, based on an idea of chalutza Manya Schochat, was first tried in experimental form on a collective farm at Sejera in 1908. It went on to set the tone for the entire pioneering *Yishuv* (agricultural and industrial labor movement component of the Jewish community in pre-state Israel).

The kibbutz carried female values that had characterized Exile communities—interdependence, altruism, consensus, mutual aid and responsibility—to their ultimate logical conclusion and institutionalized them.

In the kibbutz the concept of mutual aid was a necessary part of everyday life, and its members were interdependent, economically and psychologically. This was especially true in the small kvutza of the Second Aliyah (never more than a dozen or so members) and in the "intimate kibbutz" of the Third, where the emphasis on relationships reached its apotheosis. Members of the "intimate kibbutz" sought to create a "community of feeling" that operated by the mutual honesty and total candor of all. Members shared not only work, property and income, and ideas but also their feelings via verbal and written "confessions." While this provided a "special sort of spiritual banquet," in the words of one of its former members, it also generated tensions, which broke apart this "first community of hippies" in Eretz Israel, said Tsur. Kibbutzim subsequently established in the Third Aliyah and in later waves of immigration were composed of several hundred members who shared an ideology rather than their feelings.

All kibbutzim operated by consensus: Everything involving the personal lives of the members and the workings of the collective was debated and decided on in the *sichat chaverim* (Hebrew for members' discussion), a small-scale town meeting. All issues were picked apart, analyzed, scrutinized for how they related to basic principles and as to which principle took precedence when. If this sounds like the methodology of Talmudic analysis, it was: Everyone's opinion was heard and listened to at these meetings in the Talmudiclike "search for truth."

The kibbutz also embodied the female value of concern about ethics in relationships and the old Jewish passion for justice. For while its members were working toward that distant goal of a Socialist country, each kibbutz as a cell or precursory model-in-microcosm strived to be and saw itself as just and equal. This was an equality of poverty not only in practice—with food and clothes being shared by all—but also in philosophy and ambiance, which was that of asceticism and the renunciation of bourgeois comforts. In preventing the emergence of classes and of exploitation of labor, the kibbutz's economic egalitarianism was a return to the original vision of a just society set forth in the Five Books.

Hebrew poet Abba Kovner, who lived after World War II in a Hashomer Hatzair (left-wing Zionist) kibbutz, recognized this connection between Socialism and Jewish tradition when he wrote, "The main aim of the Jewish heritage is to build a communal reality in the face of the dangers of historical forces and egotistical human drives that recognize no *limitations* because the human being [is] . . . capable of both building and destroying," that is, of yetzer hatov and yetzer hara (italics mine). Judaism had always sought to put boundaries around those "egotistical human drives": it was, wrote Kovner, "first and foremost . . . a contradiction of petty individualism. . . . Socialism [means] restrictions on unrestrained individualism. . . . The kibbutz is the best possible place to forge that rare link between the universal ideal of righting the wrongs of the world and the Jewish heritage at its best."

Like the Jews of the traditional communities, the kibbutzniks rejected individualism and individual solutions, not only in and for their own collectives but for the entire Jewish people. Each kibbutz *and* the entire pioneering Yishuv functioned as a kind of extended family. Its altruism and mutual aid were directed toward the new national project of building a Socialist country—a secularly expressed implementation of the traditional vision of the messianic era of justice and peace—to liberate the entire nation. And indeed, A. D. Gordon, when describing the pioneer as a "redeemer," had understood that the pioneering Yishuv unconsciously saw itself and behaved as the rescuer of the Jewish people.

WOMEN RESIST THE RECAST ENABLER ROLE

The kibbutz, despite its incorporation of female values, was patriarchal, all myths to the contrary. The pioneers who struggled to achieve the "impossible dream" of an independent Jewish homeland—who overcame the obstacles of Turkish rule, British colonialism, and Arab terrorism, of environmental destruction and disease as well as problems of psychological adjustment to a rural and a collective life—lived up to the highest ideals of the Jewish nation. Unfortunately, the kibbutz men had one grievous flaw: their sexism.

There was a great deal of passionate discussion on the kibbutz about "liberating women" from traditional roles, as there had been by the Russian maskilim, and about restructuring the family. Despite all this, the kibbutz men sought to do to the family what the absolutist state had done to the autonomous Jewish communities: dismantle it so that the members' energies and loyalties could then be "reinvested" in the collective. This was particularly true in the case of the restructuring of women's roles and work.

The men sought to have the women become their enablers—by facilitating their work (agricultural labor) through back-up support in the services branch of the kibbutz economy (i.e., the same old housewifely tasks of cooking, laundry, and child care to be done by women collectively rather than on a privatized basis); and by their exclusion from the agricultural labor turf so that it could define manhood. One chalutza protested, "We were actually separated into two groups. In the one group were those who were 'building the country'; in the other were those who would take care, in everyday matters, of the 'builders of the country.'"

The men, whose revolutionary and egalitarian ethos precluded advancing an ideological rationale for excluding women from agricultural labor, fell back on claiming that women were incapable of it. Mostly they engaged in passive resistance on a case-by-case basis to those women who tried it. Although the men initially knew as little about farming as the women, they did not seem to find anything illogical in arguing that women would not be able to extract milk from a cow or wheat from a field—just as the Talmudic sages had argued that women were incapable of fathoming the subtle intricacies of scholarly learning (and, in both cases, acted to prevent women from engaging in these activities to avoid being proven wrong).

One can't help but speculate whether another motive for trying to eject women from agricultural work was the men's fear of being shown up by women who could be more efficient or better at it than them. This brings to mind the similar motivation behind the Talmudic injunction against women's reading aloud from the Torah "because of the honor of the community," that is, in order not to shame the men who could not do so.

❧ What the women wanted was simply to participate as equals with the men in the building of the new society, which they believed would resolve The Woman Question—much as they and their male comrades had once believed that The Revolution would solve The Jewish Question. It was at first inconceivable to them that their male comrades would try to track them into an enabler role, since the old national project of study, in which Jewish women traditionally functioned as enablers, no longer existed. Like the young women who immigrated to America from Russia in this period, they thought they would be able to do meaningful work at last. But like them, as well, they were to be grievously disappointed: there was now a new national project, and the men wished the women to facilitate and

withdraw from its main instrumentality of agricultural labor. Many of the chalutzot, some of whom had risked their lives in revolutionary movements in Russia
and had "experienced no distinction between men and women" in these or in the
Zionist groups there, found that in Eretz Israel "our beautiful dreams were destroyed."

The women had to fight a two-front war: to be accepted as *Jewish* laborers by
the First Aliyah settlements during the Second Aliyah and in the cities during the
Third, and to be accepted as *women* laborers by their own comrades.

They argued that there was no reason, biological or other, that they could
not and should not participate in the public role of building the new society, with
all the sacrifices it entailed. One danger this argument posed was that if logical
reasons could be advanced as to why women should not participate in, for example, hard physical labor, they could then be excluded from it. The second problem
was that the argument implied that once it was no longer necessary to build the
new society, women would have no other public role since their whole focus was
on participating as pioneers.

Their strategy was a variation of the one adopted by the male pioneers toward the First Aliyah settlers, which in turn was a variation of the strategy Jews
had long employed in the general society: They would be useful, they would be
better than the competition, they would prove themselves more efficient, more
devoted, more tenacious. They created training farms for women to learn and perfect new skills, such as vegetable gardening, poultry management, dairying, tree
planting, cereal culture, and swamp draining. In the Third Aliyah, they established urban collectives of women learning and taking on work in building construction and as carpenters and glaziers. The chalutzot also created the Council of
Working Women, now known by the acronym *Na'amat*.

Women in Third Aliyah kibbutzim initiated collective child rearing to free
themselves to participate in agricultural labor and kibbutz political life. Children
were raised collectively, sleeping, eating, and playing together in specially designated houses. It was the *metapelet* (female child-care provider) who made the decisions on the children's day-to-day lives, not the parents, with whom they visited
for an hour or two a day and on Shabbat.

The women braved hardship, harassment, and ridicule, and the charges of
being motivated by "a perverted desire to shock." When they carried heavy bas-
kets loaded with vegetables on their shoulders, none of the men would help, saying, "They want to be suffragettes—let them carry their own loads!" reported Ada
Fishman Maimon, a feminist who documented this struggle.

Even the women who did kitchen work were ridiculed for imperfect enabling.
After the women had put in sixteen-hour days preparing lunch and dinner under
extremely primitive conditions, they often had to contend with a custom "which
almost drove the hard-pressed cooks mad," wrote Maimon. If any dish turned out
badly, the men would line up the plates in a long row—called the railroad—to be

returned to the kitchen. When discussions about what was called *yachas* (Hebrew for attitude) toward women became stormy, the men, she wrote, accused the chalutzot of being "over-sensitive and of ruining the peaceful relations that should exist in the group," that is, the shalom bayit of the kibbutz-as-family.

MEN RECLAIM THE DEFENDER ROLE

The male pioneers also sought to reclaim the classic patriarchal role of defenders, fighters, and heroes. They sought to redefine themselves as able to protect not only themselves but also "their" women and children and the Jewish community-as-extended-family, something Jewish men had never been able to do in the Exile. They rejected the old Jewish definition of what it meant to be a man—a gentle scholar, charitable, intellectual, and, above all, not physically aggressive—and substituted one closer to what they believed defined the men of other nations: macho, tough, unyielding, hard, active, courageous, fearless, unsentimental; a man to be reckoned with, maybe even feared. This accounts for a great deal of the bravado, posturing, and swashbuckling that men of the Second Aliyah engaged in.

These men, some of whom had played important roles in collective self-defense against the pogroms of the early 1900s in Russia, were deeply ashamed of the Jews of the Exile, regarding their nonviolence as cowardice, their gentleness as weakness, their patience in waiting for future liberation as passivity. They were revolted by the powerlessness of the men of the Exile. Zionist leader Zev Jabotinsky, although anti-Socialist and a political opponent of the pioneering Yishuv, nevertheless captured its attitude toward physical aggression when he criticized Exile communities for having "*despised physical manhood,* the principle of *male power* as understood and worshiped by all free peoples in history." His comment on Bialik's famous epic poem about the Kishinev pogrom, "In the City of Carnage," repeats a line from it: "Great is the sorrow and great is the *shame*" (italics mine).

The pioneers' chagrin and shame over the defenselessness of the Jews in the Exile led them to wish to cast off everything associated with it, an ideology known as *Shlilat HaGalut,* the negation/devaluation of the Exile and whatever Jews had accomplished in it. They instituted a course correction, returning psychologically to the Jewish Commonwealths of several thousand years before and picking up where the men of those days had left off, as it were. They also created a chain of continuity between the heroes of yesteryear and themselves by mythologizing themselves as defenders of the homeland following in the footsteps of King David and the Maccabees. This process was similar to what the rabbis of the Talmudic era did when they created a chain of continuity between the scriptural heroes of old and the scholars of their own day.

⤏ As with agricultural labor, the men wished to exclude women from the defender turf to provide themselves a definition of masculinity.

Women served in the underground militias of Mandatory Palestine—the *Hagana* (Hebrew for defense) and the *Palmach* (its left-wing elite strike force)—but had to prove their competence again and again, because, as one later wrote, the Palmach "inscribed on its flag the principle of the equality of the sexes but didn't uphold it."

Women were accepted into the Palmach for active duty and, in the beginning, given the same training as the men. But it was eventually decided to exclude them from combat. The reason, Palmach leader Yigal Allon explained in 1971, was that

> both the Palmach and the Hagana High Command *worried about the possible aftermath of intensive combat training for women.* The girls [*sic*], for their part, stormed at any proposed discrimination, arguing that it ran counter to the spirit of the new society being built in [Eretz Israel] to restrict women to domestic chores, particularly since they had *proven their competence* as marksmen [*sic*] and snipers. In the end, the *wiser counsel prevailed;* the girls [*sic*] were trained for combat but placed in units of their own so that they would *not compete physically with the men* [italics mine].

By 1947 half of the three thousand members of the Palmach were female. But on November 29, 1947—the same day the U.N. voted to partition Mandatory Palestine, a decision that signaled the beginning of the military struggle for the future Jewish State—the women were ordered to the rear. This reduced by half the pool of available Palmach fighters at a time when every able-bodied soldier was desperately needed.

Seen against the backdrop of sexism revealed in Allon's explanation, this action demonstrates how the male leaders wished to reserve the combat turf for the men, just as the Jewish men in the Exile had arrogated to themselves the turf of study. In both of these cases of national emergency, the need for a definition of manhood superseded the need for more personnel.

❧ The pioneers could not proscribe physical aggression across the board, as traditional Jewish communities had done, because they required access to it in case the need for defense arose, which it did immediately because of attacks on villages and kibbutzim by Arab raiders. The pioneers had ruptured the delicately calibrated and synergistic system of classic Jewish communal behavior to liberate the aggression they needed to channel into the new collective and creative enterprise of building a new society and to unleash the physical aggression they required for self-defense. The problem, which became apparent only much later, was the genie-out-of-the-bottle dynamic: Once physical aggression was (again) allowed to be part of male behavior for whatever reason, how could it be kept in bounds?

What worked for the better part of sixty years was the implicit understanding on the part of the pioneering Yishuv that physical aggression, even in self-defense, had to be kept in check out of concern about political reprisals from the country's rulers—the Turks of the Ottoman Empire before World War I and the British under the Mandate given them by the League of Nations. A contributing factor was the pioneers' ideological commitment to peaceful relations with their Arab neighbors.

The pioneering Yishuv realized that not only its own survival demanded the control of physical aggression—and, indeed, the official slogan of the Hagana was *havlaga*, "restraint"—but also that of the entire national project of attaining a Jewish homeland. Moreover, the pioneering Yishuv was accountable to the entire world Zionist movement, which opposed anything that might jeopardize the chances for international acceptance of the idea of a Jewish state. The pioneering Yishuv therefore allowed the deployment of the horse of physical aggression only when harnessed to the altruistic cart of national self-defense—and only upon its approval when it deemed the context appropriate.

↩ The pioneering Yishuv lost control over physical aggression when elements outside it initiated an armed revolt against the British Mandate in 1944.

The Mandate, which had originally been welcomed by the Zionist movement and the Yishuv, had degenerated over the course of several interbellum decades into an oppressive colonialist regime. It increasingly applied a divide-and-conquer policy with regard to the Jewish and Arab communities in the country and bent over backward to appease extremist Arab elements that opposed Jewish immigration and future statehood. Its periodic limitations on Jewish immigration reached their nadir with the 1939 White Paper, a statement of British policy according to which a maximum of 15,000 Jewish immigrants a year would be allowed in over a five-year period, after which none would be admitted, and the naval blockade of "illegal" immigrant ships, which were turned back to Europe or sunk during World War II. Churchill, though he called himself a Zionist, never rescinded the White Paper.

The Labor government elected in Britain after the war obdurately closed off immigration, leaving Holocaust survivors to rot in Displaced Persons (DP) camps in Germany. The Yishuv witnessed heartbreaking scenes of refugees being forced and dragged at gunpoint off "illegal" immigrant boats and shipped from the harbor to internment camps in Cyprus (and, later, back to Germany).

While the initial response of the Hagana was to continue its wartime efforts to smuggle in "illegal" immigrants, two other underground militias, the right-wing Irgun and the Stern Group, launched an all-out revolt against the British in 1944. Most of the leaders of the Zionist movement opposed the revolt and particularly its use of violence, which included bombings of British installations and reprisal executions of military personnel. They primarily feared the loss of international support—especially from the U.S.—for a future Jewish state. The fear was in part a vestige of the old survival strategy of not antagonizing powerful forces to whom Jews looked for assistance in time of need.

By 1945–46, as British repression escalated and the government refused to consider even limited immigration, the Hagana and Palmach had joined the revolt. It is doubtful whether the British would have thrown the Mandate mess into the lap of the U.N. had the revolt not made their occupation of Palestine untenable.

After the U.N. approved Partition (1947), unofficial war broke out between Jews and Arabs in the country. The war became official in May 1948, when the armies of seven Arab countries invaded Israel following its declaration of independence. Miraculously the fledgling Israeli Army repelled the invasions, and the State of Israel became a reality.

INCONCLUSIVE VALIDATION OF MASCULINITY

After the establishment of Israel in 1948, a fundamental change occurred that affected the men and their definition of masculinity in terms of pioneering and defense. Pioneering was taken over by the state from the labor and kibbutz movements and turned over to its bureaucracy; defense was taken over from the disbanded underground militias and given over to the army. The political philosophy at the root of this institutionalization was *mamlachtiyut* (statism, from the Hebrew word for kingdom), originated and implemented by Israel's first premier, David Ben Gurion. Mamlachtiyut blocked the progress of Zionism as a revolution—the "interference of the masses into history"—by disempowering the masses and turning over their role in nation building to bureaucrats. Thus mamlachtiyut constituted the Thermidor of the Zionist revolution.

⋅❧ With state institutionalization of pioneering, the only element left from the Yishuv period's definition of the "new Jewish man" was that of defender. This now meant being a soldier in the Israeli Army. Because of The War (the various wars Israel fought, which will probably be viewed by future historians as military episodes in one long, drawn-out war) and the ongoing state of siege, the survival of the state depended on the effectiveness of the army.

Israeli society as a whole functions as a classic extended family under duress, a pattern begun in the Yishuv. It retains many of the old female values while it incorporates the legitimization of *outer*-directed physical aggression. In this variation on the classic extended family, the army collective replaces the family patriarch as defender and protector.

With statehood the Israeli citizenry became the army's altruistic-assertive enabler. Citizens had to provide it with whatever support it needed while being assertive only when this was "altruistic," that is, in the interests of the army *as the army defined those interests.* Criticism of army policy (e.g., arms sales to oppressive regimes) was considered nonaltruistic. Part of the reason for the acceptance of an uncritical attitude toward the army was that it was now the rescuer of the nation-state from its well-armed external enemies, and the usual uncritical attitude toward secular rescuers came to the fore.

The Israeli Army has enjoyed high status and has set the tone for much of the Israeli ambiance, as the kibbutz had once done. It is a people's army, not a permanent standing army, and there is no officer caste. The discouraging of formalities between officers and enlisted personnel brings to mind the scholars' limitation of the life-and-death power of the Jewish husband and father.

While the incorporation of some female values, such as cooperation and interdependence, among a group of soldiers generally obtains in warfare under patriarchy, these and other values of traditional Jewish communities, such as altruism, have characterized the entire Israeli Army to a degree unknown elsewhere. This phenomenon has helped defuse class conflict and antagonisms between individuals from different backgrounds and has promoted cohesion in the army, as it did in the traditional communities. In fact, one of the prime roles of the army is to integrate Jews from different immigrant subcultures. Group cohesion is also bolstered by the army's policy of returning to rescue soldiers trapped in enemy territory (the idea of rescue is still vital in Israeli society), securing the release of captured POW's (a continuation of the mitzvah of redeeming captives), and retrieving bodies for burial.

In addition, the fact that Israeli soldiers are involved in a collective struggle for the survival of the nation-state provides continuity with the centuries-old national Jewish project of Torah study to advance Jewish survival. There is even a faint echo of the Kalla of Babylonia in the one-month reserve duty required of male soldiers until their mid-fifties.

The difference between soldiering and the previous national projects of study and of pioneering, however, is that soldiering cannot create an organic daily lifestyle with tangible results or visible achievements. And despite the attempt to portray the army as the new rescuer and to imbue the soldier's role with spiritual content—in rituals such as the swearing-in of new recruits at Masada—soldiering provides no redemptive vision of the future. The soldier can only carry the onerous burden of defending the country in the absence of peace. Finally, the Jewish man's ability to define himself as a man by actions that he himself decided to undertake—which obtained when he could freely choose to be a scholar or a pioneer—was taken away from the Israeli man by the draft.

While Israeli men are validated by their peers and the society as a whole for serving as soldiers, the validation of their masculinity, which is defined by the *successful* fulfillment of this role, is problematic and inconclusive, and largely outside the individual man's control. Only the success of the army *collective,* in which he serves as a soldier, in protecting the state and its citizenry, validates his manhood and bolsters his feeling of masculinity. No wonder every military victory brought relief and euphoria. As Natalie Rein wrote of the Six-Day War of 1967: "The *'manhood'* of the State had been on trial and it had proved itself to be as *potent* as it had hoped it was" (italics mine).

The catch, however, is that the less successful the army is in defending the country, the less of a man the individual Israeli male feels. While the army has been successful in Israel's wars, it is not always able to prevent terrorism. Since the Israeli man's masculinity is predicated on the army's success in defending the "family," he feels less of a man every time terrorists strike.

Terrorism evokes the terrible memories of pogroms and of the Holocaust and triggers Israelis' fears of reverting to the powerlessness and defenselessness Jews experienced in the Exile. The psychological defense against the resurgence of such feelings (in addition to its perceived military necessity) is the immediate reprisal.

Reprisals, however, do not bring back the dead. Since Israel functions as an extended family, when someone's child, spouse, or parent is killed by terrorists, the whole country mourns. Israel is the only country in the world with an organization of Parents of Fallen Soldiers.

This dynamic has profound political implications. The Palestine Liberation Organization (PLO), by perpetrating terrorism against civilians, including children, took on the mantle of the age-old pogromist mob. As dovish novelist Amos Oz observed, "For many Israeli Jews, the Palestinian Arab is nothing more than a goy out to make a pogrom; an extension of the *muzhik* [Russian for peasant], of the savage goy who ... wants our property *and our [sic] women*" (italics mine). It is no coincidence that during the Intifada, teenage Palestinian boys taunted (male) Israeli soldiers with threats of raping "their" women, aiming their derision directly at the soldiers' psychological Achilles' heel.

It should not be surprising, therefore, that while Israelis have welcomed the idea of negotiating with enemy Arab nations, against whose attacks the army has successfully defended the state, many men viewed as anathema the idea of Israelis holding talks with the PLO, *the men who have been trying to destroy their "manhood."* They felt that negotiating with the PLO would imply that the army could not succeed at guaranteeing national survival and that this failure meant that all the state's soldiers are impotent.

Despite this psychological obstacle, in the fall of 1993, Israel recognized the PLO as the representative of the Palestinian people; the PLO recognized Israel's right to exist and renounced violence against it. These actions opened the way for direct negotiations over the future of the territories captured in the Six-Day War of 1967 and, possibly, the conclusion of peace agreements with various Arab countries. The yearning of the Israelis for peace and the strength of the Israeli peace movement were major factors in the Israeli government's decisions regarding negotiations with the PLO.

❧ The inconclusive nature of the men's validation of masculinity through soldiering, fluctuating as it does with the army's success in defense, has led many men to seek ersatz definitions of manhood. One of these, the domination of women, has contributed to the resurgence of classic patriarchal gender roles in Israel and, with it, misogynist violence, as we shall see presently. The validation/

domination connection clearly came to the fore during the Gulf War of 1991, when the army was not allowed to defend Israel militarily against the Scud attacks by Iraq or to retaliate for them. During this period a sharp rise in domestic violence against women was reported.

ARMY ENABLING AND PRONATALISM

When soldiering became the prime definition of masculinity, it had to be magnified, expanded, and glorified. Since women were and are still needed in the army because of the relatively small pool of individuals in each cohort of draftees, their role had to be downgraded to enabling.

In World War II, women had worked as engineers, draftspersons, drivers of trucks and ambulances, and managers of supply depots and mess halls for the British Army. Women in the Hagana and the Palmach underground militias served as wireless operators, frontline nurses, scouts, and quartermasters in the War of Independence; many also fought and died in battle.

But shortly after the end of the 1948 War, a Women's Army Corps, *Chen* (an acronym that also conveniently spells "charm" in Hebrew), separated women soldiers into an auxiliary. Their basic training was reduced to three weeks (compared with the men's three months), and their army service to two years (compared with the men's three). They were banished from combat and specifically forbidden even to hold a job, such as ambulance driving, that might bring them into contact with it.

This allowed the men to define their masculinity as combat soldiering, with the women as their enablers. Their job was to facilitate the men's important work (combat) by providing backup services as secretaries, clerks, telephone operators, signalers, teletypists, nurses, and teachers. Two job classifications were reserved exclusively for women: typing and parachute folding. They are also regarded as a moral influence on the men, like the American women who "civilized" the Wild West. (Unofficially, of course, they are seen as an ever-replenishable supply of sexual partners, and they often experience sexual harassment.)

In the event of war, women anywhere near the front lines are removed to the rear. One reason given is that female casualties would cause a drop in national morale because the army is supposed to "protect women," that is, carry out the traditional patriarchal defender role. Another rationale is the fear that women would be raped by enemy soldiers, a fear rooted in the memory of the inability of generations of men in the Exile to protect "their" women from assault by non-Jews. Israeli women's lack of protest over their exclusion from combat may derive, in part, from their acceptance of the rape rationale and their gratification over the men's new concern about extending them protection.

The real psychological motivation behind the exclusion of women from combat—to give men total control over this turf—is revealed in post-1948 Israeli fiction. In many stories women's sexual power is portrayed as a dangerous threat because it could lure the men away from their important work of combat soldiering, just as it was traditionally feared that it could lure them away from Torah study. In one story, recycling the Samson and Delilah tale, a woman's seduction of an officer on the eve of the 1973 Yom Kippur War renders him inaccessible to his men and leads to military defeat.

Because army service in Israel is the equivalent of the old-school tie, excluding women from combat, where the old-boy networks are formed, impedes their future civilian careers, including politics. Only 11 women serve in the 120-member Israeli Knesset (Parliament) elected in 1992, the same number as in the first Knesset, elected in 1949.

✦ It is important to note here, as well, the reason advanced by Ben Gurion, in his speech to that first Knesset, for excluding women from combat: "Women have a special mission as mothers. There is no greater mission in life." Elaborating on this pronatalist theme in his memoirs, Ben Gurion wrote, "If the Jewish birth-rate is not increased, it is doubtful that the Jewish State will survive. Any Jewish woman who . . . does not bring into the world at least four healthy children is shirking her duty to the nation *like a soldier who evades military service*" (italics mine). The new division of labor for Israel's survival was now men as combat soldiers, women as childbearers.

Ben Gurion's decision to take the National Religious Party (NRP) into his Labor (then called *Mapai*) Party Cabinet flows directly from his pronatalism. The NRP's quid pro quo was religious control over marriage and divorce, which means that these and other legal "personal status" matters involving Jews operate according to Halacha as interpreted by the religious authorities and their courts. There is consequently no civil marriage or divorce in Israel. Ben Gurion accepted this condition because the religious establishment's control over this arena bolstered the traditional wife and mother role. Moreover, the religious establishment's domination of "personal status," with all the sexism it has entailed, did not require the Labor Party to compromise its political virginity: The clericals were more than happy to do the dirty work, leaving the Laborites free to proclaim their abiding commitment to the equality of women. Menachem Begin, who reiterated in many a speech that Israeli women and children needed to be protected, was even more predisposed than Ben Gurion to the religious establishment's control over marriage and divorce when he became prime minister in 1977.

To ensure that women became mothers whether they liked it or not, abortions were at first made illegal; later they were partially legalized and a complicated permissions process tacked on. Illegal and legal abortions are bitterly attacked by pronatalists for cutting down on Jewish population growth.

✦ Pronatalism affected even the kibbutz. To combat the argument that there was no biological reason for excluding females from agricultural labor, the men began to spread the myth that driving tractors made women miscarry. The women accepted the tractor myth because it allowed them to retain their self-respect at a time when they were being excluded from the productive branches of agriculture and light industry and tracked into the lower-status service branches, and they were tired of fighting against it. This is reminiscent of shtetl men's downgrading breadwinning because they were unable to engage in it successfully.

With their role in the high-status productive branches shrinking, kibbutz women began to direct their emotional energy into motherhood. Largely through their initiative, the kibbutzim (with the exception of those of Hashomer Hatzair) moved away in the 1970s from collective child rearing and adopted the policy of *lina mishpachteet,* of children's sleeping in their parents' quarters. Child care, which had always been the prime responsibility of the women when it was collectivized, now became partially privatized. This made women reluctant to assume positions such as kibbutz secretary or treasurer, which necessitated periodic absences from the kibbutz and from their children.

RECRUDESCENCE OF CLASSIC GENDER ROLES

New normative gender behavior, more characteristic of classic patriarchal families than of traditional (especially East European) Jewish ones, began to emerge in Israel. The masculine man, wrote Lesley Hazleton, was defined as strong and masterful, capable and pragmatic, brash and gutsy, and emotionally tough. The feminine woman was defined as soft, emotional, in need of the man's protection, and caring and sacrificing for home and family. Israeli society also began to propagandize for women to be exceptionally nurturing wives to their soldier-husbands. Underlying this, noted a social work educator, "is the feeling that this *nurturing is necessary to the country's defense,* and that failing to carry it out means you're somehow disloyal," that is, an abandoner (italics mine). Israeli women were now charged with creating a "warm" and tranquil home as a haven from the harsh realities of Israeli life under siege.

The men also wanted and felt entitled to everything that Jewish men had had before the destruction of the Second Jewish Commonwealth and that they perceived non-Jewish men as having had in all the countries of the Exile, and as their reward for being good soldiers: nonassertive wives (and nondemanding extracurricular lovers). Female assertiveness was no longer perceived as necessary now that the national emergency that had preceded the establishment of the state was over (as it was similarly rationalized as dysfunctional in the U.S. in the twentieth century because "America is different"). Moreover, having wives who lived up to the non-Jewish patriarchal model of enabler served to validate the men's masculinity.

❧ The men's need for another ersatz definition of manhood—breadwinner—also led to intensified efforts to exclude women from the labor force. A 1992 government survey showed that only 41.5 percent of Israeli women were gain-fully employed (the figures applied to the public and financial sectors in which most worked) and that 55.2 percent worked part-time. Despite Israel's 1964 equal employment law, discrimination in pay across all job sectors (women earned 69 percent of the wages the men received) and in promotions, espe-cially to top management positions, prevails.

The exclusion of women from large sectors of the workforce contributed to their having "nothing to do" during the Yom Kippur War of 1973. Rather than let women take over *even temporarily* jobs vacated by men at the front, factories closed, hospitals turned away nonemergency patients, and public bus transporta-tion ground to a halt.

No longer threatened by women's encroaching on the labor turf, the men could afford to wax nostalgic about the women pioneers. A popular song of the 1970s, "Where Are Those Girls of Yesteryear?" actually uses the memory of the chalutzot to denigrate the Israeli women of today: "Where, oh where, are those girls / With their braids and [peasant dresses] / With their hoes and their daggers? .... They used to ride high in the saddle on guard duty. / Today they ride roughshod over their husbands."

The denigration of Israeli women is also evident in much Israeli fiction, which, observed Esther Fuchs, portrays women as profligate, materialistic, and selfish, "steeped in meaningless consumerist pursuits," an image reminiscent of the "Jewish American Princess" libel except that the Israeli woman is also pictured as over- rather than undersexed—and adulterous. Hannah, the protagonist-narrator of Oz's 1968 novel *My Michael* is careless with her husband's hard-earned money, self-destructive, and given to obsessive sexual fantasies (about Arabs yet). Signifi-cantly, the husband's surname is *Gonen*, which means protector. The subtext of the novel is that the woman has the power to destabilize the role and achieve-ments of the man as provider/protector.

❧ The novel is set in and reflects the reality of the late 1950s, when Israeli society began to become bourgeoisified. One major contributing factor was the feeling that material goodies could assuage the tension occasioned by the state of siege, the frustration born of isolation ("The whole world is against us"), and the rage at abandonment when countries regarded as allies withdrew their support (e.g., the Soviet Union in the early 1950s, France after the end of the Algerian War in 1962).

Another factor contributing to bourgeoisification was the impact of the post-1948 influx of a million and a half olim from Europe, West Asia, and North Africa. Many of these immigrants brought with them traditional Jewish attitudes favor-ing work of the mind over work of the hands, and this led to a resurgence and relegitimization of classic Jewish occupational choices. These traditional attitudes can be seen in the words of an immigrant character in *My Michael:* "I still remem-ber how Micha's friends made fun of him after the War of Independence for [studying a profession and] not going off with them *like a numbskull* to some kib-butz in the Negev. . . . The best years of their lives they have *wasted like imbeciles*" (italics mine).

The post-1948 wave of immigration, unfortunately, did not include the hun-dreds of thousands of idealistic and committed youth in the pioneering Zionist movements of Eastern Europe. Had they survived the Holocaust, they could have strengthened the labor and kibbutz sector and constituted a strong counterforce to bourgeoisification. As Ben Gurion mourned, "the millions of Jews who could have been brought" to Eretz Israel "are no more."

IMPACT OF THE HOLOCAUST TRAUMA

Nothing about Israeli society—its continuing obsession with abandonment, the glorification of the army and of soldiering, the emphasis on protecting women—can be understood without analyzing the impact of the Holocaust.

The Holocaust is a gaping wound that will not heal, especially since the acid of terrorism is constantly being poured onto it, and the salt of anti-Zionist ravings is continually being ground into it.

The Holocaust is more than a wound: It is an amputation of limbs, with bloody, inflamed stumps where those limbs—the European Jewish communities—were torn asunder, hacked to pieces, and incinerated. The phantom pain from those severed limbs is still deeply and acutely felt.

And it is in Israel where that pain and that "traumatic memory is part of the rhythm and ritual of public life," in Amos Elon's words, as it is nowhere else. Is-raelis remember how the rickety ships of Jewish refugees from Nazi genocide were barred by the British during World War II from landing in Mandatory Pales-tine and stranded on the high seas with no country willing to take them in. It was this searing memory that led Begin, in his first official act as prime minister, to offer asylum in 1977 to a group of sixty-six Vietnamese boat people. No country wanted to give them refuge. Israel did.

✤ The trauma of the Holocaust is compounded by guilt Israelis experience for their having "abandoned" the East European Jewish community, which was oblit-erated. The "abandonment" was threefold: the actual physical departure of olim from their families in Eastern Europe and from their community-as-extended-family before World War II; the rejection and negation of that community's tradi-tions, values, and lifestyle; and the Yishuv's not having done enough to rescue Jews in their hour of need even though it did more than any other Jewish com-munity. Despite its being under British rule, it organized rescue operations out of Istanbul and Romania; smuggled in thousands of "illegal" immigrants; and sent a mission of thirty-two parachutists, among them two women—kibbutzniks Chana Senesch and Haviva Reik—to organize rescue behind enemy lines.

Assuaging some of the guilt by reversing the denigration of the values of East European Jewry, which is a form of ideological abandonment, was impossible because of the Israelis' need to dissociate themselves from those values, primary among which was the proscription of physical aggression. This need dovetailed with the undercurrent of shame and anger felt by many Israelis at the European Jews' allegedly "going like sheep to the slaughter" (a subject to be dealt with in detail in chapter 15). The Holocaust "proved" to Israelis that the traditional values, especially those of the communities of Eastern Europe, had impeded the ability of the Jews to engage in mass physical resistance, just as it had done during the late-nineteenth- and early-twentieth-century pogroms. The sense of shame about the Jews' "passivity" in the pogroms had already been incorporated into official Zionist education; now it was also imposed on the Holocaust.

Guilt about the ideological abandonment of East European Jews and shame about their alleged passivity led Israel to emphasize the mass armed resistance that did take place, and the day of national remembrance of the Holocaust is officially called *Yom HaSho'ah V'Hagvurah,* the "Day of the Catastrophe and the Heroism." Identifying with the Resistance implied that Israelis were not totally abandoning their emotional connection with the Jewish culture of Eastern Europe out of which the armed revolts arose.

But glorifying resistance too much was in conflict with the need to denigrate East European Jewish values. Despite them, especially despite the negative attitude toward physical aggression, extremely courageous armed resistance did take place under the most horrific conditions. "Overly" glorifying this resistance would have thus propelled Israelis into challenging their ideological across-the-board abandonment of Exile culture. They were reluctant to do this until fairly recently because it is an agonizing process that requires the kind of psychological equanimity that does not exist under siege.

Unable to resolve the conflict, Israelis extol resistance but do not go overboard in doing so. This compromise can be seen most clearly in the choice of poet Chana Senesch to epitomize it. Senesch, a Hungarian Zionist, initially lived on a kibbutz, leaving it in 1944 to participate in the parachutists' mission to rescue European Jews. She was captured near the Hungarian border, tried for treason, and executed by the quisling government. Senesch is a safe hero because she and her actions do not activate the guilt over the "abandonment" of East European Jewry and its value system. By being a parachutist, she showed that the Yishuv had not abandoned European Jewry. That she was executed before carrying out her mission, however, "proves" that mass rescue by the Yishuv was impossible. Moreover, since she came to Europe as a pioneer, her action does not trigger the conflict over the degree of resistance by *indigenous* Jews. Because she was Hungarian and not East European–born, the conflict over the values of the latter community and guilt for "abandoning" it do not apply here, either. Finally, her capture prevented her from engaging in any physically aggressive action;

this takes the sting out of her being a woman doing the "man's work" of physical defense.

✦ It was the abandonment of Israel by every nation in the weeks before the Six-Day War of 1967 that reactivated the Israeli Jews' memories of the Holocaust, when Jews were deserted "like dogs in the street" by their neighbors, the church, and the Allies, whom so many Jews had expected to be rescuers.

The Six-Day War was precipitated when Egypt's President Nasser demanded on May 17, 1967 that UNEF, the U.N. Emergency peacekeeping Force, which had patrolled and monitored Egypt's borders with Israel since the end of the Sinai Campaign of 1956, be withdrawn. After U.N. Secretary-General U Thant acceded to that demand two days later, Egyptian troops began massing on the border with Israel; Nasser then blockaded the Straits of Tiran. This act of war evoked only silence and inaction from the world powers.

Two agonizing, terrifying weeks ensued. Israelis, watching on TV mobs in Cairo howling for their destruction in a *jihad* (Arabic for holy war), felt they were facing another Holocaust. Space was set aside in public parks for graves for the expected eighty thousand dead; civilians bought poison capsules.

Then, on June 5, 1967, the Israelis seized the ax that was about to descend on their heads and brought it down squarely on the necks of their enemy. In one strike their planes wiped out virtually all the Egyptian airplanes. Later that week the Israeli Army moved into the Sinai Desert and the Gaza Strip and repelled attacks by Egypt's allies, Syria and Jordan, capturing in the process the Golan Heights from the former and the West Bank from the latter.

The exhilarating rescue of the country by the army, the swift transition from seeming powerlessness to active and brilliant defense, the fact that the Holocaust was not repeated, and the reunification of Jerusalem with the capture of East Jerusalem, from whose holy places Jews had been forcibly separated for nineteen years—this is what caused the jubilation, not (as some anti-Zionists ranted) the conquest of land. The army's rescue of the country in 1967, and of the hostages from Entebbe in 1976, was balm for the seared souls of the Israelis. In both cases the cavalry had arrived at the last minute, as Jews had always hoped God's rescue would. These events reinforced the feeling that Israelis had only themselves to count on: No other country rated Jewish survival as its priority.

The cacophony of shrieking voices in the international left denouncing Israel for having defended itself successfully exacerbated Israelis' feelings of being misunderstood and abandoned by the sector of the political spectrum that so many had for so long regarded as their reference group. With a few exceptions—Fidel Castro said, "True revolutionaries never threaten a whole country with extermination . . . [or] deny her right to exist"—the international left and the Third World supported the Arabs, especially the Palestinians. (So did many in the Old and New Left in the U.S., as we shall see in chapter 14.) One of the first acts of

African National Congress leader Nelson Mandela upon emerging in 1990 from eighteen years' solitary confinement in a South African prison was to embrace PLO chief Yasir Arafat and "wish him success in his struggle."

Instead of trying to get both sides to the negotiating table, the international left justified and glorified Palestinian terrorism, thereby reinforcing it. Some in the left saw this terrorism against Israel as a good dress rehearsal for attacks on the First World, in the spirit of those narodniks who had hailed the 1880s pogroms in Russia as a great stirring of the masses.

The Israelis' anger and revulsion after 1967 against the left for supporting terrorism, and against the Soviets for having encouraged and supplied arms to its Arab clients, spilled over into loathing of anything that smacked of Socialism. Embittered, the Israeli public turned more and more against its own left at a time when support for the two-state solution it advanced might have made a crucial difference in government policy regarding the future of the territories captured by Israel during the 1967 War. Unfortunately, the government policy that evolved in the ensuing decades was that of "creeping annexation" through the building of settlements and land confiscation; suppression of civil liberties under military rule; and the exploitation of Palestinian labor. The international left gave no support to the Israeli peace movement, which protested these policies, and the American media provided little coverage of its activities.

BOURGEOISIFICATION AND MACHISMO

The continued occupation of the territories jolted bourgeoisification into high gear and intensified Israeli machismo. These factors have had an extremely deleterious effect on the position of women in Israel since 1967.

Within a few short years after the Six-Day War, a great deal of the manual labor that the pioneers had once been so eager to conquer was being done cheaply by Arabs, including thousands from the occupied territories. A member of a *moshav* (farm cooperative) wrote in 1972 that she and her husband and children had five Arab workers and "don't do a stitch of work on our farm. . . . My children . . . will have nothing to do with agriculture. . . . Our life-style has become that of the *effendis*" (Arabic for rich Arab landowners of the pre-state period). After 1967, as well, American ideas about work and entitlement to comfort began to seep into Israel along with increased foreign aid.

It was at this juncture that the almost moribund pioneering ethic was resurrected and reconstituted by a religious nationalist movement calling itself *Gush Emunim* (Hebrew for Bloc of the Faithful/Loyal), which advocated a "Greater Israel," that is, annexation of the territories. This was the only anti-mamlachti phenomenon to arise in Israel.

A new collective leftist pioneering movement would have been a most welcome counterforce to the state bureaucracy, whose *pkidim* (Hebrew plural for clerks, bureaucrats) have tended to treat the public contemptuously, often behaving in their official capacity like medieval nobles zealously guarding their turf from the citizenry and each other. The bureaucracy had deservedly become the object of public bitterness and cynicism—and the butt of countless jokes—because of its inefficiency, corruption, and equal-opportunity heartlessness, even to war widows. It was this bureaucracy that in the 1950s settled countless immigrants, often against their knowledge or will, in dreary development towns in the Negev and Galilee and then denied them elementary social services such as health clinics. (And its failure to plan resulted in the lack of housing and employment for hundreds of thousands of immigrants from the ex–Soviet Union in the 1990s.)

The tragedy was that the Gush Emunim counterforce, coming from the right, envisioned not the establishment of a just and egalitarian society but rather aggrandizement, conquest, and domination. Its self-styled "pioneers," who settled in cheap apartments in the territories, were characterized by swaggering machismo, self-serving insensitivity, absence of empathy or compassion for the downtrodden, total lack of interest in social justice or in humane relationships (especially with their Palestinian neighbors), and by the malignant narcissism of the "Me Decade" in the U.S., from which country many hailed.

⇥ The occupation led many Israeli men to behave like conquerors: arrogant and macho. The surge in machismo was particularly evident among men from Middle Eastern backgrounds (sometimes called Sephardic or Oriental Jews), especially the descendants of the Jews who were expelled from or forced to flee Arab countries in the population exchange that took place after the establishment of Israel. The male immigrants had felt emasculated in Israel. Many were unemployed, especially in the development towns. Successive Labor governments had denied them political power and had pressured them to adopt Ashkenazic culture, that is, to assimilate. Although their male descendants began to wield some clout in the development towns, their poor socioeconomic situation has persisted. But in the occupied territories, there were men with even less power, and many Sephardic/Oriental Jewish men enjoyed having ersatz power over them—a psychological pattern somewhat reminiscent of that of poor whites in the American South vis-à-vis blacks before the civil rights movement.

The army's "purity of arms" ideal, which dates back to the pioneering Yishuv, began to weaken. The ideal was/is that weapons were not to be used with impunity to oppress, persecute, intimidate, or terrorize—as they had been used against Jews for centuries of Exile—but only to achieve the altruistic national goal of self-defense. (This ideal is reflected in the official name of the Israeli Army, *Zahal,* an acronym for Israeli *Defense* Force.) But during the Intifada, most soldiers accepted the legitimacy of harsh reprisals, including, at one point, "breaking their bones."

The connection between military machismo and the genie-out-of-the-bottle effect regarding violence was underscored by Orthodox dove Yeshayahu

Leibowitz: "Violence, veneration of military heroism, contempt for human beings and living creatures—*all these are interconnected*" (italics mine).

Gershom Scholem, who had long been active in various peace efforts, contrasted the current reality with that of the traditional Jewish communities, which had proscribed physical aggression, including misogynist violence: "For the first time" in Jewish history, he said, there was "serious physical violence between Jews, including cases of rape." As the men became more macho, wife-battering and the physical abuse of children became phenomena of growing concern. The feminist Israel Women's Network estimated in 1992 that ten rapes take place every day and that 10 percent of Israeli women are battered regularly. Of the one hundred murders in Israel (population approximately five million) in 1991, thirty-six were of women killed by their husbands, ex-husbands, or boyfriends.

Some Israelis saw these phenomena as evidence that Israel was simply becoming the normal society that Bialik had desired when he made his "thieves and prostitutes" comment. Others, however, noted correctly that because of the ongoing state of siege, Israel is hardly a "normal" society, nor has it fulfilled the hope of most Zionists that it would be based on Jewish culture, that it would be, in the words of Orthodox Zionists, "the beginning of the flowering of our redemption."

ISRAEL AS THE WORLD'S JEW

Many Zionist theoreticians believed that much of the hostility directed against Jews derived from their being perceived as different from all other nations in not having a land they could call their own. Unconsciously accepting the idea behind the old assimilationist contract as it had been directed at individuals, they believed that once Jews behaved like all other nations, once they had a state—land, a flag, a diplomatic corps, an army—it would be treated like all the other nation-states.

Attaining "national adulthood," according to Zionist theory, was supposed to have allowed Jews to return to the family of nations as an equal—just like the adolescent, after successfully concluding the separation struggle, returns to the parents to renegotiate their relationship on an adult-to-adult basis. The instrumentality for "national adulthood" in the modern era is a state. Regrouping under the Zionist banner—what Herzl implied when he said that "Zionism is a return to the Jewish fold even before it is a return to the Jewish homeland"—they fought for and established the State of Israel.

But the separation struggle has not yet been satisfactorily resolved. Israel is not yet treated as an equal in the family of nations. Its legitimacy is rejected by many countries, subjected to debate by others. In psychological terms, this means that Israel's adulthood is not quite accepted and that it is often perceived as an illegitimate child that causes everyone else trouble and inconvenience. Like a child, too, it is constantly being monitored, its every move observed, noted, and evaluated; it is often scolded by other governments and by media pundits. This frustrates the Israelis, who long for the "normal" relationships with other nations that statehood was supposed to bring about. No matter that they call themselves Israelis; in the eyes of the world they are still ... Jews.

Judging by the attitudes of various nations, Israel should be eternally grateful simply for being allowed to exist. As Jacob Talmon put it in a related context: "The world had come to such a pass that not killing Jews and allowing them to breathe fresh air was considered a tremendous altruistic deed."

Like the scholarship student who has to get straight A's in return for his or her presence on the premises, Israel is held to standards of behavior that no other nation-state is expected to live up to. The double standard is similar to that applied to women, and, like them, Israel is often accused of "provoking" attack and of "overreacting" to threats.

Non-Jewish men are still ambivalent about Israel's ability to defend itself well militarily and remain uncomfortable with the reality and image of the Jew as warrior. Pacifist Dave McReynolds exemplified this attitude when he condemned Israel's military self-defense in 1967 thus: "After 2,000 years of pogroms, retreats, wandering and humiliation, suddenly the Jews had the guns and the capacity to be *as violent and as coldly brutal as the rest of us*" (italics mine). Thus, in refusing to be a victim and becoming a role-breaker in this regard, Israel flips over to the shadow role of brutal "imperialist" dominator. This mind-set also accounts for the warm support Israel received during the Scud missile attacks of 1991, when Israeli Jews were perceived to have reverted to the appropriate role of victims. Many non-Jews were also secretly gleeful to see Israelis getting a comeuppance during the Intifada—as role breakers should. This attitude is especially prevalant when Israelis' behavior can be condemned as unethical, because many Christians have never quite forgotten or forgiven the Chosen People countermyth of Jewish ethical superiority.

❧ Israel thus became the Jew in relation to the world. The prime difference between this condition and that of individual Jews and their communities in the Exile is that Israel is able to defend the nation-as-extended-family. In many other ways, however, the dynamics of the classic relationships with non-Jewish societies obtain.

Like Jews in the Exile, Israel got trapped between the power structure and the masses, with the First World (primarily the U.S.) playing the classic role of the ruling class and the Third World that of the oppressed and rebellious peasants. (The parallel, of course, is inexact. The U.S. did not program other countries to anti-Zionism the way the ruling classes of oppressive exiles programmed the masses to anti-Semitism.)

Israel, like Jews in the Exile, also got caught in the middle of another people's struggle: that of the Arabs against their former colonial rulers. In this variation on the classic adolescent separation struggle, the Arabs have tried to regroup against the colonial powers that have dominated them (and that have tried to impose Western culture), to coalesce a strong identity drawing on a reclaimed culture, and to renegotiate the relationship. Arab nationalists often turn to Islamic fundamentalism as a (reclaimed) cultural source "uncorrupted" by the West. That is why one Arab spokesman called Islamic fundamentalism "a defense against Western hegemony."

The Arab power structures, especially the feudal ones, feared the Yishuv, and later the State of Israel, as the cultural intermediary of the Western world. In the pre-state era, the Palestinian effendis and the religious power structure feared that the pioneers' collectivism (the kibbutzim), union organizing (the Histadrut General Federation of Labor), and secularization would influence the masses of poor Arab peasants and workers. A great deal of their antagonism to the kibbutzim stemmed from their fear that the freedom of the chalutzot would serve as a model for the women of (nearby) Arab villages. Depicting the pioneering Yishuv as Communists and as a threat to the "freedom" of the Palestinian masses, they successfully put a wedge between the two.

After Israel attained independence, the Arab leaders saw it bringing to the Mideast, along with technology, the values of the West—especially democracy, which threatens their power. Israel's touting its potential usefulness (a classic strategy) in terms of the technological assistance in agriculture and industry it could provide the Arabs if there were peace, unintentionally reinforced this fear. (The fear of Israel's serving as an example of a feisty and flourishing democracy also accounted, in part, for the "cold peace" that has prevailed between Israel and Egypt since the two countries signed a peace treaty.)

The Arab rulers recycled against Israel some of the strategies used by oppressive ruling classes against Jews in the Exile. The prime strategy was the "club": to try to destroy Israel by war and random terrorist attacks. When they failed to "drive the Jews into the sea" or even to destabilize Israel through terrorism, the leaders fell back on trying to separate Israel from their own masses. They separated Israel physically by refusing to recognize it (which meant no diplomatic relations, trade, communications, or travel) and by an economic boycott.

They also tried to separate it psychologically, as they had done in pre-state days, but had to change their line. Now they defined the threat to the Arab masses' "freedom" as deriving from Israel's being an "imperialist" power. This was a recycling of the Judeophobic myths about Jewish power and malevolence, which is why the infamous forgery *Protocols of the Elders of Zion* was published and widely disseminated in many Arab countries. The apotheosis of Arab rulers' efforts to demonize Israel and thereby isolate it from their own masses (and from other countries) was the 1975 U.N. resolution equating Zionism with racism. The myths also served to condition the Arab masses to use Israel as a lightning rod to absorb their rage against their own dictators.

Finally, the Arab states tried to make Israel invisible—referring to it not by name but as "the Zionist entity," eliminating it from their maps, and trying to exclude it from various U.N. bodies.

The international left, by denying Israel's right to exist, colluded with the Arabs in trying to render it invisible. Amos Kenan, a dovish Israeli journalist, wrote bitterly after the 1967 War,

> The New Left has investigated and found that, historically, there is no justification for the State of Israel's existence. Since it has no justification, it follows that no nation constitutes the State. Since the State has no people in it, there is no justification for this non-existent people's struggle for its existence in freedom. In short, as I do not fit somebody's intellectual image, I *do not exist* [italics mine].

◆ Because of Israel's realistic fear of military attacks by the Arabs, it recycled to some extent the traditional survival strategy of seeking the political protection of powerful authorities, in this case, the First World's leader, the U.S., just as Jews had once sought the protection of kings, nobles, and bishops. The role of Court Jew in this schema's parallel with Exile-type strategy was played by the American Jewish community, as we shall see in chapter 12.

America was not overjoyed at being identified as Israel's protector. It was concerned that this could jeopardize other, more important relationships, such as those with Arab nations. This was clearly demonstrated when the U.S. pressured Israel during the Gulf crisis and War to "keep a low profile," that is, be invisible.

Although Israel became a military power in the Mideast region, it hardly qualified for the title "superpower," and the American government was well aware of Israel's limitations. Yet it was willing to use this myth (which recycled the old one of Jewish power) as a convenient rationalization for taking actions that alarmed Israel, such as selling sophisticated weaponry to Arab nations sworn to Israel's destruction. The use of this myth also conditioned the American public to discount Israel's expression of alarm at these actions as an "overreaction."

As part of its recycling of traditional survival strategies, Israel tried to picture itself as an enabler useful to America—"the only bastion of democracy in the Mideast"—and as a strategic asset. It was occasionally pressured/maneuvered into doing its dirty work as U.S. surrogate, for example, selling arms to various tyrannical regimes the U.S. could not deal with directly. It did so, however, primarily to earn hard cash. But just as lending money to nobles was regarded by peasants and townsfolk in the Middle Ages as aiding and abetting their class enemy, so, too, Israel's actions *in its own (perceived) interests* were seen by many Third World countries as helping their colonialist enemies.

The view by some Third World nations that Israel was America's eager surrogate and the belief in the Israel-as-superpower myth legitimized their carrying out diversionary political attacks on this small state rather than against their colonialist enemies. For example, at the 1980 U.N. Mid-Decade Conference on Women in Copenhagen, some Third World delegates charged, "We have drought and famine and social injustice and inequality in our country and it is . . . because of Zionism." Israel, by its very "insistence on existing," was accused of "poisoning access to oil wells" and causing economic hardship, a recycling of the medieval Judeophobic myth that Jews caused the bubonic plague by poisoning water wells, wrote Esther Broner. The conference approved (94 to 4) a plan of action that included a paragraph listing Zionism as one of the world's main evils. Israel, concluded an American participant, was the "convenient scapegoat" for delegates of countries that were "very angry at America and at the Western world." (The attacks on Israel were also a successful diversion of attention away from serious discussion of violence against women, especially genital mutilation.)

Most Israelis did not project rescue-from-outside fantasies onto America. But the process of looking to the U.S. for some protection or assistance seemed to revive/reactivate some of the old assimilationist illusions about secular rescuer nations. One was to perceive the U.S. as distant and somewhat flawed and in need of repair to engage in protection. The repair work mostly took the form of Israel's constantly reminding the U.S. of the Jewish State's usefulness and of the "shared values" of the two democracies.

The relationship between Israel and the U.S. began to undergo a transformation with the collapse of the Soviet Union and the initiation of a new stage in the peace process. With the cold war at an end, Israel could no longer picture itself as an enabler to the U.S., facilitating some of its agenda in order to gain protection. And, should a stable peace be concluded, such protection will no longer be urgently needed, as it was in the past. A stable peace would also allow Israel, at last, to deal with all the social, economic, environmental, religious, and cultural issues that the focus on defense shunted to low-priority positions on the national agenda. And one of these issues is the condition of women in the Jewish State.

↠ While most Zionists saw attaining a state as the prerequisite for creating a country as "Jewish as England is English," they were unable to devote serious attention to the issue of its cultural content. The focus on defense and on immigrant absorption was not the only reason for this behavior; there was also an underlying psychological factor: The issue of cultural context is intertwined with the unresolved separation struggle initiated by the early Zionist movement when it rejected Exile culture and its mass rescue fantasies in order to attain "national adulthood," that is, a state.

The next stage of the separation struggle should have been the return to the tradition and the renegotiation of a new relationship with it. Kovner understood this when he told a kibbutz audience in 1984 that the Hashomer Hatzair movement had never made "an attempt to work out an attitude toward the subject of

Jewish tradition which—whether we like it or not—determines the historical continuity of the Jewish people, its very existence, and the content of its culture." The
movement, he said, did not heed the call of Ahad Ha'am, the theoretician of spiritual Zionism, to preserve the nation's ethos. It was "more involved in a process of
tearing itself away than in a process of continuation." He called for a "face-to-face
confrontation with the sources," the traditional Jewish texts.

What has primarily precluded this renegotiation phase of the separation
struggle is the incorporation of female values, especially nonviolence, in the tradition. These values were at variance with the masculinist values and behavior that
came to the fore during The War and therefore had to be rejected. Similarly, the
pioneering ethic, which drew so deeply on the female values of traditional Jewish
communities, had to be downgraded as well, and the instrumentalities of its expression—the kibbutzim, the Histadrut—stripped of much of their influence. Today
in Israel the pioneering ethic and history are treated with embarrassment, as a
naive phase of national existence with no relevance to the current reality.

Israeli men, locked in a struggle for survival against the men of the Arab nations, oppose anything that can be interpreted as a chink in the armor of their
machismo or as a sign of weakness. Efforts to resolve the separation struggle cannot get underway until Israel's survival is no longer endangered. And because
machismo is inextricably enmeshed with The War, only when there is peace will
machismo be challenged and, hopefully, overcome. Only then will a struggle for
gender equality have the possibility of succeeding.

And only when there is peace will it be possible to initiate a course correction that will allow the Zionist revolution to fulfill its original aim of building a
nation based on Jewish culture, one rooted in the female values that informed the
pioneering Yishuv.

NINE ❧ THE NO-WIN SITUATION OF THE JEWISH MOTHER IN AMERICA

> *After a Jewish youth who seeks to marry a beautiful and arrogant young woman passes all the tests she puts him through, she demands: "Bring me the heart of your mother." The young man rips out his mother's heart. As he is carrying it, dripping blood, to the woman, he stumbles and falls. His mother's heart, lying on the ground where he dropped it, calls out to him, "Did you hurt yourself, my son?"*
>
> JEWISH FOLKTALE

> *"My children must get out of this," [thought Katie]. . . . "But how?. . ." An answer came to [her]. Education! It was education that made the difference! Education would pull them out of the grime and dirt.*
>
> BETTY SMITH, *A Tree Grows in Brooklyn*

By the time the women pioneers of the Third Aliyah (1919–23) arrived in Eretz Israel and advanced the efforts of their predecessors to participate as equals in nation building, the struggle of young Jewish women immigrants to America against being retracked into enabling was going down to defeat.

They had been ejected from the turf of paid labor, and their dreams of higher education and meaningful work had been frustrated. Most were sequestered in the home—and even there the old altruistic-assertive enabler role was being rapidly eroded. As assimilationism made inroads, especially in the middle class, the work women had traditionally done in maintaining the home support system that facilitated all family members' carrying out the mitzvot shrank as Jews invented their own brands of Judaism.

Now that women were no longer required to be enablers of Jewish survival, a role that had allowed them to be assertive because it was altruistic, assertiveness was not only unnecessary, it was also counterindicated. Men felt threatened by the women's assertiveness precisely because this was a quality *they* needed to reclaim as part of recapturing the turf of paid work. Since this was behavior

Jewish men were still learning and unsure of, they needed to reduce women's assertiveness to allow their own to emerge. At the very least, the men wished to prevent their being shown up by women whose assertiveness was more visible than their own. This was the same "honor of the community" dynamic that strengthened the wish of the male pioneers in Eretz Israel to exclude women from agricultural labor. It was reinforced by the American middle-class cultural ideal of the nonassertive, subservient, dependent wife.

Highly energetic women with memories of mothers and grandmothers who had carried whole families on their backs, who had themselves slaved in the sweatshops and walked the picket lines, sought—and found—other outlets for their energies and their assertiveness. These also served as ersatz sources of validation and self-esteem.

Being a baleboosta, a quintessential homemaker, was one such outlet. In the shtetl, maintaining a household according to Jewish law and custom was extremely demanding, especially because the home was usually a one-room wooden shack with an earthen floor. On the Lower East Side and in other late-nineteenth- and early-twentieth-century immigrant ghettos, the small tenement flat lacked indoor plumbing and was overcrowded with relatives and boarders. The mother was often subjected to heavy-handed criticism from the German Jewish "ladies" who descended in teams "poking through the blocks of railroad flats, clucking about filth," in Stephen Birmingham's words.

It is no wonder that once she had the opportunity to function as a baleboosta under the improved conditions made possible by a rise in the family income, the mother overcompensated—with humongous meals, vinyl-covered couches, and spotless ("You-can-eat-off-the-floor") housekeeping serving as definitive markers of the home as her exclusive turf, the source of her identity. If she was to be in a cage, it might as well be a gilded cage.

The second and major outlet she found for her energy (as did women in kibbutzim from the 1960s on, when they were excluded from the productive branches) was mothering. The specific focus of these immigrant mothers was facilitating their children's Americanization. The boys were to be prodded and pushed toward material success, the girls into becoming wives to "successful" men and American-style enablers to them and the children. The women seized on this particular role with the desperation of a starving person coming upon a cache of diet cookies—unaware that these morsels would provide them no nourishment, although they might at first feel (ful)filled.

A third outlet for the Jewish woman's energy was volunteering in women's organizations (the subject of chapter 13). These were safe spaces in which to do useful and meaningful work and to seek validation, and in which her assertiveness was not threatening to the men.

Jewish women could channel their energy into these arenas and be strong and outspoken there because it was in the interests of others. They could be

born-again altruistic-assertive enablers. But while the old altruistic-assertive enabler role had provided women with considerable validation, the psychic rewards
of the repositioned role dwindled with every passing generation after the immigrant era until running out completely by the 1970s.

CONTRADICTIONS IN THE MOTHER'S ROLE

The Jewish family in America was child centered, or, more accurately, son centered. The father in the first few generations (immigration period and the Depression) was often the ineffectual dreamer pictured in Clifford Odets's 1935 play
Arise and Sing! Even if he did succeed to one degree or another, both parents focused on the son(s) to fulfill their dreams—the American Dream of material success and status.

The child centeredness of the Jewish home did not, of course, begin in America, nor did the concept of *naches* from the children. *Naches* is a hard-to-translate
Yiddish word that, when used in connection with children (as it usually is), de-
notes a deep and exultant, serene gratification permeated with an expansive sense
that one's life has been worthwhile, something akin to a Christian's being in a
state of grace. In the shtetl, recalled Zborowski and Herzog's interviewees, "the
shining reward a parent expects for all his [*sic*] care and sacrifice is to [derive]
naches from the child. . . . *Through the child's success the parent is validated*" (italics mine).

There were two important differences between the way shtetl and American
Jews experienced *naches fun kinder* (from the children), however, and these affected the way the woman carried out her role. One related to the definition of
the child's success. The shtetl defined success in terms of Jewish values: that she
or he become a mentsch, and a good Jew. In America success meant the son's material achievement and status and the daughter's "good marriage."

The second basic difference was that in the shtetl the woman did not depend
exclusively on the children's success for her validation and self-esteem. Other important responsibilities, such as earning a living and maintaining a Jewish household in all its infinitely complex detail, gave her a deep sense of pride and
self-worth. "She will comment constantly on the burden of it all . . . but her complaints are a kind of boasting: 'See all that is demanded of me, how everything lies
on my head. . . .' The implication is not please take it away but rather, see all I can do
and . . . don't *I deserve great credit for it,*" ex-shtetl residents reported (italics mine).

Moreover, the shtetl mother did not have the total responsibility for socializing or caring for the children. Older daughters took care of younger children; the
boys attended cheder all day from age three to thirteen; and the community itself
was a prime socializing agent.

In America the entire burden of socializing the children fell on the mother,
both because the men were busy trying to make it into the middle class and

because Jews accepted the American value that this was the woman's prime role (and carrying it out kept her out of the work turf, too). The men's role was in production, the woman's in reproduction. And, after World War II, when most Jewish neighborhoods vanished from the urban scene, as we shall see, so did their support networks, which mothers had relied on for informal child-care assistance (as well as abortion referrals). The Jewish mother, like other white American women, especially those in the middle class, now had twenty-four-hour responsibility for the children's socialization.

The Jewish mother unconsciously understood that everything—the family's future as well as her own validation and self-esteem—was riding on her children's, especially her son's, material success. If the son became a high achiever, her existence was validated, and she could boast about him ("My son the doctor") to her relatives and neighbors. Similarly if her daughter "married well." If they did not attain these objectives, it was the mother who was seen to have failed, and she was regarded with pity and scorn.

Because the Jewish woman's sense of self-worth depended so greatly on being the successful superenabler of her children, she was at high risk for depression in middle age, observed sociologist Pauline Bart in her landmark 1970 study of the "empty nest syndrome." She often became depressed when no longer able to fulfill this role, when she received little validation for having carried it out, when she felt she had not succeeded at it, and/or when her children "failed to meet her needs, either by not making what she considered 'good' marriage choices [or by] not achieving the career aspirations she had for them." The women who become clinically depressed may be a minority that is but the tip of the iceberg, or, more accurately, the canaries suffocating in the oxygen-depleted mine shaft.

✎ The Jewish mother faced a task fraught with contradictions. She was expected to facilitate her son's material success as a prerequisite for and component of his assimilation, his adopting the majority (WASP) culture, that of the middle-class reference group. At the same time, because Jews still faced economic and social discrimination, she was required to continue imparting traditional Jewish values, survival strategies, and behavior patterns to overcome it in the interest of facilitating his material success. These values, strategies, and behavior patterns included mutuality and interdependence; revulsion toward and a ban on physical aggression; intellectualism and a tendency to debate, question, and criticize; a healthy suspicion of others' motivations and the need to tread carefully and "inconspicuously"; and a respect for women's strength and a sense of marriage as a partnership and the home as a haven. All of these, being anti-assimilationist in nature, would ultimately impede the assimilation she wished the son to attain through his material accomplishments.

Moreover, at one and the same time, the mother also had to facilitate the son's assimilation as a prerequisite for his material success (as did the mother in the semi-silent 1927 film, *The Jazz Singer*.) Such behavior necessitated weakening/downgrading/relinquishing those very same values, survival strategies, and behavior patterns the mother was instilling in order to ensure the son's material success. How could he assimilate—which means giving up group values and behavior—when he is taught these values and behavior patterns in order to succeed (and thereby assimilate)? How can he give up his ethnic behavior patterns in order to assimilate (and thereby succeed) if he is taught them precisely because they are necessary for him to succeed?

In addition, the son's attempted assimilation required his trying to live up to the American definition of masculinity so that he would be validated for doing so. But the American definition of masculinity is a package deal involving not only working/providing but also a readiness to engage in physical aggression, even violence; the domination of women, even by force; "independence" and individualism; emotional "cool"; and disdain for "egghead" intellectualism. These components were antithetical to the Jewish values, survival strategies, and behavior patterns the mother was instilling to ensure the son attain material success (the middle-class variant of the masculinity definition). Having internalized these behavior patterns, the son would never feel he was living up to the total American definition of masculinity even if he did attain material success, and he would never be validated for doing so.

The Jewish mother also faced conflicts and paradoxes in raising her daughter to live up to the American definition of femininity—which included being quiet, subservient, and "ladylike"—and thereby to succeed in making a "good marriage"; we shall discuss these subsequently.

❧ In regard to children of both genders, the Jewish mother's task became even more contradictory from the 1920s on. Before World War I she was told by various advisers (e.g., in the Yiddish press) that she was the prime agent of the children's Americanization. Now she was instructed to be the transmitter of Jewish culture in the home to ensure Jewish continuity, as she was in imperial Germany.

While there was growing concern in the interbellum period about the erosion of the Yiddish immigrant culture and the "cultural defection" of the youth, this culture persisted up to the early 1950s. There were the Yiddish theaters, *landsmanshaftn* (fraternal mutual-assistance organizations of people from the same hometown), and daily Yiddish newspapers. Jewish neighborhoods also provided Jewish experiences: There were synagogues where holiday observances were held, Yiddish afternoon schools, cafés and cafeterias where people could talk for hours over a cup of coffee, numerous lecture halls and debating societies (so numerous that public school classrooms had to be made available at night). From these and from the homes, Jewish life poured into the streets and parks, which took on a Jewish ambiance. But after World War II, most urban Jewish neighborhoods disappeared. Some were deserted by Jews seeking upward mobility in the suburbs, others (like the East Bronx) fell prey to brutal urban "planning."

What was missing before and especially after World War II was the kind of universal and free quality Jewish education that had been provided to boys by the autonomous Jewish communities of the past. The communal "leaders" of American Jewry, having abdicated the prime responsibility for educating children Jewishly, were apparently unaware that the Jewish mother was already "transmitting Jewish culture" by instilling its traditional values, survival strategies, and behavior patterns. What they also wanted her to do now was to take over the community's classic role of providing education in the substance and meaning of Jewishness. Not having received this kind of in-depth education herself, she was unable to provide/transmit it. The result was that the children usually had no information about what precisely constituted authentic Jewishness, and *tended to identify everything she imparted—including assimilationist values—as Jewish.*

Moreover, the role that Jewish women had been shoehorned into—enabling the men's successful assimilation—was by its very nature counterproductive to Jewish survival, a 180-degree turn from the two-thousand-year-old role of the Jewish woman as enabler of the man's spiritual resistance, which was crucial to Jewish survival.

In the ensuing generations, the Jewish mother was blamed by communal "leaders" for her offspring's assimilation. And she was blamed by her sons for their *incomplete* assimilation. She was in a no-win situation from the outset, but she didn't realize it.

SURVIVAL SKILLS AND DOUBLE MESSAGES

The role of the mother was to push her son relentlessly to compete for high grades, to graduate high school and, later, college, to succeed in business, and, especially, to enter a profession with high status. Such goals had been impossible dreams in Czarist Russia; in America they were attainable by the men but not by the women, who sublimated their own dreams by projecting them onto their sons. The Jewish mother's ambition, wrote Zena Blau Smith, "was anything but modest. When her son began to make the first feeble sounds on his violin a *Yiddishe Mameh* already envisioned another Elman or Heifetz. If he showed scientific proficiency, she foresaw another Einstein."

The Jewish mother in America also had to make sure that the son knew exactly how far to go in his pursuit of material success. She had to ensure that the children of both genders knew that there would be certain roadblocks in their way caused by anti-Semitic discrimination (and, in the case of the girls, by sexism, as well, although the consciousness of its injustice was characteristic only of certain first-generation women). Acutely aware that her offspring would be unable to enter certain fields, she had to channel them away from such impossible goals—thus functioning and appearing as a "dream buster"—and into more accessible arenas. At the same time, she tried to boost the boys' self-confidence and their belief that they could do anything they wanted, as epitomized by the popular Jewish saying, "Anybody can become president."

Furthermore, she had to teach them whom to trust and whom not to trust, and how far to go with trusting. Pauline Bart once pointed out that Erik Erikson's view that "the successful resolution of the first stage of the development of the child is basic trust" cannot apply to women for whom, in a society where rape and other misogynist violence are rampant, "basic *mis*trust . . . [is] a successful resolution." The same has applied to Jews. The sons had to be taught, on the one hand, that America is the land of opportunity and, on the other, always to watch out for those who would deny it to them—and to watch their backs.

Of course, the classic Jewish way to get around discrimination—the old strategy of being useful—was to be so good, so valuable, that you had to get hired. But being better than the competition in and of itself causes envy, resentment, and enemies, especially if one is conspicuous about it. Therefore the sons had to be taught to walk that fine line between knowing "It's a free country" and knowing, as well, that since anti-Semitism was still present they should not be "overly" conspicuous in dealing with non-Jews. As one father wrote in 1940, "Young Jews . . . should be made to realize the advantages of unobtrusiveness."

There is a basic contradiction between the idea that if one is useful one won't be attacked (at least as long as the usefulness lasts) and the idea that if one is inconspicuous/unobtrusive one won't be attacked. How can one be outstanding without standing out? Jewish men have been torn apart by the double message that they had to be better than non-Jews in order to succeed—and better inevitably meant being conspicuous and thus triggering envy and more discrimination (which being better was supposed to overcome)—and that they also had to fade into the woodwork and not stand out "too much" lest they incur envy and invite attack. How can one walk the tightrope between the demand to be aggressive in pursuit of success and the counsel to stop short of being "too" aggressive—and, above all, of appearing too "pushy," a classic Judeophobic stereotype—in order to avoid trouble? There is also a profound contradiction between the demand of "inconspicuousness" to avoid attack and the need to be conspicuous "enough" to provide naches to the parents.

The Jewish mother, in needing to convey and instill irreconcilable assimilationist and counterassimilationist behavior at the same time, resorted to double messages: "Be a scholar, we are the People of the Book, but don't be a bookworm, and get along with the people next door and the other kids"; "Be a go-getter, become a success, but don't offend anybody."

The son was also taught to refrain from boasting and exhibiting arrogance. This was one reason Jewish mothers were/are renowned for not praising their children to their faces (but only behind their backs, to the relatives and neighbors): They didn't want them to "get a swelled head," become unwary, and learn, in turn, to boast of their accomplishments in unsafe places.

BEHAVIOR PATTERNS: INTELLECTUALISM AND EMOTIONALITY

The children absorbed in the home the patterns of verbal expressiveness—emotionality and intellectualism—perpetuated for centuries and carried over from Eastern Europe. In the shtetl, recalled ex-residents, "Everybody in the home is constantly talking with everybody else. . . . Every problem in the family, as in the community, is subject to lengthy discussion . . . and that is impossible without constant disagreement. . . . From the outset of life, the shtetl child associates verbal expression with warmth and security and silence comes to be equated with rejection and coldness."

Most East European Jews believed emotions were made to be expressed, whether in words or tears, both to achieve communication and as a catharsis. Children were expected to cry when hurt or unhappy, and boys were never told to "be brave" or "be a man."

As an oppressed people, Jews have needed to be able to express emotion freely, loudly, and even publicly without embarrassment, shame, or inhibition, and tears are not seen as a loss of control. (Moreover, violence, the other outlet for rage and frustration common under patriarchy, was forbidden.) Victims of catastrophes who express distress have been observed to exhibit less emotional disturbance. Since persecution was a constant and disaster always a possibility, emotional expression had to be an integral part of Jewish behavior so that it would be accessible when needed.

The connection between Jewish emotionality, persecution, and the Jewish passion for music is evident in what Alfred Kazin wrote about his immigrant family. Violin music could "melt their hearts" and bring them to the

> brink of tears. . . . Any slow movement . . . seemed to come to them as a reminiscence of a reminiscence. It seemed to *have something to do with our being Jews.* The depths of Jewish memory the violin could throw open apparently had no limit . . . for all slow movements fell into a single chant . . . of the great *Kol Nidré* . . . in whose long rending cry . . . [was] relived all the *Jews' bitter intimacy with death* [italics mine].

In teaching the expression of emotion, however, the Jewish mother was also teaching a value and behavior pattern that would ultimately impede the son's assimilation. The patriarchal WASP culture, which assimilationist Jews sought to live up to, required restraint of verbal expression of feelings by men to the point of emotional constipation and then allowed their release in physical aggression to the point of a diarrhea of violence.

Jews were constantly being made to feel self-conscious about being "too emotional" and "too loud." The women were especially criticized for their constant expressions of anxiety, of "worrying aloud"—behavior necessary to psychological health in "a people which lives at the best of times in a perpetual, subdued panic."

Jewish intellectual expressiveness—being critical and argumentative and challenging authority—was especially counterindicated in the corporate culture, which, as social analyst Barbara Ehrenreich noted, emphasizes "blind loyalty and intellectual timidity," discounts nonconformity, and "positively scowls at dissent." Israeli Ambassador Zalman Shoval learned just how out of sync Jewish verbal expressiveness was/is with the WASP culture when then-President Bush complained publicly in 1991 about the envoy's frank criticism of administration policy. Commented a political analyst: "In the rough and tumble of Knesset politics, where people scream at each other, to say [as Shoval did of Bush] that 'he is giving us the runaround' is the mildest form of criticism. There was a lesson for him: when you are dealing with *the boys from the country club,* you have to be more polite" (italics mine).

About two and a half decades before this, in the 1960s, radical movements provided young Jews the opportunity to attack the corporate culture that had denigrated their verbally expressive behavior; the human potential movement validated their emotionality. This accounts, in large part, for their attraction to both movements.

INTERDEPENDENCE

In Jewish families there was/is no real emotional separation between the parents, especially the mother, and the children, no matter how old they are. A combination of experiential and psychological factors caused this behavior pattern: the obsession with abandonment; the home-as-haven dynamic; and a long history of continually being uprooted from their surroundings and separated from relatives in their extended families. Jews' weak extended families were further broken down in the nineteenth and twentieth centuries by pogroms and the Holocaust in Europe; dislocations, migrations, and the closing off of U.S. immigration after 1924; and patterns of mobility, geographic and upward, the effect of the latter seen clearly in the 1990 film *Avalon.* In America the nuclear family became especially close precisely because of the absence of a classic extended family in which emotional attachments could be diffused among numerous relatives.

The emotional closeness/bonding of parents and children is also part of Jewish survival strategy. In the nuclear family the child learns the values of mutuality and interdependence, which she or he later carries into and applies to the entire Jewish community, which functions as an extended family. Separation, both in the family and in the community, is regarded as disloyalty and betrayal.

This ethos and the strength of the parent-child bond were important factors in the reluctance of many young Jews during the Holocaust to escape from ghettos and elsewhere and leave their parents behind; in some cases the parents had to push their children to flee. The bond with his mother was the main reason George Clare's father gave for remaining in Vienna when the swastikas were already on the walls. Abba Kovner, a leader in the Vilna Underground, felt enormous guilt to the end of his life for having abandoned his old mother in the ghetto when he escaped to the forest to lead a Jewish partisan unit. More often than not, family members "felt great loyalty to one another and stayed together at whatever price," said survivor Yaffa Eliach. An Auschwitz prisoner whose words were found buried after the war wrote, "This feeling of responsibility . . . turned us into one body." The Germans, of course, used this feeling against the Jews to defuse their suspicions about deportation by announcing that they were being sent to "family camps" where they would all stay together.

The abandonment by Jewish parents of adult children even when they make a mess of their lives is also alien to the normative Jewish experience. One recalls here how Lillian Roth's mother stayed by her side through her descent into and recovery from alcoholism, and how many Jewish parents of heroin addicts do not disown their grown children, either—some even going so far as to support their drug habits to keep them from a life of crime or from prison.

A situation in which children do not see their mothers and fathers for years on end and do not "call in" periodically would provoke separation anxiety in the parents, especially since history has taught Jews to expect impending doom around the corner (which is why a telegram was always expected to contain bad news). This tendency to worry about the children, no matter how old they are, is a factor in the parents' view of their children's occupational choices. A job that necessitates long absences from home and stays in locations that might be at worst dangerous and at best distant from some Jewish community—which ideally could be counted on, as in the past, to provide help in case of trouble—is not regarded as ideal for a nice Jewish boy (nor marriage to a man with such a profession for a nice Jewish girl). But the parents' real longing, to have their children live and work close by, conflicts with their wish to encourage them to choose "portable" occupations and with the American Jewish value placed on material success—going wherever there is a good job offer or business opportunity.

But even more problematic is the conflict between the Jewish value of emotional connectedness and interdependence between parents and children and the American middle-class WASP values of individuality, independence, and of the children's eventual separation from their parents. In WASP culture, "the core of the stance of being is an 'I' geared toward autonomy, self-respect and self-individuation," said psychologist Esther Perel. In the Jewish family, by contrast, "a major idea is [that of] interdependence, that what one does has implications for others." The mental health profession, which accepts the WASP value system, pathologizes behavior that is in fact normative in Jewish culture, including "fuzzy boundaries" between the self, the family, and the community.

THE APRON STRINGS

A period of adolescent transition to adulthood, when boys studied Torah (with adult support) or a trade (as apprentices), was not, as we have seen in preceding chapters, an invention of East European immigrants but characterized much of European Jewish history. Nor was this adolescent transition characterized by any "overprotectiveness" of the boy by his mother. This was especially true in the shtetl, where, former residents recalled, even children were "hurried out of baby-hood [and] urged to 'be a mentsch.'" In fact the overworked and overburdened mother of the shtetl could not always have been physically or emotionally avail-able to her children, indulgent of their whims, "overprotective," or wrapped up in their emotional lives even if she had wanted to be.

In America, where poor immigrants saw themselves as a temporary prole-tariat, the only way the son would not "work in the shop" all his life was if he re-ceived a higher secular education. This required his being given financial and emotional support by his parents during a prolonged period of study. Although many men—and women—studied in night school, the ideal was to relieve the sons of household chores, and sometimes even of responsibility for supplementing family income by after-school work, in order to allow them time and opportunity to study.

But for an adolescent boy not to go to work was contrary to the ethos and experience of the non-Jewish working class in the immigrant period. Growing up in working-class neighborhoods, Jewish boys saw their non-Jewish peers holding jobs, living up to their definition of masculinity—and being rewarded with money for nice clothes and other material goodies, plus free time to have fun. The pull in that direction was tremendous.

The boy therefore had to be kept away from "outside influence which might lure him into abandoning long-run plans for more immediate pleasures and re-wards," in Zena Blau Smith's words. (This dovetailed with the delayed gratification pattern of behavior that has long permeated Jewish life.)

It required enormous psychological strength on the part of the mother to en-sure that the boy resist this siren call. It was she who did to her son what Ulysses had done to himself: She bound him to a post to prevent his following the siren. And that post was . . . herself. She tied him to her "with her apron strings" (as the phrase went) and pulled them tight.

This pattern, once set, continued even after the parental anxiety about working-class peer influence ceased among the many Jews who moved to the suburbs and entered the middle class after World War II. Jews came to fear other kinds of peer pressures on their children, and mothers used apron-string bonding to try to overcome them.

❧ Apron-string bonding was the means by which the mother delayed the son's independence (albeit temporarily). The son identified delay of independence with/as "infantilization," especially when he contrasted it with the autonomy of his non-Jewish peers.

However, apron-string bonding was actually superimposed on the traditional generic bonding, described previously, that created interdependence between parents and children, behavior the mother also continued to instill. It was impossible for the son to discern where one type of bonding left off and the other began, and the two types became intermeshed in his mind. All bonding consequently became associated with "infantilization." Since independence was a prime element in the American definition of masculinity, the son believed that the only way to become a man was to cut the emotional bonds with his mother. Retaining these bonds would, he felt, make him a mama's boy. The mother experienced as separation the son's struggle to break what *she* considered generic bonding. She tried with every fiber of her being to maintain the bonds.

Since emotional separation usually proves to be impossible, many Jewish sons have attempted to separate themselves geographically from their parents, especially their mothers. Even this doesn't provide distance in the age of the telephone ("Why don't you ever call me?"). In too many cases, however, the final step is abandonment of the parents. The old neighborhoods of New York, Los Angeles, and Miami—vermin-infested and crime-plagued slums—are full of elderly Jews who supplement their Social Security checks by rummaging in garbage cans for half-eaten sandwiches. Their yuppie children, meanwhile, are luxuriating in split-level suburban homes hundreds of miles away, tossing the leftovers of five-course dinners into their garbage disposals. Since this abandonment obviously violates the nonseparation ethos, it is usually "justified" by the denigration of this ethos and the Jewish value system it is part of and of the parents, especially the mother who instilled it, as we shall see presently.

◆ The methodology of apron-string bonding involved the use of guilt. The mother felt she needed to find a source of power to control a situation in which she had total responsibility for the son's socialization but less control over its success because of the outside world's negative reinforcement (in contrast with the positive reinforcement the traditional community had once provided). The source of power she seized upon, guilt, is a tool that is sometimes used by the powerless to manipulate and control the behavior of an individual on whom their lives depend. This methodology, born of desperation, was an unfortunate choice that would generate an endless power struggle between mother and son.

The child was taught that doing something the mother disapproved of or refusing to do something she wanted would cause her pain, and to feel guilty for causing her pain. Only by complying could the child avoid the nasty, uncomfortable feeling of guilt. "You're killing me" was one of the mother's favorite lines. (The daughter was also apt to hear the ominous warning, "Wait until *you* have children.")

Irving Howe recounted how a Lower East Side mother reacted when she found her son, Alter, playing ball on the street. "Alter, Alter," she cried, "what will become of you? You'll end up a street bum!" Later, when Alter broke his leg, his mother wept before him in the hospital: "Alter, Alter, do you want to kill me?"

Thus the son's consciousness of his mother's feelings was linked to recognition of *her dependence on him and on his achievements for her validation and even for life itself.* This gave the son, in whom so much was invested—and on the minutiae of whose behavior so much attention was focused—tremendous power.

His chief weapon, learned practically from infancy, was withholding and withdrawal. He had observed how "withdrawal is felt as an attack"; how his parents and relatives used the "silent treatment" to torment each other; and he had experienced the form of punishment they used for children's misbehavior: sending them away from other people. Having learned this withholding technique, he used it to get his way.

As in the shtetl, he could coerce adults into "yielding on almost any point by refusing to eat" because food was a symbol of love and was the key to physical survival. This behavior metastasized to refusing to do homework or to practice the violin. Such actions could set off a series of fevered and histrionic scenes—punctuated by the mother's crying, nagging, hand-wringing, and guilt inducing—that writers of four-handkerchief Yiddish plays had only to quote verbatim to evoke high drama on the stage and wrest copious tears from the audience. Later on in life, a Jewish child's becoming a hippie or otherwise dropping out of the rat race or marrying an "unsuitable" person could propel Jewish parents, especially mothers, into despair and deep shame—and more guilt inducing ("After all I've sacrificed for you, this is how you repay me?!").

Using guilt—along with the Chinese water torture of incessant nagging—worked to create compliance. This was a Pyrrhic victory because it created a selfish rather than an altruistic personality in the son. One cannot raise a child to think only of himself and his effect on others and to interpret interdependence in terms of his power over them, to have everything revolve around his existence from day one, and to give him the weapon of withholding and withdrawal—and then expect him to emerge an altruistic adult like Athena from the head of Zeus. The American Jewish mother thus inadvertently and with the best of intentions created her own Frankenstein's monster.

FACE VALUE: CONFLICTS IN RAISING THE DAUGHTER

The strategy of delaying the son's "independence" to allow/compel him to study did not apply to the daughter. The mother in the immigrant generations did not need to encourage her daughter to study. Many young Jewish women desperately tried to pursue study and were often compelled to abandon this dream and go to work to earn money to help support the family and put their brothers through school.

Not only was there no need to delay the daughter's adulthood, but the situation was quite the opposite: She was propelled into it prematurely by the family's need for her earnings. One woman who had immigrated in the early 1900s told an interviewer eighty years later, "We were grown-ups at a very early age; our childhood was short." Working for pay led the young women to think of themselves and to be treated by their parents as "autonomous adults," commented Sydney Stahl Weinberg after analyzing immigrant interviews and memoirs.

Immigrant mothers were often ambivalent if a daughter displayed an appetite for education. One woman recollected that "when I sat reading until two or three or four o'clock in the morning, my mother used to . . . come into the dining room to say, 'The light is still on. I thought you were asleep a long time already! What do you expect to be, a doctor or a lawyer? What's the use of all this reading and writing? Don't be foolish, a woman never needs to know anything.' But under her breath I would hear her mutter, 'A talented child has hands of gold.'"

Thus, on the one hand, immigrant mothers were proud that their daughters were doing something that they themselves had been unable to do. But, on the other hand, they wished to discourage the daughters' pursuit of higher education so they would go to work. The compromise was to direct the daughters' desire for education into a practical channel: to learn skills that would get them jobs outside the sweatshops—as secretaries, sales clerks, teachers, and nurses. Training for these jobs also functioned as insurance "in case anything happened" to the husband. It also allowed the daughters to contribute more income to the family kitty.

The mother also discouraged her daughter's attending college—she felt it would impede a "good match." Fannie Hurst's aunt, for example, advised, "Don't educate yourself into a bluestocking. The more you know, the less desirable you become to men. They want a homemaker, not a superior mind." And, indeed, many of the men objected to their wives' continuing their education. One woman wrote in despair in 1910 to the *Bintel Brief* (Yiddish for bundle of letters) advice column of the *Forverts* (Yiddish daily *Forward*) to ask "whether a married woman has the right to go to school two evenings a week. My husband thinks I have no right to do this. . . . He is in favor of the emancipation of women, yet in real life, he acts contrary to his beliefs."

❧ This motivation brings us to the prime concern of the Jewish mother, especially from the 1920s through the 1960s: to mold her daughter into a marriageable female. Since the men were increasingly seeking women who fulfilled the majority culture's ideal of beauty and middle-class "ladylike" behavior, the daughter had to be trained to fulfill these assimilationist criteria.

In regard to beauty, the mother of the immigrant generations was generally too preoccupied with work and with her son(s) to pay a great deal of attention to the daughter's looks, and it was the latter who picked up quickly on the dress and hairstyles of the day. In subsequent generations, the daughter's attractiveness became a priority for the mother.

Until the 1920s there was no great disparity between the shtetl ideal of the *zaftig* (complimentary Yiddish term for full-figured) woman and the American ideal. And, indeed, immigrant children of both genders were encouraged to be fat as a perceived prophylactic against the dreaded "workers' disease" of TB. But in the 1920s, thin became fashionable, and after World War II, especially, many mothers became obsessed with their daughters' weight. The struggle over it often became a flash point of the mother-daughter conflict in America. Having a fat daughter meant the mother had failed to mold the girl to be marriageable and had therefore failed as a mother.

Being thin is a form of assimilation in several respects: living up to the American ideal of beauty, fitting in, and acceding to invisibility. It is perhaps not too surprising that the founder of Weight Watchers was a Jewish woman.

Female thinness is an American obsession that deserves the kind of in-depth feminist analysis that is outside the scope of this work. For our purposes here, however, it is important to note that thinness is a form of/step toward invisibility. As a woman becomes thinner and thinner, she takes up less space and her public presence is thus diminished, as well. Thinness is a symbolic attempt to reduce the woman's weight in order to reduce her visible public presence (and her "throwing her weight around"). This approach has existed since the onset of women's public visibility after World War I. In its current incarnation (the majority culture's body-size ideal has descended from size twelve in the 1950s to size six or even below in the 1990s), thinness is an important weapon in the backlash against the feminist movement, which has strived to make women visible—and heard—in society.

A Jewish daughter's being fat is a rejection of the invisibility the general society wishes to impose on women and has required of Jews. As a member of both groups, the Jewish woman has faced the usual double jeopardy, just as she did in the case of rape by non-Jewish men and job discrimination. Like the requirement that Jews be "inconspicuous," a Jewish woman's being thin has been experienced as a survival strategy: If she looks like everyone else and thus does not stand out, she will not be attacked.

Jewish mothers, especially from the post–World War II period, when assimilationism accelerated, tried to make sure that the daughter did not stand out in this regard, not physically (by being fat) or psychologically (by thus appearing to rebel against the majority culture and its ideals and demands). Even poet Kim Chernin's mother, an immigrant active in radical causes, said the reason she had raised her daughter to be thin was to enable her to fit into society (as the mother had not done).

❧ Feminine behavior according to the American middle-class definition began to be regarded by Jews as desirable in women primarily after World War I. A columnist for the women's page of the *Forverts* advised her readers in 1919 to give up the "outspoken" female behavior of the shtetl and tenement and adopt the "more subdued behavior of the idealized middle class American lady."

The major problem in raising the daughter to be feminine in behavior was that it was in stark opposition to an equally important (if not more important) need: to train her to be strong and resourceful, able to cope effectively with the multiple crises that the Jewish family faced, including the inability of some of the men to be "good providers." The daughter also had to be trained to be an enabler who would not only take the initiative in resolving such crises but who would also be assertive "enough" as a mother to push her son to study and attain material success.

Another problem was that the men who yearned for feminine wives were also aware of the value of having assertive and strong enablers as partners. Their own mothers, having been strong personalities, left an indelible image of what a model wife should be: assertive and outspoken with her husband, demanding of her sons, and bossy with her daughters. And this model was obviously not the ideal American middle-class feminine wife—acquiescent, quiet, subservient. The mother thus had to try to instill in her daughter two sets of obviously incompatible behavior.

Moreover, she had to impart to her daughter the various Jewish values, survival strategies, and behavior patterns we discussed previously. The girl would then be able, in turn, to pass them on to her children to ensure their success and thereby succeed herself as a mother. In the case of some of the values and survival strategies, the daughter did not face the same conflicts that the son did. Since altruism, mutuality, compassion, and cooperation were Jewish as well as female values, the daughter's behaving in accordance with these normative elements of the definition of femininity was a continuity with her socialization rather than discontinuity. Similarly, many of the Jewish survival strategies were also transferable to public feminine behavior: "Don't push yourself in where you're not wanted," always be careful and know whom to trust, and, above all, don't be "conspicuous," boastful, or arrogant.

Two major Jewish behavior patterns that were incompatible with ideal American feminine behavior were "excess" emotionalism and intellectual expressiveness. Feminine women in America were allowed to express only certain types of emotion, such as grief, and then only quietly and with "dignity" and restraint and only in the private sphere. They were not supposed to express anger or to complain, especially not in public. Therefore, while Jewish mothers were teaching their children the survival behavior of emotional expressiveness, they were also trying to tone down the daughters so assimilating Jewish men would not accuse them of being "Jewish fishwives" and *yentas* (Yiddish for loud, gossipy, opinionated busybodies).

The Jewish woman had traditionally been excluded from Jewish learning. But the patterns of expression that had characterized it and Jewish life, home and communal, had been part of her behavior, especially in Eastern Europe. This intellectual expressiveness—being argumentative and critical, engaging in debate (especially at high decibel levels)—however, was also not considered feminine behavior. Even the *Forverts,* a Socialist newspaper that encouraged women to be active in politics and in unions, advised them to be "quiet rather than talkative, agreeable rather than argumentative" and not to "dispute every point" in a conversation.

Thus the mother had to teach her daughter to value intellectual expressiveness so she could transmit this behavior to her sons and create a home where books and ideas were important but to refrain from engaging in it herself.

In raising their daughters to live up to all these contradictory demands, Jewish mothers had to weave back and forth over very fine and shifting boundaries. Their methodology involved transmitting double messages, as it did with their sons. They tried to teach their daughters to be smart enough to appreciate the man's brilliance but not "too" smart to challenge it ("Why win the argument and lose the man?"); to be resourceful without appearing dominating; to be a partner to the husband but subtle about it ("Build him up, don't throw failure in his face"); to be concerned about the man's physical well-being but not "too" concerned so as to trigger anxieties about "infantilization." The American Jewish woman would have to try to walk the tightrope suspended above this minefield without a net, knowing that any misstep would lead to her fall/failure—and then face accusations from the men of being "nervous," "too serious," and "too intense," especially in comparison with non-Jewish women, whom the men perceived as being "fun."

✦ The mother also tried to discourage her daughter's sexual emancipation. The fear was that she would be propelled into premature (i.e., premarital) sexual experiences that could preclude a "good marriage" in a society (Jewish and non-Jewish) that valued a bride's "reputation" (i.e., virginity). The value placed on reputation existed side by side with the liberalization of sexual attitudes that began in the 1920s and that found expression in the acceptance of marriages based on love and of nonchaperoned dating.

Here, again, the siren call of the general society was fierce and so was the mother's resistance to it. As with the son, her methodology involved the use of guilt, interminable nagging, and the variation of apron-string bonding many Jewish women have called the Inquisition (where are you going, who is this boy, what does he do, what kind of family does he come from). Unlike the anomalous mother in the 1987 film *Dirty Dancing*, most Jewish women rigorously monitored their daughters' comings and goings; they did not need to be asked at 10:00 P.M., "Do you know where your children are?"

Their nagging involved incessant reminders of the primacy of marriage and children and of making a suitable marriage ("It's just as easy to love a rich man as a poor man"). Remaining single was unacceptable: One would be "alone like a stone" (this also applied to men). Women unmarried past their early twenties were pitied and scorned as old maids; married women without children were bombarded with pronatalist propaganda; single motherhood and divorce were stigmatized; and lesbianism was considered beyond the pale and its very existence was often vehemently denied.

Although these attitudes also prevailed through the mid-1960s in the general society, especially among European immigrant subcultures, there were some important differences in the Jewish spin on them. One was that marriage, and especially having children, was propagandized as being "good for the Jews." Thus a young woman who rejected marriage with children was made to feel guilty for having betrayed the entire Jewish nation. This attitude, parenthetically, allowed Jewish communal "leaders" of the 1970s to attack feminism as antifamily and therefore inimical to Jewish survival, as we shall see in chapter 16.

Even a Jewish woman's premarital loss of virginity was considered a betrayal of the Jews. This message was conveyed clearly in *Marjorie Morningstar*. Marjorie's deflowering is portrayed as a surrender to the assimilationist propaganda Noel has harangued her with for two-thirds of the novel. Her seduction is pictured as leaving her bereft of her Jewish identity along with her hymen. Significantly, Marjorie rejects her lover after an intensely emotional encounter with a rescuer of German Jews casts an extremely negative light on Noel's lack of Jewish consciousness. Having retrieved her Jewish identity, she is able to transform herself into a born-again altruistic-assertive enabler and a transmitter of Jewish culture in the home.

Finally, a prerequisite for making a "good marriage" from the mid-1940s on was that a girl be popular. In the 1950s, a change occurred in the Jewish family's attitude toward the daughter's higher education: She was encouraged to go to college—to "get her MRS. degree." Now the daughter was pushed to get good grades in high school in order to qualify for admission to a good college. This created a conflict with the sexist norms of the general society, which regarded academic excellence as unfeminine. Those who attained it were unpopular with their female and male peers, especially with the intellectually competitive Jewish boys.

The Jewish adolescent female found herself torn apart by the requirement to be both popular and get high grades—even though academic success precluded popularity—because both were prerequisites for a suitable marriage. She also found herself in perpetual conflict with her mother over how far to go in either direction before hitting one or the other polar extreme—being called a tramp or a greasy grind. Girls who veered too much in either direction had to be worn down by the Chinese water torture of relentless nagging.

The conflict between mother and daughter, however tortured, did not escalate into the kind of power struggle that prevailed between mother and son. Because independence was not part of the American definition of femininity (as it was with masculinity), the daughter did not feel desperate about cutting the apron strings, although she may have tried to evade/escape her mother's iron control. She could live up to the Jewish value of interdependence/lack of separation because femininity mandated retaining rather than breaking emotional bonds with her mother. (The mental health profession, however, stigmatizes such closeness as unhealthy, a sign that the women are "too enmeshed," said Paula Caplan.) As with most descendants of European immigrants, it is the daughter and not the son who takes the prime responsibility for the care of the mother—and the father—in their old age.

❧ The American ideals of beauty and behavior have proved difficult and sometimes impossible for Jewish women to live up to. They often induce hyperstrenuous efforts at "self-improvement." A Jewish woman might manage not to be "overweight," she might bleach and tame her curly dark hair and round off her nose, but, as one young student said, "If the Jewish woman has to do all these things to be beautiful, the implication is that otherwise she is ugly." And the assertive and expressive behavior she learned in childhood, despite her mother's attempt to tone it down, is even harder to uproot than her Bronx/Brooklyn accent and her "excessive" body hair. The result is that validation for her successful assimilation in regard to the majority culture's standards of femininity is very hard to come by in the general society.

WHAT MAKES SAMMY SPRINT? (RUNNING IS NO LONGER ENOUGH)

In the past, as long as a man behaved in accordance with the community's norms, it validated his masculinity. In America, however, the man's validation was less assured because living up to the American definition of masculinity by attaining material success did not depend on his actions alone but also on circumstances beyond his control, such as a business's fortunes, a company's discriminatory hiring policies, or the stock market's gyrations. In the past a Jewish man might have lost his livelihood, but would not have been consequently deprived of validation of his masculinity, because success at breadwinning did not define it, Torah study did.

Moreover, material success fluctuates, which means that it and his masculinity *can never be finally and conclusively validated* (just as Israeli men's masculinity depends on the fluctuating success of the army and can never be conclusively validated, either). It is no wonder, then, that when Ed Koch was mayor of New York he was constantly asking, "How am I doing?" His unending quest for instant and constant validation was rooted not so much in his being an elected official concerned about popularity with voters but in the anxiety about the solidity of their material success and status common to Jewish men in America.

Another central problem with attaining validation is that it would ideally have to come from the non-Jewish men of their middle-class reference group. This, however, has collided with the requirement that Jews be "inconspicuous." American Jewish men are trapped between the Scylla of their desire to maintain a low profile so they will not be the objects of attack (leading to the possible loss of the material gains they had obtained); and the Charybdis of their equally strong yearning for validation, which requires a high profile.

Given this situation, Jewish men have tended to look to other Jewish men for validation. A man's sense of masculinity depends on how well he and they believe he is measuring up to the reference group's definition of material success in comparison with them. This makes Jewish men very competitive with each other in school, business and professional life, and in communal volunteer work.

✦ Many Jewish immigrants (and their descendants in the interbellum period) who rejected the value of material success as an ideal and as a sign of self-worth were drawn to Socialism. The goals of the Socialist movement seemed consonant with traditional Jewish messianism, and the movement embodied many of the traditional Jewish/female values that had characterized East European communities, as did some of the unions. Socialism became for many Jews a form of spiritual resistance to the crass materialism and heartlessness of American capitalism and was seen as the instrumentality for creating a just society. Socialism also provided men an alternative definition of masculinity: movement or union activist. This, of course, created the same kind of problems for the women activists as were experienced by the chalutzot in Eretz Israel in that same (pre–World War II) era.

The collapse of the Socialist movement in the 1950s left the men without a counterforce to the pressures, especially those coming from inside the community, to fall in line with the ideal of material success and status. (It also left Jews even more vulnerable to the pressures to assimilate, since the Socialists had previously constituted a strong anti-assimilationist presence in the Jewish community.)

The definition of manhood in terms of material success and the pressures on men to live up to it take their greatest toll on the men who have not made it (and on their families). Exhibiting a profound sense of failure, "they literally gag under the enormous pressure on Jewish males to succeed in this country," wrote Mary Cahn Schwartz, a social worker formerly with a Jewish family agency. "'There goes my son the doctor,' 'That's no profession for a nice Jewish boy' are gag lines . . . that give the clear message of the kind of financial and intellectual standards that are expected. . . . Given their culture, they are not mentsches, they are schleps and they know it."

It is not only these men and their families who feel a sense of shame at their "failure" but also the male-dominated Jewish community. The men are still overly sensitive about being "good providers," a role Jewish husbands had not fulfilled in the shtetl and that some had failed to fulfill in the first few generations after immigration. The shame about the "unsuccessful" men in their midst was so intense in the 1960s and 1970s that the community denied the existence of eight hundred thousand poor American Jews. When Ann Wolfe of the American Jewish Committee broke communal silence on Jewish poverty in 1971, she was excoriated by heads of other Jewish agencies for doing so.

LONGING FOR LOCKER-ROOM ACCEPTANCE

No matter how materially successful Jewish men may be, they feel insecure about their manhood because the American definition of masculinity they have internalized also includes ideal physical looks and behavior they feel/fear they cannot live up to. In America the majority cultural ideal requires a man to look like a jock—healthy ("fit"), strong and tough, able to take care of himself in a barroom brawl of the Wild West variety—and to act accordingly.

Jewish boys of the first immigration generations saw their non-Jewish peers in the neighborhood engage in a great deal of physical aggression (some of it aimed at them). Later on, the movies—produced by Jews who, in their classic role of cultural intermediary, promoted the values of the general society—and TV inundated them with images of how "real" men were supposed to look and behave.

Their attraction to the jock image manifested itself in their admiration, especially in the 1920s, of athletics and physical prowess, of circus strongmen, baseball players, and boxers (among them several Jews). Even as late as 1975, a former Jewish boxer said about prizefighter Mike Rossman (a.k.a. The Jewish Bomber): "He's tough. And he's Jewish. That makes me feel good. Everyone says Jews are pussies. . . . This Rossman ain't no pussy. No one is ever going to call him a dirty Jew. Because this dirty Jew can fight." After Rossman won a bout, a Jewish deli worker came over to thank the boxer for "*not being a nice Jewish boy* in the ring" (italics mine).

Having internalized the John Wayne images from the mass media, Jewish men today long to be accepted in the locker room as much as they yearn to be accepted in the boardroom. But they have also internalized the lessons, taught by their mothers, to devalue physicality and to refrain from physical aggression.

Physicality had long been downgraded in Jewish life, partly because it was regarded as a distraction from spiritual resistance and partly because it was regarded as a prerequisite for physical aggression, which was prohibited. In the shtetl, especially, the ideal was to be—and look—unphysical, and this ideal was "associated not with physical weakness but with spiritual vigor," wrote Zborowski and Herzog. This attitude toward physicality—and the proscription of violence—continued in America. A common admonishment in East European and American Jewish immigrant homes was *Nit mit dee hent* (Yiddish, lit., not with the hands, i.e., use words, not bodily force, to strike a blow).

Jewish boys today have continued to be taught an aversion to violence and they have learned to be careful, to play their cards close to the chest, to watch their backs, stay out of trouble, and be "inconspicuous"—and this in a society that glorifies high-profile male initiative and aggression! The son could never really charge full steam ahead without that nagging little voice in his head (his mother's voice) saying, "Are you really sure you're doing the right thing?"—causing him to do what his mother once did: pull in the reins. Thus the more a man behaves as

Jews are programmed to behave (in order to live up to the material success part of the definition of masculinity), the less he is able to feel he has lived up to the aggressiveness part of the definition. To quote Portnoy's interminable dirge to his silent shrink:

> "I am the son in the Jewish joke—only it ain't no joke! Please, who . . . made us so morbid and hysterical and *weak?* Why, why are they screaming still, 'Watch out! Don't do it! Alex—no!'. . . Doctor, what do you call this sickness I have? Is this the Jewish suffering [that] . . . has come down to me from the pogroms and the persecution? . . . Doctor, I can't stand any more being frightened like this. . . . Make me brave! Make me strong!. . . *Bless me with manhood!*" [italics mine].

MATRIPHOBIA

Since material success (inconclusively validated) and physical aggression (proscribed) are what define American manhood and, along with the domination of "his" women, make a man "sexy," Jewish men have experienced tremendous sexual inferiority. They know that their public image, like that of Asian American men, is "smart but wimpy," and they have internalized it. They "rarely employ the attributes of masculine, sexual, hot-blooded, and virile in describing themselves," observed Esther Perel. (These hang-ups may be one reason why the works of I. B. Singer, which show Jewish men—and women—as very sexy, are so popular.)

Many Jewish men blame their mothers for their sexual insecurities and are deeply angry at them for having trained them to behave in such a way as to preclude the validation of their masculinity. They feel it was their mothers who had made them into what the general society derides as wimps and nerds, thereby emasculating them. The four American Jewish authors of the 1978 "Holocaust" TV miniseries expressed this resentment when they had Inge (the "good shiksa") say to the artistic Karl, "That proper mother of yours, *she took the fight out of you*" (italics mine).

The son, having learned in childhood how to deploy the powerful weapon of withholding to get his way, to get attention, or to get even, armed it in adulthood with a nuclear warhead: withholding the validation that Jewish mothers had traditionally received for contributing to a son's success. Knowing how much public validation meant to her—how many times had he heard in childhood, "What will the neighbors say?"—he shamed his mother in public with Jewish mother "jokes" portraying her as an overbearing, pushy and controlling (a recycling of classic Judeophobic stereotypes), demanding, "overprotective," humorless *kvetch* (Yiddish for incessant complainer).

Woody Allen's omnipresent Jewish mother character who hounds her son from the sky in *Oedipus Wrecks,* while extreme in its matriphobia, is by no means a unique example of Jewish men's depiction of the Jewish mother as nagging, domineering, and infantilizing. Dan Greenburg filled his entire 1964 best seller *How to Be a Jewish Mother* with nasty libels along these lines masquerading as "jokes." Possibly the saddest thing about the book is the foreword by the author's mother, Leah Greenburg: "I only hope you will like the book" (she is still invested in her son's success, no matter how it came about). Some twenty-two years later, still in denial, she told an interviewer that "the mother [portrayed] in the book *wasn't like me*" (italics mine).

The baleboosta also came in for severe criticism. Myron Kaufman, in his 1957 novel *Remember Me to God,* compared her unfavorably with the WASP ideal: "You hesitate to invite a friend for dinner because you know she will make a whole operation out of it, and spend two days cleaning and cooking too much stuff and worrying.... A Yankee mother ... if the house is a little dusty, she still enjoys life."

This comment points to the connection between assimilationism and the insulting of Jewish mothers through so-called jokes and in other ways. Neither of these phenomena occurred among working-class men, who tried to hold on to their Yiddish culture into the early 1950s. Alfred Kazin, for example, wrote of his admiration for his mother, a home dressmaker: "Year by year, as I began to take in her fantastic capacity for labor and her anxious zeal, I realized it was ourselves she kept stitched together." Even more poignant is Michael Gold's paean to his "little East Side mother":

> She was proud of the fact that she could work hard.... She had a strong sense of reality.... How can I ever forget this dark little woman with bright eyes ... busy from morn to midnight in the tenement struggle for life. She would have stolen or killed for us. She would have let a railroad train run over her body if it could have helped us. She loved us all with the fierce painful love of a mother-wolf.... Mother! Momma!... I cannot forget you. I must remain faithful to the poor because I cannot be faithless to you!... The world must be made gracious for the poor! Momma, you taught me that!

The Jewish mother "jokes" were a phenomenon of men who were making it into the middle class who felt that their mothers had impeded their assimilation by the behavior they had imparted. These men were also embarrassed by the vestiges of anti-assimilationist behavior in the women, another variation of the anti-*Ostjuden* syndrome. The "jokes" were/are a pathetic and cruel attempt finally to separate from their mothers by denigrating them and their values.

A final note here: not only have no men of other ethnic groups insulted their mothers publicly, but never before in history have Jewish men publicly proclaimed hostility toward the women who made so many sacrifices to enable them to "make something of themselves."

◆❧ Libels/slanders about Jewish mothers as demanding, pushy, and aggressive have also sent messages to Jewish women to behave unlike them lest they, too, be smeared with this negative stereotype. Wouk's assimilationist antihero Noel Airman (the surname is a literal translation of the Yiddish *luftmentsch,* Nordau's term that came to mean a man who stumbles from one airhead castles-in-the-sky scheme to another) warns Marjorie of the dire fate awaiting her should she fail to reject her mother's bourgeois behavior: "I went out with Shirley after Shirley. . . . The respectable girl . . . all tricked out to appear gay and girlish and carefree, but . . . behind her, half the time, would loom *her mother, the frightful giveaway* . . . showing the grim horrid respectable *determined* dullness" (italics mine).

The men also projected their insecurities about not being sexy onto their Jewish wives and lovers, who, as they saw it, picked up where Mom left off (as did the young woman in *Oedipus Wrecks*). The projections reached their apotheosis in the "Jewish American Princess" ("JAP") libel/slander (to be discussed in detail in the next chapter), which stereotypes the Jewish woman as overwhelmingly materialistic, haughty, and sexually frigid once married. What the Jewish man is trying to express through this slander is this: It is not that he is not materially successful "enough"—no man could measure up to *her* hypermaterialistic criteria. It is not that he is not aggressive "enough"—it is *she* who is too pushy. It is not that he is unable to dominate—it is *she* who is indomitable/domineering. It is not that he is not sexy—she is the one who is frigid; no man could be sexy with her.

Jewish men have also deployed the "JAP" stereotype to rationalize exogamy. Their sexual insecurities cause them to yearn all the more for feminine women whose acquisition would constitute validation of their masculinity (if you can keep a "real" woman, you must be a "real" man). Their perception of non-Jewish white and Asian women as really feminine is another reason intermarriage is so attractive to Jewish men (its overall rate increased by the 1990s to about 50 percent).

JETTISONING JEWISHNESS

Since the son's struggles over achievement, success, and the definition and validation of masculinity are so painful, and since the family he has grown up in identifies itself, however vaguely and tenuously, as Jewish, he tends to believe that the cause of his angst are the Jewish values, survival strategies, and behavior patterns he learned in his family. These are viewed negatively by the reference group whose values he has also internalized.

But the values that are really at the root of the problem are not the Jewish ones. Traditional Jewish life never made material success an ideal or the basis of a definition of manhood. These alien values, however, were identified by many Jewish men as Jewish *and American Jewish.* Lacking the kind of in-depth, comprehensive Jewish education that could provide an understanding of which values are

Jewish and which not, they attribute their pain to their Jewishness. They seek to escape it, thinking they will thereby divest themselves of all the anguish they believe it causes. Since they internalized some of the old Jewish values and behavior patterns during the socialization process, what they wish to excise are those parts of themselves they consider Jewish. Insulting the Jewish mother through "jokes" is an attempt to legitimize this effort. The more un-American they make her appear, the more justification they have for excising the heart of Jewishness that she stands for, the values and behavior they learned from her that impede their becoming "real" American men.

TEN ❧ THE ROOTS AND MARITAL
REPERCUSSIONS OF LOW SELF-ESTEEM

*The blind adoration bestowed on gifted children by Jewish parents
who had divested themselves of the fear of God and had not yet
developed any deep impersonal loyalties and therefore
concentrated all their sentiment on the worship of their offspring,
has contributed not a little to fostering that type of extremely
egocentric Jew who expects all men [sic] to burn incense at his feet
and treats the world as a stage to perform and astonish upon.*

JACOB TALMON

The lack of validation of Jewish women and men in/by the general society for living up to its prescribed gender roles and other standards of behavior causes many
to experience low self-esteem. The central questions that require exploration are
how and why such outside validation came to be regarded as the main source of
their self-esteem and what precisely in the Jewish socialization process sets this
dynamic in motion. To seek answers, we first need to look at traditional Jewish
child rearing and how it changed in the modern era, and at how and why it has
differed from child rearing in classic patriarchies.

We should begin by noting that the formation of self-esteem in a child is a
complex process that involves two primary elements: a sense of being capable of
surviving and flourishing, derived from the parents' validation of the child's approved behavior; and a feeling that one deserves to be alive, derived from the parents' expression of unconditional love. A division of labor along gender lines
determines which parent provides each of these components.

The parent who provides (or withholds) validation of prescribed normative
behavior functions in the home as surrogate of the society, its demands, and its
challenges; and of the family's reference group, and its responses to these challenges, its normative standards of how to live in the society. In preliterate,
small/isolated, and most agrarian communities, the society itself was the reference group. In modern societies, the reference group is usually the family's class
and/or ethnic group.

In traditional patriarchal families, where the father is the prime breadwinner,
he fulfills this surrogate role. He teaches the son survival strategies, which in

most premodern societies included work skills, as well as the standards, values, and behavior the boy will have to live up to: He "brings the son into the world." He also provides validation and metes out punishment. The father's love is thus seen by psychologists as conditional upon behavior.

In relation to his daughter, the classic patriarchal father represents the men of the society and their demands, which she will have to deal with in the future. The mother is the surrogate of the reference group in training the girl in culturally appropriate responses to the society's norms (via behavior *and* survival strategies). The daughter then practices these responses—being useful, coy/manipulative, and often flirtatious—on her father, who validates her by his praise and presents. The mother also trains the daughter to be an enabler (in large part by modeling the role), which always includes running a household.

In addition, the classic mother under patriarchy serves as family ameliorator and as intermediary between the father and the children, trying to shield the children from the father's punishment or to mitigate it. The mother's love is usually characterized by psychologists as unconditional—it does not depend on the children's performance.

When children approach adolescence, they begin the process of individuation/differentiation from the parent of the same gender. Various societies sidestep or mitigate the individuation struggle by providing a rite of passage—for the boy, usually a task he must carry out; for the girl, a ceremony around menarche and/or marriage. The rite transforms the child into an adult, thereby changing the relationship with the parents as well.

THE JEWISH PARENT AS SURROGATE

The Jewish experience differed in that Jews have always lived in two different worlds—the general society and the Jewish community, each with a different culture: different value systems, lifestyles, customs, and behavior patterns.

As long as Jews lived among other Jews in an autonomous community—Jewish quarter, ghetto, shtetl—that small community was their society and their reference group. The parent who functioned as the surrogate of the community represented its challenges and taught the children its values and behavior patterns to enable them to live *as Jews* inside the community—the main milieu for the public expression of Jewishness. The parent surrogate of the community also imparted its survival strategies for responding to the challenges of the general society, which primarily involved physical survival and breadwinning.

Jews looked to the community to validate their behavior. But even if they lived (or traveled) far from a Jewish community, they could evaluate their own behavior by how (well) they lived up to its norms. In the words of *Pirké Avot* (Sayings of the Sages), "In a place where there is no human being," (i.e., mentsch), "try to be a human being." Jews therefore did not look to the general society or any of its classes as their reference group, nor did they wish for or expect validation from them for living up to their norms, including gender role definitions.

In traditional West European and Sephardic Jewish communities, it was the father, as prime breadwinner, who served as the surrogate of the community and of its responses to the general society. The father "brought the son into the world" of the community. He studied with the boy and/or quizzed him on his progress, taught him Jewish religious practices (such as putting on tefillin), and had him sit by his side in the synagogue to learn the prayers. He also taught the son a trade or arranged his apprenticeship or instructed him in the family business.

The father, like the community itself, was unable to offer the children physical protection from outside attack. He certainly could not protect his daughter (or wife) from rape by non-Jewish men, as we have seen. The father's unprotective behavior in this regard prepared the daughter not to expect rescue by her husband or male relatives, either.

The mother taught the daughter how to be an altruistic-assertive enabler. Traditional Jewish standards of modesty and the concomitant damper placed on physical demonstrations of affection generally precluded the girl's practicing the classic female strategies of flirtation and manipulation on her father, strategies the mother did not employ in public either.

With the destruction of the autonomous Jewish communities, this world no longer existed (except for the Orthodox minority) to bring the son into or, generally, to serve as the Jews' reference group. Individual assimilating Jews were left on their own, more or less, to face a non-Jewish world, the general society, without a community as their reference group to provide appropriate responses to the society's demands and challenges, and had to work these out alone. Their reference group now became a class within the general society, usually the middle class (and for some, the upper middle class).

What was so discontinuous with the past was that now the surrogate represented a society and a reference group that were both non-Jewish. In assimilating West European families, the surrogate was the breadwinning father. Since discrimination persisted, the father had to work out the extent to which he represented and modeled the demands of a society and the responses of a reference group that were both non-Jewish and, at the same time, ensured the family's survival. Consequently, he sometimes fell back on classic Jewish survival strategies. He, too, was unable to protect the family (or himself) from abuse by non-Jews, and this occasioned shame in some of the sons, including the young Freud.

A rite of passage exists only where there is a community to define adulthood and to absorb adults. While there was a rite of passage in traditional Jewish communities, and among Orthodox and observant Sephardic Jews today (in Israel, army service at eighteen serves this function), there obviously could be none among assimilationist Jews. In its absence, there is no mechanism to head off the son's individuation struggle with the parent who is the surrogate of the general society and the family's reference group. Kafka's long and unsuccessful struggle with his father for validation of his different lifestyle readily comes to mind here.

✦ Among East European Jews, especially in the shtetl, there was a split along gender lines in the role of community surrogate. One part was to be the model of the breadwinner relating to the general society in earning a living, a part that largely fell to the mother. She not only earned and managed the money, she also negotiated business and dealt with the peasants and the authorities in matters relating to buying and selling. (The part of the role that involved dealing with the general society over the larger issues of communal survival remained with the men of the community.)

As surrogate of the community regarding the world of work, the mother trained the daughter in what she was doing (artisanship and/or trade), as well as in the specific enabling involved in managing a Jewish household. The father served as the model of the kind of man the daughter would be doing this for when she got married, a man who often lived in an ivory tower apart from the hurly-burly of the marketplace and was unable, as well, to protect his family.

The role of surrogate and model of how to relate to and live *inside* the community remained with the father. As surrogate of the communal world of study and public performance of ritual and prayer, the spiritual resistance that was valued as the most important work for Jewish survival and which defined manhood, he supervised and socialized the son after infancy, with the community providing support and reinforcement.

These patterns did not engender conflict between mother and individuating adolescent son for three reasons. One is that while the mother was the surrogate of the community regarding the world of breadwinning, the son was not expected to enter this world. He was to enter his father's communal world of spiritual resistance. Therefore the mother did not have to teach and validate behavior related to his becoming a provider, nor, of course, in his assuming his proper role in the community; that was the father's job. Second, since the father was the surrogate and model of how to function in this communal world, conflict over individuation would have had to take place with him. But this was headed off by the rite of passage, the Bar Mitzvah, symbolizing the son's entry into this men's world and his assumption of religious responsibilities. Third, many boys in Eastern Europe were physically separated from their parents at the age of thirteen by apprenticeship, by study in a faraway yeshiva, or by teen marriage with matrilocal residence. The latter meant that the boy's adolescent individuation conflict was transferred to the in-laws, as many stories by maskilim reveal.

✦ In trying to discern who in traditional Jewish families provided the unconditional love generally associated under patriarchy with the mother, we might start by noting how Jewish books on child raising, such as one published in sixteenth-century Germany and seventeenth-century Poland, advised parents "not to reveal their love in the presence" of the children because then the offspring would not "*fear* and would not *obey* them" (italics mine). One might conclude from this advice that it was fairly common for both parents to "reveal their love" to their children, and it seems to point, along with testimonials about the "warmth" of Jewish family life, to both parents' love being unconditional. The main reason for this was that both parents were the surrogates of the community, which extended acceptance to all Jews as long as they did not abandon or betray it.

But the extreme stress from unremitting persecution and poverty in late-nineteenth-century Czarist Russia, plus deportations from villages to cities, took its toll on family life. The conflicting sources on maternal behavior in this era, viewed side by side, provide a complex picture.

Stories by maskilim and, later, Yiddish writers such as Peretz and Sholem Aleichem, describe a mother who was so overburdened with work and worry that she could not pay attention to the children's emotional needs. Ruth Adler's analysis of late-nineteenth-century Yiddish literature (mostly written by men) reveals that the complaints of the (grown) children centered on the dearth of material indulgence during childhood. (The maskilim's wish to bring the mother back to full-time homemaking, however, may have been a factor in their complaints about the working mother.) Unlike many of the other male writers Adler studied, Bialik understood the woman's burden and travail. His moving poetic tribute to his widowed mother relates how she returns in the evening every day with every penny she has earned "mired in her heart's blood and soaked with bitterness," sews by candlelight until midnight, and then "arises at dawn with the crowing of the cock" to bake bread for her children, her tears falling into the dough.

The mother's prime focus was on the children's physical survival. The recollections of Zborowski and Herzog's respondents were that the mother's love was "manifested chiefly in two ways: by constant and solicitous over-feeding and by unremitting solicitude about every aspect of her child's welfare, expressed for the most part in unceasing verbalization: 'Are you warm enough?' 'Have you had enough to eat?'" She was also experienced and portrayed—as in Sholem Aleichem's story *Gymnasia*—as making extreme sacrifices for her son's education.

As the model for the role of breadwinner, the mother had to train the daughter in all the skills this role entailed under increasingly stressful conditions. This may account for the fact that the criticism of the daughter's behavior necessitated by the role (and its difficulties in this era) escalated to the point where, wrote Adler, she was often a "target for the mother's ill-temper. . . . Her efforts were often greeted with rebuke rather than praise. . . . Her endeavors seemed unappreciated . . . [and she] could do nothing right." ·

Despite the literary testimonies that the mother neglected her children's emotional needs and nagged and criticized her daughter, it is impossible to conclude that her love was conditional upon behavior. Nor can we even be sure that the father's love, though he may have meted out stern rebukes and sometimes even corporal punishment to his son, was conditional. The recollections of former shtetl residents seem to indicate that neither parent withheld love (or food, its symbol) when a child behaved inappropriately. Even though the interviewees' nostalgia for the warmth of shtetl life as contrasted with the alienation so many immigrants felt in America probably contributed to their tendency to exaggerate the positive elements of the Old Country, especially the mother's unconditional love, the memories have too many details and too much intensity to have evolved out of whole cloth. So do the songs of that period, as epitomized by "The Yiddishe Mameh": "How holy and radiant is the home when the mother is there." Perhaps only the as-yet-untranslated writings of women in Yiddish will provide answers to the riddle of the contradictory portraits of Jewish mothers.

THE SURROGATE ROLE IN AMERICA

In America the East European immigrant men, as we have seen, tried to recapture from women the turf of breadwinning and sought to assimilate. One might therefore assume that the father would now take on the role, held by the father in assimilating West European Jewish families, of surrogate in the home of the general society and model of the reference group's appropriate responses. The mothers, and not the fathers, took on this role because they had work skills (breadwinning, negotiating, networking) honed over hundreds of years. Many of the men in Russia, wrote Simon Dubnow, were "entirely unfit for the battle of life." In many families, he continued, "energetic women took charge of the business and became wage earners." It was the women who knew how to "live in the world." No wonder the first Socialist union in Vilna, the birthplace of the Jewish labor movement of Russia, was that of *women*—sock makers—and that it was women who initiated the first strikes on New York's Lower East Side. In America many women continued to be the sole family breadwinners because they were alone. There were so many instances of desertion by husbands that a National Desertion Bureau had to be established in 1911; between then and the early 1920s, it dealt with a hundred thousand cases.

Immigrant women often played the role of economic energizers—they initiated business, made contacts, organized the operation. (This pattern had also prevailed among the German Jewish women who preceded the East Europeans. Those who went West in the second half of the nineteenth century, for example, started boardinghouses, restaurants, hotels, and stores, some of which grew into commercial empires, among them I. Magnin in San Francisco.)

In short, the women's skills, including responding appropriately to new challenges, were transferable to the new reality; the men's were usually not, although many men were a quick study. In the final analysis, the mothers trained the sons to complete the process of recapturing from women the turf of paid work, a process that necessitated and resulted in their own ejection from it.

It wasn't until the mid- to late 1950s that the father in most families became relatively secure in his role as provider. By then the pattern of the mother's being the surrogate of the family's reference group and of the general society had been set. Thus it was the mother who represented in the home the general society and its demands and replicated in some of her behavior toward the children its behavior toward the Jews, as she understood it. By learning how to respond to her demands in accordance with the reference group's norms, they learned how to respond to those they would face in the general society—how to "live in the world," by being validated or criticized by her for their behavior.

In the absence of an organic, autonomous Jewish community, she also had to work out by herself which survival strategies to instill, just like the assimilationist West European Jewish fathers had done in this surrogate role. (As we have seen in the preceding chapter, transmitting the reference group's standards and instilling classic survival strategies were intrinsically contradictory tasks.)

The parent surrogates in the past had to be acutely aware of how long a leash the Jew was on in relation to the general society and to replicate it and respond to it. If it was a very short leash—if just about anything they did could cause an outbreak of violent anti-Semitism—they had to instill behavior requiring the children (especially the sons) to be extremely cautious. That training required keeping them on a short leash. If the general society kept Jews on a long leash, parent surrogates had to instill in children behavior patterns that incorporated the knowledge of the precise points at which to hold back. This meant they had to raise the children on a long leash that could be let out and reined in as the situation required. Since American society kept Jews on a long leash, the mother kept the child on a long leash, compared with that in Europe. To the children who saw how their non-Jewish peers were being raised, however, it seemed like a short leash indeed.

The mother's withholding of praise from the children taught the son, especially, not to expect a whole lot of adulation for his achievements from/in the general society, always to be on his toes, and never to take his success for granted. The fact that for her nothing ever seemed quite good enough ("You got ninety-nine? Where is the other point?!") prepared him for the way he would have to function in the general society, where tough competition meant that yesterday's achievements were never "good enough" to ensure tomorrow's status. The withholding of praise kept the son in limbo, always unsure of whether he was measuring up, and it prepared him to ask himself, as an adult, "How am I doing?"

Even the mother's double messages—not only their specific content but also *their very existence*—were part of her training. Snaking through this minefield of double messages was an excellent *hachshara* (Hebrew for training), preparing the son for those lying in wait for Jews in the general society and teaching him to tread carefully and guard his back in the knowledge that one misstep might trigger disaster.

❧ The son's individuation/differentiation struggle took place with the mother not only because she had become the surrogate of the general society and the family's reference group but also because the father had lost his role of surrogate of the community he could bring his son into, since such a community no longer existed.

The traditional rite of passage, the Bar Mitzvah, which had headed off the son's individuation struggle in the past, lost its role as symbolizing his entry into manhood through the assumption of religious responsibilities. Like the wedding, it began to take on ersatz importance as a status symbol of the family's material success. The ostentation at these glitzy affairs, the displays of conspicuous consumption both figurative (expensive hall, banks of flowers, ice carvings) and literal (the pyramids of food eaten by guests), signaled that the family had arrived.

The daughter's individuation struggle reverted to more or less classic patriarchal form because the mother was not required to train her to be a breadwinner. This struggle could no longer be headed off by the traditional rite of passage of early arranged marriage.

The children's individuation struggles have intensified, of course, because the American value of independence collides with the Jewish view that even temporary separation constitutes abandonment and betrayal.

During the adolescents' individuation struggles with the mother, the father in America tends to provide little or no support/solace to either the son or the daughter, even though he treats the latter as his "little princess." Instead, not wishing to take on his wife in this battle, he seems to live by a noninterference directive, usually justifying his withdrawal on grounds that raising the children is the mother's job. The consequence is that children of both genders often experience the father's withdrawal as abandonment. This view is reinforced by the society's scorning of nonmacho men who do not dominate their wives or protect their families as weak and wimpy. Since the mother is experienced as overly domineering (especially in contrast with the non-Jewish mother) and the father as passive, many children often feel that neither parent is really on their side. And, indeed, it is common for both parents to take the teacher's side when a child is charged with misbehavior.

SELF-ESTEEM AND ASSIMILATIONISM

Having explored the evolution of the surrogate role, we can now return to the development of self-esteem, which, as noted earlier, requires both validation and unconditional love.

In too many homes of American middle-class non-Orthodox Jews descended from East European immigrants, despite all the emotional bonding and closeness and the absence of parent-child separation, there is no real *expression* of unconditional love. Regardless of whether the parents feel unconditional love for their children, what comes across is conditional love—the condition being performance. Love is often provided in the form of material rewards. As Brenda's father says to her in the 1969 film of *Goodbye, Columbus,* "Anything in the world that you want, you know you can have *because, Brenda, you've been a good girl"* (italics mine). The parents, especially the mother (who is involved with the day-to-day socialization), withhold expressions of love when the expected intellectual accomplishments ("producing good grades") are not forthcoming.

To appreciate fully the motivation behind this methodology, one need only recall what the mother is preparing the child to face: a general society that does not readily accept Jews and that tolerates them only when they exhibit behavior it approves. To prepare the child to succeed under (and despite) these conditions, she cannot, as the general society's surrogate, give unconditional love.

The absence of the expression of unconditional love leaves outside validation of good behavior as the only source of the child's self-esteem. Moreover, the child is specifically taught that her or his self-worth is predicated on performance. Writes Zena Blau Smith of the immigrant mothers' methodology (which has characterized those of subsequent generations, too): "At any signs of flagging effort or undue interest in activities that might divert their [sons] from serious pursuits, Jewish mothers would inquire with withering *contempt,* 'So what do you want? *To be a nothing?'"* (italics mine). Thus the flip side of the son's success is his worthlessness. Similarly with the daughter: Psychologist Leah Davidson noted that Jewish parents demand the daughter "be this way, look just so. But if you slip one little bit, you're *no good"* (italics mine).

↔ Teaching the child to derive self-esteem from outside validation is no accident. It is directly connected to the need to socialize the child according to the terms of the assimilationist contract—and its subtext.

Assimilationism, as already noted, means engaging in behavior not on the basis of one's intrinsic/authentic needs but according to what one believes will merit approval and validation in the general society. It means applying the anxiety regarding "what will the neighbors say?" to the larger society, which is why the mother surrogates asked this question of their children repeatedly during socialization.

Assimilationists are not only always looking over their shoulder to psych out what non-Jews will think of their actions; they are also always rating themselves by how they are living up to the internalized values of the reference group. This means asking oneself continually, "How am I doing?" in this regard and feeling OK only when doing something believed to merit this outside validation.

Assimilationism thus means *predicating one's self-esteem on the validation of others.* This is possibly the most psychologically pernicious aspect of assimilationism—and is obviously one of its underlying motivations.

All human beings need validation of their place in society: a certain amount of recognition every now and then for living up to normative behavior. It is a qualitatively different matter, however, to need such validation desperately *as the only source of one's self-esteem.* One's sense of self-worth then becomes a bottomless pit that can never be filled no matter how much validation is shoveled into it.

Parental withholding of expressions of unconditional love, and their providing validation only when the children live up to certain standards thus propels the children on a lifelong—and vain—search for self-esteem through outside validation.

◆ We have already noted in the previous chapter how the absence of outside validation lowers Jewish men's self-esteem to the point where many feel like wimps, nerds, and schleps. Rodney Dangerfield, for example, has made a career out of moaning, "I get no respect."

Jewish women experience multiple jeopardy in relation to self-esteem: They are plagued with the low self-worth most women experience under patriarchy and by the self-hate experienced by Jews who have internalized negative stereotypes of their group; in addition, they cannot derive self-esteem through validation in the general society for living up to its ideals of beauty and behavior. A young woman who described herself as having thick and wavy black hair, dark eyes, and olive skin wrote that she "spent 20 years as a Californian praying I could be what I was not meant to be: a beach girl blond. . . . I remember . . . crying hysterically, 'Oh, how I wish I was somebody else!'. . . . My childhood was littered with insults [and] times when I felt something was terribly wrong. I was sure my life was a tragic mistake." Many Jewish women say they feel "ugly," "fat," and "dirty" and do not define themselves as desirable or sexy. Some engage in self-destructive behavior, such as anorexia and bulimia, reported clinical psychologist Melissa Schwartz.

The difficulties of living up to the majority cultural ideals of beauty and behavior are exacerbated by the fact that the Jewish daughter is seen as the "ambassador of the family mythology" of its having "made it," said psychologist Leah Davidson. "Everyone has invested a lot in her being a *real American*" (italics mine).

This underlying parental motivation is clearly highlighted in an early scene from Marjorie Morningstar's adolescence, when her mother "was carried away by her daughter's flowering beauty. . . . At 17, Rose Kupperberg had been a Yiddish-speaking immigrant girl toiling in a dirty Brooklyn sweatshop . . . and by contrast it seemed to her that Marjorie was living the life of a fairy-tale *princess*. She . . . drew deep *vicarious delight*" from her daughter's popularity (italics mine).

This brings us to another factor predisposing Jewish women to experience low self-esteem. They are treated by their parents as "cultivated, educated, cultured, valuable *investments*," wrote Leslie Tonner, and this "embellishing" of their daughters is "accompanied by constant reminders of The Ultimate Goal: 'Get married, darling.'... Parents consider doing things for their daughters as though they were taking out some form of *matrimonial insurance*" (italics mine). Noted Davidson, "The message her family gives is, 'Make us proud by acquiring a worthwhile male. *You don't count, only what you can acquire*–a man and material symbols to show he cares'" (italics mine).

THE CHILD AS A "LIGHT UNTO THE WORLD"

Throughout history it was imperative for Jewish parents to create a strong sense of self-worth in the children as their shield (wielding a sword was impossible) against the negative messages raining down on them and threatening to seep into the psyche. The strong psychological self-defense was the idea that Jews had a special role in history, to live by God's Torah. Each child, by growing into Jewishness and observing laws and customs, could participate in this destiny and thereby feel a sense of self-worth. In the traditional communities of the past, as well, Jewish women did not ordinarily experience the low self-esteem that affects women under patriarchy. The validation they received from their families and the community for fulfilling their altruistic-assertive enabler role reinforced their own sense of its–and their–importance. (To a large extent, high self-esteem commonly obtains today among Orthodox women for this reason.)

Assimilationist Jews of Western Europe and immigrants from there and Eastern Europe to America discarded the sense of Judaism's and their own specialness as Jews, believing that this psychological shield impeded upward mobility and acceptance. But if there was no physical persecution, there was still discrimination and denigration. A lightweight replacement shield of some sort was therefore necessary.

Jewish parents, in socializing the son in America, substituted for that sense of specialness as a Jew the sense of specialness as their child. Abbie Hoffman told an interviewer, "You know you are *chosen,* especially when you are a first-born son. My father said, 'The whole world is wrong and you are right.' I didn't know *he was trying to make a point so I would assimilate.* I thought he was telling me who I was, and I'm supposed to go out and make the world right" (italics mine). Arthur Miller's Quentin (a Jewish character if ever there was one, although the assimilationist author did not identify him as such) recalls in *After the Fall* what his mother told him as a child about her pregnancy: "The first time I felt you move ... I saw a star.... And suddenly it fell, like some great man had died and you were being pulled out of me to take his place and *be a light, a light in the world!*" (italics mine). How significant it is that this description of the specialness of the son echoes (and replaces) Isaiah's description of the Jews as a "light unto the nations."

By the mid-1950s, after most Jews had made it into the middle class, the daughter, like her brother, was raised with the belief that she, too, was special. One woman wrote in 1970 that "in my home there was the unspoken conviction that I was intensely valuable; somehow, in a manner never defined, special and superior."

Bearing this in mind, it becomes possible to understand the nature and cause of the admonition children of both genders have heard for several generations: "Eat for the starving children of Europe/China/Africa." The child is urged to do something in his or her selfish interest (eat) out of some sort of responsibility to others (the starving children)—and told that his or her action (eating) in advancing self-interest (survival and pleasure) will somehow benefit starving children abroad. The children thus absorbed the feeling that they were so special that whatever was good for them was going to be good for humanity. They could actually live up to the Jewish value of altruism by being selfish and self-centered.

MALIGNANT NARCISSISM

Although it seems contradictory to describe the tendency of many American Jews to feel special on the one hand and to need continual validation to try to feed their starving self-esteem on the other, this is precisely the nature of the psychological disorder known as narcissism. The pathological narcissist's craving of adulation and praise to "inflate his [*sic*] sense of grandiosity" is seen by psychoanalysts as "protecting him from a deep feeling that his life is empty and that underneath it all, he is *worthless*" (italics mine).

Significantly, some psychologists trace individuals' narcissism to childhood experiences with parents who trained them to feel they could be loved only when they fit the parental image of perfection. The children's fear that no one loves them just as they are engenders the belief that there is something wrong with them.

In many Jewish marriages where one spouse or both suffer from narcissism, the partners have a tendency to complain about insufficient validation from each other.

What the Jewish man wishes, in the words of Quentin's first wife in *After the Fall,* is to "fly around in a constant bath of praise." He desires, feels entitled to, and demands constant adulation from his wife for his achievements and for the material goodies he gives her, made possible by his success. But the daughter in late-twentieth-century middle-class Jewish families has also been raised to believe she is special and deserves the best. Since she is thus entitled, what is there to be so appreciative about? This leads the men to complain, as did David Steinberg, that Jewish women "expect their husbands to cater to them in the same way that their mother and father did."

Thus an extreme discontinuity exists between the daughter's childhood programming to feel entitled to the best and the behavior demanded of her in a relationship with a man, when she is supposed to mutate into a female who is grateful for getting what she believes is her due.

The man complains, too, that his wife or lover is "never satisfied no matter how much I give her." "Never satisfied" actually means "never grateful." We should not be surprised that the man expresses his anger at her "insatiability" in materialistic terms ("I gave her a beautiful home, a car, jewelry—what more does she want?!") because this is what he has been taught to value. The woman may have indeed couched her demands/requests in materialistic terms, because American and American Jewish culture have taught her to see these as symbols of his validation (as the parents' presents were when she and her husband were children).

Her withholding of abject gratitude deprives the man of the validation he feels he needs to fuel his self-esteem (and is also experienced by him as a repetition of his mother's behavior in denying him praise). As Jackie Mason tells his audience, "Every Jew [sic] [is] frightened and nervous of his wife. . . . He's suffered and *struggled to become a success.* . . . But as soon as he opens the door to his own house: 'You shmuck!'" (italics mine).

The husband cannot retaliate by withholding material goodies because these are symbols of *his* success ("He treats her like a queen"). He therefore retaliates psychologically, by depriving his wife of validation for her efforts to live up to the majority cultural ideal of beauty and behavior and thereby to fuel her self-esteem.

Knowing of her feelings of inferiority to WASP women in this regard, he often gets back at her with negative comparisons of her behavior with theirs. One quintessential example comes from a self-hating article of the late 1970s that takes the form of contrasting "Gentile vs. Jewish Marriage." All the charges lobbed by the Jewish writer against his Jewish ex-wife concern her not living up to the majority culture's ideal of behavior: She was moody and volatile, her housekeeping was expressed in "a million Crazy-Kleen fetishes," and sex with her was largely nonexistent since she was never in the mood. His non-Jewish ex-wife, by contrast, never let a nasty word escape her lips, and her sexual behavior was "dynamite."

As for relationships with parents: "Jewish wives are self-generating guilt-machines. If they're not phoning their mothers every day, they have flash colitis attacks." But the non-Jewish ex-wife "had to check with Information" as to the correct phone number of her parents on the rare occasions when she called them. "Let's face it," the author comments darkly, "Gentile parents value their child's independence!" Finally, his Jewish ex-wife's relationship with her in-laws (*his* parents!) was, he writes, an "uneasy truce. . . . The wife practically has to call the auto club to get hubby out of Mama's overprotective clutches." Here he gets in a *zetz* (Yiddish for punch, hit, blow, dig) at both his ex-wife and his own mother at one go.

◆ Since the material goodies the husband provides his wife are seen by both spouses as symbols of his success and thus his masculinity, *and* of his love for her, if the man is unable to provide these, the self-esteem of both plummets and the relationship between them often becomes extremely embittered.

A major factor here is what social worker Mary Cahn Schwartz called the Jewish wife's two commandments: "The first is that 'success' identity must come primarily from what her husband does." Second, under no circumstances is she to be allowed to be vocationally more successful than her husband in money, prestige, or job satisfaction. "Thus a wife needs a successful husband simply to have room to maneuver in.... If the culture tells the wife that the normal way of achieving identity is through what the husband does, then his career, or lack of one, must become an all-consuming concern for the wife." Her desperation over her husband's lack of success and her belief in spousal interdependence lead her to try to do everything in her power to help him do better:

> And lo, the famous Jewish woman emerges, the shrew, the bitch, the nag,
> the schemer.... These wives are aware of the kind of angry, nagging people
> they are turning into. They are frightened, and often filled with self-hate.
> Anger and disappointment with the husband inevitably follow, for the one
> avenue sanctioned by society for the wife to walk forward on is being
> blocked by him.

◆➤ Many Jewish men see non-Jewish women as being lavish with their praise. As Portnoy describes to his shrink the non-Jewish woman he calls The Monkey: "But what was I supposed to be but her Jewish *savior?*... a brainy, balding, beaky Jew ... who neither drinks nor gambles nor keeps show girls on the side ... a regular domestic *Messiah!*" (italics mine).

The use of the words *savior* and *messiah* in this connection is very revealing. Given the general absence of embattled and violent homes from which Jewish women need to be saved by a good husband, the Jewish male is unable to play rescuer to Jewish females. What is there, after all, to rescue them from? Furthermore, no Jewish man who behaves as American Jewish men are raised to behave—nonviolently and as "good providers"—is going to be considered a savior to a Jewish woman, who expects/feels entitled to be treated decently and given the respect due a partner and does not think the man merits wild praise for not being abusive.

But he can symbolically act out the role of rescuer of a damsel in distress, denied Jewish men for centuries, without actually having to engage in the physical aggression that historically accompanied it, simply by being a good husband to a non-Jewish woman, especially one who did not experience decent treatment at home—or elsewhere. By being her "savior," he can receive at last the adulation/praise/gratitude he has learned he is entitled to as someone special ("a light unto the world") but feels he never extracts from a Jewish woman. (The non-Jewish wife who does feel entitled to good treatment and is not overly grateful for it does not arouse resentment in Jewish men because she is higher in status than a Jewish woman, and her very marriage to him constitutes validation in and of itself.)

THE IMPOSSIBLE DREAM OF UNCONDITIONAL
LOVE

Current psychological theory holds that most individuals are attracted to mates who have their parents' positive *and* negative traits out of an unconscious attempt to "recreate the conditions of [their] upbringing in order ... to resolve [their] unfinished business ... to heal childhood wounds," in the words of psychologist Harville Hendrix. This psychological dynamic is exacerbated in American Jewish families because the childhood "wound," the parental withholding of expressions of unconditional love, is a prime component of self-esteem. The wish for unconditional love is therefore directed at the spouse, who was chosen for resembling the parent with whom the individual experienced the greatest conflict.

The Jewish son tends to seek a wife who is strong like his mother but not domineering and demanding, as he experienced her being. This latter wish is reinforced by the majority cultural ideal of the subservient wife. The expression of unconditional love he desires is having his wife make the home a temple for the worship of the Jewish prince: to center her entire existence around him, wait on him hand and foot, and dispense endless attention to his every whim and complaint—*without making any demands for emotional reciprocity.*

The Jewish male's deeply felt but unacknowledged wish for expression of unconditional love is probably the reason behind the American Jewish myth of the all-loving, all-giving, all-nurturing Yiddishe Mameh of yesteryear's shtetl. Her positive image as dispenser of unconditional love is designed to contrast with that of the American Jewish mother, whose love is conditional upon behavior. The Yiddishe Mameh's solicitude is consequently seen as positive and legitimate, while her American counterpart's is seen as negative, linked with his "infantilization," and intrusive. (This exploitation of women from the past to denigrate those of the present is reminiscent of Israeli men's deploying the image of the idealistic pioneer "girls of yesteryear" to denigrate today's "materialistic" females.)

The daughter seeks a man who is strong like her mother (the parent with whom she, too, experienced the greatest conflict). This wish is reinforced by the majority cultural ideal of the man who is "masculine," takes the initiative, and acts decisively but (as Jewish norms mandate) nonviolently. What she means by unconditional love is being accepted for who she is without the Chinese water torture of nagging and criticism she received from her mother; and getting the kind of emotional support she never received from her father, a wish reinforced by the American cultural ideal of the protective husband. What she does not seek is a strong, silent type, silence—the absence/withdrawal of emotional expressiveness—being equated by Jews with abandonment.

Jewish women's and Jewish men's definitions of unconditional love are in complete conflict, which makes their attainment impossible. What the woman seeks as unconditional love—validation and emotional support, intimacy, and reciprocity—is precisely what the man regards as a demand whose very absence is what he defines as unconditional love. When each spouse inevitably denies the other unconditional love, their memories of how their mothers withheld it and their fathers "abandoned" them during the individuation struggle are reactivated and, with these, the old feelings of rejection, resentment, and rage.

❧ The flash points of marital conflict, therefore, are emotional intimacy and reciprocity. The American Jewish lover/husband distrusts intergender intimacy because he equates closeness with coercion. In explaining the immigrant child-raising methodology (which has persisted in later generations) Zena Blau Smith writes, "Identification with the mother became the cornerstone of the entire socialization process. . . . With no other human being did the Jewish child develop as close, as *trusting,* as free and fearless a relationship as with his mother, and therein lay the *secret of her power to gain his compliance*" (italics mine).

The American Jewish man fears emotional closeness as a kind of ploy that will inevitably lead to some demand for performance being made on him, as was the case with his mother. And he fears that intimacy has the power to make him comply with such a demand.

His wish for emotional distance is reinforced by the WASP cultural value of independence, by which spouses "have to live autonomously side by side minding your own business and leaving each other alone," in one psychologist's words. This noninterference directive is just the opposite of the traditional Jewish view of marriage, which the son absorbed in the parental home, as a partnership informed by the values of interdependence, mutuality, and reciprocity. He is torn between two incompatible value systems.

The man perceives his wife's very longing for emotional intimacy and reciprocity as a demand in and of itself, and he fears it. He often withholds emotional intimacy—a technique he mastered in his childhood power struggles with his mother—and tries to delegitimize her wish/demand for it.

One method is to accuse the woman of kvetching, a Yiddish word meaning incessant complaining in childish, whining tones. Kvetching is actually aborted protest that the complainer is unable to voice as such. He or she consequently regresses to the childlike (powerless) behavior manifest in the whining tone. The man who makes this accusation seeks thereby to denigrate the woman's demands for emotional support as being those of a child seeking pampering and not of an adult seeking reciprocity.

Another method the man uses to delegitimize demands for reciprocity is to accuse the woman of being frigid. The charge of *sexual* coldness is the only way the American culture allows a man to articulate an accusation of *emotional* withholding/withdrawal. The real meaning of the charge is that the very act of demanding emotional reciprocity is proof that the woman is cold, hard, unfeeling. Only a "frigid" woman would make such a demand; a "real" woman dispenses endless unilateral, unconditional love without expecting reciprocity.

Ever fearful that intimacy is a prelude/prerequisite to his wife's making demands, and anxious of becoming "infantilized" by giving in to them, the man ends up as infantilized by wishing for unconditional love without reciprocity, that is, without giving it himself. It is no wonder, then, that Jewish women complain that the American Jewish male, lover or husband, is immature and babyish ("always afraid there are bones in the fish") despite his putative wish for independence and autonomy; emotionally distant ("He lives up in his head"—a safe place to retreat to); commitment-phobic; and hung up on his mother ("You never take my side"). This last complaint derives from the husband's noninterventionist stance in the battles between his wife and his mother, which replicate both spouses' fathers' noninterventionist policy in the individuation battles between mother and children.

"JAP"-BASHING

The men's complaints have coalesced into and reached their apotheosis in the "Jewish American Princess" (a.k.a. "JAP") stereotype. The flip side of the ideal self-sacrificing Yiddishe Mameh, the "JAP" is described as overwhelmingly materialistic, "ostentatious," haughty and arrogant, and, above all, selfish and ungiving ("frigid").

Since most of her behavior is in fulfillment of the American Dream, which defines success in material terms—and in line with the messages of the majority culture that encourage both women and men to be self-indulgent, and with her programming to be the "ambassador" of the family's success through ostentatious display—why is it pictured as so reprehensible?

The stereotype dates to the mid- to late 1950s, with Herman Wouk's 1955 portrayal of Marjorie Morningstar and Philip Roth's 1959 depiction of Brenda Patimkin in *Goodbye Columbus*. This was a period when Jewish men were really beginning to make it in America—to attain high positions in the professions and in academia.

In the intermittently weak 1950s economy, advertisers' messages promoting consumption of material goods *as an entitlement* had the unexpected effect of unleashing a restlessness among women that got out of hand and could not be assuaged with a new fridge or vacuum cleaner, explained Barbara Ehrenreich. Women began to feel that they, too, were entitled to the same goodies—psychological as well as material—as the men.

The "JAP" stereotype arose at this juncture to warn Jewish women against such a sense of entitlement lest it lead to their breaking the role of born-again altruistic-assertive enabler. The "JAP" stereotype is of a woman who is not altruistic and not an enabler. Her assertiveness, which can be legitimately expressed only when the goal is altruistic, is therefore illegitimate ("haughty"). So is her sense of entitlement to the material goodies she does nothing (she doesn't even dispense unconditional love) to merit ("frigid").

But the "JAP" libel backfired in the ensuing decades, especially from the 1970s on. Jewish women who had not given up enabling but were attacked as if they had began to feel they had nothing to lose by acting in their own interests. Once the feminist movement had raised their consciousness and legitimized "self-actualization," they, like other white middle-class American females, went back to school and (re-)entered the job market. This was *real* role breaking, and it led to the "JAP" slander's attaining epidemic proportions.

The men were not only angry at possibly losing enablers, they were also fearful of competition from the women in the job market at a time of intermittent economic recession and cutthroat competition for the shrinking number of good jobs available. Having just begun to succeed in the corporate world, they became acutely anxious that women would overrun this new turf and outcrowd them.

The economic fear was compounded by psychological angst. Jewish women who "invaded" the work turf threatened the men's masculinity, which they defined as success at breadwinning. The angst was especially acute when the women entered fields such as law, medicine, and academia, thus cutting off control of the classic base of intellectual turf—which had always defined Jewish manhood—while invading a new one (the corporate world).

❧ Given their anxieties about loss of masculinity, it is no wonder that Jewish men recycled and incorporated into the "JAP" slander some of the elements of the Lilith libel that had addressed a similar anxiety. Like Lilith, the "JAP" is assertive in pursuing her own interests. Lilith refuses to lie beneath Adam; the "JAP" refuses to put out on demand and insists on reciprocity in the relationship. Both are described as frigid. The "JAP" is portrayed as a parasite, draining men dry with her materialistic demands as Lilith did in her nightly sperm-stealing raids. In both myths the men's anxiety is that women will obstruct their fulfilling the role that defines their masculinity. In the case of the Lilith libel, that role is spiritual resistance as a collective solution to sustain national survival; in the "JAP" slander the role is material success to promote the individual solution of making it.

Even more significantly, Lilith is attacked for behaving as a Jew (only men can be "real" Jews), but the "JAP" is attacked for living up to her assimilationist programming. The message here is that only men are entitled to the material and psychological rewards of assimilation.

This brings us back to the men's visibility/invisibility conflict. They fear that the more conspicuous their material success, the more likely it is that one day they will be pushed out. (It is this fear that leads American Jews to worry that surveys revealing the material success of the majority of the group's members will trigger the recrudescence of the old Judeophobic myth that all Jews are rich and powerful.)

Still needing validation for their self-esteem, they are unwilling to become totally invisible, as the assimilationist contract requires. They direct their demands for inconspicuousness toward the women of their group, hoping thereby to reduce their own visibility and thus avert trip-wiring the Judeophobic myth of Jewish wealth and its being directed at them, as the (presumed) providers of the material goodies the women exhibit. Their tactic is to try to intimidate Jewish women into curbing their conspicuous consumption by portraying ostentation as ugly and disgusting. Ostentation, of course, is an antidote to and the flip side of invisibility, but it must be practiced in a safe space: in the *mishpucha* (community-as-extended family). It is only when the woman's ostentation is displayed outside the mishpucha's borders that it is seen as breaking the Jewish visibility taboo.

Therefore those women who refuse to give up or at least to mitigate/reduce the display of the assimilationist symbols of material success outside the mishpucha ("ostentatious"), who are assertive in their own interests ("haughty," "arrogant"), who are unwilling to provide unending emotional labor without reciprocity ("frigid") are enemies of Jewish men. They must be treated as enemies of the Jews, just like the women of the past, epitomized by Lilith, who behaved courageously and independently in their own interests.

❧ But there is an even more sinister purpose behind libeling Jewish women as "JAPs." The men's insecurity that everything will be taken away from them by non-Jewish men leads them to recycle the anti-Semitic myth of the rich, powerful, and controlling Jewish parasite who "takes over" whenever possible—and to project it onto the women.

The purpose of this projection is to channel anti-Semitism away from the men and onto the women. This is the same lightning-rod strategy employed by ruling classes against Jews over many centuries (as seen in chapter 1).

Ruling classes tried to use anti-Semitism to promote class collaboration by fingering the Jews as the common enemy of both rich and poor and thereby deflect attacks by the latter away from themselves. Jewish men try to use the Judeophobic misogyny of the "JAP" slander to promote interethnic male bonding by fingering Jewish women as the common enemy of all men and thereby deflect attacks by non-Jewish men against themselves. By promoting the "JAP" libel, Jewish men are saying to non-Jewish men: "It's not us who are your real enemy (after your jobs and status), it's Jewish women. Don't attack us men, attack only the women." This tactic is grimly reminiscent of that pivotal scene in George Orwell's *1984* when Winston, facing the most terrifying form of torture in Room 101, cries out, "Don't do it to me, do it to Julia" (his lover).

The message of the promoters of the "JAP" slander/libel is that the men are eager to do to the women what Lot did to his daughters when he offered them to the Sodomites to "do with them what you will." They are willing to betray and sacrifice the women of their group—even to lead the attack against them—to protect/preserve the economic and social position they have attained in America. One wonders what they would do if physical danger actually threatened all the Jews.

That this is hardly a moot question can be seen from a disturbing and terrifying case: The deliberate use of the "Jewish American Princess" libel in the successful defense of a Jewish man in Arizona on trial in 1982 for premeditated murder in the multiple-stabbing death of his wife. The repeated use of the stereotype in the trial was meant to get the jury to believe that the defendant was driven to violence by the putative excessive materialism and sexual "coldness" of his late wife along the lines of "See what she is like, *that is what Jewish women are like,* that's what Jewish men have to put up with, no wonder the guy went bananas," wrote attorney Shirley Frondorf (italics mine). The tactic of blaming the victim for behavior that bigots consider specifically Jewish, while picturing the defendant as a Jew supposedly rebelling against such behavior, was successful in making the woman appear guilty of causing her own murder. (The defendant was acquitted.)

⊰ The "JAP" libel legitimizes anti-Semitism as long as it is directed "only" against females. The Jewish men who have invented and spread it prefer to believe that the virus of anti-Semitism can be contained in its deployment "only" against the women and will not spread to them, much as many heterosexual Americans believed that the AIDS virus would infect "only" homosexuals and junkies and would not spread to the population at large, that is, themselves. And, as with AIDS, the containment illusion proved cruelly mistaken. This became apparent in the 1980s, when the cry of "JAP! JAP! JAP!" on college campuses—reminiscent of the medieval hate-chant against Jews of "HEP! HEP! HEP!"—and anti-"JAP" graffiti metastasized to general anti-Semitic verbal attacks.

It was only at this point that several Jewish organizations (who had once fought for civil rights with the argument that "rights denied to one group are denied to all") began to show a modicum of concern, which mainly took the form of issuing statements critical of the "JAP"-bashing phenomenon. Nor did any Jewish organization—including the women's groups—protest Mel Brooks's 1987 movie *Spaceballs,* in which the hero comments darkly on the spoiled, inconsiderate manipulator with the fixed nose from the planet Druidia, "That's all we needed—a *Dru*ish princess." And the film did not stop there: The send-up of Yoda (the film was supposed to be a takeoff on *Star Wars*) depicts a Judeophobically stereotypical grasping, money-mad merchant who has "the *power* known throughout the universe as 'The Schwartz'—merchandising" (italics mine).

⊰ The "JAP" "jokes" are by no means the only expression of anger and hostility directed by Jewish men at Jewish women. They are described in endless "jokes" as yentas, whose most disgusting characteristic is wanting to know and having an opinion on everything—the same intellectual curiosity and disputatiousness that has always been applauded in Jewish men. Here again the men's fear of the visibility of the group's intellectuality generates warnings only to Jewish women not to show it up. (The other purpose served, of course, is to threaten women not to invade the turf of intellectuality.)

The hatred of many assimilationist Jewish men for Jewish women, which surfaces in novels by Roth, Saul Bellow, Bruce Jay Friedman, and David Evanier, among others, is most egregiously demonstrated by Norman Mailer. In his short story "The Time of Her Time," a young Jewish female finally has her first orgasm after her partner calls her a "dirty Jew," an example of projected self-hate if ever there was one.

❧ The hostility expressed by so many Jewish men aggravates/exacerbates the low self-esteem experienced by many Jewish women. Measuring themselves against the majority culture's images of beauty and behavior and often finding themselves wanting, they seek validation from the men of their own group—and find themselves wanting . . . and wanting. . . . They are in quintuple jeopardy for low self-esteem, because Jewish men withhold validation and engage instead in vilification.

Instead of finding acceptance, American Jewish women experience attack. If they are "too" altruistic, they are portrayed as intrusive "Jewish mothers" ("Why is showing concern the only way a Jewish woman can show love?" asked one man) and are at high risk for depression in middle age when they face an empty nest. If they try to be perfect homemakers (baleboostas), they are criticized for "Crazy-Kleen fetishes" and for not enjoying life. If they live up to their assimilationist conditioning, they are slapped with the "JAP" label/libel. If they are "too" successful (and thus violate the Jewish wife's "second commandment"), they are "castrators." If they are too assertive in public, they are yentas and "fishwives." If they are assertive in the volunteer sphere, they are "Hadassah ladies." If they refuse to accept the colonization of their bodies and demand reciprocity in a sexual relationship, they are "frigid." And should they not marry a Jewish man—should they remain single, stay childless, enter into a lesbian partnership, or marry a non-Jewish male—they are depicted as responsible for the destruction of the Jewish family and, with it, the entire Jewish nation.

In the past, Jewish women in actual life and in literature were criticized when the men experienced/feared them as role breakers. When they were nonaltruistic (Lilith), too assertive (Deborah), or invaded intellectual turf (Beruriah), they flipped over from enabler to *dis*abler.

In contemporary America, all Jewish women (outside traditional Orthodox and Sephardic communities) are at risk for being pictured as *dis*ablers.

ELEVEN ❧ THE BANKRUPTCY OF AMERICAN JEWISH COMMUNAL LIFE

> *To be a Jew is to belong to a Jewish organization.*
>
> WILL MASLOW

> *The community seemed hell-bent on making a hero out of the Big Giver, no matter how lacking in knowledge or how unobservant in ritual he [sic] might be.*
>
> MELVIN UROFSKY

> *In American Jewry ... we are utterly bereft of an ideological foundation for our work.... There is no forum for open discussion. And that is no accident. The reason is that the leadership of the community simply does not want to be bothered by intellectual matters, does not understand them, does not trust intellectuals, and cannot cope with a world not for sale for money or plaques and banquets and the rest.*
>
> JACOB NEUSNER

The conflicts engendered among American Jewish men by assimilationism—the inconclusive nature of the validation of their material success and definition of masculinity—has led a minority of wealthy individuals among them to create and sustain the kind of communal structure and process that allows them to capture these components of self-esteem and thus to hope to experience it at last.

The structure and process—undemocratic, hierarchical, and sexist—are geared toward providing these relatively few men with a monopoly on validation in the form of high status and with an ersatz definition of masculinity: "Jewish leader." For this plutocracy at the apex of the communal pyramid, validation also means power—both to determine and implement policy and to dispense status.

These men, usually called *machers* (Yiddish for men who run the show), dominate the Jewish community—from the local to the national level—by controlling the multiplicity of organizations, "umbrella groups," and "roof organizations" that constitute the Jewish establishment. (Synagogal, Zionist, and women's organizations are outside the Jewish establishment even though volunteer "leaders" and/or executives of some of them may sit on an umbrella group or roof organization board that is in the Jewish establishment. These three types of organizations are nevertheless considered part of the organized Jewish community. Educational and cultural organizations/institutions are not considered part of either the Jewish establishment or the organized Jewish community.)

Right below the apex of the pyramid is a thin stratum of Big Givers—men who, along with the machers, provide the bulk of financial support to the Jewish establishment organizations. The greater the amount of money a man gives to a Jewish establishment organization—really Big Givers contribute a hundred thousand dollars or more a year—the greater the likelihood of his becoming a macher should he seek power as well as status rather than simply choosing to write a check and eschew further involvement.

Below the Big Giver stratum is a large middle section of the communal pyramid: Jews with varying degrees of affiliation with Jewish organizations who contribute and/or raise smaller amounts but are not part of its power structure. And at the large base of the pyramid is a mass of individuals with varying degrees of Jewish consciousness. This stratum is constantly being eroded. A 1991–92 study of organizational affiliations revealed that fewer than one-third of American Jews reported belonging to one or more Jewish organizations other than synagogues or temples, and that these individuals were most likely to be over fifty-five and/or second-generation Americans. According to the study, only 32 percent of American Jews reported attending one or more functions of any Jewish organization during the year, and only 21 percent did volunteer work for one.

◆ The plutocracy (or "macherarchy") disenfranchises the vast majority of men—and all but a very few token women. The organizations refer to the machers as their "lay leaders" or simply "communal leaders." Since "leader" is an ersatz definition of masculinity, women must be excluded from attaining it. This accounts for the men's largely successful efforts to keep them out of the plutocracy.

The plutocracy makes and implements decisions on communal policy; on the community's dealings with the United States government and with municipalities and foreign governments (including Israel) and organizations, and with international structures such as the Catholic church, and with various national organizations; and on raising and disbursing funds. Its "leaders" claim to speak in the name of American Jewry without a body of followers, let alone a mandate to represent them.

This is an anomaly in Jewish history. In the past, as we have seen, there was usually some form of elections to communal councils. Moreover, the men who served on the councils were highly versed in Jewish education and culture—unlike today's "leaders," who are, in Rabbi Arthur Hertzberg's words, "Jewishly illiterate [and] lack a language of learning and a shared Jewish culture," whose achievements are in every field except Jewish affairs, and whose "qualification" for their high positions is wealth alone. The current situation in the U.S. is discontinuous with the democracy that obtained in immigrant mutual-aid and radical organizations in the earlier part of the century. It is also conspicuously different from the situation in other Jewish communities around the world, including Canada and Russia, where local and national leadership is elected.

The American Jewish plutocracy is accountable to no one but the members of its own exclusive club. There is no way the average Jew can learn what the plutocracy is really doing. And, indeed, most American Jews have only a vague awareness of what the work of the Jewish establishment is and certainly do not know its "leaders" by name. Nor is there any way they can have input into the plutocracy's policy decisions. No mechanism exists even to enable American Jews to express what they think are their needs and views and to have the plutocracy respond to them. There are no public forums or open hearings for the voicing of criticism of its actions. Nor do any organizations outside the Jewish establishment challenge it, except for a few marginal groups that occasionally express dissenting views. Even if an opposition group should arise, there is no *public* context where it could question/confront the "leadership," its decisions, and/or its undemocratic process.

Some of the work done by Jewish establishment organizations, as we shall see, is undoubtedly necessary and important, and many of the machers and Big Givers are sincerely committed to it. But the issue here is whether a plutocracy or the masses of Jews themselves should be making decisions on the present needs of the Jewish people and on how its future survival should be ensured.

American Jews refer to themselves as a community—and this word will therefore be used in these pages to mean the estimated 5.2 million "core Jews," those with varying degrees of Jewish identification and affiliation. But if by "community" we mean an aggregate of individuals who join together on the basis of common values and interests to discuss, debate, and decide on what direction they should take as a collective entity, what priorities and agendas they should have and how these should be implemented, and to choose leadership to do so, there is no such thing as an American Jewish community.

THE JEWISH ESTABLISHMENT

The alphabet soup of Jewish organizations that constitute the Jewish establishment can roughly be divided into those *primarily* geared for fund-raising (the Federation structure) and those involved with community relations (political advocacy).

Federations in close to 180 local communities, which operate by a United Way organizing principle, raise and disburse about 70 percent of the estimated

$1.5 billion American Jews contribute annually to Jewish causes, organizations, and projects. (This estimate was made in 1988 by Barry Kosmin, director of the North American Jewish Data Bank at the City University of New York, based on his extrapolations from some 1985 figures. No actual statistics are available.) This gives the Federations great power. Each local Federation decides pretty much unilaterally what percentage of the harvest of its annual fund-raising campaign to allocate to local social welfare service agencies, national Jewish organizations (including those involved with community relations), and to the national United Jewish Appeal (UJA).

On average, about 40 to 50 percent of the money raised by local Federation campaigns goes to the UJA. The UJA allocates these funds to foreign Jewish communities (primarily through the American Jewish Joint Distribution Committee) and Israel (through bodies that funnel it to the Jewish Agency) for social service work.

About 80 to 85 percent of the funds raised by Federations in the U.S. comes from 15 to 20 percent of the contributors, the Big Givers of $10,000 or more (a phenomenon that prevails, as well, in all major Jewish fund-raising). In 1987, 1.2 percent of Federation campaign contributors—thirteen thousand individuals—gave a total of $402 million (60 percent of the total raised); five hundred gave $100,000 or more; and twenty-two individuals gave $1 million and over.

Instead of relying on appeals for small donations from the masses—the 50 percent who give under $100 and provide only 2 percent of the total—the Federations find it "expedient, cheaper and in the short-term, more cost-effective" (in the words of one executive) to solicit the Big Givers and write off the rest, including the over 60 percent of households who give nothing.

◆ Federation fund-raising strategy is based on the "donor-directed" approach. The projects for which their campaigns raise funds are those which market research shows to be the major interest of a group of potential donors, not those which meet the needs of the Jewish people. (No one knows or seeks to determine these needs: That might prove dangerous.) "Those that rule justify the existing programs as the ones the givers are ready to support," said Judah Shapiro. "The Jewish Federation becomes for such individuals a club, exclusive and personal, rather than a communal instrument for the Jews of the locality in their pursuit of group goals." There is no mechanism whereby Federations can be accountable to the Jews they purport to serve. Rabbi Mordecai Waxman said in 1985 that never once in his thirty-eight years as a rabbi in Long Island had he ever been asked by Federation officials in New York what he thought were the needs of his community: "I don't know the people who determine funding allocations and I don't know how they are elected [sic] or whom they represent. . . . [There is no] community input . . . in determining policies."

Federations, Shapiro noted, "equate themselves with the Jewish community" and consider themselves its "central address." They believe, in the words of a former UJA executive, that "philanthropy funds and builds a Jewish community." Historically, of course, the reverse was true. Shapiro pointed out, too, that the social services apparatus was originally established to help the victims of society, "but why should there be victims? Let's eliminate the conditions that produce the victimization." Doing this, however, would eliminate the need for the structure the machers have built to provide themselves power and status. "For the sake of sustaining the establishment, you need the victims of society: this is an aberration in Jewish life."

✔ The "leadership" of the major community relations organizations is also composed of wealthy men—sometimes of the very same machers who sit on local Federation boards and committees. These organizations include the "Big Three" national "defense" organizations—the American Jewish Committee, American Jewish Congress, and the Anti-Defamation League (ADL); the Jewish Labor Committee; and B'nai B'rith International (which combines "defense" with social services). There are also organizations of organizations, the so-called umbrella groups, including the National Jewish Community Relations Advisory Council (NJCRAC) and the World Jewish Congress—American Section; and a roof organization, composed of organizations *and* umbrella groups: the Conference of Presidents of Major American Jewish Organizations.

The machers in these organizations shape policy on various matters of concern to Jews—from general issues such as health care to specifically Jewish ones such as Israel and anti-Semitism. It is they and their top executives who advocate these policies to governmental and international bodies and officials, and with American political, ethnic, labor, and religious organizations.

Much of what all of these organizations do is glorified public relations. They conduct conferences, workshops, and "fact-finding missions" for Jewish "leaders" and commission and issue policy statements, studies, and surveys on "attitudes." Their endless numbers of press releases feature the organization's president or top executive "speaking out" (that is, reacting to yesterday's news story in the *Times*) on issue X or Y. These statements make it appear that he speaks on behalf of America's Jews—an image the media accepts uncritically and validates by referring to him as a "Jewish leader."

The community relations organizations are not accountable to anyone outside them for their actions. Many American Jews were justifiably upset and disgusted when a self-selected delegation of nine men met in September 1987 with the pope after he had welcomed Austrian President (and former Nazi officer) Kurt Waldheim, a man who has blood on his hands, to the Vatican the preceding June. American Jews had no say about who, if anyone, should go on the trip or what they should say. Nor did they have any opportunity to question or criticize the nine "leaders" upon their return. Other organizational actions have also provoked outrage from many Jews: when the American Jewish Committee met with Argentina's dictators, who also had blood on their hands—the blood of the *desaparecidos,* the estimated thirty thousand people who were "disappeared" during that country's juntas' reign of terror; when the American Jewish Congress opposed government funding for parochial (including Orthodox day) schools; and when the ADL turned over information on the Jewish Defense League to the FBI.

The summer of 1993 saw the beginnings of a public debate on the accountability issue. The catalyst was New York state's report on the Crown Heights riot of two summers before, which faulted the mayor and the police for letting the violence escalate. The report brought to a boil the simmering anger of Orthodox Jews against Jewish establishment organizations for not "being there" for them during the riot, either physically or politically. (There was one exception: A small group of old men, members of the Jewish War Veterans, marched down one of the streets in Crown Heights; they went, uninvited, "to help out.") Not only did their "leaders" not take the subway to Brooklyn but many ignored the anti-Semitism of the rioters, called for restraint by blacks *and* Jews, and praised the mayor for his conciliatory efforts. Scoring these actions, a Brooklyn rabbi lambasted the "defense" organizations who "say they help Jews all over the world. So they should have been standing shoulder to shoulder with us, left their pool parties and come to Brooklyn. We're the victims, and I haven't seen them out here. They're so decoupled [sic] and detached, it's unbelievable. They have 90 percent of the money and represent no one. The grass roots don't know who they are or care."

With the exception of the ADL (whose national director, Abe Foxman, had publicly apologized in 1991 for his organization's inaction), leaders of Jewish organizations reacted defensively to the charges of abandonment, citing the "chasm" between secular and right-wing Orthodox Jews and the latter's having "distanced themselves" from the "mainstream" organizations. The debate took place mostly in the press, there being no mechanism for average Jews to challenge or confront the "leaders" face-to-face and to hold them accountable not only in this case but in general.

Furthermore, ordinary Jews have no way to seek accountability from Jewish organizations about how they spend the Jewish people's money. The Federations' umbrella group, the Council of Jewish Federations (CJF), has a Large City Budgeting Commission (LCBC). It reviews at the CJF's annual General Assembly the reports on budgets and activities submitted by the national Jewish organizations that solicit allocations from local Federations, but these reports are not available to the public. Nor is it possible in most cases to acquire the budgets of Jewish organizations from state charity registration departments because, as self-defined "religious organizations," they are exempt from filing them. (Strangely, while the New York UJA-Federation is classified by New York state as a "religious organization," the basis on which it receives various government grants is its being defined as "nonsectarian.") The only way people can find out about Jewish organizations' budgets and investments, and about the salaries of their top executives, is through the Freedom of Information Act.

THE SYMBIOTIC RELATIONSHIP

To lure Big Givers and make it appealing and worthwhile for them to part with their money, an organization must give them what they want. And what they want is the prestige that accrues from being validated by a high-status organization—plus the opportunity to meet other Big Givers who will be good business and professional contacts.

An organization's status is measured by its glamour quotient. To project an image of glamour, an organization must work on (the community relations agencies) or allocate funds to (the Federations) glamorous projects, of which more shortly. An organization that has no glamorous projects struggles to reposition itself by finding some before it goes under. It must also recruit celebrities, who are glamorous by their very nature and can sometimes make an unglamorous project glamorous by their association with it, even if all they do is sign their names to direct-mail appeals. By doing both of these things, the organization can hope to attract a great deal of media coverage, the third component of a glamorous image. Having recruited Big Givers with its glamour, the organization can amass a huge budget, the fourth component of a glamorous image and also the prerequisite for enhancing it further.

Once a Big Giver has associated himself with a particular organization and demonstrated the extent of his material success by making a large contribution, the organization needs to provide him with the validation he seeks. This validation takes the form of *koved*-fixes (*koved* is Hebrew/Yiddish for honor) to keep him "involved." One instant koved-fix for a really Big Giver and/or a man with access to other potential Big Givers is to make him president or chair of the organization. (This also ensures that he will recruit and solicit wealthy friends and colleagues.)

Another koved-fix is membership on a prestigious committee or board. When Big Givers contribute a large sum of money, said Shapiro, what they buy with it is position. And, indeed, some men will approach a macher saying, "I want to be on X board or Y committee. How much will it cost?" A Federation allocates money to various agencies, from those dealing with child welfare to those assisting the elderly. It can and does assign Big Givers to the boards of these agencies. However, this means that boards of Federation-funded agencies are composed of people beholden to the Federation, who defend its policies to the agency, rather than of people who represent the agency and advocate its needs to the Federation. This absentee board system increases Federation power.

Other koved-fixes are awards with fulsome encomiums to enhance the donors' status in their business or profession and generally; meetings with otherwise inaccessible people and with dignitaries and celebrities; having buildings, rooms, and academic chairs named for them, with name plaques prominently displayed; and having their pictures and encomium texts printed in the Jewish media. The Jewish Telegraphic (news) Agency (JTA), for example, printed verbatim the words of praise voiced in 1993 by Jewish Theological Seminary (JTS) Chancellor Rabbi Ismar Schorsch upon receiving a million-dollar check from dying ninety-three-year-old industrialist Samuel Melton: "Sam," he said, "at this moment, you remind me of Moses. Just as Moses, as he prepared for death, thought first of his community by naming Joshua to succeed him, so you have done with these gifts" (to JTS and two other institutions).

Organizational "leaders" and their hired bureaucrats bestow koved-fixes on Big Givers with the cavalier and hardened cynicism of the old-style Tammany Hall politicos when dispensing patronage.

⁌ The worth of the validation accorded the Big Giver, however, depends on the image of the organization. The more glamorous it is, the more the koved from it counts. Therefore, a great deal of the staff's time and energy is devoted to burnishing the organization's image. The big newspaper ads taken out by organizations help establish and reinforce the high status of the organization so that a Big Giver seeking prestige through association with it can point with pride to the ad and say, "I'm a member of the board." News stories about the organization, especially in the general media, serve a similar purpose.

Just as the Israeli male soldiers' validation of masculinity fluctuates with the success of the army (collective), so, too, the worth of the validation of the Big Givers and machers fluctuates with the fortunes of the organization from which they derive it. This accounts in part for their intense organizational chauvinism and for their resentment and suppression of any criticism of the organization, which could tarnish its image and thereby threaten its status—and their own.

What we have here, then, is a sick symbiotic relationship: The Big Giver uses the organization—whose structure is composed of other Big Givers, machers, and top executives (the membership, if any, is irrelevant)—for power, contacts, and status accruing from its glamour. The organization uses the Big Giver for funds and contacts to enable it to be involved with glamorous projects or issues that will attract more Big Givers. It's a self-perpetuating merry-go-round.

THE CLAMOR FOR GLAMOUR

What makes a project/issue glamorous in the Jewish community, that is, to those men who dominate it, relates primarily to the men's definition of masculinity and to the visibility/invisibility conflict. To be glamorous, a project/issue must provide the men involved with it *visible* proof that they are living up to the American definition of masculinity or part of it: of their material success and/or political aggressiveness (which is an approved substitute for physical aggressiveness). But at precisely the same time, the issue/project must also provide *visible* proof that the men are "good Americans," evidence that is derived from the fact that the work is altruistic—"good for America," as their reference group defines it.

Institutions Jews establish or maintain have greater glamour if they "serve the entire community" (that is, "not only" Jews) or if they do not have very high Jewish distinctiveness or if they are distinctive but in certain approved ways (for example, synagogues, because religion is a kosher American value). Issues Jews mobilize around have glamour if they are (portrayed as) not "only" concerning Jews. This is why organizations that engage in political aggressiveness by fighting anti-Semitism try to show that their work is for tolerance/"good intergroup relations" that will benefit all Americans. Projects in the U.S. that serve only Jews (Jewish education) or emphasize Jewish distinctiveness (Jewish culture) or issues that concern only Jews (Syrian Jewry in the 1980s) usually have no glamour in the community. Finally, if an issue has glamour in the general society, this might sometimes give it glamour by association among Jews.

◆➤ Almost all building projects are intrinsically glamorous: It has long been noted that American Jews suffer from an "edifice complex." All too often, however, while much attention is paid to constructing the building, little is dribbled out to its Jewish content. Rabbi Wolfe Kelman once observed that congregations spend hundreds of thousands of dollars on carpeting the synagogue's sanctuary and adorning it with stained-glass windows but provide no budget for the Hebrew school library.

Buildings with men's names on them are visible evidence of their material success and proclaim to all that the men are *really* here, that their presence on the American scene is neither ephemeral nor fleeting. The chair of a New York UJA-Federation capital fund-raising drive understood this motivation when he trumpeted in his sales pitch that a donor's million dollars can "leverage" ten million dollars in matching funds from the government: "So the donor *gets his name* on a $10 million building—now that's a bargain" (italics mine).

Plaques go back in American Jewish history to before 1860, but they really took off after World War II, with buildings, parks, plazas—and even air conditioners—sporting them. The plaque with the Big Giver's name on it that graces/(defaces) the outer or inner walls of a Jewish institution serves to mark it as his turf, one that defines his masculinity. This form of claiming territory goes all the way back to our animal ancestry.

◆➤ Hospitals, which are highly visible and "serve the entire community"—and especially building funds to erect or expand them—have long been the most intrinsically glamorous project in the Jewish community. And because of this and the power of building-fund contributors, a Jewish-sponsored hospital building is permanent. Unlike municipal or private hospitals, it will not be closed down; nor will it suffer the dire fate of abandonment faced by other Jewish buildings, such as synagogues and Jewish centers, when Jews desert the old neighborhood for an upscale suburb. Moreover, medicine has always had cachet with Jews.

Jewish hospitals were once needed to serve Jewish clients and provide employment for Jewish doctors. Neither need is relevant today—nor can a patient get a kosher meal from most of these hospitals' kitchens—so why should a Federation fund these institutions? The answer is that a Federation needs to have a glamorous institution listed among its beneficiaries (thus giving it glamour by association) and to have a board it can assign really Big Givers to. An executive at New York's Mount Sinai Hospital once told Shapiro that, given government funding and third-party payments, the money it receives from the city's Federation "isn't what makes or breaks the hospital, and the paperwork is not worth my time. . . . *We don't need them, they [the Federation] need us"* (italics mine).

The urge to have glamorous projects on their list of beneficiaries, whether the recipients need their money or not, is also a criterion in Federations' decisions to allocate funds to the Big Three national defense organizations. Although these organizations raise the lion's share of most of their funds through their own campaigns, Federations continue to allocate millions of dollars to them each year ($3.89 million in 1991–92).

Another problematic aspect of Federation allocation priorities derives from the requirement that a facility be "nonsectarian." This means that Federation-funded old-age homes, camps, or foster-care agencies that also receive government grants cannot be ethnically oriented; sometimes the majority of such an institution's clients are not Jews. Is it the function of a Jewish Federation to support programs that are not primarily of benefit to the Jewish community? But since the formula of "what's good for the macher and Big Giver is good for the organization is good for the community" obtains, these issues are considered "nondata."

⋰ Poverty and homelessness were unglamorous issues until the late 1980s. Anne Wolfe's 1971 revelation that the community had ignored the needs of eight hundred thousand poor Jews in the U.S. provoked a flurry of hostile and defensive reactions. Subsequent research disclosed that two-thirds of the Jewish poor were elderly and the other third comprised single people and one-parent families, many with young children. It is not surprising that the community did not exert itself to reach out to the latter population, considering, wrote Chaim Waxman, that it defined anything other than the traditional two-parent family as "deviant" and feared that adopting policies to "integrate" single-parent families might "legitimize a previously disapproved form of family life." (Discussions at the CJF's 1992 General Assembly seemed to indicate that many in the community were still struggling with this issue.)

Because New York's Federation ignored the poor, young Jewish social workers founded the Metropolitan New York Coordinating Council on Jewish Poverty in 1972; it has established two kosher homeless shelters. But in 1986–87 a confidential marketing survey of the yuppie types the New York UJA-Federation hoped to hook into their campaign revealed that they found local problems, such as homelessness and AIDS, glamorous. The Federation repositioned its campaign propaganda accordingly. A 1989 poster boasted, "We help children, the jobless, the disabled. We help the homeless and people with AIDS." Nevertheless, because the Federation does not advertise its services widely or do outreach programs, many poor and homeless Jews continue to fall through the cracks.

The Los Angeles Federation—to "involve" (that is, extract money from) the 70 percent of Jews it discovered to be unaffiliated with any Jewish institution or activity—focused on the homeless in seven of its eight 1989 newspaper ads. Even the nonestablishment Chabad (Lubavitch Hassidic) movement emphasized in its 1989, 1990, and 1991 Los Angeles telethons its apparently successful work with the homeless and with substance abusers; it sloughed over its religious programs.

The elderly have never been glamorous, especially if they are poor. In New York, where no Federation-sponsored old-age homes exist, many elderly Jews have been subjected to the abuse of private institutions run by criminally negligent owners. Although most Federations outside New York sponsor old-age homes, the American Jewish community as a whole has never grappled with the problem of long-term care for the physically and mentally disabled elderly.

Federations fund Jewish community centers and YM-YWHA's, but most of these institutions no longer serve the elderly and/or poor (and their Jewish content is often skimpy and bland). Commented Orthodox educator Marvin Schick:

> They're called Jewish centers but they're country clubs. A Jewish center used to be a Y and it used to be in the inner city.... And you used to have old Jews schlep there, and you used to have poor Jews served there ... and elderly people could get together. What does the Federation now worry about? Their Olympic-sized swimming pool, their state-of-the-art gym.... That has nothing to do with charity.

In 1991 the New York UJA-Federation closed several urban Y's while continuing to fund those in suburbia.

Day care is an exceedingly unglamorous issue, despite the fact that studies have revealed that it is the one thing Jewish parents really want from the community. Jewish day care would provide an excellent opportunity to instill Jewish values and customs in children at an impressionable age and provide them the kind of Jewish experiences many no longer have at home, especially since most Jewish families no longer have grandparents living nearby. A Jewish day care center, working with a senior citizen's center or old-age home, could also give the elderly a new lease on life by bringing them together with the kids to share their wisdom and experience. Although space exists in synagogues, most of which stand empty until after-school programs begin in the late afternoon, a 1984 CJF study revealed that a mere six thousand Jewish children in the entire U.S. were served by such community-sponsored programs. (The numbers may have increased since that date, but no official statistics are available.) The high cost of maintaining day care centers, the dwindling sources of scholarship funds, and the centers' low salaries are cited by Federations as major impediments to the expansion of Jewish day care.

✦ But the very old and the very young are not the only unglamorous constituencies. An organization of black Jews in New York called *Hatza'ad Harishon* (Hebrew for the first step) tried valiantly to get an annual ten-thousand-dollar Federation grant in the 1960s. A Federation commission was established to "deal" with the issue; this hallowed tactic in Jewish communal life works to siphon off the supplicants' energy and wear them down. The commission successfully fended off the organization for *ten years,* and it subsequently folded.

JEWISH EDUCATION AND CULTURE: THE UNGLAMOROUS STEPCHILDREN

American Federations allocate about 5 to 8 percent of their budgets to Jewish education (in contrast with their Toronto counterpart, which gave it the second highest amount of money after its allocation to Israel). The slight increase in Federation funding for education in the 1980s leveled off by the next decade.

Most of the Jewish schools that receive Federation money are of the afternoon or Sunday school genre. Their thrust is mainly to teach Hebrew (which they do poorly) rather than using the limited time available to teach Jewish history and culture, as did the old Yiddish afternoon schools of the first half of this century. A 1964–66 survey of Jewish high school and college students revealed that, as children, they had experienced instruction in these schools as "frequently dull and vapid . . . often accompanied by poor teaching and uninteresting material," which evoked paralyzing boredom and provoked desertion after the Bar/Bat Mitzvah. A 1987 study by the Board of Jewish Education in New York came up with similar conclusions, demonstrating that little had changed in the past quarter-century.

In 1967 former B'nai B'rith president Philip Klutznick said that he found it inexplicable that the community did not upgrade teacher training and salaries while it continued to kvetch publicly about the difficulty of attracting qualified people to the Jewish education field. But this inaction is not inexplicable, nor is the fact that only four out of every ten Jewish children in the U.S. receive any kind of formal Jewish education, according to a 1990 report. Both phenomena derive from the fact that the machers have never wished to make authentic Jewish education universally available. This would advance the Jewish distinctiveness they have been trying to eradicate. They have also feared that educated Jews—who had learned enough about Jewish history to realize how aberrant the current communal system is—might challenge their illegitimate power.

It is for these same reasons that the machers who run most Federations have, until recently, evinced little interest in funding Jewish day schools. Machers and their hired functionaries kvetch publicly about the decline in Jewish population and the rise in intermarriage. But they do nothing to make scholarships available to pupils in Jewish day schools, whose fees, with a few exceptions, are on par with those of good private schools and are thus prohibitive, especially for parents with several children to educate. Nor do they fund imaginative approaches to Jewish education, such as low-cost top-level Jewish high schools with excellent secular courses plus Jewish studies programs for students with no previous Jewish education. (The innovative Organization for Rehabilitation Through Training [ORT] high school in Buenos Aires provides an excellent model for such an approach.)

Of course, nobody has ever asked the masses of Jews whether they would wish the Federations to allocate more money to Jewish education and what kind of education (its philosophy, content, and structure) they would choose for their children if it existed and/or was affordable.

Jewish culture is another stepchild—neglected, shunted aside, ignored. Said a young cultural worker in 1986: "Culture is almost foreign in the Jewish community. When they think of culture, they think of Lincoln Center. Not one major Jewish organization has a cultural arm. No Jewish organization nurtures Jewish creativity. The big money people are not interested." (And, indeed, two years later, Paul Ritterband, director of the CUNY Center for Jewish Studies, told a conference that Jews are increasingly giving money to mainstream American cultural institutions because these "can give the large donor public recognition.") A few examples of the treatment of Jewish cultural endeavors will suffice:

• Jewish filmmakers receive no support from the community. One young
   filmmaker earned money to complete his work by playing violin music on
   the New York subway. Aviva Kempner received no funds from any national
   Jewish organization for her documentary *Partisans of Vilna,* possibly the
   best film ever made on the Holocaust. And, at a time of increased
   recognition of the importance of movies and videos in reaching young
   people—and a need for what can be called YidVid—the JWB (now renamed
   the Jewish Community Centers Association, JCCA) closed down its Jewish
   Media Service.

• In 1988 the Jewish Museum of New York (sponsored by the Conservative
   movement's Jewish Theological Seminary) ejected artists from basement
   rooms they had used as workshops—to create a lounge for volunteers.

• The American Jewish Congress closed down its Steinberg Center for the Arts in
   1986 after a decade of work, citing "desperate financial straits" (the center's
   annual budget was then fifty thousand dollars a year; the American Jewish
   Congress's was seven million). The AJCongress's executive director said that
   enriching Jewish cultural life was "marginal" to its "central purpose"—and an
   "inappropriate" role for the AJCongress to play.

• Jewish establishment organizations, with the exception of the AJCommittee, have no libraries, certainly none regularly accessible to the general public. There is no Jewish public library in any American city like those in Toronto and Montreal. In 1993, the JCCA dumped its Jewish Book Council and Jewish Lecture Bureau.

• There is not one Jewish publishing company in the U.S. under communal auspices (unlike Argentina, where the Mila publishing house issued ninety books between 1987 and 1991, including Spanish translations of major Jewish classics). Over 90 percent of Yiddish literature remains untranslated into English. While Jewish institutions are festooned with plaques naming Big Givers who wrote them checks, no Jewish establishment organization has ever thought of attaching plaques to the houses where great Jewish authors once lived and wrote immortal literature (e.g., Sholem Aleichem's in the Bronx).

Archives are another stepchild as far as the Jewish establishment is concerned. The YIVO Institute for Jewish Research has more than twenty-two million items, some going back centuries, chronicling the history of East European Jews and their descendants in America. After years of having to store its archives in warehouses in Brooklyn (where about one-quarter to one-third are still housed), it finally got funds from foundations and the National Endowment for the Humanities to put them on microfilm. In 1992 it received a grand total of $180,000—8 percent of its budget of $2.15 million—from Federations across the U.S. The attitudes of the Federations can be encapsulated in the response of the one in New York to YIVO's request for an emergency grant during a financial low point in the 1970s: It firmly admonished YIVO to solve the crisis by selling its landmark building. The Leo Baeck Institute, whose archives and programs on the Jews of Germany is similar to YIVO's work regarding those of Eastern Europe, had a total budget of $825,000 in 1992, of which a pitiful $60,000 (7 percent) came from Federations.

Priceless Jewish artifacts are sold at auctions and thereby lost to the Jewish people—and to the rest of the world. In the 1950s the notes of lexicographer Eliezer Ben Yehuda, the reviver of the Hebrew language, were sold scrap by precious scrap to finance publication of the remaining volumes of his dictionary.

Shapiro's concerns, expressed in 1969, about the inadequate protection of Jewish archives proved sadly prescient. Irreplaceable files of the *Vaad HaHatzala,* the Orthodox rescue agency during the Holocaust, were burned in a fire. Hundreds of Yiddish books inadequately stored by the Farband (the fraternal organization of the Labor Zionist Alliance) after it sold its building were rescued in 1981 only because a member of the Yiddish Book Center of Amherst (which has retrieved over half a million Yiddish books) happened to spot them on the street one rainy evening. He sent out an SOS. After driving all night, the center's young people arrived in New York at dawn and loaded most of the books onto their truck.

When the Jewish Forward (*Forverts*) Association sold its building on the Lower East Side and moved uptown in 1974, it tossed out on the street virtually its entire archive since the newspaper's inception in 1897, thus reducing a large part of the Jewish people's history to dust and ashes. The library of the American Section of the World Zionist Organization was forced to dump dozens of boxes of Israeli newspapers going back decades when it moved; no organization wanted them. When Hadassah moved to a new building in 1976, it threw into the garbage a mountain of material, including irreplaceable files on its work in the late 1930s for Youth Aliyah (which rescued youngsters from Nazi Germany and elsewhere in occupied Europe and took them to Eretz Israel). An employee protesting the dumping of decades of invocations from the organization's conventions was told, "Who's interested in the prayer someone said before the meal?" But it is precisely such invocations that Ellen Umansky has drawn on in her research on the religious lives of American Jewish women.

This is how the "People of the Book" treasures its historical record.

TURF BATTLES

Because involvement with glamorous projects is the key to an organization's image, and thus to its success in attracting Big Givers, Jewish organizations vie with each other for turf: capturing jurisdiction over a particular issue or project that is regarded as glamorous.

Competition for glamorous turf is particularly acute among the major community relations organizations, none of which exists or raises funds to carry out a specific, well-defined goal or aim. Rather, their stated purpose is the usual vague "Jewish survival," the motherhood-and-apple-pie of Jewish communal life.

The Big Three, for example, all claim to be struggling for Jewish rights everywhere, for "good intergroup relations," against anti-Semitism, and in political defense of Israel. Their styles of operation differ: The AJCommittee attempts to operate quietly behind the scenes as supershtadlanim, especially with the hierarchy of the Catholic church; the AJCongress works through the courts with its *amicus curiae* briefs, especially in favor of church-state separation; the ADL stresses "monitoring" extremist groups and making its information available to law enforcement agencies (and sometimes the public at large). But the work they and the other community relations organizations do involves a tremendous amount of overlap and duplication.

Their budgets are worth comparing. In 1991–92, ADL's budget was nearly $31.5 million (5 percent derived from Federations); $6.28 million went for fundraising. In that same year, the AJCommittee budget was $18 million (7 percent from Federations); it allocated $2.35 million to fund-raising. In 1992 the AJCongress's budget was $6.58 million (13 percent from Federations); it earmarked $621,000 for fund-raising. Thus these three organizations alone had over $56 million at their disposal in 1991–92 (the fiscal years varied). According to the brief "reports" they submitted to the LCBC, they spent it on fighting anti-Israel propaganda and anti-Semitism and on improving "intergroup relations" (and over $9 million on fund-raising).

One might—and should—ask: Did all this outlay of money do any good (besides support the staff)? Were their press releases worth the trees that died for them? Shouldn't there be some concern about the effectiveness of their work if the organizations' own commissioned surveys indicate that anti-Semitism has not appreciably declined for decades and that hate crimes have escalated?

For many years, the ADL projected the image of being the major organization combating anti-Semitism. The Simon Wiesenthal Center in Los Angeles has cut severely into this turf since its establishment in 1977 by projecting an activist and glamorous image, attracting celebrities, and utilizing the media effectively. A spring 1989 direct-mail piece from the center stated that "our observers *monitor* the world ... for the *earliest signs* of anti-Semitism, alert the public and take immediate, direct action through the authorities," which is precisely what the ADL claims to do. Practically the same wording was used by the World Jewish Congress (WJC) in its 1990 direct-mail piece, which stressed its "*early warning system* that provides us with a critical defense*" (italics mine).

B'nai B'rith International (BBI) used to supply most of the funding to the Hillel Foundations (considered the equivalent of local Jewish communities on college campuses). But in the early 1970s, when "the youth" became a glamorous constituency (as we shall see in chapter 14), local Federations began funding them; currently 70 percent of their support comes from Federations. This was a turf takeover ignored by BBI until it was too late. Suffering, as well, from an aging and declining membership, BBI is now struggling to project a vigorous image by having its leaders "speak out" on issues such as ... anti-Semitism.

What is obvious from all this is that Jewish community relations organizations do just about the same thing and spend a lot of their energy and time competing for jurisdictional dominance and for funds to continue competing for jurisdictional dominance and funds. (No, this is not a typographical error.)

In 1950 the NJCRAC commissioned a study of the work of the Big Three, the Jewish War Veterans, and other community relations organizations. It was conducted by Columbia University sociology Professor Emeritus Robert MacIver, and his findings still obtain today: "There ... [are] no serious inter-consultations and no cooperative planning ... with respect to programs ... [but instead] competitive conflict and discord as between agencies" and a tremendous duplication of effort. MacIver concluded that "organizational pride" rather than differing ideologies is the cause of "vexatious *disputes over jurisdiction* [involving] ... the natural tendency of every organization to *arrogate to itself as much territory and as much influence as possible*" (italics mine).

᭪ Since there is so much overlap in these organizations' work, the battles to capture and hold glamorous turf usually trigger organizational chauvinism. Each organization tries to portray itself as *the* one that deals best with issue X or Y, as the most important one working for "Jewish survival"–and as the ultimate rescuer of the Jewish people. For example, the UJA slogan "Keep the Promise" deliberately echoes the supplication to and description of God who guards/ remembers/preserves His promise to redeem the Jewish nation. The slogan thus elevates the organization that "keeps the promise," and its "leaders," to Godlike rescuer status.

A second purpose in cultivating a rescuer image for the organization is that this activates the old concept that rescuers may be flawed and that their flaws can be repaired. The standard American repair method is to throw money at problems, which is why Jewish organizations always attribute any difficulties they experience to financial problems that can be easily overcome by transfusions of cash.

A third major purpose of the rescuer image is to ensure that average Jews who contribute small sums to the organization or none at all continue to view it as legitimate *and do not challenge or criticize it*. Once an organization has successfully promoted the image of itself as a secular rescuer, Jews' critical faculty evaporates. That is why the previously cited 1991–92 organizational affiliation survey could reveal "the overall warmth . . . with which many American Jews regard Jewish organizations." The respondents, said an AJCommittee analysis of the survey, rarely expressed negative images of the organizations or criticized their agendas or activities.

The dynamics obtaining in the relationship of American Jews to Jewish establishment organizations that disempower them recapitulate/recycle those of the classic Jewish gender division of labor. The plutocracy arrogates to itself the male role of doing what it defines as the most important work, the turf of making and implementing decisions on communal policy, priorities, and programs. The masses of Jews fulfill the old female role of enabling–facilitating the plutocracy's work by providing it emotional support and legitimization and accepting exclusion from its turf. As altruistic-assertive wifelike enablers, they are supposed to speak up only when it is "altruistic," that is, in the interests of the specific Jewish organization as it defines these. They are supposed to follow a *sha-shtil* (Yiddish for keeping one's mouth shut, especially regarding anything that could make Jews look bad to "the goyim") policy otherwise–even when it may be in their own interests to question, criticize, or demand accountability. This dynamic, too, contributes to the egregious absence of debate–and democracy–in the community. Meanwhile Jews close their eyes to the contradiction between the high-minded words of Jewish "leaders" praising democracy in America but thwarting it inside their own community.

POWER PLAYGROUNDS

Struggles for power go on incessantly inside Jewish establishment organizations: macher versus macher, executive versus executive, and macher versus executive. Some organizations are dominated by the machers and some by their top executives (a.k.a. professionals); in others, there is an uneasy truce between them.

Until fairly recently, executives had considerable leeway in shaping policy. They could even suggest machers to be recruited and elevated to higher and higher positions in accordance with the escalation of their "gifts." Federation executives could also identify the young men in various local communities to be invited to join the (then-stag) national UJA Young Leadership Cabinet, where they would be primed to be future Big Givers in their hometowns.

One reason the machers allowed the professionals to set policy was that they felt the latter were more expert than themselves in community relations, law, government, and social services. Now that many machers have entered these fields, they are reclaiming the policy turf from the professionals. The result is an intensification of the power struggle between machers and professionals (one sociologist called this "the tyranny of the lay leaders"), leading to the firing and forced retirement of key executives in Jewish organizations in the 1980s and 1990s. With one exception, when told it was time to move on, none took legal action. Nor has there been any follow-up to the idea proposed some years ago to establish a kind of bet din to adjudicate such cases within the community.

The wage structure is one in which the executive director (a.k.a. executive vice-president) is paid top dollar on the grounds that it is necessary to attract the best people (the range in the late 1980s and early 1990s was $150,000 to $300,000 a year); the next in line receives about two-thirds of this; and the rest, the line workers, are "paid like peasants," said Kosmin (who also serves as CJF's research director). It goes hand in hand with rampant sexism in hiring, promoting, and working with women (to be discussed in chapter 13).

While many of the line workers (low-level professionals) are unionized, some organizations have sweetheart unions; others exclude professionals from the union by favoring only them with pension plans. Unions are also weakened by the reluctance of the workers to use the ultimate weapon, the strike. The workers of only two national Jewish organizations—Israel Bonds and the United Synagogue (Conservative congregational structure)—have gone on strike in recent decades.

Employees who contemplate a strike or legal action are castigated as traitors whose demands could cause the organization to go under and thus eliminate it as a rescuer of the Jewish nation. Striking obviously falls into the category of abandonment of and separation from the organization, in addition to being bad for its image. The workers, in short, are expected to function as altruistic enablers of the machers and the highly paid top executives, to put the interests of the organization and its lay and professional "leaders" ahead of their own.

People who have worked for Jewish organizations have experienced and observed with considerable dismay (and surprise, if they were organizationally virginal) the "leaders'" overall mean-spiritedness toward the employees—the professionals and, especially, the clerical and technical staff—for instance, forcing line workers to pay their own transportation to organizational conventions and workshops they are required to attend and harassing people to quit.

In addition, those who had expected to find a spirit of cooperation, dedication, purpose, and "Jewish warmth" there have often been shocked by the contrast between the high-minded self-image of the organization as the Jewish people's rescuer and the heartlessness of the workplace; between the stress on the employees' altruism and the machers' and executives' power-hungry and status-seeking behavior; and between the expectation of being treated like mishpucha and the reality of being treated like "peasants."

◈ In essence the Jewish organizational milieu is a safe space where machers and Big Givers can indulge in the kind of behavior that would be impossible for them in the corporate suite or in a non-Jewish upper-middle-class volunteer organization. A wannabee macher might hesitate to be superaggressive and hypercompetitive in a non-Jewish milieu because of his internal conflicts concerning inconspicuousness, especially since he would be the new kid on the block and would therefore need to tread even more carefully. But in Jewish establishment organizations, he can play the kind of power games that non-Jewish men play in their corporations and organizations. He can also behave in accordance with the Jewish expressive style of high-decibel arguing, interrupting others, and wild emotionalism—behavior non-Jews are uncomfortable with, especially in corporate America.

Above all, in Jewish organizations, a macher or a Big Giver can freely indulge in verbally aggressive behavior that a former Jewish organizational professional described as "stripping the skin off their backs." It includes brutal go-for-the-jugular insults, harassment of executives ("Why wasn't my name in the *Times* today?!"), and incessant puerile demands for koved-fixes accompanied by threats to quit and take away the piggy bank unless these are dispensed immediately.

Thus, inside the Jewish establishment, as in Portnoy's bathhouse, "there is nothing to worry about": There are "no goyim" sitting in judgment and consequently no necessity to monitor or censor one's behavior.

It is, in short, mishpucha.

The macher's and Big Giver's behavior actually resembles that of a spoiled male child in an American non-Orthodox Jewish middle-class family, who is idolized and can get away with almost anything short of violence as long as he "produces" good grades. Here, in the safe bosom of the organization, his bad-boy behavior is indulged just as it was when he was growing up—as long as he "produces" big "gifts." In an infamous incident at a public meeting of the Jewish

Agency in Jerusalem in the early 1970s (where Big Givers to Federations in the U.S. and their counterparts in other countries were assembled), a man began shouting drunkenly from the balcony at the speaker on the stage. The audience became restive, and a security guard inched toward him. Suddenly Louis Pincus, head of the Jewish Agency, called out from the stage: "Let him speak! He gives one million dollars!" (They let him speak.)

The threat of withholding—of not contributing big bucks—becomes a real weapon in Jewish organizations. If the Big Giver follows through with the threat, however, he can be punished by the machers' withholding koved, just as Jewish parents withhold expressions of love upon perusal of a bad report card.

A business management professor's description of the behavior of narcissists in the corporate world applies equally well to that of machers' and Big Givers' behavior in Jewish organizations:

> These narcissists . . . tend to try to *make their organization recreate the childhood they long for,* with themselves at the center of a loving world. . . . Many business organizations tend to reward the narcissistic fantasies of those at the upper echelons, who receive the *adulation* of those below. When the process becomes pathological, the organization becomes totalitarian, with those below fearing to do or say anything that does not fit in with the idealized view of those at the top [italics mine].

It is no wonder that the Jewish establishment is undemocratic: Democracy would destroy the entire system the machers and Big Givers have created to meet their own narcissistic needs.

◆► The power and prestige machers attain inside the community can propel some of them into acting as its ambassadors to the non-Jewish world if they are perceived by their peers in the plutocracy to be close enough to it in behavior. This ambassadorship gives them high status in the general society. The reason is that many non-Jews continue to believe the myth about Jewish (collective) power: If the community as a collectivity is so powerful, its "leaders" must be really powerful. (This is one reason the "leaders" are reluctant to puncture the power myth.) Moreover, these men can attain this high status without having to struggle for it directly in the general society with all the difficulties this entails, especially regarding breaking the visibility/conspicuousness taboo.

Nevertheless, once they function as communal ambassadors to the non-Jewish power structure, their conflict is actually intensified by the high visibility inherent in the role. (This is why their fellow machers, and even the masses of Jews, are content to let the men who are willing to take the heat in this regard do so.) They therefore attempt to reduce/dilute the Jewish distinctiveness of the organization they represent, and the community as a whole, and to align its behavior with that approved by the power structure, which identifies them with it. The less distinctly Jewish the organization is in values and public behavior, the less the ambassadors have to worry about the dangers involved in their being so visibly associated with it.

This is a prime reason that many of the values that characterized Jewish communal life for two thousand years—altruism, cooperation, empathy—are so eroded in Jewish organizations in America today. It would be against these men's interests to strengthen these values, especially since so many of them are female values denigrated by the men of their reference group. The values that now inform the Jewish establishment to a great degree are patriarchal: power, dominance, materialism, competitiveness, status seeking. But they are camouflaged by propaganda that the programs and processes of the Jewish establishment are altruistic: "good for the Jews."

THE "NEW RELIGION"

A letter in the Cairo Genizah dated 1007 C.E. reveals the antiquity of some fundraising strategy. The principal of the Babylonian yeshiva of Pumpedita sent out an emergency appeal for funds. When it reached a community in what is now Tunisia, the elders there persuaded Ben Ata, a prominent physician and courtier, to head the appeal. He made a substantial donation, others followed suit, and the campaign was a great success. Significantly, Ben Ata later received the title *nagid* (Hebrew for prince/patron: princely patron), a mark of high regard, from the Pumpedita yeshiva.

The modern-day incarnation of this time-honored strategy is to get a Big Giver to head a fund-raising campaign and thus pull in money from peers in his field. He gets the instant koved of a prestigious title. Federation campaigns are organized into "trade divisions." Men in a specific business (such as women's sportswear manufacturing), profession, or industry become members of a division composed of their peers. A popular technique, used at Federation dinners, is to honor a member of one of the trade divisions. Because the invitees are business associates of the honoree, there is no way they can refuse to attend, and they know they are expected to make pledges in his honor.

The process involves the chairman's reading off from cards the names of the guests one by one, followed by the amount they donated last year. The invitees are then expected to pledge a contribution. Wrote professional fund-raiser Milton Goldin: "None dare give less than the previous year; few dare give the same amount. Either alternative might be taken by competitors and friends alike as an indication that business is bad." Some Federations actually publish books listing each donor's "gift."

Awards and guest of honor citations, replete with fulsome encomiums and/or plaques for the honorees' great devotion to Jewish life (writing checks), are standard features of Jewish organizational dinners. One organization, for example, gave its "*Shomrim*—Guardians of Jewish Unity" award in 1989 to "four outstanding couples who share the values of family, rootedness in group, and the totality of the community. [The organization] believes that each one of these couples represents the ideal of the triumph of life: that the way to transform the world into a place where all humans can live in dignity and peace is to start with one family, then one community, then one people, and finally one world."

If the guest of honor knows that his being honored is a fund-raising technique and that the encomium is gross hyperbole, why does he find it moving nonetheless? One might ask how a guest of honor, according to Goldin's report, could have "burst into tears" at one such affair when the chairman read aloud the text on the plaque even though the man "*had written the words himself*" (italics mine).

It seems that public validation is so important that nothing else—not its cynical motivation or its obvious mendacity—matters. The encomiums, especially the oral ones, are the publicly expressed words of praise so often withheld by Jewish parents and, the men feel, by their wives as well. Hearing himself described in front of his peers as a "leader," "benefactor," "defender," "ambassador," or "a legend in his own lifetime," the macher or Big Giver can drink in the longed-for adulation—even if he did write the words himself. In fact, it is very possible that the real thrill comes from knowing that the organization had to bestow these words of praise whether it wanted to or not because he has power over it, the power to withhold his "gifts." Extracting undeserved praise may thus be more of a validation of his worth (that is, power) than receiving deserved adulation.

◆ Giving awards is also a way of attracting celebrity speakers to Jewish organizational dinners, which have all the excitement of root canal work and feel about as interminable. A celebrity is necessary to keep people in their seats after dinner—when they must endure listening to a long list of speakers, each lauded in turn—until at last the guests are rewarded by his or her speech or entertainment. (At non-Federation dinners, which raise money by charging per plate, individuals who must receive koved-fixes are often scattered between the courses.)

A celebrity speaker is usually given an award praising him or her for contributions to Jewish life even though he or she has done nothing to merit such a citation. The American Committee for the Weizmann Institute of Science, for example, lured Kirk Douglas to speak at a 1982 dinner by making him guest of honor for having "long identified himself with Israel." His "identification" consisted of making three films in that country. Some men who received awards—such as Robert Stevens of J. P. Stevens & Co., a notorious union-busting corporation—should not be invited to speak at a Jewish meeting, let alone be honored there.

The money paid out to speakers and entertainers at these functions is prodigious. In 1989, for example, former U.S. Secretary of State George Schultz was one of two men given the Defender of Jerusalem Award by the Jabotinsky Foundation. The award came with fifty thousand dollars—an amount that would have kept the Steinberg Center alive for a year. Prodigious, as well, is the amount of food thrown out after Jewish organizational dinners instead of being turned over to food banks such as City Harvest in New York, as was proposed in 1986.

The entire process of fund-raising by American Jewish organizations is a travesty of tzedakah. It violates the laws and spirit of tzedakah by intimidating and/or shaming people into "giving" via card-calling, by Big Givers' asking men who seek business contracts with them or who wish to join their country club how much they give to the campaign, by what a Chicago rabbi called the honoring of "men [sic] of questionable merit"—rather than those who exhibit "qualities of learning and character"—in order to extract their money. Giving anonymously with no expectation of recognition was considered by Maimonides to be a higher form of tzedakah, and in the past, even the poorest of the poor were expected to drop a few *kopeks* into the *pushkeh* (Yiddish for tzedakah kitty) to help those even more destitute than them. But anonymous giving would preclude the public validation the Big Givers seek so desperately.

❧ Federation campaigns embody elements reminiscent of the ancient animal sacrifice cult at the Temple. The men present their "gifts"—expected to be (how revealing is their own choice of words!) on the "sacrificial level"—to the high priests, the machers, and are thereby "absolved" of their sins of omission, of not leading an authentically Jewish life. The "sacrifice" of their money brings to mind the potlatch of Native Americans of the Northwest, who hurled blankets and other valuable property into the flames to show how much they could afford to lose. Since the contribution is seen as a sacrifice, it is not all that important where it is allocated after the campaign, as long as the recipient projects are glamorous. And, indeed, surveys of Big Givers have revealed that 50 percent could not name more than two out of the thirty to fifty agencies to which Federations allocate campaign funds.

All this is why a Cleveland Federation professional could say that "giving is the new religion," and why Jonathan Woocher, director of Jewish Education Service of North America (JESNA), could write (approvingly!) that for the vast majority of American Jews, "civil Judaism," as represented by the Federation, has taken the place of the synagogue as the dominating force in the community.

The synagogue and the traditional life of learning, prayer, and ritual observance, he said, are no longer primary: There are "*mitzvot* equally *sacred*." The Federation campaign calendar provides "occasions for *religious* exultation and inspiration which rival or surpass" Shabbat and festivals. The Federations' annual General Assembly, "where the *priests* and prophets of civil Judaism carry out their offices before its assembled *congregation*" comprising "everyone who is anyone in the Jewish world," is now the most important ritual in Jewish life, he concluded (italics mine).

The most outrageous thing Woocher said concerns the Federations' slogan for their campaigns to raise funds for both Israel and American Jewry: "'We are One' becomes a more immediate and compelling watchword of the faith than 'The Lord Is One.'" These are the last words of the Shema (Hear, O Israel) prayer that Jews down the centuries have uttered before being martyred, Al Kiddush HaShem, to Sanctify the Name of God.

THE DESPERATE SEARCH FOR CREATIVE WORK

Jewish organizational life, particularly its fund-raising processes, strangely echoes some of the patterns that obtained in the old national Jewish project of learning Torah—but without its Jewish substance. The coteries of men who are involved in giving and getting others to give money engage in a form of male bonding for what they define as an altruistic purpose ("good for the Jews," "Jewish survival"). Their activities provide them a way to cooperate in pursuit of shared goals and constitute a channel for aggressiveness and an outlet for competitiveness. The men are validated by their peers and honored with the high status once reserved for scholars.

The basic difference, of course, is that studying Torah did contribute to Jewish survival; it was a truly creative endeavor that required dedication, commitment, and respect for the life of the mind. And it gave rise to an organic lifestyle. Studying, too, was open to all men, rich and poor. No such democracy for men (forget women in both cases) exists in the Jewish establishment. Most Jews are disempowered rather than valued for their commitment to and knowledge of Jewishness or for opinions or ideas that could be instrumental in the pursuit of the putative goal of Jewish survival or, as it is now called, Jewish continuity.

What is especially discontinuous with the classic learning lifestyle is that intellectuals are shut out (and shut up) rather than sought out. As Jacob Neusner pointed out in 1975, intellectuals are "not welcome" in the Jewish community; they "have not been wanted, not been listened to and not been deemed to have anything worthwhile to contribute.... The best minds are not available to the Jewish community."

Gone are the days of debate and disputation over law, the respect for differences of opinion, the willingness to explore—and to listen to—unpopular views. The fact that "the moment you disagree, you are a traitor . . . kills all creativity in Jewish life," said then-WJC chair Nahum Goldmann in 1973. How disturbingly different this is from the traditional system in which, said Shapiro, "the heretical mentality made possible the questions" that kept the Constitution of the Jewish people, Halacha, "fresh and alive."

Nevertheless, in some desperate, unconscious way, the establishment men are groping for creative Jewish work—some project as worthwhile as studying was for centuries on end; and informed by some of the old values of altruism, cooperation, and mutuality, and by intense spirituality. The long discussions in the yeshiva have been replaced by interminable meetings; the Hassidic farbrengens where the rebbe gave a discourse, by organizational dinners with speeches by the *un*learned. It is a far cry from a group of poor and downtrodden men huddled over the Talmud in the besmedrush of a forlorn shtetl to a group of rich men in power suits poring over bank balances and computerized printouts around an oak conference table in a major metropolis. But we can see the dim, shadowy parallels.

The tragedy is what is missing from this picture: worthwhile work to satisfy the soul.

⋙ In the absence of creative work, the men must make do with the ersatz naches of finding ever-more efficient ways to harvest the Jewish people's money and to mystify the fund-raising process. That is why the UJA Young Leadership Cabinet's precampaign all-male retreat—the core of which is a session where the men disclose their incomes and make pledges—was trumpeted as "a special experience resulting in the men's returning home *spiritually* renewed," as one participant put it (italics mine).

Mystification is also the motivation behind the Jewish establishment's Orwellian vocabulary, especially at the Federations. It serves as a Jewish cover, hiding the absence of Jewish content. "Involvement," "support," and "commitment" mean giving money and withdrawing from creative Jewish activity. A "leader" means someone with no followers. The Federations' General Assembly (a term of incredible hubris when used by machers, Big Givers, and professional fund-raisers—who are certainly not "everyone who is anyone" in Jewish life—to describe their annual reunion) is the opposite of a body of *elected* delegates who represent the Jewish public.

Participation in Federation campaigns and other fund-raising and advocacy activities does not bring about the intensification of an individual's Jewish behavior; rather, it acts as a legitimized substitute for it. It allows Jews to define their Jewish identity as "being on the board of . . . " and "raising money for . . . " noted a Cleveland rabbi, and to believe they are actually leading "satisfying Jewish lives" while in reality they are engaging in behavior contrary to Jewish values.

Nevertheless, the machers and their paid propagandists continue to chant the mantra that all of these activities are the key to Jewish survival.

The process and the effects of this system—which reinforce the assimilationist values of power and status, depress expressions of Jewish distinctiveness, disenfranchise the vast plurality of Jews, and cause people to desert the community because they feel unwelcome in it—are actually counterproductive to the very Jewish survival its "leaders" claim they advance.

Only a few voices crying in the spiritual wilderness have tried to call attention to the lack of any vision of what the community and Jewish life could be like. One of them was Israel Singer (now secretary-general of the WJC), who said in 1981, "Our lives are vacuous. There are no short, middle or strategic goals—no dream. I am embarrassed to hear Martin Luther King's followers say, 'I have a dream'—when *we* don't."

TWELVE ❧ THE ENDURING–AND CONFLICTED–"MARRIAGE" BETWEEN AMERICAN JEWS AND ISRAEL

We can't have a vital Jewish culture if Jews feel they need only write out a check [to] pay for Jewishness elsewhere in the world.

HILLEL LEVINE

[The relationship is like that of] players and fans. [American Jews] think we [Israelis] are all heroes and, like good fans, they won't tolerate a negative word about us.

ZE'EV CHAFETS

Americans Jews are plugged into Israel as if it were a kidney machine, a scientific marvel that keeps them Jewishly alive.

ALEXANDER SCHINDLER

The undemocratic character of the American Jewish community—its domination by a plutocracy—has been a prime factor in the evolution of the relationship of American Jews with Israel into the enduring but troubled "marriage" it is today.

The "marriage" began with (a) passionate engagement in the immediate postwar period and a joyful honeymoon after the establishment of the State of Israel in 1948. The honeymoon, however, was disrupted when the Jewish establishment plutocracy interposed itself between the masses of American Jews and Israel in the early 1950s.

The plutocracy dammed the masses' feelings of pride and excitement over Israel's birth and accomplishments and their concern about its survival and directed these emotions into the narrow hierarchically organized canals of fundraising and political advocacy that it alone would control. It deprived the masses of any kind of say in choosing these specific activities to define their role on behalf of Israel and of a voice or a vote in how these efforts should be carried out. This stunted the growth/evolution of a genuine relationship between them and Israel based on an open and honest exchange of views/debate, the development of methods of conflict resolution, and an understanding of one another's reality.

The relationship is and was informed by many of the values of traditional Jewish communities—cooperation, mutuality, interdependence, and altruism. But elements from the behavior patterns characteristic of the men in the plutocracy seeped into it, as well: obsessive quests for validation, status seeking, power struggles.

Despite the Jewish establishment plutocracy's control over the relationship, the feelings of the masses of American Jews burst through the dams it had created and ascended to intense passion at various times when Israel was in mortal danger (1967, 1973), surprising both American Jews and Israelis with its intensity. Overall, American Jews remain genuinely committed to Israel's survival and understand that its destiny and that of Jews all over the world are intertwined. But they have never confronted intellectually or emotionally how they could relate to the new reality: the rise of a reborn Jewish commonwealth after two thousand years of national dispersion and persecution.

❧ To understand how and why the plutocracy was able to seize control of the relationship to a large extent, we need to look briefly at the character of the bond before the establishment of Israel and, specifically, at the Zionist movement, which was the parent of the Jewish State.

From its inception in Europe in the late nineteenth century, the Zionist movement was a grassroots democratic and pluralistic movement embracing *Klal Yisrael*—the multivaried totality of the body politic of Jews all over the world. Its political spectrum ranged from left to right, and from militant secularist to militant Orthodox, with all gradations in between; each ideological faction/party tried to win acceptance and adherents among Jews for its vision of what the future state should be like. Through its prime instrumentality, the World Zionist Organization (WZO), the Zionist movement as a whole engaged in a political struggle to win international support for the establishment of a "Jewish commonwealth."

The Zionist movement in America did not win a mass following until the middle of World War II. It reached its zenith of numerical and political strength in the period of 1945–48, when the pitifully few Holocaust survivors emerged from the valley of the shadow of death, sought to go to Eretz Israel, and had the door to this refuge slammed shut in their faces by the British. The passion and pain of the masses of Jews in the U.S. and their understanding of the need for a Jewish state were so great at this time that they could overcome the visibility taboo.

The movement's main activity was political advocacy; fund-raising came second; education ran a poor third. The advocacy work was conducted with mass participation in rallies, marches, and public meetings, some of them addressed by leaders in the struggle for Israeli independence. The movement's propaganda drive, which historian Melvin Urofsky described as "unparalleled in history," helped win the crucial support of the American people, Congress, and the administration for the establishment and recognition of Israel. (The women's

Zionist organizations participated in this struggle, although their prime focus in this period and after 1948 has been on practical projects in Eretz Israel, as we shall see in the next chapter. The discussion here of the politics and transformation of the Zionist movement in America concerns only the male-dominated Zionist organizations.)

The Zionist movement in America had the same political and religious divisions before the establishment of Israel as its counterparts elsewhere had, but it was internally split across party lines on the ideological question of whether America was an Exile. Those who accepted this classic Zionist concept worked for aliyah; those who rejected it engaged in activities to support the Yishuv, especially economically. And all did political work to advocate the establishment of a Jewish commonwealth/state. But none of the Zionist organizations had a domestic program with a Zionist spin on what the American Jewish community should be like. Those who believed America was an Exile worked not to change it but to generate aliyah from it; those who did not accept this concept saw no pressing need to reshape it.

The masses of Jews whose support the Zionist movement won in the post–World War II period did not believe America was an Exile. They were concerned only with the practical goal of the attainment of a Jewish state, viewing it as a place of refuge where other Jews–those who *were* persecuted–would settle. Since they did not feel persecuted or oppressed, they felt no need or obligation to settle there. They had never shared the value system of the Zionist pioneers of the Yishuv or, later, the Israelis, who "saw themselves as building a new Jewish society, ending the suffering of [Exile]," wrote Urofsky. For them, America was the Promised Land, not Israel.

After the establishment of the Jewish State in 1948, the Jewish establishment plutocracy feared that the mass-based Zionist movement, whose struggle and program had been vindicated with the birth of Israel, would take over the leadership of the community. They feared that the movement would grow through the popularity of its activities in support of the newborn state. They also feared that it would challenge the Jewish establishment's domination of the domestic scene by creating a program that would harness the intensified identification of American Jews with their Jewishness generated by the birth of Israel (and their part in it) to rejuvenate (reJEWvenate) communal life.

The plutocracy, therefore, moved quickly to prevent its loss of hegemony. It realized it had to take over the turf of the support of Israel from the Zionist movement and exploit American Jewry's commitment to Israel in the interests of enhancing and consolidating its own power. The community relations organizations took over the political defense of Israel, and, after the dust settled in 1949 following a bitter power and personality struggle, the Federations gained control over raising and allocating funds for Israeli social welfare needs.

Judah Shapiro noted that there was a clear recognition on the part of the Federations that they could now raise even more money by appealing to the Jews' emotional attachment to Israel. Here was a young struggling nation doing incredible things that excited the imagination of American Jews. The Federations presented Israel as a kind of Disney Frontierland where the Big Givers' money was helping transform drossy sand into golden wheat fields. Israel was the Jewish establishment's "leading marketable product," in Robert Spero's words, and certainly the Federation campaigns' most glamorous beneficiary—the biggest hospital, the biggest old-age home, the biggest child-care agency. Federation officials loudly emphasized Israel in their fund-raising drives and quietly piggybacked budgets for local needs onto the emotional support for the Jewish State.

One final point here about motivation: The plutocracy's takeover of pro-Israel activities was rooted not only in their wish to maintain communal dominance but also in the machers' and Big Givers' quest for self-esteem. This need intensified among all Jewish men because of the guilt and shame they felt over having failed to rescue their "extended family" in Europe. They felt emasculated by having been unable to fulfill the patriarchal male defender role.

Israel gave them a second chance to succeed in this role through defending the Jewish State politically and supporting it economically. Israel's success in self-defense before and during the War of Independence led the men in the plutocracy to glom on to Israel to bolster their self-esteem through being associated/identified with it.

❧ The plutocracy gained the acquiescence of the masses of American Jews in its turf takeover for two reasons. One was that most American Jews felt that the Zionist movement's goal had been achieved. They were not interested in its leaders' and activists' ideological struggles to influence the future direction of Israel. What they wanted was to pick up where they had left off before the war in terms of attaining upward mobility and assimilation. They were relieved that the task of organizing financial and political support for Israel, which they still regarded as necessary, was now in the seemingly capable hands of the Jewish establishment.

Moreover, the plutocracy shared and understood American Jews' anti-ideological mind-set, their belief in the efficacy of assimilation, and their resistance to aliyah. It reinforced and legitimized the unwillingness of most of them to consider aliyah seriously. It also got American Jews, and especially those who had joined the Zionist movement in the postwar era, off the hook by propagandizing the illusion that they were really participating in the unfolding of the greatest event in Jewish history without settling in Israel through supporting the plutocracy's financial and political campaigns on behalf of the Jewish State.

It is precisely because the plutocracy so successfully legitimized and validated this vicarious participation in Israel's experience that it was accepted by the masses of American Jews, who wished to see themselves as "helping suffering

Jews to escape ... persecution while they continued to build their lives in a new Zion," in Urofsky's words. The mystification of vicariousness was so complete that even as late as 1991, when the New York UJA-Federation was emphasizing the exodus of then-Soviet Jews to Israel in its campaign, it propagandized in ads and on posters featuring photos of arriving olim that "this is how it feels to come *home*" (italics mine).

The second reason for the masses' acceptance of the turf takeover was that the Israeli leadership felt it was in the best interests of the new state to legitimize it. The plutocracy's takeover of activities to support Israel paralleled that of the Israeli state's takeover of pioneering through the mamlachtiyut (statist) system. In both cases the American Jewish "leaders" and their Israeli counterparts concurred that the progress of the state required a cadre of bureaucrats rather than an ideologically committed movement, and that mass participation in state building was no longer required. The Israeli bureaucrats also felt more comfortable dealing with their counterparts in America than with activist Zionist leaders. The plutocratic "leadership" of American Jewry and the political leaders of Israel therefore formed an alliance that expanded and solidified the power of the plutocracy rather than ending or diminishing it.

THE NONINTERFERENCE DIRECTIVE

Initially Prime Minister David Ben Gurion and other Israeli Zionist leaders were not willing to let American Jews off the hook, and they demanded mass aliyah from the community, which they saw as the best way to protect and strengthen the State of Israel. When mass aliyah was not forthcoming, Israelis experienced feelings of abandonment, which they tended to express in terms of superior ideological purity ("*Real* Zionists go on aliyah"). This, plus their initial efforts to encourage aliyah from the younger generation, caused deep resentment on the part of many American Jews toward the Israelis.

Once Ben Gurion realized that American Jewry would not provide large-scale aliyah, he sought to find other sources of protection and support for Israel. One source was the non-Zionist Jewish community relations organizations, which could effectively advocate the case for crucially needed American financial and political support for Israel among their non-Jewish contacts and in Washington. Ben Gurion also sought to get American Jews to send their money on aliyah. To do this he had to reach out and touch—in both senses of the word—the wealthy non-Zionist machers and Big Givers in the Federations, who had the money and the apparatus to raise more. Many were relieved to be asked to send funds rather than their children or themselves on aliyah.

Winning over both of these sectors of the American Jewish establishment— the Federation/UJA axis and the major community relations organizations—required recasting the relationship between it and Israel along the lines of a mutual

Noninterference Directive. The terms of this directive were that the Israeli power structure and the American Jewish establishment would not try to influence each other's policies. Neither would try to influence the masses in the other country or challenge the other structure's hegemony over them.

According to the Noninterference Directive, Israel would not interfere in the internal affairs of the American Jewish community. It would not put any real efforts into propagandizing for, encouraging, or promoting large-scale aliyah; it would not challenge the American Jewish establishment's power; and it would ensure that the Zionist movement did not do so, either. In return it would receive the support of the Jewish establishment, both financial and political. Emblematic of this half of the Noninterference Directive was the agreement hammered out in a series of meetings in the summer of 1950 between Ben Gurion and the leaders of the non-Zionist AJCommittee, whose terms came to inform the relationship of Israel with the rest of the Jewish establishment as well. The agreement concluded with Ben Gurion's declaration, "We, the people of Israel, have no desire and no intention to *interfere* . . . with the internal affairs of Jewish communities abroad" (italics mine).

The corollary of the directive was that the American Jewish establishment would not interfere with Israeli policy openly or publicly. As ADL National Director Abraham Foxman said as late as 1986, "Israel's security concerns continue to require a suspension of public criticism." In return, the Jewish establishment would get a free hand in running the community and keeping American Jews in line—and its "leaders" would receive validation from Israeli leaders of the establishment's legitimacy in doing so. Meetings of American Jewish "leaders" with (and briefings by) Israeli officials—from the prime minister to army generals—and these Israelis' appearances at American Jewish organizational functions, especially fund-raising dinners, have created the dual impression that the Israelis approve of these "leaders" and their activities *and* that American Jews (putatively represented by them) support the policies of the government these Israelis represent.

◆ The Israeli and American Jewish establishments have colluded to keep the majority of Jews in both countries ignorant of one another's real lives so that they are unable to do anything that might be construed as interference.

One way has been to control communal sources of information—specifically, the approximately 120 weekly American Jewish papers, which Trude Weiss-Rosmarin criticized in 1971 as house organs pretending to be newspapers. With the majority of these owned and controlled by the Federations, as we shall see, the American Jewish public is made aware of much of the minutiae of Israeli life but not of the underlying causes of its problems or of efforts to address them seriously, including through public protest.

While the Israeli government could not exercise similar control over its free and very disputatious press, its mind-set of viewing American Jewry only as a source of support rather than as a community with its own needs came to influence the kind of news coverage the dailies provided. These papers did not and still do not print any real news about the American Jewish community, about how it functions, or about the changes that have taken place in it since the late 1960s (the subject of chapter 14), including the existence of differences of opinion on certain Israeli policies. Their U.S. correspondents (and/or their editors) do not seem to be interested in what is really going on inside the community. When *Jerusalem Post* reporter David Landau wrote a series of articles on his 1985 visit to the U.S., for example, he called the "evolution of 'Federation man' [*sic*] arguably modern American Jewry's most *remarkable contribution* to the history of our people" (italics mine), not bothering to analyze the effect of that "contribution" on communal life.

ZIONISM BETRAYED

The Noninterference Directive necessitated the deliberate declawing of the Zionist movement. The Israelis realized that the Zionist leaders and activists were too emotionally involved in the question of what kind of a society Israel should become. The movement, with its array of organizations from right to left, was not regarded as the kind of apparatus that, had it been allowed to remain strong, would have refrained from interfering in the evolution of Israeli policy.

Psychologically, what happened in the Israel–American Zionist relationship was a separation struggle: The adolescent (Israel) was trying to break away from its parent (the Zionist movement), which had been instrumental in its creation. Seeking to put a great deal of emotional distance between itself and the parent movement, it denigrated parental values and provoked nasty fights (ideological battles). What occurred next drew on one of the traditional behavior patterns that had obtained in Eastern Europe, from which the leaders of Israel had all emigrated: the shtetl arranged-marriage system. The adolescent (Israel) wanted to be independent but could not support himself. So he turned to someone other than the parent(s) to help support him. In traditional East European communities, this someone was the young wife. The wife (the American Jewish establishment) was as immature as the young husband and was not likely to be critical, to make demands for appropriate behavior, or to think she knew best (as parents do). Additionally, she (hopefully) could convince her family to advance and/or lend some money, the in-laws in this variation of the shtetl schema being the American government. (This, of course, dovetailed with the traditional female family role of interceder and drew on the old Court Jew survival strategy.)

To declaw the Zionist movement, Israelis opposed a suggestion at the 1951 World Zionist Congress that American Zionists be assigned the major responsibility for organizing the Jews of their community. The Israelis did not wish any alternative structures to challenge the Jewish establishment's hegemony. Nor did they seek any change in the status quo in the community that could cause American Jewry to direct most of its energies inward—toward building a real community—rather than outward, toward giving money to and helping Israel.

✦ American Zionist activists felt profoundly rejected. Having done so much to bring Israel into existence, they now stood "forlornly on the sidelines, shunned as inadequate by the Israelis and as outsiders by American Jewish communal leaders," wrote Urofsky. The Zionists' feeling of rejection deepened into dejection when the Israeli leaders turned down their advice and ideas and instead crisscrossed the North American continent to stroke the machers and Big Givers rather than addressing the masses of Jews in the movement.

The Zionist movement could have regrouped at this point had it been willing to analyze and confront the changed situation. It would have had to grapple with the thorny question of what living in Exile meant now that there was an independent Jewish state. Precisely because the Zionist movement embraced Jews across the entire political and religious spectrum, it could have served as the forum for genuine discussion and debate on this issue, on assimilationism, on invisibility, on the relationship of American Jewry to other ethnic groups and to Israel. It would thus have become the nucleus of a movement to democratize the community, a role taken by its predecessors after World War I.

It could also have tried to infuse the community with genuine Zionist and Jewish consciousness and content by initiating educational and cultural projects—schools, theater, films and television programs, cultural centers, exhibits, publishing, and conferences. It could have undertaken efforts to help American olim (about fifty thousand individuals settled in Israel between 1948 and 1986), such as building them rental housing, which Zionist organizations in other countries do. These olim could have served as a real bridge between American Jews and Israelis.

But the movement's leaders, overcome by feelings of abandonment and stunned by the swift appropriation of the movement's previous major functions and the Israelis' validation of the takeover, were unable to initiate such creative work or to reach out and open their ranks and leadership positions to younger people. Because of these weaknesses, they were unable to stop the erosion of the movement's mass base, and its membership rolls shrank back to prewar levels. By 1975 it had become so intellectually stagnant that its prime response to the passage of the infamous U.N. Zionism=racism resolution was to issue thousands of "I am Zionist" buttons. But the main reason the Zionists could not generate enthusiasm for initiating creative work was that they accepted the Israeli view that educational and cultural activities in the U.S. would siphon away funds from Israel. This was precisely the excuse given in 1985 by the president of the Labor-oriented Na'amat USA (then called Pioneer Women), Phyllis Sutker, for rejecting the idea of its establishing a network of Zionist day care centers in America (and the reason it stopped funding the only Zionist day school in New York, Kinneret).

This view was brutally shortsighted and betrayed Zionism and the Jewish people. For if what the Israelis really wanted was American aliyah, it would have had to come from a flourishing community, not a cultural wasteland. The fact that the majority of today's olim are Orthodox Jews, who have had the benefit of a strong Jewish education—and the support of their community—proves the connection between a flourishing Jewish environment and aliyah.

Perhaps, in the final analysis, Israel's political leaders did not really want an influx of non-Orthodox American olim skilled in organizing grassroots volunteer political action, and who could challenge the bureaucracy, the cynical deals with the clerical parties, mamlachtiyut, the electoral system, and/or other domestic and foreign policies. This is why Israeli leaders may indulge in token nagging of American Jews about aliyah (which the latter resent as an attempt to induce guilt and thereby extract more money), but its bureaucracy has continued to put logistical roadblocks in the path of American olim. Expecting to be welcomed with open arms, they have often felt they were given the back of the hand instead. Moreover, psychologically, American olim have faced a great struggle over being accepted by Israelis, who often see them through the prism of the classic Judeophobic stereotype of wealthy, materialistic, and spoiled.

Even if the Israelis really wanted only money, the way to get it was through raising generations of Jewishly committed and conscious and caring Jews. And indeed, the Federations, which have starved Jewish education and culture, found to their dismay in the late 1980s that the attitudes toward Israel of third-, fourth-, and fifth-generation American Jews with the kind of money they wished to harvest were, in the words of the confidential 1986–87 marketing survey by the New York UJA-Federation, "non-sympathetic," a subject we shall return to.

Perhaps what Israel really wanted was a mass of Jews who, lacking Jewish education, would not challenge the American Jewish establishment and would be content to let its "leaders"—who followed Israeli "guidance" on policies it wished to promote—raise money and acquire other support for Israel in their name.

It was a betrayal of Zionism, whose goal was and is Jewish liberation, for the Israelis to downgrade the American Zionist movement, which could have created Zionist consciousness and institutions to advance this goal. It was a betrayal of Zionism for the Israelis to legitimize the American Jewish establishment, which has promoted the precise opposite goal: assimilationism. And it was a betrayal of Zionism for the Israelis to sell out the Jewish masses in America and abandon them to the tender mercies of the plutocracy, and to rationalize this action on grounds that this was "good for Israel."

"COMINTERNIZATION" AND ITS METASTASIS

The Zionist movement had lost control over fund-raising and political advocacy for Israel. Neither could it engage in lobbying in the halls of Congress and with the administration because this function was given over to the American Israel Public Affairs Committee (AIPAC), established for this specific purpose in 1954. But while the Zionist movement had been shorn of control over these pre-1948 activities, the Israelis saw no reason why the movement should not continue to generate support for the Jewish State among whatever political sectors it could reach, even in its increasingly attenuated condition.

The Israel–American Zionist movement relationship began to bear an uncanny resemblance to that of foreign Communist parties (CPs) to the Comintern (Communist International) during the regime of Stalin in the Soviet Union. Although the parallel is not exact because neither the Zionist movement nor the Israeli political system is monolithic, enough similarities in process exist to call this dynamic the "Cominternization" of the Zionist movement.

The Comintern, based in Moscow and controlled by Stalin, programmed foreign CPs to be altruistic-assertive enablers of the Soviet (Stalinist) bureaucracy. In practice this meant that they subordinated the needs of their own countries' working classes for revolution to the entrenched interests of the Soviet bureaucracy as that bureaucracy defined them in "lines" handed down every few years, which they had to follow.

In the Israel–American Zionist movement relationship that operates along "Cominternization" lines, Israel plays the role the Soviet Union did in requiring political defense and deciding what it needs in this regard. The role of the Zionist movement organizations outside Israel, including in the U.S., became to defend Israel in much the same way the foreign CPs had defended the Soviet Union: to cultivate relationships with political circles willing to support it and to stifle criticism of Israel inside the community. The role of the Comintern in relation to the CPs was played in this variation of "Cominternization" by the World Zionist Organization—the elected body representing members of Zionist organizations all over the world plus those in the Zionist political parties of Israel—which is dominated by the Israeli political establishment. Unlike the one-party system in the Soviet Union before its dissolution, however, there is a multiplicity of political parties from left to right in Israel, in the WZO, and in the Zionist movements in different countries. Moreover, WZO policies are debated and voted on at Zionist Congresses, held every four years.

Each Israeli Zionist party conveys its views to the Zionist organization in the U.S. that is its ideological counterpart. Thus the left-wing Mapam Party (which advocates territorial compromise, religious freedom, and support of the labor and kibbutz sectors) conveys its "line" to Americans for Progressive Israel; the left-of-center Labor (*Avoda*) Party transmits its views (support of the peace process) to the Labor Zionist Alliance; the National Religious Party (NRP), which favors the religious establishment's policies, acts likewise in relation to the Religious Zionists of America; and the right-wing Likud Party (which advocates territorial annexation) does the same in relation to its support groups in the U.S., the right-of-center Zionist Organization of America (ZOA) and the right-wing Likud USA.

The "Cominternization" process, therefore, operates on two tracks: internal (Jewish community) and external (vis-à-vis the general society). The American Zionist organizations advance the views of the Israeli parties they are connected with as their support groups, but only inside the Jewish community. Outside it they follow the very general "line" that has emerged from the discussions and resolutions at Zionist congresses because all these organizations are united in the belief that the political defense of Israel, no matter what government is in power, is their prime function as Zionists. Therefore, when attempting to influence public opinion in the general society, each organization is involved not primarily in advancing the view of its sister party in Israel but in making the case for Israel in circles closest to it on the political spectrum.

Just as critics of Stalin and the Soviet bureaucracy and their policies were denounced by the foreign CPs as "social fascists," "infantile ultra-leftists," "counter-revolutionaries," and "Trotskyites," so, too, Jewish critics of Israel and its bureaucracy and policies were denounced by most of these organizations as "anti-Israel," "anti-Semites," "pro-PLO," "enemies of the Jewish people," and the *ne plus ultra,* "self-hating Jews."

The foreign Communist parties were enjoined from trying to create a true revolutionary consciousness in their own societies because this would jeopardize the Soviet Union's relationship with their own countries' ruling classes. Similarly, the Zionist organizations were enjoined to refrain from trying to create an authentic Zionist consciousness and politics in their own communities because this could jeopardize Israel's relationships with the Jewish establishment and possibly with those sectors of American public opinion Israel wished to cultivate.

Zionist consciousness has always meant self-liberation: a rejection of the belief in rescue-from-outside and of the classic survival strategies of cultivating powerful protectors, being useful to them, and having Court Jews plead their people's case. But it was precisely these strategies that Israel wished the Zionist (and the community relations) organizations to use on its behalf. Therefore, Zionist consciousness could not be allowed to inform Jewish communal behavior in America.

Moreover, a Zionist political program based on the concept that certain classic Exile dynamics apply in America might have led Zionists to seek alliances with other ethnic groups based on an understanding of common interests. It might have even included support for or protest of American policies that have an impact on the lives of American Jews as Americans and as Jews. But rocking the boat by being too critical of a government that is regarded as friendly to Israel, even on domestic or foreign policies that have no direct connection with Israel, might bring Jews into conflict with the American power structure, action that was considered "bad for Israel." This view, of course, is rooted in the classic Jewish survival strategy of trying to cultivate powerful protectors and not antagonizing them needlessly.

By contrast, cultivating alliances with circles regarded as supportive of Israel (for instance, certain groups on the Fundamentalist right), was generally propagandized during the Likud administration (1977–92) as being "good for Is-rael." This is why the Jabotinsky Foundation, sponsored by the right-wing Zion-ist organization Herut (now Likud) USA, gave an award to the Reverend Jerry Falwell. The question of whether it was good for American Jews to get into bed with the extreme religious right—which is, among other things, opposed to church-state separation in the U.S. (something most American Jews favor)—was considered "non-data."

The ideological rationalization accepted by American Zionists for not being engaged as Zionists with American issues, that "America is different," resembles the theory of American exceptionalism advanced in 1929 by Jay Lovestone, then head of the American Communist Party. Its implication is that because America is not an Exile where classic Exile dynamics obtain, it is not necessary to develop politics and programs to deal on a fundamental basis with these dynamics, in-cluding those of anti-Semitism and assimilationism, or even to organize large-scale aliyah.

The American exceptionalism rationale, which has always been strongly pro-moted by the Jewish establishment, is forcefully rejected by the Israelis. They con-tinue to believe the Zionist concept that America *is* an Exile—and to say this to American Zionists when the subject comes up. They see no contradiction be-tween rejecting American exceptionalism in theory and supporting it in practice by legitimizing its strongest adherents, the Jewish establishment plutocracy.

❧ What is significant is how the "Cominternization" dynamic has metastasized far beyond the confines of the weak Zionist movement to characterize much of the behavior of the community relations organizations in the Jewish establish-ment. None of these organizations was ever involved in ideological debates, as were Zionists, on what kind of society Israel should create, and some had even re-jected Zionism before 1948; they have no relationships as support groups with political parties in Israel or with the WZO. But all of them, despite having differ-ences of opinion on Israeli policies—and conveying these privately to Israeli lead-ers—engage in advocacy work to defend Israel and try to suppress public criticism of any of its policies by other Jews both inside and outside the community.

Each organization primarily tries to cultivate support for Israel in circles in the general society closest to it politically and/or appropriate to its class compo-sition, style, and/or history. For example, the AJCongress generally works with the Democratic Party; the Jewish Labor Committee with the large "mainstream" unions; the AJCommittee with the Catholic hierarchy and various ethnic mi-norities.

The community relations organizations' jealous battles over glamorous-issue turf and their puerile organizational chauvinism, however, preclude anything be-yond this vague and informal division of labor. The duplication and overlap of ac-tivities arising out of competition for glamorous issues and projects can be observed from the work in defense of Israel that various organizations reported on to the LCBC in 1992. Here are some:

- AJCommittee: Put "primary emphasis" on a major media campaign, including paid advertising; used contacts with the "international diplomatic community" to campaign for repeal of the U.N. Zionism=racism resolution; used network of contacts with organizations representing other ethnic, racial, and religious groups to "build a broad-based constituency for foreign aid, including—but not limited to—aid to Israel."

- AJCongress: Through cosponsorship of Annual Conference of Mayors in Jerusalem, obtained "endorsement" of more than forty mayors for U.S. loan guarantees to Israel; provided black media with material on Israeli cooperation with Africa and on visits to Israel by prominent African Americans; published *Boycott Report* to "monitor" Arab economic boycott of Israel.

- ADL: Conducted program to "project a positive image of Israel, develop understanding of Israel's position in the Mideast conflict and the U.S. stake in the area"; prepared background papers for use by "opinion-molders"; provided background papers with "interpretation" of threat posed by Arab boycott.

- NJCRAC: Engaged in intensive consultations to "interpret Israeli concerns in the peace process"; organized community relations field during the Gulf War to address the issues emerging from that crisis; took "central responsibility" for mobilizing community action in loan guarantee campaign.

- Jewish Labor Committee: Organized labor support for loan guarantees; arranged for AFL-CIO resolution supporting Israel during Gulf War; organized Israel study tour for eleven trade unionists.

The independent Jewish women's organizations, which are not part of the Jewish establishment, had never been involved with this kind of advocacy among their non-Jewish counterparts. Nor did the male-dominated establishment ever think those female constituencies important enough to win over. But this assessment changed dramatically after the various U.N. conferences on the status of women (Mexico City, 1975; Copenhagen, 1980) passed strong anti-Zionist resolutions. At that point, the Jewish establishment pressured the women's organizations to fall in line with this quasi division of labor and put their main energies at future U.N. conferences (e.g., Nairobi, 1985) into heading off such resolutions. Most of the women's groups did so rather than focus on the conferences' main issues, those concerning the condition of women.

While some advocacy work by Jewish organizations is undoubtedly useful, none of them, nor the community as a whole, has developed any mechanisms to evaluate its effectiveness.

❧ In this variation of the "Cominternization" schema, the role of the Comintern is played by the Israeli political establishment, which tries to set out a "line" for all to follow. In advancing the political defense of Israel, the organizations behave as the CPs did in defending the Soviet Union. The parallel is inexact, of course, because compliance is voluntary: there is no formal monolithic, hierarchical structure (like the Comintern in its heyday) that requires them to follow the "line" or else and to which they are accountable.

The closest they come to some kind of framework presenting a "line" on various policy issues exists not in Jerusalem but in New York. This is the Conference of Presidents of Major American Jewish Organizations, which also includes the Zionist ones. The Presidents Conference was originally established, Urofsky explains candidly, to "provide the *conduit* Israel needed to funnel information into the American Jewish leadership as well as secure its views on a variety of issues" (italics mine). In practice, however, this roof organization has never been a mere transmission belt. The positions it voices are those that its powerful constituent groups and personalities have promoted. Because most of these adhere to the Noninterference Directive, the Presidents Conference will never officially oppose the policy "line" advanced by the Israeli political leadership. It generally takes an official position close to that "line" and tries to sell it to its constituent organizations—or, at the very least, tries to convince them not to disagree on it in public. It does not always succeed at this. The constituent organizations are under no obligation to adhere to the Presidents Conference's positions and some of them continue to advance their own opposing views.

The years Likud was in power in Israel coincided with an era during which the American Jewish community moved to the right, as we shall see in chapter 14. In this period, therefore, there was a meeting of the minds between the Israeli leadership and the Presidents Conference, and it was easy for the latter to embrace the Israelis' hawkish position enthusiastically. Now, with the new stage in the peace process initiated by the Labor Government elected in 1992, the Presidents Conference is undergoing a difficult transition. By the terms of the Noninterference Directive, it cannot oppose Israeli government policies, but it is precisely these same policies, such as negotiating with the PLO, that were anathema for so many years. The Presidents Conference officially supports the peace process. But its lack of passion in doing so manifests itself in the coupling of support for the peace process with concerns about its possible effect on Israeli security. Israeli leaders are annoyed about Presidents Conference "leaders'" expressions of concern as being "holier than the pope." They point out that they have a handle on the security situation and have no illusions about the PLO.

A poll taken among American Jews in August 1994, sponsored by the AJ-Committee, showed that 77 percent supported the Israeli government's handling of the peace negotiations with the Arabs. The masses, however, have no input into deliberations of the Presidents Conference. The Presidents Conference is triply undemocratic, being composed of representatives of organizations nobody elected and of representatives of several umbrella groups of these organizations, such as the NJCRAC; and by being an overall roof organization of both kinds of groups that speaks for American Jewry without a legitimate mandate to do so. Nevertheless, it has come to be regarded by the non-Jewish media and by American and even Israeli government officials as the "elected representative of American Jewry" and as its unified voice not only on Israel but on other foreign policy issues as well.

CULTURAL VAMPIRISM

The "Cominternization" dynamic in Jewish organizational life has dovetailed with another phenomenon characteristic of the members of foreign CPs during the Stalinist regime in relation to the Soviet Union: vicarious participation in the life of Israel. This phenomenon characterizes the behavior not only of organizations inside and outside the Jewish establishment but also of a large part of American Jewry. It derives from cultural/spiritual malnourishment.

American Jewry has never quite matured as a community with a culture as distinguishably unique and authentically Jewish as those of the Babylonian, Spanish, Turkish, Polish, and Lithuanian communities in their heydays. It is not its relative youth that is the prime factor in the community's immaturity but its assimilationism.

Until World War II, American Jewry subsisted in large part on its gleanings from the rich fields of Yiddishkeit—the Yiddish language-based culture—and zeitgeist of Eastern Europe, particularly Poland. Despite the shutoff of mass immigration from this region after 1924, American Jews could import "spare parts"—rabbis, cantors, publications—to keep their rusty cultural machinery going instead of developing new models, new variations on the theme of being-a-Jew. American Jews could thereby focus their energies on what they really cared about—assimilating and attaining material success. They could simultaneously remain Jewishly "alive," vampire-style, via transfusions of the cultural lifeblood of the vibrant community in the Old Country. In return, and out of guilt for abandoning most of the instrumentalities for expressing the East European community's cultural values and for doing relatively well while their "extended family" abroad was suffering, they sent money. With the catastrophic annihilation of East European Jewry, American Jews could no longer look to this intensely Jewish community for cultural transfusions.

Because the Jewish culture in America up to World War II had largely been a Yiddish culture, by the third generation, when Yiddish ceased to be the lingua franca of most Jews, the culture based on it also faded away. Within several decades, most Jews could not read Yiddish, and only one daily paper, with an Orthodox orientation, survives. The Yiddish theater disappeared from New York as a cultural force by the beginning of the 1950s, when the lights of the "Yiddish Rialto," as the Second Avenue Yiddish theater row was called, dimmed forever. By contrast, the Ashkenazic Argentine community, several decades before World War II, had infused their community's institutions with a rich Jewish secular culture that could persist even after Yiddish had waned as its lingua franca by the mid-1970s. American Jews felt they did not need such institutions: The secular institutions they sought to enter were non-Jewish ones.

The few Yiddish cultural institutions that have struggled to stay afloat generally found it painful to separate the Yiddish language—which has attracted a minority, albeit a growing one, of students and young academics—from artistic expression, not realizing that educating Jews about the culture could motivate them to learn the language, too. Many workers in these institutions seemed dedicated to preserving the sacred fire and not letting the impure trample the sacred precincts where it was so lovingly tended.

Yiddish culture declined, too, because it was primarily identified with radicalism, which Jews left behind with their old neighborhoods as they moved into the middle class and, later, to the suburbs. After World War II, Yiddish became associated primarily with the right-wing Orthodox immigrants who spoke it, which few other Jews identified with.

Finally, American Jews have lacked the resources, such as a system of universal high-quality Jewish education, to nourish a new Jewish culture.

❧ In this post-Holocaust vacuum, American Jews turned to Israel to supply instant cultural content to enable them to feel connected in some way to their Jewishness. The basic problems have been that Israel has not developed many uniquely *Jewish* cultural forms; the social forms that have evolved do not mesh well with the American reality; and Israel itself increasingly looks to America for a great deal of its own popular culture.

There is an Israeli culture/lifestyle, but its religious content is skimpy and undernourished, and its secular Jewish content underdeveloped. Israel, as we have seen, never resolved its separation struggle with Judaism and consequently has never developed new forms of religious expression. Orthodox Jews in Israel continue to practice Judaism the same way they did in their countries of origin; this way does not appeal to non-Orthodox American Jews. Secular Israelis have rejected the cultural traditions of Exile communities and emphasize nationhood rather than religion as their expression of Jewish identity. In celebrating holidays, for example, they follow the practice of the pioneers, who drained off these festivals' religious substance and substituted content relating to ancient history and/or agrarian life. Such content is not readily transferable to the lives of American Jews, who primarily identify Jewishness with religion and are urban or suburban dwellers.

The unique social forms that Israel has developed, such as the kibbutz, are distinctly at odds with the temper of American capitalist society. (Actually, attempts to apply the organizing principles of kibbutz life, which reflect and institutionalize the old values of cooperation, interdependence, and altruism, to the problems of homeless people, welfare families, and the elderly would be very challenging, but no Jewish organization has contemplated such unglamorous projects.)

Finally, because Israelis rejected the cultural traditions of the Exile—viewing Yiddish culture with antipathy (as did the pioneers) and Sephardic culture as "primitive"—a vacuum was created, and American cultural forms seeped into it with the country's post-1967 bourgeoisification. Israel became more and more Americanized, and many Israelis today look to the American middle class as their reference group. "Israelis eat hamburgers at McDavid, shop at American-style supermarkets, count their wealth in dollars ... and are as likely to dress up as Rambo on ... Purim ... as they are [as] Haman and Esther," noted an American journalist. Israelis' attraction to U.S. pop culture is attested by the kind of music that has evolved in Israel. Although it could have become a unique synthesis of Ashkenazic and Sephardic melody and harmony, Israeli music largely degenerated by the 1990s into third-rate imitation pop and rock (with the possible exception of pop religious and Sephardic songs).

❧ Spiritually/culturally anemic but unable to tolerate transfusions of Israeli culture, American Jews turned to an even more extreme form of cultural vampirism than the kind previous generations had engaged in vis-à-vis Eastern Europe. They began to feed off the Israeli experience. Many focused on the day-to-day details of life in the Jewish State and obsessed about its citizens' struggles as if *they* were actually living there and participating in its history-in-the-making.

They began to believe that "being there" for Israel emotionally, politically, and financially was practically the same as actually being there physically. This vicarious existence was criticized by Rabbi Alexander Schindler, president of the (Reform) Union of American Hebrew Congregations. He warned in 1982, "We do ourselves irreparable harm ... when we *permit our Jewishness to consist almost entirely of vicarious participation in the life of the State*" of Israel (italics mine).

But living vicariously through Israel means that Israel must live up to what American Jews psychologically need it to represent. For example, Israel must be "really Jewish," which they unconsciously define as observant of Halacha. That is why American Jews with the grease of take-out treif streaming down their chins recoil in horror upon discovering that some Israelis eat pork in Tel Aviv restaurants.

It is as if Israel were a kind of theme park for American Jews to visit—or a type of zoo to preserve the "endangered species" of Judaism. American Jews can enjoy looking in on the zoo from time to time and lend it their financial support, but they certainly do not want its untamed/undomesticated (that is, unassimilated) denizens invading their *own* homes. The fund-raisers, of course, cultivate and reinforce this exploitation of Israel as a "surrogate synagogue" (Rabbi Schindler's term) with their carefully choreographed Big Giver "missions," which

JESNA director Jonathan Woocher actually hailed as "pilgrimages" whose names (such as "Next Year in Jerusalem") have "mythic overtones."

Because American Jews wish Israel to be Jewish for them, they have been fairly tolerant until recently of what most Israelis feel is religious coercion by the Orthodox authorities, such as the banning of public transportation on Shabbat, the Israelis' only day off (an inconvenience *they* do not have to endure in America or when they tour Israel in rented cars). Reform Jews have never dared hold a Reform-style (gender-integrated) prayer service at the Western Wall. (They rationalized their cancellation of plans to hold such a service in 1968, after the Orthodox had condemned the idea, by stating that they wished to avoid damage to Israel's image.) Nor did American Jews or their organizations protest when a group of women were physically attacked for praying there with the Torah in 1988 and forbidden to do so again.

This cavalier attitude toward religious coercion has contributed to the tendency not to take seriously the Orthodox domination of courts dealing with marriage, divorce, custody, and conversion. Another factor here is that those who suffer from the way these authorities interpret Halacha on family issues are mostly women, who have no clout in Israel or in the American Jewish community.

The machers in and Big Givers to Federations who are also members of the Conservative or Reform religious movements have been deeply resentful, however, of the fact that the Israeli government denies official recognition to the branches of these movements in that country. This implies that Israeli government leaders, who are secular Jews, recognize Orthodoxy as the only authentic Judaism. But their resentment has collided with their conflict over the need for Israel to be Jewish for them. This unresolved conflict has made it impossible for these men to engage in anything other than sporadic efforts to challenge Orthodox control over Jewish religious life in Israel.

◆ Finally, for many American Jews, especially the men, Israel also vicariously fulfills a psychological wish to be Jewishly visible by the very fact of its existence. Israel is visible for them, so they do not have to worry about being overly visible themselves or to confront their own conflict over visibility/invisibility in the U.S. The visibility/invisibility conflict is also the reason why American Jewish organizations agonized for such a long time over holding an annual parade in New York. They finally "resolved" the problem by holding an Israel Day Parade, which salutes Israel's existence, not their own heritage and culture and presence in the U.S., as do most annual parades of other ethnic groups.

But the conflict over visibility rears its head again when the establishment organization "leaders" engage in the high-visibility activity of political advocacy on Israel's behalf. That, said Murray Zuckoff, is why they try to portray Israel as a kind of American outpost in the Middle East: the "only democracy in the region," "America's best friend" and (until the collapse of the Soviet Union) its only true ally there in the war against Communism, and the one country in the area that shares American values. Morris B. Abram, a former AJCommittee president, actually wrote that Zionism "is the Israeli form of Americanism." The more they Americanize Israel, the less visibly Jewish it appears, the less their visibility in activities on its behalf counts against them. As Jonathan Sarna observed, the plutocracy followed in the footsteps of early American Zionists such as Louis Brandeis who had worked to create "a model state cast in the image of America." This permitted the machers and Big Givers to "bask in the reflected glory of those engaging in building the state and to boast of their own *patriotic efforts to spread the American dream outward*" (italics mine). It is precisely because work on behalf of Israel was portrayed as being "good for America" that it has had such high glamour in the community.

This mind-set accounts for the kinds of projects in Israel that American Jews raise and donate money for—not only through Federation campaigns but also in drives by "friends of" organizations for the support of universities, hospitals, and day care centers. The projects that are the most glamorous are those which "spread the American Dream outward" rather than those that the Israelis may actually need. Another factor lending Israeli projects glamour is that the buildings erected in Israel by American Jewish groups are not in danger of abandonment because of population mobility and are a permanently visible part of the landscape.

EMOTIONAL WAREHOUSING

Raising funds for Israel—the major form of American Jews' vicarious participation in its experience—involves an endless sequence of dinners, lunches, telephone solicitation sessions, and meetings.

The unconscious motivation behind all this feverish (and non-cost-effective) activity is emotional warehousing. American Jews seem to need these activities to keep busy, to cover up and avoid confronting the spiritual vacuum in their lives. And the machers of the Jewish establishment know, too, that without the myriad activities justified by Israel's need for money, American Jews might turn their attention to addressing what *they* need, materially and spiritually. This could challenge the machers' power. Better, then, to keep people busy trying to be busy.

◆ One of the questions that they might (have to)—and should—address is whether sending huge sums to Israeli institutions is always the best use of the Jewish people's money. If a community that is strong and committed is more likely to stand up for Israel—and make an effective case for American support, including foreign aid—than one whose soul is corroded by assimilation, wouldn't it make sense for the American Jewish community to plow some of the communally raised money into Jewish education and culture to strengthen itself?

Beyond this, as Bert Gold once asked when he was executive vice-president of the AJCommittee: "Who is it that determines it is more important to provide funds for higher education in Israel than funds for Jewish education in the U.S.? Who is it that decides that poor Jews in Tel Aviv need improved housing and financial aid more urgently than do the poor Jews in Miami?" (This cri de coeur was somewhat disingenuous, considering that it was Gold's own organization that insisted so strenuously on the Noninterference Directive, which reinforced the lack of accountability he decried.)

Why should American Jews sponsor fewer universities here than they support in Israel? Why do Israeli yeshivot end up getting more money from American Jews than Jewish day schools in the U.S.? Why do the Jewish aged and people with disabilities get better care in Israel than in Los Angeles or New York? Why should there be fewer Jewish day care centers for American Jewish kids than for Israelis? Why should Sutker have justified Na'amat USA's refusal to initiate day care here because "funds and energy need to be directed to Israel and don't permit the luxury of cutting down on that and elevating another aspect"? Why hasn't Na'amat USA or any other major American Jewish organization established a shelter for battered American Jewish women? Why are their needs considered less important than those of Israeli women in this regard?

Even beyond this lies the question of how this easy money encourages Israel to be dependent on American Jews—which makes the machers and Big Givers happy—rather than strive more strenuously toward economic self-sufficiency. Furthermore, with a huge chunk of Israel's social services funded by American Jews, its previous governments could allocate some of the money that would otherwise have had to be budgeted for these needs to other projects. West Bank settlements, for example, were highly questionable on ethical and practical grounds and were viewed by many Israelis as an obstacle to the peace process. They might not have been funded had not money in the budget been freed up because of American Jewish donations.

Additionally, Israelis find it hard to say no when American (or for that matter, European) Jewish machers want to build something glamorous in Israel that might otherwise not be established. This is often the case with Israeli universities (more glamorous projects than the high schools and elementary classrooms that the country really needs). This was so, as well, with the new Knesset building. Another example is Hadassah's decision to revamp its old hospital on Mount Scopus (recaptured from Jordan in the 1967 War) and reopen it, even though it had built a new facility in West Jerusalem and what Israel really needed was more and better clinics in development towns. Hadassah also decided to build a medical school on an American model of specialization and advanced technology unsuited to Israel's needs, geography, or societal orientation. "But," wrote one critic, "the Hadassah largess was irresistible.... Israeli money must [now] pay for an elite expensive research tool, its only purpose being to pump funds out of America."

The phenomenon of American Jewish machers telling Israelis what to do with the money they raise and contribute to Israeli institutions became more pronounced in the 1980s. The machers nagged the Israelis incessantly about the inefficiency of the bureaucracy of the Jewish Agency, which receives Federation campaign funds from the UJA (and from its counterparts in other countries) for immigrant absorption and other social services. (This work should have been taken over by the Israeli government after 1948 and the Jewish Agency, a pre-state institution, dismantled. This did not happen primarily because it would have made the tax-deductible status of contributions from American Jews impossible.)

The Jewish Agency had become plagued with inefficiency, corruption, featherbedding, boondoggling, and general equal-opportunity heartlessness to the point where "those who had to find their way out of [its] labyrinthine bureaucratic mazes ... developed and sustained an antipathy toward [it] bordering on hatred," in Zuckoff's words. In 1988 the machers engineered a takeover that allowed them to restructure the Jewish Agency bureaucracy along corporate lines and gave them control of its key functions. American machers are now in charge of important services that affect the lives of Israelis, who cannot vote these "benefactors" out as they can do with their elected officials.

❧ The money from abroad poisons the relationship between American Jews and Israelis. American Jewish machers and Big Givers tend to treat Israel as their exclusive country club and Israelis as welfare clients, schnorrers, and children. The Israelis resent their "benefactors" behaving as if they owned the place. Feeling that American Jews wish to infantilize them, they respond with the classic withholding behavior of Jewish adolescents. The withholding takes the form of devaluing American Jewry, especially its forms of religious expression. (The lack of interest of secular Israeli politicians in the religious authorities' delegitimization of the American Reform and Conservative religious movements may have some of its roots in their psychological need to devalue American Jews in this way.) Israeli leaders cannot, of course, go too far—that is, withhold validation from the machers and Big Givers who provide financial support. But individual intellectuals can make statements such as Amos Oz's, that "Israel is the Jewish stage and the Diaspora is the auditorium."

VICARIOUS MASCULINITY

Vicarious participation in Israeli life has another dimension: Many American Jewish men, anxious about living up to the majority culture's definition of masculinity, use Israel as their surrogate in engaging in physical aggression. A Jewish man who had raised money for arms for the Hagana in 1947–48 said at the time, "I have known Jews all my life who are waiting for this day that they could point to another *Jew that carried a gun and say, 'He represents me'"* (italics mine). Even

Jewish underworld characters opened their hearts—and wallets (to the tune of two hundred thousand dollars)—at a 1948 parlor meeting for the Irgun when kingpin Mickey Cohen said the money was "for Jews ready to knock hell out of all the bums in the world who don't like them."

When Israel (or, more accurately, Israeli men in the army) engages in military efforts, especially successful ones, American Jewish men get a rush. Israel proves conclusively that "Jewboys can fight"—and win. The male heroes (especially Ari Ben Canaan) in Leon Uris's popular 1958 novel *Exodus,* who embody the images American Jewish men have of Israeli men, said Urofsky, provided "reassurance that . . . a Jew need not be ashamed of his [sic] alleged cowardice." This novel and Arthur Koestler's *Thieves in the Night,* which preceded it, wrote Judd Teller in a burst of wishful thinking, "fixed the image of the fighting Jew in the American imagination, banishing the stereotype of the hunched student, comic opera peddler, garment center wheeler-dealer, and verbose hirsute radical."

Because Israeli men, as their surrogate, engage in physical aggression, American Jewish men do not have to act as role breakers in this regard and thereby possibly trip-wire animosity from non-Jewish men, in relation to whom they always have to be "nice."

Exploiting the men's yearning for vicarious validation of their masculinity, the UJA, on its "missions" of Big Givers to Israel, features meetings with army generals and visits to army bases. The women who participate in these missions may get a thrill, or at least a sense of satisfaction, out of seeing Jewish men willing and able at last to defend/protect "their" women. (This is partly why they are not disturbed by the Israeli women's exclusion from combat, which, as we have seen, is justified on grounds of the female soldiers' being at risk for rape by enemy troops.)

At the same time, American Jewish men envy Israeli men's ability to fight, and this envy plus their need for vicarious validation of masculinity causes them to stereotype the latter as "real cowboys, big and strong and emotionless," in Oz's words.

Even when Israel behaves "badly," American Jewish men harbor a certain secret glee that Jews can be bad boys at long last (which *they* dare not be in America). The glee is canceled out, however, by anxiety about the reaction of "the goyim." For the downside of the Israeli soldiers' being their surrogates is that American Jewish men are also identified with them when they do something that non-Jews do not approve of. If the Israelis cross a certain boundary (for instance, by being shown on TV beating up Palestinian teenagers on the West Bank), American Jewish men are propelled into cringing embarrassment and worry about how this makes them and their organizations look, especially because of their hypervisible long-term activities on behalf of civil liberties and human rights. The embarrassment of the organizational "leaders"—and the genuine concern by some of them over ethical issues—often leads them to make private ministrations to Israeli government officials about its policies. Generally they use the argument that action X or Y will downgrade the image of Israel in the eyes of the American public. The Israelis tend to dismiss such arguments as evidence of an "Exile mentality," of Jews outside Israel always looking over their shoulders to psych out "the goyim."

The machers' unwillingness to express criticism of Israel publicly derives in part from their worry about whether non-Jewish men will feel contempt for them for doing so. American Jews have accepted the Jewish establishment's equating of criticism with abandonment, the great crime in the Jewish culture, as we shall see. Since protecting and defending extended families is part of the patriarchal definition of manhood, being seen by non-Jews as abandoning the Israeli branch of the Jewish "extended family" would wipe out the sense of vicarious masculinity that had accrued to the men by identifying with the Israelis.

One final point: Because of the embarrassment factor, Israel became "deglamorized" to some extent after the Lebanon War (1982) and at the beginning of the Intifada (1987). It is primarily for this reason that the 1986–87 New York UJA-Federation marketing survey found attitudes among yuppie respondents to be "unsympathetic" to Israel. Instead of addressing the root causes of the problem—which include the absence of consciousness and understanding of the meaning of Israel's existence and reality (a direct result of the community's refusal to provide good universal Jewish education)—Federations, as we have seen, began to emphasize "glamorous" local needs in their publicity. This may also be why the 1993 Joint Program Plan of the NJCRAC, which comprises an agenda of issues of concern and policy guidelines for its constituent national organizations and local community relations councils, did not lead off, as in the preceding five years, with a section on "Israel and the Mideast." Instead its first section dealt with "Equal Opportunity and Social Justice" in the U.S.

◈ This brings us to the connection between the anxiety of the men about not measuring up to the American definition of manhood, which includes the ability and willingness to defend "their" women and children, and by extension, the entire community-as-extended-family, and their overprotectiveness of Israel.

American Jewish males had to face gangs of non-Jewish youth and union-busting goons in immigrant neighborhoods. They had to confront anti-Semites in the armed forces in World War II. They acquitted themselves well in these encounters. But they never needed to protect their own families and communities during pogroms.

Their first real test in protecting the Jewish "extended family" worldwide arose before and during the Holocaust. The rescue of European Jews was not high on the agenda of the community during World War II, and its efforts in this regard were puny and ineffective, as we shall see in chapter 15.

There is no other way to say this: American Jews failed their "extended family" in Europe.

The need of American Jews in the 1948–66 period to protect the newborn Jewish State in order to atone/compensate for having failed European Jews, *and* to believe it is they who play such a vital role in Israel's survival, was primarily rooted in their guilt for having "abandoned" European Jews during the Holocaust and their having devoted most of their energy from the middle of 1942 through 1945 into propagandizing for a future Jewish state. They felt that Israel must be preserved at all costs to justify their Draconian choice to "abandon" their grandparents to hideous deaths and to work instead to bring the fetus grandchild of the Jewish State to term.

Subsequent generations of American Jews who had not lived through the Holocaust years as adults and who had not participated in the struggle for the establishment of Israel were affected by another kind of guilt: that arising from knowing in their secret hearts that their involvement in Israel's history and experience is vicarious. More than 70 percent of American Jews have not visited Israel even once and have no wish to settle there or to send their children on aliyah. The guilt over Israel's being the source of their vicarious Jewishness and of the men's vicarious masculinity is often expressed in the anguished question, "How can we sit here in our living rooms proposing and criticizing Israeli policies that they may have to die for?"

It is also expressed in their overprotectiveness of Israel, which is reminiscent of the behavior of Jewish parents toward their children. When Israel succeeds in various endeavors—especially those from which Jews in the Exile were historically excluded (such as agriculture and the military)—and in rescue (for instance, of Ethiopian Jewry by airlift in 1992), they feel great naches. But if the rebellious teenager goes astray, they continue to shell out his allowance. And they keep mum about the kid's offenses (the sha-shtil pattern, which dovetails with the taboo on public criticism in the Noninterference Directive), defend him to the world outside the mishpucha, and often also pooh-pooh his misdeeds (boys will be boys/war is hell).

The guilt and genuine worry over Israel that fuel a great deal of American Jews' overprotectiveness toward the Jewish State serve to override the conflicts they sometimes experience over Israel's behavior. On the one hand, they harbor a gut feeling that Israel should behave more ethically than other nation-states do. But on the other hand, feeling that *they* cannot make such demands (Israel must survive at all costs), they resent it when non-Jews do so ("Who are they to preach ethics to us after persecuting Jews for two thousand years?!"). American Jews who have long been emotionally involved with Israel also resent it when assimilationist Jews who have never had the least interest in work on its behalf or the slightest involvement with the community suddenly emerge from the closet to criticize Israel in public because its engaging in hypervisible actions that non-Jews disapprove of makes *them* and their Jewishness visible.

SCATHING ON THIN ICE

The Jewish establishment capitalizes on, exploits, and reinforces the guilt and insecurities of American Jews—as well as their genuine love and concern for Israel—to stifle public criticism in its own interests. Because its "leaders" maintain the illusion of the legitimacy of their power by claiming that they "speak in the name of American Jewry," public expression of criticism by opposing voices could challenge that claim. Furthermore, the terms of the Noninterference Directive require the Jewish establishment to keep American Jews in line. Public expressions of criticism of Israel would make it appear that they were falling down on the job in this regard.

But there is an even more fundamental reason why the Jewish establishment tries to suppress public criticism of Israel in the community. While most American Jews believe that America's support of Israel derives from a common heritage and shared values, they—and especially the "leaders" among them—also think that support from the administration and Congress is primarily rooted in Jewish political clout at election time, expressed both in voting patterns and political contributions. The need to project an *image* of Jewish clout, however, collides with the anxiety over thereby detonating the old Judeophobic myth that Jews control the banks/media/industry/public opinion/the government, that "Jews have too much influence in the U.S." Thus American Jews need to convey at one and the same time that they are powerful (in terms of political clout in voting) but are not powerful (in terms of the anti-Semitic myths).

This is a difficult and nerve-wracking balancing act along a high wire with no safety net. The borderline between having political clout and having "too much influence" in political life is one so fine that it can be inadvertently crossed if hypervigilance is not exercised. That is why, regarding Israel, where the stakes are so high, it is so important that everyone know what the "line" is.

Emphasizing "unity" as the source of Jewish clout is designed to abort the triggering of the Judeophobic myth of Jewish power by projecting the idea that it is not the putative "Jewish wealth and control of the media/banks/industry" etcetera that gives Jews political power but rather their being able to pull together and act as a pressure group. While this image is bordering on negative (and makes it appear that American Jewry is a one-issue community, which it is not), it can be argued that all kinds of pressure groups are also in there slugging away, too: It's the American Way, and therefore kosher, more or less.

There is deep anxiety, therefore, that any public criticism of Israel by Jews will make it appear that there is a rupture in communal unity. Israel's enemies will move in for the kill, just as predators attack wounded prey rather than those who are whole. (This is the same kind of anxiety that causes many blacks to avoid or suppress public criticism of statements by visible African American figures even though they may privately disagree with the comments.) As one Jewish professional said early in 1991, "The Jewish community right now cannot afford to make a mistake. There are some in the [Bush] administration who will *seize on any split* in the Jewish community" (italics mine). And should the American public, Congress, and the administration get the idea that the community is not totally united behind Israel, this will mean that candidates need not try to win their electoral—and financial—support by being pro-Israel. This leads the Jewish establishment to do everything in its power to crush public expression of criticism by Jews. No matter how Jewish "leaders" feel about Israeli policy, most will not come out publicly with any views critical of Israel, behavior that ADL National Director Foxman justified as "a price to pay for maintaining a *unity which has been helpful—if not essential*—in generating support for Israel" (italics mine).

The Jewish establishment, however, has deliberately equated unity on Israel's existence and survival with unity on its specific policies. Criticism by Jews of a specific Israeli policy is presented as a threat to the image of communal unity on Israel's survival. Many American Jews have accepted this linkage of the carriage of specific Israeli policies with the horse of Israel's survival for so long that they fear that if they wish to toss out the carriage, non-Jews will think they have decided to hurl the horse over the cliff as well. This leads them to deny publicly, and sometimes even to themselves, that there is anything serious amiss with the carriage as part of keeping faith with the horse.

Finally, the Jewish establishment has for so long equated criticism with abandonment in order to suppress criticism that it has projected the belief in this equation onto non-Jews. That is why Foxman could justify the withholding of public criticism on grounds that "we have to think how we are perceived in the larger American society *if we seem to be distancing ourselves* from Israel" (italics mine).

↞ The late 1960s saw the beginnings of debate among American Jews on Israeli policies, as we shall see in chapter 14, and it increased during the Lebanon War and the Intifada. The individuals and the leaders of small Jewish organizations who have occasionally expressed opinions contrary to those of the Jewish establishment are "attacked with high emotion and ... personally attacked," said Rabbi Eugene Borowitz, founding editor of *Sh'ma,* a journal open to a variety of opinions. He described the process:

> First comes an effort to discredit the people speaking. . . . Second, their right
> to speak is challenged—what do they know about this [issue]? . . . The next
> step is the smear—they are guilty by association. "Do you know . . . that you
> are saying just what the anti-Semites say . . . ?" Finally someone will charge
> you with starting a new Holocaust.

The use of this last charge to stifle criticism demonstrates the depth of the emotional connection between American Jews' lingering guilt over "abandoning"

European Jews to their deaths during the Holocaust and their overprotectiveness of Israel.

Critics are also subjected to a latter-day form of excommunication: They are unable to get lecture engagements in the community or to have their views reported on and printed in the Federation-owned or Federation-sponsored Jewish weeklies. These papers censor anything that would harm the "campaign"—that is, show Israel "in a bad light" by reporting on problems, questionable policies, or differences of opinion, which might cause donors to shut their wallets. Editors of today's few independent weeklies have bitterly condemned "the idea that there shall be only one voice in the Jewish community which comes from the public relations people" of the Federations as a "Big Brother concept."

Most Jewish magazines are owned and operated by Jewish organizations that, with one or two rare exceptions, do not permit news unrelated to their projects, or opinions contrary to their official "line," to see the light of day. There are only seven truly independent regular periodicals: *Bridges, Jewish Currents, The Jewish Spectator, Kerem, Lilith, Moment,* and *Tikkun,* all but the last two small (plus a handful of academic and literary publications with very limited readerships). It is pathetic to compare this situation with that of interbellum Polish Jewry, a poverty-stricken population half the size of American Jewry that supported several dozen Yiddish dailies and *180 periodicals.*

◆ When Jews wish or need to express controversial opinions, they usually have to go outside the community and write for the non-Jewish media. "The modern Jew must wash his linen in public because he has nowhere else to wash it," wrote Maurice Samuel in 1931. "He has not the privacy of a national language and . . . not even the semi-privacy of intelligent Jewish publications in English." The critics' action exposes them to triple jeopardy: first for daring to say anything negative, second for what they are specifically saying, and third for where they are saying it.

The problem is that the non-Jewish media do not cover the American Jewish community even superficially; the English Jewish weeklies would have no raison d'être at all if the general media assigned reporters to this beat. Not caring to provide in-depth reportage or to investigate or analyze the community's inner workings or politics, they have uncritically bought the Jewish establishment's "line" that American Jewry's unity on Israel's existence and its unity on Israeli policies are one and the same thing. When publishing or reporting on stray expressions by Jews of opinions critical of Israeli policies, they tend to interpret and present them as signs of a rupture in the communal unity on Israel's existence and survival. This is a serious misreading of reality—and it is dangerous.

The Jewish establishment, by promoting its misleading "line," causes the very threat it seeks to avert: the impression that criticism of Israeli policies means there is a shattering of Jewish unity on Israel's right to survive. Were it not for this "line," public expression of criticism would be understood simply as a continuation of traditional Jewish disputatiousness in a community committed to Israel's survival.

The suppression of debate also poses an internal danger to American Jews, who need to be able to express differences of opinion publicly and work them out. It is precisely for this reason that debate was encouraged throughout Jewish history, and the traditional communities would not have been able to respond to the challenges facing them without it. But what prevails today, instead, is a rationale that "the Jewish people need a united front ... i.e., uniformity of opinion ... in order to survive." This, explained Rabbi Borowitz, means that "no issue can then be argued, for it would break our unity."

ULTIMATE RECYCLING OF THE
RESCUER-ENABLER DYNAMIC

The mutual feelings of abandonment, rejection, and confusion that often obtain in the relationship between American Jews and Israel derive from the variations of the classic rescuer-enabler dynamic that operates in it.

On the one hand, American Jews, especially the Jewish establishment plutocracy, see themselves as Israel's rescuer ("Keep the Promise"). They will "save" Israel (through economic support and advocacy) if the Israelis live up to their part of the contract and behave as they should, that is, as American Jews would like them to behave. Israelis see American Jewry as a flawed rescuer that, like the God of the Lurianic Kabbala, is not ... together. They try to repair this flaw by advancing communal "unity" to improve its ability to rescue, defined in terms of winning and providing support for Israel.

In this dynamic, Israel is the wife who has to function as a kind of enabler to facilitate American Jewry's, and especially its establishment's, "rescuing" by providing what wives give husbands—boosts to their egos in the form of koved: validation of their "leaders" and Big Givers. Israel also has to accept exclusion (the Noninterference Directive) from any efforts to influence the internal direction of the community, turf the Jewish establishment plutocracy claims as its own.

The view of American Jewry as a flawed rescuer obtains not only in the relationship between Israel and the Jewish establishment but also, in muted form, between political sectors of Israeli society and their supporters in the U.S. During the Likud regime, Israelis from left to right "blame[d] the powerful [sic] and populous American Jewry for failing to bail them out," wrote an American-born Israeli journalist. The left blamed the liberal American Jewish "leaders" for failing to "save" Israel from its right-wing politics. The right-wing Israelis were bitter that American Jews were not going on aliyah en masse and thereby offsetting the demographic threat from the Arabs.

❧ But at precisely the same time, both parties see the roles in this relationship in reverse. Israel sees itself as the rescuer of all Jews because it is the instrumentality of Jewish liberation. Not only does it rescue Jews in distress, but it also exists as a home for American Jews should the American exile culminate/terminate in persecution leading to stage three (which Israelis believe it will).

Israel has also allowed American Jews to hold their heads high because it proves that Jews can run a country, defend themselves, and be something other than the eternal wandering "ghosts" that Leon Pinsker wrote about, the money-grubbing, power-hungry, parasitic fiends of the Judeophobic stereotype. As an American rabbi wrote in 1942, a Jewish state would give American Jews respect in the eyes of their non-Jewish neighbors while saving them from "the demoralization and self-hatred that are the inevitable by-products of anti-Semitism"; in 1948 social psychologist Kurt Lewin called Israel a "psychological necessity." And, as the center of Jewish cultural and spiritual life that inspires and nourishes Jews in communities all over the world, Israel (ideally) infuses their lives with meaning and a sense of continuity with the past and the future.

✦ Jews in America (and elsewhere) fell in love with Israel as they had in the past with nations and revolutionary movements they saw as rescuers. This love-is-blind syndrome has contributed to the uncritical attitude that always seems to surface in these cases. Their love, like that directed to the secular non-Jewish rescuer nations and movements, was unrequited. While American Jews saw and admired Israeli men as Ari Ben Canaans—and the women saw Israeli females as chalutzot in uniform—Israelis, said Oz, were "brought up with the idea that a Diaspora Jew is an unpleasant little creature with sweating hands, somehow dishonest, somehow parasitically adapting to every system," that is, the Jew of the anti-Semitic stereotype.

✦ When Israel replaces God as rescuer in this recycled secularized dynamic, the American Jewish community, dominated by the Jewish establishment, plays the role of the Jewish people, the rescuees. This means that it is supposed to help repair the flaws of the rescuer—flaws both parties see as deriving from Israel's ongoing state of siege, and whose repair both define in terms of acquiring political and economic support for it. This role dovetails with that of Court Jew in the old survival strategy of Exile communities, with the community functioning as the interceder with the American government (a role incompatible with criticism of Israel, of course) to press it to provide some of this support.

Under the terms of the contract between them, if American Jewry behaved correctly—sent funds and withheld interference—it could look to Israel as its ultimate worst-case-scenario rescuer.

American Jews have long tried to make the Israelis regard them as equal partners ("We Are One") but, as Ben Gurion said at the twenty-third World Zionist Congress of 1951 in relation to the Zionists of the diaspora: They are not partners in the upbuilding of the state, *but only "helpers,"* that is, enablers (italics mine).

Enabling in the case of the American Jewish community requires facilitating with backup support what the Israelis have defined as their work—making and implementing all the political, economic, military, and cultural policy decisions involved in building and defending the ship of state—*and* withdrawing from this turf (the Noninterference Directive).

The division of labor between them harkens back to the normative Jewish marital relationship, especially in Eastern Europe (from which most of Israel's founders and the ancestors of most American Jews hailed). Men did the intellectual work (Israelis make policy decisions), women provided economic support (American Jews raise and send funds to Israel). Following this pattern, Israel acts as the all-knowing husband who provides direction (policy guidelines), just as Jewish men always did for Jewish women (remember how Mordechai motivated and instructed Esther). The Israelis decide what is good for Israel and argue that it is also automatically good for American Jews, who, in the role of the nonintellectual wife, shouldn't be allowed to decide on this for themselves.

The normative Jewish marriage relationship, however, was always a partnership. Although the male partner was the dominant one, the marriage was based on interdependence, and on the understanding that both worked together for a common goal and that the actions of each spouse had to be good for the relationship. This dynamic does not exist in the "marriage" between Israel and American Jewry, and it is therefore anomalous to the pattern of traditional Jewish marriages. The Noninterference Directive, which is contrary to the spirit of Jewish culture generally, aborts real mutuality and precludes the creation of any mechanism to discuss, let alone resolve, problems that arise when the interests of the parties are in conflict.

Nevertheless, the role of the American Jewish community, in recycling that of traditional Jewish women, is that of altruistic-assertive enabler. American Jews are encouraged to be assertive only when it is "altruistic," that is, when the dominant partner, Israel, decides it is in the "interests of the entire Jewish people," which of course it presumes to be consonant with its own. They are supposed to put their assertiveness on hold when it would be detrimental to Israel's interests, as the Israeli political leadership defines them. Thus American Jews are supposed to sound the alarm if something bad is about to happen to Israel but follow a sha-shtil ("Don't wash the dirty linen in public") stance if Israel does anything that in their view is either bad for it, bad for American Jews, or for both, or that is immoral, unethical, counterproductive, ineffective, suicidal, or plain downright dumb.

☙ The rescuer-enabler dynamic, "Cominternization," and the Noninterference Directive became entrenched patterns in the relationship of American Jews and Israel because of The War.

The various harbingers of peace beginning in the fall of 1993 are hopeful signs that The War may be drawing to an end. This could cause profound inner changes in the American Jewish community, which has focused so much of its energy on activities to sustain Israel, as well as in its relationship with the Jewish State.

Israel, wrote Sanford Pinsker in 1988, allows American Jewry "the luxury of postponing a confrontation with its own emptiness." Peace will make such a confrontation inevitable. American Jews will be compelled to look inward and decide on their direction and priorities and on the viability of their institutions. They will also have to think long and hard about what kind of "marriage" they wish to have with Israel and to listen to what the Israelis think about it, too.

For the first time since the birth of Israel, the possibility exists of the development of an honest and real relationship with American Jewry, one not of power struggles but of partnership.

THIRTEEN ❧ WOMEN'S VOLUNTEER ORGANIZATIONS: A CENTURY OF VICARIOUS FEMINISM

> *The second commandment [the] Jewish wife lives by, "Thou shalt not be more successful than thy husband," is obeyed by many women by doing volunteer work. In a culture in which "you get what you pay for," the unpaid wife can feel that she is not a real threat to her husband.*

MARY CAHN SCHWARTZ

> *What happened with anti-Semitism? Jews started to fight. What happened with the Blacks? A revolution went on. The same thing will have to happen in the Jewish community for [women's] issues to get solved. You are not going to do it by holding nice conferences.*

ANN WOLFE

When Rebecca bids farewell to Rowena at the end of *Ivanhoe,* she tells her rival that she will be numbered among the women who "since the time of Abraham downwards, have ... devoted their thoughts to heaven and their actions to works of kindness to men [*sic*], tending the sick, feeding the hungry and relieving the distressed."

It has been well documented that the model for Sir Walter Scott's Rebecca was one of the first and quintessential Jewish female volunteers in America, Rebecca Gratz of Philadelphia. In 1819 Gratz founded the Female Hebrew Benevolent Society; its chief work was relief. The society investigated its beneficiaries and "helped only those of good moral character who were in reduced circumstances," wrote one historian. This policy set the pattern for future lady-of-the-manor patronizing of clients by the groups Jewish women established throughout the nineteenth century in practically every American city to do social welfare work, as well as in those of the late nineteenth and early twentieth century that aimed to "uplift" (that is, Americanize) poor immigrants.

The wealthy women volunteers' patronizing/"uplifting" of the poor was intertwined with the mystification of Jewish women's organizations as unambiguously altruistic. This mystification, which prevailed well into the 1980s, was designed to address *and to mask* the psychological motivations of the women in establishing and joining these organizations.

The motivations of the women were mixed. On the one hand, there was their genuine concern for helping local (and, later, distant) Jewish poor, arising out of traditional Jewish values, including the commitment to tzedakah; this constituted continuity with the past. But, on the other hand, the women also sought in various periods the opportunity to be assertive; to attain validation to bolster their self-esteem; and to have some kind of public role in Jewish communal life.

None of these psychological motivations could be or was openly acknowledged. To admit the need for a channel for their assertiveness or for a public role would have elicited disapproval from the men, whose permission was necessary for them to engage in volunteer work outside the home. To acknowledge the need for a public role and for validation would have also meant acknowledging the absence in their lives of both. This might have propelled them to confront what was wrong with their lives, something they were most reluctant to do.

The mystification of Jewish women's volunteer work and of the organization they did it in/for as unambiguously altruistic–"good for the Jews" and Jewish survival–legitimized assertiveness by women members. It allowed them to use the organization as a safe space in which to be assertive precisely because its purpose was altruistic. In the organization they could be born-again altruistic-assertive enablers.

Mystification of the organization's and its members' altruism also allowed many women to ignore the fact that they had joined it for the purpose of attaining self-esteem through validation. Many women felt ashamed of joining an organization to achieve this end as well as others: to use their energy, to be effective, to gain some recognition, to "be someone"–all the things that patriarchal society denies women–and to ward off depression, anxiety, loneliness, and alienation, ills that patriarchy inflicts on them. The mystification allowed the women to offset their sense of shame with one of pride for serving the Jewish people.

Mystification also masked the reality that the public role the organizations themselves played was marginal to Jewish communal life. The work the organizations did, however valuable its results, was allowed by the men as a form of warehousing–of keeping women safely busy at tasks that prevented their straying either into adulterous relationships or into the workplace, and which did not threaten their marriages or challenge other power relationships in the community.

The women's organizations institutionalized the marginality of Jewish women in relation to the organized Jewish community, especially the Jewish establishment, which has remained male turf where policy on Jewish physical and cultural survival was and is decided and implemented. The segregated environment of the women's organizational sector has made women and their work invisible in the community. As sociologist Daniel Elazar noted, it "serves to exclude women from what many regard [sic] as the circle of real power and decision-making within the community."

"UPLIFTERS, NOT SISTERS"

The German Jewish women who immigrated to the U.S. after 1848 often worked side by side with their husbands, especially in the West. But as soon as the businesses they established produced enough income, the women, eager to be like their American neighbors, more often than not retired to housekeeping and child rearing. The synagogue Sisterhoods and local social welfare groups, Sunday schools, libraries, and day nurseries the women established and raised funds to support, as well as the national organizations they founded in the late nineteenth and early twentieth century, gave these women a visa out of the confines of the home and the opportunity to participate in socially useful activity that won grudging recognition from the men.

In the two decades before World War I, social welfare volunteer work by Jewish women (whose husbands were) in the upper middle class was on a parallel, though not identical, track with that of non-Jewish women of this class. The WASP women, wrote Barbara Ehrenreich and Deirdre English, sought "a project worthy of their untapped moral sensitivities and social concerns." For many a wealthy non-Jewish woman, that project was the great task of "uplifting" working-class women. In this volunteer role of "bringing the gospel of hygiene, public health, home economics, etc. to the poor, she was necessarily patronizing, at times antagonistic in her relations with poor women. . . . The relationship was not of sisters but as uplifters."

The reason the women were allowed to undertake such a project derived from the rampant anxieties during this period about the quality of the white "racial stock." The WASP upper classes feared that "society" would be contaminated by working-class women, especially immigrants, through "overbreeding" and as disease carriers via domestic service, garment manufacture, and prostitution. These anxieties fueled the popularity of the eugenics movement—self-defined as "the science of the improvement of the human race by better breeding"—and the anti–"white slavery" campaigns of this pre-World War I era.

◆ These two movements were of acute concern to Jews because of their anti-Semitism and the arguments they promoted that reinforced the strong nativism/anti-immigrant sentiment and channeled it into the drive to restrict Jewish immigration and institute other forms of discrimination, such as university quotas for Jewish students.

Many early eugenicists, noted historian Barry Mehler, were rabidly anti-Semitic. Eugenicist Madison Grant wrote in 1916 of the "problems" Americans have "with the Polish Jew, whose dwarf stature, peculiar mentality and ruthless concentration on self-interest are being engrafted upon the stock of the nation." A eugenicist colleague wrote him that "our ancestors drove the Baptists from Massachusetts Bay into Rhode Island but we have no place to drive the Jews to." The thrust, therefore, was to keep them out, and it ultimately succeeded with the restrictive immigration laws of the 1920s.

The eugenicists' propaganda struck terror into the hearts of East European Jewish immigrants, especially by 1907, when the issue of crime committed by Jews began to provide more fuel for advocates of restrictions on immigration. Their fear and rage came to the fore after New York Police Commissioner Theodore Bingham advocated the exclusion of Jewish immigrants from the U.S. because, he said, "50% of the criminals in the city were Russian Jews who numbered only 25% of the population" (phony statistics he later retracted, after the damage had been done).

A second great concern for all Jews in the pre–World War I era was the anti–"white slavery" hysteria, which was contaminated with anti-Semitism. There was widespread newspaper coverage of the Jewish involvement in the international traffic in women, which muckrakers charged was headquartered on the Lower East Side, and of the young Jewish men (called Kadets) who lured women into prostitution at the docks and in neighborhood dance halls.

Jews on the Lower East Side were well aware of the ubiquitous prostitution, and Michael Gold later wrote about it in his moving classic, *Jews Without Money*. His story about a childhood incident points to an attitude of compassion by women for women in "the life." He recalled how a gang of boys taunted Rosie, a local prostitute. His mother called him inside, where he found Rosie crying at the kitchen table. His mother slapped his face: "Murderer!" she said. "Why did you make Rosie cry?"

Prostitution had become a problem among Jews in late-nineteenth-century Russia after hundreds of thousands of Jews were expelled (1882) from the shtetls to the big cities, where poverty and unemployment were rampant, family life disrupted, and old social controls no longer effective. Large, well-organized gangs of pimps in major cities bought, sold, and transported women from the impoverished Jewish communities of Russia and elsewhere in Eastern Europe, Turkey, and Greece. Many were lured to Germany with promises of domestic jobs and then shipped to brothels in Argentina.

Bertha Pappenheim (Freud's "Anna O."), founder of the Jewish Women's Federation of Germany (*Judischer Frauenbund*), found that many Jewish religious leaders in the countries she visited to investigate the traffic in women refused to get involved in ending it. A Turkish rabbi told her that 90 percent of the prostitutes and 90 percent of the pimps in his country were Jews but added, "If we tell these merchants, 'We don't want your money, it's dirty,' our orphanages and our hospitals would close for lack of funds." As late as 1924, Pappenheim charged that the Jewish people had "never shown a desire to cooperate in solving the problem."

However, Jewish communities did try to fight prostitution. The problem, wrote Edward Bristow, was that "Jewish pimps brought on such disgrace *but so did talking about them*" (italics mine). Some Jews argued that their being involved in campaigns against the traffic in women would be an "antidote" to the anti-Semitism in the antiprostitution movement. Opponents argued that trying to deal with it directly ("washing dirty linen in public") would cause more anti-Semitism. The conflict caused a communal paralysis and impeded effective measures by Jews directed at ending the traffic in women.

✦ It was against this background that many upper-middle-class Jewish women, mostly of German descent, followed in the footsteps of WASP women of this class and made poor women (immigrants from Eastern Europe) and their families their "special project."

But their motivations in doing so were much more complex than those of their non-Jewish counterparts. They were not seeking, as did wealthy white Gentile women, to stop the "contagion" of the poor women from spreading to their class. They were seeking to clean up the poor women (and their families) so that non-Jews wouldn't accuse the poor Jews of spreading contagion and thereby taint Jews of their *own* class and national origin with this charge. Their anxiety about this accusation was undoubtedly intensified by memories of medieval pogroms triggered by the old Judeophobic myth that Jews spread disease ("poisoning the wells"), recycled in the contemporary newspaper stories about the Lower East Side's being a hotbed of prostitution and, thus, of venereal disease.

The women swooped down on the Lower East Side, shoved their way into people's cold-water flats, spouted criticism with the rapidity of machine-gun fire, and nagged the unwashed about how to tidy up their tenements. One woman urged them to stop speaking Yiddish and advised the girls "to bathe and wear clean clothes."

Such behavior was an obvious discontinuity with the patterns of tzedakah of women and men in traditional Jewish communities. In the past, the dispensing of tzedakah had involved efforts to preserve the dignity of its recipients. The women's changeover to disregarding/breaking that dignity resulted from assimilationism, from looking to upper-middle-class WASP women as their reference group and adopting what they believed was class-appropriate behavior regarding "charity work."

In "uplifting" the immigrants, the women acted as the enablers of the male German Jewish establishment in facilitating its agenda of getting the East Europeans to shape up (after it was too late to have them shipped out). This agenda took on greater urgency as a form of damage control to prevent the fallout of the anti-immigrant and anti–"white slavery" campaigns from attaching itself to *their* image. The women, wrote one historian, were "the foot soldiers who implemented the policies established by the male boards of directors."

Following the traditional Jewish pattern whereby men were responsible for the mind and women for the body, the men established institutions such as the Educational Alliance to teach immigrants English and civics; the women established vocational schools and settlement houses to teach the female newcomers pink-collar work skills and proper deportment.

In contrast to past behavioral patterns in which the enabler who implemented the male agenda remained in the background, the female social work volunteers were a highly visible—and accessible—target for the objects of their "uplifting" efforts. The German Jewish men sat at uptown board meetings and raised money for various projects to Americanize the immigrants; the women were downtown in the ghetto taking the heat. The *Forverts* voiced the antagonism of the "uplifted" in denouncing the "rich Jewish aristocratic women from uptown with their bediamonded hands [and] their delicate alabaster fingers with well-manicured nails . . . [who] shower favors upon and seek remedies for downtown Jews." This highly visible enabling by the German Jewish women harkened back to the classic Jewish roles of visible oppressor surrogate of the ruling classes and of lightning rod to absorb the oppressed masses' rage.

But whatever the women's motivations and methods, we need to use the traditional Jewish yardstick—namely, it is the deed that really counts—in order to evaluate their accomplishments. The volunteers did provide important assistance to the immigrants, particularly women. The National Council of Jewish Women (NCJW), the most active organization in this regard, set up an immigrant aid network to help female immigrants and arranged for the first Yiddish-speaking female social worker to meet incoming women at Ellis Island and find lodgings for those without relatives—thus derailing the pimps' recruiting strategy. It also established rescue facilities for victims of pimps. Thus its members aided them in the struggle against the traffic in women, just as did middle-class Jewish women in Russia, Poland, France, Germany, Hungary, and Bulgaria, and in Austrian Galicia and Bukovina.

◆ Direct social work by women volunteers ended after World War I. One reason is that the mass wave of immigrants from Europe came to a halt after restrictive immigration legislation was passed in the U.S. in 1924. The second reason is that social work became "professionalized," which meant it was claimed as male turf. The field's "professionalization" was defined by the absence of women volunteers from it. The wealthier women did not turn to volunteer work such as serving as candy stripers in hospitals or its equivalent in old-age homes and orphanages. Instead they reverted to the focus that had prevailed in women's groups in the mid-nineteenth century: fund-raising, with its time-consuming round of social activities, for practical projects mostly directed at aiding the distant poor.

The mind-body division of labor continued, with the men doing political advocacy (for instance, against anti-Semitism) through the Jewish establishment organizations they founded and the women raising money for: an international vocational school network (Women's American ORT); day care centers for the non-Jewish poor (NCJW); and aid to the poor and elderly (NCJW and B'nai B'rith Women). In the Zionist movement, the men were responsible for the high-octane ideological debates and political campaigning, and the women for the practical day-to-day realities of supporting medical and nutritional programs in Mandatory Palestine (Hadassah) and maintaining day care centers there (Pioneer Women and various women's auxiliaries of religious organizations). (Because the women's Zionist organizations were excluded from political work, they escaped the declawing of the male-dominated sectors of the Zionist movement after 1948.)

VICARIOUS FEMINISM (1920s–30s)

The prime factor in the change in the character of Jewish women's volunteering after World War I was the zeitgeist of the 1920s, the jazz-and-flapper era, which began with the granting of female suffrage and which was characterized by a general liberalization of sexual norms.

American white middle-class women faced a conflict between the liberalization of attitudes regarding women's public lives and the impossibility of their taking political and economic advantage of the new ambiance because of persistent sexism in the workplace, the universities and professional schools, and on the part of their own husbands. They tried to resolve the conflict by becoming involved in organizations that allowed them to participate in public life without threatening the sexist status quo. In the case of WASP women, this resolution led to the rise of the women's club movement.

Jewish women of the second generation of East European background whose husbands were now making it into the middle class were excluded from the turf of paid work (being) reclaimed by the men and faced double jeopardy in job discrimination. They sought to resolve the conflict by joining Jewish women's organizations, which, like the non-Jewish women's clubs, functioned in the public sphere. Additionally, their participation in this variation of a women's club was also a symbol of their middle-class status and thus of their husbands' material success.

The Jewish women's organizations also arose to resolve another contradiction in Jewish women's lives in the first half of the twentieth century. On the one hand, a liberalization of practices favoring women's participation in certain aspects of religious life seemed to be taking place. It included mixed seating in Reform (and some Conservative) synagogues and the inception of a Bat Mitzvah ceremony for girls, which had never existed before in Jewish life. But on the other hand, women continued to be excluded from active and equal participation in synagogue services and were relegated to fund-raising activities in/through the

Sisterhood. They were also excluded from active participation in the major secular Jewish organizations or were tracked into their women's auxiliaries.

The women constituted separate organizations (the independent Hadassah, NCJW, and Pioneer Women; the quasi-independent Women's American ORT; and the then-quasi-independent B'nai B'rith Women)—or accepted an auxiliary status and tried to make the most of it—to give themselves the opportunity to participate in *Jewish* public life.

Hadassah and Pioneer Women (PW) actually had to battle their male political comrades to win separate status in the Zionist movement. ZOA leader Louis Lipsky opposed Hadassah in 1928 as a "feminist" organization on these grounds: "What was formerly a Jewish women's movement—auxiliary, complementary, *aiding and comforting the main stem* of the movement—became an organization animated by the sense of women's rights. Like all other women's movements of this sort, it represented resistance to the domination of men, which resistance was turned into a demand for equality which, as soon as it was attained [*sic!*], became a desire to *dominate and control*" (italics mine).

Here we see one of the first instances in which the old anti-Semitic stereotype of the controlling Jew is recycled and used by American Jewish men against women.

It is precisely because securing a public role in the community was the women's main motivation that they needed the approval of the male "leaders." For this reason, most of the projects they chose (for instance, day care in Israel) were those which either did not compete with the glamorous ones the men were involved with or were ones for which they were men's enablers (women's auxiliaries/branches/divisions of male-dominated organizations and synagogue Sisterhoods). Another reason for eschewing projects the men considered glamorous is that the basis for their glamour—which derived from its connection with conflicts over masculinity—obviously did not obtain for women. The dynamic in the Jewish establishment by which glamour determines an organization's choice of project and an individual's choice of affiliation has been largely absent from the independent Jewish women's organizations.

❧ The woman's organization, by functioning in the public sphere, gave its members a sense of vicarious feminism. It gave the woman the opportunity to function in the public sphere through the organization. Her membership in it, and her participation in making and implementing collective decisions in and for it, gave her a public role *without her having to struggle to attain one directly as an individual.* A direct struggle would have required consciousness of the injustice of both the traditional Jewish women's exclusion from public roles in the religious and political life of the community (from, for instance, performance of public rituals, serving on communal councils) and of their repositioned enabler role, which excluded them from public *economic* life, and would have led to confrontation with the men. Both the consciousness and the willingness to be confrontational were absent.

While vicarious feminism characterized all the women's organizations, the dynamic can be observed most clearly in Pioneer Women. This Labor Zionist organization was doubly vicariously feminist in that it functioned in the public sphere and its members identified with the women pioneers of Mandatory Palestine—with the altruism, purity, and purpose of their lives, and especially with their feminism. The *chalutza* (woman pioneer), wrote Neil Mandelkern, "excited the imagination" of PW members "with what seemed to be an incredibly romantic, adventurous, and free life. She worked in the fields with the men. She carried a gun and helped to defend the isolated settlements. She was not tied down to her children because she had developed sophisticated systems of collective child care. . . . It seemed that she had achieved virtual equality with the men. . . . American women could only dream about such advances."

If they could not live such a life, they would support it by raising funds for the day care centers, urban residences for single women, and various other cooperative endeavors of the Council of Working Women, with which PW affiliated. Just as so many American Jews have supported Israel so it could be Jewish for them, the PW members supported the chalutzot so the women pioneers could be feminists for them. And just as the men drew deep vicarious satisfaction from the fact that Jewish men in Mandatory Palestine and, later, Israel were fighters and defenders, these women got secondhand naches from the fact that the female pioneers they helped support were model feminists. The chalutza, in the words of one PW member in 1927, represented "the advanced guard of our sex."

⤷ Women also sought in their organizations the opportunity to define and express their Jewishness actively, a function the synagogue and the communal organizations fulfilled only for the men. The women's organizations were thus a kind of secular shul or surrogate synagogue where prayer services were replaced with a different kind of avoda, of service to the Jewish nation. The spiritual quest that led many women to join them can be seen from the words of a veteran PW member about how she and others felt when emissaries from Eretz Israel came "from the kibbutz, the fields, the *meshek*" (farm) "they were really the *soul* of the organization. Around them there was such a *holy* feeling!" (italics mine).

Related to the secular shul dynamic was the search for sisterhood. Women looked to these organizations for the equivalent to male bonding around synagogue life (and, formerly, participation in the national project of learning Torah).

THE TWO-TIER SYSTEM (1940s–70s)

In the early stages of the women's organizations' existence, there was equality among the volunteers. But their camaraderie and cooperation eroded as they became larger, more efficient, and more businesslike in fund-raising to try to meet the needs of European Jews in the dire and threatening circumstances of the 1930s and 1940s. Pioneer Women, for example, which had "once valued the simple joys of *havershaft*" (Yiddish for comradeship) "was now . . . seeking 'formality,' 'efficiency,' and 'system,'" wrote Mandelkern. The need to raise large sums of money, especially in the post–World War II era, was a major factor in the transformation of the originally egalitarian women's organizations into hierarchical and undemocratic structures.

Gradually but inexorably, a two-tier system of volunteers coalesced. A top tier of volunteers, composed of upper-middle-class women, came to dominate the organizations at the national level, making all the major policy decisions on projects, membership, and, in some groups, fund-raising quotas for local chapters. One former Hadassah member reported that the national office "excludes its membership throughout the country from the decision-making process in much the same way men have traditionally excluded . . . women from their decision-making process."

The lower-class volunteers on the chapter level were tracked into a low tier. This involved them in the practical housekeeping type of stultifyingly tedious and endlessly repetitive scut work, the kind of work done by paid staff in the male-dominated organizations (and often by a male macher's secretary in his workplace): typing, collating, mimeographing/photocopying, envelope stuffing; and collecting and selling items at thrift shops and sales. In the case of the Houston chapter of one organization, women spent months assembling thousands of old shoes to sell; regardless of what they realized from the sale, the number of woman-hours spent on this effort was staggering. Having huge numbers of women as a cadre of unpaid labor enabled the organizations to allocate less of their budget to "administrative costs."

The low-tier volunteers thus became the altruistic-assertive enablers of the top-tier volunteers, facilitating their important work of decision making on projects and on raising and allocating funds (the intellectual labor) and accepting exclusion from it. They could be assertive only when it was "good for the organization," as defined, of course, by its "leaders."

◆ The criterion for top-tier "leadership" became, as in the male-dominated Jewish establishment organizations, the size of one's financial contribution. In the early 1970s, for example, one woman tried to become president of a large women's organization but failed. Within a year after she had remarried and her second husband had made a $200,000 donation to the organization, she got her wish.

But this example points to a crucial difference between the women's and the men's organizations. In the men's groups, the money comes from the man's earnings and his access to funds from business contacts. In the women's organizations, both money and contacts most often derive from the woman's husband.

This means, said social worker Mary Cahn Schwartz, that a woman's volunteer position is dependent on her husband's wealth and status, and if he has little, she has no chance of being on a top board or committee. "Leadership" was and is thus determined not by merit but by the *husband's class*.

This meant that working-class and lower-middle-class women were automatically relegated to the low-tier sector. Unable to attain high positions even at the chapter level, many began to compete with each other over symbols of conspicuous consumption—clothes and jewelry worn to social functions, home furnishings—and children's achievements and status ("My son the doctor"). The competitiveness caused a deterioration in the personal relationships among the women and eroded the sense of sisterhood and the female values of cooperation and compassion.

❧ The few wealthy women who came to dominate the organization used it as a vehicle for attaining a certain degree of power and status in Jewish public life. Most members were increasingly excluded from making and implementing collective decisions on policy and direction, and thus from a public role in/through the organization.

They accepted their downgraded status for two prime reasons. One was the decline of their psychological need for a sense of vicarious feminism, a need that had been important because of the zeitgeist of the 1920s and 1930s. By contrast, the zeitgeist of the mid-1940s through the 1960s was that of the feminine mystique. Rosie the Riveter and her working-class and lower-middle-class sisters who had staffed the war plants had been herded back into the home, and most accepted the propaganda glorifying their homemaker role. As their interest in having a public role through the organization declined, they were less concerned over that role's cooptation by women outside their class.

The second reason the majority of volunteer women acceded to their exclusion from a public role was that other motivations for membership in the organization began to take precedence. One need, for safe space for assertiveness, had always obtained; the other, for validation to shore up their flagging self-esteem, intensified. The need for validation grew increasingly acute as the role of the born-again altruistic-assertive enabler began to undergo a slow but inexorable breakdown. As Jewish men began to succeed economically, the family's need for this kind of enabling decreased. With educational discrimination against Jews ebbing, it was no longer quite as urgent for the mother to push her son so desperately to produce the top grades necessary to get into a good, even an Ivy League, college. Nevertheless, the Jewish mother persisted like a *golem* (Hebrew for android, robot, automaton) in carrying out her enabler role.

By this time, the sons' publicly expressed resentment of their mothers' altruistic-assertive enabling was sprouting and spreading like mushrooms after a torrential rainstorm. And these mushrooms poisoned the women's lives. No longer could they feel a sense of self-esteem, because the importance of their enabling was denied, and validation of it—and of them—was withheld. It was, in short, an era too late for the Jewish woman to derive a sense of self-esteem from altruistic-assertive enabling in the family and too early for her to experience a sense of self-worth from her own work, which had to wait for the second wave of American feminism to legitimize her reentering the turf of paid labor in the 1970s.

The validation the women's organizations provided their members to fuel their self-esteem compensated for what they were no longer receiving in the family. It also allowed them to avoid confronting the shrinkage of their enabler role at home precisely at a time when the feminine mystique mandated it as the only legitimate feminine role.

The self-esteem of the members was also bolstered by organizational chauvinism ("Our organization is doing more important work than theirs"). The prime motivations for organizational chauvinism were and are different in the male-dominated organizations and in the women's groups. In a male-dominated organization, its function was and is to address an external goal: to create an image and thereby capture glamorous turf and Big Givers. In the women's organizations, its purpose is to deal with an internal problem: the need to give members the sense that the organization is unique and to obscure its similarity with other women's organizations in ideology and in process. A woman most often joined a particular organization not because of its specific projects but because it was an auxiliary of her husband's organization or because it was nearby or one that a friend belonged to or the first one she encountered in a community the family had relocated to. She had to be made to feel that her organization was special lest she defect to another that raised money for similar projects in the same way.

Organizational chauvinism has kept the women in the different organizations isolated from one another. They were thus triply segregated: first, in the large Pale/reservation separating them from the rest of the organized Jewish community; second, in organizational ghettos; and third, in minighettos of low-tier volunteers within each organizational ghetto.

THE COMMUNAL *MECHITZAH* (PARTITION)

To understand the motivations of the top-tier "leaders" in maintaining separate women's organizations, we need to look at the position of women generally in the male-dominated organized Jewish community (which embraces the Jewish establishment with its plutocracy at the top, plus the synagogal, Zionist, and women's organizations).

Jewish organizations operate by one of two principles in regard to women: limited "integration" under male domination, or what sociologist Rela Geffen calls the counterpart system.

The boards of Federations and their agencies and those of the major community relations organizations are officially "integrated," but until the 1970s they unofficially excluded women; even today only a relatively few tokens have attained positions of power. The fund-raising bodies of many Jewish establishment organizations, including Federation campaigns, as well as the congregational structures of three of the four wings (a.k.a. "denominations") of American Judaism, operate by the counterpart system. In this system, there is a main organization composed of men and a women's auxiliary division or branch—sometimes called by one of these names and sometimes separately incorporated. Women's power is limited by the fact that the board of the main organization is virtually all male and the women's group is allowed only one representative on it.

All the women's organizations—the auxiliaries and the independents—have collective second-class citizenship in the organized Jewish community; they are not involved in shaping communal direction or policy. The women volunteers who are active in male-dominated organizations in the Jewish establishment, except for a few tokens, have second-class citizenship as individuals; they are largely excluded from positions of power. Thus, *no matter what sector of Jewish organizational life women function in, they are excluded from real power in the community.* This explains in large part why so-called women's concerns, such as the need for religious divorce reform and day care, are not taken seriously or considered essential issues for *all* Jews. Just as women had no input into the legislative processes of Halacha or the communal councils in the past, so, too, they have no input into the decision-making processes in the Jewish community in America today.

❧ Operating by the counterpart system, the Federation campaigns and the national UJA (which provides direction for them on the overseas needs they raise funds for) have Women's Divisions. Women who are earning their own incomes are discouraged from joining the trade divisions of the Federation campaigns and are instead tracked into "business and professional" women's groups within the Women's Divisions in order to bolster them. Rarely have these structures served as a conduit to move women into top leadership positions outside them. Most of the women who have made it through—and out of—these divisions are those with leadership positions in other communal organizations.

Federation "leaders" rationalize the continuation of the Women's Divisions on grounds that they encourage what they call plus-giving. This sexist term refers to the hoped-for extra amount a wife contributes to supplement her husband's donation, thereby increasing the total extracted from a couple. (The possibility that spouses might decide together what their total "gift" will be has never permeated the machers' sexist consciousness.)

Another reason advanced by the machers for the continuation of the Women's Divisions, and of the counterpart system generally, is that if various organizations are "integrated," the women will "distract" the men. This, of course, is a recycling of the rationale for quarantining women behind a mechitzah in Orthodox synagogues. In 1977, when it seemed that the stag UJA Young Leadership

Cabinet (YLC) was finally going to open its doors to women, some opponents actually argued that women's attendance at YLC retreats would lead to extramarital affairs, and that it would "destroy the Cabinet's *esprit de corps*" (male bonding) and "turn it into a social club." (The YLC was not "integrated" at that time; instead, a Young Women's Leadership Cabinet was established. The two cabinets were combined fifteen years later, in the fall of 1992.)

❧ A 1986 CJF survey revealed that three times as many women served as Federation presidents in 1986 as in 1975, but only one-fifth of Federation presidents and 28.8 percent of board members were female. "We are still getting the 'wives of' pattern—women chosen because of their husbands' volunteer roles," said Geffen. And, indeed, the survey quoted respondents as saying that "women with inactive husbands can make it in the Women's Divisions but not in the Federation as a whole"; and that the husband's involvement "will tend to pull the wife . . . up the ladder of Federation involvement," but that women with national leadership potential were often "held down by the husband's objections." Said Geffen, "A few 'superwomen' are stars. The male leadership looks around and finds a few women and puts them on every board." Only a few women are in influential positions at national UJA.

Similarly, only a handful of the "integrated" community relations organizations have had female presidents, and there are still relatively few women on their national boards. "Women are still seen as window-dressing. When it comes to something really important, women are not chosen," said Ann Wolfe, former national staff director of the Committee on the Role of Women for the AJCommittee.

The principal reason for the lack of real progress in the advancement of female volunteers is that the men have no intention of allowing women, except for a few tokens, into positions of power on their turf, where they derive power and status and an ersatz definition of masculinity. CJF research director Barry Kosmin acknowledged publicly in 1989 that Federation executives feared women volunteers would "*take over the turf*" (an obvious recycling of the old Judeophobic myth) and cause the men to "*withdraw* along with their *greater economic* resources" (italics mine). He actually added, "This is a danger which has to be considered."

A related factor of recent vintage, cited as a "problem" by Kosmin, is that the increase in women Federation volunteers has produced a "potential gender and class conflict" between the upper-class women and the middle-class male executives. Another conflict exists between these female volunteers—as well as professionals—and the Orthodox men who have increasingly been hired as professionals in Jewish organizations. Some of these men are even more uncomfortable than are non-Orthodox men with women in high positions.

The men's strategy is to talk a good game and then continue to advance other men through a promotional system that operates by male networking. This ensures that the choice of leadership is "locked in concrete," said Wolfe. Male volunteers suggest other male volunteers (and professionals); male professionals suggest other executives and often recommend volunteers for high positions. The men are neither interested in choosing women for responsible positions nor in grooming them for leadership. Another method used to exclude women from top leadership positions is the simple power play. For example, a woman vice-president of a Midwest Federation informed the male president that she intended to seek his office when his term was up. Shortly after this, she lost her vice-presidency.

The men also engage in passive resistance on a case-by-case basis, a tactic familiar to us from the history of the chalutzot in the pioneering Yishuv. A favorite method is to make endlessly recycled excuses for keeping women out of positions of power and responsibility, for example, that women will be unable to solicit contributions from men in corporations since they are not functioning in this milieu themselves. Another popular male technique is simply not to listen to what women say. One story that has circulated among women in the community for years concerns the experience of the first and only female accepted onto a local Federation board. She noticed after several months of meetings that the discussion after her presentations always picked up at the point where the previous (male) speaker had left off. As an experiment, she read a recipe into her next oral report—during which there was no visible reaction and after which the discussion resumed as if she had not spoken. Whether or not the story is apocryphal is not as significant as the fact that no surprise is evoked when it is told among women.

Finally, there is the factor of lack of democracy in the community and the choosing of "leaders" on the basis of the money they contribute from their own earnings and have access to now or expect to have in the future. This is a donation olympics in which most women are still unable to compete. It accounts for why, until the 1980s, the Major Gifts dinners of some Federation campaigns were restricted to men and had these three words printed on their menus.

⊷ Feminists have discussed the issue of increasing the number of women volunteers in high positions in the Jewish establishment since 1972. That was the year Jacqueline Levine, president of the then–Women's Division of the AJCongress, broke silence on women's second-class citizenship in the community in her address to the CJF General Assembly.

But the fundamental question that is not discussed is whether increasing the number of women in top positions would change anything for women as a whole.

The volunteers are upper-middle-class women. They are well aware that if they play by the rules of the (male-defined) game, they may be allowed to rise to positions of limited power. If and when they attain these, they continue to play by the rules. They remain committed to the organization that gave them these positions, and they reinforce the system in order to continue to hold onto them. Since most are not feminists, there are no grounds for assuming they will challenge the system to make it more responsive to the needs and concerns of women.

And, indeed, the women who have become heads of some of the "integrated" male-dominated Jewish organizations have by and large done nothing for women. For example, when Esther Leah Ritz was president of JWB (now renamed JCCA) in the 1980s, she said that nothing could be done by her organization, which supervises Jewish military chaplains, to reverse its exclusion of female rabbis from such positions. (It was only in December 1992 that a female rabbi, Chana Timoner, began a long-term assignment as a U.S. Army chaplain.)

It comes down to the old question of what the goal of the powerless group is—a bigger slice of the maggoty pie or a different and nourishing pie. Since the entire communal structure is undemocratic, allowing more women to become powerful in it will not make it "more" democratic. There is no such thing as "more" or "less" democratic: Either it is democratic or it isn't. And there is no way an undemocratic communal structure can be responsive and accountable to women—or to the majority of men, either.

WHY NETWORKING DOESN'T WORK

The situation of women professionals in "integrated" Jewish organizations is even worse than that of the female volunteers, and it has not appreciably improved since the 1970s. There is tremendous resistance to hiring and promoting women and paying them wages equal to those of the men. In small cities, where the correspondingly smaller personnel pool makes women's attaining high executive positions more likely than in large ones, "this is often seen as scraping the bottom of the barrel," said Levine.

Two consecutive studies undertaken by the National Conference of Jewish Communal Service workers showed an increase in top female executives in the Federations and their social agencies from 5 percent in 1977 to a whopping 8 percent in 1981. The first top female executive of a local Jewish family and child-care agency in the *entire* U.S. was appointed only as late as 1983. A 1979 survey by JESNA revealed that only 10 percent of women in the Jewish education field worked as principals and administrators, and there is nothing to indicate any substantive change since that time. Salary differentials between female and male workers in Federations and their agencies prove that the Federation world is not an equal opportunity employer.

As in the case of the female volunteers, the men's strategy is to pay lip service to hiring and promoting women—even passing resolutions at CJF General Assemblies—but to take no action to change anything. The men spout time-honored excuses for not hiring and advancing women professionals: "It's tough for newcomers to break in"; "professional women lack mobility"; and the oldie but goodie, "Women don't want to work at night." Another successful tactic is to make women feel uncomfortable in responsible positions by continuing to treat them in a sexist manner. One female professional told a feminist conference about the time she and a female colleague walked into a development meeting: A male campaign department head "chucked me under the chin and said, 'Hello, girls,'" thus undermining her credibility with male Big Givers.

The female professionals have so far been reluctant to confront their organizations' power structures on inequality of pay and promotion. Unlike their sisters in the turn-of-the-century sweatshops, they have been cowed into nonmilitant behavior. Discussions on affirmative action suits have come to nothing; strikes are out of the question. Even their getting together to compare salaries and conditions is too frightening. Nor are there any vehicles for citywide meetings of women professionals in the Jewish establishment. After an initial such meeting in Washington, D.C., in 1986, most of the women became so anxiety-ridden that they reported it to their supervisors. They were ordered never to attend such a meeting again, and because they acceded to this order, no subsequent meeting was ever scheduled.

A major factor here is fear of losing their jobs. Many of the women professionals were hired at midlife after years of low-level volunteer work; some do not feel they deserve as much money as men in comparable jobs. Grateful to be working for pay after coming up from the pool of unpaid volunteers, they fear being shoved back down there again, to sink under the weight of endless scut work. Single women, and women both single and married who are supporting children and/or old parents, are particularly anxious about losing their jobs, especially at a time when Jewish organizations are retrenching/downsizing in response to hard times. Younger women often secretly fear they are not being promoted because of their lack of ability (the old Jewish guilt about not being good "enough"). Women in one organization even resisted its setting up a fast track to advance female executives because this could cast doubt on whether they were being promoted on merit alone.

Finally, many Jewish women have bought into the idea that any public action, including a lawsuit, would be a *shandeh* (Yiddish for public shaming, embarrassment) that would make the organization and the entire community "look bad." Even though they are paid, their thinking is still that of altruistic-assertive enablers. They cannot be assertive except when it is altruistic, and altruistic is defined by the men.

✺ With all the talk since the inception of the women's movement about the joys and efficacy of "networking," it is as underutilized as women's talents in Jewish establishment organizations. Women volunteers do not help other women volunteers get ahead; professionals do not always aid other professionals; and, above all, women volunteers do not go out of their way to assist women professionals in their upward climb.

Women volunteers often don't feel secure enough in their positions to rock the boat by doing anything to advance other women, either as volunteers or as professionals, either inside or outside their organizations. A case in point relates to the response of women Federation campaign volunteers to discrimination against female attorneys by a Jewish men's social club in a large Mid-Atlantic city. The Federation women told the female lawyers that the issue was "trivial." Some said, "If you go after these clubs we [sic] will lose financial support from the men," an excuse that eerily echoes that of the Turkish rabbi in response to Bertha Pappenheim in her antiprostitution campaign: The communal institutions could not afford to turn away pimps because their donations were so essential.

Nor do women volunteers evince particular interest in and concern about what is happening to professional women in their own organizations (awareness might have to lead to action). Older volunteers who had a long and hard climb to the top often resent younger women, particularly professionals, who try to get on the fast track and attain the kind of power (and/or pay) they themselves have never had.

To rationalize their lack of action on behalf of women professionals, the volunteers tend to blame the women executives' failure to advance on their behavior. Ritz, for example, said in a 1986 interview that one of the greatest problems around advancement is that women "limit their own sights because they don't want to compete with men." In that very same interview, however, she reported that she had advised women professionals "not to look too eager to move up." Shoshana Cardin's rationalization for inaction on advancing women during her term as CJF president was that many women in the Federations are not "committed enough" to "lead the life" of a top executive. Pointing to several women who had left jobs to start families, she warned that "their vertical career mobility will be hampered" by this decision. The possibility of on-site day care did not enter the discussion, which took place at a time when communal "leaders" were emitting bleats of agony about the "zero population growth" among American Jews.

Asked about what these volunteers had said about women professionals, Levine was blunt: "I don't believe in blaming the victim."

Psychologically the volunteers are deeply conflicted about the professionals of their own gender: They resent them, because in a society that defines success as holding a job with pay and status, the professionals are successful and they are not. This gives the professionals higher status in the general society. But at the same time, the volunteer women's class bias makes them look down on the professional women for needing to work for pay.

The female volunteers (and top professionals) are often afflicted with the "Queen Bee" syndrome, preferring to be the only "powerful" woman around in a sea of men. This recapitulates for them the feeling of being special that obtained in their birth families, especially that of being "Daddy's little princess." It reinforces their motivation to abide by the rules ("Anything you want you know you can have because, Brenda, you've *been a good girl*").

The woman who has attained a position of power in a male-dominated Jewish organization wants to be visible as the only female good enough to have made it in this male environment. But to stay there and succeed, she needs to behave as a man, in accordance with the masculinist values of competition and power. This not only precludes empathy for other women, but it also means she cannot afford to have whatever remains of her female behavior and values called attention to by the visible presence of other women with power and especially by identifying with them—proof of which would be that she had helped them advance. In other words, she wishes to assimilate. Therefore, the same patterns obtain in her case as they do with assimilationist Jews in a non-Jewish environment, who fear that the high visibility there of Jews who retain their ethnic distinctiveness will call attention to whatever remains in them of classic Jewish values and behavior patterns, acting as a magnet to draw these hidden steel filings to the surface.

WHY WOMEN "LEADERS" NEED SEPARATE ORGANIZATIONS

The difficulties women volunteers experience in trying to attain positions of responsibility and power in the male-dominated "integrated" organizations contribute to the tenacious attempts of women's organization "leaders" to maintain the Women's Divisions, auxiliaries, and the independent and quasi-independent women's organizations.

When leaders of these organizations were interviewed in 1971 by writer-publisher Doris Gold, their justifications for the continued existence of separate women's organizations revealed their true motivations: "Women find they don't become leaders of a mixed group," said one. "Rarely do mixed groups recognize and utilize the complete talents of women," said another. Five years later, Gold reported that many women in organizations that have considered combining women's and men's chapters resisted this move because "they felt inhibited at meetings with male members."

More important, she reported, the women "leaders" know that they will lose their "leadership" roles if the organizations forfeit their separate existence. This is precisely what happened in the 1980s when the AJCongress pressured its progressive Women's Division to dissolve itself. This reduced its former female leaders to little fish in a big pond with no real possibility of becoming big fish. (The consciousness of this sequence of events was a factor in the two-year battle B'nai B'rith Women [BBW] waged with BBI for independence. The battle began in 1988, when BBI resolved to admit women. BBW, seeing this as an attempted hostile turf takeover, declared its "autonomy." After a series of threats and counterthreats, the issue was "resolved" with the upholding of BBW autonomy *and* the admission of women into BBI.)

The upper-middle-class "leaders" of the women's organizations know that, given the patriarchal structure of the organized Jewish community, they could not hold the same positions or be rewarded with the same status in an "integrated" organization. Their interests, therefore, coincide with those of the men of the Jewish establishment, who wish to keep women segregated in the volunteer ghetto and allow a few upper-middle-class women to run it in such a way that it does not threaten male power. The women "leaders" collude with the men by maintaining the ghetto so that they will be able to hold power there. Like the machers in the Jewish establishment whose positions give them status in the general society without their having to struggle for it there directly, the women volunteer "leaders" can get high status in the organized Jewish community through holding positions in their separate organizations without having to struggle for it directly within a male-dominated organization. The top-tier volunteers of the women's organizations also use these groups as a power base that can propel them into even higher positions, such as representing their group in a Jewish establishment umbrella or roof structure—or sometimes even a paid executive job.

⌁ Jewish women's organizations function as power playgrounds for the top volunteer "leaders," just as the male-dominated Jewish establishment organizations do for the machers and Big Givers. In these safe spaces, women can indulge in highly assertive behavior that they may not be able to get away with at home; that they would not dare engage in as volunteers within a male-dominated organization—where the usual double standard prevails whereby women who are assertive are criticized and men admired; and that they would feel constrained to avoid exhibiting on the job (assuming they could get one, given their lack of marketable skills in a tight job market). In these organizations, they can throw their weight around just as the men do in theirs. They can be as assertive, even as aggressive, as they please because the cause is altruistic. Looking to the plutocracy, composed of men of their own class, as their reference group, the organizations' "leaders" engage in masculinist behavior that they have long seen the men getting away with and that the women wish to emulate as symbols—and rewards—of their power.

These "leaders" have rightly acquired the reputation of being extremely aggressive—with one another, with the professional and secretarial staff, and when they represent their organizations in settings such as umbrella groups. Gold noted "the cold-blooded executive-suite style acquired by otherwise caring Jewish women when they fixate their roles as 'organization women.'" The stereotype of the "Hadassah lady"—hard-nosed, tough, known for playing dirty politics in the WZO—has a large basis in reality.

The Hadassah "leader" generally behaves like the stereotypical male corporate killer, not only with men but also with other women volunteers. But Hadassah is not alone in producing such "leaders" and in encouraging such behavior: It is common among most of the women's organizations' top volunteers to one degree or another. Their behavior toward their employees, reported by some workers to this author on condition of anonymity, has included using harassment to get people to quit; firing workers a year or two away from retirement and refusing to continue their health insurance; declawing the union; and requiring secretaries to order meat from the butcher (and, in one case, to wash a "leader's" lingerie).

In these organizations' national offices, a power struggle rages along class lines between the top-tier volunteer "leaders" and the professionals. It is fought in the psychological arena even more viciously than between women from these two groups in the male-dominated organizations. The middle-class female professionals look down on the upper-middle-class volunteers because the latter do not get paid for their work and are often even trained by them. The professionals also deeply resent the volunteers' taking credit for the work that *they* did. The volunteer women look down upon and envy the professionals and try to reduce their status by treating them as they do their secretaries—as maids—which the professionals resent and resist. All in all, women professionals in major Jewish women's organizations are on par with musicians in the court of the archbishop of Salzburg in Mozart's day.

The female professionals try hard to differentiate themselves from the secretaries, whom they fear being identified with; this is one reason they throw their power around with them and why some are as hard-boiled as the volunteers they work for. In one organization, a new female executive director summoned each staff member to her office for a get-acquainted meeting. A timer sat on her desk, set for five minutes; when the bell sounded, the getting acquainted was concluded. Another way the professionals separate themselves from the secretaries is by acceding to the organization's demand that the executives be excluded from the union. (Even in PW, renamed Na'amat USA in 1985, which is a *Labor* Zionist organization, this demand was made; in this case, however, the professionals resisted the demand and won their struggle to join the union.)

Sometimes, to avoid the messy and painful struggle with women professionals, the volunteers hire male executives, who, in the words of a former women's organization employee, are "nice to them" and usually give them "a lot of stroking." The editorship of *Hadassah* magazine has been a position held for decades by one or another man, and so was the executive director position at Women's American ORT. In some organizations the male executive has more power than the volunteers and gives the women koved-fixes, which they accept in lieu of power.

For all of these reasons, the atmosphere in the national offices of the Jewish women's organizations is generally even less "warm" (that is, informed by female values) than in the male-dominated ones of the Jewish establishment.

THE SHELTERED WORKSHOP (1940s–70s)

While the undemocratic two-tier system still functions in Jewish women's organizations, the methodology for maintaining it differed in the period of the

1940s–1970s from that in the ensuing decades, which saw the second wave of American feminism become an important movement in America.

During the earlier period, the top-tier volunteers knew that the labor of the low-tier members allowed them to play power games in the court of the national office, just as the corvée of the peasants made possible the nobles' remaining at Versailles. It was therefore necessary to keep the members from defecting. They held onto them by engendering dependency in two ways: through creating a work process and behavior that retarded rather than enhanced personal growth (growing could mean growing *away*), and through intensified mystification of the organization and of the members' role in Jewish communal life through their affiliation with it.

↔ With the prime responsibility for the organization resting in the hands of a few women at the top, and the major administrative work done by the relatively few paid professionals, the majority of the members became infantilized. Essentially the top-tier volunteers did to the low-tier ones what Jewish mothers in immigrant generations did to their sons (out of different motivations, of course): They infantilized them to delay their independence—or more accurately, in the case of the organizations, to prevent their defection.

Low-tier volunteer work came to resemble nothing so much as a distorted form of occupational therapy—more occupation than therapy—in a deformed sheltered workshop. The work*ing* (the process) rather than the work (the organization's goal/aim/purpose) became the true agenda, although everyone colluded in denying it. It was for this reason that the organizations' issue content became tangential and watery, and their Jewish content as *pareve* (Hebrew/Yiddish for bland) as that of the male-dominated establishment organizations.

A sheltered workshop, by definition, is a haven from the harsh marketplace where the rules of the "real-world" are set aside because the participants have physical or mental disabilities that preclude their being able to function by "real world" rules. The majority of Jewish women, however, had no such disabilities; nor were they even educationally deprived (by the late 1960s, most had B.A.'s, at least). And if they were/felt temperamentally unsuited to work on the outside, it was largely because of their lack of self-confidence. (Many of the men on the staffs of Jewish establishment organizations were/are also temperamentally unsuited to work on the outside and the organizations were/are *their* sheltered workshops. But no one has ever expected men to work without pay. And no one would dream of asking men with B.A.'s to do scut work.)

The women had joined one or another organization to acquire self-confidence, among other things, but the organizations—in fostering dependency and inefficient work habits—derailed its attainment. Rather, they reinforced the habit of spending an inordinate amount of time on detail ("For the last time, is it going to be tuna salad or salmon salad at the luncheon? We must decide!"), a lack of work discipline ("Sweetie, I don't think I can come in today. I'm bushed from that big dinner party we had last night"), and the terror of making a wrong decision, God forbid ("Girls, let's go over this again just one more time. It can't hurt to make sure we've covered every angle"). Thus low-tier volunteer work began to intensify rather than heal the damage patriarchal society had already inflicted on women.

❧ The "leaders" needed the sheltered workshop for its corvée, and they needed its process to prevent the personal growth that might lead to member defection. But since the work process actually impeded the attainment of the self-esteem the members thirsted for so desperately, especially during this era, the "leaders" had to employ another method of providing validation to fuel it, and to overcome the members' shame at needing it, in order to keep them within the organization.

The method they used was mystification: making the members believe that they were needed rather than needy, that what they were doing was necessary and invaluable, and that they were ably serving the Jewish people in its struggle for survival, that they were its ... rescuers. As one PW member wrote in 1939: "A duty devolves upon the American Jewish woman to *come to the aid of her people* because she is in the fortunate position to be of great *service*" (italics mine).

The sense that the work of the women in these organizations was crucial for Jewish survival could be successfully cultivated because of two historical developments. One was the reality of the physical threat to Jewish survival in the 1930s and 1940s; the other was the perception, beginning in the early 1960s, that assimilation was the threat to Jewish cultural survival.

In the 1930s the Jews in Europe faced great danger, and in the early 1940s the threat to their lives materialized into a tragic and horrific Catastrophe. During this period the Jewish women's organizations were as ineffective in the rescue of large numbers of European Jews as the men's organizations were. After the death camps were liberated, the women tried to atone for their guilt by working hard to assist the Holocaust survivors and later, to facilitate their absorption in Israel. The practical work of rehabilitating there the pitifully few survivors of the obliterated European Jewish communities—and subsequently, refugees from Arab countries—had great meaning for the women, and there is no doubt that it was invaluable.

In the late 1950s and into the 1960s and 1970s, when the threat to Jewish physical survival receded (except for that facing Jews in Syria, and, later, Iran and Ethiopia), and even Israel's continued existence seemed more or less assured, these organizations continued to harp on this malady because it could tug at the heartstrings (and the purse strings). But by this time, the organizations had gotten a shot in the arm from the new issue that had ascended onto the Jewish communal agenda: the danger of assimilation to the continued survival of the Jewish people. It became a much trumpeted subject after the alarm was sounded in a widely discussed 1964 article in *Look* magazine about "The Vanishing American Jew."

It should be pointed out here that neither then nor now has the Jewish community ever seriously considered addressing the problem of assimilation. This is evidenced from its stinginess to Jewish educational and cultural activities and its disempowerment of the masses of Jews, which has led so many to vote with their feet. But when the threat of assimilation became a great pseudo-issue, it breathed new life into Jewish organizations, providing a rationalization for their existence even as they continued to function in the same assimilationist ways as before.

With assimilation being condemned in the community and in its weeklies and from the pulpit as the new danger to Jewish survival, it became harder and harder for Jewish women to justify their instilling of assimilationist behavior in their children during the socialization process as being "good for the Jews." Many may have even felt guilty for having done so, even though this was supposed to be part of their born-again enabler role. Here the women's organizational "leaders" could provide balm to sooth the Jewish woman's troubled soul and uneasy conscience by persuading her that the organization's existence in and of itself was an anti-assimilationist act, *as was her membership in it.* Simply by being in the organization, she was automatically actively involved in combating assimilation. Because the organization supposedly promoted Jewish survival, the individual woman did not have to be agonized about whether she was doing so directly through her own efforts in her own life.

⤷ Making women believe that self-esteem could be attained by involvement with work to ensure Jewish survival by and in a specific Jewish women's organization was a stroke of genius on the part of the groups' "leaders." This mystification was another reason for propagandizing organizational chauvinism, the belief that only this particular organization could Do The Job.

The propaganda was that only through identifying with the specific organization could the women feel "OK"; outside it, they were "nothing." Like the message to the Jewish sons of their worthlessness should they fail to achieve material success, this was an either/or deal. And like Israeli men, whose validation of masculinity is linked with the success of the army, the women's sense of self-esteem was linked with the success of the particular organization. The linkage was so effective that minor criticisms of the organization were often perceived by members as personal attacks on them and on their self-worth.

The psychic reward of self-esteem went hand in hand with the psychic punishment of guilt inducing (a technique honed to razor-blade sharpness in the home) for the crime of separation or attempted or contemplated separation from the organization, equated with abandonment of the mishpucha, whose needs the organization was said to serve. Members were made to feel that the organization's work was so important to Jewish survival that the entire Jewish nation would go under if they deserted their mimeograph machines.

❧ The illusion that the members were rescuers was the flip side of the reality that they were rescuees. Some of the anecdotal material about how they came to join one or another organization bears this out. Women whose husbands changed jobs or were transferred and who moved with them to another town reported that on the very first day they had to hold the fort at home alone with infants screaming and toddlers tugging at their skirts, a woman would knock at the door, cake in hand (the Jewish female variation of the Welcome Wagon): "I'm from Hadassah/Pioneer Women/ORT/NCJW." The cavalry had arrived, providing not only an instant support network but also a group of instant acquaintances to facilitate the absorption of the new arrival and her family into the community.

Even more important, of course, the organization functioned as the members' psychic rescuer, providing validation to shore up their self-esteem. The organization's being their rescuer brought to the fore the old dynamic of wishing to repair any flaws that prevented its success, as well as that of a contract whereby they would function as altruistic-assertive enablers of its "leaders." This dynamic also triggered the usual banishment of the critical faculty that occurs in relation to secular rescuers.

VICARIOUS FEMINISM REDUX (1980s ON)

Initially feminism gave many low-tier women volunteers the feeling and confidence that they could attain self-esteem directly, through their own labor in the workplace. Young and middle-aged women left the sheltered workshops in droves, as if fleeing the Triangle (sweatshop) Fire. The narcissistic messages of the majority culture to "Look out for Number One" and "Do your own thing" served as immunization against any guilt they might have experienced for separation/defection from and abandonment of the organizations. The haste with which they jumped ship testified to their lack of commitment to the organizations' goals—to what they could do for the organizations in advancing them for the benefit of the Jewish nation—and revealed their true motivation for membership: what the organization could do for them (which was now no longer necessary). The mystification of women's organizational life was thus exploded at last.

For over a decade, most of the women's organizations could not respond constructively to the feminist challenge either ideologically or administratively. The reactions of top-tier "leaders" to feminism ranged from uptight denial of its legitimacy to outright alarm about its success. These reactions derived not only from distress over the desertion of younger members but also from fear of losing the older ones and thereby facing the final collapse of their power base. Older members could not embrace feminism because it denigrated their not working for pay; the plurality of them considered its prescription—going back to school or seeking a job—impossible. To continue to hold on to these older members, the "leaders" had to reject changes in their organization, which is why they were unwilling to discontinue the sheltered workshop process or even change their daytime meeting schedules.

Some of the women's organizational "leaders," fearing they would be totally left behind as the feminist movement picked up steam, began to issue token resolutions in favor of the Equal Rights Amendment (ERA) and reproductive choice in the mid- and late 1970s. NCJW and the Women's Division of the AJCongress (until it was disbanded) had always been strongly supportive of both, but even they did not get actively involved in winning support for these issues in the community. Only Na'amat USA agreed to participate in a women's press conference, sponsored by *Lilith* magazine, exposing pornography in Israel. None became actively involved in the struggle Jewish feminists waged from 1972 on for equal participation in Jewish religious/synagogue life.

Some of the organizations, such as Women's American ORT and Na'amat USA, have not recovered, as of 1994, from the hemorrhaging of their membership (and reduced intake of funds). Others, such as Hadassah and BBW (especially after it declared its autonomy), eventually regrouped and began to seek new members among younger women.

While tenaciously maintaining the hierarchical two-tier system, some of the organizations' "leaders" abandoned their previous sheltered workshop methodology. The low-tier members' scut work at the chapter level was reduced in many cases and given over to paid clerical workers. The chapters also changed some of their meeting hours and frequency to accommodate their (potential) younger members' busy and, for the most part, double-shift (job and home/child rearing) schedules.

More important, having understood that mystification of organizational purpose no longer worked in a narcissistic era, they abandoned trumpeting what the members could do for the organization. Instead they began to propagandize what the organization could do for new and potential members. They developed special programming in areas such as health, family issues, and Jewish studies, and in "leadership training" to recycle volunteer skills for the job market. They also appealed directly to younger women's needs for an atmosphere conductive to business networking, which has always been one of the great draws of the male-dominated organizations, especially the Federations.

To give younger members the feeling of being in a with-it outfit, some of the independent organizations began to create a new image of themselves by taking pro-feminist positions on various women's issues. For example, BBW, NCJW, Na'amat USA, Women's American ORT, and Hadassah all took part in the 1992 March for Women's Lives in Washington.

None of the organizations, however, was willing or able to go so far as to actually redefine itself and its goals as feminist. For one thing, the wealthy women volunteers at the helm feared to commit themselves and their organizations to any struggle that the male communal "leaders" smeared as a threat to Jewish survival and especially to the family, an anti-feminist strategy to be explored further in chapter 16. Nor were they interested in challenging the Jewish establishment collectively on issues such as day care or domestic violence or a role in policy making. They feared that the toehold they had staked out in the organized Jewish community might be lost if male approval of their actions were to be withdrawn.

Finally, their lack of interest in authentic feminist action stemmed from the desire of the "leaders" to perpetuate their organizations. The women's organizations' existence was predicated on the continued refusal of the organized Jewish community to allow women equality in public roles. A successful struggle against this inequality would obviously eliminate the organizations' raison d'être. The "leaders" were not willing to risk the possibility of losing the power they had already attained through the organization and to have to face struggling all over again for power as individuals in the Jewish communal structure.

❧ The "leaders'" motivation in wishing to keep their groups going is understandable, but why did older women stay and younger women begin to join some of them? The reason relates to the two things Jewish women have sought to obtain in/through the volunteer organizations during various periods of the twentieth century: validation and the feeling of having a public role.

It is easy to understand the need of the older members for validation, a need that intensified after the feminist movement began. Housewives desperately needed koved-fixes from the women's organizations because a woman who did not work for pay came to be looked down upon as a kind of parasite, a charge Jewish women were particularly sensitive to because of the old Judeophobic myth of parasitism.

As for the younger women recruits, the success they had attained as workers in business and professional life was not sufficient to build high self-esteem. Jewish women continued to experience low self-esteem because their looks and behavior were not validated in the general society and/or because of their relationship difficulties with Jewish lovers and husbands, as we have seen in chapters 9 and 10. The feeling of being excluded from the "mainstream Jewish community," which disturbed so many women, also contributed to their low self-esteem.

This brings us to the second motivation: the search for a public role in the community. The rise of feminism in the 1970s reactivated part of the conflict that had marked the 1920s and 1930s—namely, between the seeming openness toward women's assuming public roles, both in the general society and the Jewish community, and the impossibility of their doing so. While the women's movement finally opened many doors to women in the general society's economic, political, social, and cultural spheres, and Jewish feminist struggles began to result in equality in many areas of religious life, as we shall see in chapter 16, the organized Jewish community, and especially the Jewish establishment, have remained male turf, excluding most women from major public roles.

This is the prime reason that Jewish women's organizations continue to fulfill the vicarious feminism function they had done in the 1920s, albeit in reduced scope. The ongoing need for vicarious feminism was expressed by Iris Gross, executive director of NCJW, when she said in 1991 that the Jewish woman wants "a Jewish connection" and wishes "to feel that she's making a difference, that *she's having an impact in some way*. . . . I think [Jewish women] want to feel very needed and wanted, which I'm sure is *not any different than it was 10 or 15 years ago*" (italics mine).

3

THE STRUGGLE FOR A ⟨
READING OF REALITY

The Jewish faith is ancient. Through centuries and
it has come down to you. You are the product of its
of humility, of the Torah, of family bonds, of hard w⟨
love of music and art . . . traditions, above all, of bein⟨
persecuted. . . . The way you hold your head when you
the streets has our past in it. . . . Every time you speak ⟨
or nod or lift an eyebrow or express any emotion, our ⟨
doing things is in that movement of the muscles of your
The heritage is in your heart, it's a glorious heritage and
should be proud of it.

JOHN HERSEY, *The*

FOURTEEN ❧ THE SIXTIES DECADE AND ITS LEGACIES

*We could not as American Jews feel that Jewish is beautiful ... and
never have we American Jews thought, let alone asserted, "Yes, I am
beautiful ..." and we would say, "I'm not going to say that—too
arrogant" i.e., "too Jewish."*

DAVID MAMET

*I hated the middle class values and apathy of my Jewish
neighborhood, but not seeing them for what they really were, I called
that being Jewish. I internalized all of my hatred for the oppressive
state I lived in and hated my people instead.... By telling myself
that I was not Jewish, by saying that all of those [anti-Semitic
stereotypes] apply only to the Jews who came before me, I was
apologizing to fascists for them persecuting me for 4,000 years....
I am not apologizing any more. I am joining with my people and we
will determine for ourselves the character of our Jewishness.*

ANONYMOUS, *Brooklyn Bridge*

Be a Zionist in the Revolution and a Revolutionary in Zion.

RADICAL ZIONIST SLOGAN, CA. 1970

The sixties jolted American Jews out of their ethnic amnesia and compelled them
to confront their relationships with American society, Israel, and history. The
source of that jolt was not the student radicalism, antiwar activism, hippie movement, or civil rights/black power struggle of that tumultuous decade, although all
these phenomena had an important impact on Jews' emotional and intellectual
responses to it. Rather, the shock came primarily from the Six-Day War of 1967,
which made American Jews conscious of how much they cared about Israel—and
of the corollary: that it was *only* Jews who really cared about Israel.

❧ American Jews experienced the two interminable weeks in late May and early
June of 1967, after Egypt massed troops on Israel's borders and blockaded the

Straits of Tiran while the world sat idly by, as an agonizing, speeded-up replay of the kind of turn of events that had led up to the Holocaust. As they waited in wrenching anxiety to see what would happen, their inchoate feelings for Israel of what can only be called love pushed through the hard and parched soil of inertia and frustration to erupt with volcano force and passion. For the first time since the early post–World War II period, there was a confluence of emotion between American Jews and Israelis, with feelings of terror and panic pulsating back and forth across the Atlantic, drawing Jews together in their loneliness and isolation and in their mutuality of empathy and concern. For this brief moment, the later UJA slogan "We Are One" accurately reflected the emotional reality.

The Israeli victory triggered feelings of jubilation and, above all, of reprieve. Zionism had been vindicated: Having a state and an army had allowed Jews to defend themselves from their enemies and to save the nation from a second Holocaust. Most American Jews identified with Israel to the point of exulting that "*We* captured the Western Wall," and "*We* defeated the Egyptians/Syrians/Jordanians."

Their jubilation was marred, however, as the jarring shock over Israel's abandonment by many other Americans before and during the war began to sink in. The U.S. government, after doing nothing to prevent the war, announced on its first day—when Egypt's radio was trumpeting victory after victory—that it was "neutral in thought, word, and deed." With a few notable exceptions—such as Reverend Martin Luther King, Jr., and theologian Reinhold Niebuhr—leaders of Christian groups (with some of which Jews had been engaged in ecumenical dialogue) were silent. Some even attacked Israel, especially after the war. So did many activists in the antiwar movement and on the left, as well as militant leaders in the African American community, which Jews had previously regarded as their ally. Rabbi Albert Vorspan summed up Jewish feelings in the immediate postwar period: "Here were our people about to be massacred again. Where the hell was the civilized world? . . . Where are the Christian voices? . . . After all that has happened, are we Jews still alone?"

◆ American Jews' ethnic amnesia, and their fervent belief in the American Dream and in American exceptionalism, had given them delusions of false security and had left them with few intellectual or emotional resources to help them cope with the classic Jewish experiences of attack and abandonment. They had come to view their relationship with American society as contractual: cultural suicide in return for physical safety, which now seemed "illusory," said *Moment* magazine editor Leonard Fein. And despite their illusion/self-delusion that they were no different from other Americans, what happened in the Six-Day War period conclusively demonstrated that it was they and they alone who were worrying and weeping (before) and dancing with joy (after)—and nobody else really cared. The questions they would now have to deal with were: What did this difference mean? How was it to be expressed? What kind of identity should Jews strive for?

The task of working this out was undertaken not by rabbis or Jewish communal "leaders" but by young Jews, most of whom had been involved in the civil rights and antiwar struggles of the New Left and whose dormant Jewish consciousness had been awakened by the war and its aftermath. As Seattle activist Chaim Rosmarin wrote at the time: "We were still radicals, Socialists, opposed to the war, exploitation and racism, committed to building a new society. But we were also, we now perceived, Jews. What did that mean? What was the significance of this new consciousness?" Constituting themselves as "the Jewish movement," the young Jews rejected the assimilationist contract and attempted to midwife the birth of new forms of Jewish identity and cultural expression.

The mainstream Jewish community—unwilling to break the assimilationist contract—never accepted the movement's new definitions of Jewish identity nor its critique of American Jewish life. Nevertheless, the issues raised by and in the movement, including Jewish feminism, came to influence the development of Jewish life in America in the decades to come.

ABANDONED AND BETRAYED

Before, during, and after the Six-Day War, the ideological Old Left groups, including the Communist Party (CP), stuck to their "lines" that Israel was an agent/pawn/tool/ally of American imperialism in the Mideast and/or was being used by its power structure to smash Arab "revolutionary" movements.

The New Left groups had not worked out any official position on the Mideast before the war. This propelled some groups to adopt Old Left "lines" to fill the vacuum. Other groups, including the then-nonideological Students for a Democratic Society (SDS), were caught up in a Third World mystique that romanticized formerly colonized nations as leaders of "the revolution" against the First World and its leader, the United States. Since Israel looked to the U.S. for support, it was seen as the enemy of those "revolutionary" nations, including the Arabs. A similarly simplistic train of "thought" obtained among many antiwar activists, who tended to see everything through the filter of conclusions they had derived from the U.S. military intervention in Vietnam: The U.S. is suppressing a national liberation movement in Vietnam; the Arabs are involved in a struggle for liberation against imperialism; Israel is against the Arabs; the U.S. must be supporting Israel. Israel should therefore be opposed and the Arabs supported.

SDS, its members torn between the Third World mystique and the vague feeling that it would somehow be too bad if Israel were destroyed, never took an official position on the war. Other New Left groups espoused a "plague on both your houses" position or blamed Israel for initiating the war with its preemptive air-strike. Most New Leftists and antiwar activists attending the National Conference on New Politics held on the Labor Day weekend of 1967 voted for a resolution (introduced by black men identifying themselves as CP members) condemning Israel as an "imperialist aggressor."

Americans Jews' shock at their abandonment by the left was almost immediately followed by a countershock, as in the third act of a Shakespearean tragedy: the expression of virulently anti-Israel sentiments by some leaders in the emerging black power movement. Their anti-Zionism swiftly degenerated into blatant anti-Semitism.

❧ Except for the Black Muslims, the Mideast had never been an issue of great concern for African Americans. Involved for decades in a struggle for civil rights, they had concentrated on eliminating Jim Crow in civilian life and in the armed forces. But in the late 1960s, black militants redefined their goal as "black power" and began to look to African and other Third World liberation movements as their reference group. This propelled the Mideast to the top of their agenda.

Anti-Zionist propaganda began appearing in black power publications shortly after the Six-Day War. The June–July 1967 *Newsletter* of the Student Non-Violent Coordinating Committee (SNCC), an organization that had attracted a great amount of Jewish support for its civil rights activism, published a virulently anti-Zionist polemic and cartoon. Later that year, the black power conference in Newark passed with raucous acclamation a resolution condemning "Israel's oppression of the Arabs."

The position taken by the Black Panthers was perhaps the greatest shock to Jews, especially radicals and liberals (including Leonard Bernstein) who had held parlor meetings to raise money for them. The June 1967 issue of *Black Power* published a nasty anti-Semitic poem with these sentences: "The Jews have stolen all our bread / Their filthy women tricked our men into bed / We're gonna burn their towns . . . and piss upon the Wailing Wall. / . . . That will be ecstasy / killing every Jew we see."

Just as stunning was Panther leader Eldridge Cleaver's reversal of his position on Israel from 1968 to 1969. In the May 1968 issue of *Ramparts* magazine, he had pointed to how the East European Jews at the time of Herzl faced "genocide . . . and this common threat galvanized them into common action." Herzl's World Zionist Congress had enabled the Jews "to build their organization, their government and then later on they would get some land and set the government and the people down on the land, like placing one's hat on top of one's head. . . . Now Afro-Americans must do the same thing." (This brings to mind how Marcus Garvey compared the "Back to Africa" movement he led in the 1920s to Zionist efforts to secure Eretz Israel as a Jewish homeland.) But in the summer of 1969, Cleaver was quoted as saying in Algiers that in the U.S. "the Zionists are used to torpedo the struggle of our people for liberation." He declared eternal solidarity with the cause of Al Fatah, the major faction in the PLO.

In 1970 the Panthers charged that the "white left" had waffled in its support of them after the party had announced its support for the "Palestinian struggle." They asserted that the reason for this was that most of the people in the "white left are Zionists and are therefore racists." This statement, which was not only inaccurate but also a recycling of the Judeophobic myth of Jewish power, augured the infamous U.N. Zionism = racism resolution of 1975.

❧ The equation "Zionists that exploit the Arabs also exploit us in this country," in Panther official Stokely Carmichael's words, became a standard feature of much subsequent black militant propaganda and came to public attention during the 1968 New York school strike. The United Federation of Teachers (UFT), a union with a large number of Jews in its membership and which was headed by a Jew, Albert Shanker, went on strike that year against community control, which had been instituted in the Oceanhill-Brownsville (Brooklyn) School District, whose board was black dominated. As Shanker sought to win support for the UFT's position from the Jewish community, and the Oceanhill-Brownsville district attempted the same thing among blacks, the strike escalated within a few months into a full-blown Jewish-black confrontation.

Black militants enthusiastically espoused the view that Jews "dominate" the school system in which black children "are being mentally poisoned and educationally castrated" (a recycling of two Judeophobic myths at one go). A typical flyer distributed at the time read: "Zionists kill black people in their own land and in the Middle East. . . . Now here Shanker is trying to use the same tactics." Early in 1969 a black teacher read an anti-Semitic poem by one of his students on WBAI-FM radio. Dedicated to Shanker, the poem included the now-obligatory equation of how Israelis "hated the black Arabs with all their might / And you, Jew boy, said it was all right. Then you came to America, land of the free / And took over the school system to perpetrate white supremacy."

The verbal expressions of anti-Zionism and anti-Semitism by black militants, some of whom opportunistically used these as an organizing tool, propelled Jews into bleak despair and inchoate rage. The fact that the anti-Semitic bilge was coming not from illiterate lumpen types (the classic mob of pogromists) but from intellectuals meant that the prejudice was so deep-seated that education and reason could not eradicate it, just as they had not been able to do in Germany.

❧ American Jews were angry, but not distraught, over anti-Zionist statements by leftists. Their statements, as we have seen, mostly charged Israel with being reactionary and imperialistic, and while some of them may have been motivated by anti-Semitism, only the most extreme ones, which called for Israel's destruction, could be labeled Judeophobic. Too, most of these utterances did not recycle classic anti-Semitic myths, as those by some black militants did. Moreover, most American Jews, while still harboring positive memories of the left-wing antifascism of the 1930s, had no emotional investment in a relationship with the New Left. The same, however, cannot be said about African Americans, with whom most Jews felt they had had a fairly positive relationship until 1967, an alliance that blacks now seemed intent upon breaking.

RESCUE FANTASIES EXPLODED

East European refugees from Czarist persecution had empathized with blacks, and they and their descendants loathed the Ku Klux Klan (the avowed enemy of both) as latter-day pogromists. More poetry was written in Yiddish in the 1920s on the lynchings of blacks than in any other language, observed Judd Teller.

In the years following World War II, Jews put a great deal of their time, energy, money, and organizational resources into fighting for civil rights while many other Americans turned their backs. Jewish motivations were not, of course, purely altruistic, but despite this, the standard Jewish yardstick of the paramountcy of deeds applies here. The AJCommittee and the AJCongress, wrote Teller, "very nearly crippled their specific Jewish programs" by their emphasis on civil rights work. They and other groups probably hoped that through their involvement with this cause they might attract liberal and radical Jews who had become "ideological displaced persons" in the McCarthy era.

There were also profound psychological motivations behind the behavior of these organizations and their "leaders" and supporters, primarily relating to the Holocaust. American Jews believed it was unethical for them to abandon blacks to their fate as people of putative goodwill had done to the Jews of Europe. Additionally, said Teller, "Perhaps by helping [blacks] they unconsciously sought to compensate for their inadequacy when the gas chamber locks were turned on Europe's six million Jews."

There was also guilt toward the blacks because in America they had replaced the Jews as the persecuted minority of choice. The visceral kind of hatred, the persecution, exclusion and discrimination, and the humiliation Jews had experienced for centuries in Europe were directed in America at blacks. Jews therefore felt they owed it to African Americans to help them overcome this oppression and to prevent racism from escalating into a Final Solution, as it had for the Jews of Europe.

Moreover, in the anti-Semitic atmosphere of postwar America, there was a palpable fear that "it could happen here." American Jews unconsciously realized that the power structure they had been looking to for protection could not be counted on, just as it had proved it could not be relied on to help European Jewry during the Holocaust.

Jews now sought to form an alliance with African Americans to fight the discrimination perpetuated against both out-groups. While individual Jews in the 1930s, mostly left-wingers, had been active for civil rights through unions, the Communist and Socialist parties, and the NAACP, now liberal Jews also became actively involved in the struggle, primarily through Jewish establishment organizations. While forming an alliance with an oppressed group was a fundamental switch away from one classic survival strategy, seeking protection from the ruling class, its modus operandi recapitulated another survival strategy, that of being useful—through organizational lawsuits and *amicus curiae* briefs, educational activities, and programs; and through the contributions by individuals of time and money to civil rights work.

Black urban rioting in the sixties, of which many Jewish-owned mom-and-pop stores in the ghettos were the prime targets, struck fear into the hearts of Jews. This was especially true for older lower-middle-class Jewish men who owned small stores in the ghettos—and younger men who were competing with black men for civil service jobs. The riots provoked a divergence between the men of this class, for whom the blacks began to take on the mantle of pogrom-prone muzhiks, and the upper-middle-class Jewish establishment machers, whose economic interests were not threatened. The lower-middle-class men had no power or representation in the Jewish establishment organizations, which persisted in the view (expressed by the NJCRAC) that the riots were of little social significance and that Jews should remain committed to every form of assistance to blacks.

As late as May 1967, the ADL published a five-volume "study" of black anti-Semitism that claimed there was less such prejudice among African Americans than among whites. Two years later—following the anti-Zionist and anti-Semitic statements by black militants after the Six-Day War and during the 1968 school strike—journalist Richard Yaffe observed that the Jewish organizations' "studies" of the blacks "have been so wrong until now that they are worthless."

◈ One of the few American Jews who understood the dynamics of black anti-Semitism was an Orthodox rabbi, Bernard Weinberger of Williamsburg (Brooklyn). Applying a Borochovist analysis, Weinberger wrote, "The black community knows full well that their real enemy is the white establishment in this country which continues to subjugate them. They know that it is not the Jew who perpetuates white racism. But they cannot attack the real centers and power without first destroying the lower echelons of power and it is here that they encounter the Jew." The accuracy of Weinberger's analysis is evidenced by the remarks of a sixteen-year-old black student, who wrote in an introduction to the Metropolitan Museum's catalog of its Harlem exhibit in 1969 that "behind every hurdle that the Afro-American has yet to jump stands the Jew who has already cleared it."

The "lower echelons of power"—the classic oppressor surrogate role—included teaching and social and welfare work in the ghettos, administration in the union bureaucracies, and supervisory jobs in civil service. The high visibility of these positions made it possible for Jews to be maneuvered into the classic lightning rod role to absorb and deflect black rage. As Weinberger concluded, "The Jew is the buffer in the middle that the 'white establishment' is happy to project as the target for the lashing that black anger is ready to dish out."

◆➤ The underlying psychological element in the black-Jewish conflict which began in 1967 was the head-on collision between the black separation struggle and Jewish rescue fantasies.

Black militants in the late sixties initiated a struggle to forge a new identity to enable African Americans to reenter America under different terms ("Black is beautiful"). (Hispanics and some young white ethnics were also engaged in such a struggle—as were women and gay men and lesbians in the ensuing decades.) This meant a separation struggle—the adolescent individuation battle writ large—involving regrouping, working out a new self-definition, and then renegotiating the relationship with the parent/society.

Since Jews were regarded by blacks as the power structure's surrogate and cultural intermediary (in loco parentis, as it were), blacks felt they had to separate themselves first from the Jews, who functioned as the buffer between them and white society. Moreover, separating and regrouping to forge a new identity required that blacks take over their own struggle from whites, including Jews, who were among the leaders and supporters of the civil rights movement.

Jews involved with the civil rights movement through their organizations had conveyed the impression well into the militant sixties that their concern was primarily motivated by the "ethical imperative" of the Jewish tradition and a commitment to American democracy. They thus represented themselves to the blacks as rescuers. But in reality Jews had unconsciously looked to blacks as potential rescuers should a Final Solution against both groups be perpetrated in America. This rescue fantasy activated the dynamics of the classic contract with secular rescuers in which Jews tried to repair their flaws (and dovetailed with the survival strategy of usefulness). The uncritical (love-is-blind) attitude that always emerges with regard to secular rescuers led Jewish organizational "leaders" and liberal Jews generally to deny the existence of black anti-Semitism and to make allowances for the trashing of Jewish property.

But when black militants began speaking about expelling "Mr. Goldberg" from their movement (along with "Mr. Charlie"), many Jews experienced this as abandonment—for Jews, the greatest of crimes. Since Jews had outwardly behaved toward blacks as their rescuers, blacks had no clue that underneath this opaque cover was the fantasy that blacks might rescue them, or at least not abandon them. When Jews tried to hold onto the previous terms of the relationship to head off what they interpreted as abandonment, blacks experienced this behavior not as one born of desperation but as "paternalism." They thought that Jews were angry at having lost control of the civil rights movement—an interpretation informed by the old Judeophobic myth that Jews always want to control everything.

They reacted by trying to distance themselves emotionally from the Jews through words, which Jews, as "people of words," always take seriously. It will be recalled how many Jewish sons, in attempting to separate themselves from their mothers to become "independent" and thus "men," have used nasty "jokes" and insulting stereotypes to create emotional distance. Similarly, many black militants (most of them men), in attempting to become "independent" of Jews and of their support/leadership in the struggle, and ultimately to (re)gain what they themselves called their "manhood," seized upon verbal expressions of anti-Zionism and anti-Semitism to create distance from Jews.

Black anti-Semitism accomplished the separation from the Jews that some militants had sought. It also exploded/demolished the fantasy Jews had held of blacks as their rescuers. The belief—consonant with their having fallen in love with the black movement (in its civil rights stage)—that African Americans shared the same values had persisted among liberal Jews despite the black rioters' use of violence, which is so antithetical to the Jewish value system. Now this belief, too, fell by the wayside, allowing the critical faculty, long suppressed because of the secular rescuer dynamic, to emerge.

JEWISH RADICALS BECOME RADICAL JEWS

The Six-Day War, and the anti-Zionist statements by leftists and blacks in its wake, had a profoundly disturbing effect on many young Jews in the New Left.

Before the war few had had any authentic Jewish experiences, and fewer still, any positive Jewish education that could have engendered Jewish consciousness and commitment. Many Jews in the radical left movements of the sixties would have agreed with what Yippie and Chicago Eight/Seven defendant Jerry Rubin said at the time: "I am not taking responsibility for 2,000 years [of Jewish history]. . . . I have no cross to bear [sic]. If the Jews disappear tomorrow it wouldn't bother me at all."

It has been estimated that two-thirds of the Freedom Riders and one-half to two-thirds of the Mississippi Summer (voter registration) Project volunteers were Jews. With a few exceptions—such as the two youths who communicated with each other in Hebrew over the Project's tapped phones—most saw and pictured themselves as universalist radicals, not as Jews. Their attempt to hide their Jewish identity and be Jewishly invisible did not work. The southern whites knew that Andrew Goodman and Mickey Schwerner, martyred with James Chaney in 1964, were Jews, as were other civil rights activists. So did African Americans. James Jones, the black director of research for HARYOU-Act, reported in 1965 that black civil rights activists were constantly asking him: "These Jewish kids, they know union history, they know black history, but when I ask about *Jewish* history, I draw a blank. What's their game?" He described them as suffering from "inner turmoil."

Many Jews in the New Left behaved like the Jewish revolutionaries of nineteenth-century Europe who were involved in every other nation's struggle but their own, behavior both Syrkin and Borochov had derided as a form of assimilationism. They did not act out of a conscious Jewish imperative. On the contrary, they felt that Jewishness was "chauvinistic," incompatible with concern for other human beings, particularly blacks. A twenty-three-year-old chemist who took part in a 1965 panel on "The Jewish Community and the Negro Revolution" sponsored by *Jewish Currents* magazine said, "Idealistic Jewish youth have come to think of Jewishness as a restriction on their concern with the bulk of humanity who are not Jewish." A young teacher told the audience, "I react with hostility to the consciousness of my Jewish heritage ... because so often Jewish consciousness is coupled with chauvinism. The people who have a strong feeling about Israel and Jewish consciousness most often are chauvinistic to [*sic*] the Negroes or indifferent to them." Others were bitter at the "lack of action" by American Jewry—ignoring the participation of Rabbis Heschel and Kelman in the Selma march and the work of these and other rabbis and Jewish organizations for civil rights.

❧ Given their alienation from Jewish concerns, the community, and Israel, many Jewish radicals were stunned to discover how deeply touched they were by Israel's prewar trauma and its swift reprieve from destruction. They were taking their transistor radios to class, they were weeping with joy at the liberation of the Western Wall in Jerusalem. They were, in short, behaving as Jews.

They were shocked to find that their feelings about Israel were rejected by their "brothers and sisters" in the movement, including many Jews, as "reactionary" and "chauvinistic"—the very same pejoratives that they themselves had used a mere few weeks before. They found themselves isolated and vilified in the New Left, which regarded any identification with Israel as counterrevolutionary.

Gravitating to each other, these young Jewish radicals began to meet spontaneously in small groups both on and off campus all over North America to try to find some explanation for their feelings and for their comrades' rejection, to grope for some way to align or synthesize their feelings with their politics. Could they be revolutionaries and at the same time pro-Israel and committed Jews? The one group they could look to for guidance and inspiration—as their reference group in this effort of shaping an identity that was both ethnically distinctive and radical—was the blacks. By championing the legitimacy of their own ethnicity, said Rabbi Hillel Levine, blacks "reminded us that the melting pot dream was a fool's fantasy and that differences were legitimate." Since all radicals saw blacks as a revolutionary vanguard, the New Left had accepted their demand of a *hechsher* (Hebrew for seal of approval) on their ethnicity. Jewish radicals now began asking themselves why they, too, could not disinter and express their own cultural heritage.

But most of the New Left rejected the expression of Jewish ethnicity as reactionary. New Left ideology held that Jews could not be revolutionary as long as they remained conscious Jews because all Jews were middle-class oppressors—a recycling of the old Judeophobic myth of Jews as rich, powerful exploiters. To reject being an oppressor, a Jew had to reject being Jewish—a recycling of the assimilationist demand that Jews relinquish their distinctiveness in order to be accepted. If a Jew was not invisible as a Jew, she or he flipped over into the shadow role of oppressor. (A similar demand prevailed in the women's movement, when it was acceptable for black, Hispanic, Greek, and Italian women to "go ethnic" but not for Jewish women to do so.)

The young Jewish radicals who accepted the blacks' legitimization of ethnicity and who rejected the New Left's denial of this to Jews and Jews alone were electrified by an article by M. J. Rosenberg, "To Uncle Tom and Other Jews," printed in the *Village Voice* in February 1969 (and then widely photocopied and circulated). He wrote:

> The black American is the first to openly abjure the idea of assimilation, to recognize the inherent lie in the concept of the melting pot.... The young American Jew ... desperately craves assimilation; the very idea of "Jewishness" embarrasses him [*sic*].... The leftist Jewish student ... is today's Uncle Tom. He [is] ... ashamed of his identity and yet is obsessed with it.... He wants to be an "American," a leftist American talking liberation, and an aspiring WASP.... The Jew must accept his identity; and like it or not, his Jewishness is his destiny.... And thus from this point on, I will support no movement that does not accept my people's struggle. If I must choose between the Jewish cause and a "progressive" anti-Israel SDS I shall always choose the Jewish cause.... If the barricades are erected, I will fight as a Jew.

During this post-1967 period, thousands of youths drifted in and out of the dozens of groups of refugees from the New Left that sprouted up all over North America. There were so many groups that the London-based World Union of Jewish Students (WUJS) initiated the creation of a North American Jewish Students Network (informally called Network). Officially established in 1970, Network was independent of any parent organization. Its main function was to act as a resource for the various groups across the entire political spectrum, keep them au courant with each other through a newspaper and other mailings, and provide opportunities for their adherents to meet and "cross-fertilize" each other. As Network expanded and evolved, it began to see itself as the builder of a student movement that could midwife a democratic Jewish community. Network itself was run by students in a democratic fashion, and its conferences were the only forums for debate in the entire Jewish community. Network's heyday was an all-too-brief foretaste of how exhilarating communal democracy and pluralism could be.

⊷ Two distinct trends began to emerge among the groups of young leftists in what they began to call the Jewish movement: Radical Jews and Radical Zionists.

The Radical Jewish groups—several of which (e.g., Jews for Urban Justice of Washington, D.C.) antedated the 1967 war—sought to organize in the community against racism (as African Americans had demanded of them), to struggle against the Vietnam War, and to create a synthesis between Judaism and radicalism. But while caring about Israel's survival, their adherents were deeply conflicted over the legitimacy of Zionism and its concept of Israel's "centrality" to Jewish life in what they insisted on calling the diaspora. They eventually worked out a position of critical support for Israel (sometimes more critical than supportive), which essentially was that the Jewish State was alive and kicking and it was too late to contemplate a therapeutic abortion.

The second major political trend was Radical Zionism. Much of its theoretical foundation was worked out by the New York–based Jewish Liberation Project. Radical Zionists viewed Zionism as "the national liberation movement of the Jewish people," with Israel as its instrumentality. Zionism was inherently progressive, but Israel had veered off the right course, and its leaders had betrayed its fundamental principles and vision. A course correction was therefore necessary. Radical Zionists championed aliyah but also believed in creating a strong Jewish community in North America and called for its democratization, a reordering of its priorities, and its participation in revolutionary struggles.

Both kinds of groups demonstrated at Jewish organizations' offices on their policies regarding the Vietnam War and civil rights. They also expended a great deal of energy on analyzing the Israeli-Palestinian conflict and called for a two-state solution to it.

◆ Despite the New Left's rejection of Israel and of Jewish ethnicity, the young leftists looked to it as their reference group.

As the New Left moved from its Third World mystique to a search for mentors in the leftist past who could provide instant ideologies, the Jewish leftist groups found themselves seeking similarly authentic precursors—sources in the Jewish leftist and religious traditions to legitimize their politics and mentors to serve as behavior models. Radical Jewish groups began to look for inspiration to the Jewish Labor Bund of Czarist Russia with its diasporist revolutionary orientation; the Radical Zionists were drawn to Borochov and the pioneers of the Second Aliyah.

Their search inevitably led the young leftists to Jewish religious sources, where the passion for justice, peace, and social equality were originally expressed and from which both the Jewish Labor Bund and Poale Zion had drawn inspiration in late-nineteenth- and early-twentieth-century Russia. Identifying with the revolutionary elements of Judaism could serve as their visa into the revolutionary movement and as a hechsher for their politics. It also provided them some way to reach out to average North American Jews—who identified themselves primarily as a religious group—by demonstrating that Jews had a revolutionary tradition and advocating its expression through participation in the civil rights and antiwar struggles.

Turning to religious sources also became necessary because the rich Yiddish *secular* culture had long passed from the scene. Thus, while Radical Jews considered themselves neo-Bundists, they ignored the Bund's antireligious stance and

derived much of their philosophy from classic Reform Jewish concepts emphasizing the universality of the prophetic tradition of the pursuit of social justice. Radical Zionists could also emphasize the revolutionary—and proto-Zionist—elements
of the prophetic tradition. The prophets, while envisioning a peaceful and just
world, were deeply committed to the centrality of Eretz Israel (Isaiah: "Torah shall
emanate from Zion").

SEARCHING FOR COMMUNITY AND SPIRITUALITY

Young Jews' interest in Judaism in the late 1960s and early 1970s derived, as well,
from their search for community and spirituality. What the young Jews had found
in the civil rights, radical, and antiwar movements (as so many Jews had found in
the pre–World War II Socialist and union movements) were many of the values
that had once characterized the traditional Jewish communities—altruism, mutual
responsibility, compassion, and the sense of community-as-family—and a passion
for justice. When Jewish parents of Mississippi Summer Project volunteers said
that the "ethical concepts" the youths had learned at home were a significant factor in their activism, they were referring to these values, which were still being
transmitted during socialization.

Since the youths saw no way to express these values Jewishly—the community had largely depleted itself of them and no longer served as the public context
for their fulfillment—they were attracted to radical movements that seemed to embody them and provided opportunities to carry them out through deeds.

After 1967, pro-Israel young Jews were no longer able to find spirituality and
community in the New Left. The search for these began to assume even greater
importance as the New Left started to self-destruct at the end of the 1960s. The
leftist Jewish groups the young Jews were initially drawn to served as a kind of
way station/hachshara, where thousands experienced for the first time the exploration of Jewish sources; some religious and cultural expression, especially in celebrating holidays; and intellectualism and debate on Jewish concerns.

Running parallel to the Jewish leftist groups after a few years and taking on
more importance as these began to decline by the mid-1970s was the *havura*
movement. The *havura* (Hebrew sing., from the word *chaver/a*: friend/comrade/
member/colleague/study partner; pl., *havurot*) was/is a small, informal, self-constituted group meeting to study and observe holidays, perform and experiment with
rituals, and pray together, all without benefit of clergy. The havura was influenced
by the early New Left's critique of the impersonality of large institutions and by
the affinity groups of its later stages, and by the human potential movement of
the sixties. It, too, looked to the Jewish past for models and found some in Hassidism, with its emphasis on fervent prayer with the accoutrements of dance,
song, and expressive body language (e.g., swaying during praying).

The havura movement was not particularly interested in Israel or concerned about outreach, especially to Jews with little Jewish education. Its members' prime interest was creating alternative institutions. (The havura eventually became acceptable, even chic, and some synagogues reorganized themselves into groups of havurot.)

❧ The search for spirituality and community, legitimized by the fact that America was beginning to undergo one of its periodic religious revivals in the early 1970s, also led many young Jews to Orthodoxy.

The Orthodox movement, which had arisen in nineteenth-century Europe, saw itself as the inheritor and preserver of traditional normative Judaism. It was and is basically split between the left, which calls itself "Modern Orthodoxy," and the right, a spectrum of groups of Misnagdim and of Hassidim ranging from the Lubavitch/Chabad movement to various sects on the far right led by charismatic gurulike rebbes.

In the interbellum years, American Orthodoxy was dominated by the Modern Orthodox movement, which, wrote Jenna Weissman Joselit, was animated by "an ongoing romance with modernity," interpreting it in class terms of what was fashionable, decorous, mannerly, and cultured. As part of making middle-class Jews comfortable with Orthodox Judaism, it promoted the behavior, which continued into the fifties, of keeping one's religion in the closet. Boys did not wear *yarmulkes* (skullcaps) away from home or Jewish school, and one leading Orthodox day school instructed them, as well, not to let their tzitzit tassels dangle below their jackets on the street.

In the post–World War II period, Modern Orthodoxy declined. It was upstaged on the left by Conservative Judaism, which appealed to the new suburban constituency the Orthodox had hoped to recruit. On the right, it was confronted and its authenticity challenged by Central and East European adherents of various Hassidic sects who had immigrated to America. Possibly because most of them were Holocaust survivors, they were scornful of Modern Orthodoxy's "ongoing romance with modernity." These sects created a standard that those to the left of them looked to, often with anxiety and guilt. In the Orthodox world, each group's most immediate challenge in the stringency of observance comes from the group directly to its right. This means that groups on the very far right pull everyone else toward their polar point.

By the late 1960s, Modern Orthodoxy was undergoing a revival after it had regrouped and had chosen to move to the right, in the direction of increased stringency of observance. (By the 1990s the adjective *modern* would become such a pejorative that its adherents would refer to themselves as "*Centrist* Orthodox.") Never part of the power structure of the Federations nor sharing its values, and having found it unresponsive to their needs, Modern Orthodox Jews created their own network of social welfare and educational institutions, including day schools and yeshivot. They also adopted a high profile, evident in the men's wearing *kipot* (Hebrew pl. for crocheted skullcaps; sing., *kipa*) in public.

This validation of ethnicity was a prime factor in the attraction of youth to Orthodoxy, both Modern and right-wing. The Orthodox lifestyle, which had once been derided by many Jews as old-fashioned and anti-assimilationist, now appealed to those looking for their "roots" precisely because of these characteristics.

Furthermore, at a time when the country was being torn apart by the war in Vietnam and especially after a spiritual vacuum was created by the collapse of the New Left, Orthodoxy began to look more and more attractive to young Jews who wanted a community to belong to that seemed to operate by the traditional Jewish values and that provided a definitive ideology, an instant lifestyle, and a feeling of extended family.

The newly Orthodox Jews called themselves *Ba'alei Teshuva* (B.T.'s), which literally translates from Hebrew as "repenters" or "returnees to the faith," but in the context of the seventies and subsequently, it has referred to Jews who were getting involved in Orthodox life and observance for the first time.

✦ Orthodoxy's revival and growing strength had an important impact on the three other wings of American Judaism: Reform, Conservative, and Reconstructionist.

Reform Judaism was brought to America by German Jews who immigrated after 1848. Its lay leaders, wrote Rabbi Arthur Hertzberg, felt that "Judaism and the Jewish community must be reshaped and used as *instruments of the success of Jews* in American life" (italics mine). The movement continued and expanded the practices introduced in Germany: services in the language of the general society, synagogue decorum, a bare minimum of ritual and custom, and prayer books from which the Chosen People concept and proto-Zionist sentiments had been expunged.

Conservative Judaism had arisen in America at the end of the nineteenth century out of an attempt to carve out a middle road between Orthodoxy, which maintained a commitment to Halacha, and Reform, which rejected it. Its leaders, many of them noted Talmudic scholars, leaned toward Orthodoxy in accepting Halacha but amended it greatly. The Conservative movement also allowed individual congregations to make their own decisions on practices such as mixed-gender seating and the scheduling times of Friday evening services. Conservative Judaism's attraction for many American Jews who were far less observant than its religious leaders was that its ambiance was traditional (e.g., services in Hebrew using the old melodies) but also modern (services are more decorous and less noisy than in Orthodox shuls).

The Reconstructionist movement began as an offshoot of Conservative Judaism but moved so far away from it that it stood/stands at the far left of the American Jewish religious spectrum. Originated by Rabbi Mordechai Kaplan, it was initially rooted in his concept of "Judaism as a religious civilization." Like classical Reform Judaism, it rejected the Chosen People concept but, unlike it, remained committed to the principle of Jewish peoplehood. While giving Halacha "a voice but not a veto," it introduced innovations such as the Bat Mitzvah ceremony.

In the early 1970s, the regrouped Modern Orthodox movement began to have a gravitational pull on the Conservative movement to its immediate left. Conservative Judaism began moving to the right in terms of increased observance of Halacha precisely at a time when it was several years away from the feminist challenge to its left. (This accounts, in part, for its long resistance to the ordination of women rabbis, as we shall see in chapter 16.) The Reform movement, too, began moving in the direction of increased interest in traditional observances and practices, including the introduction of some Hebrew in its services. It also rejected the anti-Zionism of classic Reform Judaism and added references to Israel to its prayer books.

The move of the three major religious movements of American Judaism toward greater observance and ritual should not, however, be seen primarily in terms of a domino effect set in motion by right-wing Orthodox militancy. Mostly it had to do with the search by American Jews after the 1967 War for authentic Jewish content and forms of expression, a search that made itself felt in these movements and in Reconstructionist Judaism, as well, which accepted havurot as member congregations.

"NEVER AGAIN!"

In an era when every campus meeting had to have the word *radical* in its title to attract interest and attendance, the Jewish Defense League (JDL), which stood at the opposite end of the political spectrum, seems to have been out of sync with the zeitgeist. But it, too, was anti-establishment in its own way. And, like the Radical Zionist and Radical Jewish groups, it, too, arose out of responses to the Six-Day War, the black power movement, and the verbal attacks on Israel by black militants and leftists.

JDL members' reactions to these phenomena were shaped to a large extent by class and geography. Many were lower-middle-class young men living in city neighborhoods where there was increasing street crime by black individuals; they were also experiencing competition from blacks for civil service and white-collar jobs. By contrast, Radical Jews and havura members tended to come from middle- and upper-middle-class suburban families, and the latter, from strong Reform or Conservative backgrounds. Radical Zionists came mostly from the middle class and, like JDL members, had strong Holocaust consciousness. The difference between them, of course, is that Holocaust consciousness reinforced the Radical Zionists' leftist ideology—and the JDL's right-wing politics.

The JDL is perhaps best known for its slogan "Never Again!" The main lesson the JDL learned from the Holocaust was that anti-Semitism had to be confronted actively and militantly—violently, if necessary. The JDL came to regard any action by any non-Jew against any Jew—such as the mugging of a lower-middle-class Jew in Brooklyn by a thug who was black—or against a Jewish institution as anti-Semitism. The lack of interest in and response by the Jewish establishment, as well as all the Jewish leftist groups, to the problems of poor and lower-middle-class Jews living in high-crime neighborhoods allowed the JDL to move into this political vacuum. Establishing anticrime patrols in dangerous neighborhoods, they regarded themselves as the residents' rescuers. The Jewish establishment (ADL, NJCRAC) and the Synagogue Council of America denounced the JDL, and one Reform rabbi actually called it a "goon squad . . . [no different from] whites [in] robes and hoods standing in front of burning crosses."

The JDL was critical of the Jewish establishment, but from the right: It thought it too "liberal." And while it opposed the Jewish establishment's lack of democracy, its own style was authoritarian, anti-intellectual, and obsessed with the hero worship of its founder, Rabbi Meir Kahane.

The JDL's opposition to what it considered black anti-Semitism *and* to the Jewish establishment propelled it into paradoxical actions. One was the dispatching in 1969 of forty members, some with bats and chains, to guard (the Reform) Temple Emanu-El in New York against a (rumored) attempt by a black militant to go there to demand reparations for slavery. Many of the temple's members were machers in the same Jewish establishment the JDL opposed for being unresponsive to Jews, especially those living in high-crime neighborhoods.

⤙ Because such actions drew them into a contradictory trap, and issues such as opposing the Jewish establishment elicited a negative response in the Jewish community similar to that which the Radical Zionists received, JDL leaders seized upon the issue of Soviet Jewry. This issue had hitherto been the turf of the small and militant but nonviolent Student Struggle for Soviet Jewry (SSSJ), led by Glenn Richter and Jacob Birnbaum. SSSJ and its sister organization, the Center for Russian Jewry, were lone voices crying in the wilderness in the 1960s and 1970s. It was only when the JDL's high-visibility violent confrontations with the cops and Soviet officials over the issue hit the front page that the plutocracy moved in to prevent the JDL from upstaging it and from making it appear that American Jews were anti-establishment.

Gradually the Jewish establishment took over the Soviet Jewry issue, finding in it dividends it had somehow never perceived before. It put American Jewry squarely into the anti-Soviet camp (which showed what "good Americans" they were) and made Jews appear with-it at a time when mass rallies were de rigueur. The Soviet Jewry cause was, in short, a safe issue involving vicarious participation in a distant struggle. Such participation also helped exorcise some of the guilt

Jews felt about having "abandoned" European Jews during the Holocaust, guilt they could no longer purge by working for civil rights. As the Soviet Jewry issue became glamorous to Jewish establishment organizations, the JDL lost control of this turf.

(The Jewish establishment organizations involved with Soviet Jewry floundered with the ascent of Gorbachev and *glasnost.* They were unable to redirect their energies into providing Soviet Jews with the educational and cultural materials they thirsted for after a sixty-year drought—not surprising, considering how they had starved their own cultural institutions. The Soviet Jewry cause did not become glamorous again until the mass exodus of the 1990s. American Jewish "leaders" began to speak expansively from the safety of their cushy offices of the "miracle" of the emigration of hundreds of thousands of people terrified by emerging anti-Semitism. And funds began to flow into the coffers of Federation campaigns for the absorption of these new immigrants in Israel.)

SEEKING TO REENTER AMERICA ON NEW TERMS

The rebellion against the American bourgeois value system equating material success with personal worth, a rebellion that had fueled the hippie and radical movements of the early sixties, touched a deep nerve among young Jews. Many felt crushed between two steel vises—the double message of "producing" high grades and attaining high status (the boys through jobs, the girls through marriage) while remaining "nice." As Noel Airman wrote Marjorie Morningstar: "Your left spur has been the American idea of success and your right spur the idea of Jewish respectability." The radical movement many joined provided them with the opportunity to reject these middle-class values ideologically and to take part in high-visibility actions that were definitely not "nice" and for which they received validation from their peers.

Since material success was also perceived in their homes as an American *Jewish* value, when they rejected American middle-class values they also rejected what they considered to be "Jewishness." After some leftists had been forcefully jolted out of their assimilationist coma into Jewish consciousness by the 1967 War and its aftermath, they wanted to be Jews but sought alternative definitions to the middle-class one they had already rejected—new identities with which they and other Jews could reenter America. This motivation can be seen from Levine's remarks in 1971: "We cannot accept the way American society defines us. We have to *discover the terms [with which] we can enter American society* and be authentic to Jewish life" (italics mine).

To build new identities "authentic to Jewish life," the young leftists linked themselves emotionally and ideologically to radical Jews of the past who had forged in their own day new definitions of being a Jew. Mythologizing themselves as revolutionaries and, in the case of the Radical Zionists, Yishuv pioneers, they created a chain of continuity with past heroes the way the chalutzim had done with David's warriors and the Maccabees. Teller understood this phenomenon and its motivations when he wrote, "All the [middle-class values] against which present day American youth is rebelling the kibbutzim rebelled against generations ago."

A related definition retrieved from the Jewish past was that of intellectual/ideologist. This definition, plus their following in the footsteps of the New Left in engaging in intellectual polemic and adhering to the traditional Jewish value placed on the written word, was why virtually the first thing new Jewish leftist groups did was to start a newspaper (and there were at least fifty by 1972).

The B.T.'s had an easier time. There was a ready-made definition of Jewish identity they could adopt: scholar and fulfiller of mitzvot, including rituals performed in public. The havura members, though not stringently observant, adopted this definition in watered-down fashion, adding some elements of Hassidic religious expression. Significantly, they referred to themselves as the "new Jews."

❧ These retrieved definitions of Jewishness, however, were to cause a conflict for movement women with their male comrades similar to that experienced by the women in the pioneering Yishuv and those in the early-twentieth-century American Socialist and union movements. The sixties' movements, including the Jewish one, were for their middle-class male adherents a revolt against material success not only as a value but also as a definition of masculinity. Women in all these movements were in unconscious revolt against the middle-class enabler role, a revolt that later became conscious and that led to the second wave of American feminism.

The women in the Jewish movement faced the problem that the retrieved definitions of Jewishness (scholar, intellectual, performer of public ritual) were those that had traditionally defined Jewish masculinity, and the men in the movement wished to have exclusive control of them. This was one of the reasons for the existence of considerable male chauvinism in the Jewish movement. To their credit, Network's leaders, most of them Radical Zionists, responded positively to women's growing feminist consciousness, as we shall see in chapter 16.

❧ Seeing the attempt to redefine American Jewish manhood as a motivation for involvement in the Jewish movement throws a new light on the B.T. phenomenon. For it was Orthodoxy alone that had never bought into the middle-class material success = manhood definition. Young Jewish men who had rejected their parents' values and pressures could find great inspiration and solace in its traditional definition of Jewish masculinity as learning Torah and observing the mitzvot. Too, in the Orthodox community, men's validation and self-esteem depended on the stringency of observance, something that was under their control.

And, noted anthropologist Barbara Myerhoff, they were not "cheated of family life and intimacy." Finally, as sexual mores and gender roles began to undergo a transition that has not yet concluded in anything resembling contentment for either sex in America, many women as well as men could find relief in Orthodoxy's rigid gender division of labor and in the validation it provided for role fulfillment.

Young Jewish women who had rejected middle-class materialism and family pressure to find wealthy husbands on the one hand, and the demand during the "sexual revolution" for emotionless promiscuity on the other, could find solace in a lifestyle whose male adherents were ready to "commit" in an era of "man shortage" and commitment-phobia, and who did not judge them by the majority culture's standards of beauty and behavior. They could find comfort, as well, in living in a community in which many of the old female values survive and which provides access to child care and a support network.

They could also be validated for Orthodox-style enabling. This validation took on increasing importance after the rise of feminism—and, by the mid-1970s, the Superwoman ideal—when "housewife" and "homemaker" began to absorb the coloration of anti-Puritanical sloth and parasitism. Even working at high-status jobs did not put women on a direct collision course with Orthodox men, who do not define their manhood in terms of material success. All of these factors in the Orthodox lifestyle more than compensated many B.T. women for the lack of social and intellectual contact with men arising out of the rigid separation of the two genders in its social life. Nor were many B.T. women with little previous Jewish education disturbed about female exclusion from studying Torah and participating as equals in synagogue services and public performance of rituals. The Orthodox women who would be influenced by feminism in the ensuing decades were those who had received enough of a Jewish education to want more and to seek opportunities to express their learning in mitzvot from whose observance they were excluded. By contrast, many of the most vociferous apologists for the inequality of women in Orthodox life were B.T. women.

◆ The JDL attempted to develop a new definition of American Jewish manhood as aggressive, even physically aggressive, in defending "Jewish interests." JDL men projected an image of chutzpah, strength, pride, brashness, macho, don't-give-a-damn toughness, of being "rough and tough hoodlums," in Rabbi Kahane's words. The JDL's June 24, 1969, *New York Times* ad pictured armed Jewish men standing in front of a synagogue. The text read: "Is this any way for a nice Jewish boy to behave? Answer: Yes."

POLITICAL CONSEQUENCES OF CONFLICTS OVER MASCULINITY

American Jewish men's conflicts over the majority culture's definition of masculinity, especially its physical aggression component, constituted an important factor in their responses to black militancy and to the JDL, as well as in their attitudes toward the general society and Israel.

An unacknowledged but nevertheless deeply significant psychological factor in the Jewish response to black militancy in the 1960s was Jewish men's envy of African American men for the ease with which they engaged in physical aggression. *Commentary* editor Norman Podhoretz unconsciously made the connection between his "hatred" toward blacks and his insecurities over masculinity when he wrote in 1963 that "in childhood I envied Negroes for what seemed to be their *superior masculinity.*" The lives of blacks on the streets of his neighborhood had seemed to him, as a child, to be "free, independent, brave, *masculine,* erotic. . . . They were 'bad boys' . . . bad in a way that . . . *made one feel inadequate.* . . . They were . . . beautifully, *enviably* tough, not giving a damn for . . . the whole of the adult world that . . . *we never had the courage to rebel* against" (italics mine).

During the urban ghetto riots of the 1960s, Jewish men's envy of black men was intermixed with anger at having their own inadequacies regarding physical aggression shown up by African American males whose upbringing did not preclude their burning down whole city blocks even though they might perish, like Samson, amid the falling pillars; horror at the violence; and contempt for its mindlessness and irrationality.

❧ These feelings, plus those of abandonment and of anger over it during the post-1967 era, were a factor in American Jews' growing perception that the community's best interests did not lie in a passionate identification or alliance with the oppressed. This perception caused Jews to be less assimilationist in that they began, in Fein's words, to acknowledge that "there are such things as legitimate Jewish interests which may be in conflict with those of others, and that it is not immoral to defend them." But at the same time, it made them more assimilationist in identifying their interests with those of the ruling class and glorifying/affirming the legitimacy of its values, especially materialism and status, as Podhoretz now began to do in the pages of *Commentary* magazine (hitherto the champion of social reform) and in his autobiography, *Making It.*

The conflicts the men had long experienced over living up to the American definition of masculinity exacerbated the rage they felt toward the radicals and black militants. The radicals had attacked American Jewish men's definition of masculinity by denigrating its material success component. The blacks pointed up how Jewish men did not fulfill the physical aggression component.

Jewish men could at least retrieve and relegitimize the material success component of masculinity by rejecting the radicals and their ideologies. The need to do so was intensified by the left's rejection of Israel, whose soldiers were the surrogate of American Jewish men in engaging in physical aggression. Rejecting Israel therefore meant rejecting American Jewish men's vicarious masculinity. Significantly, one of the Jewish delegates to the 1967 National Conference on New

Politics said that in accepting its anti-Israel resolution, Jews "*castrated* ourselves and went along" (italics mine).

In addition to attacking Israel, the black power movement was engaging in the verbal expression of anti-Semitism. Experienced against the background of the violence of the urban riots, this expression reactivated the men's anxiety about their inability to defend their "extended family" and became a terrifying reminder of Jewish men's centuries-long powerlessness in this regard. By rejecting the black power movement, American Jewish men could delegitimize these assaults on their masculinity. Moreover, by doing so, they could also relinquish the historically anomalous attempt to form/maintain an alliance with an oppressed group while juggling this disintegrating bond with that of the classic survival strategy of looking to the power structure for protection. This latter strategy was increasingly regarded as necessary because of the need to win support for Israel.

Giving leftist and black militants a zetz by expressing political views antithetical to theirs could not sop up all the rage of the men. For this reason, no matter what their politics, many were buoyed when JDLers *visibly* stood up to blacks, even if their action was 90 percent bravado.

The JDL was the id of American Jewish men.

But most of them were too conflicted over physical aggression—and especially over the kind of high-visibility aggression the JDL favored—to adopt its fundamentally new definition of masculinity despite their secret attraction to it. (When it became apparent that the plurality of American Jewish men were not going to accept this definition, the JDL gave up trying to get them to adopt it as the way to reenter American society and began emphasizing aliyah to Israel, where their definition of masculinity could be more or less in sync with that of other Jewish men there.)

⮞ Young Jewish men who abhorred violence but also hated being thought of as wimps could find great comfort in Orthodox Judaism, which rejected physical aggression as a definition of manhood. This was another psychological factor in the attraction of male B.T.'s to Orthodoxy.

Moreover, Orthodox Jewish men did not envy the blacks' "masculinity" or measure themselves against it. Additionally, since they had never been part of the liberal Jews' attempt to form an alliance with blacks, nor ever looked to them as possible rescuers nor felt abandoned by them, they suffered no emotional conflicts in relation to African Americans. They felt they owed them nothing and that blacks owed them nothing.

Some American Jews who have struggled with a stew of feelings about African Americans—empathy, envy, guilt, rage over abandonment and betrayal, mistrust, pain at being misunderstood, nostalgia for the good old days of their "alliance"—have found the Orthodox perception of them as just another ethnic group on the American scene another reason to be attracted to Orthodoxy. Many non-Orthodox American Jews, male and female, still remain mired in this stew of ambivalent feelings. Not even the 1991 Crown Heights riot could make some liberal Jews give up hope of repairing the ruptured relationship.

Those Jews who still feel blacks owe them something for the civil rights work they did might consider that African Americans have more than recompensed them by legitimizing ethnicity. Perhaps in this way the blacks have (unintentionally) rescued American Jews after all, not from some anti-Semitic onslaught but from their own ethnic amnesia. The time may thus have come to mark the black "debt" to Jews "Paid in full"—and to move on to thinking of realistic ways to relate to African Americans based on present interests rather than past fantasies.

CONFRONTATION

The adherents of the Jewish movement were essentially involved in a separation struggle with the New Left. They had regrouped to work out a new identity as Jewish revolutionaries and hoped to renegotiate the relationship with their (former) comrades. They failed to reenter the New Left because by the time they had worked out a new identity (and politics), it had become so sectarian that there was nothing they could reenter. By 1971, when the Jewish movement was at its zenith, the New Left was in its death throes.

The young Jewish leftists were simultaneously involved in a separation struggle with the Jewish community. They failed to reenter the Jewish community with their new identities because it was unable/unwilling to accept them or face up to their critique of American Jewish life as a body without a soul.

The leftists in the Jewish movement—as well as members of havurot and other nonideological groups in what their adherents called "the Jewish counter-culture"—were highly critical of the character of Jewish life in America, especially its organizational structure and process. Seeing it through the prism of the contemporary hippie and the early New Left critique of bourgeois/industrial society ("the machine") and its alienation, they were revolted by its terminal boredom, heartlessness, and tunnel-vision focus on fund-raising and glamorous projects.

But the Jewish community was very uncomfortable with youth who refused to define themselves by middle-class values. While feeling uneasy with the Radical Zionists' and the JDL's advocating of aliyah, many Jews also felt uncomfortable with Radical Jews' extolling the diaspora as a "positive good" because this challenged their living vicariously through Israel.

Moreover, the community misinterpreted the movement youths' critique of its behavior as a rejection/betrayal in a time of crisis and their temporary regrouping as a permanent separation/abandonment. Emblematic of this misinterpretation was the conclusion of a New York rabbi after a heated 1970 panel discussion with movement youth: "They want to go it alone," he wrote. This misinterpretation was exacerbated by the movement's use of confrontation tactics against Jewish establishment organizations.

The movement's major confrontations were with the Federations over the issue of Jewish education. The first was the 1969 "invasion" of the CJF's General Assembly, held that year in Boston, by a group called Concerned Jewish Youth. The assembled Federation machers and bureaucrats allowed one member of the group, Hillel Levine, to speak, and it was there that he made an impassioned and much-quoted call for communal renewal through Jewish education, which, he said, was treated as the "step-son of organized Jewish philanthropies." Within the next two years, coalitions of Jewish youth—leftists, Orthodox, and havura members—took over the buildings of Federations in New York (1970) and San Francisco (1971) to demand that they "reorder their priorities" toward funding Jewish education and culture.

◆ Confrontation tactics were part of the inheritance the young Jewish critics had brought into the Jewish movement from the New Left, along with intellectual polemicizing and opposition to structure. There was a pervasive feeling in the New Left—and in the Jewish movement, as well—that "The Revolution" was imminent and that its birth could be hastened/induced by the injection of confrontational actions to leapfrog over the tedious and boring organizing work necessary to build a grassroots movement.

But with a few exceptions, the use of New Left–style confrontation tactics in the community backfired. None of the Radical Zionists or Radical Jews or those in the counterculture had stopped to consider whether this strategy was appropriate to the Jewish community; it was enough that it was used by the New Left, their reference group.

The purpose of confrontation, of course, is to drive a wedge between the establishment and the masses. Confrontation in the community, however, had precisely the opposite effect: It hurled the masses into an embrace of the Jewish establishment. Jews, feeling abandoned/beleaguered and unjustly accused by leftist and black militant critics of Israel, felt overprotective of any Jewish institution that anyone attacked.

American Jews saw themselves as essentially powerless, knowing in their secret hearts that they had been long-distance spectators to Israel's last-minute rescue from a second Holocaust. They had not managed to mobilize American support for Israel—which might have headed off the war—when Egyptians and Syrian troops were proudly and gleefully marching up to its borders. And during the war, most had responded in the only way they knew: giving money.

Their anger about their powerlessness intensified when black militants attacked them for being powerful, rich, and exploitative. Because of this, they had to tread somewhat carefully around the issue of power and keep themselves on an emotional (and political) leash precisely at a time when their anger made them want to lash out. They envied the young Jews who *were* unleashing their anger in ways most older Jews could not bring themselves to do. In 1970, for example, a group of Jewish students at the University of Washington in Seattle presented a list of demands to the administration. They told a college official, "Make no mistake about it—we are not nice Jewish boys and girls. We will not hesitate an instant to use the same means for winning our rights that any other minority group has used."

The Jewish establishment exploited the Jews' feelings of envy, abandonment, frustration, and anger, and channeled them against the movement youth, who had no power base in the community, no clout, and no mechanisms to mount an effective campaign to communicate and popularize their views. It used them as lightning rods to absorb and deflect dissatisfaction away from itself.

The Jewish establishment's real concern was the movement's challenge to the legitimacy of its power in the community with their calls for democratization and a reordering of priorities. Moreover, the machers and bureaucrats involved in fund-raising and advocacy work did not trust the authenticity and depth of the emotional response of American Jews to Israel before, during, and after the 1967 War. Perhaps they were projecting their own ambivalence onto the Jewish public at large.

Many also believed that the support for Israel, by both Jews and non-Jews, was encased in a vessel so fragile that it would shatter into tiny slivers when certain sounds—the voices of criticism—were emitted. The support would then ebb away, never to be recaptured. They harbored, as well, a deep fear that the support was based on images of Israel rather than on reality. The general public had to be kept shielded from views, other than those packaged by the Jewish establishment, that might explode/erode these images.

The Jewish establishment's strategy was to divert public attention away from the issues raised by the young critics onto the damage that criticism would do to its campaigns for political and economic support of Israel. Its methodology was to crop-dust all expressions of criticism as dangerous and noxious weeds with the toxic herbicide of the "self-hate" argument. Labeling/libeling the young critics as "self-hating Jews" and as anti-Israel provided a rationalization for not listening to their ideas about Israel or the community. The strategy worked because to most American Jews, Israel was still the vulnerable little David of the May 1967 trauma who had managed this time to maim Goliath. But the giant still lived on in all his monstrosity, battening on the repeatedly regurgitated anti-Zionist vomitus.

When the young Jews addressed Jewish gatherings, they were usually on the receiving end of verbal brickbats, especially when they criticized Israeli policies. Radical Jews were also excoriated when they called for the community to support black and Third World revolutionary struggles; most Jews rejected the call because these struggles' proponents were anti-Israel. Moreover, lacking emotional affect about Israel and a deep connectedness to the community and an appreciation of its fears, Radical Jews often rubbed other Jews' nerves the wrong way with insensitive rhetoric, such as equating Hiroshima with Auschwitz and calling Attica prison "the Warsaw Ghetto of 1971."

The anger that greeted the movement youth stunned the Radical Jews. Here they had come in from the cold, suffering emotional hypothermia after being on the front lines of a harrowing battle to counter the knee-jerk anti-Israel attacks in the New Left, where they were excoriated for being "Zionists" (when most defined themselves as "non-Zionists" and were just vaguely hopeful that Israel would not be destroyed). Then, instead of being received warmly in the Jewish community, they were given the cold shoulder for being radical and "anti-Israel." As Sol Stern wrote at the time in *Ramparts* magazine: "Where the Left has said to young Jews, 'to be for the survival of Israel is to betray the world revolution,' the Jewish establishment seems to be saying, 'if you are for the world revolution, you betray your people.'" Having one foot in the New Left and another in the community was like standing on a cracking fault line.

Radical Zionists were verbally attacked, too, but they had a slightly easier time in the community because they called themselves Zionists and many were members or graduates of pioneering Zionist youth movements, such as Hashomer Hatzair, with legendary histories of building kibbutzim in Israel and fighting in wartime ghettos and as partisans.

MOVEMENT'S END

While some American Jews felt a great deal of anger toward the movement youth, others thought they were still *unzer kinder* (Yiddish for our kiddies) who would grow up and out of their politics. Many were encouraged by the fact that these sons and daughters had "returned to the fold," even if they returned as critics. The Jewish establishment wished to co-opt "the youth," especially the Radical Zionists, to channel their criticism (the classic Jewish behavioral approach) away from the community and toward those it perceived as the enemy—New Leftist and Arab propagandists on campus.

The college campus had for some years been labeled a Jewish disaster area by "leaders" because it was there that many Jewish students left the mishpucha after their insubstantial elementary Jewish education proved no intellectual match for the sophisticated Western ideas they encountered in class. Jewish education, as the young critics pointed out, had long been suffering from anemia for lack of intellectual nourishment and transfusions of money. Content to wring their hands about the campuses, the machers had not bothered to unclasp them long enough to reach into their pockets to fund Jewish activity there to any meaningful extent. But when the danger transcended the *defection* of Jewish youth and became one of *infection* of non-Jewish youth (and academics) by anti-Israel propaganda, Jewish organizations suddenly became interested in colonizing the college campus, and this now became a glamorous project.

The Jewish establishment wanted to get the Zionist movement to co-opt the Radical Zionists (and the vaguely leftist pro-Israel campus groups) into becoming part of the unofficial division of labor schema whereby each Zionist and community relations organization attempts to influence the non-Jewish circles closest to it in ideology and/or class composition.

The tragedy was that the Zionist bureaucrats did not understand (or care) that the Radical Zionist groups were the beginnings of what could have become a vibrant American Zionist movement. Instead they colluded with the Jewish establishment and cynically tried to direct the groups' energies away from real Zionist work and toward what was in essence campus propagandizing. Success in this activity would prove that the Zionist movement was in with—that is, able to co-opt—"the youth" and was therefore still a force to be reckoned with. The Zionist movement's American Zionist Youth Foundation (AZYF) was therefore willing to provide some funding to left-leaning pro-Israel college groups so they could be a kind of left cover for Israel (and even to tolerate their radical rhetoric) as long as the campus ambiance remained radical.

AZYF coexisted uneasily with Network, with which many of these campus groups were also affiliated. While Network maintained its radical posture into the late 1970s, the campus did not. AZYF therefore became more and more unwilling to tolerate competition from Network, and in 1978 it engineered its takeover. A slate of students its bureaucrats had selected won control of Network through a delegate-manipulation and convention-packing scheme. Network was destroyed as the democratic representative of Jewish students and as the instrumentality by which they had hoped to build a strong and creative Jewish community.

◈ There is no doubt that the youth who became involved in the Jewish movement were among the best and the brightest that American Jewry had ever produced. But one of their New Left–derived failings was opposition to structure, formal membership, and anything resembling long-term commitment. The same individuals who orated endlessly about setting up communes resisted structure and resented group discipline and often confused leadership with repression. The fear in some groups that people would leave—a fear derived both from the tenuousness of many individuals' involvement and the old Jewish separation anxiety—was a factor in their reluctance to grapple with difficult and controversial issues. (Radical Jews, for example, tended to avoid confronting the ideology of Zionism for this reason.) The New Left style precluded institutionalization—the only thing that could have enabled the movement to survive after the sixties ambiance conducive to its functioning had faded from the American scene.

As for those young Jews involved in nonradical alternative countercultural groups, they were mainly disappointed in their elders' failure to measure up to "their liberal pretensions" and in their not displaying "the kind of Jewish refinement that would have made it easier for these 'nice Jewish boys' [sic] to become part of their ... system," wrote Network founding director Itzhak Epstein in an acid-dipped 1971 critique. Within a few short years, these "new Jews" succeeded in reentering the organized Jewish community. Many of their male leaders were co-opted into the Jewish establishment and hold respectable jobs there today; some have even come to behave like minimachers.

These individuals were, in essence, the R&D wing of certain circles in the Jewish establishment who held similar views but were reluctant to air them. They were glad to let the young critics be on the front lines of advancing these views and take the heat for doing so. When the ground had been cleared, the circles in the Jewish establishment who favored activities to support Jewish education and culture took over the turf and made it respectable. Observing this phenomenon, sociologist Manheim Shapiro said in 1971 that Jews had mistakenly bet on "the disappearance of differences [while keeping] Jewish education on a starvation diet," a statement that recalls Levine's remarks at the 1969 General Assembly. Now that pluralism was unexpectedly on the ascendancy in the general society, he continued, Jewish agencies that were "alienated from the Jewish interest" would have to be "imbued with some kind of Jewish character."

LEGACIES OF THE MOVEMENT

The prerequisite for the emergence of a new definition of Jewishness to enable Jews to reenter American society on different terms was the creation of a culture to provide content for and expression of such a definition. The unconscious perception of the need for a new culture was behind the movement's overwhelming concern for and emphasis on Jewish education, on retrieving Jewish cultural and religious sources/resources as a foundation to build on, and on writing new holiday ceremonies to link past and present struggles.

The movement's emphasis on Jewish education brings to mind the stress on *secular* education of the nineteenth-century Russian maskilim. While the kind of education each of the movements called for was of a different nature, both groups recognized that education was the key to redefining Jewishness in order to reenter their general societies on new terms. Movement people understood that reordering communal priorities to emphasize education would necessarily have to involve the democratization of the community, another reason democracy was high on their agenda.

The Jewish movement did create elements of a new Jewish culture that adherents wished the community to accept and develop, but the community refused to countenance cultural forms with a leftist character. Even more important, most American Jews were implacably opposed to engaging in any kind of separation struggle with the general society, even a temporary regrouping, after having devoted themselves for so long to being accepted in/by it. They were unwilling to grapple with what Jewish survival could/should mean beyond physical survival or to contemplate the purging of assimilationist values and the renouncing of invisibility. Retrieving and creating Jewish content would have also meant encouraging many different voices and views as well as debates, and this, too, would have entailed democratizing the community. American Jewry, in its circle-the-wagons mood, was not willing to challenge the Jewish establishment and its power and was unwilling to countenance debate.

The movement's attempt to create and win acceptance for a new definition of Jewishness with which to reenter American society was therefore aborted.

∻ The only discrete group within the community that has succeeded to some extent in the reentering process, although it did not consciously strive to do so, is Modern/Centrist Orthodoxy, which already possessed a culture. The more its adherents have behaved as an identifiably distinct and visible group, the easier their reentering process has been. Non-Jewish Americans know where they stand in relation to the Orthodox. Their identity is clear rather than vague, shifting, conflicted, indefinite, and muddled, as is the case with most other American Jews.

∻ While the Jewish movement, whose heyday lasted about as long as Pharaoh's years of plenty, failed to create a new culture or community, it did sow the seeds of both. The seeds did not sprout immediately; instead most went into a sporelike state and began to germinate only about a decade and a half later, when the atmosphere was more receptive.

Judah Shapiro had once stressed that disputatiousness did not mean that people would be allowed to dissent from communal policy but that they would debate it and participate in shaping it. The movement opened up debate on a variety of issues for the first time in many decades, and it slowly seeped into the interstices of Jewish communal life. During the 1970s, individuals and small groups began to break the communal taboo against criticizing Israeli policy publicly. They were excoriated and lambasted; one of the groups, *Breira* (Hebrew for choice), was taken over by opponents and voted out of existence.

After running in a thin trickle parallel to Jewish establishment views, criticism came into the open during and after the Lebanon War of 1982 and the Palestinian Intifada. The Noninterference Directive, however weakened by these activities, has never quite been broken. Nevertheless, the bastard child of debate continues to challenge the directive's legitimacy. None of this would have been possible had the movement not initiated the process of criticism and debate in the sixties and early seventies.

A second important legacy of the movement was the legitimization of the authenticity of alternative, grassroots innovation in forms of Jewish expression, including ceremony writing (which later became an important Jewish feminist activity) and experiments in collective work. The movement demonstrated that Jews need not and should not wait for someone at the top to organize an activity or to create new forms of spiritual, cultural, and political expression—or to validate these.

Third, the movement ignited the spark and flame of interest and involvement in Jewish cultural activities. These resulted in the emergence of Jewish crafts, choruses, interest in genealogy, Jewish and Yiddish studies, new Jewish scholarship, and in an upsurge in the publication of books on Jewish subjects. There are even the beginnings of Jewish film, YidVid, and several struggling Jewish theaters, including the Joseph Papp Yiddish Theatre Workshop. The popularity of *klezmer* (East European Jewish music synthesizing Hebrew liturgical, Slavic, Turkish, and Balkan elements) approaches klezmania, and there are scores of ensembles playing it. Significantly, music historian Mark Slobin called klezmer music a "statement of identity."

◆ But can the incipient cultural pluralism thrive in an undemocratic community? Most of those currently involved with alternative cultural activities feel they can sidestep the Jewish establishment like debris on the street or filter it out like toxic elements in the water. But it is more like air pollution against which neither defense works. Should alternative Jewishness become as important as breathing and should the harmful air-quality levels in the community cause/approach spiritual suffocation, they might have to confront its undemocratic climate.

Another factor in the future evolution of the emerging Jewish culture is what will happen in Israel. Until peace prospects took an unexpectedly positive turn in the fall of 1993, many young Jews involved in alternative cultural projects were turned off to Israel because of its deepening political/spiritual crisis. This put them at risk of being relegated to the far margins of a community that remains emotionally involved with Israel. Should a stable peace ensue in the near future, it may open up the prospect of a genuine cultural exchange between artists in the two countries and thus contribute to the evolution of forms of cultural expression in America that incorporate and reflect interest in the Israeli reality.

The cultural projects are, as yet, isolated pieces of a mosaic that remains to take form and shape. No new movement has yet arisen that addresses the total condition of American Jewry and that has a vision of what its future should be. Nor has any new movement emerged that provides a Zionist analysis of and program for American Jewry. The absence of such a movement, and even of any consciousness of its necessity, was glaringly obvious at the 1980 founding conference of the left-liberal New Jewish Agenda organization and at the 1988 conference, sponsored by *Tikkun* magazine, on "reconstituting" the Jewish intellectual left.

A fourth legacy of the movement was Holocaust consciousness, the subject of chapter 15. Radical Zionists and JDL people understood from the outset the link between confronting the implications of the Holocaust and forging a new Jewish identity. That link can be seen very clearly in these sentences from Rosenberg's "To Uncle Tom" piece of 1969: "In the shower rooms" (i.e., gas chambers) "it will [*sic*] little matter that one fellow was once Albert Shanker and the other was once Mark Rudd" (a sixties radical). "Their destinies and fates are intertwined, for better or for worse."

Finally, Jewish feminism was possibly the movement's most important heritage. It was the movement that served as the nursery where the tender plants of Jewish feminism grew and flourished, watered by the streams of debate and basking in the energizing sun of pluralism. By the time the nursery had shut down, Jewish feminism was sturdy enough to branch out on its own.

FIFTEEN ❧ HOLOCAUST CONSCIOUSNESS

Never Again!

> Slogan of THE JEWISH DEFENSE LEAGUE

If I were to hear one morning through bull-horns that all Jews are to report to Grand Central Station, I would not be entirely surprised.

> NAT HENTOFF

There's No Business Like Sho'ah Business.

> LUCY DAVIDOWICZ

The traumatic two-week period of impending doom that preceded the Six-Day War of 1967, when the survival of Israel seemed to be hanging in the balance, was the first crack in the iceberg of apathy in which American Jews' memories of the Holocaust had been frozen for over two decades. More fissures—shocks over abandonment by other Americans—followed apace, with each break in the iceberg releasing repressed feelings of horror, rage, helplessness, and guilt over the Holocaust. By the time the iceberg of apathy had melted down almost completely, Holocaust consciousness came to permeate every aspect of American Jewish communal life—religious, cultural, and political.

The flood of testimony by survivors and the spate of research by noted scholars since that time have continued to reveal the depth of the horror and the scope of the wartime indifference to it by non-Jewish individuals and governments. American Jews have been obsessed with agonizing over how non-Jews in nations conquered by Nazi Germany were indifferent to/collaborated in/profited from the mass murders, especially in Poland, Ukraine, the Baltics, Belarus, Hungary, and Romania; over why only the Danes rescued virtually all their Jewish compatriots; why the Vatican and Protestant church hierarchies and all but a few clergymen were silent and passive; and why no nation, including the U.S. and Canada, extended even temporary asylum to substantial numbers of Jewish refugees. Americans Jews have agonized over the horrors of the mass murders detail by excruciatingly terrifying detail.

It should be stated at the outset that there is no reason American Jews—or anyone else, for that matter—should not be obsessed with the greatest and most monstrous crime of mass murder in human history. (The reader will notice that I use "mass murder" rather than *extermination,* a term that still resonates with the Nazi recycling of the Judeophobic myth that the Jews were dangerous disease-carrying vermin.) Those who call upon American Jews to rein in the expression of their feelings of rage and pain because it might "provoke" more resentment and annoyance (code words for anti-Semitism) among non-Jews and to begin a "healing" process exhibit gross insensitivity to Jewish trauma along with a lack of trust in the ability of non-Jews ever to understand what the Holocaust means for Jews. They do not recognize, either, that obsessive review is an integral part of mourning and that it and the validation of the sufferers' feelings (a kind of emotional reparations) are prerequisites to "healing."

The key question, then, is not why Jews obsess and agonize about this great tragedy, loss, and mega-crime. The question is why the obsession is not accompanied by any attempt to analyze how and why the Holocaust happened and what its political implications are.

AVOIDANCE AND APATHY

To understand why analysis is avoided, we first need to look at the reasons American Jews of the immediate post–World War II period hardened their hearts and shut their minds to descriptions or discussions of the Holocaust. Some of the reasons for their avoidance of analysis still obtain today.

Prime among these reasons is the unconscious realization that the experiences of Jews during the Holocaust provide insight into how the dynamics that have classically prevailed in Exile societies worked, and about why the traditional survival strategies, used for centuries to try to overcome them, did not.

As an extreme but by no means aberrant example of Exile dynamics, the Holocaust testified to Jewish vulnerability everywhere. To avoid thinking what this implied for their situation, American Jews took refuge behind the shield of the theory of American exceptionalism: "America is different" and therefore exempt from these dynamics.

They bolstered American exceptionalism by grasping at "explanations" of what had "suddenly" transformed Germany, once considered the most advanced and cultured liberal country, into a nation of mass murderers. These "explanations" were that there were flaws unique to the German character ("the authoritarian personality," and the "berserk rage of which Nordic tales and Nordic songs are so full," which Heine had warned about in 1835) and that its democracy had been weak; both of these phenomena had allowed its citizens to be "brainwashed." Another favorite theory was that the Germans had undergone a "national psychosis." (This view was hard to sustain in the wake of Hannah Arendt's "banality of evil" argument that one did not have to be crazy to murder Jews.)

No such theories, however, could explain the failure of the classic survival strategies. The Holocaust conclusively demonstrated the bankruptcy of looking to any power structure for protection and rescue, of being useful to it to provide an incentive for protection, and of employing shtadlanut (quiet diplomacy/behind-the-scenes intercession) to obtain it. These strategies were impossible to employ, of course, in relation to Nazi Germany; but they also failed with collaborationist regimes (for instance, France rounded up its Jewish citizens for deportation). They also failed, as we shall see presently, in regard to Jewish efforts to motivate Allied nations to rescue European Jews.

The Holocaust exploded the fantasy of looking to liberal nations for rescue. As late as 1943, the Jewish leaders of Warsaw urged their representative in London to press Jewish leaders to obtain guarantees from Britain and the U.S. that they would save the Jews: "Let them accept no food or drink, let them die a slow death while the world looks on. This may *shake the conscience of the world*" (italics mine). That Jews in the Warsaw Ghetto still believed there was such a thing as "the conscience of the world" shows the power of the secularized rescue fantasy even among nonassimilationist Jews.

American Jews, too, had harbored expectations of the rescue of European Jews by liberal nations, including their own. They could not face the fact that their government had done little to help Jews escape annihilation. Nor were they willing to think about how the racist quota system had blocked the escape route for European Jews before, during, and after World War II. The 1924 Johnson Immigration Restriction Act had deliberately set annual quotas at 2 percent of the people from each nation present in America during the 1890 census, when relatively few people from Eastern and Central Europe, including Jews, had arrived.

Roosevelt insisted on "living up to the letter" of the immigration laws. In 1938, after *Kristallnacht* (the Night of Broken Glass) in Germany—a pogrom in which 191 synagogues were destroyed by organized mobs and thirty thousand Jews hauled away to concentration camps—the president was asked at a press conference if the laws could be relaxed to admit Jewish refugees. He replied, "That is not in contemplation. We have the quota system."

But the State Department went far beyond "living up to the letter" of the quota system laws. During the war it held *quota* immigration at 10 percent so that 6,000 Jews a year were admitted to the U.S. instead of 60,000. This, said historian David Wyman, meant that "189,000 quota slots went unused, each representing a life that could have been saved."

Nor did the government act on the various proposals to grant temporary political asylum to Jews. In 1938 FDR rejected the idea of a bill for refugee settlement in Alaska. In 1939 he turned down a plea for asylum from the more than 900 Jewish passengers on the *St. Louis,* who had been denied entry to Cuba despite strenuous bribery efforts. That year FDR also recommended "no action" on the Wagner-Rogers Bill to admit 20,000 orphaned German Jewish children over a two-year period; the bill failed. In 1944 he rejected the idea of "free ports" (in essence, temporary asylum) for refugees but allowed the token number of 1,000 to be settled in Oswego, New York. And these are but the most egregious examples of FDR's behavior.

For Jews to acknowledge that government indifference existed on such a scale would have cast serious doubts on the viability of the theory of American exceptionalism. It was too psychologically traumatic to think about what it meant for the future of American Jews that their own country had abandoned them and their "extended family" in the hour of their most urgent need.

◆ In addition, thinking about these issues might have led American Jews to raise them publicly, which thereby could have set them on a direct collision course with the American government and public. This they were determined to avoid at all costs. One reason was that in the early post–World War II era, anti-Semitism ran high and Jews feared to "provoke" more *now that they knew that it could culminate in mass murder*. Related to this was the fact that during this period—the beginning of the cold war, McCarthyism, and of the Rosenberg ordeal—any criticism of the American government was regarded as unpatriotic/un-American. Finally, the many Jews involved with the Zionist movement knew they needed the goodwill of the government in the struggle for a Jewish state. This was no time to bite the hand that might be raised at the U.N. in a "yes" vote for Partition of Mandatory Palestine. American public opinion was critically important in the struggle, and the public was in no mood to listen to accusations against the government.

◆ The only context in which the Holocaust was allowed out of the closet in the immediate postwar years was during fund-raising for the refugees and for Israel by the UJA and similar such efforts. The fund-raisers played on the guilt American Jews felt about failing to "do enough" to try to effect rescue of members of their "extended family"—another issue they refused to confront—and about not even giving shelter to survivors (as Jewish communities of the past had done after pogroms and expulsions) because they were unwilling to challenge the quota system. At the same time, the UJA and other fund-raisers channeled American Jews' guilt into a safe outlet—"sacrificing" money to "atone" for their sins of omission. *Teshuvah* (repentance) has traditionally meant making a commitment to changing one's future behavior. American Jews, however, did not wish to change the behavior that caused them to feel guilt, only to reduce or expunge the guilt. The fund-raisers colluded with them by providing instant atonement—for a price.

SABOTAGE OF RESCUE

It was the young Jews in the sixties movement, especially Radical Zionists, who raised the painful Holocaust issues requiring thought and analysis—issues American Jews had repressed for over two decades—once the apathy iceberg began to crack open in the Six-Day War period. These issues were the betrayal by putative rescuer-nations, including the U.S.; whether the wartime American Jewish community had done enough to try to rescue European Jews; and what the implications of both of these issues and the Holocaust in general were for the survival of the community.

⫸ Their generation had known little about the Holocaust until 1967. Jewish parents generally did not discuss it with their children for fear of wounding their tender psyches and thereby incapacitating them for the competitive and (in the sixties, more propitious) struggle for material success.

Nor had the Holocaust been mainstreamed (then or now) into public education. Jews are invisible in world history textbooks until World War II, when they suddenly appear on the European scene in time to be massacred. Nor is the Holocaust anything more than a subevent of World War II in these texts. This invisibility, it should be noted, makes it possible for uninformed people to give credence to the propaganda of the revisionist "historians"/Holocaust deniers that the Holocaust never took place or that the gas chambers did not exist or that the Jews who died were simply war casualties among many others.

The Jewish schools that did teach about the Holocaust did so to elicit the conclusion that the pupils were fortunate to be living in a country where non-Jews liked Jews, and where "we eat off the fat of the land," observed David Roskies in 1971. Moreover, World War II movies, in which Germans were outmaneuvered by American jocks and/or their partisan counterparts (none of the latter Jews), had conditioned young Jews to expect "happy endings, not Auschwitz," said a Jewish college student in the early seventies. It was precisely because the youth knew so little about the Holocaust that when survivors—who had been silent for so many years because no one had wanted to listen to them—finally began to speak about it, they had a tremendous impact.

The questions movement youth raised were given impetus by three other concurrent phenomena. One was the influence of the zeitgeist of the sixties, in which applying verbal battering rams of criticism against the walls of the power structure became acceptable and even laudable. The second was the use of Holocaust analogies by New Leftists and black activists. For example: Malcolm X (despite his Black Muslim–based anti-Zionism) warned that blacks live "in a society that is just as capable of building gas ovens for Black people as Hitler's society was . . . [for] the Jews." The third influence was the publication in 1967 of Arthur Morse's breakthrough book, *While Six Million Died,* the first popular work to provide solid documentation on the American government's obstruction of efforts to rescue European Jews.

⫸ In the ensuing decades, more and more information was disinterred and brought to light about how the U.S. government had sabotaged rescue efforts.

Henry Feingold's *The Politics of Rescue* was published in 1970 and David Wyman's *The Abandonment of the Jews* in 1984. Wyman's eleven years of research had led him to conclude that "the American State Department resisted every effort for rescue action.... [It] did not want rescue to occur. They did not want the Jews to get out, not in any numbers." He attributed the sabotage in part to anti-Semitism in the State Department.

A second factor in U.S. policy on rescue was its support for Britain, which was determined to obstruct rescue. The infamous reply of Lord Moyne, deputy minister of state, to a request to rescue Hungary's Jews at the eleventh hour was, "Save a million Jews? What shall we do with them?" The British feared that if masses of Jews were saved from the slaughter, Britain would be pressured to rescind the 1939 White Paper sealing the doors of Mandatory Palestine. This policy was motivated by an unwarranted fear of antagonizing the Arabs during the war and propelling them into the German camp.

Another, realistic fear, of course, was that if enough Jews survived the war, they would try to immigrate to Mandatory Palestine and might win support for this effort from other countries, which would then pressure Britain to agree to letting them in. This would jeopardize the British pro-Arab policy. The British also feared that if large numbers of Jews immigrated to Eretz Israel, they would start to struggle for its independence from colonial rule. (The British policy was undoubtedly a factor in the refusal of Canada to admit Jewish refugees during the war, a policy documented in Irving Abella and Harold Troper's 1982 work, *None Is Too Many;* similarly with Australia and other British Commonwealth nations.)

A third factor in the resistance by both the State Department and President Roosevelt to rescue efforts was their awareness of the strong and vocal opposition in Congress and among the public at large to immigration. FDR was closely attuned to this attitude and unwilling to counteract it. Had he so wished, he could easily have done so by differentiating between immigration (which even the unions resisted out of anxiety that unemployment would resume after the troops came home) and temporary asylum for the duration of the war. But his refusal to consider asylum proposals demonstrates that the pseudoissue of public opposition to immigration was not FDR's main motivation in his decisions on rescue.

Roosevelt told a delegation of Jewish leaders in 1942, "Any overt effort to rescue European Jews would harm the Allied war effort." One cannot help but speculate that this policy was rooted in his and other Allied leaders' acute awareness of the inordinate numbers of German personnel and equipment pinned down in perpetrating the mass murders. This diversion of resources from the German military effort helped the Allies prosecute the war, and they were reluctant to halt it by, for example, bombing the gas chambers and crematoria of Auschwitz and the railroad tracks leading to them. That is why, when requested to do this by Jewish leaders, the U.S. said this would impede the war effort and Britain replied, "We are conducting the war on a strategic and not a humanitarian basis."

DID AMERICAN JEWS DO "ENOUGH"?

As more and more information became available about the terrible record of the U.S. government in regard to rescue efforts, movement youth began to question whether American Jewry and its wartime "leadership" could have done more to get the government to save European Jewry. The debate that has ensued in the community has taken the form of a tangled welter of accusations and counter-accusations. Four issues can be distinguished: Was rescue a priority? Was the lack of unity among the different organizations the key impediment to action? Were despair and hopelessness about the possibility of mobilizing the general public to bring about government action a correct reading of reality? And was their shtad-lanut strategy appropriate?

On February 12, 1943, Hayim Greenberg, a Labor Zionist leader and writer, charged in his heartrending Yiddish essay "Bankrupt" that "American Jewry has not done—and has made no effort to do—its elemental duty toward the millions of Jews who are . . . doomed to die in Europe. . . . All five million of us, with all our organizations and committees and leaders, [are] politically and morally bankrupt."

No more searing words have been written on American Jewish behavior during the Holocaust—then or now.

Greenberg castigated in his "J'Accuse" all the Jewish organizations, including the Zionist ones, for failing to give priority to rescue and instead maintaining an attitude of "business as usual." Rarely was the issue of rescue on the agenda of their conferences (including the 1942 Biltmore Conference that launched the campaign for a Jewish state). Forty years later, a private group called the American Jewish Commission on the Holocaust concluded that "at no time did [the organizations] mount an all-out unified sustained mobilization for rescue."

The lack of unity was also excoriated by Greenberg, who pointed to how each organization "tried to outmaneuver the other" and to the Byzantine infighting, turf battles, and conflicts over methodology that dissipated their resources. "It seemed that they were more anxious to tear each other apart than to rescue their co-religionists," wrote Feingold many years later.

A great deal of the energy of the Jewish establishment was directed into fighting against a small group of right-wing Zionists associated with the Irgun and led by Peter Bergson (nom de guerre of Hillel Kook) from Eretz Israel. The group, which went under several names, took out dramatic full-page advertisements in daily papers and produced stirring pageants (all written by journalist Ben Hecht). In July 1943 it convened a conference of *one thousand* military, economic, and diplomatic experts to brainstorm a plan of action to rescue European Jews. The absence of any plan of action was a key impediment to rescue; the conference produced one that included the establishment of a government rescue agency.

Rabbi Stephen Wise, head of the American and the World Jewish Congress and regarded by many as the leader of American Jewry, took the lead in fighting the Bergsonites. Wise feared that the Bergsonites' actions would lead to increased anti-Semitism at a time when, in the words of Zionist leader Rabbi Abba Hillel Silver, "the Old World style of Jew-hatred had come to America." Jews were being attacked in the streets of New York and Boston and their synagogues vandalized; they claimed that the police looked the other way and that newspapers spiked the stories.

Despite the opposition from Jewish "leaders" (including efforts to get Bergson deported), the Bergsonites succeeded in having a resolution to establish a rescue agency introduced in Congress in November 1943. Meanwhile, Treasury Secretary Henry Morgenthau Sr.'s associates had completed an investigation for him about the State Department's sabotage of a plan to rescue seventy thousand Romanian Jews and had written a memo on "The Acquiescence of This Government in the Murder of the Jews." Morgenthau took the memo to the president, who feared a public scandal if the information in it became public during the upcoming congressional debate on the rescue agency resolution.

FDR signed an executive order establishing the War Refugee Board (WRB) just two days before the Senate debate was to begin. He allocated one million dollars to the WRB, which insisted American Jewish organizations contribute sixteen million dollars, the lion's share of its budget, said Wyman. The WRB's efforts, which resulted in the rescue of thousands of Jews, demonstrated what could have been accomplished had it been set up one and a half years earlier, when the government had confirmation of the German genocide plan.

Even historian Lucy Davidowicz, who loathed the Bergson group, had to acknowledge that it was "the most potent influence" in creating the WRB. The limited but palpable success of the Bergsonites in mobilizing public opinion for rescue (which is what made FDR fear a scandal), said Wyman, indicates that the impression of American Jewish establishment "leaders" that such a strategy was hopeless was an incorrect reading of reality.

The strategy of the Jewish establishment—if it can actually be dignified by that term—was classic shtadlanut. This stunningly inappropriate strategy (which had never been abandoned by the AJCommittee) came to characterize the wartime behavior of all the non-Orthodox organizations—including Wise and the AJCongress, which had not been afraid in the 1930s to employ activism, such as holding mass rallies against Nazi Germany and calling for a boycott of its exports.

What turned the roaring lion of the 1930s into the toothless and declawed cat of the 1940s? And why did the Zionist movement, in campaigning from 1942 on for a Jewish state, engage in activism rather than adhere to shtadlanut? Perhaps the answer to both questions relates to the mental state of American Jews from the time the war began in Europe. Trude Weiss-Rosmarin wrote in 1941 that they were "showing signs of cracking up under the mental and physical strain of the news from Europe" printed daily in the Yiddish press and JTA and in the English-language Jewish weeklies.

The agony and the feelings of powerlessness were felt, as well, by "leaders" of Jewish organizations. The feelings of helplessness at a time when so much was at stake caused them to revert to the tried-and-true shtadlanut strategy with which they were familiar and which they regarded as safer than an activist approach, which they feared might backfire. At the same time, their feelings of powerlessness led them to seize upon the Zionist campaign to break out of their depression. In this campaign they could take the risk of using an activist approach because it was not directly connected with the war or rescue efforts.

Shtadlanut proved an especially ignominious failure in relation to mobilizing the influential Jews who were Roosevelt's close advisers, among them Felix Frankfurter, Benjamin Cohen, Bernard Baruch, and Samuel Rosenman. These and other assimilationist Jewish men holding high government positions kept a low Jewish profile and were unwilling to advocate Jewish causes, including rescue. Most Jews, however, assumed automatically that the presence and prestige of these advisers to FDR meant an enhancement of "Jewish influence," and this reinforced their trust in the administration. The naive assumption that Jews in important positions will act in the interests of the Jewish nation rather than in their own individual interests in power and status is as sadly mistaken as the fantasy that women in high positions will always help other women individually or collectively.

❧ Assimilationist Jews in the media—those who owned and ran movie studios and newspapers and wrote plays and novels—were equally silent. The U.S. ambassador to Britain, Joseph Kennedy, told fifty leading Jewish moviemakers at a secret 1941 meeting that they must keep their Jewish rage to themselves because otherwise "it would make the world feel that a 'Jewish war' was going on," reported Hecht. Afterward "all of Hollywood's top Jews went around with their grief hidden like a Jewish fox [*sic*] under their Gentile vests." A year later, when Hecht attempted (and failed) to involve twenty Hollywood moguls in one of the Bergson group's campaigns, each of them told him that a Jew "must be very careful of angering people and very careful not to assert himself in any unpopular way . . . [and] must be as invisible as possible."

Hollywood Jews expressed their yearning for their people's rescue in one film alone, and then only indirectly. That film was *Casablanca*, which, noted Aljean Harmetz, was shaped by Jews from studio heads to scriptwriters. The film's reluctant hero, Rick Blaine, symbolizes America, and his transition from isolationism ("I stick my neck out for nobody") to self-sacrifice for a noble ideal is an expression of the Jewish rescue fantasy. That fantasy was that just as Rick saved Victor Lazlo and Ilsa Lund, the U.S. would reject its bystander stance, reaffirm its deepest values, and rescue Jews.

Jews in the print media—including those who owned the *New York Times*—did not break with the press policy of relegating accounts of the mass murders, especially those from Jewish sources, to back pages, when they published them at all. This policy was derived from and reinforced the impression that the reports were *Beyond Belief,* the title of historian Deborah Lipstadt's detailed documentation on the subject. The press's policy created a "curtain of disbelief" over the reports' accuracy, noted Feingold. And what was the public to believe when popular columnist Walter Lippmann—a Jew who had called a speech by Hitler in 1933 "the authentic voice of a genuinely civilized people"—wrote *not one single word* about the Nazi persecution of the Jews?

So much for the accuracy of the Judeophobic myth of how Jews control the media to advance Jewish causes.

FDR, THE RESCUER-PRINCE

A crucial impediment to American Jews' engaging in effective efforts for rescue was their illusion about FDR's benevolence and concern. "If there has been one president in this century with whom American Jewry has identified, to whom it gave its heart both politically and emotionally, that [man] was Franklin Roosevelt," wrote Melvin Urofsky. And they expressed their affection and trust not only by hanging his icon in their homes and sending him personal love letters but also by giving him pluralities of over 90 percent in their districts. American Jews were convinced that FDR's welfare state, "which reflected their own humanitarian proclivities, was a manifestation of [his] spirit of concern. That is why they loved him so," wrote Feingold, and they believed he shared their values.

This love, like that the Jews felt for liberal nations they believed to be cultured and enlightened, was blind, undeserved—and unrequited. FDR saw the mass murders as just another atrocity problem of the war and preferred to play down the commonality of interests between himself and the Jews out of concern about a backlash from anti-Semites.

Only some crucial domestic political reason—votes—might have propelled FDR to take the risk of building a strong counterconstituency supporting rescue, wrote Feingold. Since Jews were in love with FDR, ripping off the veils of illusion about his sharing their values and his "special love for them" was the only way Jewish "leaders" could have caused Jews to withdraw their political support. Unwilling to do this, they actually shielded the president from the Jewish public. Wise said in 1939 that "the Jews have never had a better friend in the White House," and he preferred to attack the State Department, which was being used by FDR as a lightning rod.

Jewish "leaders," therefore, had no leverage with Roosevelt: He knew he did not have to "transact business with the Jews," because their support was assured. He could keep their loyalty by following the policy of American presidents from the time of Dreyfus and the Kishinev pogrom: the "politics of gesture," said Feingold. This entailed making nice but totally ineffective statements that earned brownie points with Jews, who have always set great store by words. In December

1942, for example, FDR told a delegation led by Wise that he was "profoundly shocked" to learn that two million Jews were already dead. He reassured the delegation that the U.S. would take every step to "save those who may yet be saved." He did not, however, actually do anything until compelled by crass political considerations to create the WRB.

◆ A central clue to the psychological dynamics of the attitude of Jews to FDR emerges from Judd Teller's analysis of how "American Jewry suddenly found itself in the humiliating circumstance of dependence, like the medieval Jewish communities, upon ... the reigning prince." After anti-Semitic attacks in September 1941 by Charles Lindbergh, a leader of the isolationist America First movement, "FDR became in the Jewish imagination a pillar of fire and a pillar of smoke" (those were the pillars God gave the Jews to guide them in the desert after the Exodus), "a father and a guardian." Four years later, a rabbi eulogized FDR as a "deliverer" who had brought the world to the "border of the promised land" (that is, victory), and a Hebrew scholar wrote of his dying by a "kiss from God," as Rashi says Moses did.

These encomiums to FDR reveal the Jews' passionate fixation on the secularized rescue fantasy. This meant they believed that the rescuer-prince had some intrinsic motivation—shared values—to do right by them. But, like the God of the Kabbala, he was flawed in having his hands tied and needed to be repaired. Therefore, if he did not rescue American Jews' "extended family," it was because they had somehow not done "enough" to help untie his hands—overcome the anti-Semitic State Department bureaucrats, the latter-day Hamans, by making him aware of their plight, just like Queen Esther had done with King Ahashverosh. This explanatory style accounts for why Jewish establishment "leaders," who shared the rescue fantasy of the Jewish public, spent so much time and energy drawing up requests to be presented to high officials who could supposedly "reach" FDR.

Moreover, if the prince/president was the rescuer of Jews, then an unwritten contract obtained between them that predicated rescue on approved Jewish behavior, that is, altruistic-assertive enabling. This meant facilitating the agenda/policy of the powerful prince/president, which was defined as advancing the war effort—by doing what he wanted (such as suppressing information, stopping food shipments to occupied lands)—and accepting exclusion from efforts to shape/change policy. It meant being assertive only when it was "altruistic" as he defined it ("good for the war effort") but not otherwise. This entailed not engaging in what was called "special pleading" for Jews (propagandized after Pearl Harbor as "unpatriotic") or becoming so visible that he would have to face the horrendous charge that he was fighting the war for the Jews' benefit (a recycling of the Jewish power myth). Finally, it meant refraining from any action that could alienate or antagonize him, especially the holding of public protest demonstrations to mobilize public opinion "behind his back," criticizing his policies, or calling on Jews to vote for someone else.

This rescue fantasy and contract paralyzed the "leaders" and made them unable to come up with or implement any effective plan of action. And it led them to try to delegitimize and muzzle those Jews, like the Bergsonites (and to some extent the Orthodox), who broke the rules of the contract and could thereby anger the prince. It is why Zionist leader Nahum Goldmann, who served as the wartime representative of the Jewish Agency in Washington, said he had fought the Bergsonites: "They were very *anti-government*. . . . They encouraged the *opposition,* accusing Roosevelt [of betraying] the Jewish people" (italics mine).

Additionally, the Bergsonites aroused the terror and ire of other Jewish groups because they broke the visibility taboo. The invisibility of the Jews as victims of Nazism was an integral part of Allied policy. Before and during World War II, Jews were referred to by the camouflage terminology of "refugees" (for instance, at the 1939 Evian conference and the 1943 Bermuda conference, and by the WRB); after the war, they were called "displaced persons."

Only one of the many Allied statements on the war crimes for which the Germans would be held accountable and prosecuted after the war mentioned crimes against the Jews, and it was issued as late as March 1944. "The cattle cars rolled to Auschwitz amidst an eerie silence," wrote Feingold, and the silence reinforced the Germans' conviction that the Allies approved of the genocide and that it was unnecessary to consider curtailing it out of fear of retribution.

❧ Orthodox Jewish leaders, too, were unafraid of high visibility; four hundred Orthodox rabbis paraded through Washington in full regalia (black coats and hats) to call for rescue efforts in 1943. Nor were they loath to engage in "illegal" activities for rescue at a time when Jewish establishment "leaders" were giving Gerhart Riegner (the WJC representative in Geneva) a hard time about sending forged *schutzpasses* (protective documents) to Jews in German-occupied Europe. Through their Vaad HaHatzala, the Orthodox transmitted funds to a network of agents in Europe to save thousands of yeshiva students and teachers and other Jews.

The main reason for the difference between the behavior of assimilationist Jewish establishment "leaders" and of the Orthodox Jews was that the latter, especially those who were right-wing Orthodox, had never transferred the age-old concept of rescue-from-outside from God to Western nations and their leaders. They may have sought to get "princes" to extend help, but—and this is the key—they had never been in love with or placed their faith in them. They turned out to be more politically astute than their assimilationist brethren.

Nor were they troubled by accusations of putting Jewish interests above those of the war effort. They correctly placed *Pikuach Nefesh* (saving lives) ahead of all other considerations. This can be seen from a story told by one son of Renée

Reichman, who was herself heavily involved with rescue work from her base in Tangiers:

> A rabbi ... Abraham Kalmanowitz, he was the head of the Mirer Yeshiva, on one Yom Kippur (1943 or 1944), he took a taxi ... from Boro Park in Brooklyn with four students to Fifth Avenue in New York. He told the students to leave all the car doors open so it would be noticed ... on the holiest day in the Jewish calendar.... They went into the Reform temple [Emanu-El] and he walked up to the *bimah* [reader's platform] and he said, "For God's sake, we need money." And he fainted. People brought him water. And he said, "No water, money...." This was the *Vaad*.

DEFLECTING BLAME

While the Jewish movement put the issue of the behavior of the wartime Jewish "leadership" on the agenda of the Jewish community in the early 1970s, it did not succeed in getting American Jews to confront, as well, the implications of the government's culpability in sabotaging rescue.

American Jews' feelings of abandonment by the left and by African Americans in and after the 1967 War had, as we have seen, led their organizations to relinquish the strategy of allying with the oppressed and to seek, yet again, to look to the power structure for protection for the community and for Israel. Therefore Jews were more unwilling than ever to delve into the exhumed body of evidence about the American government's sabotage of rescue or to confront its implications for their strategy. This is why Elie Wiesel, who has called the Holocaust "the ultimate mystery, never to be comprehended," and who said that the "dead are in possession of a secret that we the living are neither worthy nor capable of uncovering," became so popular on the official Jewish lecture circuit from the mid-1970s on. What Wiesel, a Nobel Peace Prize winner, meant was that the Holocaust should not be "trivialized" by simplistic explanations and dramatizations. What American Jews chose to believe they had heard him say was that they need not and should not think about what any of the issues around the Holocaust meant for them.

Thinking about the behavior of the U.S. government was especially psychologically threatening because it involved demythologizing FDR and acknowledging that he was perfidious. This was/is especially difficult for Jews with the kind of liberal Democratic politics that FDR represented. For instance, as late at 1984, Betty Friedan named Roosevelt as the man she "most admired," adding, "I also wish he had opened these shores—without immigration quotas—and taken other steps to save more of the Six Million Jews who died in the Holocaust. But, oh, how we need a leader like him right now!" This is a good example of *not* "seeing the world through Jewish eyes."

Nor do Jews wish to challenge the secularized rescue fantasy or the classic strategy of relying on the kindness of strangers. Therefore it is far safer for most

Jews today to ignore the issue of the government's culpability and instead to put the prime blame on the wartime Jewish "leaders" for not repairing the rescuer's flaws. Thus even the debate on the behavior of the wartime "leaders" *is framed by the terms of the rescue fantasy* instead of being focused on addressing the question of whether the fantasy itself and the behavior it engendered impeded the launching of effective political action.

However distasteful it is for today's communal functionaries to listen to accusations of their organizations' poor record during the Holocaust—and some totally lose control during such debates—they still regard it as a safer outlet for Jews' anger. Here one recalls the Yiddish expression that the mother who is angry at her daughter-in-law will yell at her daughter.

Moreover, such angry accusations are usually defused by pointing, as Charles Silberman did during the 1985 Bitburg affair, to the "difference" between then and now: "In the 1930s, we were afraid to criticize Franklin Roosevelt. But in 1985, Elie Wiesel stood in the White House and over national television, as he put it, he 'spoke truth to power.'" At a White House ceremony where he was awarded a Congressional Medal of Honor, Wiesel appealed to President Reagan to cancel plans to lay a wreath at the West German cemetery where Waffen SS were buried, saying, "That place is not your place. Your place is with the victims of the SS." What Silberman ignored was that Wiesel's public pleading to Reagan bore no more results than Jews' private pleading to FDR more than forty years before.

But the main strategy Jewish organizations use to defuse the inaction accusation is to point to today's communal "unity" as the fundamental difference between past and present. Acknowledging disunity as the core flaw of the wartime community and pointing to how dangerous it was and is, they can even turn the attacks on their wartime predecessors to good advantage by justifying their own suppression of criticism on grounds that dissent incites/foments "disunity." That is why Rabbi Eugene Borowitz could write that critics in the community are so often accused of "starting another Holocaust."

❧ The Jewish establishment organizations were very successful in their objective of convincing most Jews that they would be more effective in a crisis than their wartime predecessors were. Somehow most Jews did not notice how this claim was disproved during the juntas' reign of terror in Argentina (1976–83), when about thirty thousand citizens, among them about two thousand to three thousand Jews, were "disappeared," that is, murdered.

There was no political action, not even verbal protest, by any American Jewish organization, with the exception of the ADL, which also worked to rescue some of the prisoners. The AJCongress, unlike its activist Canadian counterpart, was silent. The AJCommittee carried on its long-discredited policy of shtadlanut, actually holding meetings with junta generals who ran concentration camps and charnelhouses. To add insult to injury, its magazine, *Commentary,* took the lead in publishing scurrilous and libelous diatribes against former Argentine political prisoner Jacobo Timerman.

The aim of *Commentary*'s Neo-Conservatives (NeoCons) was to prove that Timerman and other Jewish prisoners and disappeared people had not suffered because they were Jews. This, of course, was contrary to the reality; being Jewish, noted Timerman at the time, was "a category of guilt," and anti-Semitism was central to the juntas' ideology. Nevertheless, alleging that Timerman's and other Jews' suffering was not related to anti-Semitism allowed the NeoCons to validate the juntas' denial of anti-Semitism. This enabled them to dismiss the need to take action to help Argentine Jews and to fight against the regime's atrocities in general at a time when such a struggle could have saved lives, wrote Murray Zuckoff in 1981.

REINFORCING THE RESCUERS

The glorification of rescuers—the thousands of European non-Jews who risked (and sometimes lost) their lives to save individual Jews—demonstrates the continued vitality of the secularized rescue fantasy despite everything that happened in the Holocaust.

It is, of course, ethical and fitting to honor rescuers like Raoul Wallenberg, who should be acclaimed a hero of all humanity—and awarded a posthumous Nobel Peace Prize—for saving thousands of Hungarian Jews. But some of the glorification of rescuers seems unconsciously motivated by the need to provide public reinforcement to them as an incentive to other non-Jews to engage in such decent behavior in the future . . . if and when . . .

By contrast, Jewish rescuers receive no honors. A 1991 conference of and for Jews who were hidden as children during the war, for example, honored only non-Jewish rescuers. No mention was made of the work of Recha Freier, who started Youth Aliyah in Germany and Henrietta Szold who expanded the project; Ruth Kluger in Romania; Rabbi Michael Weissmandel and Gisi Fleischmann in Slovakia; the OSE (*Oeuvre de Secours aux Enfants*) and Jewish Scout movement in France; and the parachutists from Eretz Israel, to cite but a few. Even the term *rescuer* applies only to non-Jews.

❧ Behind the glorification of (the non-Jewish) rescuers is a feeling among Jews of unfathomable terror and immutable despair that they are not really regarded as part of the human race. This makes the rescuers and their actions very unusual. If the rescuees were not Jews, there would be nothing unusual about others' treating them as human beings whose lives deserved to be saved. Of all the nations on the planet, only Israel overwhelms nonnationals with gratitude because they behaved as ethical human beings toward individuals of its group; honors them with medals, trees, and ceremonies at *Yad Vashem* (Hebrew for, lit., memorial and name; the official Holocaust Martyrs and Heroes Remembrance Authority); and calls them heroes. (No European country honors its own nationals who rescued Jewish compatriots.) If Jews feel they have to validate non-Jews for treating them like human beings, it means that they do not really expect to be treated like human beings. (Every conscious Jew longs to ask her or his non-Jewish friends, "Would you hide me?"—and suppresses the question for fear of hearing the sounds of silence.)

By contrast, the anger most Jews are able to express at the foreign bystanders and collaborators is actually a healthy phenomenon: It embodies the concept that Jews *are* real people who have every right to expect to be treated as such.

◆ The new focus on *individual* rescuers seems to imply that after the Holocaust, Jews no longer expect rescue from "enlightened"/liberal nations or movements. This is certainly true in regard to the attitude of the Israelis, who believe in their secret hearts that "the whole world is against us." Although American Jews have never confronted and repudiated the secularized fantasy of rescue by liberal nations, their new focus on individual rescuers points to pervasive despair over the possibility of developing alternative collective survival strategies, such as making alliances with other minority groups.

The despair derives in large part from what Jews regard as their rejection/ abandonment by African Americans, some of whom regard Jewish discussion of the Holocaust as a ploy/plot to upstage *their* oppression. Nation of Islam leader Reverend Louis Farrakhan, for example, said in 1985 that blacks "will never forget who sold [*sic*] our fathers into slavery. Don't push your six million down our throat when we lost 100 million." Others, including at one point the Reverend Jesse Jackson, say they are "tired" of hearing about the Holocaust. So are many white Americans.

Ironically, among African Americans, for whom the horrors of slavery are still fresh, and among southerners who have not forgotten Sherman's arson of Atlanta, there are many who do not understand why Jews are in pain over mass murders that took place just a few decades ago. Many Christians, who anguish over the crucifixion of one poor Jewish boy two thousand years ago, see no contradiction in voicing the sentiment that the murder of six million Jews took place "long ago and far away."

Nor do most Americans understand why Jews feel it is still imperative to bring perpetrators of crimes against humanity to trial. They feel that Nazi-hunter Simon Wiesenthal's pursuit of doddering old men who "only" ran gas chambers or "only" shot a few stray Jews is so relentlessly vengeful that it makes *Les Misérables'* Javier look like a sloth. Jews have apparently not been able to articulate the concept expressed so well by Lawrence Wechsler after the restoration of democracy in several Latin American countries in the 1980s. The "rehabilitation of a tortured society," he said, must involve the disclosure and acknowledgment of the truth and the "settling of accounts" with the criminal torturers and murderers through the justice process.

❧ Some notable Christian theologians (for example, Father Edward Flannery) have engaged in serious soul-searching about the role their coreligionists played during the Holocaust. Wyman, who calls the Holocaust a "Christian tragedy ... a failure of Christian civilization," said, however, that "most Christians are oblivious—they don't even know they failed."

The ease with which leading Christian personalities make insensitive comments about the Holocaust reinforces the feeling among Jews that most Christians have not really wrestled with the issue—or changed their behavior accordingly. In 1989, for example, South African Archbishop Desmond Tutu emerged from a visit to Yad Vashem. Apparently unscathed by what he had seen in its museum and oblivious of the pain of his Israeli hosts, he called for Jews to say: "We pray for those who made it happen, help us to forgive them and help us so that we in our turn will not make others suffer," which he charged Israel with doing to the Palestinians. Also in that banner year, Solidarity leader (later Poland's president) Lech Walesa asserted during a visit to the U.S. that "Auschwitz does not belong to the Jews" and complained that repeated Jewish accusations about the recrudescence of Polish anti-Semitism were unfair, exaggerated, divisive, and—in a demonstration of his firm grip on priorities—"could tarnish the mood for [U.S.] investment."

The glorification of rescuers allows Jews to "prove" that they are not tarring *all* non-Jews with the anti-Semitic brush. At the very same time, honoring those pitifully few non-Jewish individuals who—along with the Danish nation, the regime of King Boris of Bulgaria, the village of Le Chambon (France), and the Belgian, Dutch, and Italian rescue networks—did not betray their own humanity makes a very subtle point about their rarity.

Maybe the point is too subtle.

BLAMING THE VICTIM

American Jews have long been obsessed with the myth that European Jews went passively "like sheep to the slaughter" and did not resist, or did not resist "enough."

This is a slander/libel directed only at Jews. Nobody has ever blamed the Armenians, Cambodians, Bosnians, or Rwandans for being murdered. Gypsies, homosexuals, Jehovah's Witnesses, and the three million Soviet POWs—trained soldiers—murdered by the Nazis have never been held accountable for their own deaths, either.

It is mind-boggling that American Jews who are terrified to give up invisibility because being out of the closet might "provoke" anti-Semitism have the chutzpah to accuse European Jews of not resisting "enough" when the entire physical and logistical power of a totalitarian state was hurled against them.

The Jews of Europe were the target of a secret, highly organized and mechanized mass murder operation to which the Germans were even willing to sacrifice victory in the war. Unlike other nations, they had no homeland, no army, leadership, or government-in-exile, and were scattered among hostile and/or indifferent populations. Their Resistance movement, noted historian Nora Levin, was the only one that did not receive from the Allied forces the arms, funds, and technical assistance without which partisan and underground activity was impossible. That physical resistance by Jews did take place in ghettos, forests, and death camps under these circumstances is nothing short of miraculous.

Moreover, to define resistance only as taking up arms—the masculinist definition—is wrong not only ethically but also politically. Since the Nazi plan was to murder all the Jews, doesn't *whatever* Jews did to try to prevent death—from organizing soup kitchens to smuggling medicine to forging identity papers to performing abortions—constitute resistance? Doesn't sustaining the will to live among people suffering hunger, cold, disease, bereavement, terror, and mental exhaustion by conducting prayer services, schools, concerts, and theatrical performances constitute resistance? Doesn't the courage and resourcefulness inherent in all these efforts constitute resistance?

◆ It is obvious why some non-Jews might wish to believe the passivity myth (aside from ignorance of the facts): "If Jews were cowards, if they denied reality, participated in their own destruction," wrote psychologist Frances Grossman, "then the Holocaust is a Jewish issue and need not concern the rest of humanity." But why would American Jews, especially the men, need to believe the passivity myth?

One reason is that blaming the victim eliminates the necessity of analyzing the historical conditions that caused and allowed genocide, *and their implications.* The second reason is that focusing on the victims' "passivity" drains off some of the guilt felt by older Jews for having failed to be effective in saving the lives of European Jews. Most of the guilt remains, however, and it accounts in part for why American Jews do not glorify the armed resisters or even publicize their heroism. For if some Jews under impossible conditions managed to place mines and blow up trains, why couldn't American Jews have engaged in non-life-threatening political action for rescue during the war? The guilt and shame account for the absence, to date, of any biography, film, or video emanating from a major American Jewish organization on any of the Resistance fighters or movements.

The third reason for believing the passivity myth relates to the men's ongoing conflict over physical aggression and their worry over the general society's image of them as wimps and cowards. Underneath the passivity charge is unacknowledged anger at the East European Jews for having "abandoned" them. This is how children usually interpret the death of a parent, and, indeed, the East European Jews were the physical and spiritual parents and grandparents of American Jews. But American Jewish men also feel the East European Jews "abandoned" them by not serving as a (parental) model of physical resistance (even as their own fathers do not). This calls attention to Jewish men's nonviolence, making them feel even more vulnerable and their image even more wimpy now that "the world" knows their guilty little secret.

❧ Focusing on the European Jews' "passivity," however, causes the men extreme anxiety about what *they* would have done/would do if faced with such an on-slaught. Many have desperately tried to uncover some difference between them and the East European Jews, their ancestors, some fatal flaw in their cultural be-havior patterns that "invited/allowed" victimization. To alleviate the anxiety and rationalize their assimilationism at one and the same time, some assimilationist American Jewish men wish to believe that the "fatal flaw" was the East European Jews' adherence to traditional Jewish values, particularly nonviolence. Get rid of these values and take on at last those of the majority culture, especially physical aggression, and American Jewish men would finally be able to be "real" men and, by implication, defenders.

What flows from this false premise is that traditional Jewish values are bad for Jewish survival and assimilation is good. (They slough over the fact that assim-ilationist West European Jews were also murdered, because this would entail their coming to grips with the failure of assimilationism as a survival strategy.) If assim-ilation is good, then everything that goes with it—the assimilationist contract, in-visibility, faith in American exceptionalism—constitutes an appropriate response to their current reality, and *it need not be analyzed.*

❧ The use of the charge of the passivity of East European Jewry to justify assimi-lation is exhibited most egregiously in the state-of-the-art blame-the-victim theo-ries of Bruno Bettelheim. He attributed the success of the genocide to the Jews' *"unwillingness to fight* for themselves, fight for their lives and for the lives of those they loved" (italics mine). In a 1960 essay, Bettelheim attacked Anne Frank's fam-ily for planning to stay together as a family even though it was known to be "the hardest way to go underground." His arguments that nonviolence and a close and warm family life were what got the Frank family and the rest of the Six Million killed are a vicious assimilationist assault on the traditional Jewish value system.

The 1978 "Holocaust" TV miniseries, created by four Jewish men, represents the quintessential expression through drama of this "Jewish values are bad/assim-ilation is good" concept and shows how it emerges from the men's deepest long-ings. "Holocaust" contrasts the values and behavior of the East European Jewish masses, who are intensely Jewish, with those of its hero, Rudi Weiss, who admits that he is "not sure I'm much of a Jew." And that is an understatement.

The creators of "Holocaust" made Rudi the embodiment of their own assimila-tionist yearnings in several important respects. As the film opens, we see sweet, brave (and very cute) Rudi being more interested in soccer and adept at street fight-ing than at hitting the books. He subsequently abandons his mother and sister in

Germany *without guilt* and takes to the road to escape the Nazis. He then becomes a partisan, saying at one point, "They won't kill me without a fight," which scriptwriter Gerald Green cited as "the moral" of the miniseries. Rudi's ability to fight and to *separate from his family* are what make him an assimilationist model for American Jewish men.

Having contrasted the spiritual resistance of the East European Jewish masses with the physical resistance of hero Rudi Weiss, the film shows the inevitable consequences of both behaviors: the masses go "passively" to their death, but Rudi survives. This proves that Assimilation Saves: It is "good for the Jews."

At the same time, the miniseries conveys the assimilationist message that Jewish survival requires women to be subservient (another of the men's yearnings). The stubbornness of the Weiss family matriarch, Berta—the strong ("controlling") woman reminiscent of the mothers of the East European shtetl and the immigrant generations who carried whole families on their backs—is blamed in the series for preventing the family from leaving Germany until it is too late. (The charge distorts the reality, revealed by Claudia Koontz's research, that in many cases it was the women who pressed their husbands to get their families to leave Germany.) Berta's behavior proves that a domineering woman always leaves a trail of dire ruin in her wake. Rudi's lover, Helena, who tries to hold him back from partisan missions, represents the women (primarily mothers) who have instilled in the men a fear of physical aggression. Her behavior cannot be rewarded, and Helena, too, dies—significantly, when trying to do the "man's work" of being a fighter.

❧ Assimilationist men's need to glorify assimilation as a survival strategy is another reason that the community they dominate has failed to honor armed resisters. For the reality is that those Jews who engaged in armed resistance—youth primarily in Zionist and leftist movements—were steeped in Jewish culture and were deeply committed to its value system. Although raised, as were other traditional Jews, to reject physical aggression, they were able to engage in it when it was altruistic—necessary for the defense of their nation. This means that a man need not give up Jewish values, including nonviolence, in daily life during ordinary times in order to have access to the ability to engage in physical aggression when group needs demand it *in extremis*. In other words, the rationalization that Assimilation Saves because it is a prerequisite for physical national self-defense is meretricious. The truth is the exact opposite. As historian Yehuda Bauer wrote, "Those who retained some modicum of Jewish beliefs, traditions or values, whether religious or secular, usually were best able to resist the terror. For example, it may turn out to have been no accident that the 'most Jewish' Jews, those of Eastern Poland, provided a high proportion of unarmed and armed resistance."

Finally, honoring fighters would also require calling attention to the fact that women played a key role in the Resistance—as couriers, scouts, saboteurs, partisans, and rescuers. Honoring women in the Resistance would, of course, fly in the face of assimilationist men's wish for Jewish women to be subservient.

VICARIOUS MARTYRDOM AND VICARIOUS VICTIMHOOD

While the Orthodox see the Six Million as martyrs simply because they died for being Jews, Al Kiddush HaShem, other Jews have unconscious motivations for defining them thus. Martyrs, by definition, are people who died for a cause or belief they had championed and whose death had/has meaning. Therefore, once the Six Million are viewed and identified with as martyrs, the whole "sheep-to-slaughter" obsession drops away. The passivity charge can no more be lobbed at Jewish martyrs of the Holocaust than it can be hurled at early Christian martyrs of Roman tyranny.

Moreover, once the Six Million are defined as martyrs, it is impossible to see them as the exemplification of "nonaggressive" behavior that calls attention to similar "unmasculine" attributes of American Jewish men.

Finally, by identifying with those whose martyrdom resulted from having lived by the traditional Jewish values—that is, by "vicarious martyrdom"—American Jews can feel legitimized and validated for adhering to the eroded elements of these values that seeped into their behavior during childhood socialization. They need this validation because present-day American society glorifies terminal narcissism and downgrades interdependence; defines altruism as "codependency" requiring "recovery"; glorifies physical aggression by men; and accepts "compassion fatigue" as an excuse for turning away from the downtrodden. In short, it denigrates female/Jewish values. Validation of these values—and for the men, nonviolence in particular—can override/offset or at least mitigate the denigration and thereby boost their self-esteem.

The catch is that, unlike the pattern that obtains when Jews use Israel for vicarious validation, the martyrs, obviously, are dead. The only way they can, as it were, fulfill the function of embodying and validating these values is if accounts of their martyrdom are kept alive by constant repetition. This is cultural vampirism in its most shameful incarnation.

✎ The American Jews who identify with the Six Million primarily as victims (by definition, people who lost control over their lives) exhibit thereby symptoms of their anxieties about their own situation in America. Having placed their hopes in a liberal society that is, above all else, stable and lawful, they feel acutely vulnerable, especially because of the escalation of verbal expressions of anti-Semitism from both the left and the right (of which more presently) and the sharp rise in hate crimes against Jews as well as against African, Hispanic, and Asian Americans and homosexuals in recent years.

The number of anti-Semitic incidents has risen steadily, from 49 in 1978 to 1,867 in 1993, according to the ADL. And the 1991 incidents involved more attacks on Jewish individuals than on their property for the first time. The anti-Semitic incidents at American colleges increased from 114 on 60 campuses in 1992 to 122 on 81 campuses in 1993. At Queens College of CUNY in 1992, cats stolen from the animal laboratories were found dead in toilets; written on the bathroom walls was this warning: "We're going to do to Jews what we did to the cats."

But Americans Jews did not need statistics to tell them that hate crimes were escalating. They got their rude wake-up call in August 1991, when the Crown Heights disturbances took place. After a Hassidic motorist accidentally killed a black child, a mob of young blacks shouting, "Let's get a Jew!" lynched a yeshiva student, Yankel Rosenbaum. The rioters swept through the streets for four days, screaming "Heil Hitler!" and throwing bricks, rocks, and bottles through the windows of Jewish homes. The police did not act to stop the riot in the first days and even failed to respond to Jews' frantic calls to 911.

Feeling themselves victims, and needing some recognition of this status by/in the general society, Jews run up against the recycled Judeophobic myths portraying them as victimizers, as powerful and controlling. There seems to be no middle ground here: One is either a victim/powerless or a victimizer/powerful; each image is the flip side of the other.

☙ But there is another, more important reason why Jews identify with the Six Million as "vicarious victims" of the Holocaust: to use this identification as a visa to gain admittance into the constituency of groups defining their members as victims and thereby to garner the benefits of victimhood status.

The prime entitlement victimhood bestows is the right to express anger publicly and to demand a hearing on its causes. Jewish expression of anger toward/among non-Jews is usually precluded by the internalized classic survival strategy of refraining from antagonizing possible protectors and from "provoking" potential attackers.

Jews are also unconsciously aware of what sociologist Arlie Hochschild called "the doctrine of feelings": The importance of feelings varies in close correspondence with the importance of the person who feels. The lower the status, the more our manner of seeing and feeling is subject to being discredited and the less believable it becomes. Hochschild elaborates here that the feelings of the lower-status party may be discounted by considering them irrational "and hence dismissible." The belief that women are "more emotional" is used to invalidate their feelings, which are then interpreted not as a response to real events but as a sign of personal instability. Many women try to make up for the "unequal weighing of feelings" by expressing them "with more force, so as to get them treated with seriousness." But the harder they try, the more likely are their efforts to be discounted as one more example of excess "emotionalism." Hochschild's explanation of how this "doctrine" applies to women applies, as well, to Jews and other out-groups.

It was partly because of the "doctrine of feelings" that reports from Jewish sources about the mass murders were discounted by the general media, and most newspapers did not bother to check out such information. Similarly, Jews' expressions of horror and grief and their calls for rescue were not taken seriously. Lipstadt cites how British officials dismissed eyewitness accounts of massacres in 1942 with the words, "The Jews have spoiled their case by *laying it on too thick* for years past." Similarly, another official complained in 1944 about the time wasted by the Foreign Office in dealing with "these *wailing* Jews" (italics mine). The Jewish establishment "leaders" may have unconsciously felt that mass meetings during the war had to be conducted "tastefully" precisely because they feared to appear "overemotional."

Jews, aware of this "doctrine," tend to suppress the expression of anger because *the greater the intensity of emotion, the greater the degree of discreditation.*

However, it seems that *victimhood status cancels out or mitigates the "doctrine of feelings,"* and is the chief entitlement conferred by this status. Since Jews are not allowed to identify as victims or as an oppressed minority, they identify as "vicarious victims" in order to express anger among non-Jews and not have the cause of the anger dismissed or discredited.

But there is a catch: They can do so only if everybody else is aware of their "vicarious victimhood" status. Since this is derived from the Holocaust, it is primarily by linking to the Holocaust their anger over some other issue that their victim entitlement can be activated. The JDL was the first Jewish group to employ this linkage with its "Never Again!" slogan. (Many blacks regard the linkage as a cynical tactic to allow Jews to benefit illegitimately from victim entitlement. This is another reason some African Americans get furious when Jews talk about the Holocaust.) The linkage strategy means that Jews' anger over a specific group issue or concern tends not to be expressed among non-Jews without the Holocaust's being invoked to "legitimize" it.

This is a prime reason why the Holocaust is usually cited by American Jews to justify the State of Israel instead of letting the case for its right to live stand on its own very sturdy feet. This Holocaust-linked argument, noted Yad Vashem Museum director Yitzchak Mais, distorts the reality that Zionism existed for over half a century before the Holocaust took place and created "an infrastructure that allowed the survivors to be absorbed." The implication that the Holocaust caused the creation of Israel allows Arab propagandists not only to dismiss the Zionist movement along with its concept that Israel is the instrumentality of Jewish liberation. It allows them as well to portray the Arabs as victims of the Holocaust along the lines of "Europe threw you up and now *we* have to pay the bill."

Because the linkage strategy allows Jews to express anger publicly, they tend to use/abuse it. It is far easier to picture themselves or Israel as victims than as opponents of some policy or practice, such as media coverage of Israel. (Portraying Israel as victim, though, infuriates the Israelis.) And it is much easier to use the linkage strategy rather than to challenge the idea that members of out-groups can demand to be heard only if they present themselves as victims; this leads them to cultivate permanent victimhood rather than strive for self-liberation.

It is an unconscionable exploitation of the Holocaust to graft it onto other issues to legitimize the expression of anger about those other concerns.

THE HOLOCAUST INDUSTRY

Some Jews identify themselves as survivors of the Holocaust. This means that their very existence is endowed with meaning as a triumph over an enemy who tried to annihilate the entire nation. But the subtext of vicarious survivalism is that it legitimizes the fact that they are living Jews and allows them to ignore addressing how they are living *as* Jews. To quote Woody Allen, "Just showing up is enough."

Vicarious survivalism accounts in part for the proliferation of Holocaust memorials, museums, and centers in the U.S. A psychological motive beyond the simple and ethical wish to honor the memory of the Six Million is operating here: the need to make a statement that, in the words of the Jewish Partisans' Hymn, "We Are Here"—in other words, vicarious visibility.

The memorials override the visibility taboo because it is foreign dead Jews who are visible (these are the same Jews who, when they were alive, were invisible in Allied statements on war crimes and in conferences on "refugees" before and during the war). For some superassimilationist Jews, even the retrospective visibility the memorials provide is too much. Henry Kissinger, for example, warned that the U.S. Holocaust Museum on the Mall in Washington, D.C., is "*too high a profile*" for American Jews and is likely only to "reignite anti-Semitism" (italics mine).

The exploitation of the Six Million to provide American Jews vicarious visibility and, at the same time, highlight their vicarious victimhood also explains why there are so many TV "barbed-wire extravaganzas" (Robert Alter's words), mostly by Jewish producers, directors, and/or writers. Dead/dying Jews do not trigger stereotypes of Jews as pushy, controlling, dominating, powerful. The films and museums thus serve to "prove" the Judeophobic stereotypes . . . dead wrong. Actually, it is frightening to consider that Holocaust films may be so popular precisely because they show Jews being murdered en masse. The "Holocaust" miniseries was dangerous to Jewish survival precisely because its footage and photos of mass shootings and gassings were accompanied by Nazi commentary about how easy it was to murder Jews.

The American-made feature films and TV dramas on the Holocaust are careful not to go too far and actually overturn the visibility taboo. Neither the 1957 American movie about Anne Frank nor any other American feature film on the Holocaust shows Jews living vibrant, intensively Jewish lives before their deaths or—and this is especially true of "Holocaust" and the 1982 TV movie of *The Wall*—coming to grips with what it meant to be Jewish at a time when it was a death sentence. The anxiety about violating the visibility taboo explains why the director of the Jewish Film Advisory Committee (which monitored movies) hailed the director of the Anne Frank film for having given the story "a 'universal' meaning and *appeal;* it could have been an *outdated Jewish tragedy* if ... more *emotionally* handled–even a *Jewish 'wailing wall'* ..." (italics mine). (This comment is also a good example of the attempt to cope with the "doctrine of feelings.")

Ironically, Jewish moviemakers striving for Jewish cultural invisibility in the films they make on the Holocaust sometimes face charges, such as the one expressed by critic Richard Geis, that "a strong Zionist/Jewish influence" in the industry ensures the production of Holocaust dramas to keep the U.S. government feeling guilty and therefore continuing to dole out funds to Israel.

The profusion of Holocaust memorials/museums and films should be contrasted with the absence of living memorials–educational and cultural projects, including movies, which show Jews of the past and present, in the U.S. and abroad, as visibly distinctive, ethnically and culturally. As playwright/screenwriter David Mamet observed in 1991, "The only way that the Jewish experience is ever treated in American films is through the Nazi murder of the European Jews."

⤷ The proliferation of the memorials/museums/centers as well as films, lectures, and college courses on the Holocaust testifies to the emergence of a Holocaust industry. The Holocaust has now become the new Jewish glamour project, triggering the usual battles between Jewish organizations for turf jurisdiction. The Holocaust museums/centers, with a few exceptions, engage in a "ghoulish competition" for artifacts; they pay more attention to the building process than to content, purpose, and effectiveness, said Mais. The UJA and other fund-raisers continue to cite the Holocaust in appeals for contributions for Jewish olim from the ex-Soviet Union and for Israel. UJA "missions" usually begin with a now-obligatory hegira to death camp sites to soften up Big Givers en route to Israel.

Anything goes in exploiting the Holocaust. That is why in 1988 the Associates Division of the New York Holocaust Memorial Committee invited guests to "rock & roll the night away at The Hot Rod" in New York. Festivities included "cocktails, hors d'oeuvre, dessert, dancing and more (dietary laws observed)" at $100 to $125 a throw.

There were no public protests.

THE HOLOCAUST AS A SOURCE OF IDENTITY

For some American Jews, the Holocaust has come to provide the only Jewish content in their lives–the only instrumentality for their identifying as Jews and for "feeling Jewish."

To understand why, we must look at the context–the environment–in which this phenomenon occurs. The Jewish movement of the late sixties provided many Jews with authentic Jewish content for the first time in their lives and created a thirst for more. When it collapsed, Jews turned to the one element from movement days that had both reality and emotional depth: Holocaust consciousness.

Holocaust consciousness also came to permeate virtually everything in Jewish life because most of the existing communal institutions seized upon it to fill the vacuum caused by their lack of authentic Jewish content and/or spiritual substance. By the latter part of the 1970s, the atmosphere faced by Jews coming of age was already permeated with Holocaust consciousness. The Holocaust became the nexus point at which they and older Jews who were beginning to explore their Jewish identity encountered Jewishness. Composer Steve Reich, for example, after "rediscovering" his Jewish identity, based his first Jewish musical piece on Holocaust death trains. Artist Judy Chicago's first Jewish work of art is *The Holocaust Project.* Film director Steven Spielberg's first movie with Jewish content, *Schindler's List,* is the true story of a Catholic rescuer; when filming it in Cracow in 1993, he told a reporter, "This is truly my roots."

Moreover, nothing else existed in the 1970s, when this phenomenon started and spread, that could provide authentic content for young Jews to build a Jewish identity with. The havurah movement was small and elitist; Jewish feminism was in its infancy. Orthodoxy had authentic substance but its leaders alienated most Jews with their rigidity, their arrogance in insisting it was the only "real" Judaism, their failure to address social and political issues, plus this religious movement's discrimination against women.

Israel did not seem to have much to say to younger American Jews about Jewish identity, either, especially after it downgraded the kibbutz and labor movement, long the embodiment of female/Jewish values, in its rush to become a carbon copy of middle-class America. And when the sterling armor of the heroic warriors seemed to become dulled with the tarnish of the betrayal of Jewish ethics—for example, in the invasion of Lebanon—it became harder and harder for many Jewish youth to look to Israel even for vicarious Jewishness. How could Israel be Jewish for them when it was engaging in "un-Jewish" behavior?

With nothing on the scene to touch their hearts and souls, many young Americans Jews felt dead as Jews. If an individual is paralyzed in an accident, she might be very glad to begin to feel acute pain in her legs. If one has suffered from amnesia, he might be thrilled to retrieve a painful memory from the past. If someone has been depressed and then has an unhappy romance, she may welcome the emotional pain because, in Alice's words to Joe in *Room at the Top,* "I'm alive now, all of me's alive. I'm feeling things I'd forgotten. The nerve's regenerating. It hurts sometimes. I don't care."

For Jews who have suffered from an absence of Jewish emotion in their lives, and from ethnic amnesia, the arousal of painful feelings and painful ethnic memories may be a way for them to feel Jewishly alive. They will jab themselves again and again with the knifepoint of Holocaust horrors to hit the nerve ending, to keep it responding. It means the nerve is regenerating, and they are Jewishly alive.

❧ The question remains, however, as to why so many Jews identify only with the deaths of East European Jews and not with their vibrant prewar culture. The reason is that focusing on the intense Jewish lives of East European Jews before the Holocaust would be too disturbing to those Jews who do not wish to confront why their own cultural lives are so barren but who certainly do not wish to change them.

To assuage their guilt on this score, they engage in shtetl nostalgia. This is a form of tokenism by which they admit into their lives at periodic intervals a few retouched portrayals of East European life that make them feel connected to it and therefore able to believe they have not abandoned that culture. The portrayals are so sentimentalized/romanticized, however, that there is no danger that they might arouse anxieties about any similarities with the realities of their own condition. For example, the original Sholem Aleichem stories about Tevye and the 1939 Maurice Schwartz film of that name have many thought-provoking things to say to American Jews about the reality of anti-Semitism, vulnerability, and Jewish courage and perseverance in the face of disaster. The *Fiddler on the Roof* musical debittered and sugarcoated that reality and infused it with artificial flavor(ing)s to make it palatable to Jewish consumers. It goes down easily and painlessly.

Fiddler and other sentimentalized shtetl sagas domesticate Jewish ethnicity, making it seem not "clannish" but cozy and therefore safe to exhibit to non-Jews. They present Jewish culture as a precious family heirloom that can be taken out of the closet from time to time but cannot actually be put to practical use in contemporary life. It is precisely because shtetl nostalgia portrays Jewish culture as dysfunctional and quaint that it is such a safe indulgence.

❧ The need of American Jews to agonize over the horrors of the Holocaust to feel Jewishly alive, for vicarious martyrdom, and as part of the obsessive review necessary in the mourning process are not the only reasons for the immersion—and, in some cases, submersion—in the atrocities. An additional, unconscious motivation is that by dwelling on how efficiently the machine of mass murder worked, older Jews can convince themselves that there was nothing much they could have done (to get the U.S. government) to stop it. Another motivation for immersion in the horrors is the need for self-torment as a form of penance for the "abandonment" of East European Jewry (older Jews) and of its culture (younger Jews). For the Jewish establishment, American Jews' immersion in the horror stories is a form of damage control—of directing Holocaust consciousness into this channel and away from accusations (and analysis).

Finally, immersion in Holocaust horrors serves to provide American Jews a little relief from their anxieties about their own situation. The immersion serves a psychological function somewhat analogous to the watching of horror movies. The more American Jews dwell on the atrocities and the more horrific they are, the more palliative is the contrast with their own situation: What is happening here is not as bad as what happened there, so "let's not panic." Immersion in the horrors of the Holocaust thus reinforces rather than challenges American exceptionalism and justifies the resistance to analysis.

THE POLITICAL IMPERATIVE OF ANALYSIS

America is, indeed, different in many ways from the oppressive and toxic exiles Jews have lived in, especially in Eastern Europe. But certain classic social and economic dynamics do obtain here. American Jews need to look carefully at how these operate rather than ignoring them because they do not exactly resemble those that obtained in stage two in other countries where Jews once lived or because they do not precisely replicate those that preceded the Holocaust.

Silberman, once asked about the parallels with 1932 Germany, stated point-blank, "Short of changes in American society so profound as to endanger American democracy as a whole, 'it' [another Holocaust] won't happen." But looking at the harbingers of such "profound changes" is precisely what neither the Jewish establishment nor the Jewish public wishes to do. Instead they operate on the hypothesis that America is an exception to the social laws that govern the rise and growth of fascism.

It is crucial to recognize that virulent popular anti-Semitism is not necessary for genocide to succeed. Once a criminal party takes state power, noted Yehuda Bauer, most citizens will go along—as also happened in Argentina under the juntas—out of respect for the "law," out of terror for their lives, out of plain indifference, or simply because they have no idea how to resist.

A prime lesson from the Holocaust, then, is to be aware of—*and change*—the conditions that could allow such a criminal party to successfully attain state power, as it did in Germany. Under Germany's chaotic economic and political predicament in the 1930s, the ruling class saw it could no longer hold power except through fascism. The desperation of the public, after the collapse of the left-wing alternative to the chaos, was so severe that it preferred a fascist party—which promised to solve the country's economic problems—to the status quo. All other matters, such as the rest of the party's agenda, were "non-data": of little or no importance then or later, when it began to implement them.

From this disaster one must conclude that it is a prime necessity to strengthen the sociopolitical "immune system"—the public's commitment to democracy and the people's empowerment—so the society would be able to overcome conditions of economic upheaval and social desperation and resist the cancer of fascism.

The "immune system" in America is weakened by the inability of many citizens to perceive/acknowledge that there are no individual solutions. Traditional American individualism is reinforced by the power structure's promotion of malignant ("me first") narcissism. Many Americans who do believe in collective solutions define *collective* narrowly, in terms of their own ethnic or lifestyle group (identity politics) or by a focus on one issue, such as environmentalism or consumer rights.

This splintering/Balkanization impedes the emergence of any viable left-wing alternative with a *national* program that could mobilize people to try to solve together the seemingly intractable problems of crime, drugs, AIDS, racism and bigotry, poverty, homelessness, environmental destruction, deterioration of the educational system, economic depression, and the unraveling of the social fabric. Meanwhile, an array of conservative groups (some on the religious right), which lack a central program to solve these ills, divert attention from the country's real crises with campaigns on issues such as school prayer and opposition to reproductive choice and gay rights. The religious right, aiming to remold America in its image, targets the gay and feminist movements and their liberal supporters—portrayed as immoral and anti-family—as the cause of the country's malaise and decline. Its campaigns have three purposes. One is an organizing strategy: to build a power base by providing alienated and disaffected individuals an enemy they can blame for their condition and join together to oppose. The second is to discredit the philosophy of tolerance and pluralism that is so basic to American democracy by associating it with the advocacy of anti-family values. The third purpose is to make intolerance and repression respectable by portraying them as necessary weapons in a crusade for morality.

⁂ It is against this background that changes are occurring in the expression of anti-Semitism that need to be seriously analyzed and addressed.

Expressions of hate are coming at Jews from all sides of the political spectrum. On the right is the Ku Klux Klan; the "Identity Church," which preaches that Jews are "children of Satan"; the neo-Nazis; and the neo-Nazi skinheads, who have been implicated in murders and other violent crimes. Calling these skinheads "the most dangerous bigots in this country today," Morris Dees of Klanwatch reported in 1993 that they are being recruited by white supremacists (such as the White Aryan Resistance) and operate in thirty states with about thirty-five hundred members.

All of these groups are becoming more closely allied and better organized; some are well armed. Most of them support Holocaust-denial propaganda. The founder of the Liberty Lobby, which the WJC's Institute of Jewish Affairs calls the major anti-Semitic propaganda organization in the U.S., was also a key figure in the revisionist (that is, Holocaust-denying) Institute for Historical Review. New mass media technologies (public access cable) and styles (radio call-in shows, TV talk shows) have spread the views of bigots far and wide, as have computer bulletin boards, recordings, and telephone hot lines.

Black ultranationalists, including academics, have also been spewing forth anti-Semitic bilge, which African American intellectuals and political leaders, with a few exceptions, have not repudiated publicly. Farrakhan has called Judaism a "gutter religion," has said that "Hitler was a great man" and that Jews were "sucking the blood" of the black community, and has charged Jews with "giving us Aunt Jemima roles in Hollywood" and with having run the slave trade. This latter lie was enthusiastically endorsed by, among others, 1992 New York senatorial hopeful Reverend Al Sharpton and Leonard Jeffries, who chairs the black studies department at City College in New York. Jeffries charged that Jews in Hollywood colluded with the Italian Mafia to "put together a system of destruction of Black people." Steve Cokely, a former mayoral aide in Chicago, tells his audiences that Jews are building gas ovens to burn blacks. Farrakhan, Jeffries, Cokely and a host of Holocaust-deniers are invited regularly to lecture on the college circuit.

The campus has also become a prime site for vicious attacks on Jews by students and academics who define themselves as left-wing, including anti-Zionists and many of the proponents of multiculturalism, a.k.a. "a curriculum of inclusion." In the campus struggle over the creation of a multicultural curriculum, Jews, playing their classic cultural intermediary role, are trapped between the establishment and the rebels, with the usual adverse effects of being regarded with suspicion and hostility by both parties. Advocates of multiculturalism perceive Jewish academics, who are preponderant in university history departments, as proponents of "Eurocentrism." Attacking them in this oppressor surrogate role, multiculturalists ignore the invisibility of Jews in the "Eurocentric" curriculum.

They also deny that Jews are an ethnic group and a minority and that they have a unique culture, said Evelyn Torton Beck, a professor of Jewish studies. She reported facing considerable resistance to her attempts to introduce the Jewish heritage into the new multicultural curriculum. *Jews are thus condemned to invisibility in both the "Eurocentric" and the "inclusive" [sic] curricula.*

Jews on the left who support a "curriculum of inclusion" of African, Asian, and Hispanic history find themselves invisible as Jews in both the proposed new curriculum and in the struggle for it. A former Berkeley student reported in 1991 that Jews were excluded from joining *as Jews* the United Front, a local coalition advocating a multicultural curriculum, because "Jews were not perceived as oppressed."

❧ Views expressed by non-Jewish United Front members that Jews are "manipulative" and "powerful" show how accepted—and acceptable—this recycled Judeophobic myth has become. A 1978 AJCommittee survey showed that 12 percent of the American public believed "Jews have too much political influence" and in 1980, that figure had declined to 8 percent. An ADL survey, asking the slightly differently worded question of whether Jews have "too much power," got a "yes" answer in 1964 from 11 percent of the public. In 1992 the figure was 31 percent.

In 1978 the American Jewish Committee wrote that "prejudice has become disreputable in America." But in 1993 a magazine piece noted "the degree to which expressions of hate and intolerance have become acceptable." Radio and television talk shows feature racists and anti-Semites as guests—including Holocaust-deniers (who are invited to debate survivors). This not only provides them audiences in the millions but also legitimacy. Articles and ads by Holocaust-deniers are published in college newspapers (among them those at Cornell, Duke, Michigan, and Northwestern universities). Protests by Jews against this anti-Semitic propaganda are dismissed on grounds of "academic freedom." The fact that presidential hopeful Patrick Buchanan, who wrote that Jews were not gassed at Treblinka (and has voiced other anti-Semitic and anti-Israel propaganda), spoke at the Republican Party's 1992 Convention—where he warned that the U.S. was experiencing a "religious war . . . a cultural war . . . for the soul of America"—demonstrates how reputable these views and their proponents have become.

An equal, perhaps even greater, cause for concern is that there is no body of liberal opinion that publicly, forcefully, and consistently combats anti-Semitism, as the unions and the left did in the 1930s. It is useful to recall in this connection that Conor Cruise O'Brien once wrote that the German churches might well have forced the Nazi regime to stop the Holocaust had they "spoken out against the persecution of the Jews with the same vigor as they had shown in the case of 'Euthanasia,'" the gassing of the mentally and physically disabled. Church leaders, particularly Catholic bishop Clemens August von Galen, protested publicly against this atrocity, and it was stopped after August 1941. But the clergy who condemned euthanasia from the pulpit "were effective only because they represented the public will," wrote Nathan Stoltzfus. There was obviously no strong "public will" opposing the genocide against the Jews.

❧ The aforementioned 1992 ADL survey, which measured a cluster of eleven attitudes, revealed that roughly 20 percent of Americans "hold a collection of views which are unquestionably anti-Semitic," a drop of nine percentage points since 1964. (Blacks [37 percent], though, were twice as likely as whites [17 percent] to fall into the "most anti-Semitic category.") The ADL concluded that its survey "clearly reveals that the overwhelming majority of Americans reject anti-Jewish stereotypes and accept positive statements about Jews." Neither the ADL nor any other Jewish establishment organization has attempted to explain why, if this is indeed so, expressions of anti-Semitism have become so widespread and acceptable and why the hate crimes have escalated.

Jewish establishment organizations contend that the most extreme elements are exceptions/flukes not representative of mainstream America. But the fact that the recycled myth, spread in the 1970s by right-wing hate groups, that "the Jewish bankers in the East are responsible for the bankruptcy of family farms in the Midwest" could find such easy acceptance indicates the existence of a deep swamp of prejudice, where the malarial protozoa of anti-Semitism flourish. The effective approach would be to seek to drain the swamp so the mosquitoes, the extremist hate groups, cannot breed there. Instead some Jewish organizations continue to flail at the mosquitoes one by one.

And because they regard the hate groups as flukes rather than as the most visible tip of the iceberg of anti-Semitism, they do not go beyond "monitoring" to active public protest, for instance, rallies. Another reason for the lack of activism is the Jewish establishment's anxiety that highly visible protest will give the hate groups too much attention. This could encourage the perpetrators to intensify their attacks and lead others to initiate new ones precisely in order to get (more) media attention. This anti-activist approach is reminiscent of the lesson classically taught by mothers to daughters to ignore men's harassment on the street.

◆ In dealing with anti-Semitism, American Jews are trapped between their assimilationism and their anxiety. The assimilationist contract, it will be recalled, was based on the premise that giving up distinctiveness in favor of invisibility was paying off in decreased anti-Semitism. To justify continued adherence to assimilationism, therefore, Jews need to discount the significance of anti-Semitic outcroppings. But their unacknowledged anxiety prevents them from doing so. They "resolve" the conflict by believing the fluke theory but behaving as if they do not, by continuing to pour funds into the coffers of the ADL and the Wiesenthal Center. That is why these two community relations organizations, which understand the psychology of American Jews, are still thriving while others are fading.

THE REAL CAUSE OF ANTI-SEMITISM

The Holocaust goes to the very heart of the nature of patriarchy. For not only was it planned—and overwhelmingly carried out—by men, but it emerged out of a masculinist value system that glorifies power, domination, violence, the annihilation of the "useless" and the helpless, ravaging, exploitation, and cruelty. Under patriarchy, whose organizing principle is power, its possession by one gender is an abuse in and of itself, and sooner or later it is going to be egregiously abused. In a world where male violence against human beings rendered powerless, against women, against children, against animals, against the environment, is as pervasive as the air, a mega-crime such as the Holocaust should never be unexpected.

◆ It is particularly significant that the Holocaust was perpetrated against a group of people, the Jews, who were long perceived and experienced as the personification of female values: nonviolence, compassion, altruism, cooperation.

No wonder Jews were regarded as a threat to patriarchal power structures throughout the Exile.

Traditional Jewish communities were models of behavior that proved that a society based on the institutionalization of female values, resulting in a "kinder, gentler" way of life, was actually possible. It was dangerous to let this information become public knowledge. The anti-Semitic myths, expulsions, and ghettos were designed to keep Jews apart from the general society and thereby head off the possibility that dissidents would seek them out, find their way of life appealing, and decide to bring their own societies closer to that model via revolution. This, in essence, is what had happened with the Albigensians of southern France in the twelfth century. Their opposition to Pope Innocent III, wrote historian Heinrich Graetz, "was due in part to their contact with the educated Jews and with Jewish writings." Additionally, Jewish communities' perseverance in adhering to their way of life constituted in and of itself an act of resistance. By making Jews the objects of persecution, the ruling classes made abundantly clear what fate other social rebels could expect. That is why non-Jewish power structures usually persecuted converts to Judaism severely.

Non-Jewish women, in particular, had to be kept away from all Jews lest they discover the confluence/similarity of their values, as well as the commonality of their oppression by non-Jewish men. Moreover, they would also have discovered that Jewish men did not perpetrate the gynocidal and gynophobic crimes of rape, incest, suttee, genital mutilation, foot binding, witch burning, wife-beating, child abuse, or infanticide. The power structure wanted no repeat of what had happened in the early days of the Roman Empire, when many pagan women were deeply attracted to Judaism and lit candles on Shabbat eve. The late medieval "Jew in league with the devil" myth was aimed at frightening women, who were at high risk for being burned as witches, into refraining from contact with the Jewish community.

◆ The Christ-killer myth was accepted by Christians because it fulfilled a deep psychological need. The female values transmitted by a martyred Jew ("Love one another"), which his followers were very often honoring in the breach, were the normative values of Jewish communities. Christians were therefore angry at the Jews for pointing up their deficiencies in living up to their own ideals and thereby making them feel guilty and anxious. But they were also unconsciously angry at Jesus for giving them a religion with values (especially nonviolence) that they could not always live up to. This anger aroused more guilt, which spiraled into more anger over the source of the guilt. They directed their fury at the Jews.

Jews symbolized Jesus himself by living up to his ideals and being martyred for this behavior. By "killing Jesus again," Christians could symbolically free themselves of the burden of living as he had instructed them to. Similarly, Harry Golden once speculated that the Klan's cross burnings in the South symbolized the burning of Jesus, whose teachings were so obviously antithetical to the KKK's anti-Christian actions. Once they had burned Jesus "in effigy," as it were, they could feel free to torture, castrate, and lynch blacks.

At the same time, the Christian projection onto the Jews of the crime of being Christ killers made Jews the symbol of that angry part of themselves that wished to have done with Jesus and his religion and/or that was "killing Christ" by repudiating his teachings in practice. By attacking the Jews for "killing Christ," they were symbolically attacking and rejecting that murderous part of themselves—thus relieving some of their guilt.

❧ The medieval European ruling class's strategy was to eradicate Jewish visibility, either by keeping Jews separated from non-Jews (the myths) or by eliminating them through expulsions and/or pogroms. The strategy of the ruling classes of fifteenth- to eighteenth-century Europe was to quarantine Jews in ghettos, primarily in Italy and Germany (later to become the leading fascist states).

The strategy of the West European bourgeoisie from the eighteenth century on was to promote assimilationism. It was much more efficient than the strategies of the past in that it did not require expulsions or quarantines of Jews to keep non-Jews from seeing models of a humane alternative way of life: *The Jews themselves made their Jewishness invisible.* Perhaps they were unconsciously aware that it was their female values that had made them such a threat to the power structure and felt it was safer to keep them in the closet ("Be a Jew in your tent and a human being when you leave it").

❧ The ruling classes of modern European countries promoted nationalism to propagandize that their interests were the interests of the nation. The nation-state was pictured as a larger extended family (which is a reason for the late-nineteenth-century West European obsession with race and "blood") to which loyalty was due and which embodied the female values of interdependence and cooperation. This is why the capitalist ruling class, while glorifying "the family" in its propaganda, acts to break it up so that its members' loyalty will be "reinvested" in the nation-state.

Nationalism was also a successful attempt to get men of all classes (the women were considered politically irrelevant) to derive a large part of their definition of manhood and self-esteem from being members of a particular nation. The nation was propagandized as a male writ large, behaving the way a man behaved among other men—competitive, macho, violent, exploitative. If the nation did well (became dominant), the men got a shot in the arm; if it did poorly (was dominated or lost power), they got a shot to the groin: They felt . . . unmanned.

Loss of "manhood" was identified as being reduced to "effeminate" status, that is, becoming powerless like women. Therefore ruling classes of nations that had failed in the military and/or economic arenas could attribute this failure to the continued existence in their societies of female values, which impaired the full and unrestrained exercise of machismo and male power. The Nazis employed this explanatory style to account for (that is, rationalize) the country's defeat in World War I and its economic and political disasters after it and during the Depression: The Jews had "stabbed Germany in the back." The Germans were therefore not failures as men but had been weakened by a Fifth Column that embodied and promoted female values. That is why Jews were accused of "Judaizing the German spirit" through literature and science.

✍ To succeed as a criminal nation-state, Nazi Germany had to divest itself of/ eradicate whatever female values remained in the public sphere of the body politic. The Nazis regarded Jews as their main enemy: They were, in Hitler's words, "an emasculating germ," and they were perceived as powerful. The greater the amount of power they could be said to possess, the greater the importance—and the glory—of the mission of eliminating them and their influence.

It is no wonder that one of the first acts of the Nazis after attaining state power was the symbolic one of burning books "written in the Jewish spirit"—reminiscent of the various public burnings of the Talmud in the Middle Ages—wherein the female values they so hated and feared were enshrined. Later, a prime motivation for the Nazis' unspeakably fiendish cruelties in their concentration and death camps was to assault and destroy the traditional female/Jewish values of the prisoners, especially altruism, cooperation, mutuality, and interdependence. The main objective was not prisoner control but the attainment of "proof" that if these values could not be maintained under the most extreme, terrifying conditions, they were worthless.

Other enemies whom the Nazis had to eliminate were homosexuals (seen as "effeminate"); religious groups that believed in pacifism; union activists and other political opponents, especially Socialists, who believed in altruism and cooperation, whose struggle for social justice was rooted in compassion for the downtrodden, and who envisioned a society informed by these female values; and feminists. It is revealing that the Nazis campaigned against feminism as the product of a "Communist/Jewish conspiracy." Hitler stated in a 1934 speech, for example, that "the slogan 'emancipation of women' was invented by Jewish intellectuals."

✍ The Nazi persecution of the Jews in Germany began with sequential apartheid: eliminating them from one sector of public life after another and from various forms of association with non-Jews. The recycled Judeophobic myths unleashed by the Nazi propaganda machine to reinforce the separation of Jews from non-Jews included the myth of the "blackhaired Jew boy, *diabolic* joy in his face, [who] waits in ambush for [an Aryan] girl whom he defiles with his blood" (italics mine). Hitler's use of the word "diabolic" demonstrates how this myth was specifically aimed at arousing German women's fear of Jewish men, just as the medieval "Jew in league with the devil" myth did, thereby ensuring that they would avoid contact with Jews. (Later, sexual contact between Jews and "Aryans" was forbidden by the Nuremberg Laws.)

To eliminate the Jews from the public sphere, the Nazis had to make the invisible visible. The yellow star was a symbolic demonstration that the strategy of assimilationism had been scrapped in favor of older, vetted methods of getting rid of Jews and their values.

After Germany began the conquest of Central (1938), Eastern (1939), and Western (1940) Europe, it recapitulated in speeded-up fashion the chronological sequence of the West European persecution of the Jews from the High Middle Ages to the mid-eighteenth century, but more or less *in reverse order*. The Germans proceeded from incarcerating Jews in ghettos, to mass deportations (expulsions), to annihilation.

By getting rid of the Jews (one way or another), the Nazis could symbolically eradicate the female values they embodied once and for all.

Rabbi Kalonymos Shapiro understood this aim well—and expressed it in religious language—when he tried to console and fortify his congregation in the Warsaw Ghetto by telling them that the Nazis' "hatred is basically for the Torah and as a consequence, they torment us as well."

SIXTEEN ❧ THE RISE AND FUTURE OF JEWISH FEMINISM

> *My own synagogue is the only place in the world where I am not named Jew.*
>
> CYNTHIA OZICK (1979)

> *What is it after all that Jewish women seek? They do not ask to be excused or exempt. They do not wish to turn their backs on the tradition, to wash their hands of it and walk away. Rather, they desire to enter it more fully. They long to share a greater part of the tradition, to partake of its wealth of knowledge, to delight in its richness of ritual. For these reasons, their efforts should be welcomed, not scorned.*
>
> BLU GREENBERG

> *The issue is not that feminism poses insoluble problems to Jewish law but that Judaism has long ago died in the way it had existed for nearly 2,000 years. The crisis has not been brought on by feminism, but feminism clearly discloses the morbid condition of Judaism that has continued untreated throughout the modern period.*
>
> SUSANNAH HESCHEL

When the Jewish feminist movement began its struggle to bring women into Jewish public life, most Jews, women and men, unconsciously assumed that they would aim to reintroduce the female values of altruism, cooperation, compassion, and interdependence into the community.

Of the three pillars that had upheld traditional Jewish public life—the value system, Halacha, and the autonomous communal structure—only the value system remained after the onset of the assimilationist period. This pillar, unable to support Jewish public life without the other two, buckled under the strain and began to crumble. The female values, now deinstitutionalized with the abandonment of Halacha and the dismantling of the autonomous communities, flowed back to their original source, women—the "bride" who had brought this "dowry" into traditional communal life but had been excluded from developing or enforcing the laws based on them. Women now became the repository for these values and had the responsibility of transmitting them in the home.

When Jewish feminists began demanding the right to equal participation in Jewish life, assimilationist men feared that the "bride" would bring the values "dowry" from the home back into the community and would play a key role in creating new ways to express them. This possibility is what Barry Kosmin alluded to when he said that Federation "male leadership and staff often fear that the women will *take over.* They perceive [that] the women . . . challenge the tradition [*sic*] whereby the term 'leader' is used in such circles as a synonym for large donor. . . . They are less willing to be the *passive* 'front men' [*sic*]. . . . Perhaps this is because they have *failed to be socialized fully* into the 'big giver equals leader' model" (italics mine).

Translation: Women live by different values and will operate by them in Jewish organizations if allowed to assume major responsibilities on this turf. Moreover, adherence to these values would lead them to demand responsiveness to unglamorous concerns such as day care and education, which would compel the community to reorder its priorities. The fear of this happening was so deep that it precluded the recognition of the dynamics that militate against its occurrence: most present upper-middle-class female "leaders" do not wish to change the rules by which they attained and maintain their positions.

But the male fear of a takeover by upper-middle-class female volunteers was only one example of a pervasive terror that such behavior would characterize all women allowed to function in the public sphere, and it arose long before Kosmin wrote about it in 1989. What is more, the roots of the fear went deeper than the specter of a female takeover and the evolution of new models of leadership and accountability.

The terror was that the reintroduction and reinstitutionalization of female values in the community would involve and represent the breaking of the assimilationist contract, resulting in dire consequences.

Western Jews had originally accepted its terms out of an inchoate understanding that they had been persecuted because their communities and they themselves were experienced by non-Jews as living by female values. Giving up visible behavior based on these values ("Don't behave as Jews always behaved") seemed like an advantageous opportunity ("you won't be treated as Jews were always treated") rather than the *continuation of oppression by a more sophisticated methodology.*

Jews should have learned from the Holocaust that assimilation is not a viable survival strategy. Instead many Jews unconsciously accepted as its lesson the corollary of the assimilationist contract: behaving as Jews *had* resulted in their being treated as Jews were always treated. They had, in short, not assimilated

(Eastern European Jews) or not assimilated *enough* (Western Jews). Therefore what they needed to do was try harder to be more ethnically and culturally invisible and thereby avert future persecution.

It is not surprising, therefore, that it is precisely after World War II that the internalization of this lesson caused American Jews to give up most of what remained from their eroded culture.

Thus it is terror, the terror of renewed persecution, that fuels assimilationism. And the terror has increased exponentially since the Holocaust because the *list of ways of "being treated as Jews were always treated" now includes mass murder.*

While the 1967 War and its aftermath regenerated Jewish consciousness, it also had the effect of increasing the terror. Jews felt abandoned and without allies and were in no mood to listen to Jewish movement youth who urged them to confront the power structure instead of looking to it for protection for themselves and for Israel. And seeking its protection meant not antagonizing it unduly by "behaving as Jews have always behaved," by breaking the assimilationist contract.

The communal "leadership," especially, feared that the community would be perceived as doing so as a collectivity if it encouraged the reclaiming of the Jewish cultural heritage. This is what a San Francisco Federation executive meant when he said during the 1971 takeover of its building by movement people, "My reading of Jewish history is that any time we've become more ethnic, we've opened ourselves to destruction."

The Jewish movement failed to motivate the community to take full advantage of the legitimization of ethnicity because, lacking a feminist perspective, its activists did not understand the nature of the terror of renouncing assimilationism and were therefore unable to address it effectively.

❧ Jewish feminism sprang out of the Jewish movement and shared its anti-assimilationist ethos. The Jewish establishment feared that Jewish feminism, if its ethos were legitimized and accepted, would succeed in breaking assimilationism where the sixties movement had failed. The plutocracy realized that while the movement had incorporated many female/Jewish values, it was largely composed of men, who were also affected by other factors, such as sexism; women, by contrast, lived by these values on a daily basis. Moreover, unlike the young Jewish leftists of the sixties, Jewish feminists were adults; they could not be dismissed with the "kids will be kids" put-down. Nor, being highly Jewishly identified, could they be denigrated as "self-hating Jews." Finally, they were seen as being allied with the entire women's movement, which was reaching all women and thus preparing them to be receptive to the application of feminist views to Jewish life. They were thus a real threat.

The fear that the Jewish feminist movement would seek to reintroduce female values into the community was, unfortunately, an incorrect reading of reality.

Jewish feminists spoke occasionally of the "feminization of culture," and many hoped that women, as Conservative Rabbi Amy Eilberg put it in relation to the rabbinate, would bring in "a model of leadership that will be cooperative and empowering." But they did not focus their efforts on this goal. Nor did they wish to challenge the main impediment to its attainment: the patriarchal communal structure. They concentrated, instead, on winning acceptance in/by the community and were loath to engage in any activity that might jeopardize it.

EQUAL ACCESS

To understand the inner dynamics of the Jewish feminist movement, we must first look at its history and leadership. The movement has always been amorphous and pluralistic, consisting of self-constituted small groups all over the North American continent, some lasting only as long as a college semester. No mechanism has (yet) evolved to allow these groups to keep in touch with one another consistently, nor has any means been created for the determination of goals or the selection of leadership. The women who were considered movement leaders, all Jewishly well-educated, religiously oriented feminists, were mainly those whose scholarship was widely respected. While they sought to accomplish certain goals, they did not try to mobilize other women to join them in doing so actively.

From the outset, these leaders sought to attain "equality of access": full participation by women in all areas of Jewish life, religious and secular. This goal was stated in a manifesto presented by a group of about a dozen women to the annual convention of the Rabbinical Assembly (RA) of the Conservative movement in March 1972. The group, called *Ezrat Nashim*, had sprung a half-year before out of the New York Havurah. Its name translates from Hebrew as "women's aid" but also echoes with deliberate irony the name of the separate women's section in the traditional synagogue.

At the time Ezrat Nashim was founded, women in Radical Zionist and Radical Jewish groups were also grappling with issues raised by the feminist movement. Women from these groups, from havurot, and from Ezrat Nashim encountered one another for the first time at a 1971 cultural conference sponsored by Network and WUJS and held in Zieglerville, Pennsylvania. To mollify the men, who were annoyed that the women had "separated themselves" for several days to discuss their concerns, the women agreed to present the issues they had discussed in caucus to a coed session. There the men, from left to right on the movement's political spectrum, shouted them down, hurled verbal insults, and loudly and angrily charged that the changes the women wanted were "bad for the Jews."

But the shock—and the sexism in the movement generally—did not propel the women to drop out, regroup, and create a separate women's movement, as women in the New Left had done. Deeply influenced by the women's liberation movement, they already defined themselves as feminists and could discuss their situation in feminist terms. Moreover, they were able to bring up feminist issues inside the movement because, despite the sexism of some of the men, the movement, and especially Network, welcomed diversity, and its leaders tried to be au courant with every emerging trend as an organizing/recruiting strategy.

This was a prime motivation for Network's organizing the First National Jewish Women's Conference in February 1973 in New York. The more than five hundred North American women (with a sprinkling from abroad) who attended the conference were preoccupied with reform of Halacha, particularly in the area of divorce; with equal participation in synagogue life, including the ordination of women rabbis; and with the writing of rituals. Equal access to the secular organized Jewish community was not a burning concern at the conference. Later in the decade, after the Radical Zionist and Radical Jewish groups as well as Network had faded from the scene, there were few Jewish feminists who were interested in this issue, either. The prime focus of activity of Jewish feminists was equal access to religious life, and it absorbed most of their energies for over a decade.

⮜ Two of Ezrat Nashim's demands were the inclusion of women in the minyan and their receiving aliyot; a third was the ordination of female rabbis and cantors. The demands were directed primarily toward the Conservative and Reform movements. There was general consensus that an attempt to make these demands of Orthodoxy would be fruitless because of the obduracy of its opposition.

The class of the congregants and leaders of the Conservative and Reform movements was an important factor in determining their responses to women's demands for equal access. The lower the class of most of a movement's membership and the farther removed it was from the Federation structure and the rest of the Jewish establishment, the greater was its opposition to equal access, including women's ordination.

The reason goes back to how the men's validation for living up to the American definition of material success fluctuates and is never conclusive. Many men, therefore, use the Jewish establishment organizations for an ersatz definition of masculinity and for validation, status, and power. The more successful a man is at obtaining these in a Federation or other Jewish establishment organization, the less likely he is to seek them in the synagogue, which has less status than the secular sector. The men who lack the wealth to become "leaders" in the Jewish establishment are more likely to use the synagogue as a kind of consolation prize. It provides them, as well, with the placebo of ersatz power over the women and over the synagogue's decision-making processes (e.g., building plans, membership regulations, dress code rules). Sexism in the synagogue is thus a form of co-optation of the men, designed to siphon off any resentment they may have for being disempowered in the secular sector, particularly the Jewish establishment, and for not being able to use it to obtain validation because of their lower class.

Reform Jewish men, who are generally part of the upper middle class, tend to derive their status from their positions in the general society and to use the Jewish establishment organizations for ersatz validation when necessary. They need the synagogue only for worst-case-scenario backup validation and power. They consequently did not resist women's equal participation in their movement's religious activities.

The Reform movement had long officially approved women's being included in the minyan and receiving aliyot, although it was not until the 1970s that these practices became socially acceptable in its temples. (Its motivations bore some similarity to those of its predecessors in nineteenth-century Germany, who, wrote Marion Kaplan, made some cosmetic reforms regarding women's roles because they were "embarrassed lest gentile society should observe the Oriental customs evident in the relegation of Jewish women to second-class status.") However, since Reform temple leaders were often also machers in the Jewish establishment, some resisted equal access for women to religious life because they feared that if male hegemony in the synagogue were eliminated, the men would search for empowerment in the secular sphere, a subject we will return to.

The Conservative Jewish men ranged from lower-to-middle middle class. The lower their class, the more vulnerable they were/are to the effects of fluctuating validation in the general society and the less likely they were to attain it, as well as status, in the Jewish establishment. In addition, the lower their class, the more likely were the men to use the synagogue for validation and power and to oppose women's access to the activities there that served as an ersatz definition of manhood.

The Conservative movement had allowed women to get aliyot as far back as 1955 and to be included in the minyan in 1973 but left decisions on these options to individual congregations. This led to congregational battles and a kind of crazy-quilt effect in North America. Some synagogues, particularly those on the West Coast, became completely "integrated"; others allowed one practice but not others; and some adopted complex Byzantine rulings, such as allowing women aliyot on certain occasions, for instance, at their children's Bar/Bat Mitzvahs.

❧ Class was not a factor in Orthodox men's opposition to any reform in the status of women. Because they had never accepted material success as a definition of manhood, they did not need to seek ersatz validation in the organized Jewish community or to look to the synagogue as a consolation prize. The prime reason for their opposition to equal access for women to the synagogue was that the public performance of prayer and ritual was a component of their definition—the traditional definition—of masculinity, along with Torah study.

The synagogue, moreover, was and is central to Orthodox life, a status it has never achieved among Conservative and Reform Jews. As Orthodoxy kept moving toward greater stringency in observance, one marker of this stringency was the synagogue's mechitzah. Only Orthodox synagogues have such partitions between worshipers of the two genders, and many reinstated them in the 1970s and 1980s. Depending on the position of the synagogue on the left-to-right spectrum of Orthodoxy, the mechitzah may be a waist-high drape separating the male and female sections of pews (Modern/Centrist Orthodox) or a curtain separating the back section, where the women sit, from the main area of the sanctuary (right-wing Orthodox). In some Orthodox synagogues, women sit in the balcony, as they did in the late Middle Ages. Orthodox women may participate in prayer but are not counted in the minyan, not even one organized to mourn a parent, and they do not perform any of the synagogue rituals, such as reading aloud from the Torah or having aliyot.

THE ORDINATION BATTLE

The struggle that encapsulated and epitomized all the equal-access issues and provoked heated and often acrimonious debate in the Jewish community for eleven years was over the ordination of women as Conservative rabbis.

There was no struggle in the Reform movement over ordination, which began in 1972; in the Orthodox world, this issue did not even ascend to the agenda. The battle was in the Conservative movement because of the synagogue/validation dynamic and because it was the largest denomination and wished to remain so. Many leaders in the Conservative movement were fearful of losing recruits at a time when Orthodoxy was attracting new adherents. Said one JTS (Jewish Theological Seminary) professor during the ordination battle: "When the entire Jewish world is moving to the right, should we move to the left to *satisfy the needs of a handful of women* and their male supporters?" (italics mine). Others believed that a negative decision on ordination would confirm the "rigidity" of the Conservative movement in the eyes of young people who were both traditional and egalitarian.

The arguments advanced in the Conservative movement against female ordination were not theological, as is often the case in Christian denominations. They derived primarily from two prohibitions in Halacha, one that excluded women from certain time-bound mitzvot, among them daily prayer in the synagogue, and the other from being witnesses in a bet din (except in a few limited circumstances). These prohibitions were of particular significance in the Conservative movement because of the changed role of the rabbi in America.

Traditionally the rabbi's function was to be a teacher and religious arbiter. Unlike the Catholic priest, the rabbi is not an intermediary between humans and God or responsible for the flock's good behavior. Nor is the rabbi like a Protestant minister, one of whose major functions is to conduct prayer; any observant adult Jew (traditionally meaning a man, of course) is supposed to be able to do that. Nor is a rabbi necessary to "sanctify" a marriage: two "kosher" (i.e., observant male) witnesses to the groom's declaration to the bride are sufficient.

One argument against female ordination was heightened by the fact that in the West, most non-Orthodox Jews are incapable of leading services (a result of their poor Jewish education), and it is the rabbi who does so. The rabbi (or the cantor) thus functions as the congregation's "agent." The argument here was based on the law in the Mishnah that "anyone who is not obligated for a matter cannot be the agent through whom others fulfill their obligations."

The second argument related primarily to the fact that the state has invested the rabbi with the function of "witnessing" a marriage. (The rabbi also signs religious divorce documents.) Halacha prohibits women from being witnesses. The witness problem, however, should not even have been at issue in Conservative Judaism because the RA had already voted in 1974 to allow women's testimony (but as a nonbinding option).

A final argument against ordination was that it "goes against custom"–a position vitiated by Conservative synagogues' having accepted mixed seating and driving to shul on Shabbat, which are not in accordance with custom–or with Halacha.

◆ The ordination issue was discussed at various conventions of the rabbinical and congregational organizations of the Conservative movement. In 1977 the JTS chancellor appointed a special commission to study the issue. It held eight public hearings in major North American cities–the first time any issue of importance to the community was discussed openly, publicly, and democratically in/by a mainstream Jewish organization. After years of debate, during which time the commission recommended ordination and the JTS tabled it (1979), it was finally approved in 1983. (Four years later, the JTS decided to ordain female cantors but the Cantors Assembly waited until 1990 to accept women members.)

The few women ordained at the JTS as Conservative rabbis–like their several hundred Reform and Reconstructionist colleagues–continue to struggle for full congregational acceptance, advancement, equal pay, and solo pulpits in large synagogues. A 1991 survey found that the incomes of women Reform rabbis was 5 to 25 percent lower than those of male counterparts in comparable positions. Seventy percent of the female rabbi respondents to an AJCongress survey, released in 1993, reported having experienced sexual harassment in connection with their work. Women rabbis told a reporter that they are often viewed as novelties and are reminded of this in remarks and "jokes" by congregants, especially by comments focused on their bodies. Rabbi Eilberg, for example, reported that congregants in her first pulpit avidly discussed whether she should be permitted to cross her legs on the *bima* (reader's platform).

THE ESTABLISHMENT FIGHTS BACK

Although Jewish feminists did not actively and consistently challenge the Jewish establishment and its sexism, its "leaders" feared that feminist consciousness would inspire female encroachment on their domain. Women would transform this turf from one where the men played power games and derived status and validation into one where female values of cooperation, altruism, and consensus prevailed. They therefore moved to protect this turf by making sure the battle over feminism took place elsewhere: in the religious sector, over equal access to synagogue life. They accomplished this goal by leaping into the fray to delegitimize feminism and Jewish feminism with arguments over how equal access in the synagogue and Conservative female ordination were issues for the entire community because they were "bad for the Jews."

Once the battle was firmly entrenched in the religious sphere, the Jewish establishment men could leave it in the hands of the religious (Orthodox and Orthodox-leaning Conservative) men, who feared the loss of hegemony in the synagogue and were eager to protect this turf. Thus the secular plutocracy used the religious men to do a lot of its dirty work just as the Israeli Laborites used the religious hierarchy to advance their party's own goal of encouraging pronatalism and traditional roles for women by giving it control over marriage and divorce.

Even more shamefully, the Jewish establishment exploited the synagogue as a lightning rod to deflect attack from itself. In this recycling of the classic dynamic of oppressive exiles, the synagogue took on the role of the Jewish community that the disenfranchised rebels were allowed to attack. They did so, unconsciously following the classic social activist strategy of striking (first) at the weakest link of the opposition—in this case, the synagogue, which is at the bottom of the power pyramid in Jewish communal life.

The Jewish establishment regarded the religious sector as expendable. After years of tortuous struggle, the establishment relented in its opposition to equal access in the synagogue but only very gradually, grudgingly agreeing to the religious movements' doling out of concessions in small doses after fighting so long to make sure they were withheld.

It was brilliant military strategy on the part of the Jewish establishment to hold off its enemies at positions it could afford to relinquish in order to keep them pinned down and preoccupied with besieging those strongholds for years. This allowed the Jewish establishment to fortify and protect its power base inside impenetrable boundaries. The eventual abandonment of the expendable religious-sphere positions to the enemy thus appeared to be a great victory for the attackers, the majority of whom then believed the war was over and ignored the few who wished to besiege the fortified bastion of the Jewish establishment, where the real power lies.

❧ The strategy of picturing equal access as a threat to Jewish survival can be seen in the illogical, mean-spirited, and pseudopsychological arguments advanced against it.

One genre of arguments was designed to arouse/intensify anxiety about how equal access and ordination would ruin the synagogue. This was the argument that if women got equality there, they would "take over" and, in the words of sociologist Daniel Elazar in 1973, "further *reduce* the presence of men in synagogue activities ... and enhance the image of Judaism as 'women's work,' *i.e., less important,*" presumably the same way real estate loses value in a racist society when the percentage of nonwhites passes the tipping point (italics mine). The anxiety that the men would defect in droves if women participated in services as equals should have been perceived by the men as an insult to the integrity of their religious commitment, but somehow it was not.

Historian Lucy Davidowicz went even further when she fulminated on "*the threat of female power, female usurpation of the synagogue.* Women are efficient; they can turn the shul into a Hadassah chapter.... I do not like the idea of [Hadassah] ladies ... *taking over* the synagogue" (italics mine). It is passing strange that this obvious recycling of the old Judeophobic power myth, projected onto women, should have flowed from the pen of an author of scholarly works on the Holocaust.

A related slew of arguments was that women's equal participation in synagogue life would fatally undermine the men's self-esteem. Mortimer Ostow, chair of the JTS Department of Pastoral Psychiatry [*sic*], said in 1974 that "the synagogue serves traditionally as a *refuge* from the struggles of the marketplace, struggles for a *sense of self-worth* as well as for economic survival. And in these struggles, women are coming to play a more active role.... The new aggressiveness of women ... has distinctly increased the frequency of impotence.... One would not wish to ... convert the synagogue from a refuge to an arena where a man will feel that he must struggle again to *defend his self-esteem* ... [and] will be awed and *humiliated* by the women whose competence in religious matters clearly exceeds [his] own" (italics mine).

This, of course, recapitulates that Talmudic statement, which Ostow quoted, about how women should not be allowed to read publicly from the Torah because of the "honor of the community," that is, damage to men's egos and erosion of their definition of masculinity. An implication of Ostow's argument—which went unchallenged in the Conservative movement—is that men go to shul not to pray but to get validation-fixes. Here again was a denigration of male religious commitment and spirituality that the men did not repudiate.

Ostow's primary argument was that men use their domination of the synagogue to define their masculinity when they cannot otherwise live up to the American definition. If women "invade" the synagogue and thereby deprive the men of the ability to define themselves as men, they will have nobody but themselves to blame if the men react by becoming detumescent in bed. Thus women have the power to cause male impotence if they refuse to accept exclusion from equality in the synagogue, just as they have the power, according to the Lilith myth, to destroy Jewish life by refusing to stay in the enabler role. *If women are full and complete Jews, men cannot be full and complete men.*

❧ The second basic genre of arguments against equal access and feminism in general was that these constituted an assault on the Jewish family and therefore a threat to Jewish survival. "What happens to family life if women accept ritual obligations on an equal footing with men? . . . What would happen if we created a new family pattern in which competition might rear its ugly head?" whined a member of Ostow's department during the ordination debate.

It was not a coincidence that the Jewish community became preoccupied during this period of the ordination debate with the decline of Jewish fertility, a pattern that had generated no alarm in the preceding few decades. Hysteria about American Jews' "zero population growth" was whipped up by anti-feminists, some attempting to legitimize their arguments by linkage with the Holocaust. The terms "genocide" and "preventive Holocaust" of the unborn were shamelessly—and shamefully—bandied about.

It was unconscionable to exploit the tragedy of the Holocaust to try to generate a pronatalist panic to stampede women back to the home and nursery.

Calls by Jewish "leaders" for women to have more children reached fever pitch in the 1970s, with secular organizations convening conference after conference on Jewish fertility at which feminism was charged with causing the Jewish population to plummet. Typical of the arguments was one in *The Reconstructionist* magazine, voicing alarm that "even mothers of small children with *successful husbands* arbitrarily [*sic*] elect to return to the labor pool" (italics mine).

The pronatalists refused to recognize that bringing increased numbers of Jewish children into the world provided no guarantee that they would lead Jewish lives or even identify as Jews, given the lack of quality Jewish education and the absence of authentic Jewish content in communal institutions, as well as the dynamics of intermarriage.

THE PEN-ULTIMATE TOOL

At no time during the long years of the battle over ordination did Jewish feminists organize themselves politically to struggle for this goal or for equality of access in other areas of the religious sector or in the secular sphere.

The approach—it can hardly be dignified by the name "strategy"—of most Jewish feminists was to influence (male) "leaders" to schlep the rest of the community up the path of righteousness and to motive these men to create solutions and tactics, rather than to struggle politically themselves for self-defined goals.

Appealing to "leaders" with conflicting interests or other priorities—and most of the time appealing indirectly, through writing articles—rather than organizing the public to demand change is classic shtadlanut with eerie parallels to that used by American Jewish "leaders," with tragically unsuccessful results, during the Holocaust. Jewish feminists appealed to communal and intellectual leaders to "lead" just as the Jewish establishment appealed to FDR to rescue European

Jewry; both refrained from mobilizing public opinion. Jewish feminists refused to ask women to withhold or to put in escrow contributions to Jewish organizations until equality was achieved just as the Jewish establishment refused to ask the Jewish public to withdraw votes from the Democrats. Jewish feminists never worked out a strategy or plan of action; Jewish wartime "leaders" were unable to do so, either. Jewish feminists did not protest male "leaders'" lip service to equal access just as Jewish "leaders" went along with the "politics of gesture" of FDR. The only elements missing from the parallel were the tragic urgency and the interorganizational fighting that had prevailed in the long, dark night of the Holocaust.

Neither did Jewish feminists do what the Vaad HaHatzala had done during the war: organize alternative institutions/mechanisms to carry out their goals. Jewish feminist day care could have been one such alternative institution, yet there is not a single such center in the U.S. under Jewish feminist auspices. Nor did Jewish feminists establish any Jewish battered women's shelters. They did not even sponsor their own off-campus conferences (with three or four local exceptions in the early 1970s; a major one, "Jewish Women's Voices," was organized by Canadians and held in Toronto in 1993).

✦ Jewish feminists have never insisted that the secular Jewish organizations or the women's organizations support any of their demands or concerns or those they share with the general women's movement, such as reproductive choice. Nor did they attempt to mobilize themselves or the Jewish establishment to support issues such as affirmative action and the ERA.

Had any of the major Jewish organizations mobilized for the amendment in Illinois and Florida—unratified states with large Jewish populations—they might have midwifed state ratification at a time when only three more ratified states were needed for the ERA to become law. While most Jewish organizations made official statements in favor of the ERA, not a single one—including the women's groups—put the full force of its organizational, lobbying, and political machinery behind it. When some organizations held conventions in unratified states, no protests ensued from Jewish feminists. Nor did they protest or mobilize protest against "JAP"-bashing on campus, in the popular culture (e.g., in the film *Space-balls*), or in the community. They made no attempt, either, to win political or financial support in the community for Israeli feminists, who are primarily involved with combating rape, battering, sexual harassment, and the proliferation of pornography and struggling for divorce reform, abortion rights, economic equality, and political representation.

✦ By far the most popular activity of Jewish feminists has been writing, with public speaking running a close second. This pattern is in stark contrast with those of the general women's movement—and with the activities of Jewish women involved in it. Jewish feminists have relied almost exclusively on words to be their surrogate, their champion, their advocate. They send out their written work like Noah dispatched the dove from the ark, hoping it will bring back a conciliatory olive branch.

Jewish feminists' use of words to attain their goals has obviously derived from both their belief in the power of words and their wish to claim intellectual turf. The latter is a key reason why their writings have provoked such a prodigious number of written counterarguments in which words are used to reaffirm the men's exclusive claim to intellectual turf. It also accounts for the resistance to female scholars (and rabbis) by their male peers. The male intellectuals had/have no intention of giving up this classic instrumentality for the definition of their manhood.

◆ Going beyond polemics, Jewish feminists in academia have begun to generate considerable scholarship, although historical research is still rather skimpy. There is as yet no good text for adults, children, or youth in which Jewish women's history is mainstreamed, just as there is no general history textbook in which *Jewish* history is mainstreamed. Meanwhile, Jewish scholarly works by men still distort reality by ignoring the existence of women and not grappling with how their experiences differed in many ways from those of the men in various historical periods.

The endowment of university-level chairs in Jewish women's history and the establishment of an international central archive for scholars in this area would provide great impetus to historical research on women and toward Jewish women's studies becoming an academic discipline. Such projects are the prerequisite for mainstreaming Jewish women's history into Jewish history books, general history texts, and feminist works.

SEPARATION ANXIETY REDUX

The unwillingness of Jewish feminists to organize politically to attain religious equality of access or to challenge the Jewish establishment, their shtadlanut approach, and their lack of fire and of ire are rooted in classic Jewish conflicts over separation and abandonment. (This behavior was especially prevalent during the equal-access struggle but it and the reasons for it have continued into the nineties.)

Jewish feminists, said academic Paula Hyman, a founder of Ezrat Nashim, "are always treading that line—are we going to do something that will *cut us off from our people?*" (italics mine). Jewish feminists have been afraid to do anything that might be perceived/criticized as abandoning the community—the great crime in Jewish life. They have been afraid, as well, of doing anything that could be interpreted as betraying the community; this could lead it to retaliate by ejecting them from the fold.

Like all groups involved with social change, Jewish feminists needed to re-group to organize themselves to advance their cause. They were unable to do so during the equal-access struggle because of their profound fear of thereby appearing to separate themselves from the community. They had to be careful not to go too far and had to create boundaries (and "fences" outside them) to make sure that they did not do anything that could create the impression that what they were attempting or doing was "separating."

Challenging/confronting religious hierarchies or the Jewish establishment was an act skirting perilously close to betrayal in the eyes of American Jews. Jewish feminists were well aware that Jewish movement youth were often regarded as traitors for criticizing Israeli policies, American Jewish establishment politics, communal behavior, and especially for engaging in confrontational actions.

Moreover, while the media paid scant attention to feminist tracts or lectures, they might have covered Jewish feminists holding a mass rally or chaining themselves to the gates of the JTS to protest yet another tabling of ordination. This would have been not only a betrayal but one that was a *shandeh far dee goyim,* one that puts Jews in a bad light before non-Jews. This is a major reason why Jewish feminists have engaged primarily in writing, a low-profile activity compared with physical expression, especially the high-visibility kind that gets attention in the general society.

Public confrontations would also be experienced as weakening the image of communal "unity" which was so important to present to the general society, as we have seen in chapter 12. That is why Francine Klagsbrun, a Conservative Jewish feminist, when asked why there was "no uprising" when ordination was tabled by the JTS in 1979, gave this instructive answer: "Women were scared, mostly, of causing divisiveness in the community."

◆ But there was an even deeper reason for the timidity of Jewish feminists: the fear of facing the charge that what they really wanted was to "take over" power from the men. The charge was paranoid: Jewish feminists were not interested in power, not even in sharing it; the word was not in their vocabulary, which was replete with terms like "responsibility" and "burden." But the men perceived them as wishing to take over, and they and many women as well regarded this eventuality as "bad for the Jews."

The reason is that under patriarchy, it is the men whose classic role is to defend the group, politically and, if need be, physically. Therefore a vulnerable minority with a history of persecution perceives that the stronger and more powerful its men, the stronger the group and its ability to defend itself. The corollary of this view is that any perceived diminution of male power or numbers makes the group feel less able to constitute a strong presence in the patriarchal general society; its image also becomes one of weakness.

Jewish men living in the traditional communities of past eras had also been affected by this dynamic of needing to strengthen their patriarchy against that of the general society, but they had done so by reforming it to incorporate female values. They had also redefined male power as spiritual resistance, and masculinity as engaging in it, as we have seen. But assimilationist American Jewish men had internalized the values of the majority culture, including its definition of masculinity in terms of physical aggression. They were anxious about their ability to defend the community-as-extended-family, especially during the post-1967 era, when Jews felt abandoned and betrayed. The more anxious they became about this, the more obsessed they became over anything that seemed to reduce male power inside the group—such as women's increased public presence and active participation in it. (Feminists in the black community, which is also afflicted with this minority dynamic, face a similar problem and similar charges from "the brothers" of their actions' serving to weaken the group.)

❧ Jewish feminists did not seem to be able to win acceptance for their case that feminism was a positive development that would enhance Jewish survival. As late as 1983, Hyman could still observe that the feminist issues raised by Jewish women were seen either as incidental or "potentially dangerous for Jewish survival." Therefore they used defensive tactics, seeking to avoid any behavior that could "prove" that their opponents were right in charging that feminist activities were "bad for the Jews."

Jewish feminism was born at the tail end of the sixties ambiance and on the cusp of the narcissism of the seventies. On the one hand, that narcissism worked to the advantage of Jewish feminists on religious equal-access issues. The demand for equal access was perceived as one of "self-actualization," an argument advanced by feminists in the mid-1970s that was powerful precisely because it was in tune with the general culture, noted Hyman. The advances in religious equality of access may have been more the result of the ripple effect of the achievements of the general women's movement and its impact on the Jewish community than of the actual work of Jewish feminists.

But on the other hand, the circle-the-wagons mood of American Jews, almost a kind of group narcissism, worked against Jewish feminism. Jewish feminists did not employ the self-actualization argument. On the contrary, like the chalutzot, they asked only to assume the responsibilities that come with being Jewish. But they were identified with the general women's movement and seen through the prism of its adherents' being primarily involved with individual "self-actualization." Therefore they were often perceived as being wrapped up in their petty selfish concerns, as narcissistic rather than altruistic, at the expense of the community. (Portraying them as selfish—in essence, deploying the female value system of altruism, mutuality, and interdependence as a battering ram *against* feminists—was another excellent strategy on the part of the opponents of Jewish feminism.)

↦ The actions Jewish feminists were afraid of carrying out were precisely those regarded as aggressive or assertive, traditionally precluded unless linked to altruism (as defined, of course, by men) as part of enabling.

This brings us to the question of Jewish feminists' lack of righteous anger—the kind of ire that fuels the fire of public action. The reason for its absence lies, perhaps, in the inchoate recognition that Jewish women had not suffered from the kind of oppression that women have faced under classic patriarchy, particularly misogynist violence. How angry could they be?

This, of course, is one of the standard arguments of the anti-feminist apologists. Perhaps Jewish feminists feared that if they started to behave "aggressively," as non-Jewish feminists were perceived as doing, they would be treated as non-Jewish women have always been treated. There may have been some anxiety that assertiveness/aggressiveness would unleash physically gynophobic behavior in Jewish men, escalating beyond the unprecedented verbal misogyny exemplified by their vicious attacks on Jewish women as "JAPs" and "Jewish mothers."

Of course, the unconscious presumption that what restrained Jewish men from engaging in misogynist violence was the women's invisibility as quiet, modest little altruistic enablers is a dangerous distortion of history. Not only were Jewish women not generally quiet/quiescent, but Jewish men's rejection of violence had other roots, as we have seen in chapter 4. Moreover, violence against women has increased in Israel even as the women have become *more* subservient. Invisibility can no more keep Jewish women safe from male violence than it can keep assimilationist Jews safe from anti-Semitic violence.

In the final analysis, therefore, it would not have mattered very much that Jewish feminists were perceived as being nonaltruistically assertive. The very fact that they were rejecting the role of enabler was enough to flip them over immediately to the shadow role of *dis*abler. As Hadassah founder Henrietta Szold had once observed: "To the Jews, accustomed from time immemorial to regarding Jewish women as symbols of loyalty, a daughter's *insubordination* is nothing short of a catastrophe" (italics mine).

NOWHERE ELSE TO GO

Being outside the community—either through voluntary separation or ejection—has never been an option for Jewish feminists. As Hyman said, Jewish feminists "are reluctant to get too far away from the Jewish community . . . or to say 'women should walk out of these institutions.'" Beyond their devotion to Judaism, they wished to stay inside the community because it continued to function as a deformed extended family in which enough of a residue of female values still remained for Jewish women to feel safer and more comfortable there than practically anywhere else: a haven, in other words. Despite its having been polluted by the industrial effluence of assimilationist values, it was still possible to navigate in this lake, and there was hope that the toxic wastes would yet be extracted.

The religiously oriented Jewish feminists also had nowhere else to go. With a few exceptions, they did not feel altogether comfortable in the general women's movement. Their unease was heightened as reports began to seep out regarding the stereotyping of Jewish women, their invisibility, and about the proliferation of writings blaming Jews for inventing patriarchy.

The stereotyping went public in 1971 when *Off Our Backs,* which defines itself as a radical feminist paper, published a cartoon charging that "Jewish princesses now grow up to be movement heavies." Four years later, feminist author Phyllis Chesler wrote that "it was feminist comrades who reintroduced me to anti-Semitism ... in its more primitive and undisguised forms: 'dirty Jew,' 'Jew bitch,' 'smart New York Jew' ... those were the words that reminded me as Jews have always been reminded." By the late 1970s/early 1980s, Jewish women in the general feminist and lesbian-feminist movements had begun to speak out about anti-Semitism there, and Letty Cottin Pogrebin exposed it in a groundbreaking 1982 article in *Ms.* magazine. She quoted the Jewish radical lesbian-feminist author Andrea Dworkin as saying that other feminists made her feel self-conscious about being "an intellectual." Other Jewish women reported being stereotyped as loud, pushy, domineering, and middle class.

❧ At this time, as well, authors Judith Plaskow, Susannah Heschel, and Annette Daum called attention to anti-Semitism in Christian feminist and "post-Christian"/matriarchalist writings. A myth attaining considerable circulation in some Christian feminist circles was that the ancient Hebrews had invented patriarchy, dislodging "the Goddess [who] had reigned [before] in matriarchal glory" and foiling Jesus, who had tried to restore the original egalitarianism. Heschel pointed out how "blaming Judaism provided a convenient explanation for patriarchy, together with a prescription for its cure: just get rid of the Jewish influences and Christianity will be rescued in all the pristine feminist glory of Jesus." Many "post-Christian feminists" blamed Jews for destroying the Goddess and Goddess worship and thereby causing the ensuing suffering of women. This, of course, is a recycling of the old Judeophobic Christ-killer myth.

Some Christian feminists who advance the "Jesus was a feminist" myth do so to avoid engaging in a painful separation struggle with Christianity. If God/Jesus can be portrayed as inherently feminist—and the patriarchal characteristics of Christianity as barnacles of malignant Jewish influence that can be scraped off—one can remain in the Christian community as a feminist. The post-Christian matriarchalists, for their part, need to picture the religion of the Father-God as more patriarchal to justify their permanent abandonment of it. If the Father-God is identified not as the Gospels' "God of love" but as a continuation of the Jewish Scriptures' "God of wrath" (a classic anti-Jewish motif of dichotomy in Christian thought) whose followers murdered the Goddess who embodied female values, they can feel amply justified in and less guilty over rejecting the religion.

Early in 1980 Plaskow said she hoped that Christian feminists "will be my allies as a Jew if there is a general outbreak of anti-Semitism in this country. And it frightens me that, instead, feminism may become an excuse for oppressing me as a Jew."

Her fears materialized at the 1980 U.N. Mid-Decade Conference on Women held in Copenhagen, where Jewish women were subjected to virulent verbal anti-Semitic assault. During many panels, there were constant and uninterrupted chants by pro-PLO women of "Jews must die! Israel must die!" Some women were overheard saying, "The only good Jew is a dead Jew," and "The only way to rid the world of Zionism is to kill all the Jews." The Jewish women in Copenhagen, including the Israelis, "could not believe that there would be so loud a chorus of hatred against Israel and against Jews *that would not be interrupted*," reported one participant (italics mine). Non-Jewish feminists, including those in the American delegation, were silent. Calling Copenhagen a "psychological pogrom," a noted Jewish feminist long active in the women's movement wrote upon her return to the U.S. that "in Copenhagen, I saw my grandmother's wig askew and her legs in the air and Cossacks riding off and nobody noticed and nobody cared."

◄• Another aspect of anti-Semitism in the women's movement was that of Jewish women's invisibility as Jews, of Jews being "omitted from the feminist litany of 'the oppressed' . . . [which includes] every other female whose struggle is complicated by an extra element of 'outness,'" wrote Pogrebin. Jewish women's lives have been absent from the majority of introductory women's studies texts and from most feminist and lesbian-feminist anthologies, even those on religious issues.

Jewish invisibility also obtains among feminist therapists, according to testimony by female mental health professionals and academics at the 1992 conference on Judaism, Feminism, and Psychology. A common assumption in therapy theory and practice, said lesbian-feminist academic Evelyn Torton Beck, is that Jewish identity is "insignificant." As a result, behavior considered in Jewish culture to be healthy and normative, such as intense interdependence among family members, is viewed as pathological.

The reverse of the coin is also true: Emotional disorders experienced by Jewish women, such as "chronic terror," extreme anxiety, and "hypervigilance"—being suspicious, distrustful, and continually needing to check out who can be trusted—are seen as *individual* pathologies, said another therapist. Neither anti-Semitism nor the Holocaust is factored in as a cause of this behavior, even though, said Beck, "the Holocaust has marked the psyche of every Jew the world over. I walk around with a subliminal fear of anti-Semitism the way women walk around with a subliminal fear of rape."

The fear of anti-Semitism often leads many Jewish women to accede to pressures to become invisible, to "put themselves down in public," especially about their accomplishments. They repeatedly find themselves in situations where "they have to decide whether to show their Jewishness or to hide it," said psychotherapist Rachel Josefowitz Siegel. The demand for Jewish invisibility has also led many feminists to avoid writing on Jewish themes out of anxiety that their work would be perceived as "marginal" and would go unnoticed and unread, and to refrain from protesting the scheduling of events on Shabbat and Jewish holidays.

Some Jewish women in the feminist movement have acceded to invisibility for fear of flipping over to the shadow role of dominator—"When Jews have made ourselves visible as Jews, we have been seen as wanting to take over," said Beck—and to avoid being criticized, as some have been, for being "too Jewish."

The rationale for delegitimizing Jewish ethnicity parallels that which had obtained in the New Left. Many feminists regard Judaism as *inherently* patriarchal, just as New Leftists regarded Jewishness as *inherently* reactionary. To be a radical (then) or a feminist (later), a Jew has to relinquish cultural distinctiveness. Many Jewish women in the feminist movement have done so, replicating not only the behavior of Jews in the pre-1967 New Left but also of those in the revolutionary movements of the nineteenth and early twentieth centuries.

Many have also accepted uncritically the feminist dismissal of Judaism as the epitome of patriarchal religion and as not being amenable to reform. This denigration is based primarily on their generalizing from the narrow base of the sexist morning prayer in which Orthodox men thank God for not having created them as women. Lacking a solid Jewish education, and apparently uninterested in acquiring even its rudiments, many Jewish women in the movement are unaware that historically Jewish patriarchy was a reformed patriarchy and that its communal life was infused with female values. Moreover, since these Jewish women were not in contact with the Jewish community or with Jewish feminists, they did not know about the struggles for and victories in the attainment of equal access to participation in religious life. Without the intellectual resources to resist the attacks, many Jewish women have internalized the denigration of Jewish culture and experience low self-esteem and even self-hate. One noted feminist leader, a Jew, justified refusing her dying mother's request to say the Shema ("Hear, O Israel") with her on grounds that it was a "chauvinist prayer."

An unconscious factor that operated here up to a point was the depression of the critical faculty, which, as we have seen, occurs when Jews regard movements or nations as secular rescuers. As Plaskow's comment demonstrates, many Jewish feminists looked to the women's movement for rescue. It was only after the Copenhagen events exploded the love-is-blind rescue fantasy that the critical faculty reemerged, and Jewish women in the movement began to protest its anti-Semitic phenomena publicly (as only a few had done before).

But Beck also reported that when the issue of anti-Semitism was finally raised in the feminist and lesbian-feminist movements, it was not taken seriously. It was not, for example, included by name in the list of -isms against which the lesbian-feminist movement had pledged itself to struggle. Jewish women, she said, were given the message to forget about and ignore anti-Semitism.

Jewish lesbians began to realize that they were deeply involved in advancing the lesbian-feminist movement's diversity without dealing with their own distinctiveness. Grassroots groups of Jewish lesbians emerged in the seventies and eighties all over the U.S. to enable them to "reclaim their roots" through learning Jewish history, celebrating holidays, and fighting anti-Semitism.

Perhaps because Jewish lesbians had long forfeited the possibility and rewards of being considered "nice Jewish girls," they were less likely to fear being confrontational. Unfortunately, because the Jewish lesbians and the Jewish religious feminists lacked any mechanism for meeting, discussing issues, and working out a direction for an organized, pluralistic Jewish women's movement, the lesbians' activism did not influence the way the religious feminists operated.

ORTHODOXY

The Orthodox leadership, as we have seen, was in the forefront of the ideological/Halachic battle against equality of access in the synagogue. While this has not (yet) become a burning issue for most Orthodox women, access to education has. Modern Orthodoxy was compelled by pressure from the increasing number of well-educated women to allow the study of classic Jewish legal texts, including the Gemara, in its high schools and colleges. (The world of the yeshivot, however, remains closed to women.) Orthodox feminist Blu Greenberg described in 1992 the "explosion of women's learning" in the Orthodox movement and the emerging cadre of female teachers of Talmud and Halacha. She believes that the confluence of this phenomenon with the model of female rabbis in the other wings of American Judaism will lead to women becoming Orthodox rabbis, although probably not pulpit rabbis, "in the not-too-distant future."

Greenberg called the impact of feminism on Orthodoxy "a revolution of small signs": These include individual women chanting the blessing over wine and the Havdalah at home and reciting some "words of love," usually from the Song of Songs, at their weddings; and saying the mourner's prayer daily at the synagogue during the year-long mourning period. "Slowly but surely," Greenberg said, "a female presence in sacred settings is becoming normal, natural, familiar, everyday. The taboos against seeing and hearing women perform communal acts of holiness are steadily being lifted."

She also cited in this connection a second change instituted by Orthodox women in the 1980s and 1990s: their forming grassroots *tefillah* (Hebrew for prayer) groups to allow women to participate actively in services. The tefillah groups received support from some individual male rabbis, among them Saul Berman and Avi Weiss of New York.

They were condemned as prohibited by Halacha in a 1984 responsum by five Yeshiva University (YU) (Modern/Centrist Orthodox) scholars. It stated, "All these customs are coming from the movement for the emancipation of women, which in this area is only for licentiousness." This, of course, echoes Rabbi Eliezer's statement in the Talmud that whoever teaches his daughter Torah is teaching her *tiflut* (immorality). These rabbis ignored the fact that Jewish women in the Middle Ages had their own prayer meetings in special rooms of the synagogue and were led by "female precentors," some of whom (e.g., Urania of thirteenth-century Worms) attained a considerable reputation. One of the YU Orthodox scholars said, "What are they doing it for? A psychological lift? . . . If they want to get their kicks, there are other ways to get it" [*sic*]. This nasty comment is reminiscent of the charge by some of the male pioneers in pre–World War I Eretz Israel that the women were plowing in the fields only out of a "perverted desire to shock."

When a Brooklyn women's tefillah group approached the (Modern/Centrist Orthodox) Rabbinical Council of America (RCA) for Halachic guidelines, it was turned away. Rivka Haut, founder of the Women's Tefillah Network, commented that this might be the first time in history that "Jews turned to rabbis for Halachic advice and were refused." Three years later, when women from all the religious movements tried to pray as a group with the Torah at the Western Wall in Israel, some Israeli and American Orthodox rabbis called this "a desecration"; one said that the women's chief motivation was "truly to uproot everything." The "everything" the Orthodox men feared women were uprooting by conducting prayer services, whether in tefillah groups or at the Western Wall, was, of course, the men's domination of this turf, which has traditionally defined their masculinity.

◄ The area of least progress for women in the Orthodox community for two decades after the beginnings of Jewish feminism was that of divorce reform. Halacha stipulates that only the husband can give the wife the *get* (divorce document). Today there is no way a bet din can actually compel him to adhere to its decision that he do so, as it could in the traditional autonomous communities. This has led to a situation where the husband can extort huge sums of money from the wife, and even get custody of the couple's children, in return for the get. If the husband refuses, the woman becomes an aguna (pl., *agunot*), unable to remarry. There are at present an estimated fifteen thousand agunot in New York State alone and between five thousand and ten thousand in Israel, where Halacha is state law in "personal status" matters.

A simple solution, of course, would be a takkanah that would allow the woman to give the get to the man, but even the Conservative movement has been unwilling to consider what JTS professor Boaz Cohen once called "engraft[ing] upon the tree of Jewish law a foreign branch" such as this. Conservative scholars came up instead with various Halachic solutions, such as inserting provisions into the marriage contract allowing a bet din to grant a get if the husband refuses. But the Orthodox rabbis were unwilling to consider any such solutions by non-Orthodox scholars.

Instead, Orthodox communities stepped up communal pressure against recalcitrant husbands. Orthodox rabbi Haskel Lookstein urged his colleagues in 1986 to withhold synagogue membership and honors from them. In one Canadian community, Orthodox women initiated a successful Lysistrata-type solution: They refused to go to the mikvah (the prerequisite for resumption of sexual relations after Niddah) unless the community compelled a recalcitrant husband to give his wife a get.

The Orthodox also became less reluctant to let the secular courts take the problem off their hands. Both New York State and the Province of Ontario now have laws that imply the granting or accepting of a get during divorce actions. The Canadian law had the unanimous support of the entire Jewish community, from secular to religious, including the Orthodox, and all the women's organizations.

It was only in June 1993—twelve years after Rabbi Berman's prediction that a Halachic solution on divorce was imminent—that one finally emerged from the RCA. The organization endorsed at its convention the use of a two-part prenuptial agreement. The first part, an extension of the ketubah, mandates a cost-of-living-linked sum a husband will pay for his wife's support in the event that they separate and until they conclude a religious divorce. The second part is an agreement by both partners to adhere to the arbitration of a bet din regarding the divorce. The decision was a direct result of a struggle by Orthodox feminists, among them Norma Baumel Joseph, a founder of the International Coalition for Agunah Rights (ICAR), and Haut, founding director of Agunah, Inc. The RCA also formalized sanctions to be imposed by synagogues whose rabbis are RCA members against spouses who refuse to appear before a bet din in a divorce proceeding. These include not allowing the sanctioned individual to be a synagogue member, official, or employee, or to receive an aliyah.

✦ The lack of progress on amending divorce law by the time the equal access battle had ended (1983) was a factor in the declining interest by most Jewish feminists in Halachic reform. Trude Weiss-Rosmarin, a pioneer Jewish feminist, believed to the end of her days that Halachic reform was the key to women's liberation in Judaism. Of course, Halacha has the "machinery" to change the official status of women in Judaism with a few sweeping takkanot. These could have abolished the classic concept that defines the normative contractor of the Covenant as male, with the female, in Rachel Adler's words, being nothing more than a "partial and diminished participant." Adler cited as evidence the scriptural account of the preparations for the revelation at Mount Sinai, when "Moses tells the people, 'Be ready for the third day, do not go near a woman.'" She commented, "Clearly, 'the people' does not mean [women]." Religious arbiters could have published an enactment specifying that women *are* contractors of the Covenant and are required to fulfill all the mitzvot, including the time-bound ones from which they were exempted, and especially the study of Torah. But, as Ozick noted, Halacha's principles have not been applied to changing the status of women, and, as a result, "justice is not being done." Obviously the problem lies with the men at the controls of the Halachic "machinery."

Throughout the 1970s some Jewish feminists believed that learning Halachic texts would enable them to become religious arbiters and make necessary reforms themselves, possibly through a women's bet din. But even as Halachic rulings were becoming more accessible (e.g., on computerized databases), most Jewish feminists lost interest in Halachic reform. Orthodox women, except for feminists such as Greenberg, Haut, and Joseph, did not see such reform as desirable; the feminists in the Conservative movement did not believe it possible; and those in Reform Judaism (which does not accept Halacha as binding) and among the Reconstructionists (who, in the words of the movement's founder, Rabbi Mordechai Kaplan, give Halacha "a voice but not a veto") did not see it as necessary.

THE JEWISH FEMALE CULTURE PROJECT
(1983+)

Getting equal access to participation in non-Orthodox synagogues meant, in essence, that women were now "officially" considered adult Jews. No longer were they to be exempted, as were children, from responsibilities such as being part of a minyan of worshipers.

But being an adult, by the very nature of that concept, means having a distinct identity, being one's own person. This status is in contrast with that of a child, whose identity is unformed and untested, who is defined only in terms of who she or he is in relation to parents: X's daughter, Y's son. In Judaism a woman has always been referred to by the tender but nonetheless demeaning phrase "Jewish daughter," someone "whose identity is linked to and defined by another's role. 'Jew' signifies adult responsibility. 'Daughter' evokes immaturity and a dependent and subordinate connection," wrote Ozick.

Jewish women, therefore, needed some way to symbolize their new, adult status in Judaism. It was not enough for them simply to engage in various ritual activities required of adult Jews (in the past, men). Without forging a visible adult identity, they would still be seen through the prism of the patriarchal tradition as

"Jewish daughters" even while fulfilling responsibilities commensurate with the definition of adult Jew. They would, in short, appear to be impostors.

For this reason the Jewish feminist enterprise had to proceed along the same lines as that of ethnic minorities in the 1960s (and, in later decades, out-groups such as women and gays) to reenter society after many of their civil rights goals had been attained. Jewish feminists now sought to retrieve their culture as the content for a new self-definition, a new *and adult* identity with which to reenter the Jewish religious community. (The Bat Mitzvah ceremony became popular among older women at this time to symbolize their new adult Jewish identity.)

❧ Jewish feminists soon discovered, however, that there was no Jewish female culture that could be retrieved to serve as the basis for their new self-definition. Its absence can be seen from a study of the folktales on themes of specific concern to women. In these tales, transmitted by women—and probably originating with them—they are pictured as clever, resourceful, and brave. They outwit demons or the Angel of Death to save their husbands, and outwit their husbands to save their marriages. In other words, they behave as classical altruistic-assertive enablers.

There are also a great many folk songs in Yiddish about women's experiences in nineteenth-century Eastern Europe of being abandoned by their lovers or husbands; separated from husbands gone for soldiers or to America, and from children and other family members; about poverty, hunger, despair, and prostitution; and about toiling night and day over the sewing machine. Many of these songs and the lullabies were undoubtedly composed by women.

The folktales and folk songs, however, cannot be regarded as evidence of a Jewish female *culture* substantively different from that of the rest of Jewish society. They are unmistakably Jewish in values, philosophy, ambiance, and context, and in having a Jewish "twist."

Nor was there any substantial body of spiritual practices or literature by and unique to Jewish women and shared by those of all eras and locales. Recent oral history has revealed that Sephardic women engaged in certain gender-specific activities—a musical tradition in Yemen, dance in Kurdistan. Jewish women in Europe recited *techinot* (Hebrew pl.; sing., *techina*), prayers before lighting the Shabbat candles, separating the portion of the Shabbat challah bread, immersion in the mikvah, and childbirth, among other occasions. These prayers were ad-libbed or written by others. But there is considerable debate as to whether the authors of many of the techinot in the popular published collections were women or pseudonymous male hacks whose heartrending prayers were reviled by scholars for their lack of literary worth. The controversy points to the absence of spiritual writings by Jewish women on par with the poetry of Christian mystic Teresa of Avila.

In sum, the reality is that there never was a separate women's culture within Judaism rooted in female values because these values were mainstreamed into Jewish communal life.

In America, after the values had flowed back to the women, they lacked specific forms of female expression to sustain, nourish, and enrich both the value system and themselves as its repository. They lacked, as well, the kind of support systems non-Jewish women built around female relatives because their already weak extended families were further broken down by dislocations and migrations.

Nor were there any religious institutions Jewish women could turn to for spiritual/emotional sustenance, as Catholic women do the church, with its nunneries, female saints, and Maryology. Women were excluded from the synagogue minyan, which served as a support group for the men who participated in it every day. They turned to synagogue Sisterhoods and other women's organizations for friendship, a sense of self-worth, and as the instrumentality for expressing their Jewish identity, as we have seen in chapter 13. But these groups were focused on "uplifting" or fund-raising for others; their becoming hierarchical and evolving into a locus for status competition precluded their being strong support groups for their participants. One can only wonder what far-reaching advances could have been achieved had Jewish women's organizations nurtured female values and provided an institutional base for the development of a Jewish female culture.

❧ Jewish feminists gravitated toward developing a religious/spiritual female culture, rather than a secular one, for two substantive reasons. One involved the issue of which sphere of Jewish society women should reenter or reenter first. Obviously the synagogue world, unlike the secular sphere, was the only place where the traditional values still received some respect to one degree or another. Jewish feminists could make a case there that feminism was an ethical issue and that by carrying it forward, Jews were living up to the Jewish ideal of justice, enshrined in the Scriptures. In the secular sphere, where participation was based on money and power, it was impossible to have an appeal for justice taken seriously.

The second major reason for developing a religious culture is that the secular Yiddish and radical cultures had long faded from the American Jewish scene. The untranslated works of the hundreds of women who wrote poetry and prose in Yiddish, both in Czarist Russia and North America, much of it permeated with feminist consciousness, were inaccessible. But even had these works been retrieved, there was no sector of American Jewish society that would have welcomed women whose self-definition was based on Yiddish culture or on the radical consciousness and actions of the women of revolutionary movements in Czarist Russia or in the unions of the immigrant generations.

It was mainly Jewish lesbian-feminists who focused on retrieving the history of Jewish women in the radical and labor movements of Eastern Europe and immigrant-generation North America. The reason is that they were primarily involved in developing a new self-definition with which to reenter the lesbian-feminist movement as authentic Jews with a revolutionary history, not in reentering the Jewish community as lesbian-feminists.

❧ Having discovered that there was little to retrieve from the past besides the custom of the New Moon's designation as a day women were not to work, Jewish feminists began to accelerate their writing of new rituals, midrashim, and prayers. The writing of new rituals had actually run parallel to the equal-access struggle in a thin trickle, receiving much of its inspiration and impetus from ceremony writing in the Radical Jewish, Radical Zionist, and havura groups. The event for which ceremonies were already being written in the early 1970s was the birth of a daughter. Although such ceremonies have not yet attained the importance of the *bris* (Yiddish, from the Hebrew *brit,* Covenant), the ceremony that physically and spiritually initiates a baby boy into Judaism, they have become acceptable even in Centrist Orthodox circles.

Jewish feminists began to put their energy into writing rituals/ceremonies for holidays as well as life-cycle events such as menarche and menopause, pregnancy, giving birth, and mourning a miscarriage; heterosexual marriage and lesbian partnership ("commitment ceremonies"); and coming to terms with a divorce. Many also began to "take back the waters" of mikvah, a ceremony they had previously regarded as degrading (a view still held by non-Orthodox Israeli feminists).

The midrashim, mostly on women in the Scriptures, had two purposes. One was to provide a kind of retroactive proof of women's participation in history in order to validate/legitimize their own active participation in current Jewish life. The second was to imbue the scriptural female characters with protofeminist tendencies to validate Jewish women's new roles. This activity had the same motivation as that of the Talmudic sages when they reshaped scriptural heroes into scholars to legitimize their new definition of masculinity.

❧ Reentering the community under new terms/definitions had to involve a variation of the classic adolescent separation struggle. Jewish feminists began to regroup around ritual to forge and dramatize a new identity—a far less assertive activity than struggling for equal access or against communal sexism. This regrouping provoked some criticism from Jewish men that the women were abandoning the community. But significantly, the criticism (e.g., of feminist seders) was at its height during the time when ritual writing was (seen to be) linked with the equal-access struggle.

(It is precisely because the Orthodox tefillah groups are seen by some rabbis as a hachshara for a struggle over equality of access in the synagogue that they have triggered fear and loathing. Attempts to prohibit these groups were aimed at creating an outer "fence" around the synagogue to prevent the breaching of its inner walls of custom.)

After the ordination victory, when equal access was no longer regarded as an issue in the non-Orthodox movements, opposition to ritual writing de-escalated considerably. It was almost as if rituals were no longer regarded as weapons to strengthen women in that struggle (now supposedly over) but as a diversion/

distraction from active confrontation over the still remaining discrimination. The one exception to the lessening of opposition has been in the area of God-language in prayer.

PRAYER AND PATRIARCHY

The sexist language of the traditional prayer book contradicted and delegitimized women's equal participation as adults in the synagogue. As Ellen Umansky wrote, "As long as God is only the God of our fathers and not our mothers, men will be perceived as having (and will perceive themselves as having) both a closer relationship with God and a higher religious status." A struggle ensued to add "God of our mothers" to "God of our fathers" in the prayers, and the names of the foremothers (a.k.a. Matriarchs)—Sarah, Rebecca, Leah, and Rachel—to those of the forefathers (a.k.a. Patriarchs)—Abraham, Isaac, and Jacob.

This problem, though it has occasioned congregational battles, was relatively minor compared with that of God-language. In the Hebrew prayer book, God is addressed in the second person masculine and is always referred to as "He." All the descriptions of God (e.g., Creator) are in the masculine gender; they employ male images—King of the Universe, man of war—as do their English translations.

The pervasiveness of the male images became shockingly apparent only after feminists began writing prayers where God's male attributes were replaced with female ones, such as "Her voice comforted our people in their despair," and "She soothes those in pain and cradles the abandoned," to quote from Naomi Janowitz's and Rabbi Maggie Wenig's *Siddur Nashim* (women's prayer book) for Shabbat.

Some feminists began writing/amending prayers to address God as "She" and as "Queen" of the universe; others directed prayers toward the Schechinah. The belief that the transformation of God-language is linked with the reentry dynamic can be seen in Rita Gross's argument that "the ability to say 'God-She' is the sign of Jewish women's authentic *entrance* in their own right *into the ritual covenant community* of Israel" (italics mine).

The corollary is the belief that without transforming the image of God to female or, at the very least, adding female attributes to God, women will not be able to reenter the Jewish religious community as equals. Weiss-Rosmarin disagreed with this thesis, arguing that goddess worship in Greece and Rome had had no salutary effect on the misogynist treatment of women in these patriarchal societies. Moreover, there is something disquietingly sacrilegious about cobbling together a new image of God by selecting some qualities from Column A and others from Column B. The concept of God in all religions, including Judaism, emerged out of intense spiritual experiences. Yet for all the talk in the feminist movement about spirituality, evidence and expression of such an inspired experience is sorely lacking in all its liturgy.

The more immediate question is that of Jewish authenticity. How far can Jewish feminists go in changing the image of God, the gender-linked attributes of God, and especially the gender of God ("God-She") and remain within the parameters of authentic Judaism?

This brings us to consider the reasons behind the fierce resistance by congregants, women as well as men, to changes in the liturgical language, especially those that picture and address God as female. Jewish feminists believe that the resistance is at best an unwillingness to relinquish language familiar from childhood and at worst a symptom of unreconstructed sexism.

Although both of these are motivations for the resistance, the most important factor is psychological, and it goes back to why Jews experienced God as male in the first place: They perceived themselves as powerless and vulnerable and in need of rescue, which under patriarchy could only come from a powerful male. As long as they continue to feel vulnerable, Jews—even learned individuals who know that in Judaism God is neither male nor female—will continue to feel comfort and solace from praying to a male rescuer God.

If patriarchy is abolished and power is no longer the organizing principle of society, Jews will no longer be and feel powerless or need to see God as a powerful male rescuer. Maybe by then Jews and non-Jews, women and men, will experience God in ways we—with our imagination impoverished and our spirituality imprisoned by patriarchal constructs—cannot now even begin to conceive.

WHAT IS TO BE DONE?

As the twentieth century draws to a close, the Jewish feminist movement in America stands at a crossroads. While it is no longer regarded as an alien threat or a bizarre joke, neither is it a strong and active force in the American Jewish community. It must now decide what role to play in the future.

The movement pioneered in raising consciousness among American Jews about how women had been excluded from participating in the religious responsibilities of adult Jews. It gained equal access for women in non-Orthodox synagogues and began creating a Jewish female culture to legitimize and reinforce their presence there as adults.

Most Jewish feminists are aware of the contradiction implicit in winning (partial) acceptance into a community that is patriarchal in values and structure. But they have been unwilling to challenge the patriarchy or even the sexism of its secular sector, where the real power lies. Instead they have operated on the assumption that the feminist values in the new rituals and prayers will osmose from the synagogue into the rest of the community and magically cause its patriarchal character to wither away. It is far more likely, however, that the ritual activities will be allowed to coexist with the patriarchal structure to siphon off discontent and energy into what the Jewish establishment regards as a relatively harmless enterprise. Should these activities attain mass popularity, the Jewish establishment can even use them as its R&D wing, as circles within it did with some of the attitudes toward Jewish education and culture that emerged in the Jewish movement of the sixties.

Moreover, in focusing on God-language in prayer, Jewish feminists (mostly the rabbis among them) have moved farther and farther away from activities that touch the lives of and involve the vast plurality of women. Thus, while Jewish women evince a great deal of interest in Jewish feminism—as attendance at conferences demonstrates—the range of activities they can actively take part in is narrow and limited.

✥ Jewish feminists are in danger of becoming marginal and irrelevant in the community because they have not given serious attention to the changes that are going on in America in general and among Jews in particular. Increasing numbers of Americans are seeking to deepen and intensify their ethnic identification and revive their cultures, and America is moving toward becoming a multicultural society. While a small number of American Jews are becoming more intensely involved with cultural and religious activities, larger numbers of Jews are moving in the opposite direction—away from meaningful involvement with other Jews and with Jewish forms of expression, including religion.

The prime reason for this disaffiliation is, of course, assimilationism, of Jews' acceding to the assimilationist contract and the demands for their cultural invisibility. But it is not the only reason. For there are many Jews wavering between assimilation and affiliation, struggling with the terror of breaking the assimilationist contract, seeking some group to join that provides meaningful content and support. At one point or another, many turn to the Jewish community—to the synagogues of the major religious movements or the most visible secular organizations. And what they invariably report is that the community is "cold" and "unwelcoming."

These descriptions are particularly significant because they contrast so vividly with the descriptions of the "warmth" of the traditional Jewish community of yesteryear. What had made the community of the past function as a "warm" extended family was its having reformed itself by incorporating female values, creating the instrumentality of Halacha to institutionalize them, and serving as the context for their expression.

✥ A course correction is urgently needed in American Jewish life, which is careening toward spiritual and cultural suicide.

The course correction cannot entail a return by American Jews to the autonomous community of the past—which cannot be reconstituted under present conditions. But it does mean pulling themselves out of the quicksand of assimilation and charting a new, postassimilationist direction.

Jewish feminism—the only new idea to have emerged among American Jews since their arrival on these shores in 1654—provides the only hope for such a constructive course correction, because feminism is intrinsically anti-assimilationist, democratic, and empowering.

Feminism means the transformation of all society so that its organizing principle is not power and domination but rather the female values that are at the core of Judaism. What, after all, is Isaiah's vision of a world where "the wolf and the lamb will dwell together" but a metaphor for a nonhierarchical society where relationships between nations, among individuals, and between humans and the natural world are based on respect and compassion, on cooperation and nonviolence, and on the interdependence of all Creation in the web of life?

Patriarchy, the antithesis of this vision, has proved extremely lethal for Jews throughout history. Jewish communities living in oppressive exiles reformed their own patriarchy to strengthen it against those of the surrounding general societies by incorporating and institutionalizing female values. But being a powerless minority unable to change the dynamics of Exile, they obviously could not unilaterally abolish their own patriarchy.

The reformed Jewish patriarchal communities were terribly weakened by their exclusion of women from active participation in their public intellectual, spiritual, and communal spheres. This exclusion drastically reduced—by half—the body of individuals contributing to the shaping of communal responses to the challenges that faced them. Despite this fundamental flaw, the traditional communities were committed to Jewish survival and tried the best they could under extremely trying conditions to ensure it.

Today's patriarchal communities are incapable of working out collective solutions to ensure Jewish survival. In America the structure of the organized Jewish community operates by the assimilationist masculinist values of power, dominance, prestige, and worship of the golden calf of material success. And while the pseudoleaders of the community engage in ritualized kvetching over the disaffiliation of so many Jews, they do not wish to see the restoration of the old female/Jewish values in the community, which could stem/reverse this process. Such restoration would threaten their assimilationism and their hegemony. It is precisely because these values permeate Jewish religious and cultural literature, and because a knowledge of history would allow the youth to see how anomalous the community is in its lack of democracy, that the Jewish establishment has never supported universal quality Jewish education.

✧ The community must be transformed into one that is able to respond to the physical, political, spiritual, and cultural needs of all Jews. The transformation requires the dismantling of the current patriarchal structure and institutions and their replacement by those whose organizing principle is not power but the female value system that characterized traditional Jewish communities. And, unlike those communities of the past, the Jewish community of the future must enfranchise women. In short, the community must be feminized. This feminization/refeminization of communal life will rejuvenate (reJEWvenate) it.

Democratizing the community is the prerequisite for carrying out this refeminization. Only democratization will make possible the active participation of female and male Jews of all classes, ages, affectional orientations, countries of origin, political views, and religious affiliations, and the development of a diversity of forms of expression. Through "cross-fertilization" involving revivified discussion and debate, a distinctively American Jewish culture will be able to evolve, providing substance, content, and meaning for Jewish identity. Democratization will also enable all Jews to determine their political agenda and create instrumentalities whereby the community can work out relationships with other groups in society to develop collective solutions for meaningful social change: moving toward the feminization of America.

Israel, when it attains a stable peace with its neighbors, will be able to turn its attention to shaping a society in accordance with Jewish values and thus to fulfill the Zionist vision. It will be able to pioneer, as did Socialist and Labor Zionists during the Yishuv era, in creating forms of and mechanisms for social, political, and cultural expression that are possible only in an independent Jewish state. These will serve as inspiration and models for Jewish communities outside Israel. As both Israel and communities abroad move toward feminization, they will be able to work out a relationship based on mutuality and interdependence—a true "marriage" and partnership.

The course correction in Jewish life the world over from assimilationism to feminization is the only possible alternative for an authentic and creative Jewish future.

Will the Jewish feminist movement continue to strive ever more strenuously for acceptance in/by an intellectually stagnant and spiritually bankrupt patriarchal community? Or will it dedicate itself to the feminization of Jewish life?

Jewish feminists—or, as some now call themselves, feminist Jews—face the one question that is crucial to Jewish survival. That question is whether they will decide to undertake this transformation of the Jewish community out of the realization that if there is to be a Jewish future, it will have to be a feminist future.

NOTES

> *Whoever quotes with attribution brings redemption to the world.*
>
> *Pirké Avot* (SAYINGS OF THE SAGES), 6:6.

All English-language books cited in the Notes are listed in full detail in the Selected Bibliography. Citations are given in the Notes with the author's surname (and an identifying part of the title of the work in question, when the Bibliography lists several books by her or him). Frequently cited works, marked with an asterisk in the Bibliography, are listed by the following abbreviations:

ENGLISH-LANGUAGE BOOKS

B/W: Baron and Wise anthology, *Violence and Defense in the Jewish Experience.*
BHM: Baum, Hyman, and Michel, *The Jewish Woman in America.*
BOW: *Maimonides, Code of* (Mishneh Torah), *Book 4: The Book of Women.*
D/R&P: Dubnow's 3-vol. *History of the Jews in Russia and Poland.*
EJ: *Encyclopedia Judaica.*
ET: Abraham Cohen's *Everyman's Talmud.*
F&S: Elon's *The Israelis: Founders and Sons.*
G-H: Grossman-Haut anthology, *Daughters of the King.*
H/G: Howe and Greenberg anthology, *Voices from the Yiddish.*
M&M: Margolis and Marx, *A History of the Jewish People.*
OVS: Booklet edited by Yehezkel Landau, published by Oz Veshalom.
P&D: Porter and Dreier anthology, *Jewish Radicalism.*
S/E: Ben-Sasson and Ettinger anthology, *Jewish Society Through the Ages.*
wmt: Nora Levin's *While Messiah Tarried.*
z&h: Zborowski and Herzog, *Life Is with People.*
ZI: Arthur Hertzberg's *The Zionist Idea.*
Z&S: Mitchell Cohen's *Zion and State.*

ENGLISH-LANGUAGE PERIODICALS

AJH: *American Jewish History*
JP: *Jerusalem Post*
JR: *Jerusalem Report* (magazine)
JTA-CNR: Jewish Telegraphic Agency *Community News Reporter*
JTA-DNB: Jewish Telegraphic Agency *Daily News Bulletin*

NYRB: *New York Review of Books*
NYT: *The New York Times*
NYTBR: *Sunday NYT Book Review Section*

HEBREW AND ARAMAIC SOURCES

BT: Babylonian Talmud
JT: Jerusalem Talmud
PA: *Pirké Avot* (Sayings of the Sages), a tractate of the Mishnah.

Note: All nonpolitical individuals quoted in this work by name, unless otherwise indicated (e.g., by title or occupation), are authors.

INTRODUCTION

1 **Rabbi Tarfon quote** PA 2:21.
2 **Heine quote** 433.

PART I. PATTERNS OF TRADITIONAL
JEWISH CULTURE

11 **Memmi epigraph** *Portrait,* 201–2.

CHAPTER 1: POWERLESS UNDER PATRIARCHY

13 **Pinsker** Russian Zionist precursor of Herzl (1821–1891). Bio: ZI, 178–81. Avineri, chap. 7. Quote: Pinsker, 12.

13 **B.C.E.** Before the Common Era, the form Jews prefer over B.C., which means "Before Christ." C.E. means "Common Era," the Jewish equivalent of A.D., and is used for the same reason.

13 **Eretz Israel** Term used in this work to refer to the land Jews lived in during scriptural times (a.k.a. Canaan), the First Commonwealth (Judea, Israel), the Second Commonwealth (Judea, Galilee), and in small communities there throughout the centuries of the third exile, when it was called Palestine, until the establishment of Israel in 1948.

14 **club, yoke, leash** Essay of same title by author, *Ms.,* August 1983.

14 **"enemy territory"** 1893 letter, quoted in Elon, *Herzl,* 115. Herzl (1860–1904) was the founder of political Zionism and of the modern Zionist movement. Bios: Elon; Pawel; ZI, 200–204.

14 **withdraw** Janeway, 48.

15 **"defenseless pen"** Abrahams, 83; **sadism, crimes** 84, 94; Dubnow, *History,* 3:559, 560.

15 **"bear pit"** Jacob Robinson, quoted by Ben Halperin in "Self-Denial and Self-Preservation," B/W, 269; see 282 n. 17.

15 **"ferae naturae"** Robert Freitas, "The Legal Rights of Extra-Terrestrials," *Analog,* April 1977, 64.

15 **Luther's call** Made in 1543: Dubnow, *History,* 3:679.

15 **Exile as good thing** Dimont, 414–21; **a natural condition** essentially the ideology of the Jewish Labor Bund: Baron, 141–44; see also historian Simon Dubnow in Davidowicz, *Golden,* 55–56; **mystics' view** chap. 2, below; **Reform Judaism's** chap. 7.

16 **classes in medieval society** Keller, 218; M&M, 365, 405; Pirenne, 195; Leon, 96ff, 105, 115, 128, 130; Ben-Sasson, 485.

16 **Western bourgeoisie** Keller, 410; Bein, 263, and 624 n. 62 a and b.

16 **Borochov** Socialist Zionist theoretician and Yiddishist (1881–1917). Bio: ZI, 353–54; Borochov, 11–16, 179–82; Nadia Borochov, "My Brother, Ber Borochov," *Jewish Liberation Journal,* Summer 1971; Mitchell Cohen, introductory essay to *Ber Borokhov: Class Struggle and the Jewish Nation: Selected Essays in Marxist Zionism,* ed. M. Cohen (New Brunswick, NJ: Transaction Books, 1984); Avineri, chap. 13.

17 **on marginality** Borochov, 69, 79.

17 **job choices** Richard Israel, "Is This a Job for a Nice Jewish Boy?" *Dimensions,* Summer 1969, 33–35.

17 **Borochov on immigrants** 184–85.

17 **Pirenne on merchants** 11.

18 **interstitial** See Robert J. Marx, "The People in Between," *Dimensions,* Spring 1969.

18 **money lending** M&M, 365, 405; Keller, 218; Bein, 98–103.

18 **cultural intermediaries** Werner J. Cahnman, intro. to Wischnitzer (hereinafter Cahnman), xxi–xxii; Abrahams, 233; I. Twersky, "Aspects of the Social and Cultural History of Provençal Jewry," S/E, 203.

18 **Paul Mayer and Maximilian Harden,** in Bein, 628.

18 **Gabler on movie moguls** 5.

18 **Jewish journalists** Mayer and Harden in Bein, 628. See also Wistrich, 84–85.

18 **Salon Jewesses** See Herz; and Jacobs, 299–300.

19 **Kurtzman** Obit., NYT, February 23, 1993.

19 **smallest shtetl** Patai, *Mind,* 532.

19 **Communist countries** See, for example, Istvan Deak, "Hungary, The New Twist." NYTBR, August 19, 1988.

19 **Czech national movement** Hillel Kieval, "Autonomy and Independence: The Historic Legacy of Czech Jewry," in Altschuler.

19 **middle range** Bauer, *Emergence,* 4.

20 **"king's persons"** Keller, 209, 217.

20 **"sponges"** Abrahams, 243; see also Leon, 119, and Bein, 103–4.

20 **Polish Jews' occupations** M&M, 551–52; **Chmielnitzki revolt** 552–56.

20 **statue** Bein, 193.

20 **atrocities** M&M, 552.

21 **"stabbed infants"** Nathan Hannover, quoted in Keller, 304.

21 **"buried alive"** Contemporary letter quoted in Potok, 337.

21 **Kautsky letter** Wistrich, 227.

21 **Bebel** Wistrich, 131–39. Quote: in "Socialism," EJ, 15:26.

21 **"battering ram"** Robert Wistrich, quoting from the *Arbeiterzeitung,* 1892, in "Socialism and Anti-Semitism in Austria Before 1914," *Jewish Social Studies,* Summer–Fall 1975, 326.

21 **mass stirring** WMT, 55.

21 **Narodnaya Volya faction** WMT, 54.

22 **Jeffries** James Traub, "The Hearts and Minds of City College," *The New Yorker,* June 7, 1993, 42–53.

22 **badges** M&M, 375.

22 **Innocent III** Quoted in Solomon Grayzel, *The Church and the Jews in the Thirteenth Century* (Philadelphia: Dropsie College, 1933), 115.

22 **repudiation** "Nostra Aetate," promulgated by Vatican II, October 28, 1965.

22 **matriarchalists' charge** quoted in Susannah Heschel, "Anti-Judaism in Christian Feminist Theology," *Tikkun,* May–June 1990, 25.

22 **Apion** Greek rhetorician, in "History of Egypt," EJ, 3:178.

22 **blood libel** Trachtenberg, 124–58.

22 **"Jewish abortionists"** Jackson Katz, "Abortion Foes Target Jews," *Journal of the North Shore Jewish Community,* Swampscott, MA, July 13, 1989.

22 **host desecration** Trachtenberg, 109–23; **parasites** Bein, 323, 364–72; **poison Christians** Trachtenberg, 97–108.

22 **bubonic plague** M&M, 404; Gottfried, 52, 73–74, 350.

22 **"dangerous carriers"** Trachtenberg, 240 n. 38.

23 **LaRouche organization** Dennis King, *Lyndon LaRouche and the New American Fascism* (New York: Doubleday, 1989), 282–83; **blacks told** "Fascism in America: A Turning Point," in *The Generation After* (newsletter), Spring 1980, 1.

23 **rock star** Professor Griff of Public Enemy, quoted by R. J. Smith, "The Enemy Within," *Village Voice*, May 20, 1989, 102–3.

23 **physicians** Trachtenberg, 97–100.

23 **Doctors' Plot** Baron, 277.

23 **Steve Cokely** Quoted by Eugene Kennedy, "Anti-Semitism in Chicago: A Stunning Silence," NYT Op-Ed, July 26, 1988.

23 **enemies of nations** Trachtenberg, 40, 183–86.

23 **Rashi/Fifth Column** Commentary on Exod. 1:9–10. Rashi (acronym for Rabbi Shlomo Yitzhaki, 1040–1105) was the author of popular commentaries on Scripture and Talmud. Bio: M&M, 356–57. See also Steinsaltz, 67–69.

23 **Elders of Zion** Bein, 337–43.

23 **Argentine juntas** Timerman, 69, 73–74, 101–3, 130–31, 155.

23 **"Beat the Jews" current slogan** Alexander Belenki, quoted by Douglas Martin, "Room 910: Where Emigres Find a Home," NYT, September 9, 1989.

23 **"killed God"/Stalinism** John Garrard and Carol Garrard, NYT, letter, May 27, 1989.

24 **Japanese best seller** Willy Stern, "Anti-Semitic Books May Spark a Backlash," New York *Jewish Week*, July 22, 1989, 17.

24 **"gain the affection"** Finance Minister Ikeda's argument, December 1938, quoted in Tokayer-Swartz, 59.

24 **Glemp's warning** "Remarks by Cardinal at Mass in Czestochowa," NYT, August 29, 1989, A7.

24 **Capote's charge** In *Playboy* interview, March 1968, 169.

24 **black leaders on Hollywood** Leland Clegg, president of the Coalition Against Black Exploitation, spoke on July 12, 1990, of "Jewish Racism in Hollywood" at panel on blacks in the entertainment industry. Reported in NYT, July 13, 1990.

24 **Gen. Brown** Speech, October 10, 1974, at Duke University.

24 **banks and farmers** *The American Farmer and the Extremists: An ADL Special Report*, January 1986.

24 **De Gaulle's description** Quoted in Israel Schenker, *Coat of Many Colors* (New York: Doubleday, 1985), 301–2.

25 **"let us first . . . revenge"** Keller, 202.

25 **10,000 dead** M&M, 363; **records burned** Keller, 218.

25 **blood libel, Poland** M&M, 529, 541–44, 579–81.

25 **Kielce** Sachar, 425.

25 **Semana Trajica** Robert Weisbrot, *The Jews of Argentina: From the Inquisition to Peron* (Philadelphia: JPS, 1979), 200–202.

25 **atrocities during pogroms** Elbogen, 201–5, 378–83, 386.

25 **"We were drunk"** Z&H, 156.

26 **"mothers' milk"** See, for example, remark by then-Premier Itzhak Shamir of Israel, in interview in JP int'l ed., September 6, 1989, 5.

26 **Black Hundreds** M&M, 714.

26 **interior minister** Wencelas von Plehve, quoted by Elbogen, 393.

26 **post-WWI pogroms** Elbogen, 485–500. See also Shalom Schwartzbard, "Memoirs of an Assassin" in Davidowicz, *Golden*, 453–57.

26 **Red Cross report** Elbogen, 500.

26 **Bein on pogroms** *95–96.*

27 **Ben-Sasson quote** "The Northern European Jewish Community" in s/e, 217. See also Nordau, 107.

27 **attitude to Franz Josef** Quoted from Robert Wistrich, *The Jews of Vienna in the Age of Franz Joseph* (New York: Oxford Univ. Press, 1989), in boxed excerpt accompanying Leon Botstein's review, "Blooming While the Sun Went Down," NYTBR, January 18, 1990, 14.

27 **Court Jews** D. Biale, *Power,* 98–99.

28 **Spain** D. Biale, *Power,* 45; M&M, 308–10, 313–17, 312–24; Abrahams, 57.

28 **court factors** M&M, 342–43; Dubnow, *History,* 3:683; Keller, 339–46; Bein, 539–40.

28 **flip side** Janeway, 129, 122–23, 125, where she uses this concept in relation to prescribed roles and negative "shadow roles."

28 **Polish monarchy** M&M, 585, 588.

28 **Jews and Ferdinand and Isabella** M&M, 470–76.

29 **"overnight hotels"** *"Nachsayl,"* in Nordau's words: Sachar, 359. Nordau (1849–1923), a Zionist leader and one of Herzl's first and prime supporters, was known for his "state of the Jews" addresses to World Zionist Congresses. Bio: ZI, 232–34.

29 **Buber** Zionist, philosopher, and advocate of Jewish-Arab rapprochement (1878–1965). Bio: ZI, 451–53. Quote: from 1934 address, "The Jews in the World," ZI, 453.

30 **Jabotinsky** Leader of right-wing Zionist Revisionist Party (1880–1940). Bio: ZI, 557–59. Quoted by Lionel Kahan, "European Jewry in the Nineteenth and Twentieth Century," in Kedourie, 273.

31 **expulsions** England, 1290; France, 1394: M&M, 479.

31 **"seeing the world"** "What Our Literature Needs" in H/G, 26. Isaac Laybush Peretz (1852–1915) was a much-loved Yiddish writer, journalist, and folklorist; he was pro-Socialist, pro-feminist, and pro-Zionist. Bio: Madison, 99–133.

CHAPTER 2: SPIRITUAL RESISTANCE

33 **Horia quote** *God Was Born in Exile* (New York: St. Martin's Press, 1961), 269.

33 **Memmi quote** Memmi, *Liberation,* 147.

33 **Havdalah** Saturday evening ceremony marking the end of Shabbat, which, like all Jewish holidays, begins the preceding evening.

34 **Maimonides** Philosopher, physician, law codifier (1138–1204). Bio: M&M, 337–45. **Longing for "Andalusian homeland," "back home in"** quoted in Abraham J. Heschel, *Maimonides* (New York: Doubleday, 1982), 173.

34 **Sephardic folktales** The Sephardim are Jews descended from those expelled in 1492 from *Sefarad,* the Hebrew name for Spain. (Ashkenazim are Northern, Central, and East European Jews.) Dov Noy, head of the Folklore Department of the Hebrew University of Jerusalem, at Institute on Jewish Folklore, sponsored by 92d Street YM-YWHA, February 26, 1989. From author's notes (hereinafter Noy/Institute).

34 **nostalgia for shtetls** Howe, 71–72, 250; Glanz, 118.

34 **"panic"** Samuel, 23.

34 **anxiety and depression** Memmi, *Liberation,* 267.

34 **explanatory style** Martin E. P. Seligman used this term regarding individuals. His work is described in Robert J. Trotter, "Stop Blaming Yourself," *Psychology Today,* February 1987.

34   **maturation**   Buber, *Moses: The Revelation and the Covenant* (New York: Harper & Row, 1968), 181.

34   **Moses' strategy**   Described by Itzhak Epstein in the *Jewish Liberation Hagada* (New York: Jewish Liberation Project, 1971, 1972).

35   **ethical content**   The idea of one God of justice and mercy for the weak and strong alike: Eisenstadt, 24.

35   **times of danger**   William Orbach, "The Four Faces of God: Toward a Theology of Powerlessness," *Judaism,* Spring 1983, 240.

36   **other nations rejected Torah**   *Sifré* (commentary on Numbers and Deuteronomy attributed to Rabbi Ishmael) Deuteronomy 33:2; *Numbers Rabba* on 14:10; *BT Sota* 35b.

36   **all Jews at Sinai**   *Midrash Tanhuma Yitro,* quoted in Emil Fackenheim, *God's Presence in History* (New York: Harper Torchbooks, 1972), 16.

36   **Berditchever Rebbe's Kaddish**   Ausubel, 29 and 726–77. The Kaddish is an Aramaic prayer affirming faith said at funerals, *yahrzeits* (Yiddish for annual anniversaries of an individual's death), and at services during the mourning period.

37   **Fishkeh film**   Based on a novel by Mendele Mocher Sforim, Mendele the Bookseller, pen name of Sholem Jacob Abramovitch (b. ca. 1836–1917). Writer in Hebrew and Yiddish, satirist, and reformer. Bio: Madison, 33–60. Novel summarized in Madison, 53–57.

37   **Samuel and king**   See Eisenstadt, 56–59.

37   **First Temple/Commonwealth**   The First Jewish Commonwealth, a.k.a. the monarchy, began with King Saul, in 1028 B.C.E.; the Temple was built during the reign of Solomon (973–33). After his death, the monarchy split into two states: Judea and Israel. The First Commonwealth and Temple were destroyed by Babylonia in 586 B.C.E.

38   **prophets as social thinkers and activists**   Eisenstadt, 17, 22.

38   **reform under Hezekiah**   M&M, 100–101; **under Josiah**   Eisenstadt, 114–17.

38   **pleasant exile**   M&M, 116.

39   **take Torah seriously**   M&M, 115.

39   **Second Temple/Commonwealth**   The rebuilding of the Temple began in 520 B.C.E. while Judea was under Persia. Judea was conquered by Alexander the Great in 331 B.C.E., Egypt in 320, and the Hellenistic Syrians in 198 B.C.E. A revolt led by the Maccabees succeeded in the establishment of an independent state in 142 B.C.E. It ended de facto when Pompey attained control of Judea for Rome in 63 B.C.E. and de jure in 6 C.E. The Temple was destroyed in 70 C.E. after a revolt, crushed in 73 C.E., which marks the official end of the Second Commonwealth.

39   **Pharisees**   M&M, 153–60, 174–75. The Pharisees were unfairly maligned in the New Testament. For an accurate description, see Ahad Ha'am's essay, "Flesh and Spirit" (1904), in *Basic Writings*.

40   **Akiva**   See Finkelstein biography and M&M, 213.

40   **Akiva and Bar Kochba**   JT Taanit 68b; M&M, 213–14.

40   **Maimonides' principles**   In *High Holyday Prayer Book,* translated and annotated by Philip Birnbaum (New York: Hebrew Publishing Co., 1951), 879–80.

40   **discouraged messianism**   D. Biale, *Power,* 39; Zeitlin, 187.

40   **mass movement**   Patai, *Goddess,* 113–16; Scholem, *Mysticism,* 229.

40   **"cosmic law"**   Scholem, *Mysticism,* 14. See also A. J. Heschel, "The Mystical Element in Judaism," in Finkelstein, *Jews,* 166–68.

40   **Zohar**   Authored by Moshe de Leon of Spain (1256–1305): Scholem, *Mysticism,* 190–204; M&M, 432–34.

40   **Ein Sof, sefirot**   Scholem, *Mysticism,* 207–9, 225. **faces**   213.

40   **evolution of Kabbalah and merging with messianism**   Scholem, *Mysticism,* 247.

40   **"hastening the End"**   Scholem, *Mysticism,* 247.

40   **the Ari**   Acronym of Ashkenazi Rabbi Yitzhak (1534–1572), and meaning "lion" in Hebrew: Scholem, *Mysticism,* 253–59; Dubnow, *History,* 3:507.

40   **Lurianic Kabbala, as "great myth of Exile"**   Scholem, *Mysticism,* 286.

41   **"This is the secret"**   Rabbi Hayim Vital Calabrese (1543–1640), a leading disciple of Rabbi Luria, *Book of Gleanings,* quoted in Scholem, *Mysticism,* 284.

41   **when good and evil separated**   Vital, quoted in Scholem, *Mysticism,* 305. **symbol of tikkun**   Scholem, *Mysticism,* 274.

41   **pre-Lurianic martyrologies**   Orbach, "Four Faces of God," 243.

41   **"redeemer of captives"**   In the *Shmoneh Esray (18 Benedictions),* the prayer said at daily and holiday synagogue services.

41   **Chosen People in Scriptures**   See ET, 58–63 and Ahad Ha'am's 1898 essay, "The Transvaluation of Values" in *Basic Writings,* 175–76.

41   **"self-stereotype"**   Patai, *Mind,* 461–62; see also BT *Yevamot* 79a.

42   **"shackles His omnipotence"**   Berkovits, *Faith,* 108–9.

42   **absent medieval husbands**   Abrahams, 89.

42   **home-based mother**   See Z&H, 333.

42   **Schechinah**   See Heschel in Finkelstein, *Jews,* 162–66.

42   **Schechinah approachable**   Patai, *Goddess,* 139.

42   **Shechinah in Exile**   Patai, *Goddess,* 103; BT *Megillah* 29a.

42   **maternal**   Scholem, *Mysticism,* 230; Patai, *Goddess,* 116.

43   **Schechinah in Talmud**   Patai, *Goddess,* 99–102; **"manifestation"**   105.

43   **Schechinah in desert**   Patai, *Goddess,* 99; **Tabernacle**   100–101; **First Temple** 101; **Second Temple**   102; **worthy individuals**   103, 104; **comforter**   103; **houses of study**   *Pesikta Rabati,* 160a.

43   **identified with Knesset Israel**   Scholem, *Mysticism,* 230, 233; Patai, *Goddess,* 108, 110, 129.

43   **would remain in Exile until redemption**   Patai, *Goddess,* 159–60.

43   **grammatical gender**   Patai, *Goddess,* 107.

43   **Matronit**   Patai, *Goddess,* 115; **Mother Rachel**   128, 145–46; **Mother Zion** 212–14; **Shabbat bride**   267–69; **Widow Jerusalem**   Scholem, *Mysticism,* 230.

43   **interceder**   Patai, *Goddess,* 106, 115; Scholem, *Mysticism,* 105.

43   **Matronit and King as sefirot**   Patai, *Goddess,* 128–29.

43   **separated when "bedchamber" destroyed**   Patai, *Goddess,* 129–42, 144.

43   **to reunite**   Scholem, *Mysticism,* 232, 275; see also Patai, *Goddess,* 162, 168; **yichudim**   Patai, *Goddess,* 161–72.

44   **folk idea**   Patai, *Goddess,* 158–60, 168.

44   **her importance**   Scholem, *Mysticism,* 229; Patai, *Goddess,* 160.

44   **doctrine of tikkun**   Scholem, *Mysticism,* 274, 284.

44   **prayer with kavannah**   Patai, *Mind,* 205; Scholem, *Mysticism,* 277–78; and Heschel, in Finkelstein, *Jews,* 168–71.

44   **Zohar on marital sex**   Patai, *Goddess,* 142–43; Scholem, *Mysticism,* 235.

44   **three-part meditation**   Written by Jacob ben Hayyim Tzemach (d. after 1665): Patai, *Goddess,* 146.

45   **folk heroes**   For example, Joseph della Reyna, in Ausubel, 206–15.

45   **"responsible for . . . Exile"**   Scholem, *Mysticism,* 274. See also 276.

45   **two perfect Sabbaths**   BT *Shabbat* 118b.

45   **false messiahs**   *Jewish Almanac,* 584–89, 592–94; **Shabbetai Zvi**   M&M, 558–67, and Scholem, *Sabbetai Sevi.*

45   **Herzl as Messiah**   Elon, *Herzl,* 382–84, 182.

46   **maskilim and absolutist states**   D. Biale, *Power,* 101–9; **"redeemer"**   107.

46   **secularized version**   See Bein, 273 and 578 n. 211.

46   **The Jewish Question**   See Bein.

46   **"true Messiah"**   Gold, 309.

46   **Steinthall**   Scientist and professor at the University of Berlin, in 1890. Quoted by Gordon Craig in book review, "Outsiders." NYRB, June 13, 1985, 4; **cultural intermediaries transmitted**   3.

46   **enlightenment values replaced by nationalism**   Craig, "Outsiders," 3. Craig, in his review, summarizes views expressed by George Mosse in *German Jews Beyond Judaism* (Bloomington: Indiana Univ. Press and Cincinnati: HUC Press, 1985).

47   **anti-Semitic parties**   Ben-Sasson, 870–78.

47   **Dreyfus**   M&M, 702–3; See also Nordau, 79–84.

47   **"Death to the Jews!"**   Elon, *Herzl,* 129. See also Talmon, 111.

48   **Syrkin**   Socialist Zionist writer and activist (1867–1924). Bio: ZI, 331–32, WMT, 377–99, and Avineri, chap. 12. Quote: 1898 essay, "Internationalism vs. Nationalism," reprinted in Syrkin, *Essays,* 16–17. See also Memmi, *Liberation,* chap. 15.

48   **Luxembourg's rebuke**   In 1917 letter quoted in J. P. Nettl, *Rosa Luxembourg* (London: Oxford Univ. Press, 1966), 2:860.

48   **Jewish revolutionaries**   See Talmon, chap. 1.

48   **Russian Jewish revolutionaries**   See WMT.

48   **Second Front**   Personal testimony of Lillian Elkin to author.

48   **"unpatriotic"**   Marie Syrkin, "What American Jews Did During the Holocaust," *Midstream,* October 1982, 5.

49   **acting in its best interests**   See Judd Teller, "Failures and Prospects of U.S. Zionism," *Israel Horizons,* April 1970, 25.

49   **Soviet Yiddish writers**   Baron, 269–74.

49   **Slansky**   Secretary of post–WWII Czech CP, executed after 1952 show trial charging him (and thirteen others) with participating in a worldwide Jewish conspiracy against the state: EJ, 14:1654.

49   **Cinderella**   See Memmi, *Liberation,* 152.

50   **triumphed**   The parent-child metaphor appears in some prayers (e.g., Yom Kippur liturgy).

50   **whoring as rebellion**   Adler, "Feminine Imagery in Judaism," *J. Almanac,* 513.

50   **midrash on Lamentations**   *Lamentations Rabba* 3:21.

50   **Song of Songs**   "The holiest of the holies": *Mishnah Yadayim* III.5; **Akiva's view of** Finkelstein, *Akiva,* 187, 191.

51   **Gerchunoff**   Quoted from his 1910 novel, *Los Gauchos Judios,* by Edna Aisenberg in "Resurgent Anti-Semitism in Argentina," JTA-DNB, August 7, 1975.

51   **German Jews' unrequited love**   Scholem, *Crisis,* 86. See Memmi, *Oppression,* 214.

51   **dowry**   *Portrait,* 75.

52   **Trotsky's definition of revolution**   *History of the Russian Revolution* (New York: Simon & Schuster, 1937), xvii.

52 **"auto-emancipation"** Title of Pinsker's pamphlet, 1882.

52 **"If you will it"** Epigraph in *Altneuland,* 1902; Eng. trans.: *Old-New Land* (New York: Bloch, 1941), i.

CHAPTER 3: EVOLUTION OF *HALACHA,* JEWISH CONSTITUTIONAL LAW

53 **Ahad Ha'am** ("One of the people"), pen name of Asher Zvi Ginsberg (1856–1927), founder of Spiritual Zionism, which conceived of a Jewish homeland's becoming the spiritual center for the Jews. Bio: ZI, 248–51; Avineri, chap. 2; Zipperstein; and Hans Kohn's intro. to *Basic Writings,* 7–33. Quote: "Shabbat in Zionism," *Collected Works of Ahad Ha'am* (Heb.) (Jerusalem: Hotza'a Ivrit, 1947), 286.

53 **Heine quote** 435.

53 **Moses Hess** Early German Socialist Zionist (1812–1875), author of *Rome and Jerusalem* (1862). Bio: Meyer Waxman's intro. to *Rome and Jerusalem,* 11–33; see also ZI, 117–18; Avineri, chap. 3; and Talmon, 94–103. Quote: *Rome and Jerusalem,* 92.

53 **"responsible"** BT *Shevuot,* 39a.

54 **practical matters** Steinsaltz, chap. 13.

55 **Yannai** JT *Sanhedrin* 22a.

55 **link through interpretation** Judah Shapiro, class on "The American Jewish Establishment" at the Jewish Liberation School (JLS), February–March 1972, from author's tapes (hereinafter Shapiro/JLS). Shapiro (1912–1980) was also a Labor Zionist leader, author, and radio commentator.

56 **synods** Abrahams, 37–39; **Councils' legislation** 58–61.

56 **Yavneh** Academy/legislature/court (Sanhedrin) established by Rabbi Yochanan ben Zakkai. It made important decisions dealing with problems arising from the destruction of the Temple and the exile of the plurality of Judeans: Zeitlin, 161–214.

56 **evolution of Mishnah** Steinsaltz, 24–55; ET, xxxi–xxvi; Tamari, 14–15; **Six Orders** ET, xxvii–xxx; Steinsaltz, chap. 12.

56 **evolution of Gemara** Steinsaltz, 56–63; ET, xxxi–xxxvii; Tamari, 16–19.

56 **Babylonian Talmud** 5,894 folio pages: Potok, 239. About one quarter to one third consists of *Agada.* See Steinsaltz, chap. 32.

56 **Oral Law** Tamari, 12. According to Jewish tradition, the law given at Sinai included the Oral Law: BT *Brachot* 5a.

56 **the word "Torah"** Z&H, 108.

56 **post-Talmud evolution** Steinsaltz, 64–73.

57 **responsa** Freehof, 16–17, 199–200, 222–23.

57 **educated laypersons, economic interests** Shapiro/JLS.

57 **"state of disputation"** Shapiro/JLS.

57 **conflicting opinions** Tamari, 12–13.

57 **conflict ... consensus** Murray Zuckoff calls this process the "dialectic of *Halacha.*"

57 **legal methods** Blu Greenberg, "Women's Liberation and Jewish Law," *Lilith* no. 1 (1976): 16–17. A basic principle in Talmudic literature is that every age is justified in disregarding, and is even duty-bound to disregard, the Written Law whenever reason and conviction demand its nullification: *Mishnah Rosh Hashana* II.9.

57 **Irving Greenberg's suggestion** Address to the First National Jewish Women's Conference, April 1973, from author's notes.

58 **"One wonders"** Gershon Mamlak, "How Religious Zionism Lost Its Values," JP, November 6, 1988.

58 **Graetz on Talmud** 2:448. See also Steinsaltz, chap. 34.

59 **"partner"** Heschel, "The East European Era in Jewish History" in H/G, 74. See also Steinsaltz, chap. 30.

59 **"workshop of thought"** Graetz 2:447.

59 **avoidance of generalizations** Z&H, 122; **models** Steinsaltz, 228 and chap. 28.

59 **labor on Shabbat** *Mishnah Shabbat* VII.2. See Steinsaltz, 12, 108–9.

59 **categories of damage** *Mishnah Bava Kamma* VIII.1; **fines substituted** BT *Bava Kamma* 83bff.

59 **"evidence . . . search for truth"** Steinsaltz, 231–32; **from life experience** 99.

59 **reconcile differences** Steinsaltz, 232.

59 **Midrash** Compiled at various dates between the fifth and twelfth centuries C.E. The most important collection is *Midrash Rabba* (the Great Midrash) of commentaries on verses in the Five Books and the five Scrolls: ET, xxxvi–vii.

60 **"attitudes and thought habits"** Z&H, 121, 123. This 1952 work, which attempted an ethnographic reconstruction of shtetl life, though problematic in being based totally on recollections by an unrevealed number of unidentified individuals from the hindsight of anywhere from several decades to over a half-century after, is nevertheless an invaluable source.

60 **resemblance to discussions in yeshiva** Z&H, 121.

60 **house-painting incident** Z&H, 122.

60 **patients' worry** Richard A. Sternbach, director of Pain Treatment Center of Scripps Clinic and Research Foundation, La Jolla, CA, quoted in NYT Personal Health column on "Pain—For Millions of Americans It Remains a Daily Reality," April 22, 1981, C12.

61 **Durants** *The Story of Civilization.* III: *Caesar and Christ* (New York: Simon & Schuster, 1944), 548. For accurate description of exegetical methodology, see Steinsaltz, 221–26.

61 **never mainstreamed** Hopefully Steinsaltz's new translation of the Talmud will make the Talmud more accessible.

61 **Noy's observation** Noy/Institute.

61 **Arab hyperbole** See Joel Kraemer, "Use of Words Is an Arab Art," JP magazine, August 18, 1972, 13.

61 **Palestinian Covenant** "Words Israelis Insist PLO Drop in Pact" include "Armed struggle is the only way to liberate Palestine. . . . The establishment of the State of Israel [is] entirely illegal. . . . The liberation of Palestine will destroy the Zionist and imperialist presence": NYT, September 8, 1993, A15.

61 **Irish chief's words** Hugh Lanigan to Rabbi David Small in *Friday the Rabbi Slept Late* (New York: Crown, 1974), 132.

62 **Freud on unpopularity** 1926 letter to his B'nai B'rith lodge, quoted in Erikson, 281.

62 **Samuel quote** 28.

62 **"keep warm"** Quoted by Myerhoff, 188.

62 **debate in Tikva** Piercy, *He, She and It* (New York: Fawcett Crest/Ballantine, 1991), 403–4.

63 **Spinoza** Shapiro/JLS. See M&M, 497, and Dubnow, *History,* 3:641.

63 **Latin America** See Murray Zuckoff, "Who Is a Jew in Latin America," JTA-DNB, September 1, 1976.

63 **Foster's confession** *Square One: A Memoir* (New York: Donald I. Fine, 1988), 128.

64 **Yohanan on Resh Lakish** BT *Bava Metzia* 84a.

64 **"no matter how wise"** Z&H, 120.

64 **"Seek no intimacy"** PA 1:10.

64 **tradition of resisting authority** See Uriel Simon, "Biblical and Rabbinic Passages of the Jewish Ethics of Warfare," OVS, 18–26; and Emanuel Rackman, "Violence and the Value of Life: A *Halakhic* View," OVS, 42–54.

64 **Israeli soldiers** "The Appellate Military Court enjoined all soldiers to disobey a manifestly illegal order" a few years after the court-martial of soldiers who carried out a mass killing in Kfar Kassem in 1956: F&S, 231.

64 **Weizmann's comment** Quoted by his nephew, Ezer Weizmann (who took office as Israel's president in fall 1993), in Eric Silver, "All the People's President," JR, January 27, 1994, 19.

65 **"If Not Higher"** Peretz, 174.

65 **"If only"** Rabbi Hiya's comment in JT *Hagiga* 76b on Jeremiah's lament (16:11) in God's name that "they have abandoned Me and not kept My Torah."

66 **Heavenly voice tale** BT *Bava Metzia* 59b.

66 **similarity with Chinese tradition** Lecture, January 1, 1959, by Jacob L. Talmon, professor of history, Hebrew University of Jerusalem, in course "History of Imperialism, 1879–1914," from author's notes.

66 **three inviolable laws** BT *Sanhedrin* 74 a+b.

66 **"Whoever saves one life"** *Mishnah Sanhedrin* IV.5.

66 **Pikuach Nefesh and holidays** BT *Shabbat* 84b–85b.

66 **David and famine midrash** Ginzberg, 4:11.

66 **O'Connor statement** In Trude Weiss-Rosmarin, "The Absurdity of Theologizing the Holocaust," *Jewish Spectator*, Spring 1988, 8.

66 **Borowitz on sickness** Confirmed in phone conversation with Tamara Cohen, December 1993.

67 **contraception** Discussed throughout Feldman; **and painful births** 240, 293; **abortions** 275–84, 291; **and woman's psychological health** 285–94. The principle, Feldman sums up on 294, is that "her pain comes first."

67 **abortion in Kovno Ghetto** August 28, 1942, responsum of Rabbi Y. Lieman, quoted in translation of his responsa by Ephraim Oshry, *Responsa from the Holocaust* (New York: Judaica Press, 1983), 81.

67 **children** Z&H, 372.

67 **Shaw on food** Quoted by Evelyn Keyes, *Scarlett O'Hara's Younger Sister* (New York: Fawcett Crest, 1977), 251.

67 **"kill him first"** BT *Sanhedrin* 72a. See Steinsaltz, 173.

67 **war and context** See essays in OVS.

68 **proof in murder case** Steinsaltz, 167–68. See *Tosefta* (supplement)—collection of laws parallel to Mishnah but with added material, ca. fifth cent. C.E.—*Sanhedrin* VIII.3.

68 **bloodthirsty court** Steinsaltz, 169.

68 **theft** Tamari, 40.

68 **kashrut** See Samuel Dresner and Seymour Siegel, *The Jewish Dietary Laws* (New York: Burning Bush Press, 1959, 1966).

69 **Soler's thesis** "The Dietary Prohibitions of the Hebrews," NYRB, June 14, 1979, 28–29; **ban on intermixing** 29.

69 **Berman's views** Lecture on "Ecology and the Jewish Torah" at Conference on "Judaism and the Environment," New York, March 13, 1988, from author's notes.

69 **"sanctuary in time"** Heschel, "Beyond Civilization," in *The Sabbath—Its Meaning for Modern Man* (New York: Farrar, Straus and Giroux/Noonday, 1951), 29.

69 **mandated for all** Harvey Cox, interviewed by Sherman Goldman, "Lost in Wonderland," *East-West Journal,* May 1978.

69 **utopia in time** Eisenstadt, 46.

70 **two yetzers** See ET, 88–93.

70 **definition of yetzer hara** Feldman, 88.

70 **"Were it not for"** *Gen. Rabba* 9:7. Concept dramatized in the *Star Trek* episode "The Enemy Within," by Richard Matteson.

70 **"fences"** For example, Ashkenazic rabbis placed a "fence" of six hours' wait between eating meat and eating dairy.

70 **Emden on sex** Quoted in Feldman, 89.

70 **rabbis with "temporary wives"** Rav and Rav Nachman: BT *Yoma* 18a. See Isaiah M. Gafni, "The Institution of Marriage in Rabbinic Times," in Kraemer, 24.

71 **wealthy man living on crusts** Quoted in Ausubel, 130.

71 **attitude on pursuing material possessions** Tamari, 28–32, 38–40, 50.

71 **fraud, cheating, etc.** Tamari, 46–48, 49–50, and chap. 5.

71 **price controls, etc.** Adena Berkowitz, in "Business and Ethics: An Odd Couple," points out that over 100 of the 613 commandments deal with economic matters: *Barnard Alumnae Magazine,* Winter 1990.

71 **labor laws** ET, 196–97; Wischnitzer, 36–38; Tamari, chap. 6.

71 **payment of wages** *Mishnah Bava Metzia* IX.12; see Tamari, 135–36.

71 **alternative dispute resolution** See Fein, 295–96.

71 **"central principle"** Tamari, 36–37.

71 **tzedakah** Tamari, chap. 9, 242–62; ET, 219–26; Patai, *Mind,* 530–33; **obligation of community** Tamari, 260.

71 **anonymous giving and dignity** ET, 224, 249; Tamari, 260.

71 **Persia** The Jewish community of Meshhed in Northeast Persia, early twentieth century: Patai, *Mind,* 531.

71 **closed coffins** Shapiro/JLS.

71 **entitlement** Tamari, 260; Patai, *Mind,* 525.

72 **"deed . . . that counts"** PA 1:7.

72 **repentance** BT *Taanit* 16a.

72 **not doing . . . doing for own sake** BT *Brachot* 16b; *Sanhedrin* 105b.

72 **Ladder of Tzedakah** In English translation: Ausubel, 124.

73 **Zweig on Vienna Jews** *The World of Yesterday* (Lincoln: Univ. of Nebraska Press, 1964), 21–22.

74 **"every man . . . equally among all"** "Poetry, Books and Readers," in Peretz, 320.

74 **new reality of classes** M&M, 85–87; Eisenstadt, 64–67.

75 **no vision of gender equality** Cynthia Ozick calls this "The Missing Commandment" of "Thou shalt not lessen the Humanity of Woman": "Notes Toward the Right Question," *Lilith* no. 6 (1979): 27–29.

75 **"Do not impose a decree"** BT *Bava Kamma* 89b.

76 **rabbis and leaders** D. Biale, *Power,* 47–52.

76 **Islam, 900–1200 C.E.** S. D. Goitein, "Jewish Society and Institutions Under Islam," in S/E, 184.

76 **medieval Spain** Haim Beinart, "Hispano-Jewish Society," in S/E, 227 and 230–37 generally. See also Cahnman, xviii.

76 **synod's takkanah** Finkelstein, *Self-Government,* 33.

76 **European High Middle Ages** Abrahams, 43.

76   **Poland**   Katz, *Tradition and Crisis,* 82, 102, 105.

76   **poor Jews**   See D. Biale, *Power,* 82.

76   **artisans' revolts: Spain**   Cahnman, xix; **eighteenth-century Poland**   Wischnitzer, 258–59 and chap. 23, passim.

77   **Raya Mehemna**   Believed to have been written in thirteenth-century Spain under Christian rule. Interpretation: Gershom Scholem's course on *Kabbalah* at the Hebrew University of Jerusalem, lectures given February 4, 1959, and February 18, 1959, from author's notes.

77   **prayer interruption**   Finkelstein, *Self-Government,* 15–17. See also S. D. Goitein, *A Mediterranean Society,* vol. 2 (Los Angeles: UCLA Press, 1971), 324; and Abrahams, 7.

77   **in Italy**   Howard Adelman, "Italian Jewish Women," in Baskin, 144.

77   **"same effect"**   Finkelstein, *Self-Government,* 15–16, 33.

CHAPTER 4: FROM MACHO TO MENTSCH

79   **"Scholars increase peace"**   BT *Brachot* 64a.

79   **"Jerusalem was destroyed"**   BT *Shabbat* 119b.

79   **"My town"**   Quoted from his book, *Mein Shtetl in Ukrayne,* in Abraham Menes, "The East Side and the Jewish Labor Movement" in H/G, 207. Olgyn bio: Howe, 240.

79   **Barzini on family**   190; see also 191, 219.

79   **medieval community**   Abrahams, 24. Similarly, in the shtetl: Z&H, 306; see also 228–30, 421–24.

80   **"always concerned"**   Z&H, 230.

80   **"felt as an attack"**   Z&H, 227. See also Myerhoff, 171–73.

80   **Hillel's instructions**   PA 2:5.

80   **Talmud on mine/yours**   PA 5:13. **Sodomites' crimes**   Ausubel, 366–68.

80   **"mutual responsibility"**   Zuckerman, quoted in Christopher Browning, "He Out-fought the Holocaust," review of *A Surplus of Memory: Chronicle of the Warsaw Ghetto Uprising* (Los Angeles: Univ. of California Press, 1993), NYTBR, May 23, 1993, 22.

80   **"Do we have the right"**   Quoted in Fackenheim, 221.

81   **M. K.'s statement**   Ehud Olmert, quoted in George Gruen, *The Not-So-Silent Partnership: Emerging Trends in American Jewish–Israel Relations* (New York: American Jewish Committee, 1988), 19.

81   **scholars**   See discussion on Pharisees in Ahad Ha'am's "Flesh and Spirit" (1904) in *Basic Writings,* 188–205; Yitzhak F. Baer, "The Social Ideals of the Second Jewish Commonwealth," and E. E. Urbach, "The Talmudic Sage—Character and Authority," in S/E.

81   **resisting tyranny militarily**   Against Babylonia: M&M, 109–13; against Rome, Zealots: 194–204, Masada: 203–4; against Rome, Bar Kochba revolt: 213–15, Betar: 215.

81   **Eisenstadt on Isaiah**   97.

82   **condemned Zealots**   BT *Gittin* 56a; see Zeitlin, 136–37.

82   **Bar Keziva**   A pun on his name, Bar Koziba: D. Biale, *Power,* 39; see also BT *Gittin* 57a.

82   **physical resistance**   Salo Baron, "Review of the History" of the ancient and medieval period, in B/W, 32; M&M, 366.

82   **Tulczyn, events at**   M&M, 366; **leaders' address**   Quoted by Rackman, "Violence and the Value of Life," in OVS, 34.

82   **factor in Underground decisions**   See author's interview with Vitke Kempner of the United Partisan Organization (FPO) of Vilna, "She Fought Back," in *Lilith,* no. 16 (Spring 1987): 23.

82 **Vilna martyr** FPO leader Itzik Wittenberg: Kowalski, 142–44.

83 **cut out of prayer book** Abraham E. Millgram, *Jewish Worship* (Philadelphia: JPS, 1971), 453.

83 **banned Haman effigy** Dubnow, *History,* 3:418.

83 **class war, food** M&M, 201; Zeitlin, *99,* 434 n. 44.

84 **"Only against rioters"** Beinart in S/E, 223.

84 **violence-free zones** See Roth, 58.

84 **self-image** Patai, *Mind,* 461. See also Teller, 204.

84 **tzaar ba'alei chayim** For laws and traditions, see author et al., "Kindness to Animals" in *Jewish Catalog 3;* Richard H. Schwartz, *Judaism and Vegetarianism* (Marblehead, MA: Micah Press, 1988), chap. 2; Abrahams, 138–39; Z&H, 341.

84 **schechita** Ronald L. Androphy, *"Shehitah,"* in *Jewish Catalog 3,* 298–305; ET, 237.

84 **"animal sagged . . . down"** Hersey, 226.

84 **animals fed first** BT *Brachot* 40a.

84 **Rosenberg story** Quoted in Berkovits, *Faith,* 168.

85 **Sholem Aleichem** Pen name of Sholom Rabinovitch (1859–1916), beloved Yiddish writer, known for his compassionate portrayal of the common people. Bio: Madison, 61–98. Story: *"Tzaar Ba'alei Chayim"* in Sholem Aleichem's *Works for Jewish Children* (Yiddish) (New York: Tageblatt, 1912), 3:121.

85 **Dina** Aschkenasy, 124–31; midrash on: 130.

85 **traveling around** See, for example, Roth, 44.

85 **rape legislation** See Rachel Biale, chap. 10.

85 **two angles** R. Biale, 240.

85 **unattached woman** R. Biale, 242, 243; **protection** 242.

85 **crime of passion** R. Biale, 254; **way of compelling a match** 241, 243, 254.

85 **Maimonides' ruling** R. Biale, 242.

86 **fines in Talmud** R. Biale, 243–45.

86 **duress** R. Biale, 249, 255.

86 **marital rape** R. Biale, 252–53, quoting BT *Eruvin* 100b.

86 **Rabad's definition of** R. Biale, 253–54.

86 **rape of three-year-old** BT *Ketubot* 11a, b. The context was a discussion on whether the child's virginity was destroyed, which would halve her dowry; the rabbis decided the hymen grew back. **Adler's comment** "I've Had Nothing Yet So I Can't Take More," *Moment,* September 1983, 25.

86 **premarital pregnancies** Rabbi Ovadiah di Bertinoro, a traveler in fifteenth-century Sicily, quoted in Roth, 45.

86 **Kempner testimony** Author's notes for interview, "She Fought Back," *Lilith.*

87 **Korczak** Testimony obtained during research on *Partisans of Vilna* film, provided to author by its producer, Aviva Kempner.

87 **double jeopardy** The Hebrew terms for rape and rape victim, and for forced converts, derive from the same grammatical root.

87 **Belle Juive** Sartre, 48–49.

87 **discussions** *Mishnah Ketubot* II.5 and IV.9.

87 **dress as men** Abrahams, 93; **false beards** 274–75.

87 **defined by mother** The Orthodox were incensed about the Reform movement's unilateral decision in 1983 to approve what has been misnamed "patrilineal descent": defining a Jew as a person born to a Jewish father or mother, in contradistinction to Halacha.

88 **rape during the Holocaust** Testimony of women survivors at 1983 conference on "Women Surviving: the Holocaust," recorded in Katz/Ringelheim, *Proceedings.* See also

Joan Ringelheim, "Women and the Holocaust: A Reconsideration of Research," in Baskin, 263 n. 6.

88 **prostitution** See Ka-Tzetnik 135633 (pseud.), *House of Dolls* (Chicago: Academic Press, 1982).

88 **sterilization** See accounts in Mavis Hill and L. Norman Williams, *Auschwitz in England: A Record of a Libel Action* (New York: Stein & Day, 1965).

88 **sadism** Fackenheim writes, "One characteristic action of the Holocaust world was the most painful public murder of Jewish babies conducted whenever possible in the hearing or sight of their mothers": 212–13.

88 **rape in Argentina** Jacobo Timerman, quoted by Jack Newfield, "Anti-Semitism and the Crime of Silence," *Village Voice,* June 17–23, 1981, 14.

88 **live cats** M&M, 552.

89 **Bart's conclusion** In Susan Weidman Schneider's interview with her in *Lilith,* no. 15 (Summer 1986): 8.

89 **David's motive** Cited in David S. Shapiro, "The Jewish Attitude Toward War and Peace," OVS, 70.

89 **"take care of herself"** Z&H, 132.

89 **Dina's "promiscuity" and "motive"** Aschkenasy, 129–30.

89 **"pleasure with uncircumcised man"** *Gen. Rabba* 80:11.

89 **"a pogrom"** Quoted in Schneider, 222.

89 **"In the City of Carnage"** In *Complete Poetic Works of Chayim Nachman Bialik* (Heb.) (Tel Aviv: Dvir, 1939), 82–85 (hereinafter Bialik/Dvir). Bialik (1873–1934) was a noted Hebrew poet, Zionist, folklorist. Bio: Sanders, 269–74.

90 **Kishinev pogrom** D/R&P 3:69–75. **"They saw"** "Carnage," 83.

90 **"Three Gifts"** In Peretz, 182ff; sum. in Madison, 123–25.

90 **Medieval Spanish account** In Rabbi Abraham Ibn David, *Sefer Ha-Quabbalah* (Philadelphia: JPS, 1967), 64.

90 **Kurdish account** From oral history recounted by Susan Starr Sered in "The Synagogue as Sacred Space for the Elderly Oriental Women of Jerusalem," G-H, 209.

90 **Brahilov** Recounted in Belinfante-Dubov, *An-Sky,* 103–4.

90 **Venice tale** Related by Leone de Modena, in *Tzemach Tzaddik* as "The Chaste Maiden." In English translation: Ausubel, 120ff.

92 **"most potent" means** Urbach, "The Talmudic Sage," in S/E, 138.

92 **"school of fighting"** Heine, 327.

93 **Resh Lakish's transformation** BT *Bava Metzia* 84a.

93 **"just as in Bible times"** Abrahams, 171–72.

93 **"Study was a technique"** Heschel, in H/G, 74.

93 **"nothing worthwhile"** Paul Goodman, "Youth in the Organized Society," *Commentary,* February 1960, page 10 of reprint.

93 **excluded from "life of mind"** "The Image and Status of Women in Classic Rabbinic Judaism," in Baskin, 85; **"learning-based culture"** 92 n. 41.

93 **democratized** See Abrahams, 357, and Heschel, in H/G, 72.

93 **God studies Torah** Three hours a day: BT *Avoda Zara* 3b.

94 **respect for books** Abrahams, 353. It was customary to kiss a book that fell to the floor: Z&H, 360. See also Elon, *Herzl,* 383.

94 **Ibn Tibbon's advice** Quoted in Abrahams, 354.

94 **ignoramus** PA 2:6. See discussion in Zeitlin, 319–22.

94   **Torah lishma**   BT *Sukkah* 49b and BT *Taanit* 7a.

94   **"Sholom Bayis" story**   "An Idyllic Home," Peretz, 146–54.

94   **"learned rather than wealthy"**   Samuel, 196.

95   **"songs of learning"**   Samuel, 196. See Rubin, 32, 132.

95   **"The Calf"**   In Irving Howe and Eliezer Greenberg, eds., *A Treasury of Yiddish Stories*, rev. ed. (New York: Viking, 1989), 97–111.

95   **ruddy look**   Comment by Ruth Adler, 171. See Z&H, 358.

95   **"muscular Judaism"**   Nordau, address to the fifth World Zionist Congress, 1901: 138.

95   **community's support of education**   Abrahams, 349; Simon Greenberg, "Jewish Educational Institutions" in Finkelstein, *Jews,* 386–91; see also Dubnow, *History,* 3:421, and Tamari, 269–74.

95   **Joshua ben Gamala**   BT *Bava Batra* 21a.

95   **"One does not suspend"**   BT *Shabbat* 119b.

95   **universality**   Simon Greenberg, "Jewish Educational Institutions," in Finkelstein, *Jews,* 387.

95   **Ozick on Tevye**   "Sholem Aleichem's Revolution," *The New Yorker,* February 28, 1988, 104.

95   **interbellum Poland**   Simon Greenberg, "Jewish Educational Institutions," 392–93.

95   **Image Before My Eyes**   Produced by YIVO Institute for Jewish Research; Josh Waletzky, director; 1980.

96   **Talmudic academies**   Simon Greenberg, "Jewish Educational Institutions," 402–4.

96   **Kalla**   Simon Greenberg, "Jewish Educational Institutions," 404–5; See also Wischnitzer, 41.

96   **yeshiva in Europe, eating days**   Simon Greenberg, "Jewish Educational Institutions," 405–6, and testimony of author's father, Joseph Cantor, z"l, who studied at the Volozhin Yeshiva. See also Abraham Menes, "Patterns of Jewish Scholarship in Eastern Europe," in Finkelstein, *Jews.*

96   **primary aim**   Simon Greenberg, "Jewish Educational Institutions," 406.

96   **home or besmedrush study**   Menes, "Jewish Scholarship," in Finkelstein, *Jews,* 209.

96   **Chevreh Shas**   *Shas,* an acronym for the Hebrew words for *Six Orders,* is commonly used to mean the Talmud; **study circle**   Samuel, 194.

96   **"one is permitted"**   Quoted by Simon Greenberg, "Jewish Educational Institutions," 403.

96   **"creative house / foundry"**   Poem, "*Hamatmid*" (roughly translated as "The Diligent Torah Student") in Bialik/Dvir, 75.

97   **"Should You Wish to Know"**   Bialik/Dvir, 17–18, trans.: author.

97   **Yochanan ben Zakkai**   *Gittin* 56b; **Role in Legislation**   Zeitlin, 259–62, 179–84.

97   **Ten Martyrs**   M&M, 216; Ausubel, 154–56.

97   **"worthy of ... Plato"**   Finkelstein, "The Ten Martyrs" in *Essays and Studies in Memory of Linda R. Miller,* ed. Israel Davidson (New York, 1939), 48–49.

97   **God revealed to Abraham**   Ginzberg, 1:292.

97   **fulfilled mitzvot**   BT *Yoma* 28b.

97   **Jacob, after thirteenth year**   Ginzberg, 1:316.

98   **"prepare his meal"**   319.

98   **Rashi on "lived with Lavan"**   Commentary on Gen. 32:4.

98   **613 mitzvot**   BT *Makkot* 24a.

98   **David stories**   Ginzberg, 4:101.

98 **Solomon** See Ausubel, 448–49, 492–94; **analyzed laws** Ginzberg, 4:130.

98 **Elijah, disguised as beggar** Ausubel, 193, 448; **adviser to scholars** Ginzberg, 4:217, 223, 229–33.

98 **Torah portion** The Pentateuch is divided into sections. One section is read aloud per week in sequence (except for holiday weeks, when special portions relevant to the holiday are read). Parts of the portion are read at services on Mondays and Thursdays; the complete portion is read on Shabbat, together with a section from the Prophets on a related theme. The reading cycle begins and ends on Simchat Torah, the holiday of "Rejoicing in the Law," the last day of Succot (Tabernacles).

98 **arguably closest to philosopher-king ideal** Expansion of an idea expressed by Baer in "Social Ideals," in s/e, 84.

CHAPTER 5: THE JEWISH WOMAN AS ALTRUISTIC-ASSERTIVE ENABLER

99 **"liberated from Egypt"** BT *Sota* 11b.

99 **"carried on her shoulders"** J. Polia, *"Dee Yiddishe Froi"* (The Jewish Woman) in issue no. 1; quoted in Glanz, 152 n. 1.

99 **"The truth is"** "Notes," 25.

100 **Rabbi Akiva and Rachel stories** BT *Ketubot* 62b, 63a. Also in Bialik-Rabinsky, *Sefer HaAgada* (The Agada Book), 179; recounted by Ausubel, 33–36.

100 **"everything . . . is hers"** BT *Nedarim* 50a.

101 **Rachel "typical"** Finkelstein, *Self-Government,* 44; see also 68.

101 **"mother is responsible"** z&h, 292.

101 **baleboosta** z&h, 292.

101 **Marranos** Etymology obscure; refers to those *conversos* who practiced Judaism in secret. Mass conversion by the sword and out of terror began in Spain after the pogrom of March 15, 1391, in Seville initiated a century of massacres: m&m, 446. The Spanish Inquisition (1233–1808) executed at least thirty thousand conversos charged with "backsliding": Lee Levinger, *Anti-Semitism: Yesterday and Tomorrow* (New York: Macmillan, 1936), 48–50.

101 **only context/center** Renée Levine Melammed, "Mediterranean and Early Modern Sephardi Women," in Baskin, 126.

102 **Enriques and Mendez** Seymour Liebman, *The Jews in Spain: Faith, Flame and the Inquisition* (Coral Gables, FL: Univ. of Miami Press, 1970); **Enriques** 63, 226, 228–30, 232–33; **Mendez** 154, 158, 263.

102 **"burden"** In his fall class on "The Holocaust: The Nazi Ghetto as a Means of Genocide," YIVO Weinreich Institute, from author's notes.

102 **nutrition, housekeeping skills** Sybil Milton at 1983 conference, "Women Surviving," and testimony of survivor Luba Gurdus there, from author's notes.

102 **ghetto soup kitchens, house committees** Trunk class, from author's notes.

102 **couriers, ghetto "mothers"** Syrkin, *Match,* 191–92.

102 **lagershvesters** Testimony by women at 1983 conference "Women Surviving," and Ringelheim in Baskin, 248.

102 **Kogon** Paraphrased by Tillion from his work *The Theory and Practice of Hell* (New York: Farrar, Straus & Giroux, 1949), 230.

102 **"entry ritual"** Levi, *The Drowned and the Saved,* 39.

102 **Tillion on women** 230.

102 **never been incorporated** Ringelheim in Baskin, 243ff.

102   **not legally forbidden**   Women were exempted from Torah study: BT *Kiddushin* 29a–b. By late Talmudic times, women could study if they chose to. Most leading medieval and modern scholars discouraged such study.

103   **women scholars in various eras**   Abrahams, 342–47; Brayer, 2:83–114, 121–29; Adelman in Baskin, 142–43; and Taitz-Henry.

103   **what females were taught**   Z&H, 124–25; **what to ask**   130; **prayer reading**   124.

103   **stories in Yiddish**   The prime source was the *Tsena U'rena* (Hebrew for go forth and see) by Jacob ben Isaac Ashkenazi of Janov, first published in Lublin ca. 1615: Dubnow, *History,* 3:743.

103   **"family purity"**   Laws and rituals on menstrual and postmenstrual separation.

103   **"light-headed"**   BT *Kiddushin* 80b and *Shabbat* 33b.

103   **Mishnah, Gemara discussion on women learning**   BT *Sota* 20a, 21b.

103   **R. Eliezer**   A Shammaite. See Zeitlin, 186, 193, 197.

103   **"Torah"**   See discussion on meaning in context, in Wegner, 161.

103   **"be burned"**   JT *Sota* 19a.

103   **exempted from some time-bound mitzvot**   For example, the Mishnah exempts women (as well as slaves and minors) from putting on *tefillin* (two small leather cases with straps attached, in each of which is a parchment inscribed with four biblical passages); they are obligated in prayer (but not in the synagogue): *Mishnah Brachot* III.3, *Kiddushin* I.7. They must say grace after meals but cannot be included in the quorum of three required for it to be an official service: *Mishnah Brachot* VII.2.

103   **minyan**   See Zeitlin, 309; **exclusion of women from it**   BT *Brachot* 47b, *Sanhedrin* 74b.

103   **aliyah**   BT *Megillah* 23a. See R. Biale, 24–29.

104   **three female mitzvot**   *Mishnah Shabbat* II.6.

104   **challah**   Since the destruction of the Temple made a tithe for priests impossible, all bakers had to burn a symbolic amount (1/24th) of this bread. See Brayer, 1:97.

104   **Chanukah and Passover**   Women were required to be present at ceremonies conducted during these holidays even though these are technically "time-bound."

104   **morning prayer**   BT *Menachot* 43b; **Rashi on**   Same page.

104   **apologists**   The first, David ben Joseph Abudarham, of mid-fourteenth-century Seville, explained that women were exempted to avoid conflicts over obligations to God and to their husbands: R. Biale, 13–14. See Wegner in Baskin, 90 n. 19; Zucrow, 79; and Zeitlin, 313.

104   **witness disqualification**   JT *Yoma* 43b. The Mishnah allows women to bring and defend lawsuits: *Mishnah Bava Kamma* I.3; but denies them the right to testify personally in a bet din: *Mishnah Shevuot* IV.1.

104   **women witnesses**   Rabban Gamliel II ruled that women's testimony was acceptable in certain matters affecting them personally (including identifying a child's father): Zeitlin, 205. They could be witnesses in cases where they were more likely to have observed an incident: *Shulchan Aruch Choshen Mishpat* 35:14.

104   **Egypt**   Cited in Erwin R. Goodenough, *The Jurisprudence of the Jewish Courts in Egypt: Legal Advice by the Jews Under the Early Roman Empire as Ascribed by Philo Judaeus* (New Haven, CT: Yale Univ. Press, 1929), 92, 98.

104   **Renaissance Italy**   Adelman in Baskin, 142.

104   **men disqualified by trade**   JT *Yoma* 43b; **usurers**   *Mishnah Sanhedrin* III.3.

104   **testimony on rape**   See discussion in Freehof, 110–11; **battering**   See chap. 6, below.

105   **"Woe unto you"... promise**   Scholem, *Sabbetai Sevi,* 404.

105   **calling women for aliyah**   Scholem, *Sabbetai Sevi,* 403.

105   **dream of radical reform**   Scholem, *Sabbetai Sevi,* 403, 404.

105   **"neglects ... study"**   PA 1:5. See also Z&H, 134.

105   **as prophylactic**   BT *Kiddushin* 30b; similarly, BT *Avoda Zara* 5b.

105   **Akiva on palm tree**   Aschkenasy, 48; **Meir on bridge**   BT *Kiddushin* 81a.

105   **Hassidic story**   On Rabbi Yaakov Yitzhak of Pshycha, Poland: Aschkenasy, 52.

105   **mechitzah**   Debate rages among scholars as to precisely when and where the separation of the two genders during prayer originated. See Abrahams, 25, and articles by Hannah Safrai and Sara Reguer in G-H and by Ross Kraemer and Melammed in Baskin.

106   **"honor of the community"**   BT *Megillah* 23a.

106   **"should have their sons taught"**   "And thereby acquire merit": BT *Brachot* 17a.

106   **Beruriah**   See Leonard Swidler, "Beruriah—Her Word Became Law," *Lilith,* no. 3 (1977); and Wegner in Baskin, 76.

106   **stories about, in Talmud**   *Mishnah Bava Metzia* I.6; *Tosefta Kelim Bava Metzia* I.6 and *Bava Kamma* IV.17; BT *Eruvin* 53a&b; BT *Brachot* 10a; BT *Pesachim* 62b.

107   **"the incident"**   BT *Avoda Zara* 18a (Rashi is on same page).

107   **exemplary marriage**   See midrash on Prov. 30:10 retold in Ausubel, 114–15.

107   **Rashi**   Student of Rabbi Jacob ben Yakar: M&M, 356.

107   **transmits midrashim**   Potok, 302; **modesty**   M&M, 358.

107   **source of Rashi story**   Zeitlin theorizes that Rashi "based his account [*sic*] on a medieval midrash which has been lost": 470 n. 17.

107   **economic position and ritual**   I. Epstein, "The Jewish Woman in the *Responsa:* 900 C.E.–1500 C.E.," *Response* magazine, Summer 1973, 24–25.

107   **Bruna**   Epstein, "Jewish Woman in the *Responsa,*" 31 n. 17.

107   **Rashi's daughters**   Taitz-Henry, 88. See M&M, 363.

108   **R. Abraham's daughters and R. Simcha's wife**   Epstein, "Jewish Woman in the *Responsa,*" 31 n. 21.

108   **Janeway's argument**   119–126, 202.

108   **"sexless"**   Z&H, 131; **"marketplace"**   132.

108   **silk embroiderers**   Wischnitzer, 65. See also 139.

108   **work in Eretz Israel**   Walter Duckat, "The Jewish Working Woman." FEGS (New York Federation Employment and Guidance Service) reprint of article from *Hadassah* magazine, September 1971, first three pages; **spinning and weaving**   Wegner in Baskin, 82; **cosmeticians**   BT *Bava Kamma* 82a.

109   **Jews as artisans in Exile**   Cahnman, xvi.

109   **occupations in Exile countries**   Wischnitzer: Palermo, 81; Rhodes, 72, 136; Salonika, 129; Prague, 174–75 and Adelman in Baskin, 142. Rome: Duckat, fourth page; **as beauticians:** Wischnitzer, 146.

109   **blind ... disorders**   Wischnitzer, 147, 148. See also Cahnman, xxii–xxiii.

109   **Navarre**   Wischnitzer, 104.

109   **ritual slaughterers**   Adelman in Baskin, 141.

109   **copyists**   S. D. Goitein, "The Jewish Family in the Days of Moses Maimonides," *Conservative Judaism,* Fall 1974, 32 (hereinafter Goitein/*CJ*).

109   **in printing industry**   Duckat, fourth page; Brayer, 2:119–21.

109   **physicians Italy**   Adelman in Baskin, 142; **medieval Spain**   Melammed in Baskin, 120; **Prague**   Wischnitzer, 174–75. Women also worked as midwives: Duckat, third to fourth pages.

109   **diamond industry** Wischnitzer, 198.

109   **chenvanit** *Mishnah Ketubot* IX.4. See comment by Wegner, 127.

109   **stalls, Second Temple era** Duckat, second page.

109   **fairs: Navarre** Melammed in Baskin, 121; **Lombardy** Adelman in Baskin, 142; **Cracow** Wischnitzer, 211.

109   **merchants   Asia Minor** Kraemer in Baskin, 45–46; **Islamic Spain** Melammed in Baskin, 121, 122; **England** Judith Baskin, "Jewish Women in the Middle Ages," in Baskin, 109; **Renaissance Italy** Adelman in Baskin, 142; **Turkey** Melammed in Baskin, 123–24; **Poland** See notes below.

109   **husband's absences** Abrahams, 172; Epstein, "Jewish Woman in the *Responsa*," 26.

109   **Gluckel** See *Gluckel, Life of* (1646–1724), and Bein, 565.

110   **Mirele Efros** Yiddish play, originally called *The Jewish Queen Lear:* Sandrow, 156.

110   **expectation in match** Immanuel Etkes, "Marriage and Torah Study Among the *Lomdim* [Torah students] in Lithuania in the Nineteenth Century," in Kraemer, 167.

110   **"doing . . . handiwork"** Ovadiah of Bertinaro, quoted in Roth, 18.

110   **wives of Hassidic rabbis** Rabinowicz, 207.

110   **non-Hassidim** Etkes in Kraemer, 169.

110   **shtetl diet** Jane Kinderlehrer, *Cooking Kosher: The Natural Way* (Middle Village, NY: Jonathan David Publishers, 1980), 125; Z&H, 257, 369, 371.

110   **chicken "joke"** Actually, kashrut laws forbid the eating of an animal that died a natural death.

110   **orange** Yuri Suhl, quoted in Jean Roth, "You Don't Have to Be Ill to Eat an Orange," *Forward,* March 11, 1994.

111   **Czarist oppression** M&M, 669; Pale: D/R&P: 1:314, 317, 342; 2:39. Jews were restricted to certain provinces and, within them, to certain locales: Wirth, 93.

111   **roundups** D/R&P, 2:342–46; **livelihood** 346–48.

111   **expulsions** D/R&P, 3:57; see also M&M, 696.

111   **draft** D/R&P, 2:15–29, 145–50; **"military martyrdom"** 22.

111   **Herzen** *My Past and Thoughts* (New York: Alfred A. Knopf, 1973), 169–70.

111   **nineteenth-century pogroms** D/R&P, 2:191, 247–69, 280–83, 299, 358, 411; 3:52. Also see M&M, 693–95.

111   **alcoholism** D/R&P, 2:124–25; see also Patai, *Mind,* 202.

111   **"play the man"** Abrahams, 156.

111   **view of peasants** See Z&H, 152–58, 339.

112   **"Skin a carcass"** BT *Shabbat* 118a, *Pesachim* 113a.

112   **Vilna Gaon** Rabbi Elijah, son of Solomon (1720–1797), leader of the opponents of Hassidism: M&M, 586–87. Quoted from his commentary on Proverbs by Etkes in Kraemer, 154 and 174 n. 5.

112   **Hassid in Smolenskin novel** Smolenskin: D/R&P, 2:234–36. Novel: *Wanderer on the Paths of Life* (Heb.) (Warsaw, 1905), 3:22ff.

112   **guidebook** *Brantshpiegl* by Moshe Henoch Yerushalmi Altschuler (Prague, 1602), which also circulated in Eastern Europe. Quoted in Dubnow, *History,* 3:749.

112   **privilege and honor** Etkes in Kraemer, 170.

113   **"antidote"** D/R&P, 2:125. See also WMT, 7.

113   **turn-of-century movements** D/R&P, 3:40–65.

113   **"sledgehammer . . . iron constitution"** D/R&P, 3:40.

114   **Midrash on Esther's secret observance** See Ginzberg, 4:386–87. Esther was a symbol of loyalty for the Marranos: Baer, 95.

114   **"redeemer"**   Midrash on Lamentations in Ginzberg, 4:385.

114   **consummate strategist**   See commentaries in Art Scroll edition of Esther, M. Zlotowitz, ed., and Ginzberg, 4:429, 430.

115   **blames Adam**   BT *Sanhedrin* 29a.

115   **women in early Scriptures**   Susan Niditch, "Portrayals of Women in the Hebrew
Bible" in Baskin, 32–34; **Miriam**   See Plaskow, 38–39.

115   **apologetics on Deborah**   Brayer, 2:108, 152, 200.

116   **midrashim on Deborah**   Ginzberg, 4:36.

116   **Hulda and Josiah's reform**   Eisenstadt, 114–15. See also Niditch in Baskin, 35,
and Plaskow, 39.

116   **"nasty animals"**   BT *Megillah* 14b.

116   **Hannah in 2 Maccabees**   Chap. 7; **"wonderful"**   7:20; **"manly courage"**   7:21.

116   **in 4 Maccabees**   14:11–17; 18:6–19.

116   **Agada martyr**   BT *Gittin* 57b.

116   **tenth-century work**   *Yosiphon,* cited by Shlomo Noble, "The Jewish Woman in
Medieval Martyrology" in *Studies in Jewish Bibliography, History, and Literature in Honor of
I. Edward Kiev* (New York: Ktav, 1971), 353 (hereinafter Noble).

117   **"contempt for self-interest"**   Noble, 353.

117   **"finest hour"**   Noble, 349.

117   **"noble women," 1007**   Noble, 349. See Baskin in Baskin, 114 n. 52.

117   **Rhineland communities**   Noble, 349; M&M, 361.

117   **"bid farewell"**   Noble, 349.

117   **"strangled their children"**   Noble, 349; **"knowing the greed"**   350.

117   **Spanish chronicler**   Rabbi Joseph Yaavez, quoted in Noble, 352.

117   **Crusaders blamed**   Noble, 350–51; **first to perceive nature of onslaught ...
"Quite early"**   350.

117   **Koontz on German Jewish women**   "Reading the Writing on the Wall," *Lilith,* no.
17 (Fall 1987): 12–14.

117   **names known**   Minna of Speyer: Noble, 349; Minna of Worms: M&M, 361; Dulcie
of Worms: Ivan G. Marcus, "Mothers, Martyrs and Money-makers: Some Jewish Women in
Medieval Europe," *Conservative Judaism,* Spring 1986, 40–42.

118   **Eve in Midrash**   Aschkenasy, 44. See also *Midrash HaGadol* on Gen. 3:4.

118   **Eve in Judaism and Christianity**   Ozick, "Notes," 20.

118   **enabler/disabler**   Point made by Murray Zuckoff.

118   **Midrash on "First Eve"**   *Gen. Rabbah* 22:7.

118   **Lilith in Talmud**   BT *Eruvin* 100b, *Niddah* 24b, *Shabbat* 151b, *Bava Batra* 72a. See
Judy Weinberg, "Lilith Sources," *Lilith,* no. 1 (Fall 1976).

118   **Adam and Lilith in Alphabet**   23a–b; see Aschkenasy, 183–85.

118   **Lilith in Zohar**   1, 19b; see Aschkenasy, 50–51.

118   **later Kabbalistic works**   Aschkenasy, 5 and 75 n. 23.

119   **folktale endings**   Noy/Institute.

120   **lower conversion rates**   Noble, 347–48 and 351.

120   **endured torture**   Melammed in Baskin, 126.

120   **midrash or midwives**   *Exodus Rabba* 1:16; Ginzberg, 2:250–53.

CHAPTER 6: THE INSTRUMENTALITY OF DOMESTIC TRANQUILLITY

123   **"nation ... themselves"**   BT *Shabbat* 62a.

123   **"Woman's weapons"**   BT *Yevamot* 115a.

123   **Ruppin quote**   *Sociologie der Juden* (Berlin, 1931), 2:108–9.

123   **national emergency**   By 63 B.C.E., the Pharisees had come to believe that the Commonwealth would not long survive: Zeitlin, 156. Many of the changes they instituted in Judaism were in preparation for the expected "national emergency."

123   **marriage a mitzvah**   Quoted in Feldman, 33.

123   **blessings**   BT *Ketubot* 8a; Feldman, 35–36.

123   **JT definition**   Cited in Mordechai A. Friedman, "Marriage as an Institution: Jewry Under Islam," in Kraemer, 35.

123   **in Geniza documents**   Friedman, "Marriage," 34–5. The Cairo Geniza was discovered in 1896.

124   **tateh-mameh**   Z&H, 291.

124   **couples, Egypt**   Goitein/*CJ*, 32; **early modern Europe**   Paula Hyman, intro. to Cohen and Hyman anthology, citing Katz: 6.

124   **extrinsic**   For exceptions, see Baskin in Baskin, 71.

124   **pair-bond and sex**   The Saadya Gaon (882–942) of Sura, the religious leader of Babylonian Jewry and the major arbiter of the era (M&M, 264–65, 267–72), acknowledged that erotic expression was a means of deepening the husband-wife bond: Feldman, 70.

124   **discouraging polygamy**   Sages argued, for example, that "Two women at home—conflict at home": *Midrash Tanhuma*, 491.

124   **no polygamous rabbis**   Feldman, 37 nn. 85, 86.

124   **Babylonia**   Jews abandoned farming then because of high taxes and rural insecurity: Cahnman, xiv–xv.

124   **Gershom's ban**   Zucrow, 89; Feldman, 38–39; **synod**   Potok, 300.

124   **Sephardic Jews**   Dubnow, *History,* 3:416; Goitein, *Med. Society,* 3:150, 205; Melammed in Baskin, 118; Abrahams, 120–21.

124   **kinyan**   A discussion with Rachel Adler played an important role in my conceptualization of the kinyan-partnership conflict. See also Wegner, 95, 170, 173.

125   **"Every man is a king"**   *Mishneh Torah Hilchot Ishut* 15:20 (BOW, 98).

125   **"respect his wife"**   BT *Bava Metzia* 59a.

126   **sociologist on family violence, U.S.**   Richard Gelles, associate professor of sociology and anthropology, University of Rhode Island, quoted by Celeste Durant of *Los Angeles Times* in "Violence: A Family Tradition," *Arizona Republic,* June 6, 1979, D1.

126   **"haven of rest"**   Abrahams, 113.

127   **"respects her more"**   BT *Yevamot* 62b.

127   **Greeks and Romans**   See George Steiner's "Poor Little Lambs," book review of John Boswell's *Kindness of Strangers* (New York: Pantheon, 1988), *The New Yorker,* February 6, 1989, 104.

127   **Tacitus**   *Complete Works* (New York: Modern Library, 1942), 657–60.

127   **loyalty forged**   Abrahams, 127, 140.

127   **guidebooks' laments**   Abrahams, 126.

128   **entitlements in ketubah**   BT *Ketubot* 5a. See Zucrow, 51–53.

128   **Shimon ben Shetach**   Leader of the Pharisees and brother of Queen Shlomit Alexandra, Hasmonean (Maccabean) dynasty ruler, 76–67 B.C.E.; **marriage laws**   BT *Ketubot* 82b; **education laws**   BT *Bava Batra* 21a.

128   **laws on property, earnings**   Zucrow, 54–61; Wegner, 88, 91, 139.

128   **tailor-made ketubot**   Rabbi Emanuel Rackman, lecture, "Jewish Family Law—From Status to Contract and Then From Status to Contract Again," NYU Law School, September 11, 1990, from author's notes. See Goitein/*CJ*, 33; and Friedman in Kraemer, 36–37.

128   **Geniza documents on women**   Goitein/*CJ*, 33ff.

128 **reason for clothing provisions** Goitein, *Med. Society,* 3:134.

128 **decline of tailored ketubot** Rackman lecture, "Jewish Family Law."

129 **R. Landau's responsum** Landau (1713–1793) was the leading arbiter of the era: M&M, 598; **responsum** Quoted in Zucrow, 62.

129 **Mishnah rules** *Mishnah Ketubot* VII. 2–3, 4–5.

129 **"spend above his means"** BT *Hullin* 84b; **"honor wives"** BT *Bava Metzia* 59a.

129 **"counts her tears"** BT *Shabbat* 22a–b.

129 **"not to be a terror at home"** Abrahams, 88.

129 **ethical will** Rabbi Eliezer Halevi of Mainz, quoted in Dubnow, *History,* 3:428.

129 **"monstrosity"** Abrahams, 88.

129 **R. Tam on battering** Quoted in Abrahams, 89.

129 **R. Peretz's words** In Finkelstein, *Self-Government,* 216–17.

129 **why not dealt with in Talmud** Zucrow, 63.

129 **batei din, ninth, tenth centuries** Abrahams, 88.

129 **Simhah of Vitry** (d. 1105), in Zucrow, 64.

130 **R. Meir's view, synod** Zucrow, 64.

130 **Peretz's takkanah** In Finkelstein, *Self-Government,* 217.

130 **sided with wife** Goitein/*CJ,* 33.

130 **Maimonides** *Mishneh Torah Hilchot Ishut* 21:10 (BOW, 133).

130 **R. Isserles** (1530–1572); **on wife-beating and wife's testimony** quoted in R. Biale, 95.

131 **Polish (and Russian) expression** Noy/Institute.

131 **synagogue decorum** Abrahams, 24–25.

131 **"divine Tetrad," emotional satisfaction** Patai, *Goddess,* 131.

131 **"not called a man"** BT *Yevamot* 63a; **the Schechinah rests only on a married man** *Zohar Hadash* 4:50b, quoted in Feldman, 35.

131 **the King without the Matronit** Patai, *Goddess,* 129, 145.

131 **tzimtzum** Patai, *Goddess,* 158.

131 **"consecrated unto me ... "** *Mishnah Kiddushin* I.1; formalized at Yavneh: Zeitlin, 311.

132 **"cannot ... destabilize"** Wegner, 50.

132 **sell daughters** Zucrow, 3–4, 8–9.

132 **redemption at puberty** BT *Kiddushin* 4a, 18a. See Zucrow, 27–29.

132 **forbade immigration** Zucrow, *28.*

132 **"I want this man"** BT *Ketubot* 102b, *Kiddushin,* 41a. The sages at Yavneh also legislated that a woman could reject, and have annulled when she reached her majority, a marriage that her father had forced her into *Mishnah Yevamot* XIII.1–2.

132 **"wife of one's youth"** BT *Sanhedrin* 22a.

132 **contentment with first wife** BT *Yevamot* 53b, *Brachot* 32b.

132 **"altar sheds tears"** BT *Gittin* 90b.

132 **"not be a slight matter"** BT *Ketubot* 11a. See also 82b.

132 **Blu Greenberg's view** "Jewish Divorce Law: If We Must Part, Let's Part as Equals," *Lilith,* no. 3 (Spring, Summer 1977): 26 and 27.

132 **hasty action** B. Greenberg, "Jewish Divorce Law," and BT *Bava Batra* 160b.

132 **with, without consent** BT *Yevamot* 112b.

132 **R. Gershom's takkanah** M&M, 354. See also Zucrow, 68–69.

133 **R. Peretz on child marriage** Quoted in Abrahams, 169.

133 **Shammai-Hillel debate** B. Greenberg, "Jewish Divorce Law," 27; Finkelstein, *Akiva,* 188–89; R. Biale, 73–79; Zucrow, 67.

133 **economic conditions** Finkelstein, *Akiva,* 188–89.

133 **prettier woman** BT *Gittin* 25b.

133 **"beautiful in her deeds"** BT *Shabbat* 25b.

133 **R. Akiva and marriage** Finkelstein, *Akiva,* 189–91.

133 **conditions: conjugal rights** BT *Ketubot* 61b–62b; **impotence** BT *Yevamot* 65b– the burden of proof was on the man; **disease or odor** BT *Ketubot* 77a; see also R. Biale, 85–86; **support** BT *Ketubot* 77a; **licentiousness** B. Greenberg, "Jewish Divorce Law," 28; **tyrannies** Maimonides, *Mishneh Torah Hilchot Ishut* 14.5 (BOW, 88).

133 **procedure** B. Greenberg, "Jewish Divorce Law," 28.

134 **coercion** *Mishnah Arachin* V.6; Maimonides, *Mishneh Torah Laws of Divorce,* 2.20 (BOW, 177).

134 **Genizah contracts, third and fourth centuries** Riskin, xii.

134 **eleventh-century documents** Friedman in Kramer, 43 n. 14.

134 **Babylonia** Haut, 51.

134 **"not a captive"** *Mishneh Torah Hilchot Ishut,* 14.8 (BOW, 89).

134 **Ahad Ha'am's view** "Judaism and the Gospels," in *Basic Writings,* 312.

134 **Ashkenazic arbiters' debate** R. Biale, 88–91. See Riskin, xiii.

134 **too much power** R. Biale, 90.

134 **Meir on requiring wife-batterer to divorce** R. Biale, 93.

134 **Renaissance Italy courts** Adelman in Baskin, 147.

134 **Meir's opposition to property restoration** Finkelstein, *Self-Government,* 67–69; Finkelstein's rationale 68.

134 **insane** R. Biale, 93.

135 **conditional divorces** Abrahams, 90. Married Israeli soldiers are required to sign such documents: B. Greenberg, *Tradition,* 134.

135 **Shulchan Aruch law** *Orach Chayim,* 339.

135 **one witness's testimony** Wegner, 124. See Maimonides *Laws of Divorce* 13.29 (BOW, 261).

135 **responsum by Rabbi Avigdor** Quoted in Freehof, 198–99.

135 **Emden on sex** Quoted in Feldman, 102.

135 **"Judeo-Christian" ethic and sex** Feldman, 102–3.

135 **Iggeret** Quoted in Feldman, 179.

136 **motive for creation from rib** *Gen. Rabba* 18:2.

136 **woman's nature** See Bialik and Rabinsky, 488–91, and ET, 160–61.

136 **"passion is greater"** BT *Bava Metzia* 84a.

136 **"life of poverty . . . "** BT *Sota* 20a.

136 **Nachmanides** Spanish physician, commentator, and Kabbalist (d. 1270), known for triumph in forced public religious disputation in Barcelona, 1263: M&M, 422–27.

136 **Nachmanides on Eve's curse** Quoted in R. Biale, 124.

136 **shalom bayit ideal** Feldman, 43.

136 **sex as its instrumentality** BT *Shabbat* 152a.

136 **Onah** See Feldman, 60–61, and R. Biale, 126–28.

136 **Mishnah's timetable** In R. Biale, 130.

137 **R. Feinstein's ruling** R. Biale, 134.

137 **before trip** BT *Yevamot* 62b.

137 **Rabad** Quoted in R. Biale, 132.

137 **"bodily contact"** Quoted in R. Biale, 128–29.

137 **not in emnity, intoxication** Feldman, 72.

137 **not by force** Feldman, 64 and 72.

137 **"Engage her first"** Quoted in R. Biale, 142.

137 **"insemination" first** R. Biale, 142–43.

137 **Genizah letter** In S. D. Goitein, *Letters of Medieval Jewish Traders* (Princeton, NJ: Princeton Univ. Press, 1973), 222.

137 **abstinence during: period** Lev. 18:19 and 20:18; **half-day before** Feldman, 64; **white days** BT *Niddah* 66a.

137 **no-contact laws** R. Biale, 161; See also B. Greenberg, *Tradition,* 116, 121.

138 **Portnoy in bathhouse** Roth, *Portnoy,* 48.

138 **legally acceptable reason** R. Biale, 129–30.

138 **Ben Azzai's statement** BT *Kiddushin* 29b–30a, *Yoma* 71b. See also BT *Yevamot* 63b, and BT *Ketubot* 61b–62a.

139 **children** See "The *Mitzvah* of Procreation," which was incumbent on the man, in Feldman, chap. 3.

139 **Orthodox view of Niddah** Brayer, 1:90. See also B. Greenberg, *Tradition,* 107.

139 **"deferred gratification" and sex** Patai, *Mind,* 503.

140 **"sexual hardship"** See R. Biale, 122–25.

140 **owes his wife . . . sex** Rabad, *Ba'alei HaNefesh* (roughly translated as "Mastering One's Desires"), popular guidebook, ca. 1180, quoted in D. Biale, *Eros,* 95–96.

141 **"Woman was created . . ."** 96.

141 **"whatever a man wishes"** BT *Nedarim* 20b and Maimonides, *Mishneh Torah Issurei Bi'ah* 21:9, quoted in R. Biale, 145–46.

141 **"expend . . . to no purpose"** See below (both text and notes). This rule is a factor in rulings on contraception. See Feldman 67, 75–76, 103–5, and chap. 6.

141 **Talmud stories** For example, BT Nedarim 20b. Paraphrased in Zucrow, 47–49 and 51; R. Biale, 138.

142 **"wife is his home"** Rabbi Yossi in BT *Shabbat* 118b.

142 **Adler on menstrual blood and impurity** "*Tum'ah and Taharah*" (ritual impurity and purity) in Koltun, 66.

142 **Douglas** *Purity and Danger* (Middlesex, U.K.: Penguin, 1970).

142 **"white days" rules** "*Niddah*" in EJ, 12:1145.

142 **R. Akiva and mikvah** BT *Shabbat* 64b.

142 **sperm slaughter** See Feldman, chap. 6.

142 **mystical tradition and its effects** Feldman, 114–22.

142 **seminal emissions** Feldman, 118.

142 **Zohar: "sin more serious . . ."** Feldman, 114 and 115 n. 37; **"murder"** 115 and n. 40.

143 **"true representatives"** Scholem, *Mysticism,* 229.

143 **Sabbath bride** Patai, *Goddess,* 268.

143 **Sabbath prayers welcoming bride** For example, "*Lecha Dodi*" (Come my beloved, to welcome the bride), written by Shlomo ben Moshe Halevi Alkabetz (ca. 1505–1584) of Safed: Patai, *Goddess,* 268–69.

143 **Iggeret on Shabbat eve** Feldman, 100; Patai, *Goddess,* 271–72.

143 **Talmud on marital sex then** *Mishnah Ketubot* V.6.

143 **first marriage ages: Babylonia** M&M, 234; **W. Europe to sixteenth century** Abrahams, 167–68; Dubnow, *History,* 3:413.

143   **W. Europe, sixteenth century on**   Jacob Katz, "Marriage and Marital Life at the End of the Middle Ages" (Hebrew) in *Zion,* no. 10 (1945–46): 36.

143   **(Russian) Poland into nineteenth century**   Etkes in Kraemer, 155; **Russia**   see D/R&P, 3:112.

143   **kest and absence of need for job training**   Katz, "Marriage," 24–25; **future leaders**   32–33; **religious reason**   23, 29.

144   **no concept of adolescence**   One of the theories of Philip Aries, *Centuries of Childhood* (New York, 1962).

144   **no independence model**   Katz, "Marriage," 38.

144   **servants**   Katz, "Marriage," 44.

144   **Jabotinsky on passion**   Intro. to Bialik's translated *Poems from the Hebrew,* ed. C. V. Snowman (London: HaSefer, 1924), xiii.

144   **David's abuse of Michal**   See Aschkenasy, 140–45.

145   **"act of liberation"**   Alberoni, 84; **smash institutional control**   24, 108–9, 129, and passim.

145   **love after marriage**   Similarly in shtetl: Z&H, 271.

146   **Prohibition on Christians' sexual relations with Jews**   Salo Baron, *A Social and Religious History of the Jews,* V, *Religious Controls and Dissensions* (New York: Columbia Univ. Press, 1957), 133.

146   **persecution of converts to Judaism**   See EJ, "Proselytes," 13:1187–88.

146   **"I set aside ... "**   Arthur Miller, *After the Fall* (New York: Viking, 1964), 35.

146   **Talmud on purpose of Niddah**   BT *Niddah* 31b.

147   **Spanish Hebrew poets**   Moses Ibn Ezra (1070–?1139): M&M 324, Abrahams, 163–64. Yehuda Halevi (1086–?1141), also a philosopher: M&M, 329–31; Abrahams, 164.

147   **ballads**   Abrahams, 361–62.

147   **folk songs**   D. Biale, *Eros,* 166; Rubin, 70–71, 73–78, 85–91. **Love songs, lullabies** *Eros,* 68–69 nn. 29 and 31. Rubin writes that the folk songs on love emerged from the lower stratum: 72, 81.

147   **clandestine marriages with servants**   David Biale, "Love, Marriage, Modernity and the Jews," *Jewish Spectator,* Spring 1984, 13. See also D. Biale, *Eros,* 65.

147   **Legislation: Council of Four Lands**   D. Biale, *Eros,* 64; **Lithuania**   64 n. 10.

147   **read clandestinely**   Ruth Adler, 109. See also Z&H, 126, Madison, 38.

147   **predestination theme**   See D. Biale, *Eros,* 170, and his *Childhood, Marriage and Family,* 9. Central to Sh. An-Sky's play *The Dybbuk.*

147   **restless youth**   D. Biale, "Childhood, Marriage," 3–4.

PART II. THE IMPACT OF ASSIMILATIONISM ON JEWISH PUBLIC AND PRIVATE LIFE

149   **epigraph**   Samuel, 9–10.

CHAPTER 7: THE NEW MARRANOS

151   **Gordon**   Maskil poet (1830–1892). See bio: D/R&P, 2:228–31. Quote: from "Awake My People" (1863); in D. Biale, *Power,* 106.

151   **Fein quote**   Address to opening session of YIVO annual conference, June 6, 1971, from author's notes. He amended his views somewhat in his book: 4. See also Bein, 270.

151   **Borochov quote**   85.

152 **"best powers**   Nordau, in address to first WZC, 71.

152 **ethnic amnesia**   Term coined by Murray Zuckoff.

152 **domestication**   Documentary, *The Ultimate Slavery,* CBC, 1985. Aired on Channel 13 in NYC, May 7, 1991.

153 **assimilation impossible**   Memmi, *Liberation,* 66–67.

153 **"get out as Jews"**   "Escaping Jewishness," Peretz, 378.

153 **Golden Age**   M&M, 307–29.

153 **Ozick quote**   "Sholem Aleichem's Revolution," *The New Yorker,* February 28, 1988, 103.

154 **Shabbetai Zvi movement**   See Scholem, *Sabbetai Sevi;* M&M, 558–67; Bein, 196–200; **effects of failure on W. Jews**   Bein, 202–3.

154 **Fein quote**   4.

155 **absolutist states' motivations**   D. Biale, *Power,* 89–95; **strategies**   Katz, *Emancipation,* 5.

155 **"reinvest . . . in . . . secular state"**   D. Biale, *Power,* 112.

155 **bourgeois states**   Bein, 223–29.

155 **National Assembly delegate**   Count Stanislaw de Clermont-Tonnere in 1789: M&M, 608–10, 613–15; Bein, 215–17.

156 **Mamet quote**   "A Plain Brown Wrapper," in *Some Freaks,* 17–18.

156 **hypervisible economic roles**   Bauer, *Emergence,* 44; Bein, 220–21.

156 **Marx on Judaism**   *Early Writings* (New York, 1964), 40. See Memmi, *Liberation,* 240–41.

156 **Voltaire**   Quoted in Katz, *Emancipation,* 201 and 167 n. 2. See discussion in Bein, 186–89.

157 **"unreal"**   Nordau address to first WZC, 71.

157 **Gruenberger**   Quoted in Terence Prittie's review of his *The Twelve-Year Reich* (New York: Holt, Rinehart & Winston, 1971), in NYTBR, August 15, 1971, 23.

157 **critics**   Bein, 179–86, 206, 214–15, 559–64; **Voltaire**   Katz, *Emancipation,* 50. For Kant, see Bein, 562.

157 **occupations**   See Keller, 371.

157 **peddling as "morally dangerous"**   Katz, *Emancipation,* 65.

158 **citizens' rights**   M&M, 616–26, 654–58; Bein, 213–14; Wirth, 113–16; Katz, *Emancipation,* 23. **Rome ghetto**   Wirth, 114.

158 **internalization of stereotypes**   See Bein, 265–67, 270–71; Katz, *Emancipation,* 51–52.

158 **self-hate**   Bein, 269 and 633–34; **Lessing quote**   in Bein, 634. See also Oring, 109–10, 112–13.

158 **Weininger**   Quoted in Patai, *Mind,* 463. See also Oring, 110–12.

159 **Samuel quote**   119.

159 **hatred for Ostjuden**   Kurt Lewin, "Bringing up the Jewish Child" (1940) in Lewin, 176. See Bein, 708–9; Oring, 42, 43, 47, 49.

159 **right-wing Orthodox**   The term *right-wing,* when used in this work in connection with Orthodoxy, refers not to politics but to stringency of religious observance. The degree of stringency determines a group's position on the right-to-left spectrum of observance in American Judaism. See chapter 14 for discussion of this issue.

159 **maskilim**   D. Biale, *Power,* 100–102; Katz, *Emancipation,* 15.

159 **"occupational redistribution"**   Katz, *Emancipation,* 66–68.

159 **give up distinctiveness**   Katz, *Emancipation,* 13, 70.

159 **allies of absolutists**   D. Biale, *Power,* 106–7, 109.

160   **Reform Judaism**   Bein, 271–72; M&M, 634, 659–63. **Hebrew language**   Bein, 271.

160   **"mission"**   Michael A. Meyer, *Response to Modernity: A History of the Reform Movement in Judaism* (New York: Oxford Univ. Press, 1988), 137–38.

160   **Ahad Ha'am critique**   "Slavery in Freedom," *Basic Writings,* 63.

160   **"Mosaic persuasion"**   Keller, 463.

160   **family to fill void**   Marion Kaplan, "Women and Tradition in the German Jewish Family," in Cohen and Hyman, 69; **secluded from "front lines," expected to "cushion family"**   Kaplan in Baskin, 204. See also 207.

160   **"new Marranos"**   Nordau address at first WZC, 72.

161   **Christian character**   Katz, *Emancipation,* 79.

161   **Hassidism**   See S. Ettinger, "The Hassidic Movement—Reality and Ideals," in S/E, 251ff; Patai, *Mind,* chap. 8.

161   **Ba'al Shem Tov**   Patai, *Mind,* 191–95.

161   **joy**   Patai, *Mind,* 218–20; **music, dance**   214–16; **study**   220.

161   **effect cosmic repair**   Scholem, *Mysticism,* 341; Patai, *Mind,* 205.

161   **looked down on the unlearned**   WMT, 6.

161   **new ... religious leader**   See Hyam Maccoby's critical essay "Judaism in Extremis—The Messiah of Bratslav," *Commentary,* September 1980, 49, 54. See also Patai, *Mind,* 206ff+.

161   **intermediary**   Patai, *Mind,* 210.

162   **male bonding**   Potok, 355; Aschkenasy, 120.

162   **"Maid of Ludomir"**   (1805–1892): Rabinowicz, 206–7. See also Nehemia Polen, "Miriam's Dance: Radical Egalitarianism in Hasidic Thought," in *Modern Judaism* no. 12 (1992).

162   **Hassidic leadership and Misnagdim**   D. Biale, *Power,* 100–101.

162   **revival of learning**   Finkelstein, *Jews,* 405.

162   **obsession with "separatism"**   D/R&P, 2:184–198.

162   **special commission**   D/R&P, 2:191.

162   **disbanded councils (Kahals)**   D/R&P, 2:59–61; **schools**   51–54, 174–77; see also Baron, 34–37.

162   **dress code, shaved heads**   D/R&P, 2:144.

162   **wig custom**   See Z&H, 136; Schneider, 237; Abrahams, 281.

163   **entrepreneurs**   Baron, 88–94.

163   **class interests**   See D/R&P, 2:158–61, 166–68, 214–16.

163   **differences between Haskalahs**   D/R&P, 2:137; WMT, 10–11.

163   **Russian Haskalah**   Baron, 124–31; D/R&P, 2:132–38, 224–33.

163   **its aims**   D. Biale, *Childhood,* 5.

163   **original naiveté**   D/R&P, 2:130–32, 136–37; M&M, 671–72.

163   **attitude to occupational structure, agricultural labor**   Baron, 77; Biale, *Power,* 131.

163   **Warshawsky**   Baladeer (1845–1907); see Rubin, 273; **"Song of Bread"**   "Songs of Gebirtig and Warshawsky," Doyres Records (New York: Dr. Chaim Zhitlovsky Foundation, n.d.), LP 520497.

164   **Green Fields**   Based loosely on 1916 play by Peretz Hirschbein (1880–1948): Madison, 274–75.

164   **Jews as farmers**   Baron, 77–80, 218–24, 254; M&M, 700–701; D/R&P, 2:419–21; WMT, 47–52; **Crimea**   Goldin, 89–90, Sachar, 382–83.

164   **in U.S.**   Manners, 157–91; Howe, 84–87; Glanz, 12–14. See also documentary by Gertrude Dubrowsky, *The Land Was Theirs,* aired on NYC's Channel 13, September 19, 1993.

164   **maskilim's propaganda**   D. Biale, *Childhood,* 10–13.

164   **Russification**   D/R&P, 2:206–14.

164   **narodniks**   WMT, 20–26; **Jews and**   26–37 and 492 n. 26; D/R&P, 2:221–24; Talmon, 26–38.

164   **Jewish women narodniks**   WMT, 17, 32; Talmon, 45; **Cherikover on**   206–7.

164   **masses vs. maskilim**   Talmon, 27. See D/R&P, 2: 112; WMT, 8.

165   **"Whither?"**   In English in his *Whither? and Other Stories* (Philadelphia: JPS, 1973), 31ff.

165   **brutal shock**   D/R&P, 2:324–37; reaction of Jewish narodniks: WMT, 53–62.

165   **collective solutions**   D/R&P, 3:40–58, 143–48.

165   **"led them to conclude"**   Eli Ginzberg, "Jews in the American Economy," *Jewish Digest,* July–August 1979, 31; Birmingham, 318–19.

165   **"To speak Yiddish . . . "**   Shapiro, *Friendly Society,* 22.

165   **nasty stories**   Goldin, 52. See also Birmingham, 38–39.

166   **Mead quote**   Shapiro, *Friendly,* 22. See Howe, 273.

166   **Fiedler quote**   Confirmed by author in 1994 phone conversation.

166   **"only disgrace"**   August Levy, secretary of the Hebrew Emigrant Aid Society, established 1881, quoted in Goldin, 52.

166   **attempts to limit and redirect immigrants**   Goldin, 49–52, 54–55, 56–59, 61; **Americanize them**   Goldin, 61; Birmingham, 317–22; Manners, 107–14.

166   **clean the immigrants up . . .**   Birmingham, 320.

166   **delousing stations**   Birmingham, 320, and Shapiro/JLS.

166   **purpose of Y's and centers**   Manners, 133; Birmingham, 320.

166   **attitude to Yiddish**   Birmingham, 319.

166   **stamp out Socialism, unions**   Goldin, 61; Birmingham, 320.

166   **economic interests**   As factory owners: Howe, 155; Goldin, 60; Birmingham, 320. As landlords: Manners, 135.

166   **Educational Alliance**   Adam Bellow, *The Educational Alliance* (1990), 75; Howe, 230–35; Manners, 133–38; **no Yiddish books at**   Glanz, 167 n. 108.

166   **German Jews' fears**   Birmingham, 318; Manners, 111; Teller, 46.

166   **Lippmann quote**   Essay, "Public Opinion and the American Jew," in *The American Hebrew* (1922), quoted in Silberman, 64.

166   **paternalism**   Birmingham, 321–22; Goldin, 61.

166   **set up own institutions**   Shapiro/JLS; Goldin, 62–64; Howe, 183–90; Manners, 134; Teller, 15.

166   **resentment**   Manners, 112, 115, 134; Birmingham, 322.

166   **hierarchical character**   Goldin, 64–68. See chap. 11 of this book.

167   **wished to be Americanized**   Goldin, 60; Howe, 121, 128.

167   **marginality of synagogue**   Howe, 191–93.

167   **NJPS**   Barry Kosmin et al., *Highlights of the CJF 1990 NJPS* (New York: CJF, 1991), 35, 36.

167   **M.B.A.'s**   American Jewish Committee press release, September 7, 1988, 2, citing results of survey conducted by Samuel Z. Klausner, professor of sociology at the University of Pennsylvania.

168   **Shapiro on Jews-Judaism relationship, past and present**   JLS.

168   **"America is different"**   Silberman, 24, 40–41, 112–14.

168   **hospitality myth**   Shapiro, *Friendly,* 11.

168   **moguls and invisibility**   Howard Suber, "Hollywood's Closet Jews," *Davka,* Fall 1975, 12.

168 **"accidental Jews" and casting** Michael Blankfort, quoted by Tom Tugend, "The Hollywood Jews," *Davka,* 5.

169 **Jewish men on TV** See Michael Elkin, "Better Deception: TV Changes Its Depiction of Jewish Men," *Palm Beach Jewish-World,* April 8–14, 1988; and John O'Connor, "They're Funny, Loveable, Heroic—and Jewish," NYT, July 15, 1990. Jewish male TV writers, directors, and producers are too conflicted about Jewish women to be able to portray them with any authenticity.

169 **Days of Our Lives** Naomi Pfefferman, "Star-Crossed Romance, 1987, NBC," *Lilith,* no. 18 (Winter 1987–88): 16–17.

169 **Locate the Landsman** Albert Vorspan, *My Rabbi Doesn't Make House Calls* (Garden City, NY: Doubleday, 1969), 4–6.

169 **Widawer quote** Hertzberg, 156.

170 **Tevye on "being poor"** From *Fiddler on the Roof,* book by Joseph Stein, lyrics by Sheldon Harnick (New York: Crown, 1965), 16.

170 **communal tzedakah statistics** Goldin, 45.

170 **proof of worth** See Mendele, quoted in Howe-Libo, 5.

170 **Marjorie's father** Wouk, *Marjorie Morningstar,* 448.

171 **recapture** Howe actually writes, "The successful entry of the immigrant Jew [*sic*] into the American business world would require a reassertion of the 'male principle'": 174. See Glanz, 16.

171 **Yezierska's father** Described in *Bread Givers.*

171 **invested hopes in sons** Howe, 251, 252, 253, 254–55.

171 **temporary proletariat** Howe, 143.

171 **"natural gravitation"** Borochov, 64.

171 **"my son ... "** Howe, 252.

172 **breakdown of arranged marriage system; love marriages** Glanz, 77–80. See also Ari Lloyd Fridkis, "Desertion in the American Jewish Family," AJH, December 1981, 288.

172 **"native cadres"** Khrushchev's term, 1958, quoted in Judd Teller, "Negroes and Jews: A Hard Look," *Conservative Judaism,* Fall 1966, 19–20.

172 **"helping"** See BHM, 191.

172 **home work** BHM, 111–12; **boarders** 103–9; **pushcarts** 100–101, and Glanz, 156 n.8; **mom-and-pop stores** BHM, 98–99; Glanz, 118.

172 **status symbol** See BHM, 193.

172 **sacrifice for brothers** BHM, 123; **"ladies of leisure"** 199.

172 **younger immigrant women** Howe, 266–67; Hapgood, 79; **as factory workers** Glanz, 21–22, 27–28.

172 **night school** BHM, 129–30.

172 **unionists** Alice Kessler-Harris's intro. to *Bread Givers,* xvi; Howe, 297–300; Glanz, 54–55; **Lemlich** Sparked the 1909 shirtwaist strike: Glanz, 51–53, and Howe, 298–99; **Schneiderman** Howe, 305–6, BHM, 152–62; **Malkiel** Sally M. Miller, "From Sweatshop Worker to Labor Leader: Teresa Malkiel, A Case Study," AJH, December 1978.

173 **Hapgood's description** 83.

173 **their reference group** Hapgood, 84–85; Howe, 266–67.

173 **job discrimination** Howe, 167; **college quotas** Eli Ginzberg, "Jews in the American Economy," 34.

173 **women writers in Yiddish radical subculture** Norma Fain Pratt, "Culture and Radical Politics: Yiddish Women Writers 1890–1940," AJH, September 1980. See also Glanz, chap. 11.

174 **chose the son** Howe, 266; **black families** Schneider, 152.

174 **expected to be married** BHM, 227.

174 **ideal feminine behavior** BHM, 193–95.

174 **shed wigs** BHM, 205.

174 **competition with non-Jewish women** BHM, 223.

175 **"conquering" America** Roth, *Portnoy,* 235; **"love . . ."** 147.

175 **decline of observance of ritual purity laws** Joselit, 60.

175 **sexual practices** Interviews by author.

175 **"around the house"** Roth, *Portnoy,* 153.

175 **marriage and limited economic opportunity** BHM, 233. See also Glanz, 71 and 176 n. 38.

CHAPTER 8: ISRAEL: "NEW JEWS" AND RECYCLED GENDER ROLES

177 **Heschel quote** In essay "Engagement to the Land," in *An Echo of Eternity* (New York: Farrar, Straus & Giroux, 1967), 59.

177 **Bialik quote** Prof. Shlomo Shva of Israel, an expert on the poet's life, confirmed in a 1989 phone conversation with Nina Natelson that Bialik expressed this sentiment among friends.

177 **"Feminism has the power"** Interview with Chesler by author, *Lilith,* no. 2 (Winter 1976–77): 28.

178 **Ozick on attitude to Yiddish** "Sholom Aleichem's Revolution," 100. Mendele Mocher Sforim called Yiddish the "rejected daughter": Madison, 42.

178 **Hebrew** F&S, 96–98, 110–111; Z&S, 55–57.

178 **Mapu** WMT, 13–14; *Love of Zion:* 1853; *Shame of Samaria:* 1865.

178 **"new Jew"** F&S, 121, 237; Z&S, 97.

179 **Bilu** F&S, 70, 98.

178 **narodniks** WMT, 54–55.

178 **abandonment** Baron, 51. Tolstoi and Turgenev, the two contemporary giants of Russian literature, did not protest the pogroms. The one exception among Russian writers was the satirist Shchedrin-Saltykov: D/R&P, 2:325.

178 **"Where are . . ."** Writer in *Raszvet* (Dawn), quoted in Louis Greenberg, *The Jew in Russia* (New Haven, CT: Yale Univ. Press, 1951), 2:58.

178 **Bilu history** F&S, 94–96, 98–102; Z&S, 61–62.

179 **despair . . . didn't leave rooms** Muki Tsur, Jewish Liberation School (JLS) class, "History of the Yishuv," February–March 1972, from author's tapes (hereinafter Tsur/JLS).

179 **Bund** WMT, 219–373, 409–11.

179 **Zionist movement in Russia** F&S, 70–71, 74–75; **impetus** 73.

179 **WZC** Elon, *Herzl,* 234–47; **Basle Progam** 242.

179 **as "Jewish as England is English"** In Weizmann's statement at the 1919 Paris Peace Conference, paraphrased in F&S, 195.

179 **Poale Zion** F&S, 75; Z&S, 90–92; WMT, 394–95, 408–9, 411–13; Borochov, 179–82; 101.

179 **PZ analysis and program** See "Our Platform," in Borochov, 183–205; and WMT, 413–17, 418–19.

179 **Labor Zionists** Z&S, 92–98; A. Duker, intro. to Borochov, 52–54.

179 **disciples . . . tendency** F&S, 121–22. See also Z&S, 93; and WMT, 402.

179   **statistics on Second, Third Aliyah**   Tsur/JLS; F&S, 122.

179   **starved**   WMT, 403–4; **malaria and suicide**   F&S, 144.

180   **suicide**   Tsur/JLS.

180   **chalutzim**   F&S, 111–12.

180   **"magic key"**   F&S, 113; **"worshipped"**   114.

180   **Gordon**   (1856–1922); bio: E. Silbershlag in Gordon, xi–xiv; WMT, 404–6; Avineri, chap. 14.

180   **"lack ... labor"**   Gordon, 52; **"Our entire structure"** ... **"Then we can consider"** ... **"Labor will heal us"**   56.

180   **mystical connection ... Tolstoy**   F&S, 113.

180   **in love with the earth**   F&S, 142–43.

180   **adulation of obschchina**   Z&S, 101.

180   **aliyah**   F&S, 111; **avoda**   114.

180   **"hymns to labor"** ... **"vision of glory"** ... **"blessing descends"** ... **"returned to the earth"**   *"Avoda, Adama"* (Work, Earth) by Sh. Shalom and A. Mindlin, "We Sing for You," Hed Artzi Records, 1975; **"to be regenerated"**   from pioneer song *"Anu Banu Artza"* (We Have Come to the Land of Israel), anon.: F&S, 229.

180   **rabbis' manual trades**   For example, Joshua was a charcoal burner (BT *Brachot* 28a); Yossi ben Chalafta, a leather worker (BT *Shabbat* 49b); Yohanan, a sandal maker (PA 4:14). See Steinsaltz, 58.

180   **"all study ..."**   PA 2:2; **"a blessing"**   *Tosefta Brachot* VII.8.

181   **adulation of road builders**   Testimony by David Horowitz, co-head of the left-wing faction of the Labor Brigade, in part 5 of *Pillar of Fire: A TV History of Israel's Rebirth, 1896–1948,* created by Yigal Lossin. See also F&S, 138–40, and Maimon, 70.

181   **Ben Gurion in census**   Z&S, 135.

181   **"with our very own hands"**   Gordon, 55.

181   **pioneering Yishuv**   One sector of the entire Jewish community of Mandatory Palestine, called "the Yishuv."

181   **Schochat**   See biography by Ben-Zvi; and WMT, 424–25.

181   **set the tone**   While not all olim founded or settled on kibbutzim, the kibbutz was the "seismograph" of the Yishuv, its members symbolizing "the new Jews": F&S, 131.

181   **"intimate kibbutz," "community of feeling"** ... **confessions**   Tsur/JLS; F&S, 140–43.

181   **"banquet"**   Horowitz on *Pillar,* part 5.

181   **tensions**   Tsur/JLS. Part of the reason for its failure may have been its radical discontinuity with the attitudes in the shtetl; "most thoughts and feelings ... [were] not freely shared" there: Z&H, 347.

181   **debating**   F&S, 136.

182   **poverty**   F&S, 139, 144; **asceticism**   116–17, 133.

182   **Kovner quote**   "Bridging the Cultural Chasm," *Israel Horizons,* March–April 1984, 11.

182   **"redeemer"**   Gordon, 18.

183   **family**   See Hazleton, 117, 119.

183   **enabling**   Maimon, 26, 37, 38, 51.

183   **"We were ... separated"**   Zipporah Bar-Droma, "Comrade So-and-So's Wife," in Katzenelson-Rubashow, *The Plough-Woman* anthology, 182.

183   **milk from cow**   Maimon, 27.

183   **what the women wanted**   Maimon, 21, 37.

184 **"no distinction . . . our beautiful dreams"** Sarah Malchin, "The Woman Worker in Kinneret" (1913), quoted in Maimon, 23.

184 **two-front war** Maimon, 22, 69. First Aliyah villagers worried that their daughters would be influenced by the chalutzot.

184 **cities** Maimon, 73–83. Men argued that building trades were harmful to women and that their buildings would fall: 75–80.

184 **strategy** See film *"Anou Banou": The Daughters of Utopia* (France, 1982, Edna Politi, director).

184 **training farms** Maimon, 29–31, 48, 64–67, 96–101, 104–9; Rein, 40–41; WMT, 442–43.

184 **learning, working collectives** Maimon, 81–82, 101–4.

184 **Council** Rein, 45.

184 **collective child rearing** Maimon, 50–51, 53–54.

184 **"desire to shock"** Leveled at the women plowing in Sejera in 1908: Maimon, 23–24.

184 **"let them carry . . . "** Maimon, 32.

184 **sixteen-hour days** Maimon, 24.

185 **the railroad . . . "oversensitive . . . ruining peaceful relations"** 25.

185 **swashbuckling** See F&S, 123.

185 **veterans of self-defense in Russia** WMT, 402; see Borochov, 180.

185 **"despised . . . manhood"** Intro. to Bialik, *Poems from the Hebrew,* xiii. See Z&S, 137.

185 **"great is the shame"** Intro. to Bialik, *Poems from the Hebrew,* xiv; **"In the City"** Bialik/Dvir, 84.

185 **mythologizing themselves** See D. Biale, *Power,* 146, 148.

186 **Hagana, Palmach** Hazleton, 20; Maimon, 217–19. Women also served in the right-wing Irgun and the Stern Group.

186 **"inscribed on its flag," 1947 order** Netiva Ben-Yehuda, quoted in Ruth Beizer-Bohrer, "Images of Women in Israeli Literature—Myth and Realities," *Judaism,* Winter 1984, 99.

186 **Allon's "explanation"** *Shield of David, The Story of Israel's Armed Forces* (London: Weidenfeld & Nicolson, 1970), 128.

186 **raiders** WMT, 425. There were also Arab pogroms against religious Jews in 1921 and 1929 and terrorist attacks in the cities and on settlements in 1936–39.

187 **ideological commitment** Several groups worked actively for Jewish-Arab rapprochment, including *Brit Shalom* (Covenant of Peace) and the *Ichud* (Union).

187 **havlaga** Urofsky, 205; Syrkin, *Match,* 314.

187 **oppressiveness of Mandate** Talmon, 145; Ben-Sasson, 1042–43, 1045, 1053; **limits on immigration** Sanders, 123–22.

187 **White Paper** May 17, 1939 Talmon, 152; Sanders, 136.

187 **Labor goverment** Lacqueur, 565; F&S, 212–13; Urofsky, 134.

187 **"illegal" vessels** Lacqueur, 567–70; Ben-Sasson, 1048–51.

187 **Hagana and immigrants** Syrkin, *Match,* 337–53.

187 **Irgun-Stern revolt** Sanders, 159; **Irgun** 156–57; **Stern** 157–58.

187 **opposition in WZO** Sanders, 159; Ben-Sasson, 1053.

188 **Hagana joined** Lacqueur, 572; Ben-Sasson, 1049.

188 **U.N. role** Urofsky, 135–46; **from Partition to armistice** Lacqueur, 582–86; F&S, 191–92; Ben-Sasson, 1055–62; Urofsky, 179–91.

188   **mamlachtiyut**   Mitchell Cohen gives a germinal analysis of it in z&s. See 210–18.

188   **disbanded militias**   z&s, 231–34.

188   **The War**   War of Independence, 1948–49; Sinai Campaign, 1956; Six-Day War, 1967; Yom Kippur War, 1973; Lebanon War, 1982. Israelis also add the unofficial "War of Attrition" (intensified attacks and terrorism), 1967–70.

188   **uncritical attitude**   Rein, 49, 73.

189   **set the tone**   Rein, 73; **discouraging formalities**   f&s, 253.

189   **captured POWs**   See, for example, Hirsch Goodman, "3 POWs Freed for 1,150 Terrorists," jp, May 21, 1985, 1.

189   **swearing-in at Masada**   f&s, 288.

189   **"'manhood' . . . on trial"**   Rein, 75.

190   **terrorism**   See Joel Brinkley, "Years of Bloodletting Scar Israeli-PLO Relations," nyt, September 11, 1993, A6.

190   **"For many Israeli Jews"**   "More Nightmares Per Square Mile," interview with Oz, part 1, by Steve Shaw and David Twersky, Jewish Student Press-Service (JSPS) (feature packet), March 1973, 2.

191   **domestic violence in Gulf War**   Amy Avgar, "The Gulf War–What Price Did Israeli Women Pay?" *Na'amat Woman,* September–October 1991, 29.

191   **needed in army**   Hazleton, 138.

191   **WWII**   Hazleton, 139; Maimon, 220.

191   **War of Independence**   Maimon, 228–29; Hazleton, 21.

191   **basic training**   Hazleton, 144–45; **combat exclusion**   140.

191   **work in army**   Hazleton, 139, 149; **moral influence**   146; **sexual partners**   147; **sexual harassment**   Bruria Avidan-Breer: "Sisters in Arms," *WIZO Review,* fall–winter 1994, 9.

191   **"protect women," fear of rape**   Hazleton, 140.

192   **post-1948 fiction**   Fuchs, 24–33; **Samson and Delilah type story**   "Nicole" by Yizhak Ben Ner (1976), cited on 28.

192   **old-boy network and civilian life**   Alice Shalvi, chair, Israeli Women's Network, quoted in Cynthia Mann, "Pioneer Image of Women's Equality Was a Myth, Says Israeli Feminist," jta-cnr, August 6, 1993, 4.

192   **Ben Gurion to first Knesset**   David Ben Gurion, *Israel, A Personal History* (New York: Funk & Wagnalls, 1971), 375; **memoirs**   8.

192   **Begin's speeches**   Hazleton, "Post-Election Blues–Begin's Victory, Feminism's Defeat," *Lilith,* no. 4 (Fall–Winter 1977–78): 22.

192   **religious control over marriage, divorce**   Instituted under the Rabbinical Courts Jurisdiction Law of 1953: Hazleton, 23.

192   **abortion**   A clause in the reformed law introduced by MK Chaika Grossman of Mapam (a ghetto fighter from Bialystok), allowing pregnancy termination for "social" (i.e., economic) reasons, was repealed under the Begin government.

192   **pronatalists**   Hazleton, 83. Their aim was to increase what some called "internal aliyah" to offset the high Arab birthrate. Hazleton also writes that many women have more children to "cover their bets," i.e., just in case sons get killed in wars: 66–67.

193   **tractor myth**   Testimonies to author.

193   **women's acceptance of it**   Hazleton, 27, 154–55.

193   **shrinkage of production role**   Hazleton, 152, 156–57; and interview with Mordechai Cafri of Kibbutz Gal-On by author, 1972.

193   **mothering**   Hazleton, 160; **lina mishpachteet**   157–58.

193   **reluctance**   Hazelton, 159–60, and interview with Cafri.

193   **sex role stereotypes**   Hazleton, 107, 109.

193   **nurturing is necessary**   Joyce Rosman Brenner, "The Wounds of War," *Lilith,* no. 11 (Fall–Winter 1983), 15.

194   **equal employment law**   Hazleton, 25.

194   **statistics on employment**   JR, "Story of the Sexes," March 26, 1992, 22.

194   **Yom Kippur War**   Ruth Seligman, "Womanpower Unused," *Hadassah,* March 1974; Rein, 87–91. Similarly, during the Gulf War: "Women in Times of National Emergency," *Networking for Women* (publication of the Israeli Women's Network) 5, no. 4 (1992): 3.

194   **"Where Are Those Girls?"**   Lyrics, Yossi Gamzu, in Talma Alyagon-Roz and Rafi Pesahzon, *Erets, Erets–Sixty Favorite Israeli Songs* (Ramat Gan: Kinneret, 1986), 56.

194   **portrayal of women in fiction**   Fuchs, 16.

195   **"I still remember"**   Oz, *Michael,* 112–13.

195   **Ben Gurion's lament**   In March 1944 speech to Mapai Council, quoted in Teveth, 862.

195   **"part of the rhythm and ritual"**   F&S, 199.

195   **Begin and boat people**   "Begin, the Humanitarian," sidebar to obit., New York *Jewish Week,* March 13–19, 1992, 2.

195   **guilt for abandonment**   F&S, 124, 128, 199.

195   **rejection of values**   See Yehuda Litani, "Memories of a Family I Never Knew," JP int'l ed., January 6, 1990, 12–13.

195   **not done enough**   F&S, 210, 211. See also Teveth, 348–62.

195   **Istanbul**   Syrkin, *Match,* 81–89; **Romania**   see Kluger.

195   **parachutists**   The plan, by Yitzhak Sadeh of the Palmach, was reluctantly accepted by the British in 1944 only on condition that the parachutists' main mission would be intelligence. See Harriet Parmet, "Haviva Reik–A Woman of Valor," *Midstream,* April 1990, 24; F&S, 210–11; Ben-Sasson, 1043; Syrkin, *Match,* 13–21, 33–42, 65–76.

196   **shame about "passivity" during pogroms**   See school text quoted in F&S, 209.

196   **until recently**   See Yossi Klein Halevi, "Who Owns the Memory?" JR, February 25, 1993, 29.

196   **safe hero**   Term coined in this connection by Grace Weiner.

197   **origins of Six-Day War**   Herzog, 145–51.

197   **facing another Holocaust**   F&S, 216.

197   **parks, capsules**   Personal testimonies to author.

197   **military prosecution of war**   Herzog, 151–91.

197   **holy places**   During the Jordanian occupation of 1948–67, Jews were not allowed at the Western Wall. The Jordanians destroyed Jewish tombstones, cemeteries, manuscripts, and houses: Shipler, 175–76.

197   **Entebbe**   Herzog, 328–36.

197   **no other country**   Paraphrase of quote by.Yitzchak Mais, director of Yad Vashem Museum, in A. C., "'Americanizing the Holocaust' Worries Israelis Doing Holocaust Research," JTA-DNB, April 24, 1987.

197   **Castro**   Quoted in Sol Stern, "My Jewish Problem–And Ours," *Ramparts,* August 1971, 32.

198   **Mandela**   Sheila Rule, "Old Allies Greet Mandela in Zambia," NYT, February 28, 1990.

198   **moshavnik's letter**   Dvorah Namir of Kfar Vitkin, published in *Yediot Acharonot* (Hebrew daily), October 6, 1972.

199 **war widows** See Shamgar-Handelman, 19–51, 179–81.

199 **American-born settlers** It was generally those with hawkish views who were interviewed on American television.

199 **population exchange** This is the term used in J. Schechtman's article "Arab Refugees" in the *Encyclopedia of Zionism and Israel,* Raphael Patai, ed. (New York: Herzl Press and McGraw Hill, 1971), 1:56. The article estimates that in 1948-49 about 519,000 Arabs fled the areas of Mandatory Palestine that became Israel to Jordan and the West Bank (which it annexed unilaterally in 1950), Syria, Lebanon, and Gaza. (No census of the refugees and their descendants has ever been taken and no accurate figures are available.) A comparable number of Jewish refugees fled Arab countries (Yemen, Iraq, Morocco, Tunisia, Algeria, Libya) to Israel between 1949 and 1952 because of intensified persecution.

199 **condition of Sephardim** F&S, 307.

199 **assimilation of** See Kovner, "Cultural Chasm," 15.

199 **"purity of arms"** Fein, 89.

200 **Leibowitz** Professor emeritus, Hebrew University of Jerusalem: "Judaism, the People of Israel and Violence," *Jewish Spectator,* Spring 1987, 40; **"living creatures"** an issue addressed by CHAI, Concern for Helping Animals in Israel (Alexandria, VA).

200 **Scholem quote** In David Biale, "The Threat of Messianism: An Interview with G.S." NYRB, August 18, 1980, 22.

200 **wife-battering** See Hazleton, 177; **10 percent battered** "Women's Rights," JR, July 2, 1992, 18.

200 **estimated rapes** JR, July 2, 1992, 18. There were thirty-two recorded cases of Arab women raped in the wars of 1948 (twenty), 1956 (six), and 1967 (six), according to criminologist Menahem Amir: Shipler, 3.

200 **child abuse** Author interview with Hanita Zimrin, founding director of the Israeli Association for Child Protection, for JTA, reprinted in *Omaha Jewish Press,* July 19, 1985, 3.

200 **1991 murders** *Newsletter* of US-Israel Women to Women, Fall 1992, 3. Of the thirty-six women, thirty were Jews, six Arabs.

200 **approximately five million** Only an estimate is possible, given the politicization of population statistics by Israel, the U.N., and the U.S. government. The estimate for Israel proper (i.e., inside the Green Line) is extrapolated from the figure of 5,195,000 for the end of 1992 (Jerusalem: Central Bureau of Statistics: *Statistical Abstract of Israel,* 1993, 47, table 2.5). That figure includes the population of Israel proper as well as the 105,400 Jewish settlers in the administered territories (i.e., outside the Green Line). Subtracting the latter provides the estimate.

200 **"beginning . . . of our redemption"** Phrase used in the "Prayer for the Peace of the State" of Israel, written by the Chief Rabbinate and included in the Daily Prayer Book: *HaSiddur HaShalem,* translation by Philip Birnbaum (New York: Hebrew Pub. Co., 1949), 789.

200 **"return to the Jewish fold"** Address to first WZC, quoted in Elon, *Herzl,* 240. See Memmi, *Liberation,* 293.

201 **"come to such a pass"** Talmon, 78.

201 **McReynolds's condemnation** "The Destiny of Israel: A Minority View," *Village Voice,* June 29, 1967.

202 **"uncorrupted . . . Western hegemony"** Mohammed Mehdi, director of the American-Arab Relations Committee (NY), interviewed on Channel 11, New York, March 5, 1992, from author's notes.

202 **effendis' fear of kibbutz women** Melanie Kaye/Kantrowitz, address to Second Texas Jewish Feminist Conference, held in Houston, October 23–25, 1992, from author's

notes. Arab "traditionalists" opposed "the bare-armed and bare-legged Jewish pioneer girls [*sic*] . . . and the participation of women in public affairs": *Falastin* (1924), quoted in Esco Foundation for Palestine, *Palestine, A Study of Jewish, Arab and British Policies* (New Haven, CT: Yale Univ. Press, 1947), 1:529–30.

202   **called them Communists**   For example, Arab propagandist M. E. T. Mogannam said, "A strong bolshevik element has already established itself in the country and has produced an effect on the population . . . especially the poorer classes": Esco 1:529.

202   **imperialism charge**   See note on "Palestinian Covenant" on p. 453.

202   **economic boycott**   Imposed by the Arab League in 1951 at Cairo meeting and until mid-1994 observed by twenty countries (not including Egypt since the peace treaty with Israel was signed). The primary boycott was of recognition and trade with Israel; the secondary boycott, a blacklist of companies conducting business with the Jewish State; the tertiary boycott, a blacklist of companies dealing with businesses on the original blacklist. Following Israel's signing a peace treaty with Jordan (October 1994) an economic conference was held in Casablanca with participation of politicians and business executives from all Mideastern and North African countries but five. There, Foreign Minister Shimon Peres told a reporter, "The boycott has died even if it has not been formally buried": Naomi Segal, "Casablanca Conference Ends with Pronouncements That Boycott Is Over," JTA-DNB, November 2, 1994. Saudi Arabia and five other Gulf states terminated the secondary and tertiary boycotts in September: Jennifer Batog, "Jews Debate Value of Anti-Boycott Provisions in Upcoming GATT Bill," JTA-DNB, November 24, 1994, 1.

202   **Protocols**   Bein, 707; F&S, 217.

202   **1975 U.N. resolution**   Adopted November 11, 1975 (rescinded December 16, 1991).

203   **Kenan on New Left**   "New Left, Go Home," *Jewish Liberation Journal,* no. 2 (1969): 1.

203   **arms sales**   Israel, for example, sold arms to Argentina when it was under the juntas' reign of terror (1976–83).

204   **"we have drought and famine"**   Quoted by Regina Schreiber (pseud.), "Copenhagen, One Year Later," *Lilith,* no. 8 (1981): 30.

204   **"oil wells . . . water wells"**   Sidebar to Schreiber, "Copenhagen," 31.

204   **"scapegoat"**   Schreiber, "Copenhagen," 30; **mutilation**   34.

205   **Kovner on kibbutz and Jewish tradition**   "Cultural Chasm," 13; **"more involved"** . . . **"confrontation"**   19.

CHAPTER 9: THE NO-WIN SITUATION OF THE JEWISH MOTHER IN AMERICA

207   **Jewish folktale**   Retold, with changes, in Maurice Tamerlin, *Lucy, Growing up Human* (New York: Bantam, 1977), 26–27.

207   **quote from A Tree**   184–85.

208   **shtetl housekeeping**   Z&H, 361–65, 369–70, 373–76.

208   **"ladies . . . poking"**   Birmingham, 322.

208   **overcompensated**   See Howe, 175–76, and BHM, 201.

209   **ineffectual dreamer**   Ellen Schiff, "What Kind of Way Is That for Nice Jewish Girls to Act: Images of Jewish Women in Modern American Drama," AJH, September 1980, 108.

209   **naches . . . "shining reward"**   Z&H, 297; **"validated"**   298.

209   **success = becoming a mentsch**   Z&H, 331–32.

209   **in America**   See Kazin, 21–22.

209   **"She will comment"**   Z&H, 132.

209   **older daughters' role**   Z&H, 331, 353; **cheder**   348–52.

210   **Bart study**   "Portnoy's Mother's Complaint: Depression in Middle-Aged Women," in Koltun; **"failed to meet her needs"**   76.

211   **"she was told"**   Lecture by Paula Hyman at panel at the Jewish Museum (NY) on "What Is Jewish About the Jewish Home?" September 18, 1990, from author's notes.

211   **"cultural defection"**   Many Yiddish women writers taught in Yiddish afternoon schools, focusing their energies on preventing it: Pratt, "Culture and Radical Politics," 82.

211   **Jewish neighborhoods**   Deborah Dash Moore at Jewish Museum panel, from author's notes. See also Howe, 131.

211   **lecture halls, classrooms opened**   Harry Golden, *For Two Cents Plain* (New York: World, Permabook, 1960), 81.

211   **streets and parks**   Moore, at Jewish Museum panel, from author's notes.

212   **Jewish education**   See S. Greenberg, "Jewish Educational Institutions," in Finkelstein, *Jews,* 393–94, and Moshe Davis, "Jewish Religious Life and Institutions in America," in Finkelstein, *Jews,* 355–56.

212   **blamed for offspring's assimilation**   Hyman lecture at Jewish Museum panel, from author's notes.

212   **impossible in Czarist Russia**   A 10 percent quota for Jewish gymnasia and university students was instituted in 1887: Ben-Sasson, 885. See also Graetz, 6:192–93.

212   **Jewish mother's ambition**   Zena Blau Smith, "In Defense of the Jewish Mother," *Midstream,* February 1967, 45.

212   **"dream buster"**   Schiff, "Nice Jewish Girls," 108–9.

213   **Bart on Erikson, women and Jews**   Schneider interview with Bart in *Lilith,* 11.

213   **inconspicuous**   Olga Silverstein, in interview in *Lilith,* Spring 1989, 8.

213   **"unobtrusiveness"**   Adam Hochchild's father, Harold's, secret 1940 memo, quoted in Janice L. Booker, *The Jewish American Princess and Other Myths* (New York: Shapolsky, 1991), 71.

213   **torn apart by double message**   Observation by Ruth Grunzweig Roth at 1970 meeting of the Jewish Liberation Project, from author's notes.

213   **"Be a scholar . . ."**   Tamerlin, *Lucy,* 28, 34.

214   **"Everybody . . . talking"**   Z&H, 325; see also 301, 363; **"Every problem"**   301; **"From the outset of life"**   325.

214   **emotions to be expressed**   Z&H, 294, 314, 328, 355, 414. See also Howe, 221–22.

214   **children expected to cry, never told "be brave"**   Z&H, 325.

214   **less emotional disturbance**   See Daniel Goleman, "Those Who Stay Calm in Disasters Face Psychological Risk, Studies Say," NYT April 17, 1994, I:20.

214   **Kazin on music, emotion**   62–63.

215   **corporate culture**   "A Class Divided," *Utne Reader,* July–August 1990.

215   **political analyst**   Martin Indyk, director of the Institute for Near East Policy, Washington, D.C., quoted in Clifford Kraus, "Israel's Man, Scorched Once, Adjusts to Life in the Diplomatic Minefield," NYT, May 10, 1991, A8.

215   **no separation**   See discussion in Memmi, *Portrait,* 308–11.

215   **Clare's father**   G. Clare, *Last Waltz in Vienna* (New York: Avon, Discus, 1983), 159.

216   **Kovner's mother**   His testimony in film *Partisans of Vilna.*

216   **Eliach quote**   A. C., "Silent No More: The Hidden Child of the Holocaust," *Na'amat Woman,* September–October 1991, 8; **inmate**   8.

216   **parents of addicts**   Interviews for A. C., "Drug Addiction in New York," London *Jewish Chronicle,* March 19, 1965.

216   **A situation**   See Diana Trilling, "Intellectuals in Love: My Speak-Easy Romance with Lionel Trilling," NYTBR, October 13, 1993, 15.

216   **Perel on WASP and Jewish families**   Interview by Susan Weidman Schneider in *Lilith,* no. 17 (Fall 1987): 17.

216   **"fuzzy boundaries"**   Melanie Kaye/Kantrowitz believes these can be a "sign of health" in the Jewish culture: A. C., "Therapy and the Jewish Woman: Exploring the Connections" (report on Conference on Judaism, Feminism and Psychology, Seattle, October 1992), *Na'amat Woman,* January–February 1993 (hereinafter A.C./Therapy), 11.

217   **"hurried out of babyhood"**   Z&H, 328; **"be a mentsch"**   331.

217   **"outside influence"**   Smith, "In Defense of the Jewish Mother," 47. See Kazin, 21.

217   **"delay of independence"**   Blau Smith, "In Defense of the Jewish Mother," 47. Irving Howe wrote the following misogynist passage about this dynamic: "Learning to *relish the privileges of suffering,* the Jewish mother had become *absurdly,* outrageously protective. From that condition, especially if *linked, as it well might be, with contempt for her husband,* she could decline into a brassy scourge, with her *grating bark* or soul-destroying whine, silver-blue hair and unfocussed aggression. Nor was it unusual for her to employ ingenuity in order to keep her brood in a state of prolonged dependency as she grew expert at groaning, cajoling, intimidating. Daughters paled, sons fled": 176–77 (italics mine). See also 254.

218   **old neighborhoods**   See Goldin, 222, on elderly in Miami.

218   **guilt as tool of powerless**   See Tamerlin, *Lucy,* 27–28.

218   **"Alter, Alter"**   Quoted in Howe, 261.

219   **"silent treatment"**   Z&H, 302.

219   **isolation as punishment**   Berman, 428.

219   **"refusing to eat"**   Z&H, 303, 338.

220   **"We were grown-ups"**   Etta Byer, interviewed by Sydney Stahl Weinberg, "Working Daughters," *Lilith,* no. 8 (1981): 20, 22. See Yezierska in Glanz, 176 n. 48.

220   **as "autonomous adults"**   Weinberg, "Working Daughters," 22.

220   **"when I sat reading"**   Unpublished immigrant autobiography no. 92 in YIVO archives, quoted in Weinberg, "Working Daughters," 22.

220   **jobs outside sweatshops**   Howe, 266; Teller, 87–88.

220   **Hurst's aunt**   Hurst, *Anatomy of Me* (New York: Doubleday, 1958), 105.

220   **Bintel Brief letter**   Quoted in Isaac Metzker, ed., *A "Bintel Brief": Sixty Years of Letters from the Lower East Side to the "Jewish Daily Forward"* (New York: Doubleday, 1971), 109–10.

220   **styles**   See BHM, 223–27.

220   **zaftig**   Golden writes how around 1916 "young women practiced sitting postures to simulate double chins": Golden, *Plain,* 60. See also Z&H, 138.

221   **encouraged to be fat**   Golden, *Plain,* 60–61. He also wrote, "A stout girth was accounted a sure sign of success": 60.

221   **TB**   By 1906 TB afflicted twelve out of every thousand Jews on the Lower East Side: Howe, 149. See Golden note in Hapgood, 94.

221   **Weight Watchers founder**   Jean Nidetch of Long Island, NY.

221   **Chernin's mother**   Comment by Chernin to author (from author's notes).

221   **Forverts columnist's advice**   Regina Freshwater, August 31, 1919. Quoted in Maxine S. Seller, "Defining Socialist Womanhood: The Woman's Page of the *Jewish Daily Forward* in 1919," AJH, June 1987, 436.

222   **complain**   Another behavior criticized by Freshwater, quoted in Seller, "Defining Socialist Womanhood," 436.

223   **"quiet ... not to dispute"**   Freshwater in Seller, "Defining Socialist Womanhood," 436.

224   **guilt for not marrying**   Numerous testimonies at women's conferences (from author's notes). See also Silverstein, *Lilith* interview, 9.

225   **"too enmeshed"**   Quoted in A.C./Therapy, 11.

225   **"If the Jewish woman has to do all these things"**   Wendy Marks, A.C./Therapy, 28.

226   **Socialism as spiritual resistance**   See Abraham Menes, "The East Side and the Jewish Labor Movement" in H/G. Menes writes, "Socialist intellectuals ... were in the forefront of the struggle against the culture of success": 214.

226   **"they literally gag"**   Mary Cahn Schwartz, "The High Price of Failure," *Lilith,* no. 1 (1976): 21; **"There goes ... expected" ... "Given their culture"**   21.

226   **Wolfe's revelations**   Her 1971 paper "The Invisible Jewish Poor" was delivered at the annual meeting of the Chicago chapter of the American Jewish Committee and was later published in the *Journal of Jewish Communal Service (JJCS),* Spring 1972.

226   **excoriation of**   She was accused of "scare tactics" and "sociological overkill," *JJCS,* Summer 1972.

227   **admiration in 1920s**   Teller, 89–91.

227   **"He's tough"**   Solly Krieger, quoted in Mark Jacobson, "Mazel Tough," *Village Voice,* March 10, 1975, 12; **deli worker**   13.

227   **physicality downgraded**   Z&H, 330, 354, 357; **prerequisite**   An example of the methodology of making "fences."

227   **shtetl ideal**   Z&H, 358.

227   **nit mit dee hent**   See Z&H, 343; Smith, "In Defense of the Jewish Mother," 44.

228   **"I am the son"**   Roth, *Portnoy,* 36–37.

228   **matriphobia**   See BHM, 245–46, 247–51.

228   **Asian American men's image**   Katherine Bishop, "For Asian Men, A Calendar for Change," NYT, December 24, 1990.

228   **"rarely employ"**   Perel interview in *Lilith,* 16.

228   **Holocaust miniseries**   Inge to Karl in part 1. See A. C., "TV's 'Holocaust': The Selling of Assimilation," *Lilith,* no. 5 (1978).

229   **How to Be a Jewish Mother**   Subtitled *A Very Lovely Training Manual* (Los Angeles: Price, Stern, Sloan, 1964).

229   **foreword**   *How to Be a Jewish Mother,* 9; **"wasn't like me"**   quoted in interview with Fred A. Bernstein in *The Jewish Mother's Hall of Fame* (New York: Doubleday, 1986), 10.

229   **Kaufman novel**   (Philadelphia and New York: J. B. Lippincott, 1957), 84–85.

229   **Kazin quote**   67; **Gold's mother**   Gold, 157–58.

230   **luftmentsch**   Nordau, 126. Nordau was speaking with concern of the huge population of Jews who seemed to subsist "from the air," somehow eking out a precarious living by insubstantial means. See Z&H, 258.

230   **"Shirley after Shirley"**   Wouk, *Marjorie Morningstar,* 171–72.

230   **intermarriages**   1964–84 rise: "Intelligence" column, *Parade,* December 13, 1984, 25. Current rate: Kosmin et al., *Highlights of NJPS,* 13–14.

231   **excise part of themselves**   Perel interview in *Lilith,* 19.

CHAPTER 10: THE ROOTS AND MARITAL REPERCUSSIONS OF LOW
SELF-ESTEEM

233   **Talmon quote**   93.

234   **"try to be a human being"**   PA 2:5.

235   **damper on demonstrativeness**   See Z&H, 332–33, 359.

235   **model of appropriate responses**   The mother in imperial Germany, argues Marion Kaplan, played the role of "cultural administrator" in middle-class homes. She was a "shaper and guardian of bourgeois respectability" and had to restrain the children from "behavior attributed to Jews by anti-Semites—being noisy, undisciplined, dirty, unmannerly": presentation at a panel on "Gender and Assimilation in Modern Jewish History" sponsored by Leo Baeck Institute at JTS, May 1, 1994 (from author's notes).

235   **young Freud**   "The Interpretation of Dreams," *The Basic Writings of Sigmund Freud* (New York: Modern Library, 1938), 260.

236   **mother negotiated**   Z&H, 132.

236   **taught daughter**   Z&H, 346, 366–67, 369–76.

236   **lived in ivory tower**   Z&H, 341; **unable to protect**   341.

236   **enter father's world of study**   Z&H, 329, 348–49; **Bar Mitzvah**   350–52.

237   **child-raising manual**   *Lev Tov* (A Good Heart) by Yitzhak ben Eliakim of Poznan (1620); similarly, in *Brantshpiegl.* Quoted by Gershon David Hundert, "Jewish Children and Childhood in Early Modern East Central Europe," in Kraemer, 82–83; see also 88.

237   **Ruth Adler's analysis**   "The 'Real' Jewish Mother?" *Midstream,* October 1977, 38–40; "complaints" 38.

237   **Bialik poem**   "My Song," in Bialik/Dvir, 117–18.

237   **manifestations of solicitude**   Z&H, 293.

237   **Gymnasia**   *The Complete Works of Sholem Aleichem* (Yid.) (New York: Forverts, 1944), 7:175–93.

237   **mother and daughter**   Adler/*Peretz,* 87.

238   **corporal punishment**   Z&H, 337.

238   **never withheld love**   Z&H, 337; **or food**   338. The mother demonstrated her affection more readily to the son than to the daughter, according to shtetl interviewees (Z&H, 332). The father was more affectionate with the daughter, although physical demonstrativeness declined when she became preteen (Z&H, 332). The reason is that the father did not need to train the daughter nor the mother, the son, in breadwinning or in Jewish religious practice. In Orthodox families today, father-daughter closeness is a common behavior pattern, according to testimony to the author.

238   **"Yiddishe Mameh" song**   By L. Pollack and Y. Yellen, "Spirit of a People," Decca, London Records, 1974, LP SP44026.

238   **Dubnow quote**   D/R&P, 2:113.

238   **sock makers' union**   Glanz, 188 n. 18; **first strikes**   Howe, 297–302.

238   **desertion**   Howe, 179–80; Glanz, 62, 63, 70; Goldin, 59; Fridkis, "Desertion."

238   **100,000 cases**   Hertzberg, 199.

238   **economic energizers**   Irene D. Neu, "The Jewish Businesswoman in America," AJH, September 1976, 147.

238   **German Jewish women in West**   Harriet Rochlin, "Riding High: Annie Oakley's Jewish Contemporaries," *Lilith,* no. 14 (Fall–Winter 1985–86): 14–18. See also Harriet and Fred Rochlin, *Pioneer Jews.*

241   **"... To be a nothing?"**   Smith, "In Defense of the Jewish Mother," 45.

241   **Davidson**   Quoted in Marsha Dubrow's untitled Reuters news feature (slugged "Princess") no. RNR 739–741, dispatched on wire February 13, 1977; **"you're no good"** Reuters no. RNR741.

242   **ex-Californian**   Gloria Averbuch's untitled piece in "The Ways We Are" cluster, *Lilith,* no. 2 (Winter 1976–77): 7.

242   **Schwartz's report**   Quoted in A.C./Therapy, 28.

242   **"ambassador ... real American"**   Davidson, Reuters no. RNR739.

242   **Marjorie's mother's "vicarious delight"**   Wouk, *Marjorie Morningstar,* 44.

243   **Tonner quote**   "The Truth About Being a Jewish Princess," *Cosmopolitan,* September 1976, 212.

243   **"The message"**   Davidson, Reuters no. RNR740.

243   **Hoffman quote**   In interview with Benny Avni, *Tikkun,* July–August 1989, 16.

243   **Quentin as "light in the world"**   Miller, *Fall,* 73.

244   **"special and superior"**   Barbara Mayer, "Sex and the Jewish Girl," *Cosmopolitan,* December 1970, 70.

244   **pathological narcissist's motivation and childhood**   Daniel Goleman, "Narcissism Looming Larger as Root of Personality Woes," NYT, November 1, 1988, C16.

244   **narcissism and marriage**   Psychiatrist David A. Berkowitz said, "In marriage, a couple ... tend to reenact early relationships with parents who failed to give them enough love." This, he said, is especially difficult for individuals with the "emotional vulnerabilities of the narcissist": Goleman, "Narcissism."

244   **"bath of praise"**   Betty to Quentin, Miller, *Fall,* 46.

244   **Steinberg's complaint**   Quoted in Julie Baumgold, "The Persistence of the Jewish American Princess," *New York* magazine, May 3, 1971, 25.

245   **"Every Jew is frightened ... You shmuck!"**   Jackie Mason, *The World According to Me* (New York: Simon & Schuster, 1987), 82.

245   **"Gentile vs. Jewish Marriage"**   By Rubin Carson, *Cosmopolitan,* December 1972.

245   **moody and volatile**   Carson, 104; **"Crazy-Kleen fetishes"**   106; **sex nonexistent** 114; **"guilt-machines" ... "check with Information" ... "value their child's independence ... uneasy truce"**   108.

246   **two commandments**   Mary Cahn Schwartz, "The High Price of Failure," 21–22.

246   **"room to maneuver in"**   Schwartz, "The High Price of Failure," 22.

246   **"And lo ..."**   Schwartz, "The High Price of Failure," 22.

246   **"domestic Messiah!"**   Roth, *Portnoy,* 153.

247   **Hendrix's thesis**   *Getting the Love You Want: A Guide for Couples* (New York: Harper & Row, 1990), 36, 46.

247   **reciprocity**   See Nikki Stiller, "The Shiksa Question," *Moment,* July–August 1980, 25.

247   **Yiddishe Mameh myth**   See Adler, "The 'Real' Jewish Mother?" 39–40.

248   **"Identification with the mother"**   Smith, "In Defense of the Jewish Mother," 44.

248   **"live autonomously"**   Silverstein in interview in *Lilith,* 8.

249   **Jewish women's complaints**   William Novak, "Are Good Jewish Men a Vanishing Breed?" *Moment,* January–February 1980, 19 and 20.

249   **Ehrenreich's thesis**   In *Fear of Falling: The Inner Life of the Middle Class* (New York: Pantheon, 1989).

251   **emotional labor**   Arlie Hochschild's term, used in her book *The Managed Heart.*

252   **"See what she is like"**   Frondorf, 229; see also 277.

252   **behavior bigots consider specifically Jewish**   Frondorf, 278.

252   **cry of "JAP! JAP! JAP!"**   Sherry Chayat, "JAP-Baiting on the College Scene," *Lilith,* no. 17 (Fall 1987): 7; and Judith Rubinstein, "The Graffiti Wars," *Lilith,* no. 17 (Fall 1987): 8.

252   **"HEP! HEP! HEP!"**   Bein, 590–92. Also revived in nineteenth-century Germany: 228; Ben-Sasson, 804.

252   **metastasized**   Rubinstein, "Graffiti Wars," 8; Newfield, "Anti-Semitism and the Crime of Silence," *Village Voice,* 13.

252   **Jewish organizations' protests**   After the *Lilith* exposé on "JAP"-baiting appeared, the American Jewish Committee followed up on the initiative of its Houston chapter in condemning the phenomenon. The ADL did so, as well.

253   **Mailer story**   In *Advertisements for Myself* (New York: Putnam/Berkeley, 1966), 464.

253   **Evanier**   In his novel *The One-Star Jew,* Evanier wrote of how "Jewish Feminists have set up a booth on the Holocaust and hold up signs to advertise a rally 'In Memory of the 3 Million,'" (San Francisco: Northpoint Press, 1983), 208.

CHAPTER 11: BANKRUPTCY OF AMERICAN JEWISH COMMUNAL LIFE

255   **Maslow**   Quoted in Robert Spero, "Speaking for the Jews: Who Does the Conference of Presidents of Major American Jewish Organizations Really Represent?" *Present Tense,* January–February 1990 (hereinafter Spero), 17.

255   **Urofsky quote**   226.

255   **Neusner**   Letter in Boston *Jewish Advocate,* November 20, 1975. He is professor of religious studies at Brown University.

256   **eschew further involvement**   Norbert Fruehauf, director of Campaign Planning Services, CJF, in paper "The Bottom Line: Major Gifts to Federation Campaigns," submitted to Conference on Jewish Philanthropy in Contemporary America, held June 15–16, 1988, at the Center for Jewish Studies of CUNY. Published by the University Center of CUNY and CJF in Information Series no. 2 of North American Jewish Data Bank (hereinafter *NAJDB*), 36.

256   **1991–92 study**   Renae Cohen and Sherry Rosen, *Organizational Affiliations of American Jews: A Research Report* (New York: American Jewish Committee, 1992); **one-third** 2.

256   **over fifty-five**   53; **second generation**   11; **32 percent attended functions**   8; **21 percent volunteered**   9.

257   **"Jewishly illiterate"**   Speech at meeting of NYC chapter, AJCommittee, December 12, 1989, from author's notes.

257   **"in every field except Jewish affairs"**   Judah Shapiro, "The Philistine Philanthropists: The Power and Shame of Jewish Federations," *Jewish Liberation Journal,* no. 4 (October 1969), 4.

257   **5.2 million "core Jews"**   Kosmin et al., *Highlights of NJPS,* 4, 6.

257   **United Way principle**   For evolution, see Goldin, 66.

258   **Kosmin's estimate**   Paper, "The Dimensions of Contemporary American Jewish Philanthropy," submitted to 1988 Philanthropy Conference: *NAJDB,* 7, 17, 19.

258   **40–50 percent**   Declining from 60 percent in the early 1980s: Spero, 27.

258   **UJA**   National organization (not to be confused with local Federations, which often have "UJA" in their names or those of their campaigns). For evolution from 1914, see Goldin, 146–51.

258   **80–85 percent from 15–20 percent**   Silberman, 194.

258   **Big Givers = donors of $10,000+**   Kosmin, *NAJDB,* 15.

258   **13,000 gifts totaling $402 million**   Fruehauf, *NAJDB,* 28.

258   **500 give $100,000, 22 give $1 million**   "22 UJA Donors Give Million or More," *National Jewish Post-Opinion,* October 7, 1987.

258   **50 percent under 100 = 2 percent of total**   Fruehauf, *NAJDB,* 27. This is in stark contrast to the situation in 1947, when gifts of $100 and under accounted for 92.6 percent of the total raised by UJA: Goldin, 180.

258   **"expedient"**   Fruehauf, *NAJDB,* 37.

258   **60 percent give nothing**   Kosmin, *NAJDB,* 14.

258   **"donor-directed" approach**   Charles Hoffman, "The 'Me Generation' and Israel," JP int'l ed., June 17, 1989, 17.

258   **"Those that rule justify ... club"**   Shapiro/JLS.

258   **Waxman**   Rabbi of Temple Israel in Great Neck, Long Island, quoted in Stewart Ain, "Waxman Urges Synagogual Input—Federations Should Raise Funds, Not Determine Communal Policy," *L.I. Jewish World,* January 11–17, 1985, 2.

258   **"central address"**   Shapiro/JLS.

259   **"philanthropy ... builds a Jewish community"**   Irving Bernstein, then-executive vice-chairman of UJA, in panel on "The Future of Jewish Philanthropy," January 28, 1980, held at Brandeis University. In transcript booklet it printed, n.d., 4.

259   **"why should there be victims?"**   Shapiro/JLS.

259   **NJCRAC**   Comprising 117 local community relations agencies and 13 national organizations.

259   **Conference of Presidents**   See Spero, and chap. 12 of this book.

259   **image accepted uncritically by media**   Spero, 17.

259   **meeting with pope**   September 1, 1987, reported in Edwin Eytan, "An Historic Meeting," JTA-DNB, September 2, 1987, 1–2; **pope's meeting with Waldheim**   June 25, 1987.

260   **AJCommittee meetings with junta generals**   Press release no. 81–960–83, dated March 19, 1981, on March 18, 1981, meeting with Roberto Viola at Waldorf; and AJCommittee, "The Jewish Community in Argentina: A Foreign Affairs Department Background Memorandum," July 7, 1981, 3.

260   **AJCongress opposition to government funding of parochial schools**   Joint statement with the ADL and the (Reform) Central Conference of American Rabbis (CCAR): Goldin, 219.

260   **ADL action on JDL**   "ADL Scored for Giving File to FBI; ADL Rejects 'Invidious Interpretation,'" JTA-DNB, May 19, 1971, 3.

260   **NYS Report**   Released July 20, 1993. Debra Nussbaum Cohen, "Jewish Groups Learn Painful Lessons in Aftermath of Crown Heights Riots," JTA-DNB, July 22, 1993, 1.

260   **anger by Orthodox Jews**   Lucette Lagnado, "The Jewish Non-Defense League: How Mainstream Jews Failed the Hasidim of Crown Heights," *Village Voice,* August 10, 1993, 13–14; **JWV**   13.

260 **ignored anti-Semitism, called for restraint, praised mayor** Jonathan Mark, "Turning Inward: Jewish Leaders and Groups Could Stand a Bit of Soul-Searching on the Crown Heights Tragedy," New York *Jewish Week,* July 30–August 5, 1993, 29.

260 **Brooklyn rabbi** Jacob Goldstein, Lubavitch (Chabad) rabbi in Cohen, "Jewish Groups Learn Painful Lessons," 1.

260 **Foxman's apology** J. J. Goldberg, "Mixed Messages," JR, October 31, 1991, 26.

260 **LCBC** Reports by most national organizations contain only very general statements about their work (some recycled from previous years' reports).

260 **state charity registration departments** For example, New York State's Office of Charities Registration (OCR) exempts organizations "operated by, supervised, controlled by or in connection with a religious corporation or agency" from filing annual statements: Carol Palmer of the OCR, interviewed by Rochelle Saidel, August 5, 1981.

261 **glamour** See comment by Goldin, 182.

261 **koved-fix** A term coined by Judith Sokoloff. Similarly, Trude Weiss-Rosmarin wrote that the drug of most big donors is "communal honor": "The Subject Is Fraud," *Jewish Spectator,* December 1970, 5. See also Goldin, 181.

261 **make him president or chair** Goldin, 176.

261 **what they buy is position** Shapiro/JLS.

261 **approach machers** Mimi Alpern, then-chairperson of the AJCommittee's Interreligious Affairs Committee, paraphrased from quote in A. C., "The Missing Ingredients—Power and Influence in the Jewish Community," *Present Tense,* Spring 1984 (hereinafter A.C./*PT*), 11.

261 **absentee boards** Shapiro/JLS.

262 **Schorsch to Melton** Quoted in "Benefactor Samuel Melton Dead at 93; Dedicated Life to Jewish Education," JTA-CNR, July 9, 1993, 4.

262 **ads** Shapiro/JLS.

263 **Kelman's observation** Quoted by Trude Weiss-Rosmarin, "The Editor's Quarter," *Jewish Spectator,* January 1970, 5.

263 **sales pitch** Alvin H. Einbender, chairman, capital building campaign, NY UJA-Federation, quoted in Kathleen Teltsch, "$1.2 Billion Fund Drive Opened by Jewish Appeal," NYT, November 21, 1989.

263 **plaques before WWII** Goldin, 36; **after** 176.

263 **hospitals' glamour and reasons originally founded** Shapiro/JLS.

263 **abandoned buildings** Goldin, 175.

264 **kosher meals** See Goldin, 218.

264 **"We don't need them"** Quoted by Shapiro/JLS.

264 **Federations' allocations to Big Three** See budgets, in text below.

264 **nonsectarian** See AJCongress, *Report of Task Force on Public Funding of Jewish Social Welfare Institutions* (1986), 2.

264 **poverty unglamorous** See Goldin, 220–21.

264 **two-thirds elderly** Anne Wolfe, *JJCS,* Summer 1972, 7.

264 **statistics** Wolfe, "The Invisible Jewish Poor," 263.

264 **nontraditional = deviant** Chaim I. Waxman, *Single-Parent Families: A Challenge to the Jewish Community* (New York: AJCommittee National Jewish Family Center, 1980), 9.

264 **marketing survey** Fruehauf, *NAJDB,* 38–39.

265 **1989 poster** David Landau, "Agency Chairman Heads for U.S. Showdown Over Soviet Aid," JTA-DNB, April 10, 1989, 1.

265   **L.A. Federation, motives and ads**   JTA-CNR, March 3, 1989, 3.

265   **elderly unglamorous**   Silberman, 142.

265   **never grappled**   The Baycrest Center in Toronto is a model for care of elderly.

265   **critique of Jewish centers**   Schick, then-chair of the Community Relations Commission of the Union of Orthodox Jewish Congregations of America (UOJCA), quoted in Spero, 27.

265   **closed Y's**   The Flushing Y (closed in June 1992) and the Gustav Hartman Y (in June 1991), both in Queens: Larry Feinstein of the Associated Y's, in 1994 phone conversation with Tamara Cohen.

265   **parents' wish for day care**   Rela Geffen study, cited in Ruth Mason, "Jewish Day Care," *Na'amat Woman,* January–February 1989, 28.

265   **synagogue space**   Neil Rubin, "Who Cares for Day Care?" *Jewish Monthly*, March 1991, 35.

265   **1984 CJF study**   Mason, "Jewish Day Care," 28.

266   **impediments cited**   Rubin, "Who Cares for Day Care?" 35–36.

266   **Hatza'ad Harishon**   Story filed by author to the London *Jewish Chronicle,* August 6, 1964; subsequently followed up, from author's notes.

266   **5–8 percent**   In 1991, for example, UJA-Federation of New York announced that allocations to Jewish education and culture together will constitute 8.8 percent of its allocations (compared with 4.6 percent in 1950): Stewart Ain, "Hospitals Lose, Education Gains in Funding Shift," New York *Jewish Week,* June 21–27, 1991.

266   **Toronto**   Gil Kezwer, "Ontario's Class Struggle," JR, December 5, 1991, 7.

266   **1964–66 survey**   Joseph Schechtman, *Jewish Education in the U.S.: A Working Paper on Facts and Problems* (New York: Jewish Agency–American Section, Inc. Research Dept., n.d.), 7.

266   **1987 study**   Alvin I. Schiff, *Jewish Supplementary Schooling: An Educational System in Need of Change* (New York: Board of Jewish Education, 1988).

266   **Klutznik's 1967 statement**   Quoted in Schechtman, *Jewish Education,* 19.

266   **1990 report**   *A Time to Act,* issued by the Commission on Jewish Education in North America: "$2.5 Million in Grants Awarded to Help Revive Jewish Education," JTA-CNR, September 27, 1991, 1.

266   **day schools**   An estimated 130,000–160,000 children and youth attend over 500. Most are under Orthodox auspices, 71 are affiliated with the Conservative movement, and 12 with Reform Judaism. Lisa Hostein, "The Cost of Jewish Education," *NCJW Journal,* Fall 1992, 4.

267   **their fees** $3,500 to $10,000 per year; most are in the $4,000–6,500 range: 4.

267   **ORT school in B.A.**   A. C. series, "The Jews of Argentina: Not Strangers in the Land," part 4, JTA-DNB, September 28, 1987, 3–4.

267   **"Culture is almost foreign"**   Chava Miller, acting director of Steinberg Center (see text and note below), interviewed by author, May 1986.

267   **Ritterband**   Paper, "Generation, Age and Income Variability," written with Richard Silberstein, submitted to 1988 Philanthropy Conference: *NAJDB,* 62.

267   **filmmakers, museum**   Personal testimony to author; **Jewish Media Service** headed by Eric Goldman, closed in 1987.

267   **Steinberg Center**   Begun in 1976 and headed by Jeff Oboler; **"desperate"**   Letter from Evan Bayer, then-director of field operations, May 6, 1986, to members protesting its closing.

267 **"marginal," "inappropriate" role**   Rabbi Henry Siegman, in phone interview with author, May 1986.

268 **Mila**   Noga Tarnopolsky, "Thriving in the Shadow of Fear," JR, July 18, 1991, 42–43.

268 **YIVO archives' locations**   Author's discussion with YIVO head librarian Zachary Baker.

268 **budget, allocations**   LCBC *Budget Digest,* no. 8E, March 1992, 21.

421 **NY Federation and YIVO**   Testimony of Sam Norich, then-executive director of YIVO, to author.

268 **Leo Baeck Institute**   LCBC *Budget Digest,* no. 8D, March 1992, 17.

268 **Ben Yehuda's notes**   Personal experience of author.

268 **Shapiro's concerns**   "Philistine Philanthropists," 4.

268 **Vaad's files**   The Vaad was the Orthodox-sponsored rescue agency during the Holocaust. An electrical fire destroyed files of Rabbi Yitzchok Sternbuch, its representative in Switzerland in WWII, on May 6, 1988: Tamara Cohen's 1994 phone conversation with Agudath Israel.

268 **Farband books' rescue**   Reported by author on WEVD-FM radio, 1981.

268 **Yiddish Book Center**   Founded by Aaron Lansky. A. C., "A Treasure Trove of Jewish Books," JTA-DNB, May 9, 1984, 4.

269 **Forverts**   Testimony of staffer to author.

269 **WZO library newspapers**   Librarian Esther Togman desperately tried to find some institution willing to accept them but failed.

269 **Hadassah**   Staffer testimony to author.

269 **Big Three claims**   Stated in their LCBC reports. *Budget Digest,* March 1992: AJ-Committee: no. 10; AJCongress: no. 11; ADL: no. 12.

269 **Big Three budgets**   *Budget Digest,* March 1992.

270 **direct mail appeals**   All solicitations cited in these pages were received by author in the years stated.

270 **Federation and Hillel funding**   David Makovsky, "B'nai B'rith on the Brink: Searching for a Focus," *Moment,* January–February 1989, 48; **membership**   29–30; **project image**   31–32.

270 **NJCRAC**   Then called NCRAC; **MacIver Report**   researched with Jessie Bernard (New York: NCRAC, 1951). It recommended expansion of the powers of the NCRAC, combining some of the organizations' overlapping activities and enforcing a division of labor.

270 **"no serious inter-consultations"**   MacIver, 48; **"competitive conflict"**   54; **"organizational pride," jurisdictional disputes**   56.

271 **"Keep the Promise"**   *Keeping the Promise* is the title of UJA's *The First Fifty Years—A Pictorial History (1939–1989).*

271 **view it as legitimate**   "Fighting" anti-Semitism is one way Jewish establishment organizations win support for their legitimacy in the Jewish public (discussed in chap. 15).

271 **"warmth"**   Cohen and Rosen study, *Organizational Affiliations,* 24.

272 **uneasy truce**   See *Sh'ma,* January 22, 1988, 41–47.

272 **professionals' past role**   Daniel Elazar, "Decision-Making in the American Jewish Community," in *The Future of the Jewish Community in America,* ed. David Sidorsky (Philadelphia: JPS, 1973), 300–302.

272 **executive-macher relationship, YLC, "tyranny of the lay leaders"**   Sociologist Elihu Davison, in discussions with author.

272   **time to move on**   Michael Berenbaum in *Sh'ma,* January 22, 1988, 41; Spero, 23.

272   **salary range**   Organizations' IRS Form 990, obtained via FOIA.

272   **Kosmin on wage structure**   Quoted in Spero, 24.

272   **Israel Bonds strikes**   There were several such actions in the 1960s and 1970s, according to Ann Roberts of District 1701 AFCSME (phone conversation with author); **United Synagogue strike** the employees struck in January 1990 over a health coverage issue: AFL-CIO strike flyer.

273   **mean-spirited actions**   Reported to author by staffers on condition of anonymity.

273   **"stripping the skin" type of behavior**   Staffer's anonymous testimony.

274   **Jewish Agency incident**   Staffer's anonymous testimony.

274   **"recreate the childhood"**   Howard S. Schwartz, professor of management at the Oakland University School of Business Administration, Rochester, MN, paraphrased in Goleman, "Narcissism," C12; **"reward the narcissistic fantasies"** C12.

274   **ambassadors**   Phenomenon described by Kurt Lewin in "Self-Hatred Among Jews" (1941), Lewin, 196.

274   **close enough to it in behavior**   See z&H, 235; Samuel, 118.

275   **Genizah letter**   Story filed by author to London *Jewish Chronicle* December 7, 1963.

275   **trade divisions**   See Silberman, 89, and Urofsky, 227–28.

275   **card-calling**   Goldin, 178–80; **"None dare"**   179.

276   **Shomrim award**   Made by CLAL and reported on in CLAL *News and Perspectives,* September 1989, 4.

276   **"burst into tears"**   Goldin, 178.

276   **Douglas**   Awarded the Weizmann Medallion for "Services to Science, Israel and the Jewish People" at dinner of ACWIS's Florida Division, December 11, 1992: press release, November 29, 1982.

276   **Stevens**   In 1970 the Merchants Council of the UJA of Greater New York (then separate from the Federation) gave him an award for "humanitarian endeavor." J. P. Stevens & Co. was previously cited by the NLRB for illegal anti-union activity. *Jewish Liberation Journal,* no. 8 (November 1970), 2.

277   **Jabotinsky Foundation**   Sponsored by Herut, USA (now called Likud USA).

277   **food bank proposal**   By Robert Kohler, then-executive director of the Metropolitan Coordinating Council on Jewish Poverty (NYC). A. C., "A Moveable Feast," JTA-DNB, May 27, 1986, 2.

277   **country club membership**   Goldin, 179; Doron P. Levin, "Anguished Appeal: Jewish Charities Raise Huge Sums in U.S. But Resistance Grows," *Wall Street Journal,* April 1, 1983.

277   **"questionable merit"**   Rabbi Eric Friedland, "Milking the Diaspora," *Chicago Jewish Sentinel,* July 26, 1973, 9.

277   **"sacrificial"**   See Goldin, 176.

277   **surveys of Big Givers**   Shapiro/JLS; see also Goldin, 182.

277   **"new religion"**   Barbara Rosenthal, chair, Cleveland Federation Department of Community Relations, quoted in David Landau's series "Faces of American Jewry," part 2, "The Religion of Giving," JP magazine, March 15, 1985, 4.

277   **Woocher on "civil Judaism"**   *Sacred Survival: The Civil Religion of American Jews* (Indianapolis: Indiana Univ. Press, 1987), quoted in Weiss-Rosmarin, "The Editor's Quarter," *Jewish Spectator,* Spring 1987, 3; **"mitzvot equally sacred"** ... **Federation calendar** 3; **GA** 4.

278 **"We are One"** Quoted in Weiss-Rosmarin, "The Editor's Quarter," spring 1987, 3.

278 **Neusner** *Boston Jewish Advocate* letter.

278 **Goldmann quote** Speech at dinner of the Union of American Hebrew Congregations (UAHC), November 10, 1973, from author's notes.

278 **"heretical mentality"** JLS.

279 **"spiritually renewed" at YLC retreat** Amy Stone, "The Locked Cabinet," *Lilith,* no. 2 (Winter 1976–77), 19.

279 **"being on the board"** Rabbi Daniel Jeremy Silver of The Temple, Cleveland, quoted in Landau, "The Religion of Giving," 5.

280 **"Our lives are vacuous"** Singer (now WJC secretary-general) address in Toronto, quoted in Tammy Karol, "American Jewish Leader Says: We Have No Goals, No Dreams," *Canadian Jewish News,* April 7, 1981.

CHAPTER 12: THE ENDURING–AND CONFLICTED–"MARRIAGE" BETWEEN AMERICAN JEWS AND ISRAEL

281 **Levine quote** At youth symposium on the "American Jewish Counter-Culture" at YIVO annual conference, June 7, 1971, from author's notes.

281 **"players and fans"** Quoted in Thomas L. Friedman, "America in the Mind of Israel," NYT magazine, May 25, 1986, 29.

281 **Schindler** Speech to Board of UAHC, quoted in Kenneth A. Briggs, "Reform Leader Cautions Jews on Israel Ties," NYT, May 5, 1982, A16.

282 **mid-WWII** Urofsky, 1–2, 10–12, 20–28; Teller, 200.

282 **zenith of strength** In 1945 one-fifth of American Jews belonged to the Zionist movement: Urofsky 32–33, 125, 126, 279.

282 **its activities** Urofsky, 285, 290; **education** Judd Teller, "The Failure and Prospects of U.S. Zionism," *Israel Horizons,* April 1970 (hereinafter Teller/*IH*), 25.

282 **propaganda drive** Urofsky, 147; **"unparalleled"** 32; **won support** 34–39, 80, 94, 124.

283 **no shared value system ... building a new society** Urofsky, 290.

283 **America was Promised Land** Teller/*IH,* 26.

283 **community relations organizations** Their main focus until 1967 war was fighting bigotry.

283 **bitter struggle** Urofsky, 280–84, 286.

284 **clear recognition** Shapiro/JLS.

284 **"marketable product"** Spero, 26.

284 **glamorous beneficiary** Shapiro/JLS.

284 **piggy-backed** Tom Tugend, "Jewish Federation [L.A.] Launches Controversial Ad Campaign," JTA-CNR, March 31, 1989, 3.

284 **guilt** See Urofsky, 240–43.

284 **pick up where left off** Urofsky, 125.

284 **resistance to aliyah** Urofsky, 258–77.

285 **"new Zion"** Urofsky, 290. See also Howe, 207.

285 **"... to come home" ad** *New York Jewish Week,* November 16, 1990, 49.

285 **demanded mass aliyah** Urofsky, 265–68, 288; **felt abandoned** 323.

285 **"Real Zionists"** View of Golda Meir: Urofsky, 268, and of Ben Gurion: 288.

285 **encourage children's aliyah** Urofsky, 193, 268; **resentment about this** 269–70.

285 **reach out to wealthy** Urofsky, 291.

286   **1950 meetings and agreement**   Urofsky, 193–94; Goldin, 195; **BG's declaration** Urofsky, 194.

286   **Foxman, 1986**   "To Speak or Not to Speak," JP, April 28, 1986, 8.

286   **house organs**   Weiss-Rosmarin, "The Unfreedom of the American Jewish Press," *Jewish Spectator,* May 1971, 4.

287   **Israeli dailies**   Yossi Klein Halevi, "A World Filled with Strangers," Philadelphia *Jewish Exponent,* December 16, 1988, 3.

287   **"Federation man"**   Landau, "The Religion of Giving," 5.

287   **suggestion at 1951 WZC**   Urofsky, 287–88.

288   **"on the sidelines"**   Urofsky, 297.

288   **post-WWI**   Teller, 12.

288   **fifty thousand olim**   Friedman, "America in the Mind of Israel," 22.

288   **buttons**   Moshe Zedek, "Jewish Power in America: Illusion or Reality?" *Israel Horizons,* April 1979, 9–10.

288   **Sutker's excuse**   A. C., "Pioneer Women Will Be Marking Their Sixtieth Anniversary Next Week," JTA-DNB, November 8, 1985, 4.

289   **Orthodox olim**   Urofsky, 272; Friedman, "America in the Mind," 29.

289   **given back of hand**   Urofsky, 272–73, 402–3.

289   **stereotypes**   Urofsky, 273, 276.

289   **survey**   Charles Hoffman, "The 'Me' Generation," 17.

289   **betrayal**   See Jeremy Berson and S. Brent, "Zionism Betrayed," *Jewish Liberation Journal,* no. 11 (Summer–Fall 1972): 1–4.

290   **AIPAC**   Urofsky, 456, and Silberman, 214.

290   **Mapam**   United Workers Party, mainly an outgrowth of pre-1948 Hashomer Hatzair, now part of Meretz coalition.

290   **ZOA**   Often misidentified as *the* Zionist movement rather than one group in it.

292   **Falwell's award**   Editors' intro. to "Jerry Falwell's View of Israel" (interview) in *Israel Today,* May 16, 1986, 1.

292   **American exceptionalism**   See Urofsky, 258–62.

292   **rejected by Israelis**   Urofsky, 258; Fein, 106–8, 112–14, 121–22.

293   **activities for Israel**   LCBC *Budget Digest,* March 1992: AJCommittee: no. 10; AJCongress: no. 11; ADL: no. 12; NJCRAC: no. 13; JLC: no. 14.

293   **women's groups**   Testimonies of staffers to author.

294   **Conference of Presidents' members**   Spero, 18–19.

294   **why established**   Urofsky, 300; see also Goldmann, 325.

294   **1994 poll**   Larry Yudelson, "U.S. Jews Still Support Peace Process," *New York Jewish Sentinel,* September 23–29, 14.

295   **regarded by media**   Spero, 17. **regarded by officials**   When Likud was in power, Israeli officials often cited the expression of the views of the Presidents Conference as evidence of the support they claimed to have for their policies in the American Jewish community. Its views, though, were on the hawkish end of the spectrum of the diverse opinions of American Jews, opposing negotiations with the PLO, while 70 percent of the respondents in sociologist Stephen M. Cohen's survey said Israel should talk to it if it recognized Israel and renounced terrorism: *Attitudes of American Jews Toward Israel and Israelis* (New York: American Jewish Committee, 1983), 18. Conference leaders, wrote Cohen, thus verged on a "misrepresentation of American Jewry both to Israel and to important American policymakers": Stephen M. Cohen, "Who Speaks for American Jewry?" JP, February 16, 1984, 8.

295   **guilt**   Goldin, 139.

295   **one daily**   The *Algemeiner Journal* of Brooklyn. See Howe, 518–51.

296   **Argentine community**   See A. C. series, "The Jews of Argentina: Not Strangers in the Land," part 2, JTA-DNB, September 23, 1987, 3–4.

297   **"eat hamburgers"**   Friedman, "Israel in the Mind," 25.

297   **pop culture**   Urofsky, 409.

297   **"harm ... surrogate synagogue"**   Schindler, speech, quoted in "Reform Leader Cautions," 29.

297   **"missions"**   Silberman, 198.

298   **"pilgrimages ... mythic overtones"**   Woocher, quoted from *Sacred Survival,* in Weiss-Rosmarin, "The Editor's Quarter" (Spring 1987), 3–4.

298   **Reform prayer service and its cancellation**   Urofsky, 400–401.

298   **women at the Wall**   On December 1, 1988, several dozen delegates to the International Jewish Feminist Conference held a morning service, with a Torah reading, on the women's side of the Western Wall. Male worshipers on the other (and larger) side of the mechitzah hurled insults, chairs, and stones: "Feminist Service at Western Wall Ires Male Worshipers," JP, December 2, 1988, 1. Attacks continued at subsequent services. On January 26, 1994, the Supreme Court rejected the petition filed by the Israeli Women of the Wall in 1989 for the right to pray peacefully at the Wall: Cynthia Mann, "Court Rules Against Women at Wall, Says Councils Can't Bar Non-Orthodox," JTA-DNB, January 27, 1994, 1.

298   **Zuckoff's view**   Discussions with author.

299   **Abram**   Letter to NYT, July 27, 1980. **Sarna's observation**   He is professor of American Jewish history at Brandeis University. Cynthia Mann, "U.S. Jewry's Attachment to Israel Has Not Diminished, Study Reports," JTA-CNR, June 25, 1993, 3.

299   **corroded by assimilation**   Friedland, "Milking the Diaspora."

300   **Gold's cri**   Quoted by Goldin, "Plaques and Flattery Will Get You Nowhere," *Present Tense,* Spring 1977, 25–26.

300   **fewer universities**   Israel has six—Bar Ilan, Ben Gurion, Haifa, Hebrew of Jerusalem, Tel Aviv, Technion—plus the Weizmann Institute of Science. In the U.S. there is Yeshiva University.

300   **yeshivot in Israel vs. day schools in U.S.**   Marc Lee Raphael, associate professor of history at Ohio State University, quoted in "We Give Money to Israeli Yeshivas But Not to Our Own Day Schools," *Jewish Post and Opinion,* November 28, 1975. See also Friedman, "America in the Mind," 29.

300   **aged, people with disabilities**   Raphael, quoted in "We Give Money."

300   **day care**   75 percent of Israel's two-year-olds, 96 percent of three-year-olds, and 99 percent of four-year-olds are in day care or kindergarten: Moshe Hartman and Harriet Hartman, "How Equal is Equal? A Comparison of Gender Equality Among Israeli and American Jews," *Israel Horizons,* Autumn 1993, 10, 11.

300   **Sutker**   JTA interview, "Pioneer Women Will Be Marking."

300   **battered women's shelter**   The one such shelter in the U.S., at the Hartman Y in Queens, went underground when that Y closed in 1991: Nadine Lavi, "When 'Nice Jewish Boys' Start Hitting Their Wives," *Forward,* April 1, 1994, 1. There are half a dozen Jewish "safe houses" in the United States that offer kosher food and yeshivot for the children: Rochelle Siegel, "Domestic Abuse and Jewish Women: Opening the Shutters." *The Jewish Women's Journal,* Summer 1994, 18.

300   **major chunk**   American Jews were "expected to contribute more than half of the Jewish Agency's $511 million 1993 budget... ": Larry Yudelson, "Dinitz Controversy Highlights Dual Nature of the Jewish Agency," JTA-DNB, July 27, 1993, 4.

300 **critique of Hadassah** George A. Silver, "Love Is Not Enough: Hadassah and Israel's Medical Care Dilemma," *Midstream,* March 1978, 50–55; **"largess"** 52; **"pump funds"** 55. Silver speculated that a prime factor in Hadassah's creating an American type of medical school in Israel was that the organization and its supporters "visualized Israel as a 'little America':53

301 **nagged Israelis about inefficiency** Silberman, 216–18.

301 **Jewish Agency history** Silberman, 217; Urofsky, 283. **U.S. tax factor** Goldin, 197–98.

301 **"bordering on hatred," takeover** Murray Zuckoff, "How Jewish 'Leaders' Are Eroding the Ideals of Israel's Founders," *Women's American ORT Reporter,* Spring 1988, 9.

301 **poisons the relationship** See Clyde Haberman, "An Israeli Anxiety: Should Charity Stay at Home?" NYT, February 1, 1994, A3.

301 **resent benefactors** Urofsky, 263; **devaluing American Jews** 263.

301 **delegitimization of American religious movements and views of politicians** The Orthodox rabbinate and its law courts do not recognize marriages, divorces, or conversions performed by non-Orthodox (Reform, Conservative, Reconstructionist) rabbis. The bitterness by American Conservative and Reform rabbis and laity over this situation came to the fore during various (unsuccessful) attempts by Orthodox political parties to amend the Law of Return, which does not define "Jew." The Orthodox amendment to add the words "according to Halacha" would mean that the Law of Return would not apply to Jewish olim converted by non-Orthodox rabbis. What shocked American Jewish "leaders" in 1988 was that Premier Shamir and Shimon Peres (then head of the Labor Party) were prepared to accept the amendment, wrote Yossi Klein Halevi: "Who Is a Jew: Why American Jews Are Failing," *Washington Jewish Week,* January 5, 1989, 11.

301 **"stage . . . auditorium"** Quoted from speech at B'nai Zion meeting in Andrew Silow Carroll, "Israel and American Thinkers Debate Viability of Diaspora," JTA-DNB, December 7, 1987, 4.

301 **"I have known Jews all my life"** Quoted in Urofsky, 155.

302 **underworld types and M. Cohen** Hecht, *Child,* 612.

302 **provided "reassurance"** Urofsky, 242.

302 **"fixed the image"** Teller, 260.

302 **generals, army bases** Silberman, 198.

302 **"cowboys"** Oz 1973 JSPS interview, 4.

302 **cringing embarrassment** Rabbi Arthur Schwartz, for example, said about the beatings of Palestinians who attacked soldiers that "American Jews are sitting in their home, seeing the hand-to-hand fighting and saying no matter how justified it is, that's them on the screen and their homeland and they don't like it." Quoted in Geraldine Baum, "Jewish Community Is Strained," *NY Newsday,* February 1, 1988, 5.

302 **civil liberties factor** For example, Schindler said he had publicly criticized the beatings because "as American Jews we can't remain silent about the civil rights we talk about here and that have protected us. We'd lose credibility": Baum, "Jewish Community Is Strained," 14.

303 **"unsympathetic"** Hoffman, "The 'Me' Generation," 17.

303 **NJCRAC Plan** Larry Yudelson, "New Jewish Communal Policy Plan Shifts Focus to Domestic Concerns," JTA-DNB, July 7, 1993, 1.

303 **gangs** See Howe, 123–24, and Gold, 47, 187–89, 261.

304 **guilt** Urofsky, 359.

304 **over 70 percent haven't visited Israel once** Study by David Mittelburg of Haifa University: Hugh Orgel, "Do U.S. Jews Visit Israel? Not Most!" JTA-DNB, October 6, 1994, 2.

304 **behavior of Jewish parents** For example, the 1988 UJA Speakers and Writers Resource Kit, "Israel at Forty" (hereinafter "Kit") speech for a community gathering, includes the following sentiments: "When he was born, our long-awaited *baby* was *shown off* to everyone on the block. . . . Like all parents, but especially Jewish ones, we wanted only the best for *our child.* . . . And we shared, we ourselves *were exalted,* by the lustre of his achievements. . . . As he lived through his twenties, our little boy . . . outgrew us. . . . Then, to his amazement and ours, our tough, cocky son . . . was almost overwhelmed by his enemies . . . and learned . . . that he was, after all, related to us, and *needed our love and support*": 2–3 (italics mine).

305 **belief about administration support** The reality, however, is that its policy is determined by foreign policy interests. One example: The Truman administration refused to lift its arms embargo until after the War of Independence: Urofsky, 164.

305 **contributions, votes** For example, Jews contributed about 60 percent of President Clinton's noninstitutional 1992 campaign funds and gave him about 80 percent of their votes: Thomas L. Friedman, "Clinton Nominees Disturb Some Jews," NYT, January 5, 1993, A11.

305 **one-issue community** This is another misreading of reality. Jews are divided on many issues, from affirmative action to credits for parochial school education to nuclear power to gay rights.

306 **African Americans** See comment on Jesse Jackson in Fein, 254.

306 **"seize on any split"** William Rapfogel, then–executive director of the Institute for Public Affairs of the UOJCA, quoted in Debra Nussbaum Cohen, "The Need to Show Support for Israel Dominated This Year's NJCRAC Plenum," JTA-DNB, February 22, 1991, 4.

306 **Foxman on unity** "To Speak or Not to Speak," 8.

306 **"seem to be distancing ourselves"** "ADL: Siegman Sounded the Wrong Note," JP, July 21, 1990.

306 **beginnings of debate** There is more open discussion in the community about Israel since the new phase in the peace process began in the fall of 1993.

306 **Borowitz quote** "Are American Jews Allowed to Dissent on the Policies of Israeli Governments?" *Israel Horizons,* October 1976, 16. **unable to get lectures** 14.

307 **unable to get views printed** Hertzberg, a former AJCongress president, at roundtable discussion on "What's a Jew to Do?" *Village Voice,* May 18–24, 1988.

307 **"only one voice . . . Big Brother"** Rabbi Yale B. Butler, executive editor of the *B'nai B'rith Messenger* of Los Angeles (no relation to BBI), quoted in Robert Lindsey, "Jewish Press Is Divided on Influence of Charities," NYT, March 3, 1984.

307 **do not permit opinions** The major exception is *Commentary,* which is considerably to the right of the AJCommittee, which sponsors it and allocates it $1.647 million a year (1991–92 budget): LCBC *Budget Digest,* no. 10, 4.

307 **180 periodicals** Kahan in Kedourie, 272.

307 **"wash his linen"** Samuel, 23.

307 **non-Jewish media** Murray Zuckoff (JTA editor, 1970–1987), "Jewish News Isn't News in the Daily Press," JTA feature, January 15, 1971, 2–3.

308 **"united front"** Borowitz, "Are American Jews Allowed," 17.

308 **"failing to bail them out"** Klein Halevi, "A World Filled with Strangers," 3.

309 **hold their heads high** B.G., quoted in Urofsky, 242.

309 **rabbi, 1942** Jacob Weinstein, quoted in Urofsky, 126.

309 **Lewin** Quoted in Urofsky, 126.

309 **"brought up with the idea"** Oz in JSPS interview, 4.

309 **to regard them as partners** "Kit" speech for campaign workers states, "For 40 years, we've been steadfast partners in the task of nation-building": 3.

309 **"We Are One"** UJA slogan used repeatedly, e.g., on back cover of brochure, "UJA 1939–1977," n.d.

309 **"only 'helpers'"** Quoted in Urofsky, 288.

310 **provided economic support** "Kit" fund-raising speech for a leadership group begins by describing how a Jewish marriage "doesn't become legal until the groom gives something of value to the bride" and goes on to state that in contributing "we give something of value to seal the contract": 1.

311 **"postponing a confrontation"** Sanford Pinsker, "Surviving History: Updated Notes on the American-Jewish Dream," *Jewish Spectator,* Summer 1988, 21.

CHAPTER 13: WOMEN'S VOLUNTEER ORGANIZATIONS: A CENTURY OF VICARIOUS FEMINISM

313 **"second commandment"** Schwartz, "The High Price of Failure," 22.

313 **"What happened . . ."** Wolfe, quoted in A.C./*PT,* 12.

313 **R. Gratz** *Jewish Encyclopedia,* 6:83.

313 **"helped only those"** Jacob Rader Marcus, *The American Jewish Woman, 1654–1980* (New York: Ktav, 1980), 47; **nineteenth-century groups** 48–51.

315 **Elazar** Quoted in A. C., "Power Plays: Breaking the Male Monopoly of Jewish Community Leadership," *Lilith,* no. 14 (Fall–Winter, 1985–86) (hereinafter A.C./"Power Plays"): 10.

315 **German Jewish women after 1848** Neu, "Businesswoman," and Rochlin, "Riding High."

315 **eager to be** Neu, "Businesswoman," 144.

315 **sought "a project"** Ehrenreich and English, 70–71; **"uplifting"** 71; **"bringing the gospel"** 72; **"uplifters"** 63.

315 **anxieties** Ehrenreich and English, 45–62; **racial stock** Bristow, 41–42.

315 **definition of eugenics by eugenicists** Barry Mehler, "The New Eugenics: Academic Racism in the U.S. Today," *Israel Horizons,* January–February 1984, 22.

315 **restricting immigration** Ehrenreich and English, 62.

316 **eugenicists' anti-Semitism** Mehler, "The New Eugenics," 22.

316 **Grant** In his work *The Passing of the Great Race* (New York: Scribners, 1916), quoted in Ehrenreich and English, 24.

316 **colleague** C. B. Davenport in 1925, quoted in Stephen Jay Gould, "Science and Jewish Immigration," *Natural History,* December 1980, 14.

316 **restrictive immigration laws** Gould, "Science," 19; Bristow, 220.

316 **crime issue** Manners, 241.

316 **fear and rage** Manners, 241–44.

316 **Bingham** Howe, 133, and Shapiro, *Friendly Society,* 61.

316 **coverage of prostitution** Manners, 248–49; Glanz, 110–12 and 190 n. 38; Bristow, 44.

316 **awareness** Glanz, 189–90 n. 33; BHM, 172.

316 **Gold's mother and Rosie** 18–19; see also 34 and 290.

316 **reasons for and organization of traffic** Bristow, chap. 4.

316 **Pappenheim and Frauenbund** Marion Kaplan, "Bertha Pappenheim: Founder of German-Jewish Feminism," in Koltun, 149–63.

316 **travels, investigation** Freeman, 101–15.

317 **Turkish rabbi** 104. **charge, 1924** Freeman, 143.

317 **"disgrace"** Bristow, 228–29; see also Glanz, 110–12.

317 **debate** Bristow, 230.

317 **swooped** Birmingham, 322.

317 **"bathe and wear clean clothes"** Minnie Louis quoted in Goldin, 61.

318 **"foot soldiers"** Sochen, 51.

318 **vocational schools** Paula Hyman, "The Immigrant Jewish Experience in the U.S.," in Baskin, 227; Manners, 114; Glanz, 28; **settlement houses** Glanz, 32–41.

318 **taking the heat** BHM, 183.

318 **Forverts on rich women** Manners, 113. See BHM, 182–83.

318 **NCJW** Ellen Umansky, "Spiritual Experiences: Jewish Women's Religious Lives in the Twentieth-Century U.S.," in Baskin, 271.

318 **NCJW's aid to immigrant women, Ellis Island worker** Paula Hyman, "The Volunteer Organizations: Vanguard or Rear Guard?" *Lilith,* no. 5 (1978): 17; BHM, 165–68. It organized similar efforts in 250 cities: BHM, 174. See also Glanz, 42.

318 **lodgings** BHM, 169; **rescue facilities** 170; Glanz, 43; Bristow, 234.

318 **middle-class Jewish women, Europe** Bristow, 232–34.

318 **professionalization of social work** Hyman, "The Volunteer Organizations," 22.

319 **escaped declawing** Women's Zionist organizations with specific projects were no threat to Israel's political leadership, wrote Urofsky, 286.

319 **joining Jewish women's organizations** Nick Mandelkern, "The Story of Pioneer Women," part 1, *Pioneer Woman,* September 1980, 28–29.

320 **Lipsky vs. Hadassah** Quoted in Sochen, 65.

321 **identification with chalutzot** Mandelkern, "The Story of Pioneer Women," part 2, *Pioneer Woman,* November 1980, 8.

321 **"excited the imagination … advances"** Mandelkern, "The Story of Pioneer Women," part 2, 8; **"they would support it"** 7–8.

321 **model feminists** Mandelkern, "The Story of Pioneer Women," part 2, 8; **"advanced guard"** 8.

321 **define and express Jewishness** See Doris B. Gold, "Beyond the Valley of the Shmattes" (Yiddish for rags), *Lilith,* no. 1 (1976) (hereinafter Gold/Shmattes): 30.

321 **emissaries** Devorah Rothbard, quoted in Mandelkern, "The Story of Pioneer Women," part 2, 7.

322 **havershaft to efficiency** Mandelkern, "The Story of Pioneer Women," part 4, *Pioneer Woman,* March–April 1981, 8.

322 **Hadassah ex-member quote** Betty Lieberman, *Lilith,* no. 5 (1978): 21.

322 **Houston case** Testimony told to author. See also Gold/Shmattes, 31.

322 **case of president** Testimony told to author by staffer, on condition of anonymity.

323 **dependent** Schwartz, "The High Price of Failure," 22.

323 **competitiveness** Testimony by members told to author.

323 **discrimination ebbing** Urofsky, 324.

324 **counterpart system** A.C./*PT,* 8. The UOJCA has its Women's Branch; the (Conservative) United Synagogue has the Women's League for Conservative Judaism (WLCS); the (Reform) UAHC has its Women of Reform Judaism.

325 **women on Federation boards** Barry Kosmin and Jeffrey Scheckner, *The Place of Women in the Leadership of Federations* (New York: CJF Research Department, 1986), 4.

325 **women on community relations organization boards** A.C./*PT,* 9.

325   **one representative on board**   Geffen, quoted in A.C./*PT,* 11.

325   **women's issues**   For example, in 1993, AJCommittee chapters were informed by the national office that women's issues were no longer a priority for the organization.

325   **tracked into business and professional groups in Women's Division**   A.C./*PT,* 11; **how leaders made it**   11.

325   **plus-giving**   A.C./*PT,* 11. See also Barry Kosmin, "The Political Economy of Gender in Jewish Federations," *Contemporary Jewry,* Spring 1989, 26–27.

325   **distraction**   Gold/Shmattes, 31.

326   **YLC arguments**   Stone, "The Locked Cabinet," 19.

326   **YLC integration**   The process was set in motion by Yael Septee when she became executive director of Young Leadership at the UJA.

326   **CJF study**   Table 3, Kosmin and Scheckner, *The Place of Women,* 12.

326   **"wives of"**   Quoted in A.C./*PT,* 9.

326   **influence of husbands**   Kosmin and Scheckner, *The Place of Women,* 10.

326   **"superwomen"**   Quoted in A.C./*PT,* 9.

326   **"window-dressing"**   Quoted in A.C./*PT,* 10.

326   **"take over the turf"**   Kosmin, "Political Economy," 29.

326   **"potential ... conflict"**   Kosmin, "Political Economy," 29.

326   **Orthodox men**   Esther Leah Ritz, then-president of JWB (now renamed JCCA), quoted in A.C./"Power Plays," 11.

327   **"locked in concrete"**   Quoted in A.C./*PT,* 10.

327   **Midwest case**   From author interviews for *PT* article.

327   **unable to solicit from corporate men**   A.C./*PT*

327   **recipe story**   From author interviews for *PT.*

327   **restricted to men**   From author interviews for *PT.*

327   **Levine's speech**   Kosmin, "Political Economy," 21.

328   **Ritz on chaplaincy question**   In interview with author for *PT.*

328   **Timoner**   "Woman Awaits Posting as a Rabbi in the Army," NYT, December 29, 1972.

328   **professionals**   Reena Sigman Friedman, "The Professional Sphere," *Lilith,* no. 14 (Winter 1985–86), 11.

328   **"bottom of the barrel"**   Quoted in A.C./*PT,* 10.

328   **NCJS studies   1977**   Amy Stone, "The Jewish Establishment Is Not an Equal Opportunity Employer," *Lilith,* no. 4 (Fall–Winter 1977–78), 25; **1981**   Friedman, "The Professional Sphere," 11.

328   **family and child care agency**   Philadelphia, 1983: A.C./*PT,* 10.

328   **JESNA, 1979**   Eddi Wolk, "Discrimination Against Women Educators," *Lilith,* no. 6 (1979): 5.

328   **not an equal opportunity employer**   Report by Albert Chernin, executive vice-chairman of NJCRAC, "Status of Women in Jewish Community Relations as Professionals and Lay Leaders," presented January 22, 1979 (Cincinnati, n.d.).

328   **GA resolutions**   See, for example, 1979 resolution, in Stone, "Not Equal Opportunity Employer," 26.

328   **excuses**   A.C./*PT,* 11.

329   **"Hello, girls"**   11.

329   **D.C. meeting**   A.C./"Power Plays," 12.

329   **feel undeserving**   Evan Bayer, quoted in A.C./"Power Plays," 12; **grateful**   12–13.

329   **fear of inability charge, fast track**   Reported to author by staffers on condition of anonymity.

330 **female lawyers case** A.C./"Power Plays," 13.

330 **Ritz quotes, Cardin's excuse** A.C./"Power Plays," 11.

330 **Levine on "blaming the victim"** Quoted in A.C./"Power Plays," 11.

331 **1971 justifications** Doris B. Gold, "Jewish Women's Groups: Separate—But Equal?" *Congress Bi-Weekly,* February 6, 1970, 9–10; **"don't become leaders"** Diana Coran, JWB staffer, 10; **"mixed groups"** Betty Shapiro, then-BBW president, 10.

331 **"inhibited"** Gold/Shmattes, 32; Kosmin, "Political Economy," 27.

331 **lose leadership roles** Gold/Shmattes, 32.

331 **AJCongress Women's Division case** The Division, which had been very active on women's issues, folded in 1980–81 under pressure from the organization. The Commission for Women's Equality (CWE), constituted in 1984, lacks autonomy.

331 **BBW, BBI battle** Documented in Elena Neuman, "B'nai B'rith Move to Cut Ties to Women's Group Draws Protest," JTA-DNB, December 7, 1989, 4; Neuman, "BBW Votes to Retain Separate Status Despite a Warning from B'nai B'rith," JTA-DNB, December 20, 1989, 4; Andrew Goldsmith, "B'nai B'rith Decides to Admit Women After Reaching Agreement with BBW," JTA-CNR, August 31, 1990, 1.

332 **double standard** Mimi Alperin, A.C./"Power Plays," 10.

332 **"cold-blooded . . . style"** Gold/Shmattes, 32.

333 **the timer story** Testimony told by staffer to author on condition of anonymity; **Na'amat case, "nice to them"** anonymous staffer testimony.

333 **Hadassah magazine** Edited by Jesse Zel Lurie, followed by Alan Tigay; **WAO executive director** Nathan Gould.

334 **"tuna or salmon salad"** Reported to author by a WAO member from New York, not for attribution.

335 **"A duty devolves"** Alta Sher, 1939, quoted in Mandelkern, "The Story of Pioneer Women," part 4, 8.

335 **Look article** Thomas B. Morgan, "The Vanishing American Jew," May 5, 1964.

337 **Welcome Wagon approach** Testimony told to author by Lillian Elkin.

337 **Triangle Fire** March 25, 1911, the Triangle Waist Company, a sweatshop on the top three floors of a Greenwich Village building, burned, claiming the lives of 146 Jewish and Italian women workers. The sweatshop had numerous fire code violations, including keeping the doors locked from outside. Most of the victims burned or suffocated to death; some died jumping from windows. An unknown number of the 500 workers in the building that day were crippled for life. News stories reported how the desperate women leaped out of windows; some managed to escape to roofs of other buildings. BHM, 148–52; Howe, 304–5.

338 **ERA** *Lilith,* no. 1 (1976): 32.

338 **NCJW and ERA** Pearl Water (pseud.), *Lilith,* no. 5 (1978): 18.

338 **Lilith's antipornography conference** After *Lilith* published Judith Bat-Ada's "Porn in the Promised Land" (issue no. 11, Fall–Winter, 1983), it invited all the Jewish women's organizations to join it at a news conference on the issue. All but Na'amat USA (then called PW) refused, on grounds that this was bad for Israel.

338 **WAO and Na'amat** Testimony by persons close to these organizations on condition of anonymity.

338 **Hadassah** Elena Neuman, "Hadassah Revamping Its Image to Add Concerns of the '90's," jta-cnr, July 27, 1990, 3.

338 **Hadassah and B'rith women** Linda Ostrow Schlesinger, "New Women, New Approaches—Women's Groups Adapt to Changing Times," *Jewish Monthly* (a BBI

publication), February 1991, 16; **scheduling**   17; **special programs**   15–17; **networking opportunities**   15.

338   **1992 March**   *Forward,* April 10, 1992.

340   **Gross's statement**   Quoted in Schlesinger, "New Women," 15.

PART III. THE STRUGGLE FOR A CORRECT READING OF REALITY

341   **epigraph**   Rabbi Goldflamm to Mauritzi Apt, 188.

CHAPTER 14: THE SIXTIES DECADE AND ITS LEGACIES

343   **Mamet**   "The Decoration of Jewish Houses," *Some Freaks,* 11.

343   **Brooklyn Bridge**   "Self-Hate," February 1971, 20. (This was the publication of the BB "radical nationalist" collective organized in the early seventies by Lee Weiner of the Chicago Eight/Seven.)

343   **interminable weeks**   Urofsky, 345–49; **another Holocaust**   350–52.

344   **"We captured"**   Congregants quoted by Rabbi Martin Siegel, "Diary of a Suburban Rabbi," *New York,* January 18, 1971, 26–27.

344   **"neutral"**   State Department spokesman Robert J. McCloskey, quoted in "U.S. 'Neutral' in Conflict," JP, June 6, 1967, 1.

344   **Niebuhr and King**   Hertzberg, 374.

344   **Christian reactions**   Urofsky, 364, 382–3; Silberman, 203.

344   **Vorspan's cri**   "Days of Exaltation—A Letter from Israel, July, 1967," in untitled collection of mimeographed material distributed in Reform movement, 1967, 9.

344   **Fein**   At 1971 YIVO conference.

345   **Rosmarin**   "America's New Jewish Left," *New Outlook,* April 1971 (hereinafter Rosmarin/*N.O.*), 38.

345   **Old and New Left**   A. C., "The Left and the Six-Day War," *Israel Horizons,* November–December 1967.

345   **CP**   Its position was repudiated by the Communist *Freiheit* (Freedom) and the left-wing *Jewish Currents* magazine.

345   **antiwar activists**   A. C., "The Left," 32–33.

345   **SDS**   Testimony told to author by activists.

345   **NCNP**   Rosmarin/*N.O.,* 36.

346   **Black Muslims**   Robert G. Weisbord and Arthur Stein, "Black Nationalism and the Arab-Israel Conflict," *Patterns of Prejudice* (periodical; London: Institute of Jewish Affairs), November–December 1969, 3–5.

346   **Jewish support for SNCC**   Weisbord and Stein, "Black Nationalism," 7.

346   **Newark conference**   Testimony told to author by participants.

346   **anti-Semitic poem**   Cited in *The Black Panther Party—The Anti-Semitic and Anti-Israel Component* (New York: AJCommittee, 1970), 2.

346   **Cleaver in Ramparts**   Quoted in Moshe Zedek, "Rebuttal," in *Arab-Israel Debate—Toward a Socialist Solution* (New York: Times Change Press, 1970), 43.

346   **similarity to Garvey**   Weisbord and Stein, "Black Nationalism," 1–2.

346   **Cleaver from Algiers**   NYT, July 23, 1969. Cited in Itzhak Epstein, "Open Letter to the Black Panther Party," *Jewish Liberation Journal,* no. 3 (September 1969): 1.

347   **1970 charges**   Connie Matthews (international coordinator, BPP), "Will Racism or International Proletarian Solidarity Conquer?" *The Black Panther,* May 25, 1970, 16.

347   **Carmichael**   Quoted from 1968 speech in Weisbord and Stein, "Black Nationalism," 6.

347   **"dominate ... poisoned"**   John F. Hatchett, "The Phenomenon of Anti-Black Jews and the Black Anglo-Saxon: A Study in Educational Perfidy," *African-American Teachers Forum* (Brooklyn, NY: African American Teachers Association [AATA]), November–December 1967, 1.

347   **flyer**   Entitled "Shanker This Is Not Egypt–You Ain't Coming In Here!" calling for Harlem rally December 8, 1968.

347   **anti-Semitic poem**   By Sia Berhan. Henry Raymont, "Teachers Protest Poem to FCC," NYT, January 16, 1969.

347   **from intellectuals**   Silberman, 339.

348   **KKK**   Jack Nelson, *Terror in the Night: The Klan's War Against the Jews* (New York: Simon & Schuster, 1993).

348   **Yiddish poetry**   Teller, 46–47; **"crippled"**   293.

348   **ideological displaced persons**   Judd Teller, "Negroes and Jews: A Hard Look," *Conservative Judaism (CJ)*, Fall 1966, 14.

348   **"sought to compensate"**   Teller, "Negroes and Jews," 14.

348   **post-WWII anti-Semitic atmosphere**   Arnold and Caroline Rose wrote in *America Divided: Group Relations in the U.S.* (New York: Harper, 1948) that "among Jews the feeling has become widespread that the outside world is bent on their destruction": Urofsky, 126.

349   **divergence**   Rabbi Bernard Weinberger, "The Negro and the (Orthodox) Jew," *Jewish Observer,* September 1968, 12.

349   **NJCRAC**   Hertzberg, 366; **ADL study**   366.

349   **Yaffe**   "Anti-Semitism: The Rude Awakening," *Israel Horizons,* February 1969, 8.

349   **Weinberger's analysis**   "A Reply to Some Critics," *Jewish Observer,* January 1969, 8. (Teller's article in *CJ* also provided a Borochovist analysis: 20.)

349   **"behind every hurdle"**   Candice Van Ellison, quoted in Yaffe, 10.

349   **Weinberger's conclusion**   "A Reply," 8.

350   **"ethical imperative"**   Teller, "Negroes and Jews," 14–15.

350   **paternalism**   Hatchett equated liberal Jews' support of the black liberation movement with paternalism, adding, "Black men have been systematically castrated in this society. Paternalism is one of the forms of castration": Letitia Kent, "Hatchett at NYU: What Makes Racism," *Village Voice,* August 8, 1968, 37–38.

350   **"people of words"**   Zvi Sobel, quoted in "Black-Jewish Talks Produce Angry Clash But Some Hope," NYT, April 9, 1989.

351   **Rubin quote**   J. Anthony Lukas, "The Making of a Yippie," *Esquire,* November 1969, 127.

351   **Freedom Riders**   Arthur Liebman, quoted in Lenni Brenner, *Jews in America Today* (Secaucus, NJ: Lyle Stuart, 1986), 227; **Mississippi**   Lucy Davidowicz, quoted in intro. to P&D, xxi–xxii.

351   **two youths**   Testimony to author.

351   **Jones**   Quoted in A. C., "Is Jewishness Chauvinistic?" *Israel Horizons,* December 1965, 11.

352   **chemist, teacher**   A. C., "Is Jewishness Chauvinistic?" 11.

352   **touched**   Testimony told to author; **transistors, weeping**   Bonnie Anker, testimony told to author, describing situation at Berkeley.

352   **shocked ... vilified**   Testimony told to author.

352   **small groups**   Rosmarin/*N.O.,* 38.

352   **"melting pot dream"**   Levine, speech "To Share a Vision," at November 1969, GA, *Response,* Winter 1969; reprinted in P&D, 185.

353   **"The black American ... WASP"**   Reprinted in P&D, 6; **"must accept ... destiny"** 9; **"And thus from this point on"**   10.

353   **Network's role and self-image**   Edwin Freedman, "This is a Defeat of Jewish Students," in *Call for Justice* (New York: Committee for AZYF Accountability), vol 1, no. 1 (March 1978), 2.

355   **community and spirituality**   Comment by anthropologist Barbara Myerhoff in Lynn Littman's 1985 film *In Her Own Time.*

355   **parents of Mississippi volunteers**   A. C. story filed January 29, 1965, to London *Jewish Chronicle* about AJCongress Women's Division honoring seventeen mothers of civil rights workers.

356   **Hassidim**   Teller, 246–47; **Chabad**   247–48.

356   **"romance"**   Joselit, 20; **interpreting it**   20; **closet**   21. The yarmulke was seen as an "indoor garment": 21, and Blu Greenberg, *Tradition,* 23.

356   **tzitzit at day school**   Author's experience at Ramaz, 1950s.

356   **Conservative Judaism's appeal**   Joselit, 81; **challenged**   80.

356   **created own institutions**   Teller, 168.

357   **Reform**   Urofsky, 222–23.

357   **"must be reshaped"**   Hertzberg, 117.

357   **expunged**   Teller, 163.

357   **Conservative Judaism, history**   Teller, 240; Urofsky, 223–24.

357   **amended**   For example, allowing driving on Shabbat if it was to the synagogue; **make own decisions**   Teller, 240.

358   **Reconstructionism**   Teller, 163–64.

358   **Reform interest in tradition**   Teller, 163; Ari Goldman, "Reform Jews Are Returning to Ritual," NYT, June 26, 1989, A14. (The process began in the WWII era: Teller, 163.)

358   **radical**   At this time the word meant left-wing and antiestablishment, not (as today) extremist.

359   **Jewish establishment denounced JDL**   "The Jewish Defense League: A Fact Sheet," (New York: Commission on Social Action of Reform Judaism, n.d.), 2; **"goon squad"** Rabbi Maurice N. Eisendrath, UAHC president, 1.

359   **critical of Jewish establishment**   Kahane, in interview in *The Flame,* Winter 1971. Reprinted in P&D, 278.

359   **lack of democracy**   A JDL ad called for an American Jewish Parliament representative of the "total thinking of American Jewry": NYT, October 14, 1975.

359   **Temple Emanu-El action**   May 1969. SNCC executive secretary James Forman never showed up there.

360   **"miracle"**   Word used by Shoshana Cardin in address to the eighty-fourth annual dinner of the AJCommittee, May 17, 1990 (from author's notes).

360   **Noel to Marjorie**   Wouk, *Marjorie Morningstar,* 430.

360   **"We cannot accept"**   At YIVO 1971 symposium.

361   **Teller on values**   Teller/*IH,* 21.

361   **student papers**   Bill Novak and Robert Goldman, "The Rise of the Jewish Student Press," *Conservative Judaism,* Winter 1971 10–19.

361   **male chauvinism**   Vivian Silver, "Sexism in the Jewish Student Community," *Response,* Summer 1973, 55.

362   **Myerhoff**   Stated in film *In Her Own Time.*

362   **apologists**   See Gitelle Rappaport, "Women Sing Praises to an Orthodox Life," JTA feature, January 18, 1991.

363   **Podhoretz on blacks**   "My Negro Problem—And Ours," *Commentary,* February 1963; **"hatred" ... "superior masculinity"** 99; **"free ... erotic"** 97; **"tough ... rebel against"** 98.

363   **Fein**   Speech at 1971 YIVO conference.

363   **legitimacy of its values**   See Bernard Avishai, "Breaking Faith: *Commentary* and the American Jews," *Dissent,* Spring 1981, 242–43 and passim. Podhoretz began publishing articles in support of the Vietnam War and Israeli hawks; and, later, against the feminist and gay liberation movements (the latter were particularly vicious attacks by his wife, Midge Decter) and the Jewish counterculture (many by Ruth Wisse).

364   **"castrated ourselves"**   Delegate quoted in Rosmarin/*N.O.,* 36.

365   **owe them something**   Teller warned against the "self-pitying complaints about Negro 'ingratitude for all the Jews have done' for the Civil Rights struggle": "Negroes and Jews," 15.

365   **recompensed**   Fein wrote that if black militancy succeeds, "it will succeed because Americans will have learned to live with difference. If, therefore, it succeeds, we ourselves will be among *the unintended beneficiaries*" (italics mine): "Negro and Jew: A 'Special Relationship,'" *Israel Horizons,* November 1968, 8.

365   **diaspora as "positive good"**   Arthur Waskow, "Judaism and Revolution Today," *Judaism,* Fall 1971; reprinted in P&D, 16.

365   **"go it alone"**   Rabbi Myron Fenster, "The Dialogue That Failed," *Congress Bi-Weekly,* January 23, 1970, 18.

366   **"invasion" of 1969 GA**   Itzhak Epstein, "Confrontation in Boston: Demand Funds Act on Jewish Education," *Jewish Liberation Journal,* no. 5 (November–December 1969), 1, 7; intro. to P&D, xxxv.

366   **"step-son"**   "Vision," in P&D, 187. Levine thus recapitulated Schechtman's comment that Jewish education "is still the stepchild of the organized Jewish community": Jewish Agency paper, *Jewish Education in the U.S.,* 31.

366   **NY Federation takeover**   April 8, 1970. "Forty-five Busted: Youth Occupy Federation," *Jewish Liberation Journal,* no. 7 (April–May 1970): 1, 4–5.

366   **San Francisco takeover**   April 30–May 1, 1971. Sherman Rosenfeld, "Shabbat Sit-In: Jews Liberate the Federation," *The Jewish Radical* (Berkeley), Spring 1971, 2, 4.

366   **giving money**   Urofsky, 355–56.

367   **Seattle, 1970**   Rosmarin/*N.O.,* 35.

368   **Hiroshima and Auschwitz**   Waskow, "Judaism and Revolution Today," 24.

368   **Attica**   Flyer of Brooklyn Bridge collective, calling for rally September 18, 1971.

368   **Stern on Radical Jews**   "My Jewish Problem—And Ours," *Ramparts,* August 1971. Reprinted in P&D, 368.

368   **campus ... no intellectual match**   See Irving Greenberg, "Jewish Survival and the College Campus," *Judaism,* Summer 1968.

369   **Network takeover**   Documented in Neil Reisner, "Death of the Jewish Student Movement?" in *Call for Justice,* 4.

369   **precluded institutionalization**   The opinion of sociologist Elihu Davison, in conversation with author.

369   **Epstein's critique**   "Unrepresentative View of a Unique Phenomenon," review of James Sleeper and Alan Mintz's *The New Jews,* in *WAO Reporter,* March–April 1972, 6.

370   **minimachers**   Term coined by Bob Lamm.

370   **R&D wing**   The concept is that of William Irwin Thompson, in "We Become What We Hate," excerpted from *Evil and World Order* in *East-West Journal,* September 1976, 9.

370   **Manheim Shapiro**   "Survival and Services: Who? What? Why? How?" *JJCS,* Fall 1971; **bet on "disappearance"**   33; **Jewish education's starvation**   34; **pluralism**   33; **"alienated" agencies**   34; **be "imbued"**   35.

371   **Shapiro on disputatiousness**   JLS.

371   **Breira**   See William Novak, "Dynamics of American Jewish Dissent: The Breira Story," *Genesis II* (Boston), March 16, 1977.

372   **klezmania**   "Klezmer Music Revival in Full Swing Across U.S.," JTA-CNR, May 9, 1986, 2; **Slobin**   professor of music at Wesleyan University: Ben Rose, "Professor Sees Klezmer Music as a Statement of Identity Rather Than Rehash of Tunes," *Canadian Jewish News,* September 7, 1983, Rosh Hashanah Supplement, 8.

373   **"shower rooms"**   In P&D, 10.

CHAPTER 15: HOLOCAUST CONSCIOUSNESS

375   **Hentoff quote**   From piece in *Village Voice,* confirmed in phone conversation with author.

375   **"No Business"**   Attributed to Davidowicz. *Sho'ah* is Hebrew for the Holocaust and is the term used in Israel.

375   **only the Danes**   See Harold Flender, *Rescue in Denmark* (New York: MacFadden Books, 1964). Also see note for 391, on Bulgaria, on p. 510.

376   **those who call**   This is the implication of Anne Roiphe's argument in *A Season for Healing.*

376   **hardened their hearts**   Photographer Roman Vishiac (1897–1990), who took thousands of pictures of East European Jews between 1932 and 1940, was told by Jewish organizations to whom he showed some of his photos upon arrival in the U.S. in 1940 to burn the collection: testimony of colleague told to author.

376   **"explanations"**   Mais in A. C., "Americanizing the Holocaust," 4.

376   **"authoritarian personality"**   See T. W. Adorno, *The Authoritarian Personality* (New York: Harper, 1950).

376   **Heine's warning**   Heine, 331.

377   **Warsaw leaders' plea**   Communicated to Smull (Arthur) Zygelbojm, representative to the Polish government-in-exile in London. Quoted in Henry Feingold, "Who Shall Bear Guilt for the Holocaust: The Human Dilemma," AJH, March 1979, 265.

377   **1924 Act**   See Mehler, "The New Eugenics," 24.

377   **Kristallnacht: 191 synagoges, 30,000 incarcerated**   Gilbert, 69–70.

377   **"letter of the law"**   Morse, 148; **"not in contemplation"**   149.

377   **10 percent**   David Wyman, address to the first Conference of Holocaust Studies Alumni, February 13, 1988. Reported in "Professor David Wyman on the Abandonment of the Jews," *Alumni Newsletter* (New York: Holocaust and Jewish Resistance Summer Fellowship Program), Summer 1988, 2. Wyman said the quota would have allowed 210,000 in during the war; instead, 21,000 were admitted: transcript of address tape (hereinafter Wyman/Transcript), 26.

377   **Alaska bill**   Feingold, 94.

377   **St. Louis**   Morse, 270–82; Irwin F. Gellman, "The St. Louis Tragedy," AJH, December 1971.

377   **Wagner-Rogers Bill**   Morse, 252–69.

378 **free ports, Oswego** 341–42.

378 **cold war** It was in this period that American government agencies began recruiting Nazi war criminals to work on military, intelligence, and scientific projects under "Project PaperClip": Charles Allen, Jr., "Why U.S. Monopoly Capitalism Imported Nazi War Criminals," *Israel Horizons,* May–June 1984, 10–15.

379 **suddenly appear** View of teacher Barbara Grau, reported in *Alumni Newsletter,* 5.

379 **subevent** Joel Epstein, professor of history at Olivet College, quoted in Jack Fischel, "Strategies for Holocaust Studies," *Midstream,* December 1988, 59.

379 **Roskies on Jewish schools** Symposium on "American Jewish Youth and the Holocaust" at YIVO conference, May 8, 1972, from author's notes.

379 **"happy endings"** Arthur Samuelson, YIVO symposium, May 8, 1972, from author's notes.

379 **Malcolm X's warning** Quoted in Weisbord and Stein, "Black Nationalism," 5.

380 **"resisted," "did not want rescue to occur"** Wyman/Transcript, 19–20; **"did not want Jews to get out"** *Alumni Newsletter,* 2; **anti-Semitism** 2.

380 **Britain determined to obstruct** Wyman/Transcript, 20.

380 **Moyne** Henry Feingold, "Roosevelt and the Holocaust: Reflections on New Deal Humanism," *Judaism,* Summer 1969, 272.

380 **British fear of pressure** Wyman/Transcript, 21–22, 23.

380 **opposition to immigration** Wyman/Transcript, 24; **unwilling to counteract** 25. Wyman said Roosevelt feared a backlash from anti-Semites on this issue but "could have built a counter-constituency among the one-third" of the nation that was not anti-Semitic: author's interview with Wyman, "The Holocaust as Christian Tragedy," JTA-DNB, February 4, 1985, 4.

380 **"Any overt effort"** At meeting December 9, 1942: Alex Grobman, "What Did They Know? The American Jewish Press and the Holocaust, Sept. 1, 1939–Dec. 17, 1942," AJH, March 1979, 349.

380 **bombing Auschwitz and railroad tracks** Wyman, "Why Auschwitz Was Never Bombed," *Commentary,* May 1978, 37–46.

380 **requests by Jewish leaders** Author's interview with Gerhart Riegner, WJCongress representative in Geneva during WWII, "The Long Night," part 2, JTA-DNB, April 7, 1983, 4.

380 **impede the war effort** See Wyman, "Why Auschwitz Was Never Bombed," 40–41.

380 **British reply** Herman Landau (Vaad HaHatzala executive director during WWII), letter in *Canadian Jewish News,* April 12, 1979.

381 **Hayim Greenberg** Bio: Howe, 511–13. Eng. trans. of "Bankrupt" was published in *The Inner Eye* (New York: Jewish Frontier Assn., 1964), 2:193ff. **"American Jewry has not done"** 194; **"bankrupt"** 202; **"business as usual"** 199–200.

381 **"at no time"** Richard Bernstein, "Report Contends U.S. Jews Reacted Slowly to Nazi Peril," NYT, February 9, 1983.

381 **"outmaneuver"** H. Greenberg, "Bankrupt," 195.

381 **"more anxious"** Feingold, "Roosevelt," 267.

381 **Bergsonites** Sarah Peck, "The Campaign for an American Response to the Nazi Holocaust, 1943–45," *Journal of Contemporary History,* April 1980.

381 **conference** Neil Barsky, "Jewish Organizations Versus the Bergson Group," Long Island *Jewish World,* July 15–21, 1983, 14.

382 **Wise's fear** Goldmann told a State Department official that Wise regarded Bergson "equally an enemy of the Jews as Hitler for the reason that his activities could only lead to increased anti-Semitism": State Department document quoted in Barsky, "Jewish Organizations," 14.

382   **Silver**   Quoted in Urofsky, 45.

382   **attacked, vandalism**   Godfrey Perrett, *Days of Sadness, Years of Triumph* (Madison: Univ. of Wisconsin Press, 1973), 362.

382   **resolution in Congress**   Feingold, "Roosevelt," 268.

382   **Morgenthau, memo, fear of scandal, WRB establishment**   Wyman/Transcript, 27–34. See also Riegner, "The Long Night" part 2, 4.

382   **American Jewish contributions to WRB**   Wyman/Transcript, 36. Wyman commented that it is unparalleled in American history "that a policy of that importance is established and then the government goes to one tiny minority ... and says, it's your responsibility to pay for the most part of this U.S. government policy": Wyman/Transcript, 36–37. See also Shlomo Shafir, "Roosevelt: His Attitude Toward American Jews, the Holocaust and Zionism," *Forum* 44 (1982): 45.

382   **rescued thousands**   Wyman calculated it played a vital role in saving 200,000 Jews: Transcript, 34.

382   **Davidowicz's loathing**   She called them "an embarrassment" to the organized Jewish community: "American Jews and the Holocaust," NYT magazine, April 18, 1982, 48; **"most potent"**   quoted in Barsky, "Jewish Organizations," 14.

382   **incorrect reading**   Interview with author for "Christian Tragedy" article, from author's notes.

382   **shtadlanut**   Edward Pinsky, "American Jewish Unity During the Holocaust–the Joint Emergency Committee, 1943," AJH, June 1983, 484, and 485–92. He quotes an AJCommittee leader saying that he was able to convince Wise to "follow the policy of cooperating with government officials," including having no protests over government policy at public mass rallies: 484.

382   **"cracking up"**   Quoted from May 1941 issue of the *Jewish Spectator* in Grobman, "What Did They Know?" 350; **news printed**   351.

383   **advisers**   Henry Feingold, "Courage First and Intelligence Second: The American Jewish Secular Elite, Roosevelt and the Failure to Rescue," AJH, June 1983. See Leonard Dinnerstein, "Jews and the New Deal," AJH, June 1983.

383   **kept low profile**   Davidowicz wrote that they were "vilified ... because they were Jews. Understandably [*sic*] they tried to keep their Jewishness out of their public lives": "American Jews and the Holocaust," 102.

383   **unwilling to advocate Jewish causes**   Feingold, "Courage," 432.

383   **most Jews assumed**   Feingold, "Courage," 433.

383   **trust**   Shafir, "Roosevelt," 40.

383   **Joseph Kennedy and Hollywood Jews' reaction**   Hecht, *Child,* 520.

383   **"as invisible as possible"**   Hecht, *Child,* 538–39.

383   **Casablanca shaped by Jews**   *Round up the Usual Suspects: The Making of Casablanca* (New York: Hyperion, 1992), 53.

383   **Jews in media**   Hecht, *Child,* 519.

383   **back pages or at all**   Wyman/Transcript, 17, and Lipstadt.

384   **"curtain of disbelief"**   Feingold, "Guilt," 275. Polls showed that by December 1944, 75 percent of Americans believed the Germans had murdered about 100,000 people in concentration camps; "the public was oblivious to the fact that the victims were largely Jewish": Feingold, "Roosevelt," 278.

384   **Lippman**   Lipstadt, 45–47. **on Hitler speech**   Cited by Anthony Lewis in his review of Ronald Steel, *Walter Lippman and the American Century* (Boston: Little, Brown, 1980), in NYRB, Oct. 9, 1980, 6. **wrote nothing**   6.

384   **"one president"**   Urofsky, 46; **love letters, pluralities**   46. See Feingold, "Courage," 427 and 429, and Feingold, "Roosevelt," 273.

384   **"spirit of concern"**   Feingold, "Guilt," 279.

384   **blind love**   Feingold, "Roosevelt," 270.

384   **just another atrocity**   Feingold, "Courage," 456.

384   **play down commonality**   Shafir, "Roosevelt," 41.

384   **concern about anti-Semitism**   Wyman, "Christian Tragedy" interview, 4.

384   **only votes**   Feingold, "Courage," 430; Teller, 195.

384   **belief in "special love"**   Hertzberg, 282.

384   **shielded the president**   Teller, 194–95.

384   **"friend"**   Speech at Waldorf-Astoria, quoted by journalist Arno Herzberg in unpublished manuscript.

384   **preferred to attack State Department**   Feingold, "Roosevelt," 270.

384   **no leverage**   Feingold, "Courage," 430; **"transact business"**   450.

384   **"politics of gesture"**   Feingold, "Courage," 427.

385   **"profoundly shocked" . . . take every step**   Statement December 8, 1942 to delegation led by Wise: Morse, 20.

385   **"humiliating circumstance"**   Teller, 191.

385   **Lindbergh attacks**   In a September 1941 speech in Des Moines, he warned that "Britain, the Jews and the Roosevelt Administration" were plotting to bring the U.S. into the European war: Feingold, "Guilt," 277.

385   **"pillars," father, guardian**   Teller, 191.

385   **eulogies: "border of the promised land"**   Rabbi Robert Gordis in *National Jewish Monthly,* June 1945, quoted in Haskel Lookstein, "The Public Response of American Jews to the Liberation of European Jewry, January to May, 1945," in Gurock, 149; **"kiss"**   Menachem Ribalow in *Hadoar,* April 20, 1945, in Gurock, 149. **Rashi on Moses' death**   commentary on Deut. 34:5.

385   **advancing the war effort**   Urofsky, 44–45. See also Feingold, "Courage," 453.

385   **suppress information**   The State Department did not give Wise the cable Riegner sent him August 8, 1942, about the Final Solution plan until August 28, with the request that he not publicize the information until it had been "confirmed," which was at the end of November. Wise had no choice but to suppress the information, said Riegner, because he and the AJCongress "wanted action from the government [and] felt they should not act against their advice from the beginning": "The Long Night" part 1, April 6, 1983, 3.

385   **food shipments**   The British announced a blockade of occupied Europe in October 1939. The State Department told the AJCongress in 1940 that sending food packages to Poland "was not in the interest of the Allies." Wise agreed to stop the shipments "for the good of England": Aryeh Tartakower (in charge of AJCongress aid work), quoted in letter by Lenni Brenner in *Moment,* November 1987, 4. "Nobody dared to raise the question of changing the immigration laws," which "were absolutely sacrosanct," said Riegner: "The Long Night" part 1, 4. See also Goldin, 96.

385   **"special pleading . . . unpatriotic"**   Marie Syrkin, "What American Jews Did During the Holocaust," *Midstream,* October 1982, 5.

385   **fighting for Jews' benefit**   The suppression of information on the mass murders and the refusal to bomb Auschwitz "all stemmed from [the] fear" of that charge: Shafir, "Roosevelt," 44.

386   **Goldmann on Bergsonites**   In Lawrence Jarvik's documentary, *Who Shall Live and Who Shall Die?* quoted in Barsky, "Jewish Organizations," 14.

386   **integral part of Allied policy**   None of the conferences that worked out war aims and strategy had anything to say about the Jews: Feingold, "Guilt," 264; **"camouflage term"**   264.

386   **Evian**   July 6–15, 1938: Thirty-two nations met there on U.S. invitation to deal with the "refugee situation" but, with the exception of the Dominican Republic, none made any asylum offers: Feingold, "Roosevelt," 260–61.

386   **Bermuda**   Opened on the first day of the Warsaw Ghetto Uprising, April 19, 1943, its primary objective "was to deflect the growing agitation over rescue policy": Feingold, "Roosevelt," 267. See also Urofsky, 51.

386   **by WRB**   Feingold, "Guilt," 264.

386   **Allied statements**   The November 1, 1943, joint statement by the U.S., Britain and the USSR, issued in Moscow, condemned war crimes and promised retribution for them. Every conceivable nationality and local group in occupied Europe was mentioned except the Jews. "Crimes against Jews were consistently omitted from war-crimes statements": Feingold, "Roosevelt," 271. See also Feingold, 228–29.

386   **March 1944 statement**   Issued by the U.S., under pressure from the WRB: Feingold, 229.

386   **"cattle cars"**   Feingold, "Roosevelt," 271; **reinforced German conviction**   272, citing Goebbels's diary entry.

386   **rabbis' march**   They marched from the Capitol to the White House on October 6, 1943, to call attention to the mass murders and presented a petition about rescue to Vice-President Henry Wallace: Davidowicz, "American Jews and the Holocaust," 111.

386   **Vaad's illegal and legal activities**   See Efraim Zuroff, "Rescue Priority and Fundraising as Issues During the Holocaust: A Case Study of the Relations Between the Vaad HaHatzala and the Joint, 1939–1941," AJH, March 1979, 313–14.

386   **schutzpasses**   Interview with author for "The Long Night."

387   **Renée Reichmann**   Elaine Dewar, "The Mysterious Reichmanns: The Untold Story," *Toronto Life,* November 1987, 161–85, passim.

387   **her son**   Edward, on Vaad: Dewar, "Mysterious Reichmanns," 183–84.

387   **Wiesel on Holocaust**   "The Trivialization of the Holocaust," NYT, April 16, 1978.

387   **Friedan on FDR**   "The Men I Most Admire," *Parade,* August 12, 1984, 4.

388   **1930s, 1985 difference**   "Glad Tidings: A *Moment* Interview with Charles Silberman," *Moment,* September 1985, 30.

388   **White House, Wiesel**   April 19, 1985: Silberman, 360–62.

388   **disappeared numbers**   A. C., "A Nightmare Continues in Argentina," part 1., JTA-DNB, May 21, 1986, 4.

388   **no protest by any American Jewish organization**   "Nightmare," part 3, JTA-DNB, May 23, 1986, 4; and A. C., "My Children Are Disappeared—A Jewish Mother's Struggle Against Argentine Fascists," *Lilith,* no. 15 (Spring 1986): 19–20.

388   **Canadian Jewish Congress**   "My Children," 20.

388   **ADL**   "Nightmare," part 3, 4, and "My Children," 20. Rabbi Mort Rosenthal, director of the ADL Latin American Affairs Department, created an Argentine Prisoners Project.

389   **Commentary attacks on Timerman**   For example, Mark Falcoff, "The Timerman Case," July 1981.

389   **NeoCons**   See Murray Zuckoff, "Who Hates Ya, Baby," JTA-DNB, September 24, 1981, 3.

389   **"category of guilt"**   Timerman in Newfield, "Anti-Semitism and the Crime of Silence," 14.

389   **NeoCon motivation**   Zuckoff, "Who Hates Ya," 4.

389 **Wallenberg** Sent by the Swedish Foreign Ministry to Budapest in July 1944, he established safe houses and issued protective passes for Jews to keep them from being deported; on many occasions he intervened to pluck Jews from the jaws of death: EJ, 16:255–56.

389 **1991 conference** A. C., "Silent No More," 26.

389 **Jewish rescuers Kluger** See autobiography; **Weissmandel** coleader with Fleischmann of the Working Group in Slovakia that rescued Jews through bribery and smuggled out information: Abraham Fuchs, *The Unheeded Cry* (New York: Mesorah, 1984); **Fleischmann** Joan Campion, *Gisi Fleischmann and the Jewish Fight for Survival* (Bethlehem, PA: Dvorion Books, 1983); **OSE** A. C., "Silent No More," 26; **French Jewish Scout movement,** *Eclaireurs Israelites* Nora Levin, "Resistance and Rescue: Jewish Partisan Groups During the Holocaust," *Midstream,* August–September 1988, 29. See also Syrkin, *Match,* 295–301.

390 **upstage** Letty Cottin Pogrebin, "Anti-Semitism in the Women's Movement," *Ms.,* June 1982, 71.

390 **Farrakhan, 1985** Quoted in Kenneth S. Stern, *Farrakhan and the Jews in the 1990's* (New York: American Jewish Committee, 1992), 7.

390 **Jackson** Quoted in Newfield, "Anti-Semitism and the Cry of Silence," 16.

390 **Southerners on Sherman** Donald W. Shriver, Jr., "The Presence of the Past," *Los Angeles Times,* July 7, 1990, B7.

390 **doddering** See Dirk Johnson, "Anger in Ohio over a Death-Camp Conviction," NYT, April 27, 1988, A21.

390 **Wechsler** Author of *A Miracle, A Universe: Settling Accounts with Torturers* (New York: Pantheon, 1990), in lecture on "Transition to Democracy in Latin America" at Center for American Cultural Studies, Columbia University, February 7, 1990, from author's notes.

391 **Flannery** See his *Anguish of the Jews: Twenty-three Centuries of Anti-Semitism* (New York: Paulist Press, 1985).

391 **"Christian tragedy"** A. C., "Christian Tragedy" interview, 4.

391 **Tutu** Alan Cowell, "Tutu Urges Israelis to Pray for and Forgive Nazis," NYT, December 27, 1989, A5.

391 **Walesa's comments** Neil A. Lewis, "Walesa's View of Glemp Irks [*sic*] Jewish Leaders," NYT, November 18, 1989, A7.

391 **Bulgaria** Michael Bar-Zohar, professor of history at Emory University, writes that Bulgaria refused to turn over its 50,000 Jews in March 1943: letter to NYT, October 16, 1993. See qualification by Yehuda Bauer, professor of Holocaust Studies at the Hebrew University: NYT letter, October 23, 1993.

391 **rescue networks** See A. C., "Silent No More," and Eva Fogelman, *Conscience and Courage: Rescuers of Jews During the Holocaust* (New York: Anchor/Doubleday, 1994), chap 11.

391 **slander directed only at Jews** And only those of the Holocaust era.

391 **Gypsies** The murder machinery had been created to murder the Jews, but as long as it was in place, the Germans could and did deploy it against the Romani.

392 **target ... sacrifice victory** Levin, "Resistance and Rescue," 27–28.

392 **Unlike other nations ... no aid from Allies** Levin, "Resistance and Rescue," 28.

392 **ghettos, forests, death camps** See summary in Yehuda Bauer's booklet *They Chose Life—Jewish Resistance in the Holocaust* (New York: AJCommittee, 1973); and in books, listed in the bibliography, by Eckman and Lazar, Gilbert, Levin, Nirenstein, Suhl, and Syrkin.

392 **resourcefulness** Yitzchak Mais, interview on Jerusalem-On-Line, aired May 9, 1993, in NY, on CUNY TV, from author's notes.

392   **Grossman's view**   "Blaming the Victim: Bettelheim's Theories and the Holocaust,"
Israel Horizons, May–June 1984, 25.

393   **"unwillingness"**   Quoted by Michiko Kakutani in review of Bettelheim's *Freud's Vienna and Other Essays* (New York: Alfred A. Knopf, 1989), NYT, December 27, 1989, C21.

393   **1960 essay**   "The Ignored Lesson of Anne Frank" in *Surviving and Other Essays* (New York: Alfred A. Knopf, 1979); **"hardest way"**   248, 250–51, 257.

394   **Green's moral**   Quoted from *TV Guide,* March 15, 1978, in A. C., "'Holocaust,'" 36.

394   **Koontz's research**   "Reading the Writing on the Wall," *Lilith,* no. 17.

394   **failed to honor resisters**   For example, the fiftieth anniversary of the October 17, 1943, Sobibor revolt was not marked in the U.S. (Nor was the excellent docu-drama, "Escape from Sobibor" [originally shown on CBS-TV April 12, 1987], rebroadcast then.)

394   **Bauer quote**   *They Chose Life,* 57.

394   **women**   See Hay, Laska, Masters, Syrkin, *Match,* and listings in A. C., *The Jewish Woman,* under "Women in the Holocaust and Resistance." See also "The Fate of Women," in Nehama Tec, *Defiance: The Bielski Partisans: The Story of the Largest Armed Rescue of Jews During WWII* (New York: Oxford Univ. Press, 1993), 154–69.

395   **Al Kiddush HaShem**   This can be seen from the practice by cantors when chanting *El Malay Rachamim* (God of Mercy, prayer said at funerals and memorial services) during commemorations of *Yom HaShoah* (Day of the Catastrophe) of adding a line about the murdered Six Million who perished *Al Kiddush HaShem.*

395   **rise in hate crimes**   Howard Ehrlich, director of the National Institute Against Prejudice (Baltimore), quoted in Daniel Goleman, "As Bias Crime Seems to Rise, Scientists Study Roots of Racism," NYT, May 29, 1990, C1.

395   **anti-black, anti-Asian, anti-gay**   Goleman, "Bias Crime," C5, and J. J. Goldberg, "How Much Anti-Semitism," JR, February 20, 1992, 24.

395   **rise in anti-Semitic incidents   1978**   Newfield, "Anti-Semitism and the Crime of Silence," 13, citing ADL study.

395   **1993**   AP: "Assaults on Jews Increased in 1993," NYT, January 25, 1994, A12.

395   **1991 incidents, more attacks on individuals than on property**   AP: "Anti-Semitic Attacks in '91 Called a Record," NYT, February 16, 1992, A33.

395   **at colleges, 1992**   Stewart Ain, "Anti-Semitism," New York *Jewish Week,* February 5–11, 1993, 3.

396   **1993**   Larry Yudelson, "Anti-Semitic Assaults in U.S. Up, But Vandalism Is Down, ADL Reports," JTA-DNB, January 25, 1994, 3.   **Queens, 1992**   Ain, "Anti-Semitism," 3.

396   **"doctrine of feelings"**   Hochschild, 172. Hochschild, in a 1994 phone conversation with the author, cited H. E. Dale's comment in *The Higher Civil Service of Britain* as the source of the term. **the lower the status … emotions … instability**   173; **try to make up**   174.

396   **did not check out**   Grobman, "What Did They Know?" 333.

397   **"laying it on too thick"** … **"wailing Jews"**   Lipstadt, 277.

397   **"tastefully"**   Pinsky, "American Jewish Unity," 484.

397   **not allowed to identify as minority**   Evelyn Torton Beck, quoted in Jenny Milner and Donna Spiegelman, "Carrying It On: A Report from the [1991] New Jewish Agenda Conference on Organizing Against Racism, and Anti-Semitism," *Bridges,* Spring–Summer 1992, 139.

397   **Mais**   A. C., "'Americanizing the Holocaust.'"

398   **Partisans' Hymn**   "Never Say," written by Hirsh Glick of the FPO (Vilna underground); he died in a concentration camp in Estonia. In *Let's Sing a Yiddish Song* (New York: Kinderbuch Pub., 1970), 136–37.

398 **"too high a profile"** Quoted in Judith Miller, "The Holocaust Museum, A Troubled Start," NYT magazine, April 22, 1990, 48.

398 **"extravaganzas"** Robert Alter, "Deformations of the Holocaust." *Commentary,* February 1981, 48.

399 **hailed director** Quoted in Doneson, 72; see also 69.

399 **Geis's charge** In Spring 1985 issue of *Science Fiction Review,* quoted in Sheldon Teitelbaum, "SF Reviews and News," JP magazine, September 13, 1985, 18.

399 **living memorials** A proposal made in the 1960s by one of my teachers, Rabbi Nathan (Nachum) Dunn.

399 **"The only way"** Quoted in Peter Brunette, "Mamet Views Cops Through a New Lens," NYT, February 10, 1991, Arts & Leisure, 13.

399 **proliferation** The 1988 Directory of Holocaust Institutions in North America, published by the U.S. Holocaust Memorial Council, has ninety-eight listings in twenty-three states, Washington, D.C., and Canada: Yitzchak Mais, "Institutionalizing the Holocaust," *Midstream,* December 1988, 16.

399 **glamour project** This is why realtor Harvey Meyerhoff negotiated to donate $6 million to the Holocaust Museum on condition that the entrance plaza be named in memory of his father: Robert Greenberger, "The Politics of Building a Holocaust Memorial," Long Island *Jewish World,* April 28–May 4, 1989, 8.

399 **"ghoulish competition"** James Young, author of *The Texture of Memory: Holocaust Memorials and Meaning in Europe, Israel and America* (New Haven, CT: Yale Univ. Press, 1993), quoted in S. T. Meravi, "Whose Holocaust?" JP int'l ed., June 24, 1989, 12.

399 **pay more attention** Mais, "Institutionalizing the Holocaust," 20.

399 **cited in appeals** For example, a UJA-Federation Operation Exodus ad with a yahrzeit candle had the text, "A Million Soviet Jews Don't Want to Be Remembered This Way," NYT, October 22, 1990, A9.

399 **"missions"** Silberman, 198.

399 **Associates Division** Invitation to October 23, 1988, event.

400 **Steve Reich** K. Robert Schwartz, "For Reich War [*sic*] and Rediscovery," NYT, May 28, 1989, Arts & Leisure, 21.

400 **Judy Chicago** Subtitled *From Darkness into Light,* her book about the project was published by Viking Penguin in 1993.

400 **"truly my roots"** Jane Perlez, "Spielberg Grapples with the Horrors of the Holocaust," NYT, June 13, 1993, Arts & Leisure, 17.

402 **Silberman** *Moment* interview, 24.

402 **social laws** Murray Zuckoff, "The Need to Look Homeward: Anti-Semitism in the U.S. Today," JTA-DNB, September 3, 1980, 2.

402 **Bauer's argument** Paraphrased from A. C., "Leading Historian Says It Is 'Dangerous' to Rely on Public Opinion Polls That Popular Anti-Semitism Is Declining in the U.S.," JTA-DNB, October 30, 1985, 2; **once a criminal party** Bauer interview for "Leading Historian," from author's notes.

403 **religious right** See David Cantor, *The Religious Right: The Assault on Tolerance and Pluralism in America* (New York: Anti-Defamation League, 1994).

403 **Klan, "Identity Church," Nazis, skinheads** *Anti-Semitism World Report 1992* (London: Institute of Jewish Affairs, 1992), 110.

403 **neo-Nazi skinheads** Kenneth Stern, *Skinheads: Who They Are and What They Do When They Come to Town* (New York: AJCommittee, 1990), and ADL *Special Report: Young and Violent: The Growing Menace of America's Neo-Nazi Skinheads,* n.d. (ca. 1989).

403   **Dees's view and report**   "Young, Gullible and Taught to Hate," NYT Op-Ed, August 25, 1993, A15.

403   **IJA on Liberty Lobby and IHR**   *Report,* 110.

403   **Holocaust-denying**   See Kenneth S. Stern, *Holocaust Denial* (New York: AJCommittee, 1993), and Deborah Lipstadt, *Denying the Holocaust: The Growing Assault on Truth and Memory* (New York: Free Press, 1993).

404   **exceptions**   In Stern, *Farrakhan and the Jews,* 7.

404   **"gutter religion," "Hitler . . . great man"**   Stern, *Farrakhan and the Jews,* 5–6.

404   **"sucking the blood"**   Speech quoted in Mitchell G. Bard, "Poison on Campus," *Midstream,* June–July 1993, 10.

404   **"Aunt Jemima roles," slave trade**   Stern, *Farrakhan and the Jews,* 1; **endorsed by Sharpton**   13.

404   **by Jeffries**   Speech, July 20, 1991, at Empire State Black Arts and Culture Festival, Albany, NY, quoted in Kenneth S. Stern, *Dr. Jeffries and the Anti-Semitic Branch of the Afrocentrism Movement* (New York: AJCommittee, 1991), 3–5; **his Hollywood Jews charge**   1, 3.

404   **Cokely's charge**   Quoted in Bard, "Poison on Campus," 10.

404   **campus attacks**   Bard, "Poison on Campus," 9–11.

404   **deny Jews are a minority**   Jews are not included in the Civil Rights Act of 1964: Beck, "The Politics of Jewish Invisibility," *NWSA Journal,* Autumn 1988.

404   **deny Jews' ethnicity**   Beck, quoted in Milner and Spiegelman, "Carrying It On," 139; **resistance to inclusion in multicultural curriculum**   139.

404   **Berkeley student**   Milner and Spiegelman, "Carrying It On," 140; **United Front**   140.

404   **"political influence," 1978, 1980**   *Anti-Semitism in America: A Balance Sheet* (New York: AJCommittee, 1981), 5.

404   **"power," 1964, 1992**   *Highlights from an ADL Survey on Anti-Semitism and Prejudice in America* (New York: ADL, 1992), 18.

404   **"disreputable"**   Rose Feitelson and George Salomon, *The Many Faces of Anti-Semitism* (New York: AJCommittee, 1978), 39. Similarly, the AJCongress National Governing Council declared February 1, 1981, that "in all sectors of American life, anti-Semitism has become shabby, *disreputable,* and abhorrent." This "is the legacy left to us by those martyred by the Nazis" [*sic*]: Phil Baum, *Where We Stand: Anti-Semitism* (New York: AJCongress, 1981), 9 (italics mine).

405   **1993 magazine piece**   Craig Horowitz, "The New Anti-Semitism," *New York,* January 11, 1993, 23.

405   **ads by Holocaust-deniers**   Placed by Bradley Smith, who has ties to the IHR: *IJA Report,* 112; **academic freedom**   112. Jewish student groups do not confront these phenomena as they did anti-Zionist campus activities in the late 1960s and early 1970s. They lack a strong Jewish student movement to back them up and provide ideological and moral support—an unfortunate consequence of the destruction of Network.

405   **Buchanan on Treblinka**   Cited in *New York Post* editorial, September 19, 1990, and reported in Debra Nussbaum, "Patrick Buchanan Tumult Continues as Jewish Leaders Ponder Response," JTA-DNB, September 28, 1990, 4; **other propaganda**   4.

405   **O'Brien**   Quoted in Nathan Stoltzfus, "Dissent in Nazi Germany," *Atlantic Monthly,* September 1992, 94; **von Galen's protest**   92.

405   **Stoltzfus's conclusion**   Stoltzfus, "Dissent," 93.

405   **20 percent, down from 1964**   35–40 million adults: *Highlights from an ADL Survey on Anti-Semitism and Prejudice in America,* 2; **blacks, whites**   30.

405   **"clearly reveals"**   *Highlights of ADL Survey* (1992), 2. The AJCommittee released a

study in January 1992 claiming "anti-Semitism is at an historic low compared to the last 40 years": Goldberg, "How Much Anti-Semitism," 24.

405 **no attempt to explain** AJCommittee Research Director David Singer said, "We don't have the money to do a proper comprehensive survey of public attitudes": Goldberg, "How Much Anti-Semitism," 24.

405 **flukes** Zuckoff, "Look Homeward," 3.

405 **bankers/farm myth** After a Kansas City Jewish Community Relations Board (JCRB) delegation went to Chillicothe, MO, to talk with farmers and work with them to save their farms, farmers told JCRB executive director David Goldstein, "It's wonderful you are helping us because with your ownership of banks, the media and government, you bring a great deal of power to our struggle": Walter Ruby, "Farm Crisis: As Families Fight to Cope, Extremists Make a Pitch," Philadelphia *Jewish Exponent,* January 9, 1987, 35–37.

405 **its easy acceptance** Bauer, interview for "Leading Historian" (author's notes).

406 **thriving, fading organizations** The ADL and the Wiesenthal Center have a definite purpose; most of the other community relations organizations do not. Many have lost most of their membership (AJCongress) and power (AJCommittee) although they continue to function as if they hadn't. The main problem is their inability to conceptualize relevant approaches in response to the changes in the world, the United States, and the community since the early 1990s. See Jacob Neusner, "The New Jewish Era," *Forward,* November 6, 1990, 6.

407 **Albigensians** Graetz, 3:297. In the Crusade against the Albigensians in 1209, 20,000 were massacred and the Jews of those French provinces were also murdered: 299–300.

407 **pagan women** M&M, 290. See Bein, 527–28; Zeitlin, 281.

407 **Golden on KKK** 150–51.

408 **obsession with race and "blood"** Carlton J. H. Hayes, *A Generation of Materialism, 1871–1900* (New York and London: Harper & Bros., 1941), 258 and 255–61 generally.

409 **"Judaizing" charge** Samuel, 18.

409 **"emasculating germ"** Quoted in Erickson, 341.

409 **burning of Talmud** M&M, 378; Trachtenberg, 178–79.

409 **"Communist/Jewish conspiracy"** Quoted in Gloria Steinem, "The Nazi Connection: Authoritarianism Begins at Home," *Ms.,* November 1980, 14; **1934 speech** 19.

409 **"blackhaired Jew boy"** Quoted from *Mein Kampf* in Erich Goldhagen, "Nazi Sexual Demonology," *Midstream,* May 1981, 9.

410 **R. Kalonymos Shapiro** (1889–1943), a Hassidic rabbi known for innovations in Hassidic education. He buried in 1943 the manuscript of his discourses—*Esh Kodesh* (Fire of Holiness)—delivered on Shabbat and festival services, and it was published in Israel after the war. The quote is from his penultimate discourse, delivered July 11, 1942: Nehemia Polen, "Divine Weeping: Rabbi Kalomymos Shapiro's Theology of Catastrophe in the Warsaw Ghetto," *Modern Judaism,* October 1987, 258.

CHAPTER 16: THE RISE AND FUTURE OF JEWISH FEMINISM

411 **Ozick quote** "Notes," 21.

411 **Blu Greenberg** Keynote address to the First National Jewish Women's Conference, 1973, from author's notes.

411 **Susannah Heschel quote** Heschel, intro. to *On Being a Jewish Feminist* (hereinafter Heschel, *Feminist*), xxiv.

412 **takeover fear** Kosmin, "Political Economy," 28–29.

413 **San Francisco Federation executive** John H. Steinhart, chairman, executive committee, quoted in sidebar to Rosenfeld, "Shabbat Sit-In," 2.

414 **Eilberg on rabbinate** "Exploring the Link Between Womanhood and the Rabbinate," interview in *Lilith,* no. 14 (Fall-Winter, 1985): 22.

414 **Ezrat Nashim manifesto** "Call for Change," distributed at RA convention, March 12–16, 1972: Enid Nemy, "Young Women Challenge Their Second Class Status in Judaism," NYT, June 12, 1972, 43.

414 **origin of Ezrat Nashim** See "The Jewry Is Still Out," interview in *Lilith,* no. 11 (Fall–Winter 1983), with founding members Arlene Agus and Paula Hyman.

414 **Zieglerville** The intense male bonding at the conference, and part of the session on women's issues, chaired by Sheryl Baron, can be seen in David Kaufman's film, *Encounters in the Month of Elul*

415 **class factor** A. C., "Women Rabbis and the Conservative Movement," *WAO Reporter,* November–December 1980, 10–11.

416 **Reform men** The movement seminary ordained Sally Priesand, the first American woman ordained at such an institution, in 1973.

416 **Kaplan's argument** In Baskin, 211.

416 **minyan decision, 1973** Announced by RA Committee on Jewish Law and Standards: "Women's Lib," *Newsweek,* September 17, 1973, 63.

416 **crazy-quilt effect** In a Women's League for Conservative Judaism (WLCJ) survey, 68 percent of the 700 responding congregations said they counted women in the minyan and 66 percent said women had aliyot: "Religion Notes," NYT, December 1, 1990, A14; **Byzantine rulings** the survey revealed that an additional 7 percent of the responding congregations gave women aliyot on such special occasions.

417 **mechitzah** It has become a symbol of "allegiance" to the Orthodox community, wrote Norma Baumel Joseph in "Mechitzah–Halachic Decisions and Political Consequences," in G-H, 129. In 1979, JTS Prof. Israel Francus noted that just as the mechitzah distinguished between Orthodoxy and Conservatism, male-only ordination was the "symbolic dividing line" between Conservatism and Reform: quoted in Reena Sigman Friedman, "The Politics of Ordination," *Lilith,* no. 6 (1979), 11.

417 **"When the entire Jewish world"** Francus, quoted in Friedman, "Politics of Ordination," 13.

417 **confirm the "rigidity"** Rabbi Stephen Lerner, in Friedman, "Politics of Ordination," 14. Other advocates of ordination were Rabbi Wolfe Kelman, executive vice-president of the RA; and Rabbi Seymour Siegel, professor of theology and ethics at the JTS: Amy Stone, "Gentlemen's Agreement at the Seminary," *Lilith,* no. 3 (Spring–Summer 1977).

418 **Mishnah law** *Rosh Hashana* III.8 (BT 29a). See Samuel, 190.

418 **cantors' ordination** Sheldon Engelmayer and Toby Axelrod, "Cantors Assembly Rejects Women as Cantors," New York *Jewish Week,* May 6, 1986, 3; **membership in Cantors Assembly** approved August 30, 1990: executive vice-president Cantor Samuel Rosenbaum (phone conversation with Tamara Cohen).

418 **1991 survey** By CCAR, cited in Debra Nussbaum Cohen, "Women Rabbis Still Struggling," *Forward,* August 16, 1991, 20.

418   **1993 survey**   CWE report, September 21, 1993.

418   **views of women rabbis, Eilberg**   Cohen, "Women Rabbis," 20.

420   **Elazar's statement**   "Women in American Jewish Life," *Congress Bi-Weekly,* November 23, 1973, 11.

420   **Davidowicz's view**   Quoted by Susannah Heschel in intro. to Heschel, *Feminist,* xx.

420   **Ostow's "analysis"**   In symposium on "Women and Change in Jewish Law," *Conservative Judaism (CJ),* Fall 1974, 11–12. See also Berman, 354.

421   **"What happens to family life"**   Louis Linn in *CJ,* Fall 1974, 16–17.

421   **decline of Jewish fertility**   Uziel Schmelz and Sergio Della Pergola, in *Basic Trends in American Jewish Demography,* emphasize that Jewish fertility has always lagged behind overall white American fertility and that no major change took place between 1970 and the early 1980s (New York: AJCommittee, 1988), 6.

421   **preoccupation with fertility issue**   Shirley Frank, "The Population Panic—Why Jewish Leaders Want Jewish Women to Be Fruitful and Multiply," *Lilith,* no. 4 (Fall–Winter 1977–78).

421   **"preventive Holocaust"**   Various quotes in sidebar to Frank, "Population Panic," 16.

421   **Reconstructionist view**   H. L. Roberts, "Endogenous Jewish Genocide—the Impact of the ZPG-Nonparental Movement," November 1974.

422   **conferences**   For example, those of Network, 1973, 1974; the NY Section of NCJW, 1983, 1989, 1993; AJCongress, 1987, 1988.

422   **conventions in unratified states**   Reena Sigman Friedman, "Protest CCAR Arizona Convention," *Lilith,* no. 6 (1979): 7.

423   **resistance of male rabbis, scholars**   Testimony told to author.

423   **children's texts, literature**   Schneider, 167–69.

423   **mainstreaming**   See Irene Fine's essay in "How to Get What We Want by the Year 2000" section in *Lilith,* no. 7 (1980), 21; Maxine Seller, "Reclaiming Jewish History," *Lilith,* no. 7, 23, 26; and Shulamit Magnus, "Out of the Ghetto: Integrating the Study of Jewish Women into the Study of 'the Jews,'" *Judaism,* Winter 1990, 28–30.

423   **distort reality**   See Magnus, "Out of the Ghetto"; and Susannah Heschel, "Women's Studies," *Modern Judaism,* 1990, 243–58.

423   **"treading that line"**   "The Jewry" *Lilith* interview, 22.

424   **Klagsbrun**   At Oct., 1983 NCJW conference, reported in A.C., "Jewish Feminism 'Coming of Age!'" *WAO Reporter,* Winter 1984, 4.

425   **perception of feminism**   Hyman in "The Jewry" *Lilith* interview, 23; **"in tune with general culture"**   22.

425   **perceived as narcissistic**   See Daniel Elazar on their "self-indulgence" and "personal gratification" in symposium, "Does Judaism Need Feminism?" *Midstream,* April 1986, 40.

426   **anti-feminists**   See, e.g., Ruth Wisse, "The Feminist Mystery," JR, January 9, 1992, 40.

426   **Szold on daughter**   "The Education of the Jewish Girl [*sic*]," *Maccabean,* no. 5 (1903), 7, quoted in Glanz, 153 n. 1. It is interesting to note here, as well, that the Yiddish production of Ibsen's *The Doll's House* in the U.S. added a fourth act in which Nora returns home: Glanz, 176 n. 38.

426   **"reluctant"**   In "The Jewry," 22.

427   **"Jewish princesses" in** *OOB*   April 15, 1971, 5 (anon.).

427   **Chesler's report**   Letter in *Majority Report,* May 31, 1975.

427   **lesbian-feminist movement**   Irena Klepfisz, "Anti-Semitism in the Lesbian/Feminist Movement," *OOB,* April 1982, 8.

427   **Pogrebin's article**   "Anti-Semitism," 45–72.

427   **Dworkin**   Quoted in Pogrebin, "Anti-Semitism," 66; **loud, pushy, etc.**   66. Pogrebin cited "slurs, Jew-baiting and outright persecution": 65; and the stereotypes of "exotic Jewess" and Jew as moneymaker: 66.

427   **dislodging "the Goddess," foiling Jesus**   Judith Plaskow, "Christian Feminism and Anti-Judaism," *Cross-Currents,* Fall 1978, 306.

427   **"convenient explanation"**   Susannah Heschel, "Anti-Judaism in Christian Feminist Theology," *Tikkun,* May–June 1990, 26.

427   **destroying the Goddess, recycling Christ-killer myth**   Annette Daum, "Blaming Jews for the Death of the Goddess," *Lilith,* no. 7 (1980): 22.

428   **"will be my allies"**   Plaskow in "Feminists and Faith," discussion with Daum in *Lilith,* no. 7 (1980), 16.

428   **"Jews must die!"**   In Regina Schreiber (pseud.), "Copenhagen," 31; **"only good Jew"**   32.

428   **"The only way"**   Testimony on quote provided by Sonia Johnson in sidebar, "Bitter Fruit," *Ms.,* June 1982, 48. See discussion on anti-Zionism in the women's movement in Pogrebin, "Anti-Semitism," 46.

428   **"could not believe"**   Schreiber, "Copenhagen," 33.

428   **"psychological pogrom"**   Schreiber, "Copenhagen," 32; **"I saw"**   35.

428   **"omitted from the feminist litany"**   Pogrebin, "Anti-Semitism," 46.

428   **absence from texts**   Beck, "Jewish Invisibility," 84; **religion texts, anthologies** 98–99.

428   **invisibility among feminist therapists**   A.C./Therapy, 11.

428   **identity "insignificant"**   Beck, quoted in A.C./Therapy, 11.

428   **behavior seen as pathological**   A.C./Therapy, 11. Rachel Josefowitz Siegel said this is especially true in regard to the family: 11.

428   **emotional disorders**   Melissa Schwartz in A.C./Therapy, 12.

429   **"the Holocaust has marked ... fear of rape"**   A.C./Therapy, 12.

429   **"put themselves down in public"**   Schwartz in A.C./Therapy, 12; **"have to decide"**   12.

429   **avoid writing on Jewish themes**   Beck, "Jewish Invisibility," 96–7. This bears resemblance to a phenomenon of the 1950s/early 1960s whereby "many Jewish social scientists actively avoided research on Jewish life lest they become too closely identified with their subject": Urofsky, 338.

429   **"wanting to take over"**   Beck, interviewed by author in *Lilith,* no. 10 (Winter 1983), 11.

429   **"too Jewish"**   For example, Nancy Polikoff actually wrote that a story in Julia Mazow's *The Woman Who Lost Her Names* "seemed too Jewish": *OOB,* April 1982, 10.

429   **Shema story**   In unsolicited ms. rejected by *Lilith.*

429   **rescue**   Beck called the lesbian-feminist movement "a place of refuge," *Lilith* interview, 12.

430   **anti-Semitism not taken seriously or included in -isms**   Beck intro. to *Nice Jewish Girls,* excerpted in *Lilith,* no. 10, 13.

430   **without dealing with own distinctiveness**   Beck interview, *Lilith,* no. 10, 10; **grassroots groups**   10–11.

430   **study of Gemara, "explosion of women's learning"**   Blu Greenberg, "Feminism Within Orthodoxy: A Revolution of Small Signs," *Lilith,* Summer 1992, 16.

430   **confluence**   Blu Greenberg, "Feminism," 16; **examples of "small signs"**   13–16; **"Slowly but surely"**   16.

431   **tefillah groups**   Blu Greenberg, "Feminism," 13.

431   **Berman and Weiss**   Berman, associate professor of Jewish studies at YU's Stern College for Women, reviewing Weiss's *Women at Prayer,* JTA book review (in features packet), August 9, 1991; both conclude the groups are Halachically acceptable. Rabbi Eliezer Berkovits also supported them.

431   **1984 responsum**   Rivka Haut, "Women's Prayer Groups and the Orthodox Synagogue," in G-H, 145.

431   **meetings in Middle Ages, Urania**   Abrahams, 26.

431   **"What are they doing it for?"**   Quoted from Long Island *Jewish World,* in "Orthodox Women's Prayer Groups," *Lilith,* no. 14 (Fall–Winter 1985–86), 5; **RCA, "first time in history"**   6.

431   **"desecration"**   Rabbi Shlomo Goren, quoted in *Newsletter* of the International Committee for the Women of the Wall, February 1991, 3; **"uproot everything"**   Rabbi Herschel Schacter (one of the five YU rabbis), 3.

431   **extortion**   Adena Berkowitz, "The Prisoners of Divorce," *Lilith,* no. 18 (Winter 1987), 18.

431   **agunot, New York State**   Berkowitz, "Prisoners," 18; **agunot, Israel**   Debra Nussbaum Cohen, "Orthodox Rabbis Adopt Resolution Making Pre-Nuptial Pacts Mandatory," JTA-DNB, June 22, 1993, 2.

432   **"engraft"**   Boaz Cohen, professor of Codes at the JTS, quoted in Trude Weiss-Rosmarin, "Wanted: Equality for Jewish Women," *Jewish Spectator,* Winter 1978, 7.

432   **Conservative solutions**   One was the Lieberman Clause, devised in 1954 by JTS professor Saul Lieberman (later the prime Halachic opponent of female ordination): Berkowitz, "Prisoners," 20.

432   **unwillingness to accept non-Orthodox solutions**   Berkowitz, "Prisoners," 22.

432   **Lookstein's call**   "Prisoners," 19.

432   **Lysistrata action**   Reported by social worker Sarah Silver Bunim at NY Federation's Task Force on the Jewish Woman conference, NY, October 1979: A. C., "Jewish Women and the Communal Agenda," *WAO Reporter,* January–February 1980, 16. The tactic has apparently spread: see Blu Greenberg, "Feminism," 13.

432   **Orthodox and secular courts**   Berkowitz, "Prisoners," 20. **New York State and Ontario**   20; "Two Get Provisions Become Law in Ontario," JTA-CNR, March 7, 1986, 1–2.

432   **Berman's prediction**   Interview with Shulamith Magnus, *Response,* no. 40 (Spring 1981): 8.

432   **RCA solution, 1993**   Cohen, "Orthodox Rabbis Adopt," 2.

432   **Joseph, Haut**   Viva Hammer, "No More Chains!" *Na'amat Woman,* March–April 1993, 19.

432   **Weiss-Rosmarin's belief**   Discussions with author. Similarly, Ozick, "Notes," 27.

433   **"partial and diminished"**   Rachel Adler, "I've Had Nothing Yet," 23; **"clearly the people"**   27.

433   **"justice not ... done"**   "Notes," 27.

433   **Halacha on computer**   The Responsa Computer Project at Bar-Ilan University, linked to YU in NY.

433   **Conservatives didn't believe it possible**   See, for example, comment by Eilberg in *Lilith* interview, 23.

433   **"voice not veto"**   Quoted in the "Report of the Committee on the Status of Women in Jewish Life" of the NCJW by Ethel Cohen, its chair, May 17, 1966, 2.

433   **"Jewish daughter . . . Jew"**   Ozick, "Notes," 21.

434   **reenter after civil rights struggle**   Plaskow described the Jewish women's movement of the 1973–83 decade as a "civil rights" rather than a "liberation" movement: "The Right Question Is Theological," in Heschel, *Feminist,* 223–24.

434   **women in folktales**   Noy/Institute and conversations with author.

434   **folk songs on women**   A central theme in Ruth Rubin's book; **abandoned**   82, 83, 85; **separated from soldiers**   212–213, 215; **from immigrating husbands**   343, 344; **poverty and hunger**   282; **toil**   290; **prostitution**   334–35.

434   **Sephardic women**   Sered, G-H, 209–10.

434   **techinot**   Chava Weissler, "Prayers in Yiddish and the Religious World of Ashkenazic Women," in Baskin, 159–81.

434   **debate on their authorship**   Ozick contends they were written by men using women's pseudonyms: "Notes," 23. Weissler argues that some in eighteenth- and early-nineteenth-century Eastern Europe were "written or reworked by women": Weissler in Baskin, 161.

436   **New Moon**   The Talmud says this was an acceptable custom: BT *Megillah* 22b. Arlene Agus, in "This Month Is for You: Observing Rosh Hodesh as a Women's Holiday," argues that this custom was widely observed: Koltun, 87. No written ceremonies, however, have come down to us.

436   **daughter's birth**   See Reifman.

436   **life-cycle events**   Rahel Musleah, "New Rituals and Ceremonies for Jewish Women," *Na'amat Woman,* March–April 1992, 5ff. See Adelman and Fine.

436   **mikvah**   Elyse Goldstein, "Taking Back the Waters," *Lilith,* no. 15 (Summer 1986).

436   **midrashim**   See, for example, Jane Sprague Jones, ed., *Taking the Fruit: Modern Women's Tales of the Bible* (San Diego: Women's Institute for Continuing Jewish Education, 1989).

437   **"As long as God"**   "(Re)Imaging the Divine," *Response,* Fall–Winter 1982, 116.

437   **Siddur Nashim**   Excerpted in *Lilith,* no. 4 (Fall–Winter 1977–78). **"Her voice"**   28; **"She soothes"**   29.

437   **Weiss-Rosmarin on Greece, Rome**   "Is God 'She' and So What?" *Commonweal,* 374 (undated reprint distributed by TWR).

440   **incapable**   See Jacob Neusner, "The New Jewish Era."

SELECTED BIBLIOGRAPHY

Code:

F: work of fiction

pbk.: paperback edition of work

*: see abbreviation listed at beginning of the Notes.

Abella, Irving, and Troper, Harold. *None Is Too Many*. New York: Random House, 1983.

Abrahams, Israel. *Jewish Life in the Middle Ages*. Cleveland, OH, and New York: Meridian Books, World Publishing Co.; Philadelphia: JPS, 1958. (pbk.)

Adelman, Penina. *Miriam's Well: Rituals for Jewish Women Around the Year*. Fresh Meadows, NY: Biblio Press, 1986.

Adler, Ruth. *Women of the Shtetl Through the Eyes of Y. L. Peretz*. Cranbury, NJ: Associated Univ. Presses, 1980.

Ahad Ha'am. *Nationalism and the Jewish Ethic. Basic Writings*. New York: Herzl Press, 1962.

Alberoni, Francesco. *Falling in Love*. New York: Random House, 1983.

Altshuler, David, ed. *The Precious Legacy: Judaic Treasures from the Czechoslovak State Collections*. New York: Summit Books, 1983.

Aschkenasy, Nehama. *Eve's Journey: Feminine Images in Hebraic Literary Tradition*. Philadelphia: Univ. of Pennsylvania Press, 1986.

Ashkenazy, Jacob ben Isaac. *Tzenah Ur'enah*. 3 vols. Brooklyn, NY: Mesorah, 1983–84.

Ausubel, Nathan. *A Treasury of Jewish Folklore*. New York: Crown, 1948.

Avineri, Shlomo. *The Making of Modern Zionism*. New York: Basic Books, 1981.

Baer, Yitzhak F. *Galut*. New York: Schocken, 1947.

Baron, Salo W. *The Russian Jew Under Tsars and Soviets*. New York: Schocken, 1987.

*Baron, Salo W., and Wise, George S., eds. *Violence and Defense in the Jewish Experience*. Philadelphia: JPS, 1977.

Barzini, Luigi. *The Italians*. New York: Atheneum, 1964.

Baskin, Judith R., ed. *Jewish Women in Historical Perspective*. Detroit: Wayne State Univ. Press, 1991. (pbk.)

Bauer, Yehuda. *The Jewish Emergence from Powerlessness*. Toronto: Univ. of Toronto Press, 1979.

*Baum, Charlotte; Hyman, Paula; and Michel, Sonya. *The Jewish Woman in America*. New York: Dial, 1976.

Beck, Evelyn Torton, ed. *Nice Jewish Girls: A Lesbian Anthology*. Boston: Beacon Press, 1989.

Bein, Alex. *The Jewish Question. Biography of a World Problem*. Cranbury, NJ: Associated Univ. Presses, 1990.

Belinfante, Judith, and Dubov, Iga, eds. *Tracing An-Sky: Jewish Collections from the State Ethnographic Museum in St. Petersburg*. Amsterdam: Jewish Historical Museum, 1992–94.

Benedict, Ruth. *Patterns of Culture*. New York: Penguin, 1934.

Ben-Sasson, H. H., ed. *A History of the Jewish People.* Cambridge, MA: Harvard Univ. Press, 1976. (pbk.)

*Ben-Sasson, H. H., and Ettinger, S., eds. *Jewish Society Through the Ages.* New York: Schocken, 1971. (pbk.)

Ben-Zvi, Rachel Yanait. *Before Golda: Manya Shochat.* New York: Biblio Press, 1989.

Berkovits, Eliezer. *Faith After the Holocaust.* New York: Ktav, 1973.

——. *Jewish Women in Time and Torah.* Hoboken, NJ: Ktav, 1990.

Berman, Lewis A. *Jews and Intermarriage: A Study in Personality and Culture.* New York: Thos. Yoseloff, 1968.

Biale, David. *Childhood, Marriage and the Family in the East European Jewish Enlightenment.* Pamphlet. New York: American Jewish Committee, 1983.

——. *Eros and the Jews—From Biblical Israel to Contemporary America.* New York: Basic Books, 1992.

——. *Power and Powerlessness in Jewish History.* New York: Schocken, 1986.

Biale, Rachel. *Women and Jewish Law: An Exploration of Women's Issues in Halachic Sources.* New York: Schocken, 1984.

Bialik, Chaim Nachman. *Collected Writings.* (Heb.) Tel Aviv: Dvir, 1939.

Bialik, Chaim Nachman, and Rabinsky, Y. Ch., eds. *Sefer HaAgada.* (Heb.) Tel Aviv: Dvir, 1955.

Bieber, Hugo. ed. *Heinrich Heine: A Biographical Anthology.* Philadelphia: JPS, 1956.

Birmingham, Stephen. *Our Crowd.* New York: Harper & Row, 1967.

Bitton-Jackson, Livia. *Madonna or Courtesan? The Jewish Woman in Christian Literature.* New York: Seabury Press, 1982.

Borochov, Ber. *Nationalism and the Class Struggle.* New York: Poale Zion, 1937.

Brayer, Menachem M. *The Jewish Woman in Rabbinic Literature.* 2 vols. Hoboken, NJ: Ktav, 1986. (pbk.)

Breines, Paul. *Tough Jews—Political Fantasies and the Moral Dilemma of American Jews.* New York: Basic Books, 1990.

Bristow, Edward J. *Prostitution and Prejudice: The Jewish Fight Against White Slavery, 1879–1939.* New York: Schocken, 1983.

Brownmiller, Susan. *Against Our Will: Men, Women and Rape.* New York: Simon & Schuster, 1975.

Buber, Martin. *Israel and the World: Essays in a Time of Crisis.* New York: Schocken, 1948.

Cantor, Aviva. *The Egalitarian Hagada.* New York: Beruriah Books, 1992.

——. *The Jewish Woman 1900–1985, A Bibliography.* Fresh Meadows, NY: Biblio Press, 1987.

Cherikover, Eliahu. *Jews in Revolutionary Eras.* (Heb.) Tel Aviv: Am Oved, 1957.

*Cohen, Abraham. *Everyman's Talmud.* New York: Schocken, 1975. (pbk.)

*Cohen, Mitchell. *Zion and State: Nation, Class and the Shaping of Modern Israel.* New York: Columbia Univ. Press, 1992.

Cohen, Stephen M., and Hyman, Paula, eds. *The Jewish Family—Myths and Realties.* New York: Holmes & Meier, 1986.

Cuddihy, John Murray, *The Ordeal of Civility.* New York: Basic Books, 1974.

Dash, Joan. *Summoned to Jerusalem: The Life of Henrietta Szold.* New York: Harper & Row, 1979.

Davidowicz, Lucy S. *The Golden Tradition: Jewish Life and Thought in Eastern Europe.* New York: Holt, Rinehart & Winston, 1967.

Deloria, Vine, Jr. *Custer Died for Your Sins—An Indian Manifesto.* Norman: Univ. of Oklahoma Press, 1988.

Dershowitz, Alan. *Chutzpah*. Boston: Little, Brown, 1991.

Deutscher, Isaac. *The Non-Jewish Jew and Other Essays*. London: Oxford Univ. Press, 1968.

Dimont, Max I. *Jews, God and History*. New York: Signet/New American Library, 1962. (pbk.)

Doneson, Judith E. *The Holocaust in American Film*. Philadelphia: JPS, 1987.

Dubnow, Simon. *History of the Jews*. 3 vols. New York: Thos. Yoseloff, 1967–69.

*——. *History of the Jews in Russia and Poland*. 3 vols. Philadelphia: JPS, 1916–20.

Eckman, Lester, and Lazar, Chaim. *The Jewish Resistance: The History of the Jewish Partisans in Lithuania and White Russia During the Nazi Occupation, 1940–1945*. New York: Shengold, 1977.

Ehrenreich, Barbara, and English, Deirdre. *Complaints and Disorders: The Sexual Politics of Sickness*. New York: Feminist Press, 1973.

Eisenstadt, Shmuel. *The Prophets*. New York: Yiddisher Kultur Farband, 1971.

Elbogen, Ismar. *A Century of Jewish Life*. Philadelphia: JPS, 1944.

Elon, Amos. *Herzl*. New York: Schocken, 1986. (pbk.)

*——. *The Israelis: Founders and Sons*. New York: Holt, Rinehart & Winston, 1971.

Erikson, Erik K. *Childhood and Society*. 2d ed. New York: W. W. Norton, 1963. (pbk.)

Esther, Scroll of. See Zlotowitz.

Fackenheim, Emil L. *To Mend the World: Foundations of Post-Holocaust Jewish Thought*. 2d ed. New York: Schocken, 1989. (pbk.)

Fein, Leonard. *Where Are We? The Inner Life of America's Jews*. New York: Harper & Row, 1988.

Feingold, Henry L. *The Politics of Rescue: The Roosevelt Administration and the Holocaust, 1938–1945*. New Brunswick, NJ: Rutgers Univ. Press, 1970.

Feldman, David M. *Birth Control in Jewish Law: Marital Relations, Contraception, and Abortion as Set Forth in the Classic Texts of Jewish Law*. New York: NYU Press, 1968.

Fine, Irene. *Midlife: A Rite of Passage* and *The Wise Woman: A Celebration*. San Diego: Women's Institute for Continuing Jewish Education, 1988.

Finkelstein, Louis. *Akiva: Scholar, Saint and Martyr*. Cleveland, OH: World Publishing Co., 1936.

——. *Jewish Self-Government in the Middle Ages*. Philadelphia: JPS, 1924.

——. *The Pharisees: The Sociological Background of Their Faith*. 2 vols. Philadelphia: JPS, 1946.

Finkelstein, Louis, ed. *The Jews: Their Religion and Culture*. New York: Schocken, 1971. (pbk.)

Forman, Frieda, et al., eds. Found Treasures: Stories by Yiddish Women Writers. Toronto: Second Story Press, 1994. (F)

Freehof, Solomon B. *The Responsa Literature*. Philadelphia: JPS, 1955.

Freeman, Lucy. *The Story of Anna O*. New York: Walker & Co., 1972.

Frondorf, Shirley. *Death of a "Jewish American Princess."* New York: Villard Books, 1988.

Frymer-Kensky, Tikva. *In the Wake of the Goddesses: Women, Culture and the Biblical Transformation of Pagan Myth*. Boston: Beacon Press, 1992.

Fuchs, Esther. *Israeli Mythogynies: Women in Contemporary Hebrew Fiction*. Albany, NY: SUNY Press, 1987.

Gabler, Neal. *An Empire of Their Own: How Jews Invented Hollywood*. New York: Crown, 1988.

Gilbert, Martin. *The Holocaust*. New York: Owl Books/Holt, 1985. (pbk.)

Gilligan, Carol. *In a Different Voice*. Cambridge, MA: Harvard Univ. Press, 1982.

Ginzberg, Louis. *The Legends of the Jews*. 5 vols. Philadelphia: JPS, 1909.

Glanz, Rudolf. *The Jewish Woman in America: Two Female Immigrant Generations, 1820–1929*. Vol. 1: *The East European Jewish Woman*. New York: Ktav and the National Council of Jewish Women, 1976.

Gluckel of Hameln, Life of, Written by Herself. New York: Thos. Yoseloff, 1963.

Goitein, Shlomo Dov. *Mediterranean Society.* Vol. 3: *The Family.* Berkeley: Univ. of California Press, 1978.

Gold, Michael. *Jews Without Money.* New York: Horace Liveright, 1930.

Golden, Harry. *Only in America.* Cleveland, OH, and New York: World Publishing Co., 1958.

Goldin, Milton. *Why They Give: American Jews and Their Philanthropies.* New York: Macmillan, 1976.

Goldmann, Nahum. *The Autobiography of Nahum Goldmann.* New York: Holt, Rinehart & Winston, 1969.

Gordon, A. D. *Selected Essays.* New York: League for Labor Palestine, 1938.

Gottfried, Robert S. *The Black Death.* New York: The Free Press/Macmillan, 1983.

Graetz, Heinrich. *Popular History of the Jews.* 6 vols. New York: Hebrew Publishing Co., 1919, 1949.

Greenberg, Blu. *On Women and Judaism: A View from Tradition.* Philadelphia: JPS, 1981.

*Grossman, Susan, and Haut, Rivka, eds. *Daughters of the King—Women and the Synagogue.* Philadelphia: JPS, 1992.

Gurock, Jeffrey, ed. *Ramaz: School, Community, Scholarship and Orthodoxy.* Hoboken, NJ: Ktav, 1989.

Hamelsdorf, Ora, and Adelsberg, Sandra. *Jewish Women and Jewish Law: A Bibliography.* Fresh Meadows, NY: Biblio Press, 1980.

Hapgood, Hutchins. *The Spirit of the Ghetto.* New York: Funk & Wagnalls, 1902.

Haut, Irwin H. *Divorce in Jewish Law and Life.* New York: Sepher-Hermon, 1983.

Hay, Peter. *Ordinary Heroes: Chana Szenes and the Dream of Zion.* New York: Putnam, 1986.

Hazleton, Lesley. *Israeli Women: The Reality Behind the Myths.* New York: Simon & Schuster, 1977.

Heary, Maurice. *Hebraic Literature: Translations from the Talmud, Midrashim and Kabbala.* New York: Tudor, 1936.

Hecht, Ben. *A Child of the Century.* New York: Donald I. Fine, 1954.

——. *Perfidy.* New York: Julian Messner, 1961.

Heine, Heinrich. See Bieber.

Heller, Celia S. *On the Edge of Destruction: Jews of Poland Between the Two World Wars.* New York: Columbia Univ. Press, 1977.

Henry, Sondra, and Taitz, Emily. *Written out of History: Our Jewish Foremothers.* Rev. ed. Fresh Meadows, NY: Biblio Press, 1983. (pbk.)

Hersey, John. *The Wall.* New York: Alfred A. Knopf, 1950. (F)

Hertz, Deborah. *Jewish High Society in Old Regime Berlin.* New Haven, CT: Yale Univ. Press, 1988.

Hertzberg, Arthur. *The Jews in America—Four Centuries of an Uneasy Encounter: A History.* New York: Simon & Schuster, 1989.

*Hertzberg, Arthur, ed. *The Zionist Idea.* New York: Doubleday & Herzl Press, 1959.

Herzog, Chaim. *The Arab-Israeli Wars.* New York: Random House, 1982.

Heschel, Susannah, ed. *On Being a Jewish Feminist: A Reader.* New York: Schocken, 1983.

Hess, Moses. *Rome and Jerusalem.* New York: Bloch, 1945.

Hirsch, Richard G. *The Way of the Upright: A Jewish View of Economic Justice.* Pamphlet. New York: Union of American Hebrew Congregations, 1973.

Hite, Shere. *Women and Love: A Cultural Revolution in Progress.* New York: Alfred A. Knopf, 1987.

Hoch-Smith, Judith, and Spring, Anita, eds. *Women in Ritual and Symbolic Roles.* New York: Plenum, 1978.

Hochschild, Arlie Russell. *The Managed Heart—Commercialization of Human Feeling.* Berkeley: Univ. of California Press, 1983.

Howe, Irving. *World of Our Fathers.* New York: Touchstone Books/Simon & Schuster, 1983. (pbk.)

*Howe, Irving, and Greenberg, Eliezer, eds. *Voices from the Yiddish.* Ann Arbor: Univ. of Michigan Press, 1972.

Howe, Irving, and Libo, Kenneth, eds. *How We Lived: A Documentary History of Immigrant Jews in America.* New York: Richard Marek, 1979.

Hunt, Morton M. *The Natural History of Love.* New York: Alfred A. Knopf, 1959.

Ichud Habonim. *Sisters of Exile—Sources on the Jewish Woman.* Booklet. New York: Ichud Habonim Labor Zionist Youth, n.d. [1971].

Jacobs, Joseph. *Jewish Contributions to Civilization.* Philadelphia: Conat Press, 1920.

Janeway, Elizabeth. *Man's World, Woman's Place: A Study in Social Mythology.* New York: William R. Morrow, 1971.

Jewish Almanac. See Siegel.

Jewish Catalogue. See Strassfeld.

Joselit, Jenna Weissman. *New York's Jewish Jews: The Orthodox Community in the Interwar Years.* Indianapolis: Indiana Univ. Press, 1990.

Kaplan, Marion A. *The Jewish Feminist Movement in Germany: The Campaigns of the Judischer Frauenbund, 1904–1938.* Westport, CT: Greenwood Press, 1979.

Katz, Esther, and Ringelheim, Joan, eds. *Proceedings of the Conference on "Women Surviving: The Holocaust."* New York: Institute for Research in History, 1983.

Katz, Jacob. *Exclusiveness and Tolerance.* London: Oxford Univ. Press, 1973.

———. *Jewish Emancipation and Self-Emancipation.* Philadelphia: JPS, 1986.

———. *Out of the Ghetto: The Social Background of Jewish Emancipation, 1770–1970.* Cambridge, MA: Harvard Univ. Press, 1973.

———. *Tradition and Crisis: Jewish Society at the End of the Middle Ages.* Glencoe, IL: Free Press of Glencoe, 1961.

Katzenelson-Rubashow, Rachel, ed. *The Plough Woman: Records of the Pioneer Women of Palestine.* New York: Nicholas L. Brown, 1932.

Kaye/Kantrowitz, Melanie, and Klepfisz, Irena, eds. *The Tribe of Dina: A Jewish Women's Anthology.* Boston: Beacon Press, 1986.

Kazin, Alfred. *A Walker in the City.* New York: Harcourt Brace, 1951.

Kedourie, Elie, ed. *The Jewish World.* New York: Harry N. Abrams, 1979.

Keller, Werner. *Diaspora: The Post-Biblical History of the Jews.* New York: Harcourt Brace & World, 1969.

Klein, Judith Weinstein. *Jewish Identity and Self-Esteem: Healing Wounds Through Ethnotherapy.* Booklet. New York: American Jewish Committee, 1980.

Kluger, Ruth, and Mann, Peggy. *The Last Escape.* Garden City, NY: Doubleday, 1973.

Kobler, Franz, ed. *Her Children Call Her Blessed: A Portrait of the Jewish Mother.* New York: Stephen Daye Press, 1955.

Koltun, Elizabeth, ed. *The Jewish Woman: New Perspectives.* New York: Schocken 1976. (pbk.)

Kowalski, Isaac. *A Secret Press in Nazi Europe: The Story of the Jewish United Partisan Organization.* 3d ed. New York: Shengold Publishers, 1978. (pbk.)

Kraemer, David, ed. *The Jewish Family—Metaphor and Memory.* New York: Oxford Univ. Press, 1989.

Kramer, Sydelle, and Masor, Jenny. *Jewish Grandmothers.* Boston: Beacon Press, 1976.

Lacks, Roslyn. *Women and Judaism: Myth, History and Struggle.* New York: Doubleday, 1980.

*Landau, Yehezkel, ed. *Violence and the Value of Life in Jewish Tradition.* Booklet. Israel: Oz Veshalom Publications, n.d. [after 1975].

Laqueur, Walter. *A History of Zionism.* New York: Holt, Rinehart & Winston, 1972.

Laska, Vera, ed. *Women in the Resistance and in the Holocaust: The Voices of Eyewitnesses.* Westport, CT: Greenwood Press, 1983.

Lazare, Bernard. *Job's Dungheap.* New York: Schocken, 1948.

Lazarus, M. *The Ethics of Judaism.* Philadelphia: JPS, 1900.

Lebeson, Anita. *Recall to Life: The Jewish Woman in America.* New York: Thos. Yoseloff, 1970.

Leon, Abraham. *The Jewish Question: A Marxist Interpretation.* Mexico City: Ediciones Pioneras, 1950.

Levi, Primo. *The Drowned and the Saved.* New York: Vintage/Random House, 1989. (pbk.)

——. *Survival in Auschwitz.* London: Collier Books/Collier-Macmillan, 1961. (pbk.)

Levin, Nora. *The Holocaust.* New York: Schocken, 1973.

*——. *While Messiah Tarried: Jewish Socialist Movements, 1871–1917.* New York: Schocken, 1977. (pbk.)

Levine, Amy-Jill, ed. *Women Like This—New Perspectives on Jewish Women in the Greco-Roman World.* Atlanta: Scholars Press, 1991.

Lewin, Kurt. *Resolving Social Conflicts.* New York: Harper & Row, 1948.

Lewis, Bernard. *The Jews of Islam.* Princeton, NJ: Princeton Univ. Press, 1984.

Lipstadt, Deborah E. *Beyond Belief: The American Press and the Coming of the Holocaust, 1933–1945.* New York: The Free Press/Macmillan, 1986.

Madison, Charles A. *Yiddish Literature: Its Scope and Major Writers.* New York: Schocken, 1971.

Maimon, Ada Fishman. *Women Build a Land.* New York: Herzl Press, 1962.

*Maimonides. *The Code of Maimonides: The Book of Women.* New Haven, CT: Yale Univ. Press, 1972.

Mamet, David. *Some Freaks.* New York: Viking, 1989.

Manners, Ande. *Poor Cousins.* New York: Coward, McCann & Geoghegan, 1972.

*Margolis, Max L., and Marx, Alexander. *A History of the Jewish People.* Philadelphia: JPS, 1953.

Masters, Anthony. *The Summer That Bled: The Biography of Hannah Senesh.* New York: St. Martin's Press, 1972.

Mazow, Julia Wolf, ed. *The Woman Who Lost Her Names: Selected Writings by American Jewish Women.* San Francisco: Harper & Row, 1980.

Memmi, Albert. *The Liberation of the Jew.* New York: Orion Press, 1966.

——. *Portrait of a Jew.* New York: Orion Press, 1962.

Morse, Arthur P. *While Six Million Died: A Chronicle of American Apathy.* New York: Random House, 1967.

Myerhoff, Barbara. *Number Our Days.* New York: Touchstone/Simon & Schuster, 1980. (pbk.)

Nirenstein, Albert. *A Tower from the Enemy.* New York: Orion Press, 1959.

Nordau, Max. *Max Nordau to His People—A Summons and a Challenge.* Addresses. New York: Nordau Zionist Society/Scopus Publishing Co., 1941.

Oring, Elliott. *The Jokes of Sigmund Freud: A Study in Humor and Jewish Identity.* Philadelphia: Univ. of Pennsylvania Press, 1984.

Oz, Amos. *My Michael.* London: Chatto & Windus, 1972. (F)

Patai, Raphael. *The Hebrew Goddess.* 3d ed. Detroit: Wayne State Univ. Press, 1990. (pbk.)

——. *The Jewish Mind.* New York: Scribner's, 1977. (pbk.)

Pawel, Ernst. *The Labyrinth of Exile—A Life of Theodor Herzl.* New York: Farrar, Straus & Giroux, 1989.

Peretz, Isaac Leib. (Untitled translation of stories and essays). Sol Liptzin, ed. New York: YIVO, 1947.

Pinsker, Leo. *Auto-Emancipation.* Pamphlet. New York: Masada Youth Zionist Organization of America, 1939.

Pirenne, Henri. *Economic and Social History of Medieval Europe.* New York: Harvest Books/Harcourt, Brace & Co., 1937. (pbk.)

Plaskow, Judith. *Standing Again at Sinai.* San Francisco: Harper & Row, 1990.

Pogrebin, Letty Cottin. *Deborah, Golda and Me: Being Female and Jewish in America.* Garden City, NY: Doubleday, 1991.

Porter, Jack Nusan, ed. *The Sociology of American Jews.* 2d ed. Lanham, MD: Univ. Press of America, 1980.

*Porter, Jack Nusan, and Dreier, Peter, eds. *Jewish Radicalism.* New York: Grove Press, 1973.

Potok, Chaim. *Wanderings.* New York: Alfred A. Knopf, 1978.

Rabinowicz, H. *The World of Hasidism.* Hartford, CT: Hartmore House, 1970.

Reifman, Toby Fishman, ed. *Blessing the Birth of a Daughter: Jewish Naming Ceremonies for Girls.* Booklet. Englewood, NJ: Ezrat Nashim, 1978.

Rein, Natalie. *Daughters of Rachel: Women in Israel.* Middlesex, UK, and New York: Penguin, 1980. (pbk.)

Riskin, Shlomo. *Women and Jewish Divorce: The Rebellious Wife, The Agunah and the Right of Women to Initiate Divorce in Jewish Law, a Halakhic Solution.* Hoboken, NJ: Ktav, 1989.

Rochlin, Harriet, and Rochlin, Fred. *Pioneer Jews: A New Life in the Far West.* Boston: Houghton Mifflin, 1984.

Roiphe, Anne. *Generation Without Memory.* New York: Simon & Schuster/Linden, 1981.

——. *A Season for Healing.* New York: Summit Books, 1988.

Rosmarin, Trude. *Jewish Women Through the Ages.* Pamphlet. New York: Jewish Spectator, 1940.

Roth, Cecil. *Jews in the Renaissance.* Philadelphia: JPS, 1959.

Roth, Philip. *Portnoy's Complaint.* New York: Random House, 1967. (F)

Rubin, Ruth. *Voices of a People: The Story of Yiddish Folksong.* 2d ed. New York: A. S. Barnes, 1963.

Sachar, Abram L. *A History of the Jews.* 5th ed. New York: Alfred A. Knopf, 1966.

Samuel, Maurice. *Jews on Approval.* New York: Liveright, 1932.

Sanders Ronald. *Israel—The View from Masada.* New York: Harper & Row, 1964.

Sandrow, Nahma. *Vagabond Stars: A World History of the Yiddish Theatre.* New York: Harper & Row, 1977.

Sartre, Jean-Paul. *Anti-Semite and Jew.* New York: Schocken, 1965.

Schappes, Morris U., ed. *A Documentary History of the Jews in the United States, 1654–1875.* New York: Schocken, 1971.

Schneider, Susan Weidman. *Jewish and Female: Choices and Changes in Our Lives Today.* New York: Simon & Schuster, 1984.

Scholem, Gershom G. *Major Trends in Jewish Mysticism.* New York: Schocken, 1961. (pbk.)

——. *On Jews and Judaism in Crisis.* New York: Schocken, 1976. (pbk.)

——. *Sabbetai Sevi—The Mystical Messiah.* Princeton, NJ: Princeton Univ. Press, 1973.

Schulberg, Budd. *What Makes Sammy Run?* New York: Random House, 1941. (F)

Schwartz, Gwen Gibson, and Wyden, Barbara. *The Jewish Wife.* New York: Paperback Library, 1969.

Shamgar-Handelman, Lea. *Israeli War Widows—Beyond the Glory of Heroism.* South Hadley, MA: Bergin & Garvey, 1986.

Shapiro, Judah J. *Contemporary Jewish Community Life and the Zionist Movement: Dangers and Challenges.* Booklet. Jerusalem: World Zionist Organization, 1965.

——. *The Friendly Society: A History of the Workmen's Circle.* New York: Media Judaica, 1970

Shipler, David K. *Arab and Jew: Wounded Spirits in a Promised Land.* New York: Times Books/Random House, 1986.

Siegel, Rachel Josefowitz, and Cole, Ellen, eds. *Seen But Not Heard: Jewish Women in Therapy.* New York: Harrington Park Press, 1991.

Siegel, Richard, and Rheins, Carol, eds. *The Jewish Almanac.* New York: Bantam, 1980.

Silberman, Charles. *A Certain People: American Jews and Their Lives Today.* New York: Summit Books/Simon & Schuster, 1985. (pbk.)

Sleeper, James A., and Mintz, Alan, eds. *The New Jews.* New York: Vintage/Random House, 1971.

Smith, Betty. *A Tree Grows in Brooklyn.* New York: Harper & Bros., 1943. (F)

Sochen, June. *Consecrate Every Day: The Public Lives of Jewish American Women, 1880–1980.* Albany, NY: SUNY Press, 1981.

Spiro, Melford E. *Gender and Culture: Kibbutz Women Revisited.* New York: Schocken, 1980.

Steinsaltz, Adin. *The Essential Talmud.* New York: Basic Books/Bantam, 1976. (pbk.)

St. John, Robert. *Tongue of the Prophets.* Garden City, NY: Doubleday, 1952.

Strassfeld, Michael and Sharon. *Jewish Catalog 3: Creating Community.* Philadelphia: JPS, 1980.

Suhl, Yuri. *They Fought Back!* New York: Crown, 1967.

Swidler, Leonard. *Women in Judaism: The Status of Women in Formative Judaism.* Metuchen, NJ: Scarecrow Press, 1976.

Syrkin, Marie. *Blessed Is the Match: The Story of Jewish Resistance.* Philadelphia: JPS, 1947.

——. *The State of the Jews.* Washington, DC: New Republic Books, 1980.

Syrkin, Nachman. *Essays on Socialist Zionism.* Pamphlet. New York: Young Poale Zion of America, n.d.

Talmon, J. L. *Israel Among the Nations.* New York: Macmillan, 1970.

Tamari, Meir. *"With All Your Possessions": Jewish Ethics and Economic Life.* New York: The Free Press/Macmillan, 1986.

Tax, Meredith. *Rivington Street.* New York: William R. Morrow, 1982. (F)

——. *Union Square.* New York: William R. Morrow, 1988. (F)

Teller, Judd L. *Strangers and Natives: The Evolution of the American Jew from 1921 to the Present.* New York: Delacorte, 1968.

Teveth, Shabtai. *Ben Gurion: The Burning Ground, 1886–1946.* Boston: Houghton Mifflin, 1987.

Tiger, Lionel, and Shepher, Joseph. *Women in the Kibbutz.* New York: Harvest/Harcourt Brace Jovanovich, 1976. (pbk.)

Tillion, Germaine. *Ravensbruck.* New York: Anchor/Doubleday, 1947.

Timerman, Jacobo. *Prisoner Without a Name, Cell Without a Number.* New York: Alfred A. Knopf, 1981.

Tobias, Henry J. *The Jewish Bund in Russia from Its Origins to 1905.* Palo Alto, CA: Stanford Univ. Press, 1972.

Tokayer, Marvin, and Swartz, Mary. *The Fugu Plan: The Untold Story of the Japanese and the Jews During World War II.* New York: Paddington Press, 1979.

Trachtenberg, Joshua. *The Devil and the Jews: The Medieval Conception of the Jew and Its Relation to Modern Anti-Semitism.* Cleveland and New York: Meridian Books, World Publishing Co. and Philadelphia: JPS, 1961. (pbk.)

Trunk, Isaiah. *Jewish Responses to Nazi Persecution.* New York: Stein & Day, 1979.

——. *Judenrat: The Jewish Councils in Eastern Europe Under Nazi Occupation.* New York: Macmillian, 1972.

Umansky, Ellen, ed. (with Diane Ashton). *Four Centuries of Women's Spirituality.* Boston: Beacon Press, 1992.

Urofsky, Melvin I. *We Are One! American Jewry and Israel.* New York: Anchor Press/Doubleday, 1978.

Waskow, Arthur I. *The Bush Is Burning.* New York: Macmillan, 1971.

Waxman, Meyer. *A Handbook of Judaism as Professed and Practiced Through the Ages.* 2d ed. Chicago: L. M. Stein, 1953.

Wegner, Judith Romney. *Chattel or Person? The Status of Women in the Mishnah.* New York: Oxford Univ. Press, 1988.

Weinberg, Sydney Stahl. *The World of Our Mothers.* Chapel Hill: Univ. of North Carolina Press, 1988.

Weiss, Avraham. *Women at Prayer: A Halakhic Analysis of Women's Prayer Groups.* Hoboken, NJ: Ktav, 1990.

Wirth, Louis. *The Ghetto.* Chicago: Univ. of Chicago Press, 1928.

Wischnitzer, Mark. *A History of Jewish Crafts and Guilds.* New York: Jonathan David, 1965.

Wistrich, Robert S. *Socialism and the Jews: The Dilemmas of Assimilation in Germany and Austria-Hungary.* East Brunswick, NJ: Associated Univ. Presses, 1982.

Wouk, Herman. *Marjorie Morningstar.* Garden City, NY: Doubleday, 1955. (F)

Wyman, David S. *The Abandonment of the Jews.* New York: Pantheon, 1984.

Yezierska, Anzia. *Bread Givers.* New York: Persea Books, 1925. (F)

——. *Red Ribbon on a White Horse.* New York: Persea Books, 1981.

Yutang, Lin. *My Country and My People.* New York: John Day, 1935.

*Zborowski, Mark, and Herzog, Elizabeth. *Life Is with People.* New York: International Universities Press, 1952.

Zeitlin, Solomon. *The Rise and Fall of the Judean State: A Political, Social and Religious History of the Second Commonwealth.* Vol. 3: *66 CE–120 CE.* Philadelphia: JPS, 1978.

Zipperstein, Steven J. *Elusive Prophet: Ahad Ha'am and the Origins of Zionism.* Berkeley: Univ. of California Press, 1993.

Zlotowitz, Meir, trans. and compiler. *The Megillah: The Book of Esther with Commentaries.* New York: Artscroll, 1976.

Zucrow, Solomon. *Women, Slaves and the Ignorant in Rabbinic Literature.* Boston: Stratford, n.d.

(Space considerations limited the scope of this bibliography. For a listing of feminist classics of the second wave of American feminism, see *Ms.,* July–August 1992, 64–65. For works on Jewish women, see A. C., *The Jewish Woman.*)

INDEX